Dean Ferguson

W9-BAJ-609

READINGS IN THE HISTORY OF
ECONOMIC THOUGHT

READINGS *in the* HISTORY

OF

ECONOMIC THOUGHT

BY

S. HOWARD PATTERSON, A.M., Ph.D.

Professor of Economics, Wharton School, University of Pennsylvania;
Author of "Family Desertion and Non-support," "Social Aspects
of Industry;" co-author of "Economics Problems of Modern
Life," "American Social Problems," "Problems of
American Democracy"

FIRST EDITION
SIXTH IMPRESSION

McGRAW-HILL BOOK COMPANY, INC.

NEW YORK AND LONDON

1932

Copyright, 1932, by the
McGraw-Hill Book Company, Inc.

Printed in the United States of America

*All rights reserved. This book, or
parts thereof, may not be reproduced
in any form without permission of
the publishers.*

TO THE HONORED MEMORY OF TWO OF MY FORMER
TEACHERS

Robert Ellis Thompson

AND

Simon Nelson Patten

WHOSE SCHOLARSHIP AND ORIGINALITY GRACED THE EARLY
TEACHING OF ECONOMICS IN AMERICA

PREFACE

In the history of political theory a number of excellent books of selected readings are available for the beginning student. Such is not the case in the comparable field of economics. Although the student of the history of economic thought has access to several texts in that field, there is no volume of selected readings which traces the continuity of economic thought and the rise and fall of various schools of economists. The need of such a companion volume in courses in the history of economic thought has been evident to the author from his classroom experience in teaching this subject for a number of years at the University of Pennsylvania.

The author's first intention was the preparation of a comprehensive work of at least two volumes. But the existence of excellent, cheap editions of the great masters, as well as abridged economic classics, seemed to make such an effort as useless as it would have been expensive. Each student of the history of economic thought can easily provide himself with Smith's "Wealth of Nations," Ricardo's "Principles of Political Economy and Taxation," and John Stuart Mill's "Principles of Political Economy." Moreover, to provide adequate selections from the masterpieces of these great giants of the past would of itself have taken at least one stout volume of readings. Consequently, these three great economists are not represented, except for a few selections, generally taken from their less important and less familiar works.

It will be noted also that recent writers are not included. There are many reasons for this, one of which is that they are generally treated in a course in recent developments, rather than in one in the history of economic thought. Thus, Alfred Marshall and John Bates Clark, the two great modern defenders of the faith, have been omitted. Their work is too recent and their present importance is too great to permit of selection. Moreover, each has been a great system builder, whose economic philosophy seems to stand or fall in its unified entirety.

The various selections in Monroe's readings in "Early Economic Thought" carry the story from its beginnings down to and through the Physiocrats. Consequently, it seemed wise in this volume to omit the early writers and to begin with the immediate predecessors of Adam Smith. Even François Quesnay and David Hume have not been included here because selections from them are to be found in the work of Professor Monroe.

In short, this volume of "Readings in the History of Economic Thought" covers the long period from the Father of Economics down to

Neo-classicism. It stresses the minor rather than the major prophets, and perhaps economic heresies rather than economic orthodoxies. The reasons for this lack of balance have just been given. Our attempt is merely to put between two covers important economic literature, some of which can be found only in large libraries. Even there, the available copies of these old and rarely used books, many of which have long since been out of print, are so few that students in large classes are forced to suffer considerable inconvenience and to lose much valuable time in the preparation of their assignments.

Selections have been made from the point of view of English speaking students, particularly those of America. For this reason, the British Historical School has been stressed and the German Historical School has been omitted, even thought it was the earlier and the more important of the two branches.

The classification of the various writers into different schools of thought seemed better than a rigorous adherence to the chronological method. The grouping followed is a compromise arrangement, which is somewhat arbitrary and overlapping. Nevertheless, it seemed to offer a fairly logical and workable approach to the long and complex history of economic thought.

Selections from each writer are preceded by brief editorial notes in order to give continuity to the volume, to indicate the significance of the following selections, and to provide a ready reference for dates and titles. Such notes are necessarily brief. Complete information is easily accessible in Palgrave's "Dictionary of Political Economy," the "Encyclopaedia of Social Science," or any one of the several available histories of economic thought. With one or two economists, such is not the case, and specific references have been made to the source material.

S. HOWARD PATTERSON.

PHILADELPHIA,
January, 1932.

CONTENTS

V. OPTIMISTS AND NATIONALISTS

VI. BRITISH HISTORICAL SCHOOL

VII. SOCIAL REFORMERS AND IDEALISTS

VIII. RISE OF SOCIALISM AND ECONOMIC RADICALISM

IX. MISCELLANEOUS AMERICAN WRITERS

APPENDIX. POPULARIZATIONS OF ENGLISH CLASSICAL ECONOMY

PART I

ADAM SMITH AND HIS GROUP

1. Bernard de Mandeville: "Fable of the Bees."
2. Francis Hutcheson: (*a*) "An Inquiry into the Original of Our Ideas of Beauty and Virtue."
   (*b*) "A System of Moral Philosophy."
3. Adam Smith: (*a*) "Theory of the Moral Sentiments."
   (*b*) "Lectures on Justice, Police, Revenue and Arms."
4. Jean Baptiste Say: "A Treatise on Political Economy."

BERNARD DE MANDEVILLE

(1670?–1731)

Mandeville was born in Holland, but the exact date is uncertain. He practiced medicine there before his migration to England. Little is known of his subsequent career in his adopted country beyond his authorship of the " Fable of the Bees." His chief claim to fame is that of a satirist, who succeeded in making his wares popular in an age of pamphleteering.

Mandeville is of interest to students in the history of economic thought because of the "Fable of the Bees" and because of its direct influence on Adam Smith. This piece of verse, for poetry it is not, was published as early as 1705 in a six-penny pamphlet under the title of "The Grumbling Hive." A second edition under the name of "The Fable of the Bees or Private Vices Publick Benefits" was put out in 1714. It was accompanied by numerous and lengthy notes expounding the moral, which the verse had apparently not succeeded in making clear. Because of these notes, or in spite of them, the second edition was far more popular than the first. As is still the case, prosecutions and denunciations succeeded merely in selling more copies of the work. The "Fable of the Bees" continued to increase in popularity, and edition after edition continued to come off the presses for the next century.

The paradox of Mandeville rests on the economic fallacy of making work, which has been denounced in economics texts from Adam Smith to the present time, but which still persists, apparently undisturbed, in popular opinion and public policy. This popular pamphlet of Mandeville no doubt had often been brought to the attention of the serious young Scotch student at Glasgow, and in the maturity of his powers he attacked its economic fallacy in defense of luxury and leisure. Again, Mandeville's "Fable of the Bees" contained certain suggestions of division of labor, which may have had an influence on Smith, who made this great economic principle the starting point of "Wealth of Nations."

BERNARD DE MANDEVILLE

SELECTIONS FROM "THE FABLE OF THE BEES, OR PRIVATE VICES, PUBLICK BENEFITS"

THE PREFACE

Laws and Government are to the Political Bodies of Civil Societies, what the Vital Spirits and Life it self are to the Natural Bodies of Animated Creatures; and as those that study the Anatomy of Dead Carcases may see, that the chief Organs and nicest Springs more immediately required to continue the Motion of our Machine, are not hard Bones, strong Muscles and Nerves, nor the smooth white Skin that so beautifully covers them, but small trifling Films and little Pipes that are either over-look'd, or else seem inconsiderable to Vulgar Eyes; so they that examine into the Nature of Man, abstract from Art and Education, may observe, that what renders him a Sociable Animal, consists not in his desire of Company, Good nature, Pity, Affability, and other Graces of a fair Outside; but that his vilest and most hateful Qualities are the most necessary Accomplishments to fit him for the largest, and, according to the World, the happiest and most flourishing Societies.

The following Fable, in which what I have said is set forth at large, was printed above eight Years ago in a Six Penny Pamphlet, call'd, *the Grumbling Hive; or Knaves turn'd Honest;* and being soon after Pirated, cry'd about the Streets in a Half-Penny Sheet. Since the first publishing of it I have met with several that either wilfully or ignorantly mistaking the Design, would have it, that the Scope of it was a Satyr upon Virtue and Morality, and the whole wrote for the Encouragement of Vice. This made me resolve, whenever it should be reprinted, some way or other to inform the Reader of the real Intent this little Poem was wrote with. I do not dignify these few loose Lines with the Name of Poem, that I would have the Reader expect any Poetry in them, but barely because they are Rhime, and I am in reality puzzled what Name to give them; for they are neither Heroick nor Pastoral, Satyr, Burlesque nor Heroi-comick; to be a Tale they want Probability, and the whole is rather too long for a Fable. All I can say of them is, that they are a Story told in Dogrel, which without the least design of being Witty, I have endeavour'd to do in as easy and familiar a manner as I was able: The Reader shall be welcome to call them what he pleases. 'Twas said of *Montagne*, that he was pretty well vers'd in the Defects of Mankind, but unacquainted with the Excellencies of human Nature: If I fare no worse, I shall think my self well used.

3

What Country soever in the Universe is to be understood by the Bee-Hive represented here, it is evident from what is said of the Laws and Constitution of it, the Glory, Wealth, Power and Industry of its Inhabitants, that it must be a large, rich and warlike Nation, that is happily govern'd by a limited Monarchy. The Satyr therefore to be met with in the following Lines upon the several Professions and Callings, and almost every Degree and Station of People, was not made to injure and point to particular Persons, but only to shew the Vileness of the Ingredients that all together compose the wholesome Mixture of a well-order'd Society; in order to extol the wonderful Power of Political Wisdom, by the help of which so beautiful a Machine is rais'd from the most contemptible Branches. For the main Design of the Fable, (as it is briefly explain'd in the Moral) is to shew the Impossibility of enjoying all the most elegant Comforts of Life that are to be met with in an industrious, wealthy and powerful Nation, and at the same time be bless'd with all the Virtue and Innocence that can be wish'd for in a Golden Age; from thence to expose the Unreasonableness and Folly of those, that desirous of being an opulent and flourishing People and wonderfully greedy after all the Benefits they can receive as such, are yet always murmuring at and exclaiming against those Vices and Inconveniences, that from the Beginning of the World to this present Day, have been inseparable from all Kingdoms and States that ever were fam'd for Strength, Riches, and Politeness, at the same time.

To do this, I first slightly touch upon some of the Faults and Corruptions the several Professions and Callings are generally charged with. After that I shew that those very Vices of every particular Person by skilful Management, were made subservient to the Grandeur and worldly Happiness of the whole. Lastly, by setting forth what of necessity must be the consequence of general Honesty and Virtue, and National Temperance, Innocence and Content, I demonstrate that if Mankind could be cured of the Failings they are Naturally guilty of, they would cease to be capable of being rais'd into such vast, potent and polite Societies, as they have been under the several great Commonwealths and Monarchies that have flourish'd since the Creation.

If you ask me, why I have done all this, *cui bono?* and what Good these Notions will produce? truly, besides the Reader's Diversion, I believe none at all; but if I was ask'd, what Naturally ought to be expected from 'em, I wou'd answer, That in the first Place the People, who continually find fault with others, by reading them, would be taught to look home, and examining their own Consciences, be made asham'd of always railing at what they are more or less guilty of themselves; and that in the next, those who are so fond of the Ease and Comforts, and reap all the Benefits that are the Consequence of a great and flourishing Nation, would learn more patiently to submit to those Inconveniences, which no Government upon Earth can remedy, when they should see the Impossibility of enjoying any great share of the first, without partaking likewise of the latter.

This I say ought naturally to be expected from the publishing of these Notions, if People were to be made better by any thing that could be said to them; but Mankind having for so many Ages remain'd still the same, notwithstanding the many instructive and elaborate Writings, by which their Amendment has been endeavour'd, I am not so vain as to hope for better Success from so inconsiderable a Trifle.

Having allow'd the small Advantage this little Whim is likely to produce, I think my self oblig'd to shew, that it cannot be prejudicial to any; for what is published, if it does no good, ought at least to do no harm: In order to do this I have made some Explanatory Notes, to which the Reader will find himself referr'd in those Passages that seem to be most liable to Exceptions.

The Censorious that never saw the *Grumbling Hive*, will tell me, that whatever I may talk of the Fable, it not taking up a Tenth part of the Book, was only contriv'd to introduce the *Remarks:* that instead of clearing up the doubtful or obscure Places, I have only pitch'd upon such as I had a mind to expatiate upon; and that far from striving to extenuate the Errors committed before, I have made Bad worse, and shewn my self a more bare-faced Champion for Vice, in the rambling Digressions, than I had done in the Fable it self.

I shall spend no time in answering these Accusations; where Men are prejudiced, the best Apologies are lost; and I know that those who think it Criminal to suppose a necessity of Vice in any case whatever, will never be reconcil'd to any Part of the Performance; but if this be thoroughly examin'd, all the Offence it can give, must result from the wrong Inferences that may perhaps be drawn from it, and which I desire no body to make. When I assert, that Vices are inseparable from great and potent Societies, and that it is impossible their Wealth and Grandeur should subsist without, I do not say that the particular Members of them who are guilty of any should not be continually reprov'd, or not be punish'd for them when they grow into Crimes.

There are, I believe, few People in *London*, of those that are at any time forc'd to go a-foot, but what could wish the Streets of it much cleaner than generally they are; while they regard nothing but their own Clothes and private Conveniency: but when once they come to consider, that what offends them is the result of the Plenty, great Traffick and Opulency of that mighty City, if they have any Concern in its Welfare, they will hardly ever wish to see the Streets of it less dirty. For if we mind the Materials of all Sorts that must supply such an infinite number of Trades and Handicrafts, as are always going forward; the vast quantity of Victuals, Drink and Fewel that are daily consum'd in it, the Waste and

Superfluities that must be produced from them; the multitudes of Horses and other Cattle that are always dawbing the Streets, the Carts, Coaches and more heavy Carriages that are perpetually wearing and breaking the Pavement of them, and above all the numberless swarms of People that are continually harassing and trampling through every part of them: If, I say, we mind all these, we shall find that every Moment must produce new Filth; and considering how far distant the great Streets are from the River side, what Cost and Care soever be bestow'd to remove the Nastiness almost as fast as 'tis made, it is impossible *London* should be more cleanly before it is less flourishing. Now would I ask if a good Citizen, in consideration of what has been said, might not assert, that dirty Streets are a necessary Evil inseparable from the Felicity of *London*, without being the least hindrance to the cleaning of Shoes, or sweeping of Streets, and consequently without any Prejudice either to the *Blackguard* or the *Scavingers*.

But if, without any regard to the Interest of Happiness of the City, the Question was put, What Place I thought most pleasant to walk in? No body can doubt but, before the stinking Streets of *London*, I would esteem a fragrant Garden, or a shady Grove in the Country. In the same manner, if laying aside all worldly Greatness and Vain-Glory, I should be ask'd where I thought it was most probable that Men might enjoy true Happiness, I would prefer a small peaceable Society, in which Men, neither envy'd nor esteem'd by Neighbours, should be contented to live upon the Natural Product of the Spot they inhabit, to a vast Multitude abounding in Wealth and Power, that should always be conquering others by their Arms Abroad, and debauching themselves by Foreign Luxury at Home.

Thus much I had said to the Reader in the First Edition; and have added nothing by way of Preface in the Second. But since that, a violent Out-cry has been made against the Book, exactly answering the Expectation I always had of the Justice, the Wisdom, the Charity, and Fair-dealing of those whose Good-will I despair'd of . . . It has been presented by the Grand-Jury, and condemn'd by thousands who never saw a word of it. It has been preach'd against before my Lord Mayor; and an utter Refutation of it is daily expected from a Reverend Divine, who has call'd me Names in the Advertisements, and threatened to answer me in two Months time for above five Months together. What I have to say for my self, the Reader will see in my Vindication at the End of the Book, where he will likewise find the Grand-Jury's Presentment, and a Letter to the Right Honourable Lord C. which is very Rhetorical beyond Argument of Connexion. The Author shews a fine Talent for Invectives, and great Sagacity in discovering Atheism, where others can find none. He is zealous against wicked Books, points at the Fable of the Bees, and is very angry with the Author: he bestows four strong Epithets on the Enormity of his Guilt, and by several elegant Innuendo's to the Multitude, as the Danger there is in suffering such Authors to live, and the Vengeance of Heaven upon a whole Nation, very charitably recommends him to their Care.

Considering the length of this Epistle, and that it is not wholly levell'd at me only, I thought at first to have made some Extracts from it of what related to my self; but finding, on a nearer Enquiry, that what concern'd me was so blended and interwoven with what did not, I was oblig'd to trouble the Reader with it entire, not without Hopes that, prolix as it is, the Extravagancy of it will be entertaining to those who have perused the Treatise it condemns with so much Horror.

THE GRUMBLING HIVE, OR KNAVES TURN'D HONEST

A Spacious Hive well stockt with Bees,
That liv'd in Luxury and Ease;
And yet as fam'd for Laws and Arms,
As yielding large and early Swarms;
Was counted the great Nursery
Of Sciences and Industry.
No Bees Had better Government,
More Fickleness, of less Content:
They were not Slaves to Tyranny,
Nor rul'd by wild *Democracy:*
But Kings, that could not wrong, because
Their Power was circumscrib'd by Laws.

These Insects Liv'd like Men, and all
Our Actions they perform'd in small:
They did whatever's done in Town,
And what belongs to Sword or Gown:
Tho' th' Artful Works, by nimble Slight
Of minute Limbs, 'scap'd Human Sight;
Yet we've no Engines, Labourers,
Ships, Castles, Arms, Artificers,
Craft, Science, Shop, or Instrument,
By they had an Equivalent:
Which, since their Language is unknown,
Must be call'd, as we do our own.
As grant, that among other Things,
They wanted Dice, yet they had Kings;
And those had Guards; from whence we may
Justly conclude, they had some Play;
Unless a Regiment be shewn
Of Soldiers, that make use of none.

Vast Numbers throng'd the fruitful Hive;
Yet those vast Numbers made 'em thrive;
Millions endeavouring to supply
Each other's Lust and Vanity;
While other Millions were employ'd,
To see their Handy-works destroy'd;
They furnish'd half the Universe;
Yet had more Work than Labourers.
Some with vast Stocks, and little Pains,
Jump'd into Business of great Gains;
And some were damn'd to Sythes and Spades,
And all those hard laborious Trades;
Where willing Wretches daily sweat,
And wear out Strength and Limbs to eat:
While others follow'd Mysteries,
To which few Folks bind 'Prentices;
That want no Stock, but that of Brass,
And may set up without a Cross;
As Sharpers, Parasites, Pimps, Players,
Pick-pockets, Coiners, Quacks, South-sayers,
And all those, that in Enmity,
With downright Working, cunningly
Convert to their own Use the Labour
Of their good-natur'd heedless Neighbour.
These were call'd Knaves, but bar the Name,
The grave Industrious were the same:
All Trades and Places knew some Cheat,
No Calling was without Deceit.

The Lawyers, of whose Art the Basis
Was raising Feuds and splitting Cases,
Oppos'd all Registers, that Cheats
Might make more Work with dipt Estates;
As wer't unlawful, that one's own,
Without a Law-Suit, should be known.
They kept off Hearings wilfully,
To finger the refreshing Fee;
And to defend a wicked Cause,
Examin'd and survey'd the Laws,
As Burglars Shops and Houses do,
To find out where they'd best break through.

Physicians valu'd Fame and Wealth
Above the drooping Patient's Health,

Or their own Skill: The greatest Part
Study'd, instead of Rules of Art,
Grave pensive Looks and dull Behaviour,
To gain th' Apothecary's Favour,
The Praise of Midwives, Priests, and all
That serv'd At Birth or Funeral.
To bear with th' ever-talking Tribe,
And hear my Lady's Aunt prescribe;
With formal Smile, and kind How d'ye,
To fawn on all the Family;
And, which of all the greatest Curse is,
T' endure th' Impertinence of Nurses.

Among the many Priests of *Jove*,
Hir'd to draw Blessings from Above,
Some few were Learn'd and Eloquent,
But thousands Hot and Ignorant:
Yet all pass'd Muster that could hide
Their Sloth, Lust, Avarice and Pride;
For which they were as fam'd as Tailors
For Cabbage, or for Brandy Sailors:
Some, Meagre-look'd, and meanly clad,
Would mystically pray for Bread,
Meaning by that an ample Store,
Yet lit'rally received no more;
And, while these holy Drudges starv'd,
The lazy Ones, for which they serv'd,
Indulg'd their Ease, with all the Graces
Of Health and Plenty in their Faces.

The Soldiers, that were forc'd to fight,
If they surviv'd, got Honour by't;
Tho' some, that shunn'd the bloody Fray,
Had Limbs shot off, that ran away:
Some Valiant Gen'rals fought the Foe;
Others took Bribes to let them go:
Some ventur'd always where 'twas warm,
Lost now a Leg, and then an Arm;
Till quite disabled, and put by,
They liv'd on half their Salary;
While others never come in Play,
And staid at Home for double Pay.

Their Kings were serv'd Knavishly,
Cheated by their own Ministry;

Many, that for their Welfare slaved,
Robbing the very Crown they saved:
Pensions were small, and they liv'd high,
Yet boasted of their Honesty.
Calling, whene'er they strain'd their Right,
The slipp'ry Trick a Perquisite;
And when Folks understood their Cant,
They chang'd that for Emolument;
Unwilling to be short or plain,
In any thing concerning Gain;
For there was not a Bee but would
Get more, I won't say, than he should;
But than he dar'd to let them know,
That pay'd for't; as your Gamesters do,
That, tho' at fair Play, ne'er will own
Before the Losers what they've won.

But who can all their Frauds repeat?
The very Stuff, which in the Street,
They sold for Dirt t'enrich the Ground,
Was often by the Buyers found
Sophisticated with a quarter
Of good-for-nothing Stones and Mortar;
Tho' *Flail* had little Cause to mutter,
Who sold the other Salt for Butter.

Justice her self, fam'd for fair Dealing,
By Blindness had not lost her Feeling;
Her Left Hand, which the Scales should hold,
Had often dropt' em, brib'd with Gold;
And, tho' she seem'd Impartial,
Where Punishment was corporal,
Pretended to a reg'lar Course,
In Murther, and all Crimes of Force;
Tho' some, first pillory'd for Cheating,
Were hang'd in Hemp of their own beating;
Yet, it was thought, the Sword she bore
Check'd but the Desp'rate and the Poor;
That, urg'd by meer Necessity,
Were ty'd up to the wretched Tree
For Crimes, which not deserv'd that Fate,
But to secure the Rich and Great.

Thus every Part was full of Vice,
Yet the whole Mass a Paradise;

Flatter'd in Peace, and fear'd in Wars,
They were th' Esteem of Foreigners,
And lavish of their Wealth and Lives,
The Balance of all other Hives.
Such were the Blessings of that State;
Their Crimes conspir'd to make them Great;
And Virtue, whom from Politicks
Had learn'd a Thousand Cunning Tricks,
Was, by their happy Influence,
Made Friends with Vice: and ever since,
The worst of all the Multitude
Did something for the Common Good.

This was the State's Craft, that maintain'd
The Whole of which each Part complain'd:
This, as in Musick Harmony,
Made Jarrings in the main agree;
Parties directly opposite,
Assist each other, as 'twere for Spight;
And Temp'rance with Sobriety,
Serve Drunkenness and Gluttony.

The Root of Evil, Avarice,
That Damn'd ill-natur'd baneful Vice,
Was Slave to Prodigality,
That noble Sin; whilst Luxury
Employ'd a Million of the Poor
And odious Pride a Million more:
Envy it self, and Vanity,
Were Ministers of Industry;
Their darling Folly, Fickleness,
In Diet, Furniture and Dress,
That strange ridic'lous Vice was made
The very Wheel that turn'd the Trade.
Their Laws and Clothes were equally
Objects of Mutability;
For, what was well done for a time,
In half a Year became a Crime;
Yet while they alter'd thus their Laws,
Still finding and correcting Flaws,
They mended by Inconstancy
Faults, which no Prudence could foresee.

Thus Vice nurs'd Ingenuity,
Which join'd with Time and Industry,

Had carry'd Life's Conveniencies.
It's real Pleasures, Comforts, Ease,
To such a Height, the very Poor
Liv'd better than the Rich before,
And nothing could be added more.

How Vain is Mortal Happiness!
Had they but known the Bounds of Bliss;
And that Perfection here below
Is more than Gods can well bestow;
The Grumbling Brutes had been content
With Ministers and Government.
But they, at every ill Success,
Like Creatures lost without Redress,
Curs'd Politicians, Armies, Fleets;
While every one cry'd *Damn the Cheats*,
And would, tho' conscious of his own,
In others barb'rously bear none.

One, that had got a Princely Store,
By cheating Master, King and Poor,
Dar'd cry aloud, *The Land must sink
For all its Fraud;* And whom d'ye think
The Sermonizing Rascal chid?
A Glover that sold Lamb for Kid.

The least thing was not done amiss,
Or cross'd the Publick Business;
But all the Rogues cry'd brazenly,
Good Gods, Had we but Honesty!
Merc'ry smil'd at th' Impudence,
And others call'd it want of Sense,
Always to rail at what they lov'd:
But *Jove* with Indignation mov'd,
At last in Anger swore, *He'd rid
The bawling Hive of Fraud;* and did.
The very Moment it departs,
And Honesty fills all their Hearts;
There shews 'em, like th' Instructive Tree,
Those Crimes which they're asham'd to see:
Which now in Silence they confess,
By blushing at their Ugliness:
Like Children, that would hide their Faults,
And by their Colour own their Thoughts:

Imag'ning, when they're look'd upon,
That others see what they have done.

But, Oh ye Gods! What Consternation,
How vast and sudden was th' Alteration!
In half an Hour, the Nation round,
Meat fell a Peny in the Pound.
The Mask Hypocrisy's flung down,
From the great Statesman to the Clown:
And some in borrow'd Looks well known,
Appear'd like Strangers in their own.
The Bar was silent from that Day;
For now the willing Debtors pay,
Ev'n what's by Creditors forgot;
Who quitted them that had it not.
Those, that were in the Wrong, stood mute,
And dropt the patch'd vexatious Suit:
On which since nothingless can thrive,
Than Lawyers in an honest Hive,
All, except those that got enough,
With Inkhorns by their sides troop'd off.

Justice hang'd some, set others free:
And after Goal delivery,
Her Presence being no more requir'd,
With all her Train and Pomp retir'd.
First march'd some Smiths with Locks and Grates,
Fetters, and Doors with Iron Plates:
Next Goalers, Turnkeys and Assistants:
Before the Goddess, at some distance,
Her chief and faithful Minister,
'Squire CATCH, the Law's great Finisher,
Bore not th' imaginary Sword,
But his own Tools, an Ax and Cord:
Then on a Cloud the Hood-wink'd Fair,
JUSTICE her self was push'd by Air:
About her Chariot, and behind,
Were Serjeants, Bums of every kind,
Tip-staffs, and all those Officers,
That squeeze a living out of Tears.

Tho' Physick liv'd, while Folks were ill,
None would prescribe, but Bees of skill,
Which through the Hive dispers'd so wide,

That none of them had need to ride:
Wav'd vain Disputes, and strove to free
The Patients of their Misery;
Left Drugs in cheating Countries grown,
And us'd the Product of their own;
Knowing the Gods sent no Disease
To Nations without Remedies.

Their Clergy rous'd from Laziness,
Laid not their Charge on Journey-Bees;
But serv'd themselves, exempt from Vice,
The Gods with Pray'r and Sacrifice;
All those, that were unfit, or knew
Their Service might be spar'd, withdrew:
Nor was there Business for so many,
(If th' Honest stand in need of any),
Few only with the High-Priest staid,
To whom the rest Obedience paid:
Himself employ'd in Holy Cares,
Resign'd to others State-Affairs.
He chas'd no Starv'ling from his Door,
Nor pinch'd the Wages of the Poor;
But as his House the Hungry's fed,
The Hireling finds unmeasur'd Bread,
The needy Trav'ler Board and Bed.

Among the King's great Ministers,
And all th' inferior Officers
The Change was great for frugally
They now liv'd on their Salary:
That a poor Bee should ten times come
To ask his Due, a trifling Sum,
And by some well-hir'd Clerk be made
To give a Crown, or ne'er be paid,
Would now be call'd a downright Cheat
Tho' formerly a Perquisite.
All Places manag'd first by Three,
Who watch'd each other's Knavery,
And often for a Fellow-feeling,
Promoted one another's stealing,
Are happily supply'd be One,
By which some thousands more are gone.

No Honour now could be content,
To live and owe for what was spent;

Liv'ries in Brokers Shops are hung,
They part with Coaches for a Song;
Sell stately Horses by whole Sets:
And Country-Houses, to pay Debts.

　　Vain Cost is shunn'd as much as Fraud;
They have no Forces kept Abroad;
Laugh at th' Esteem of Foreigners,
And empty Glory got by Wars;
They fight, but for their Country's sake,
When Right or Liberty's at Stake.

　　Now mind the glorious Hive, and see
How Honesty and Trade agree.
The Shew is gone, it thins apace;
And looks with quite another Face.
For 'twas not only that They went,
By whom vast Sums were Yearly spent;
But Multitudes that liv'd on them,
Were daily forc'd to do the same.
In vain to other Trades they'd fly;
All were o'er-stock'd accordingly.

　　The Price of Land and Houses falls;
Mirac'lous Palaces, whose Walls,
Like those of *Thebes*, were rais'd by Play,
Are to be let; while the once gay,
Well-seated Household Gods would be
More pleas'd to expire in Flames, than see
The mean Inscription on the Door
Smile at the lofty ones they bore.
The building Trade is quite destroy'd,
Artificers are not employ'd;
No Limner for his Art is fam'd,
Stone-cutters, Carvers are not nam'd.

　　Those, that remain'd, grown temp'rate, strive,
Not how to spend, but how to live,
And, when they paid their Tavern Score,
Resolv'd to enter it no more;
No Vintner's Jilt in all the Hive
Could wear now Cloth of Gold, and thrive;
Nor *Torcol* such vast Sums advance,
For *Burgundy* and *Ortelans*;

The Courtier's gone, that with his Miss
Supp'd at his House on *Christmas* Peas;
Spending as much in two Hours stay,
As keeps a Troop of Horse a Day.

The haughty *Chloe*, to live Great,
Had made her Husband rob the State:
But now she sells her Furniture,
Which th' *Indies* had been ransack'd for;
Contracts th' expensive Bill of Fare,
And wears her strong Suit a whole Year:
The slight and fickle Age is past;
And Clothes, as well as Fashions, last.
Weavers, that join'd rich Silk with Plate,
And all the Trades subordinate,
Are gone. Still Peace and Plenty reign,
And every Thing is cheap, tho' plain:
Kind Nature, free from Gard'ners Force,
Allows all Fruits in her own Course;
But Rarities cannot be had,
Where Pains to get them are not paid.

As Pride and Luxury decrease,
So by degrees they leave the Seas.
Not Merchants now, but Companies
Remove whole Manufactories.
All Arts and Crafts neglected lie;
Content, the Bane of Industry,
Makes 'em admire their homely Store,
And neither seek nor covet more.

So few in the vast Hive remain,
The hundredth Part they can't maintain
Against th' Insults of numerous Foes;
Whom yet they valiantly oppose:
'Till some well-fenc'd Retreat is found,
And here they die or stand their Ground.
No Hireling in their Army's known;
But bravely fighting for their own,
Their Courage and Integrity
At last were crown'd with Victory.

They triumph'd not without their Cost,
For many Thousand Bees were lost.

Hard'ned with Toils and Exercise,
They counted Ease it self a Vice;
Which so improv'd their Temperance;
That, to avoid Extravagance,
They flew into a hollow Tree,
Blest with Content and Honesty.

THE MORAL

Then leave Complaints: Fools only strive
To make a Great an Honest Hive
T' enjoy the World's Conveniencies,
Be fam'd in War, yet live in Ease,
Without great Vices, is a vain
EUTOPIA seated in the Brain.
Fraud, Luxury and Pride must live,
While we the Benefits receive:
Hunger's a dreadful Plague, no doubt
Yet who digests or thrives without?
Do we not owe the Growth of Wine
To the dry shabby crooked Vine?
Which, while its Shoots neglected stood,
Chok'd other Plants, and ran to Wood;
But blest us with its noble Fruit,
As soon as it was ty'd and cut:
So Vice is beneficial found,
When it's by Justice lopt and bound;
Nay, where the People would be great,
As necessary to the State,
As Hunger is to make 'em eat.
Bare Virtue can'st make Nations live
In Splendor; they, that would revive
A Golden Age, must be as free,
For Acorns, as for Honesty.

THE INTRODUCTION

One of the greatest Reasons why so few People understand themselves, is, that most Writers are always teaching Men what they should be, and hardly ever trouble their Heads with telling them what they really are. As for my Part, without any Compliment to the Courteous Reader, or my self, I believe Man (besides Skin, Flesh, Bones, &c. that are obvious to the Eye) to be a compound of various Passions, that all of them, as they are provoked and come uppermost, govern him by turns, whether he will or no. To shew, that these Qualifications, which we all pretend to be asham'd of, are the great Support of a flourishing Society, has been the

Subject of the foregoing Poem. But there being some **Passages** in it seemingly Paradoxical, I have in the Preface promised some explanatory Remarks on it; which to render more useful, I have thought fit to enquire, how Man, no better qualify'd, might yet by his own Imperfections be taught to distinguish between Virtue and Vice: And here I must desire the Reader once for all to take notice, that when I say Men, I mean neither Jews nor Christians; but meer Man, in the State of Nature and Ignorance of the true Deity.

FRANCIS HUTCHESON

(1694–1746)

Francis Hutcheson was a Scotch philosopher who lectured at the University of Glasgow. His chief works of interest to the student of the history of economic thought were "An Inquiry into the Original of Our Ideas of Beauty and Virtue" (third edition of 1729) and "A System of Moral Philosophy" (1755), from which the following brief selections have been taken. Hutcheson taught and deeply influenced Adam Smith, both by his writings and by his personal influence, while the latter was a student at the University of Glasgow in the years from 1737 to 1740, as may be discovered in the following brief selections from Hutcheson.

Although Hutcheson had some lingering traces of mercantilism, he openly advocated the natural system of individual liberty and private enterprise. His writings radiate the optimism which is associated with Adam Smith, in contrast to the Malthusian pessimism and the Ricardian conflict. The "invisible hand" begins to make itself felt even in the pages of Hutcheson. The following selections stress self-interest and universal benevolence.

Hutcheson's work also is characterized by the philosophy of utilitarianism, which blossomed in full bud in the writings of Bentham, and which bore ripe fruit in the work of Ricardo, Mill, and Jevons. It also foreshadows the psychology of hedonism.

FRANCIS HUTCHESON

SELECTIONS FROM "AN INQUIRY INTO THE ORIGINAL OF OUR IDEAS OF BEAUTY AND VIRTUE"

TREATISE II. AN INQUIRY CONCERNING MORAL GOOD AND EVIL

Section 2

III. *Benevolence disinterested.*

As to the *Love* of *Benevolence*, the very Name excludes *Self-Interest*. We never call that Man *benevolent*, who is in fact useful to others, but at the same time only intends his *own Interest*, without any ultimate desire of the *Good* of *others*. If there be any *Benevolence* at all, it must be *disinterested;* for the most useful Action imaginable, loses all appearance of *Benevolence*, as soon as we discern that it only flowed from *Self-Love*, or *Interest*. Thus, never were any human Actions more *advantageous*, than the Inventions of *Fire*, and *Iron;* but if these were casual, or if the *Inventor* only intended his *own Interest* in them, there is nothing which can be call'd *Benevolent* in them. Where-ever then *Benevolence* is suppos'd, there it is imagin'd *disinterested*, and design'd for the *Good* of others. To raise Benevolence, no more is required than calmly to consider any *sensitive Nature* not pernicious to others. *Gratitude* arises from Benefits conferred from Good-will on our selves or those we love; *Complacence* is a perception of the moral Sense. Gratitude includes some *Complacence*, and Complacence still raises a stronger Good-will than that we have toward indifferent Characters, where there is no opposition of Interests. Self-Love join'd with Benevolence.

But it must be here observ'd, That as all Men have *Self-Love*, as well as *Benevolence*, these two Principles may jointly excite a Man to the same Action; and then they are to be consider'd as two Forces impelling the same Body to Motion; sometimes they conspire, sometimes are indifferent to each other, and sometimes are in some degree opposite. Thus, if a Man have such strong *Benevolence*, as would have produc'd an Action without any Views of *Self-Interest;* that such a Man has also in View *private Advantage*, along with *publick Good*, as the Effect of his Action, does no way diminish the *Benevolence* of the Action. When he would not have produc'd so much *publick Good*, had it not been for Prospect of *Self-Interest*, then the Effect of *Self-Love* is to be deducted, and his *Benevolence* is proportion'd to the remainder of *Good*, which pure *Benevolence* would have produc'd. When a Man's *Benevolence* is hurtful to himself, then *Self-Love* is opposite to *Benevolence*, and the *Benevolence* is porportion'd to the Sum of the *Good* produc'd, added to the Resistance of *Self-Love* surmounted by it. In most Cases it is impossible for Men to know how far their Fellows are influenc'd by the one or other of these Principles; but yet the general Truth is sufficiently certain, That this is the way in which the *Benevolence* of Actions is to be computed.

Section 7. A Deduction of Some Complex Moral Ideas, viz: of Obligation, and Right, Perfect, Imperfect, and External, Alienable, and Unalienable, from This Moral Sense

I. *To conclude this Subject, we may, from what has been said, see the true Original of moral Ideas, viz. This moral Sense of Excellence in every Appearance, or Evidence of Benevolence. It remains to be explain'd, how we acquire more particular Ideas of Virtue and Vice, abstracting from any Law, Human, or Divine.*

Obligation.—If any one ask, Can we have any Sense of OBLIGATION, abstracting from the *Laws* of a *Superior?* We must answer according to the various Senses of the Word *Obligation.* If by Obligation we understand *a Determination, without regard to our own Interest, to approve Actions, and to perform them; which Determination shall also make us displeas'd with our selves, and uneasy upon having acted contrary to it:* in this meaning of the word *Obligation,* there is *naturally* an *Obligation* upon all Men to *Benevolence;* and they are still under its Influence, even when by false, or partial Opinions of the natural Tendency of their Actions, this *moral Sense* leads them to *Evil;* unless by long inveterate Habits it be exceedingly weaken'd. For it scarce seems possible wholly to extinguish it. Or, which is to the same purpose, this *internal Sense,* and *Instinct* of *Benevolence,* will either influence our Actions, or else make us very uneasy and dissatisfy'd; and we shall be conscious that we are in a base unhappy State, even without considering any *Law* whatsoever, or any external Advantages lost, or Disadvantages impending from its Sanctions. And farther, there are still such Indications given us of what is in the whole *beneficent,* and what not; as may probably discover to us the true Tendency of every Action; and let us see, some time or other, the evil Tendency of what upon a partial View appear'd *good:* or if we have no Friends so faithful as to admonish us, the Persons injur'd will not fail to upbraid us. So that no Mortal can secure to himself a perpetual Serenity, Satisfaction, and Self-approbation, but by a *serious Inquiry* into the Tendency of his Actions, and a *perpetual Study* of *universal Good,* according to the justest Notions of it.

But if by *Obligation,* we understand *a Motive from Self-Interest, sufficient to determine all those who duly consider it, and pursue their own Advantage wisely, to a certain Course of Actions;* we may have a Sense of such an *Obligation*, by reflecting on this *Determination* of our *Nature* to approve *Virtue*, to be pleas'd and happy when we reflect upon our having done *virtuous Actions*, and to be uneasy when we are conscious of having acted otherwise; and also by considering how much superior we esteem the Happiness of *Virtue* to any other Enjoyment. We may likewise have a Sense of this Sort of *Obligation*, by considering those Reasons which prove a constant Course of *Benevolent* and *social Actions*, to be the most probable means of promoting the *natural Good* of every *Individual;* as CUMBERLAND and PUFENDORF have prov'd: And all this without Relation to a *Law*.

But farther, if our *moral Sense* be suppos'd exceedingly weakned, and the *selfish Passions* grown strong, either thro' some general Corruption of Nature, or inveterate Habits; if our *Understanding* be weak, and we be often in danger of being hurry'd by our *Passions* into precipitate and rash Judgments, that *Malicious Actions* shall promote our Advantage more than *Beneficence;* in such a Case, if it be inquir'd what is necessary to engage Men to *beneficent Actions*, or induce a steady sense of an *Obligation* to act for the *public Good;* then, no doubt, "A *Law* with Sanctions, given by a *Superior Being*, of sufficient Power to make us happy or miserable, must be necessary to counter-balance those apparent Motives of *Interest*, to calm *Passions*, and given room for the recovery of our *moral Sense*, or at least for a just View of our *Interest*."

II. *How far Virtue can be taught.*

Now the principal Business of the *moral Philosopher* is to shew, from solid Reasons, "That *Universal Benevolence* tends to the Happiness of the *Benevolent*, either from the Pleasures of *Reflection*, *Honour*, *natural Tendency* to engage the good Offices of Men, upon whose Aid we must depend for our Happiness in this World; or from the Sanctions of *divine Laws* discover'd to us by the Constitution of the *Universe*"; that so no apparent Views of *Interest* may counteract this *natural Inclination:* but not to attempt proving, "That Prospects of our *own* "*Advantage* of any kind, can raise in us the *virtuous Benevolence* toward others." Let the Obstacles from *Self-love* be only remov'd, and NATURE it self will incline us to *Benevolence*. Let the Misery of *excessive Selfishness*, and all its Passions, be but once explain'd, that so *Self-love* may cease to counteract our *natural Propensity* to *Benevolence*, and when this noble Disposition gets loose from these Bonds of *Ignorance*, and false Views of *Interest*, it shall be assisted even by *Self-love*, and grow strong enough to make a *noble virtuous Character*. Then he is to inquire, by *Reflection* upon human Affairs, what Course of Action does most effectually promote the *universal Good*, what universal Rules or Maxims are to be observ'd, and in what Circumstances the Reason of them alters, so as to admit Exceptions; that so our *good Inclinations* may be directed by *Reason*, and a *just*

Knowledge of the *Interests* of *Mankind*. But *Virtue* it self, or *good Dispositions* of *Mind*, are not directly taught, or produc'd by *Instruction;* they must be originally implanted in our Nature, by its *great* AUTHOR and afterwards strengthen'd and confirm'd by our own Cultivation.

III. *Objection.*

We are often told, "That there is no need of supposing such a *Sense* of *Morality* given to Men, since *Reflection*, and *Instruction* would recommend the same Actions from Arguments of *Self-Interest*, and engage us, from the acknowledg'd Principle of *Self-love*, to the Practice of them, without this *unintelligible Determination* to *Benevolence*, or the *occult Quality* of a *moral Sense*."

It is perhaps true, that *Reflection* and *Reason* might lead us to approve the same Actions as *advantageous*. But would not the *same* Reflection and Reason likewise, generally recommend the same *Meats* to us which our *Taste* represents as pleasant? And shall we thence conclude that we have no *Sense* or *Tasting?* Or that such a *Sense* is *useless?* No: The use is plain in both Cases. Notwithstanding the mighty *Reason* we boast of above other Animals, its Processes are too slow, too full of doubt and hesitation, to serve us in every Exigency, either for our own Preservation, without the *external Senses*, or to influence our Actions for the *Good* of the *Whole*, without this *moral Sense*. Nor could we be so strongly determin'd at all times to what is most conducive to either of these Ends, without these *expeditious Monitors*, and *importunate Sollictors;* nor so nobly rewarded, when we act vigorously in pursuit of these Ends, by the calm dull Reflections of *Self-Interest*, as by those delightful Sensations.

This *natural Determination* to approve and admire, or hate and dislike Actions, is no doubt an *occult Quality*. But is it any way more mysterious that the Idea of an Action should raise *Esteem*, or *Contempt*, than that the motion, or tearing of Flesh should give *Pleasure*, or *Pain;* or the Act of Volition should move *Flesh* and *Bones?* In the latter Case, we have got the Brain, and elastic Fibres, and animal Spirits, and elastic Fluids, like the *Indian's* Elephant, and Tortoise, to bear the Burden of the Difficulty: but go one step farther, and you find the whole as difficult as at first, and equally a Mystery with *this Determination* to love and approve, or condemn and despise *Actions* and *Agents*, without any Views of *Interest*, as they appear *benevolent*, or the contrary.

When they offer it as a Presumption that there can be no such *Sense*, antecedent to all Prospect of *Interest*, "That these Actions for the most part are really *advantageous*, one way or other, to the *Actor*, the *Approver*, or *Mankind* in general, by whose Happiness our own State may be some way made better"; may we not ask, supposing the DEITY intended to impress such a *Sense* of something *amiable* in Actions, (which is no impossible Supposition) what sort of Actions would a *good* GOD determine to *approve?* Must we deny the possibility of such a Determination, if it did not lead us to admire Actions of no *Advantage* to *Mankind,* or to love *Agents* for their being *eminent Triflers?* If then the Actions which a wise and good GOD must determine us to approve, if he give us any such *Sense* at all, must be Actions *useful* to the *Publick,* this *Advantage* can never be a Reason against the *Sense* it self. After the same manner, we should deny all *Revelation* which taught us *good Sense, Humanity, Justice,* and a *rational Worship,* because *Reason* and *Interest* confirm and recommend such *Principles,* and *Services;* and should greedily embrace every *Contradiction, Foppery,* and *Pageantry,* as a *truly divine Institution.* without any thing *humane,* or *useful* to *Mankind.*

FRANCIS HUTCHESON

SELECTIONS FROM "A SYSTEM OF MORAL PHILOSOPHY"

BOOK I. CONCERNING THE CONSTITUTION OF HUMAN NATURE, AND THE SUPREME GOOD

Chapter I. Of the Constitution of Human Nature and Its Powers, and First of the Understanding, Will and Passions

I. *Moral Philosophy, what.*

The intention of moral philosophy is to direct men to that course of action which tends most effectually to promote their greatest happiness and perfection; as far as it can be done by observations and conclusions discoverable from the constitution of nature, without any aids of supernatural revelation: these maxims, or rules of conduct are therefore reputed as laws of nature, and the system or collection of them is called the LAW OF NATURE.

* * * * *

VI. *The two calm determinations of will.*

Self-love.—There are two calm natural determinations of the will to be particularly considered on this occasion. First, an invariable constant impulse toward one's own perfection and happiness of the highest kind. This instinct operates in the bulk of mankind very confusedly; as they do not reflect upon, or attend to, their own constitution and powers of action and enjoyment; few have considered and compared the several enjoyments they are capable of, or the several powers of action. But whosoever does so will find a calm settled desire of the perfection of all our active powers, and of the highest enjoyments, such as appear to us, upon comparison, of the greatest importance to our happiness. Those who have not made such reflections and comparisons, naturally desire all sorts of enjoyments they have any notion of by their senses or any higher powers they have exercised, as far as they are consistent with each other, or appear to be so; and desire the perfection of such powers as they attend to. Where several enjoyments appear inconsistent, the mind, while it is calm, naturally pursues, or desires in preference to other, those which seem of the greatest importance to its happiness. So far all agree.

Benevolence.—The other determination alleged is toward the universal happiness of others. When the soul is calm and attentive to the constitution and powers of other beings, their natural actions and capacities of happiness and misery, and when the selfish appetites and passions and desires are asleep, 'tis alleged that there is a calm impulse of the soul to desire the greatest happiness and perfection of the largest system within the compass of its knowledge. Our inward consciousness abundantly testifies that there is such an impulse or determination of the soul, and that it is truly ultimate, without reference to any sort of happiness of our own. But here again, as few have considered the whole system of beings knowable by men, we do not find this determination exerted generally in all its extent; but we find natural desires of the happiness of such individuals, or societies, or systems, as we have calmly considered, where there has intervened no prejudice against them, no notion that their happiness is any way opposite to our own.

Affections extensive or limited.—As the notion of one's own highest happiness, or the greatest aggregate or sum of valuable enjoyments, is not generally formed by men, it is not expressly desired or intended. And therefore we cannot say that every particular calm desire of private good is aiming directly at that sum, and pursuing its object under the notion of a necessary part of that sum. Men naturally desire, even by calm motions of the soul, such objects as they conceive useful or subservient to any valuable enjoyment, such as wealth, power, honour, without this conception of their making a part of this greatest sum. In like manner we have calm benevolent affections toward individuals, or smaller societies of our fellows, where there has not preceeded any consideration of the most extensive system, and where they are not considered formally as parts of this largest system, nor their happiness pursued as conducing to the greatest sum of universal happiness. Such are our calm benevolent affections to friends, countries, men of eminent worth, without any reference in our thoughts to the most extensive system. We can make these references of all selfish enjoyments pursued by us to the greatest sum of private happiness, whenever we please; and we can in like manner refer all our calm particular kind affections to the general extensive benevolence; and 'tis of great consequence to have these large conceptions, and to make these references. But 'tis plain the several particular affections, whether selfish or benevolent, operate, and that too without turbulent or passionate commotions, where no such references have preceeded.

Chapter IX. The Duties toward God; and First, of Just Sentiments Concerning His Nature

V. *The moral dispositions of the original Mind.*

When the existence of original boundless art and power is ascertained, the next point is the moral character, or the dispositions of will toward other beings capable of happiness or misery; which must be the foundation of all piety, and all joy in religion.

That it is benevolent, as this imports pure perfection.—Here first, if we can any way reason concerning the *original Nature* from what we feel in our own, or from any of our notions of excellency or perfection, we must conceive in a *Deity* some *perceptive power* analogous to our *moral sense*, by which he may have self-approbation in certain affections and actions rather than the contrary. Such a *power* must bring a large addition of happiness, and that of the noblest sort, along with it; and, in an omnipotent Mind, cannot be inconsistent with any other perfection or source of enjoyment. The ultimate determinations or affections of the *Divine Being*, which can be approved by himself, must either be *that* toward his own happiness; or a desire of the greatest universal happiness; or a desire of the greatest universal misery. The desire of his own happiness cannot be the sole ultimate desire or determination; because the desire of the happiness of others being distinct from himself would be another source of sublime pure happiness, distinct from the former, but perfectly consistent with it, in a mind which always has it in its power to gratify this desire to the utmost, without obstructing any other source of happiness. The approbation and delight in this kind determination must be quite excluded from the *Divine Mind*, if there is no such original determination in it. And 'tis inconceivable that the *original Mind* can want any source of pure enjoyment or happiness, consistent with every other sort of excellence, while yet in other beings formed by the counsels of that which is original we experience such sources of happiness.

* * * * *

VI. *Proofs of goodness from the effects of Divine Power.*

In judging of the design of any mechanism, where we tolerably understand it, we can always discern the *natural intention*, the *proper end* or *effect* of the contrivance; and distinguish it from events which may casually ensue, or be the necessary attendants or consequents of it, tho' they are no part of the end aimed at by the contriver. The finest statue may hurt one, by falling on him: the most regular and convenient house, must obstruct the inhabitant's prospect of the heavens and the earth, more than a field does; and must put him to some trouble and expence in supporting it. By the most benign and wisely contrived course of the sun some severe weather must happen in some places. Some evils may be so essentially connected with the means of the supreme good, that *Omnipotence* cannot make it attainable to some beings, without them. Such evils therefore must exist in a world contrived by perfect Goodness. The goodness therefore of the author of a system, in which some evils appear, may be sufficiently proved, if the natural design of the structure appears to be good and benign, and the evils only such as must ensue upon laws well calculated for superior good. This reasoning will be exceedingly confirmed if we find a great superiority of pleasure, or happiness, actually enjoyed by means of the constitution and laws established in nature. Creatures who have no immediate intuition of the Creator, nor a compleat knowledge of the whole plan and all its parts, can expect no better evidence; nor should they desire it.

The whole contrivance good.—Now all the curious mechanism observed, has conservation of life, pleasure, happiness, in some species or other, for its natural end. The external senses of animals recommend things salutary, and reject what is destructive: and the finer powers of perception in like manner recommend to every one what is beneficial to the system, as well as to the individual; and naturally raise aversion to what is pernicious. The whole inward constitution of the affections and *moral faculty* above explained, is obviously contrived for the universal good, and therefore we only hint at it in this place. Some kinds of animals are plainly subordinate to some others, and the powers and instincts of the superior species may be destructive to the inferior; but they are the means of good to the species in which they reside. The effects of them on the inferior is indeed the depriving some of them sooner of their existence; but not in a worse manner than they must have lost it however in a natural death: nay the suddeness of the violent death, to a creature of no forethought, makes it preferable to the tedious sort we call natural. And many of such low kinds must have perished as early by want of sustenance, had not nature provided other causes more gentle than famine. An *original malicious being* would have exercised its art in proper engines of torture, in parts formed for no other purposes, in appetites and senses leading ordinarily to what would be useless or pernicious, even in a moderate degree; in impatient ardours for what gave no pleasure of use; in excrescences useless for life or action, but burdensome and tormenting; and in affections pernicious to society, approved by a perverse taste.

* * * * *

XIII. *If God be good he is perfectly good.*

Since then the whole contrivance of nature, directly intended for good, and the prevalence of happiness in consequence of it, proves the *original Mind* to be benevolent; wherever there is any real goodness, a greater happiness must be more desired than a less; and where there is sufficient power, the desire shall be accomplished. If God be omnipotent and wise, all is well: the best order obtains in the whole: no evil is permitted which is not necessary for superior good, or the necessary attendant and consequent upon what is ordered with the most benign intention for the greatest perfection and happiness of the universe.

Unreasonable to demand the particular purposes of all evils.—'Tis arrogant to demand a particular account how each evil is necessary or subservient to some superior good. In the best possible scheme many things must be inexplicable to imperfect knowledge. The ends and connexions must be hid, as some steps in the oeconomy of the parent, or the practice of the physician must be dark to the child, or the patient. 'Tis enough that we discern the natural end to be good in all the mechanism of nature which we understand; that happiness is prevalent, and our state very eligible. All new discoveries increase our evidence by shewing the wise purposes of what before seemed an imperfection. A candid mind must conclude the same to be the case of parts whose uses are yet unknown. The very anxieties of men about this grand point, help to confirm it, as they shew the natural determination of the soul to wish all well in the universe; one of the clearest footsteps of our benevolent Creator imprinted in our own hearts. This truth must be acceptable to all, where vanity, affectation of singularity and of eminent penetration, or an humour of contradiction, hath not engrossed the heart.

Chapter XI. The Conclusion of This Book, Shewing the Way to the Supreme Happiness of Our Nature

I. *The sum of human happiness.*

Having thus considered the several sources of happiness our nature is capable of; and, upon a full comparison, found that the noblest and most lasting enjoyments are such as arise from our own affections and actions, and not the passive sensations we receive from those external things which affect the body: having also compared the several sort of affections and actions, whether exerted toward our fellows in narrower or more extended systems, or toward the *Deity*, whose nature and grand intention in the administration of the universe we have also endeavoured to discover: and having found that, as our *moral faculty* plainly approves in an higher degree, all the more extensive affections toward our fellows than it approves the more confined affections or passions; that these extensive affections are also more noble sources of enjoyment; and that our love of moral excellence; our knowledge, veneration, and love of the Deity, conceived as perfectly good and wise and powerful, and the fountain of all good; and an entire resignation to his will and providence is the source of our sublime happiness, the grand foundation of all our tranquility or security as to any other object of the most honourable desires: 'tis plain our supreme and compleat happiness, according to the universal doctrine of the wisest men in all ages, must consist in the compleat exercise of these nobler virtues, especially that entire love and resignation to *God*, and of all the inferior virtues which do not interfere with the superior: and in the enjoyment of such external prosperity as we can, consistently with virtue, obtain.

Book II. Containing a Deduction of the More Special Laws of
Nature, and Duties of Life, Previous to Civil
Government, and Other Adventitious States

*Chapter III. The General Notions of Rights, and Laws, Explained; with
Their Divisions*

X. *How the law of nature is perfect.*

As the laws of nature comprehend not merely the original moral
determinations of the mind, but likeways the practical conclusions made
by the reasoning and reflection of men upon the constitution of nature,
shewing what conduct is worthy and tends to publick good, there needs
be little controversy about their perfection, as all must own that the
reason even of the most ingenious and most improved is still imperfect.
And that it may be very possible that a superior being could see a certain
rule of conduct to be conducive to the publick good, which none of human
race could ever have discovered to be useful: and as to the bulk of mankind, they may indeed easily discover the general and most necessary
rules, but they seldom can find out or even apprehend well the reasons
upon which some of the more special laws which yet have a substantial
foundation in nature are built. If one by the system of the laws of nature
means the very constitutions of nature itself, or the objective evidence
laid before rational beings in the whole; this no doubt is perfect: but its
perfection does not supersede the usefulness of the revelation of laws to
mankind by words or writing, or of the discoveries of the wise human
legislators or moralists, or of precepts positive as to their matter; since
so few of mankind can attain any great knowledge of this constitution,
and none can pretend to understand it compleatly.

We should not censure providence on account of this imperfection, for
reasons mentioned above, any more than we censure it for our small
bodily strength, or the shortness of our lives. If we use our powers and
opportunities well, the condition of human life in this world will be in the
main an agreeable and happy state; and yet by divine revelation, or even
by accurate reasonings of wise men, much may be discovered for the
improvement of this life; and many fine institutions contrived, the reasons
for which neither any one in the ruder nations, nor the populace in the
more civilized, shall ever apprehend.

But this holds in general, that all wise and just laws have some tendency to the general happiness, or to the good of some part of the system
subservient to and consistent with the general good. The moral good is
obedience and consists in either a direct intention of this good and proposed by the law, whether we know it fully ourselves, or implicitly trust
to the goodness of the legislator; or in some grateful affection toward the
legislator: where obedience flows only from fear of punishment, or hope
of reward, it has no moral excellency. tho' in some cases it may be
innocent.

ADAM SMITH

(1723–1790)

Adam Smith, "the Father of Economics," was born in the little Scotch village of Kirkcaldy. At the age of fourteen he went to Glasgow where he came under the influence of Hutcheson. Next we find him on a scholarship at Oxford, although his years there apparently were not so profitable as those spent at Glasgow. Between 1748 and 1751 he lectured at Edinburgh, after which he became a professor at Glasgow, first of logic and then of moral philosophy. Smith was a close friend of David Hume. On his travels to the continent of Europe, he met Quesney, Tourgot, and numerous others among the physiocrats. The life and work of Adam Smith are so important that they are treated completely in all histories of economic thought. They need not be discussed at length here.

The writings of Adam Smith include "Theory of the Moral Sentiments" (1759) and "Wealth of Nations," or, to be more exact, "An Inquiry into the Nature and Causes of the Wealth of Nations" (1776). Another work of Adam Smith was prepared by Dr. Edwin Cannan almost a century after Smith's death from the university notes of a student at Glasgow. It appeared under the title of "Lectures on Justice, Police, Revenue and Arms." Indeed, one of the best, if not the best, editions of "Wealth of Nations" is that by Cannan.

"Wealth of Nations" is available in numerous cheap editions and should be in the library of every student in the history of economic thought. Because of its familiarity and accessibility, no selections have been taken from this great classic. The following selections are taken from Smith's "Theory of the Moral Sentiments" and "Lectures on Justice, Police, Revenue and Arms." The student is asked to compare the views and statements contained therein with those in "Wealth of Nations."

ADAM SMITH

SELECTIONS FROM "THEORY OF THE MORAL SENTIMENTS"

Chapter II. Of the Order in Which Societies Are by Nature Recommended to Our Beneficence

The same principles that direct the order in which individuals are recommended to our beneficence, direct that likewise in which societies are recommended to it. Those to which it is, or may be of most importance, are first and principally recommended to it.

The state or sovereignty in which we have been born and educated, and under the protection of which we continue to live, is, in ordinary cases, the greatest society upon whose happiness or misery, our good or bad conduct can have much influence. It is accordingly, by nature, most strongly recommended to us. Not only we ourselves, but all the objects of our kindest affections, our children, our parents, our relations, our friends, our benefactors, all those whom we naturally love and revere the most, are commonly comprehended within it, and their prosperity and safety depend in some measure upon its prosperity and safety. It is by nature, therefore, endeared to us, not only by all our selfish, but by all our private benevolent affections. Upon account of our own connexion with it, its prosperity and glory seem to reflect some sort of honour upon ourselves. When we compare it with other societies of the same kind, we are proud of its superiority, and mortified in some degree, if it appears in any respect below them. All the illustrious characters which it has produced in former times (for against those of our own times envy may sometimes prejudice us a little), its warriors, its statesmen, its poets, its philosphers, and men of letters of all kinds; we are disposed to view with the most partial admiration, and to rank them (sometimes most unjustly) above those of all other nations. The patriot who lays down his life for the safety, or even for the vain-glory of this society, appears to act with the most exact propriety. He appears to view himself in the light in which the impartial spectator naturally and necessarily views him, as but one of the multitude, in the eye of that equitable judge, of no more consequence than any other in it, but bound at all times to sacrifice and devote himself to the safety, to the service, and even to the glory of the greater number. But though this sacrifice appears to be perfectly just and proper, we know how difficult it is to make it, and how few people are capable of making it. His conduct, therefore, excites not only our entire approbation, but our highest wonder and admiration, and seems to merit all the applause which can be due to the most heroic virute. The traitor, on the contrary, who, in some peculiar situation, fancies he can promote his own little interest by betraying to the public enemy that of his native country; who, regardless of the judgment of the man within the breast, prefers himself, in this respect so shamefully and so basely, to all those with whom he has any connexion; appears to be of all villains the most detestable.

The love of our own nation often disposes us to view, with the most malignant jealousy and envy, the prosperity and aggrandisement of any other neighbouring nation. Independent and neighbouring-nations, having no common superior to decide their disputes, all live in continual dread and suspicion of one another. Each sovereign, expecting little justice from his neighbours, is disposed to treat them with as little as he expects from them. The regard for the laws of nations, or for those rules which independent states profess or pretend to think themselves bound to observe in their dealings with one another, is often very little more than mere pretence and profession. From the smallest interest, upon the slightest provocation, we see those rules every day, either evaded or directly violated without shame or remorse. Each nation foresees or imagines it foresees, its own subjugation in the increasing power and aggrandisement of any of its neighbours; and the mean principle of national prejudice is often founded upon the noble one of the love of our own country. The sentence with which the elder Cato is said to have concluded every speech which he made in the senate, whatever might be the subject, "It is my opinion likewise that Carthage ought to be destroyed," was the natural expression of the savage patriotism of a strong but coarse mind, enraged almost to madness against a foreign nation from which his own had suffered so much. The more humane sentence with which Scipio Nasica is said to have concluded all his speeches, "It is my opinion likewise that Carthage ought not to be destroyed," was the liberal expression of a more enlarged and enlightened mind, who felt no aversion to the prosperity even of an old enemy, when reduced to a state which could no longer be formidable to Rome. France and England may each of them have some reason to dread the increase of the naval and military power of the other; but for either of them to envy the internal happiness and prosperity of the other, the cultivation of its lands, the advancement of its manufactures, the increase of its commerce, the security and number of its ports and harbours, its proficiency in all the liberal arts and sciences, is surely beneath the dignity of two such great nations. These are all real improvements of the world we live in. Mankind are benefited, human nature is ennobled by them. In such improvements each nation ought, not only to endeavour itself to excel, but from the love of mankind to promote, instead of obstructing the excellence of its neighbours. These are all proper objects of national emulation, not of national prejudice or envy.

The love of our own country seems not to be derived from the love of mankind. The former sentiment is altogether independent of the latter, and seems sometimes even to dispose us to act inconsistently with it. France may contain, perhaps, near three times the number of the inhabitants which Great Britain contains. In the great society of mankind, therefore, the prosperity of France should appear to be an object of much greater importance than that of Great Britain. The British subject, however, who, upon that account, should prefer upon all occasions the prosperity of the former to that of the latter country, would not be thought a good citizen of Great Britain. We do not love our country merely as a part of the great society of mankind: we love it for its own sake, and independently of any such consideration. That wisdom which contrived the system of human affections, as well as that of every other part of nature, seems to have judged that the interest of the great society of mankind would be best promoted by directing the principal attention of each individual to that particular portion of it, which was most within the sphere both of his abilities and of his understanding.

National prejudices and hatreds seldom extend beyond neighbouring nations. We very weakly and foolishly, perhaps, call the French our natural enemies; and they perhaps, as weakly and foolishly, consider us in the same manner. Neither they nor we bear any sort of envy to the prosperity of China or Japan. It very rarely happens, however, that our good-will towards such distant countries can be exerted with much effect.

The most extensive public benevolence which can commonly be exerted with any considerable effect, is that of the statesmen, who project and form alliances among neighbouring or not very distant nations, for the preservation either of, what is called, the balance of power, or of the general peace and tranquillity of the states within the circle of their negotiations. The statesmen, however, who plan and execute such treaties, have seldom any thing in view, but the interest of their respective countries. Sometimes, indeed, their views are more extensive. The Count d'Avaux, the plenipotentiary of France, at the treaty of Munster, would have been willing to sacrifice his life (according to the Cardinal de Retz, a man not over-credulous in the virtue of other people) in order to have restored, by that treaty, the general tranquillity of Europe. King William seems to have had a real zeal for the liberty and independency of the greater part of the sovereign states of Europe; which, perhaps, might be a good deal stimulated by his particular aversion to France, the state from which, during his time, that liberty and independency were principally in danger. Some share of the same spirit seems to have descended to the first ministry of Queen Anne.

Every independent state is divided into many different orders and societies, each of which has its own particular powers, privileges, and immunities. Every individual is naturally more attached to his own particular order or society, than to any other. His own interest, his own vanity, the interest and vanity of many of his friends and companions, are commonly a good deal connected with it. He is ambitious to extend its privileges and immunities. He is zealous to defend them against the encroachments of every other order of society.

Upon the manner in which any state is divided into the different orders and societies which compose it, and upon the particular distribution which has been made of their respective powers, privileges, and immunities, depends, what is called the constitution of that particular state.

Upon the ability of each particular order or society to maintain its own powers, privileges, and immunities, against the encroachments of every other, depends the stability of that particular constitution. That particular constitution is necessarily more or less altered, whenever any of its subordinate parts is either raised above or depressed below whatever had been its former rank and condition.

All those different orders and societies are dependent upon the state to which they owe their security and protection. That they are all subordinate to that state, and established only in subserviency to its prosperity and preservation, is a truth acknowledged by the most partial member of every one of them. It may often, however, be hard to convince him that the prosperity and preservation of the state require any diminution of the powers, privileges, and immunities of his own particular order of society. This partiality, though it may sometimes be unjust, may not, upon that account, be useless. It checks the spirit of innovation. It tends to preserve whatever is the established balance among the different orders and societies into which the state is divided; and while it sometimes appears to obstruct some alterations of government which may be fashionable and popular at the time, it contributes in reality to the stability and permanency of the whole system.

The love of our country seems, in ordinary cases, to involve in it two different principles; first, a certain respect and reverence for that constitution or form of government which is actually established; and secondly, an earnest desire to render the condition of our fellow-citizens as safe, respectable, and happy as we can. He is not a citizen who is not disposed to respect the laws and to obey the civil magistrate; and he is certainly not a good citizen who does not wish to promote, by every means in his power, the welfare of the whole society of his fellow citizens.

In peaceable and quiet times, those two principles generally coincide and lead to the same conduct. The support of the established government seems evidently the best expedient for maintaining the safe, respectable, and happy situation of our fellow-citizens; when we see that this government actually maintains them in that situation. But in times of public discontent, faction and disorder, those two different principles may draw different ways, and even a wise man may be disposed to think some alteration necessary in that constitution or form of government, which, in its actual condition, appears plainly unable to maintain the public tranquility. In such cases, however, it often requires, perhaps, the highest effort of political wisdom to determine when a real patriot ought to support and endeavour to re-establish the authority of the old system, and when he ought to give way to the more daring, but often dangerous spirit of innovation.

Foreign war and civil faction are the two situations which afford the most splendid opportunities for the display of public spirit. The hero who serves his country successfully in foreign war gratifies the wishes of the whole nation, and is, upon that account, the object of universal gratitude and admiration. In times of civil discord, the leaders of the contending parties, though they may be admired by one-half of their fellow-citizens, are commonly execrated by the other. Their characters and merit of their respective services appear commonly more doubtful. The glory which is acquired by foreign war is, upon this account, almost always more pure and more splendid than that which can be acquired in civil faction.

The leader of the successful party, however, if he has authority enough to prevail upon his own friends to act with proper temper and moderation (which frequently he has not), may sometimes render to his country a service much more essential and important than the greatest victories and the most extensive conquests. He may re-establish and improve the constitution, and from the very doubtful and ambiguous character of the leader of the party, he may assume the greatest and noblest of all characters, that of the reformer and legislator of a great state; and, by the wisdom of this institution, secure the internal tranquility and happiness of his fellow citizens for many succeeding generations.

Amidst the turbulence and disorder of faction, a certain spirit of system is apt to mix itself with that public spirit which is founded upon the love of humanity, upon a real fellow-feeling with the inconveniences and distresses to which some of our fellow-citizens may be exposed. This spirit of system commonly takes the direction of that more gentle public spirit; always animates it, and often inflames it even to the madness of fanaticism. The leaders of the discontented party seldom fail to hold out some plausible plan of reformation which, they pretend, will not only remove the inconveniences and relieve the distresses immediately complained of, but will prevent, in all time coming, any return of the like inconveniences and distresses. They often propose, upon this account, to new model the constitution, and to alter, in some of its most essential parts, that system of government under which the subjects of a great empire have enjoyed, perhaps, peace, security, and even glory, during the course of several centuries together. The great body of the party are commonly intoxicated with the imaginary beauty of this ideal system, of which they have no experience, but which has been represented to them in all the most dazzling colours in which the eloquence of their leaders could paint it. Those leaders themselves, though they originally may have meant nothing but their own aggrandisement, become many of them in time the dupes of their own sophistry, and are as eager for this great reformation as the weakest and foolishest of their followers. Even though the leaders should have preserved their own heads, as indeed they commonly do, free from this fanaticism, yet they dare not always disappoint the expectation of their followers; but are often obliged, though contrary to their principle and their conscience, to act as if they were under the common delusion. The violence of the party, refusing all palliatives, all temperaments, all reasonable accomodations, by requiring too much frequently obtains nothing; and those inconveniences and distresses which, with a little moderation, might in a great measure have been removed and relieved, are left altogether without the hope of a remedy.

The man whose public spirit is prompted altogether by humanity and benevolence, will respect the established powers and privileges even of individuals, and still more those of the great orders and societies, into which the state is divided. Though he should consider some of them as in some measure abusive, he will content himself with moderating what he often cannot annihilate without great violence. When he cannot conquer the rooted prejudices of the people by reasoning and persuasion, he will not attempt to subdue them by force; but will religiously observe what, by Cicero, is justly called the divine maxim of Plato, never to use violence to his country no more than to his parents. He will accommodate, as well as he can, his public arrangements to the confirmed habits and prejudices of the people; and will remedy as well as he can, the inconveniences which may flow from the want of those regulations which the people are averse to submit to. When he cannot establish the right, he will not disdain to ameliorate the wrong; but like Solon, when he cannot establish the best system of laws, he will endeavour to establish the best that the people can bear.

The man of system, on the contrary, is apt to be very wise in his own conceit; and is often so enamoured with the supposed beauty of his own ideal plan of government, that he cannot suffer the smallest deviation from any part of it. He goes on to establish it completely and in all its parts, without any regard either to the great interests, or to the strong prejudices which may oppose it. He seems to imagine that he can arrange the different members of a great society with as much ease as the hand arranges the different pieces upon a chess-board. He does not consider that the pieces upon the chess-board have no other principle of motion besides that which the hand impresses upon them, but that, in the **great** chess board of human society, every single piece has a principle of motion of its own, altogether different from that which the legislature might choose to impress upon it. If those two principles coincide and act in the same direction, the game of human society will go on easily and harmoniously, and is very likely to be happy and successful. If they are opposite or different, the game will go on miserably, and the society must be at all times in the highest degree of disorder.

Some general, and even systematical, idea of the perfection of policy and law, may no doubt be necessary for directing the views of the statesman. But to insist upon establishing, and upon establishing all at once, and in spite of all opposition, every thing which that idea may seem to require, must often be the highest degree of arrogance. It is to erect his own judgment into the supreme standard of right and wrong. It is to fancy himself the only wise and worthy man in the commonwealth, and that his fellow-citizens should accommodate themselves to him and not he to them. It is upon this account, that of all political speculators, sovereign princes are by far the most dangerous. This arrogance is perfectly familiar to them. They entertain no doubt of the immense superiority of their own judgment. When such imperial and royal reformers, therefore, condescend to contemplate the constitution of the country which is committed to their government, they seldom see any thing so wrong in it as the obstructions which it may sometimes oppose to the execution of their own will. They hold in contempt the divine maxim of Plato, and consider the state as made for themselves, not themselves for the state. The great object of their reformation, therefore, is to remove those obstructions; to reduce the authority of the nobility; to take away the privileges of cities and provinces, and to render both the greatest individuals and the greatest orders of the state, as incapable of opposing their commands, as the weakest and most insignificant.

Chapter III. Of Universal Benevolence

Though our effectual good offices can very seldom be extended to any wider society than that of our country; our good-will is circumscribed by no boundary, but may embrace the immensity of the universe. We cannot form the idea of any innocent and sensible being, whose happiness we should not desire, or to whose misery, when distinctly brought home to the imagination, we should not have some degree of aversion. The idea of a mischievous, though sensible, being, indeed, naturally provokes our hatred: but the ill-will which, in this case, we bear to it, is really the effect of our universal benevolence. It is the effect of the sympathy which we feel with the misery and resentment of those other innocent and sensible beings, whose happiness is disturbed by malice.

This universal benevolence, how noble and generous soever, can be the source of no solid happiness to any man who is not thoroughly convinced that all the inhabitants of the universe, the meanest as well as the greatest, are under the immediate care and protection of that great, benevolent, and all-wise Being, who directs all the movements of nature; and who is determined, by his own unalterable perfections, to maintain in it, at all times, the greatest possible quantity of happiness. To this universal benevolence, on the contrary, the very suspicion of a fatherless world, must be the most melancholy of all refections; from the thought that all the unknown regions of infinite and incomprehensible space may be filled with nothing but endless misery and wretchedness. All the splendour of the highest prosperity can never enlighten the gloom with which so dreadful an idea must necessarily overshadow the imagination; nor, in a wise and virtuous man, can all the sorrow of the most afflicting adversity every dry up the joy which necessarily springs from the habitual and thorough conviction of the truth of the contrary system.

The wise and virtuous man is at all times willing that his own private interest should be sacrificed to the public interest of his own particular order or society. He is at all times willing, too, that the interest of this order or society should be sacrificed to the greater interest of the state or sovereignty, of which it is only a subordinate part. He should, therefore, be equally willing that all those inferior interests should be sacrificed to the greater interest of the universe, to the interest of that great society of all sensible and intelligent beings, of which God himself is the immediate administrator and director. If he is deeply impressed with the habitual and thorough conviction that this benevolent and all-wise Being can admit into the system of his government, no partial evil which is not necessary for the universal good, he must consider all the misfortunes which may befall himself, his friends, his society, or his country, as necessary for the prosperity of the universe, and therefore as what he ought, not only to submit to with resignation, but as what he himself, if he had known all the connexions and dependencies of things, ought sincerely and devoutly to have wished for.

Nor does this magnanimous resignation to the will of the great Director of the universe, seem in any respect beyond the reach of human nature. Good soldiers, who both love and trust their General, frequently march with more gaiety and alacrity to the forlorn station, from which they never expect to return, than they would to one where there was neither difficulty nor danger. In marching to the latter, they could feel no other sentiment than that of the dulness of ordinary duty: in marching to the former, they feel that they are making the noblest exertion which it is possible for man to make. They know that their general would not have ordered them upon this station, had it not been necessary for the safety of the army, for the success of the war. They cheerfully sacrifice their own little systems to the prosperity of a greater system. They take an affectionate leave of their comrades, to whom they wish all happiness and success; and march out, not only with submissive obedience, but often with shouts of the most joyful exultation, to that fatal, but splendid and honourable station to which they are appointed. No conductor of an army can deserve more unlimited trust, more ardent and zealous affection, than the great Conductor of the universe. In the greatest public as well as private disasters, a wise man ought to consider that he himself, his friends and countrymen, have only been ordered upon the forlorn station of the universe; that had it not been necessary for the good of the whole, they would not have been so ordered; and that it is their duty, not only with humble resignation to submit to this allotment, but to endeavour to embrace it with alacrity and joy. A wise man should surely be capable of doing what a good soldier holds himself at all times in readiness to do.

The idea of that divine Being, whose benevolence and wisdom have, from all eternity, contrived and conducted the immense machine of the universe, so as at all times to produce the greatest possible quantity of happiness, is certainly of all the objects of human contemplation by far the most sublime. Every other thought necessarily appears mean in the comparison. The man whom we believe to be principally occupied in this sublime contemplation, seldom fails to be the object of our highest veneration; and though his life should be altogether contemplative, we often regard him with a sort of religious respect much superior to that with which we look upon the most active and useful servant of the commonwealth. The Meditations of Marcus Antoninus, which turn principally upon this subject, have contributed more, perhaps, to the general admiration of his character, than all the different transactions of his just, merciful, and beneficent reign.

The administration of the great system of the universe, however, the care of the universal happiness of all rational and sensible beings, is the business of God and not of man. To man is allotted a much humbler department, but one much more suitable to the weakness of his powers, and to the narrowness of his comprehension; the care of his own happiness, of that of his family, his friends, his country; that he is occupied in contemplating the more sublime, can never be an excuse for his neglecting the more humble department; and he must not expose himself to the charge which Avidius Cassius is said to have brought, perhaps unjustly, against Marcus Antoninus; that while he employed himself in philosophical speculations, and contemplated the prosperity of the universe, he neglected that of the Roman empire. The most sublime speculation of the contemplative philosopher can scarce compensate the neglect of the smallest active duty.

ADAM SMITH

SELECTIONS FROM "LECTURES ON JUSTICE, POLICE, REVENUE AND ARMS"

DELIVERED IN THE UNIVERSITY OF GLASGOW AS REPORTED BY A STUDENT IN 1763

PART II: POLICE

Chapter II. Cheapness or Plenty

1. *Of the Natural Wants of Mankind.*

In the following part of this discourse we are to confine ourselves to the consideration of cheapness or plenty, or, which is the same thing, the most proper way of procuring wealth and abundance. Cheapness is in fact the same thing with plenty. It is only on account of the plenty of water that it is so cheap as to be got for the lifting; and on account of the scarcity of diamonds (for their real use seems not yet to be discovered) that they are so dear. To ascertain the most proper method of obtaining these conveniences it will be necessary to show first wherein opulence consists, and still previous to this we must consider what are the natural wants of mankind which are to be supplied; and if we differ from common opinions, we shall at least give the reasons for our non-conformity.

* * * * *

2. *That all the Arts are subservient to the Natural Wants of Mankind.*

* * * * *

3. *That Opulence arises from the Division of Labour.*

In an uncivilized nation, and where labour is undivided, everything is provided for that the natural wants of mankind required; yet, when the nation is cultivated and labour divided, a more liberal provision is allotted them; and it is on this account that a common day labourer in Britain has more luxury in his way of living than an Indian sovereign. The woollen coat he wears requires very considerable preparations—the wool-gatherer, the dresser, the spinster, the dyer, the weaver, the tailor, and many more, must all be employed before the labourer is clothed. The tools by which all this is effectuated employ a still greater number of artists—the loom-maker, miln-wright, ropemaker, not to mention the bricklayer, the tree-feller, the miner, the smelter, the forger, the smith,

&c. Besides his dress, consider all his household furniture, his coarse linens, his shoes, his coals dug out of the earth or brought by sea, his kitchen utensils and different plates, those that are employed in providing his bread and beer, the sower, the brewer, the reaper, the baker, his glass windows and the art required in preparing (them), without which our northern climate could hardly be inhabited. When we examine the conveniences of the day labourer, we find that even in his easy simple manner he cannot be accommodated without the assistance of a great number, and yet this is nothing compared with the luxury of the nobility. An European prince, however, does not so far exceed a commoner, as the latter does the chief of a savage nation. It is easy to conceive how the rich can be so well provided for, as they can direct so many hands to serve their purposes. They are supported by the industry of the peasant. In a savage nation every one enjoys the whole fruit of his own labour, yet their indigence is greater than anywhere.

It is the division of labour which increases the opulence of a country.

In a civilized society, though there is a division of labour, there is no equal division, for there are a good many who work none at all. The division of opulence is not according to the work. The opulence of the merchant is greater than that of all his clerks, though he works less; and they again have six times more than an equal number of artisans, who are more employed. The artisan who works at his ease within doors has far more than the poor labourer who trudges up and down without intermission. Thus, he who as it were bears the burden of society, has the fewest advantages.

4. *How the Division of Labour multiplies the Product.*

We shall next show how this division of labour occasions a multiplication of the product, or, which is the same thing, how opulence arises from it. In order to do this let us observe the effect of the division of labour in some manufactures. If all the parts of a pin were made by one man, if the same person dug the ore, (s)melted it, and split the wire, it would take him a whole year to make one pin, and this pin must therefore be sold at the expense of his maintenance for that time, which, taking(it) at a moderate computation, would at least be six pounds for a pin. If the labour is so far divided that the wire is ready-made, he will not make above twenty per day, which, allowing ten pence for wages, makes the pin a half-penny. The pin-maker therefore divides the labour among a great number of different persons; the cutting, pointing, heading and gilding are all separate professions. Two or three are employed in making the head, one or two in putting it on, and so on, to the putting them in the paper, being in all eighteen. By this division every one can with great ease make 2,000 a day. The same is the case in the linen and woollen manufactures. Some arts, however. there are which will not admit of this division, and therefore they cannot keep pace with other manufactures and arts. Such are farming and grazing. This is entirely owing to the return of the seasons, by which one man can only be for a short time employed in any one operation. In countries where the season(s) do not make such alterations it is otherwise. In France the corn is better and cheaper than in England. But our toys, which have no dependence on the climate, and in which labour can be divided, are far superior to those of France.

When labour is thus divided, and so much done by one man in proportion, the surplus above their maintenance is considerable, which each man can exchange for a fourth of what he could have done if he had finished it alone. By this means the commodity becomes far cheaper, and the labour dearer. It is to be observed that the price of labour by no means determines the opulence of society; it is only when a little labour can procure abundance. On this account a rich nation, when its manufactures are greatly improven, may have an advantage over a poor one by underselling it. The cotton and other commodities from China would undersell any made with us, were it not for the long carriage, and other taxes that are laid upon them. We must not judge of the dearness of labour by the money or coin that is paid for it. One penny in some places will purchase as much as eighteen pence in others. In the country of the Mogul, where the day's wages are only two-pence, labour is better rewarded than in some of our sugar islands, where men are almost starving with four or five shillings a day. Coin, therefore, can be no proper estimate. Further, though human labour be employed both in the multiplication of commodities and of money, yet the chance of success is not equal. A farmer, by the proper cultivation of an acre, is sure of increase; but the miner may work again and again without success. Commodities must therefore multiply in greater proportion than gold and silver.

But again, the quantity of work which is done by the division of labour is much increased by the three following articles: first, increase of dexterity; secondly, the saving of time lost in passing from one species of labour to another; and thirdly, the invention of machinery. Of these in order:

First, when any kind of labour is reduced to a simple operation, a frequency of action insensibly fits men to a dexterity in accomplishing it. A country smith not accustomed to make nails will work very hard for three or four hundred a day, and those too very bad; but a boy used to it will easily make two thousand, and those incomparably better; yet the improvement of dexterity in this very complex manufacture can never be equal to that in others. A nail-maker changes postures, blows the bellows, changes tools, &c., and therefore the quantity produced cannot be so great as in manufactures of pins and buttons, where the work is reduced to simple operations.

Secondly, there is always some time lost in passing from one species of labour to another, even when they are pretty much connected. When a person has been reading he must rest a little before he begin to write. This is still more the case with the country weaver, who is possessed of a little farm; he must saunter a little when he goes from one to the other. This in general is the case with the country labourers, they are always the greatest saunterers; the country employments of sowing, reaping, threshing being so different, they naturally acquire a habit of indolence, and are seldom very dexterous. By fixing every man to his own operation, and preventing the shifting from one piece of labour to another, the quantity of work must be greatly increased.

Thirdly, the quantity of work is greatly increased by the invention of machines. Two men and three horses will do more in a day with the plough than twenty men without it. The miller and his servant will do more with the water miln than a dozen with the hand miln, though it, too, be a machine. The division of labour no doubt first gave occasion to the invention of machines. If a man's business in life is the performance of two or three things, the bent of his mind will be to find out the cleverest way of doing it; but when the force of his mind is divided it cannot be expected that he should be so successful. We have not, nor cannot have, any complete history of the invention of machines, because most of them are at first imperfect, and receive gradual improvements and increase of powers from those who use them. It was probably a farmer who made the original plough, though the improvements might be owing to some other. Some miserable slave who had perhaps been employed for a long time in grinding corn between two stones, probably first found out the method of supporting the upper stone by a spindle. A miln-wright perhaps found out the way of turning the spindle with the hand, but he who contrived that the outer wheel should go by water was a philosopher, whose business is to do nothing, but observe everything. They must have extensive views of things, who, as in this case, bring in the assistance of new powers not formerly applied. Whether he was an artisan, or whatever he was who first executed this, he must have been a philosopher. Fire machines, wind and water-milns were the invention of philosophers, whose dexterity too is increased by a division of labour. They all divide themselves, according to the different branches, into the mechanical, moral, political, chemical philosophers.

Thus we have shown how the quantity of labour is increased by machines.

5. *What gives Occasion to the Division of Labour.*

We have already shown that the division of labour is the immediate cause of opulence; we shall next consider what gives occasion to the division of labour, or from what principles in our nature it can best be accounted for. We cannot imagine this to be an effect of human prudence. It was indeed made a law by Sesostris that every man should follow the employment of his father, but this is by no means suitable to the dispositions of human nature, and can never long take place; every one is fond of being a gentleman, be his father what he would. They who are strongest and, in the bustle of society, have got above the weak, must have as many to defend them in their station. From necessary causes, therefore, there must be as many in the lower stations as there is occasion for, there must be as many up as down, and no division can be over-stretched. But it is not this which gives occasion to the division of labour; it flows from a direct propensity in human nature for one man to barter with another, which is common to all men, and known to no other animal. Nobody ever saw a dog, the most sagacious animal, exchange a bone with his companion for another. Two greyhounds, indeed, in running down a hare, seem to have something like a compact or agreement betwixt them, but this is nothing else but a concurrence of the same passions. If an animal intends to truck, as it were, or gain anything from man, it is by its fondness and kindness. Man, in the same manner, works on the self love of his fellows, by setting before them a sufficient temptation to get what he wants. The language of this disposition is, 'Give me what I want, and you shall have what you want.' It is not from benevolence, as the dogs, but from self love that man expects anything. The brewer and the baker serve us not from benevolence, but from self love. No man but a beggar depends on benevolence, and even they would die in a week were their entire dependence upon it.

By this disposition to barter and exchange the surplus of one's labour for that of other people, in a nation of hunters, if any one has a talent for making bows and arrows better than his neighbours, he will at first make presents of them, and in return get presents of their game. By continuing this practice he will live better than before, and will have no occasion to provide for himself as the surplus of his own labour does it more effectually.

This disposition to barter is by no means founded upon different genius and talents. It is doubtful if there be any such difference at all, at least it is far less than we are aware of. Genius is more the effect of the division of labour than the latter is of it. The difference between a porter and a philosopher in the first four or five years of their life is, properly speaking, none at all. When they come to be employed in different occupations, their views widen and differ by degrees. As every one has this natural disposition to truck and barter, by which he provides for himself, there is no need for such different endowments; and accord-ingly, among savages there is always the greatest uniformity of character. In other animals of the same species we find a much greater difference than betwixt the philosopher and porter, antecedent to custom. The

mastiff and spaniel have quite different powers, but though these animals
are possessed of talents they cannot, as it were, bring them into the
common stock and exchange their productions, and therefore their different talents are of no use to them. It is quite otherwise among mankind;
they can exchange their several productions according to their quantity
or quality; the philosopher and the porter are both of advantage to each
other. The porter is of use in carrying burdens for the philosopher, and
in his turn he burns his coals cheaper by the philosopher's invention of
the fire machine.

Thus we have shown that different genius is not the foundation of this
disposition to barter which is the cause of the division of labour. The
real foundation of it is that principle to persuade which so much prevails
in human nature. When any arguments are offered to persuade, it is
always expected that they should have their proper effect. If a person
asserts anything about the moon, thought it should not be true, he will
feel a kind of uneasiness in being contradicted, and would be very glad
that the person he is endeavouring to persuade should be of the same way
of thinking with himself. We ought then mainly to cultivate the power of
persuasion, and indeed we do so without intending it. Since a whole life
is spent in the exercise of it, a ready method of bargaining with each other
must undoubtedly be attained. As was before observed, no animal can
do this but by gaining the favour of those whom they would persuade.
Sometimes, indeed, animals seem to act in concert, but there never is
anything like bargain among them. Monkeys, when they rob a garden,
throw the fruit from one to another, till they deposit it in the hoard, but
there is always a scramble about the division of the booty, and usually
some of them are killed.

6. *That the Division of Labour must be proportioned to the Extent of
   Commerce.*

From all that has been said we may observe that the division of labour
must always be proportioned to the extent of commerce. If ten people
only want a certain commodity, the manufacture of it will never be so
divided as if a thousand wanted it. Again, the division of labour, in order
to opulence, becomes always more perfect by the easy method of conveyance in a country. If the road be infested with robbers, if it be deep
and conveyance not easy, the progress of commerce must be stopped.
Since the mendings of roads in England forty or fifty years ago, its
opulence has increased extremely. Water carriage is another convenience,
as by it 300 ton can be conveyed at the expense of the tear and wear of
the vessel, and the wages of five or six men, and that too in a shorter time
than by a hundred wagons which will take six horses and a man each.
Thus the division of labour is the great cause of the increase of public
opulence, which is always proportioned to the industry of the people, and

not to the quantity of gold and silver, as is foolishly imagined, and the industry of the people is always proportioned to the division of labour.

Having thus shown what gives occasion to public opulence, in farther considering this subject we propose to consider:

First, what circumstances regulate the price of commodities:

Secondly, money in two different views, first as the measure of value, and then as the instrument of commerce.

Thirdly, the history of commerce, in which shall be taken notice of the causes of the slow progress of opulence, both in ancient and modern times, which causes shall be shown either to affect agriculture or arts and manufactures:

Lastly, the effects of a commercial spirit, on the government, temper, and manners of a people, whether good or bad, and the proper remedies. Of these in order.

7. *What Circumstances regulate the Price of Commodities.*

Of every commodity there are two different prices, which though apparently independent, will be found to have a necessary connexion, viz. the natural price and the market price. Both of these are regulated by certain circumstances. When men are induced to a certain species of industry, rather than any other, they must make as much by the employment as will maintain them while they are employed. An arrow-maker must be sure to exchange as much surplus product as will maintain him during as long time as he took to make them. But upon this principle in the different trades there must be a considerable difference, because some trades, such as those of the tailor and weaver, are not learned by casual observation and a little experience, like that of the day-labourer, but take a great deal of time and pains before they are acquired. When a person begins them, for a considerable time his work is of no use to his master or any other person, and therefore his master must be compensated, both for what maintains him and for what he spoils. When he comes to exercise his trade, he must be repaid what he has laid out, both of expenses and of apprentice fee, and as his life is not worth above ten or twelve years' purchase at most, his wages must be high on account of the risk he runs of not having the whole made up. But again, there are many arts which require more extensive knowledge than is to be got during the time of an apprenticeship. A blacksmith and weaver may learn their business well enough without any previous knowledge of mathematics, but a watchmaker must be acquainted with several sciences in order to undertake his business well, such as arithmetic, geometry, and astronomy with regard to the equation of time, and their wages must be high in order to compensate the additional expense. In general, this is the case in all the liberal arts, because after they have spent a long time in their education, it is ten to one if ever they make anything by it. Their wages therefore must be higher in proportion to the expense they have been at, the risk of not living long enough, and the risk of not having dexterity enough to manage their business. Among the lawyers there is not one among twenty that attains such knowledge and dexterity in his business as enables him to get back the expenses of his education, and many of them never make the price of their gown, as we say. The fees of lawyers are so far from being extravagant, as they are generally thought, that they are rather low in proportion. It is the eminence of the profession, and not the money made by it, that is the temptation for applying to it, and the dignity of that rank is to be considered as a part of what is made by it.

In the same manner we shall find that the price of gold and silver is not extravagant, if we consider it in this view, for in a gold or silver mine there is a great chance of missing it altogether. If we suppose an equal number of men employed in raising corn and digging silver, the former will make more than the latter, because perhaps of forty or fifty employed in a mine, only twenty make anything at all. Some of the rest may indeed make fortunes, but every corn man succeeds in his undertakings, so that upon the whole there is more made this way than the other. It is the ideal acquisition which is the principal temptation in a mine.

A man then has the natural price of his labour, when it is sufficient to maintain him during the time of labour, to defray the expense of education, and to compensate the risk of not living long enough, and of not succeeding in the business. When a man has this, there is sufficient encouragement to the labourer, and the commodity will be cultivated in proportion to the demand.

The market price of goods is regulated by quite other circumstances. When a buyer comes to the market, he never asks of the seller what expenses he has been at in producing them. The regulation of the market price of goods depends on the three following articles:—

First, the demand, or need for the commodity. There is no demand for a thing of little use; it is not a rational object of desire.

Secondly, the abundance or scarcity of the commodity in proportion to the need of it. If the commodity be scarce, the price is raised, but if the quantity be more than is sufficient to supply the demand, the price falls. Thus it is that diamonds and other precious stones are dear, while iron, which is much more useful, is so many times cheaper, though this depends principally on the last cause, viz:—

Thirdly, the riches or poverty of those who demand. When there is not enough produced to serve everybody, the fortune of the bidders is the only regulation of the price. The story which is told of the merchant and the carrier in the deserts of Arabia is an evidence of this. The merchant gave 10,000 ducats for a certain quantity of water. His fortune here regulated the price, for if he had not had them, he could not have given them, and if his fortune had been less, the water would have been cheaper. When the commodity is scarce, the seller must be content with that degree of wealth which they have who buy it. The case is much the same as in an auction. If two persons have an equal fondness for a book, he whose fortune is largest will carry it. Hence things that are very rare go always to rich countries. The King of France only could purchase that large diamond of so many thousand pounds value. Upon this principle, everything is dearer or cheaper according as it is the purchase of a higher or lower set of people. Utensils of gold are comeatable only by persons in certain circumstances. Those of silver fall to another set of people, and their prices are regulated by what majority can give. The prices of corn and beer are regulated by what all the world can give, and on this account the wages of the day-labourer have a great influence upon the price of corn. When the price of corn rises, wages rise also, and *vice versa;* when the quantity of corn falls short, as in a sea-voyage, it always occasions a famine, and then the price becomes enormous. Corn then becomes the purchase of a higher set of people, and the lower must live on turnips and potatoes.

Thus we have considered the two prices, the natural and the market price, which every commodity is supposed to have. We observed before that however seemingly independent they appear to be, they are necessarily connected. This will appear from the following considerations. If the market price of any commodity is very great, and the labour very highly rewarded, the market is prodigiously crowded with it, greater quantities of it are produced, and it can be sold to the inferior ranks of people. If for every ten diamonds there were ten thousand, they would become the purchase of everybody, because they would become very cheap, and would sink to their natural price. Again, when the market is overstocked, and there is not enough got for the labour of the manufacture, nobody will bind to it, they cannot have a subsistence by it, because the market price falls then below the natural price. It is alleged that as the price of corn sink(s), the wages of the labourer should sink, as he is then better rewarded. It is true that if provisions were long cheap, as more people would flock to this labour where the wages are high, through this concurrence of labour, wages would come down, but we find that when the price of corn is doubled, the wages continue the same as before, because the labourers have no other way to turn themselves. The same is the case with menial servants.

From the above we may observe that whatever police tends to raise the market price above the natural, tends to diminish public opulence. Dearness and scarcity are in effect the same thing. When commodities are in abundance, they can be sold to the inferior ranks of people, who can afford to give less for them, but not if they are scarce. So far, therefore, as goods are a conveniency to the society, the society lives less happy when only the few can possess them. Whatever therefore keeps goods above their natural price for a permanency, diminishes (a) nation's opulence. Such are

First, all taxes upon industry, upon leather, and upon shoes, which people grudge most, upon salt, beer, or whatever is the strong drink of the country, for no country wants some kind of it. Man is an anxious animal, and must have his care swept off by something that can exhilarate the spirits. It is alleged that this tax upon beer is an artificial security against drunkenness, but if we attend to it, (we shall find) that it by no means prevents it. In countries where strong liquors are cheap, as in France and Spain, the people are generally sober, but in northern countries, where they are dear, they do not get drunk with beer, but with spirituous liquors; nobody presses his friend to a glass of beer, unless he choose it.

Secondly, monopolies also destroy public opulence. The price of the monopolized goods is raised above what is sufficient for encouraging the labour. When only a certain person or persons have the liberty of import- ing a commodity, there is less of it imported than would otherwise be; the price of it is therefore higher, and fewer people supported by it. It is the concurrence of different labourers which always brings down the price. In monopolies, such as the Hudson's Bay and East India companies, the people engaged in them make the price what they please.

Thirdly, exclusive privileges of corporations have the same effect. The butchers and bakers raise the price of their goods as they please, because none but their own corporation is allowed to sell in the market, and therefore their meat must be taken, whether good or not. On this account there is always required a magistrate to fix the prices. For any free commodity, such as broad cloth, there is no occasion for this, but it is necessary with bakers, who may agree among themselves to make the quantity and price what they please. Even a magistrate is not a good enough expedient for this, as he must always settle the price at the out- side, else the remedy must be worse than the disease, for nobody would apply to these businesses, and a famine would ensue. On this account bakers and brewers have always profitable trades.

As what raises the market price above the natural one diminishes public opulence, so what brings it down below it has the same effect.

It is only upon manufactures to be exported that this can usually be done by any law or regulation, such as bounty allowed by the govern- ment upon coarse linen, by which it becomes exportable, when under twelve pence a yard. The public paying a great part of the price, it can be sold cheaper to foreigners than what is sufficient for encouraging the labour. In the same manner, by the bounty of five shillings upon the quarter of corn when sold under forty shillings, as the public pays an eighth part of the price, it can be sold just so much cheaper at a foreign market. By this bounty the commodity is rendered more comeatable, and a greater quantity of it produced, but then it breaks what may be called the natural balance of industry. The disposition to apply to the production of that commodity is not proportioned to the natural cause of the demand, but to both that and the annexed bounty. It has not only this effect with regard to the particular commodity, but likewise people are called from other productions which are less encouraged, and thus the balance of industry is broken.

Again, after the ages of hunting and fishing, in which provisions were the immediate produce of their labour, when manufactures were introduced, nothing could be produced without a great deal of time. It was a long time before the weaver could carry to the market the cloth which he bought in flax. Every trade therefore requires a stock of food, clothes, and lodging to carry it on. Suppose then, as is really the case in every country, that there is in store a stock of food, clothes, and lodging, the number of people that are employed must be in proportion to it. If the price of one commodity is sunk below its natural price, while another is above it, there is a smaller quantity of the stored stock left to support the whole. On account of the natural connexion of all trades in the stock, by allowing bounties to one you take away the stock from the rest. This has been the real consequence of the corn bounty.

The price of corn being sunk, the rent of the farms sinks also, yet the bounty upon corn, which was laid on at the time of the taxes, was intended to raise the rent, and had the effect for some time, because the tenants were assured of a price for their corn, both at home and abroad. But though the effects of the bounty encouraging agriculture brought down the price of corn, yet it raised the grass farms, for the more corn the less grass. The price of grass being raised, butchers' meat, in consequence of its dependence upon it, must be raised also, so that if the price of corn is diminished, the price of other commodities is necessarily raised. The price of corn has indeed fallen from forty-two to thirty-five, but the price of hay has risen from twenty-five to near fifty shillings. As the price of hay has risen, horses are not so easily kept, and therefore the price of carriage has risen also. But whatever increases the price of carriage diminishes plenty in the market. Upon the whole, therefore, it is by far the best police to leave things to their natural course, and allow no bounties, nor impose taxes on commodities.

Thus we have shown what circumstances regulate the price of commodities which was the first thing proposed.

8. *Of Money as the Measure of Value and Medium of Exchange.*

We come now to the second particular, to consider money, first as the measure of value and then as the medium of permutation or exchange. When people deal in many species of goods, one of them must be considered as the measure of value. Suppose there were only three commodities, sheep, corn, and oxen, we can easily remember them comparatively, but if we have a hundred different commodities, there are ninety-nine values of each arising from a comparison with each of the rest. As these cannot easily be remembered, men naturally fall upon one of them to be a common standard with which they compare all the rest. This will naturally at first be the commodity with which they are best acquainted. Accordingly we find that black cattle and sheep were the standard in Homer's time. The armour of one of his heroes was worth nine oxen, and that of another worth an hundred. Black cattle was the common standard in ancient Greece. In Italy, and particularly in Tuscany, everything was compared with sheep, as this was their principal commodity. This is what may be called the natural measure of value. In like manner there were natural measures of quantity, such as fathoms, cubits, inches, taken from the proportion of the human body, once in use with every nation. But by a little observation they found that one man's arm was longer or shorter than another's, and that one was not to be compared with the other, and therefore wise men who attended to these things would endeavour to fix upon some more accurate measure, that equal quantities might be of equal values. This method became absolutely necessary when people came to deal in many commodities, and in great quantities of them. Though an inch was altogether inconsiderable when their dealings were confined to a few yards, more accuracy was required when they came to deal in some thousands. We find, in countries where their dealings are small, the remains of this inaccuracy. The cast of the balance is nothing thought of in their coarse commodities.

Since, then, there must of necessity be a common standard of which equal quantities should be of equal values, metals in general seemed best to answer this purpose, and of these the value of gold and silver could best be ascertained. The temper of steel cannot be precisely known, but what degree of alloy is in gold and silver can be exactly found out. Gold and silver were therefore fixed upon as the most exact standard to compare goods with, and were therefore considered as the most proper measure of value.

*   *   *   *   *

9. *That National Opulence does not consist in Money.*

We have shown what rendered money the measure of value, but it is to be observed that labour, not money, is the true measure of value. National opulence consists therefore in the quantity of goods, and the facility of barter. This shall be next considered.

The more money that is necessary to circulate the goods of any country, the more is the quantity of goods diminished. Suppose that the whole stock of Scotland in corn, cattle, money, &c. amounts to twenty millions, and if one million cash is necessary to carry on the circulation, there will be in the country only nineteen millions of food, clothes, and lodging, and the people have less by one million than they would have if there were no occasion for this expedient of money. It is therefore evident that the poverty of any country increases as the money increases, money being a dead stock in itself, supplying no convenience of life. Money in this respect may be compared to the high roads of a country, which bear neither corn nor grass themselves, but circulate all the corn and grass in the country. If we could find any way to save the ground taken up by highways, we would increase considerably the quantity of commodities, and have more to carry to the market. In the same manner as (the worth of) a piece of ground does not lie in the number of highways that run through it, so the riches of a country does not consist in the quantity of money employed to circulate commerce, but in the great abundance of the necessaries of life. If we could therefore fall on a method to send the half of our money abroad to be converted into goods, and at the same time supply the channel of circulation at home, we would greatly increase the wealth of the country.

Hence the beneficial effects of the erection of banks and paper credit. It is easy to show that the erection of banks is of advantage to the commerce of a country. Suppose as above that the whole stock of Scotland amounted to twenty millions, and that two millions are employed in the circulation of it, (and) the other eighteen are in commodities. If then the banks in Scotland issued out notes to the value of two millions, and reserved among them £300,000 to answer immediate demands, there would be one million seven hundred thousand pounds circulating in cash, and two millions of paper money besides. The natural circulation however is two millions and the channel will receive no more. What is over will be sent abroad to bring home materials for food, clothes, and lodging. That this has a tendency to enrich a nation may be seen at first sight, for whatever commodities are imported, just so much is added to the opulence of the country. The only objection against paper money is that it drains the country of gold and silver, that bank notes will not circulate in a foreign market, and that foreign commodities must be paid in specie. This is no doubt the case; but if we consider it attentively we will find that this is no real hurt to a country. The opulence of a nation does not consist in the quantity of coin, but in the abundance of commodities which are necessary for life, and whatever tends to increase these tends so far to increase the riches of a country.

Money is fit for none of the necessaries of life. It cannot of itself afford either food, clothes, or lodging, but must be exchanged for commodities fit for these purposes. If all the coin of the nation were exported, and our commodities proportionably increased, it might be recalled on any sudden emergency sooner than anyone could well imagine. Goods will always bring in money, and as long as the stock of commodities in any nation increases, they have it in their power to augment the quantity of coin, if thought necessary, by exporting their stock to foreign countries. This reasoning is confirmed by matter of fact. We find that the commerce of every nation in Europe has been prodigiously increased by the erection of banks. In this country everybody is sensible of their good effects, and our American colonies, where most of the commerce is carried on by paper circulation, are in a most flourishing condition.

* * * * *

10. *Of Prohibiting the Exportation of Coin.*

* * * * *

11. *Of the Balance of Trade.*

The idea of public opulence consisting in money has been productive of other bad effects. Upon this principle most pernicious regulations have been established. Those species of commerce which drain us of our money are thought disadvantageous, and those which increase it beneficial, therefore the former are prohibited and the latter encouraged. As France is thought to produce more of the elegancies of life than this country, and as we take much from them, and they need little from us, the balance of trade is against us, and therefore almost all our trade with France is prohibited by great taxes and duties on importation. On the other hand, as Spain and Portugal take more of our commodities than we of theirs, the balance is in our favours, and this trade is not only allowed, but encouraged. The absurdity of these regulations will appear on the least reflection. All commerce that is carried on betwixt any two countries must necessarily be advantageous to both. The very intention of commerce is to exchange your own commodities for others which you think will be more convenient for you. When two men trade between themselves it is undoubtedly for the advantage of both. The one has perhaps more of one species of commodities than he has occasion for, he therefore exchanges a certain quantity of it with the other, for another commodity that will be more useful to him. The other agrees to the bargain on the same account, and in this manner the mutual commerce is advantageous to both. The case is exactly the same betwixt any two nations. The goods which the English merchants want to import from France are certainly more valuable to them than what they give for them. Our very desire to purchase them shows that we have more use for them than either the money or the commodities which we give for them. It may be said indeed that money lasts for ever, but that claret and cambrics are soon consumed. This is true: but what is the intention of industry if it be not to produce those things which are capable of being used, and are conducive to the convenience and comfort of human life? Unless we use the produce of our industry, unless we can subsist more people in a better way, what avails it? Besides, if we have money to spend upon foreign commodities, what purpose serves it to keep it in the country? If the circulation of commodities require it, there will be none to spare; and if the channel of circulation be full, no more is necessary. And if only a certain sum be necessary for that purpose, why throw more into it?

Again, by prohibiting the exportation of goods to foreign markets, the industry of the country is greatly discouraged. It is a very great motive to industry, that people have it in their power to exchange the produce of their labour for what they please, and wherever there is any restraint on people in this respect, they will not be so vigorous in improving manufactures. If we be prohibited to send corn and cloth to France, that industry is stopped which raises corn and prepares cloth for the French market. It may be said indeed that if we were allowed to trade with France we would not exchange our commodities with theirs, but our money, and thus human industry is by no means discouraged; but if we attend to it, we shall find that it comes to the same thing at last. By hindering people to dispose of their money as they think proper, you discourage those manufactures by which this money is gained. All jealousies therefore between different nations, and prejudices of this kind, are extremely (hurtful) to commerce, and limit public opulence. This is always the case betwixt France and us in the time of war.

In general we may observe that these jealousies and prohibitions are most hurtful to the richest nations, and that in proportion as a free commerce would be advantageous. When a rich man and a poor man deal with one another, both of them will increase their riches, if they deal prudently, but the rich man's stock will increase in a greater proportion than the poor man's. In like manner when a rich and a poor nation engage in trade, the rich nation will have the greatest advantage, and therefore the prohibition of this commerce is most hurtful to it of the two. All our trade with France is prohibited by the high duties imposed on every French commodity imported. It would, however, have been better police to encourage our trade with France. If any foreign commerce is to be prohibited, it ought to be that with Spain and Portugal. This would have been most advantageous to England. France is much more populous, a more extensive country, farther advanced in arts and manufactures of every kind, and the industry which a commerce with that country would have excited at home would have been much greater. Twenty millions of people perhaps in a great society, working as it were to one another's hands, from the nature of the division of labour before explained, would produce a thousand times more goods than another society consisting only of two or three millions. It were happy therefore, both for this country and for France, that all national prejudices were rooted out, and a free and uninterrupted commerce established.

It may be observed in general that we never heard of any nation ruined by this balance of trade. When Gee published his book, the balance with all nations was against us, except Spain and Portugal. It was then thought that in a few years we would be reduced to an absolute state of poverty. This indeed has been the cry of all political writers since the time of Charles II; notwithstanding all this, we find ourselves far richer than before, and, when there is occasion for it, we can raise much more money than ever has been done. A late minister of state levied in one year twenty-three millions with greater ease than Lord Godolphin could levy six in Queen Anne's time. The French and Dutch writers, embracing the same principle, frequently alarmed their country with the same groundless terror, but they still continue to flourish. It is to be observed that the poverty of a nation can never proceed from foreign trade if carried on with wisdom and prudence. The poverty of a nation proceeds from much the same causes with those which render an individual poor. When a man consumes more than he gains by his industry, he must impoverish himself unless he has some other way of subsistence. In the same manner, if a nation consume more than it produces, poverty is inevitable; if its annual produce be ninety millions and its annual consumption an hundred, then it spends, eats, and drinks, tears, wears, ten millions more than it produces, and its stock of opulence must gradually (go) to nothing.

12. *Of the Opinion that no Expense at Home can be hurtful.*

There is still another bad effect proceeding from that absurd notion, that national opulence consists in money. It is commonly imagined that whatever people spend in their own country cannot diminish public opulence, if you take care of exports and imports. This is the foundation of Dr. Mandeville's system that private vices are public benefits: what is spent at home is all spent among ourselves, none of it goes out of the country. But it is evident that when any man tears, and wears, and spends his stock, without employing himself in any species of industry, the nation is at the end of the year so much the poorer by it. If he spend only the interest of the money he does no harm, as the capital still remains, and is employed in promoting industry, but if he spend the capital, the whole is gone. To illustrate this let us make a supposition, that my father at his death, instead of a thousand pounds in cash, leaves me the necessaries and conveniences of life to the same value, which is precisely the same as if he left it in money, because I afterwards purchase them in money. I get a number of idle folks about me and eat, drink, tear, and wear, till the whole is consumed. By this, I not only reduce myself to want, but certainly rob the public stock of a thousand pounds, as it is spent and nothing produced for it. As a farther illustration of the hurt which the public receives from such practices, let us suppose that this island was invaded by a numerous band of Tartars, a people who are still in the state of shepherds, a people who lead a roving life, and have little or no idea of industry. Here they would find all commodities for the taking, they would put on fine clothes, eat, drink, tear, and wear everything they laid their hands upon. The consequence would be that from the highest degree of opulence the whole country would be reduced to the lowest pitch of misery, and brought back to its ancient state. The thirty millions of money would probably remain for some time, but all the necessaries of life would be consumed. This shows the absurdity of that opinion that no home consumption can hurt the opulence of a country.

Upon this principle that no public expense employed at home can be hurtful, a war in Germany is thought a dreadful calamity, as it drains the country of money, and a land war is always thought more prejudicial than a sea one for the same reason; but upon reflection, we will find that it is the same thing to the nation, how or where its stock be spent. If I purchase a thousand pounds' worth of French wines, and drink them all when they come home, the country is two thousand pounds poorer, because both the goods and money are gone; if I spend a thousand pounds worth of goods at home upon myself the country is only deprived of one thousand pounds, as the money still remains; but in maintaining an army in a distant war it is the same thing whether we pay them in goods or money, because the consumption is the same at any rate. Perhaps it is the better police to pay them in money, as goods are better fitted for the purposes of life at home. For the same reason there is no difference between land and sea wars, as is commonly imagined.

From the above considerations it appears that Britain should by all means be made a free port, that there should be no interruptions of any kind made to foreign trade, that if it were possible to defray the expenses of government by any other method, all duties, customs, and excise should be abolished, and that free commerce and liberty of exchange should be allowed with all nations, and for all things.

But still further, and on the same principles as above, an apology is made for the public debt. Say they, though we (owe) at present above a hundred millions, we owe it to ourselves, or at least very little of it to foreigners. It is just the right hand owing the left, and on the whole can be little or no disadvantage. But (it) is to be considered that the interest of this hundred millions is paid by industrious people, and given to support idle people who are employed in gathering it. Thus industry is taxed to support idleness. If the debt had not been contracted, by prudence and economy the nation would have been much richer than at present. Their industry would not be hurt by the oppression of those idle people who live upon it. Instead of the brewer paying taxes which are often improper, the stock might have been lent out to such industrious people as would have made six or seven per cent by it, and have given better interest than the government does: this stock would then have been employed for the country('s) welfare. When there are such heavy taxes to pay, every merchant must carry on less trade than he would otherwise do; he has his taxes to pay before he sell any of his commodities. This narrows, as it were, his stock, and hinders his trade from being so extensive as it otherwise would be. To stop this clamour, Sir Robert Walpole endeavoured to show that the public debt was no inconvenience, though it is to be supposed that a man of his abilities saw the contrary himself.

13. *Of the Scheme of Mr. Law.*

* * * *

14. *Of Interest.*

We have only two things further to mention relating to the price of commodities, to wit, interest and exchange.

It is commonly supposed that the premium of interest depends upon the value of gold and silver. The value of these are regulated by their quantity, for as the quantity increases, the value diminishes, and as the quantity decreases, the value rises. If we attend to it, however, we shall find that the premium of interest is regulated by the quantity of stock. About the time of the discovery of the West Indies it is to be observed that common interest was at 10 or 12 per cent, and since that time it has gradually diminished. The plain reason is this. Under the feudal constitution there could be very little accumulation of stock, which will appear from considering the situation of those three orders of men, which made up the whole body of the people: the peasants, the landlords, and the merchants. The peasants had leases which depended upon the caprice of their masters; they could never increase in wealth, because the landlord was ready to squeeze it all from them, and therefore they had no motive to acquire it. As little could the landlords increase their wealth, as they lived so indolent a life, and were involved in perpetual wars. The merchants again were oppressed by all ranks, and were not able to secure the produce of their industry from rapine and violence. Thus there could be little accumulation of wealth at all; but after the fall of the feudal government these obstacles to industry were removed, and the stock of commodities began gradually to increase.

We may further observe that what one trade lends to another is not so much to be considered as money, as commodities. No doubt it is generally money which one man delivers another in loan, but then it is immediately turned into stock, and thus the quantity of stock enabled you to make a greater number of loans. The price of interest is entirely regulated by this circumstance. If there be few who have it in their power to lend money, and a great number of people who want to borrow it, the price of interest must be high; but if the quantity of stock on hand be so great as to enable a great number to lend, it must fall proportionably.

15. *Of Exchange.*

* * * * *

16. *Of the Causes of the slow Progress of Opulence.*

We come now to the next thing proposed, to examine the causes of the slow progress of opulence. When one considers the effects of the division of labour, what an immediate tendency it has to improve the arts, it appears somewhat surprising that every nation should continue so long in a poor and indigent state as we find it does. The causes of this may be considered under these two heads: first, natural impediments; and secondly, the oppression of civil government.

A rude and barbarous people are ignorant of the effects of the division of labour, and it is long before one person, by continually working at different things, can produce any more than is necessary for his daily subsistence. Before labour can be divided some accumulation of stock is necessary; a poor man with no stock can never begin a manufacture. Before a man can commence farming, he must at least have laid in a year's provision, because he does not receive the fruits of his labour till the end of the season. Agreeably to this, in a nation of hunters or shepherds no person can quit the common trade in which he is employed, and which affords him daily subsistence, till he have some stock to maintain him, and begin the new trade. Every one knows how difficult it is, even in refined society, to raise one's self to moderate circumstances. It is still more difficult to raise one's self by those trades which require no art nor ingenuity. A porter or day-labourer must continue poor for ever. In the beginnings of society this is still more difficult. Bare subsistence is almost all that a savage can procure, and having no stock to begin upon, nothing to maintain him but what is produced by the exertion of his own strength, it is no wonder he continues long in an indigent state. The meanest labourer in a polished society has in many respects an advantage over a savage: he has more assistance in his labour; he has only one particular thing to do, which, by assiduity, he attains a facility in performing; he has also machines and instrument which greatly assist him. An Indian has not so much as a pickaxe, a spade, or a shovel, nor anything else but his own labour. This is one great cause of the slow progress of opulence in every country; till some stock be produced there can be no division of labour, and before a division of labour takes place there can be very little accumulation of stock.

The other cause that was assigned was the nature of civil government. In the infancy of society, as has been often observed, government must be weak and feeble, and it is long before its authority can protect the industry of individuals from the rapacity of their neighbours. When people find themselves every moment in danger of being robbed of all they possess, they have no motive to be industrious. There could be little accumulation of stock, because the indolent, which would be the greatest number, would live upon the industrious, and spend whatever they produced. When the power of government becomes so great as to defend the produce of industry, another obstacle arises from a different quarter. Among neighbouring nations in a barbarous state there are perpetual wars, one continually invading and plundering the other, and though private property be secured from the violence of neighbours, it is in danger from hostile invasions. In this manner it is next to impossible that any accumulation of stock can be made. It is observable that among savage nations there are always more violent convulsions than among those farther advanced in refinement. Among the Tartars and Arabs, great bands of barbarians are always roaming from one place to another in quest of plunder, and they pillage every country as they go along. Thus large tracts of country are often laid waste, and all the effects carried away. Germany too was in the same condition about the fall of the Roman Empire; nothing can be more an obstacle to the progress of opulence.

We shall next consider the effect of oppressive measures, first, with regard to agriculture, and then with regard to commerce.

Agriculture is of all other arts the most beneficent to society, and whatever tends to retard its improvement is extremely prejudicial to the public interest. The produce of agriculture is much greater than that of any other manufacture. The rents of the whole lands in England amount to about 24 millions, and as the rent is generally about a third of the produce, the whole annual produce of the lands must be about 72 millions. This is much more than the produce of either the linen or woollen manufactures, for, as the annual consumption is computed to be about 100 millions, if you deduce from this the 72 millions, the produce of agriculture, there will remain only 28 millions for all the other manufactures of the nation. Whatever measures therefore discourage the improvement of this art are extremely prejudicial to the progress of opulence.

* * * * *

The slow progress of arts and commerce is owing to causes of a like kind. In all places where slavery took place, the manufactures were carried on by slaves. It is impossible that they can be so well carried on by slaves as by freemen, because they can have no motive to labour but the dread of punishment, and can never invent any machine for facilitating their business. Freemen who have a stock of their own, can get anything accomplished which they think may be expedient for carrying on labour. If a carpenter think that a plane will serve his purpose better than a knife, he may go to a smith and get it made; but if a slave make any such proposal he is called a lazy rascal, and no experiments are made to give him ease. At present the Turks and Hungarians work mines of the same kind, situated upon opposite sides of the same range of mountains, but the Hungarians make a great deal more of them than the Turks, because they employ free men, while the Turks employ slaves. When the Hungarians meet with any obstacle every invention is on work to find out some easy way of surmounting it; but the Turks think of no other expedient but to set a greater number of slaves to work. In the ancient world, as the arts were all carried on by slaves, no machinery could be invented, because they had no stock; after the fall of the Roman Empire, too, this was the case all over Europe.

* * * * *

All taxes upon exportation and importation of goods also hinder commerce. Merchants at first were in so contemptible a state that the law, as it were, abandoned them, and it was no matter what they obliged them to pay. They, however, must lay the tax upon their goods, their price is raised, fewer of them are bought, manufactures are discouraged, and the division of labour hindered.

All monopolies and exclusive privileges of corporations, for whatever good ends they were at first instituted, have the same bad effect. In like manner the statute of apprenticeship, which was originally an imposition on government, has a bad tendency. It was imagined that the cause of so much bad cloth was that the weaver had not been properly educated, and therefore they made a statute that he should serve a seven years apprenticeship before he pretended to make any. But this is by no means a sufficient security against bad cloth. You yourself cannot inspect a large piece of cloth, this must be left to the stampmaster, whose credit must be depended upon. Above all other causes the giving bounties for one commodity, and the discouraging another, diminishes the concurrence of opulence, and hurts the natural state of commerce.

JEAN BAPTISTE SAY

(1767–1832)

Jean Baptiste Say was a Frenchman whose life covered the interesting periods of the French Revolution, the Napoleonic era, the Restoration of the Bourbons, and the Revolution of 1830. He was a business man, a soldier, a journalist, an important political figure in his troubled times, and a member of the First Tribunate in 1799. After his early editorial experiences, Say became manager of a cotton mill for a number of years. Finally he turned economist and gave one of the first courses of lectures on political economy, ever given in France, and after the accession of Louis Philippe, he was made a professor of political economy at the College of France.

The works of Say included: "A Treatise on Political Economy" (1803); "A Catechism of Political Economy" (1817); "A Complete Course in Practical Political Economy," in six volumes (1828–29).

Say is commonly classified as the continental disciple of Adam Smith and is regarded as the founder of the French classical school, just as Ricardo may be said to have founded the English classical school. Nevertheless, he made numerous important original contributions, including Say's law. In the famous arguments with Sismondi, he naturally took the position that a general overproduction was an impossibility. Just as Ricardo made the landlord the center of his economic system, so Say made the *entrepreneur* the center of his economic philosophy. Perhaps this may be attributed to his early business experiences.

The following selection is taken from Say's "A Treatise on Political Economy," (3d American Ed., 1827). Note that Say regarded immaterial services as wealth, a different position from that of the English classicists. On the other hand, there is the same opposition to governmental regulation of business as characterized Adam Smith. It is particularly important that the student scrutinize Say's analysis of the nature and sources of demand.

JEAN BAPTISTE SAY

SELECTIONS FROM "A TREATISE ON POLITICAL ECONOMY"

BOOK I. OF THE PRODUCTION OF WEALTH

Chapter I. Of What Is to Be Understood by the Term, Production

If we take the pains to inquire what that is, which mankind in a social state of existence denominate wealth, we shall find the term employed to designate an indefinite quantity of objects bearing inherent value, as of land, of metal, of coin, of grain, of stuffs, of commodities of every description. When they further extend its signification to landed securities, bills, notes of hand, and the like, it is evidently because they contain obligations to deliver things possessed of inherent value. In point of fact, wealth can only exist where there are things possessed of real and intrinsic value.

Wealth is proportionate to the quantum of that value: great, when the aggregate of component value is great; small, when that aggregate is small.

The value of a specific article is always vague and arbitrary, so long as it remains unacknowledged. Its owner is not a jot the richer, by setting a higher ratio upon it in his own estimation. But the moment that other persons are willing, for the purpose of obtaining it, to give in exchange a certain quantity of other articles, likewise bearing value, the one may then be said to be worth, or to be of equal value with, the other.

The quantity of money, which is readily parted with to obtain a thing, is called its *price*. *Current price*, at a given time and place, is that price which the owner is sure of obtaining for a thing, if he is inclined to part with it.

The knowledge of the real nature of wealth, thus defined, of the difficulties that must be surmounted in its attainment, of the course and order of its distribution amongst the members of society, of the uses to which it may be applied, and, further, of the consequences resulting respectively from these several circumstances, constitutes that branch of science now entitled Political Economy.

The value that mankind attach to objects originates in the use it can make of them. Some afford sustenance; others serve for clothing; some defend them from the inclemencies of the season, as houses; others gratify their taste, or, at all events, their vanity, both of which are species of wants: of this class are all mere ornaments and decorations. It is universally true, that, where men attribute value to any thing, it is in consideration of its useful properties: what is good for nothing they set no price upon. To this inherent fitness or capability of certain things to satisfy the various wants of mankind, I shall take leave to affix the name of utility. And I will go on to say, that, to create objects which have any kind of utility, is to create wealth; for the utility of things is the ground-work of their value, and their value constitutes wealth.

Objects, however, can not be created by human means; nor is the mass of matter, of which this globe consists, capable of increase or diminution. All that man can do is, to re-produce existing materials under another form, which may give them an utility they did not before possess, or merely enlarge one they may have before presented. So that, in fact, there is a creation, not of matter, but of utility; and this I call *production of wealth.*

In this sense then, the word production must be understood in political economy, and throughout the whole course of the present work. Production is the creation, not of matter, but of utility. It is not to be estimated by the length, the bulk, or the weight of the product, but by the utility it presents.

Although price is the measure of the value of things, and their value the measure of their utility, it would be absurd to draw the inference, that, by forcibly raising their price, their utility can be augmented. Exchangeable value, or price, is an index of the recognised utility of a thing, so long as human dealings are exempt from every influence but that of the identical utility: in like manner as a barometer denotes the weight of the atmosphere, only while the mercury is submitted to the exclusive action of atmospheric gravity.

In fact, when one man sells any product to another, he sells him the utility vested in that product: the buyer buys it only for the sake of its utility, of the use he can make of it. If, by any cause whatever, the buyer is obliged to pay more than the value to himself of that utility, he pays for value that has no existence, and consequently which he does not receive.

This is precisely the case, when authority grants to a particular class of merchants the exclusive privilege of carrying on a certain branch of trade, the India trade for instance; the price of Indian imports is thereby raised, without any accession to their utility or intrinsic value. This excess of price is nothing more or less than so much money transferred from the pockets of the consumers into those of the privileged traders, whereby the latter are enriched exactly as much as the former are unnecessarily impoverished. In like manner, when a government imposes on wine a tax, which raises to 15 *sous* the bottle what would otherwise be sold for 10 *sous,* what does it else, but transfer 5 *sous* per bottle from the hands of the producers or the consumers of wine to those of the tax-gatherer? The particular commodity is here only the means resorted to for getting at the tax-payer with more or less convenience; and its current value is composed of two ingredients, *viz.* 1. Its real value originating in its utility: 2. The value of the tax that the government thinks fit to exact, for permitting its manufacture, transport, or consumption.

Wherefore, there is no actual production of wealth, without a creation or augmentation of utility. Let us see in what manner this utility is to be produced.

Chapter XIII. Of Immaterial Products, or Values Consumed at the Moment of Production

A physician goes to visit a sick person, observes the symptoms of disease, prescribes a remedy, and takes his leave without depositing any product, that the invalid or his family can transfer to a third person, or even keep for the consumption of a future day.

Has the industry of the physician been unproductive? Who can for a moment suppose so? The patient's life has been saved perhaps. Was this product incapable of becoming an object of barter? By no means; the physician's advice has been exchanged for his fee; but the want of this advice ceased the moment it was given. The act of giving was its production, of hearing its consumption; and the consumption and production were simultaneous.

This is what I call an immaterial product.

The industry of a musician or an actor yields a product of the same kind: it gives one an amusement, a pleasure one can not possibly retain or preserve for future consumption, or as the object of barter for other enjoyments. This pleasure has its price it is true: but it has no further existence, except perhaps in the memory, and no exchangeable value, after the instant of its production.

Smith will not allow the name of products to the results of these branches of industry. Labour so bestowed he calls unproductive; an error he was led into by his definition of wealth, which he defines to consist of things bearing a value capable of being preserved, instead of extending the name to all things bearing exchangeable value: consequently, excluding products consumed as soon as created. The industry of the physician, however, as well as that of the public functionary, the advocate or the judge, which are all of them of the same class, satisfies wants of so essential a nature, that without those professions no society could exist. Are not, then, the fruits of their labour real? They are so far as to be purchased at the price of other and material products, which Smith allows to be wealth;

and by the repetition of this kind of barter, the producers of immaterial products acquire fortunes.

Chapter XV. Of the Vent or Demand for Products

It is common to hear adventurers in the different channels of industry assert, that their difficulty lies not in the production, but in the disposal of commodities; that produce would always be abundant, if there were but a ready demand, or vent. When the vent for their commodities is slow, difficult, and productive of little advantage, they pronounce money to be scarce; the grand object of their desire is, a consumption brisk enough to quicken sales and keep up prices. But ask them what peculiar causes and circumstances facilitate the demand for their products and you will soon perceive that most of them have extremely vague notions of these matters; that their observation of facts is imperfect, and their explanation still more so; that they treat doubtful points as matter of certainty, often pray for what is directly opposite to their interests, and importunately solicit from authority a protection of the most mischievous tendency.

To enable us to form clear and correct practical notions, in regard to the vents for the products of industry, we must carefully analyse the best established and most certain facts, and apply to them the inferences we have already deduced from a similar way of proceeding; and thus perhaps we may arrive at new and important truths, that may serve to enlighten the views of the agents of industry, and to give confidence to the measures of governments anxious to afford them encouragement.

A man, who applies his labour to the investing of objects with value by the creation of utility of some sort, can not expect that the value to be appreciated and paid for, unless where other men have the means of purchasing it. Now, of what do these means consist? Of other values, of other products, likewise the fruit of industry, capital, and land. Which leads us to a conclusion, that may at first sight appear paradoxical; viz: that it is production which opens a demand for products.

Should a tradesman say, "I do not want other products for my woollens, I want money," there could be little difficulty in convincing him, that his customers can not pay him in money, without having first procured it by the sale of some other commodities of their own. "Yonder farmer, he may be told, will buy your woollens, if his crops be good, and will buy more or less according to their abundance or scantiness; he can buy none at all, if his crops fail altogether. Neither can you buy his wool or his corn yourself, unless you contrive to get woollens or some other article to buy withal. You say, you only want money; I say, you want other commodities, and not money. For what, in point of fact, do you want the money? Is it not for the purchase of raw materials or stock for your trade, or victuals for your support? Wherefore, it is products that you want, and not money. The silver coin you will have received on the sale of your own products, and given in the purchase of those of other people, will the next moment execute the same office between other contracting parties, and so from one to another to infinity; just as a public vehicle successively transports objects one after another. If you can not find a ready sale for your commodity, will you say, it is merely for want of a vehicle to transport it? For after all, money is but the agent of the transfer of values. Its whole utility has consisted in conveying to your hands the value of the commodities, which your customer has sold, for the purpose of buying again from you; and the very next purchase you make, it will again convey to a third person the value of the products you may have sold to others. So that you will have bought, and every body must buy, the objects of want or desire, each with the value of his respective products transformed into money for the moment only. Otherwise, how could it be possible, that there should now be bought and sold in France five or six times as many commodities, as in the miserable reign of Charles VI? Is it not obvious, that five or six times as many commodities must have been produced, and that they must have served to purchase one or the other?

Thus, to say that sales are dull, owing to the scarcity of money, is to mistake the means for the cause; an error that proceeds from the circumstances, that almost all produce is in the first instance exchanged for money, before it is ultimately converted into other produce: and the commodity, which recurs so repeatedly in use, appears to vulgar apprehensions the most important of commodities, and the end and object of all transactions, whereas it is only the medium. Sales can not be said to be dull because money is scarce, but because other products are so. There is always money enough to conduct the circulation and mutual interchange of other values, when those values really exist. Should the increase of traffic require more money to facilitate it, the want is easily supplied, and is a strong indication of prosperity—a proof that a great abundance of values has been created, which it is wished to exchange for other values. In such cases, merchants know well enough how to find substitutes for the product serving as the medium of exchange or money: and money itself soon pours in, for this reason, that all produce naturally gravitates to that place where it is most in demand. It is a good sign when the business is too great for the money; just in the same way as it is a good sign when the goods are too plentiful for the warehouses.

When a superabundant article can find no vent, the scarcity of money has so little to do with the obstruction of its sale, that the sellers would gladly receive its value in goods for their own consumption at the current price of the day: they would not ask for money, or have any occasion for that product, since the only use they could make of it would be to convert it forth-with into articles of their own consumption.

This observation is applicable to all cases, where there is a supply of commodities or of services in the market. They will universally find the most extensive demand in those places, where the most values are produced; because in no other places are the sole means of purchase created, *i.e.* values. Money performs but a monentary function in this double exchange; and when the transaction is finally closed, it will always be found, that one kind of produce has been exchanged for another.

It is worth while to remark, that a product is no sooner created, than it, from that instant, affords a market for other products to the full extent of its own value. When the producer has put the finishing hand to his product, he is most anxious to sell it immediately, lest its value should vanish in his hands. Nor is he less anxious to dispose of the money he may get for it; for the value of money is also perishable. But the only way of getting rid of money is in the purchase of some product or other. Thus, the mere circumstance of the creation of one product immediately opens a vent for other products.

For this reason, a good harvest is favourable, not only to the agriculturist, but likewise to the dealers in all commodities generally. The greater the crop, the larger are the purchases of the growers. A bad harvest, on the contrary, hurts the sale of commodities at large. And so it is also with the products of manufacture and commerce. The success of one branch of commerce supplies more ample means of purchase, and consequently opens a vent for the products of all the other branches; on the other hand, the stagnation of one channel of manufacture, or of commerce is felt in all the rest.

But it may be asked, if this be so, how does it happen, that there is at times so great a glut of commodities in the market, and so much difficulty in finding a vent for them? Why can not one of these superabundant commodities be exchanged for another? I answer, that the glut of a particular commodity arises from its having outrun the total demand for it in one of two ways; either because it has been produced in excessive abundance, or because the produce of other commodities has fallen short.

It is because the production of some commodities has declined, that other commodities are superabundant. To use a more hackneyed phrase, people have bought less, because they have made less profit; and they have made less profit for one of two causes; either they have found difficulties in the employment of their productive means, or these means have themselves been deficient.

It is observable, moreover, that precisely at the same time that one commodity makes a loss, another commodity is making excessive profit. And since such profits must operate as a powerful stimulus to the cultivation of that particular kind of produce, there must needs be some violent means, or some extraordinary cause, a political or natural convulsion, or the avarice or ignorance of authority, to perpetuate this scarcity on the one hand, and consequent glut on the other. No sooner is the cause of this political disease removed, than the means of production feel a natural impulse towards the vacant channels, the replenishment of which restores activity to all the others. One kind of production would seldom outstrip the rest, and its products be disproportionately cheapened, were production left entirely to itself.

Should a producer imagine, that many other classes, yielding no material products, are his customers and consumers equally with the classes that raise themselves a product of their own; as, for example, public functionaries, physicians, lawyers, churchmen, &c., and thence infer, that there is a class of demand other than that of the actual producers, he would but expose the shallowness and superficiality of his ideas. A priest goes to a shop to buy a gown or a surplice; he takes the value, that is to make the purchase, in the form of money. Whence had he that money? From some tax-gatherer who has taken it from a tax-payer. But whence did this latter derive it? From the value he has himself produced. This value, first produced by the tax-payer, and afterwards turned into money, and given to the priest for his salary, has enabled him to make the purchase. The priest stands in the place of the producer, who might himself have laid the value of his product on his own account, in the purchase, perhaps, not of a gown or surplice, but of some other more serviceable product. The consumption of the particular product, the gown or surplice, has but supplanted that of some other product. It is quite impossible that the purchase of one product can be effected, otherwise than by the value of another.

From this important truth may be deduced the following important conclusions:—

1. That, in every community the more numerous are the producers, and the more various their productions, the more prompt, numerous, and extensive are the vents for those productions; and, by a natural consequence, the more profitable are they to the producers; for price rises with the demand. But this advantage is to be derived from real production alone, and not from a forced circulation of products; for a value once created is not augmented in its passage from one hand to another, nor by being seized and expended by the government, instead of by an individual. The man, that lives upon the productions of other people, originates no demand for those productions; he merely puts himself in the place of the producer, to the great injury of production, as we shall presently see.

2. That each individual is interested in the general prosperity of all, and that the success of one branch of industry promotes that of all the others. In fact, whatever profession or line of business a man may devote himself to, he is the better paid and the more readily finds employment,

in proportion as he sees others thriving equally around him. A man of talent, that scarcely vegetates in a retrograde state of society, would find a thousand ways of turning his faculties to account in a thriving community that could afford to employ and reward his ability. A merchant established in a rich and populous town, sells to a much larger amount than one who sets up in a poor district, with a population sunk in indolence and apathy. What could an active manufacturer, or an intelligent merchant, do in a small deserted and semi-barbarous town in a remote corner of Poland or Westphalia? Though in no fear of a competitor, he could sell but little, because little was produced; whilst at Paris, Amsterdam, or London, in spite of the competition of a hundred dealers in his own line, he might do business on the largest scale. The reason is obvious: he is surrounded with people who produce largely in an infinity of ways, and who make purchases, each with his respective products, that is to say, with the money arising from the sale of what he may have produced.

This is the true source of the gains made by the towns' people out of the country people, and again by the latter out of the former; both of them have wherewith to buy more largely, the more ample they themselves produce. A city, standing in the centre of a rich surrounding country, feels no want of rich and numerous customers; and, on the other side, the vicinity of an opulent city gives additional value to the produce of the country. The division of nations into agricultural, manufacturing, and commercial, is idle enough. For the success of a people in agriculture is a stimulus to its manufacturing and commercial prosperity; and the flourishing condition of its manufacture and commerce reflects a benefit upon its agriculture also.

The position of a nation, in respect of its neighbours, is analogous to the relation of one of its provinces to the others, or of the country to the town; it has an interest in their prosperity, being sure to profit by their opulence. The government of the United States, therefore, acted most wisely, in their attempt, about the year 1802, to civilize their savage neighbours, the Creek Indians. The design was to introduce habits of industry among them, and make them producers, capable of carrying on a barter trade with the States of the Union; for there is nothing to be got by dealing with a people that have nothing to pay. It is useful and honourable to mankind; that one nation among so many should conduct itself uniformly upon liberal principles. The brilliant results of this enlightened policy will demonstrate, that the systems and theories really destructive and fallacious are the exclusive and jealous maxims acted upon by the old European governments, and by them most impudently styled *practical truths,* for no other reason, as it would seem, than because they have the misfortune to put them in practice. The United States will have the honour of proving experimentally, that true policy goes hand in hand with moderation and humanity.

3. From this fruitful principle, we may draw this further conclusion, that it is no injury to the internal or national industry and production to buy and import commodities from abroad; for nothing can be bought from strangers, except with native products, which find a vent in this external traffic. Should it be objected, that this foreign produce may have been bought with specie, I answer, specie is not always a native product, but must have been bought itself with the products of native industry; so that, whether the foreign articles be paid for in specie or in home produce, the vent for national industry is the same in both cases.

4. The same principle leads to the conclusion, that the encouragement of mere consumption is no benefit to commerce; for the difficulty lies in supplying the means, not in stimulating the desire of consumption; and we have seen, that production alone, furnishes those means. Thus it is the aim of good government to stimulate production, of bad government to encourage consumption.

For the same reason, that the creation of a new product is the opening of a new vent for other products, the consumption or destruction of a product is the stoppage of a vent for them. This is no evil, where the end of the products has been answered by its destruction, which end is the satisfying of some human want, or the creation of some new product designed for such a satisfaction. Indeed, if the nation be in a thriving condition, the gross national reproduction exceeds the gross consumption. The consumed products have fulfilled their office, as it is natural and fitting they should; the consumption, however, has opened no new vent, but just the reverse.

Having once arrived at the clear conviction, that the general demand for produce is brisk in proportion to the activity of production, we need not trouble ourselves much to inquire towards what channel of industry production may be most advantageously directed. The products created give rise to various degrees of demand, according to the wants, the manners, the comparative capital, industry, and natural resources of each country; the article most in request, owing to the competition of buyers, yield the best interest of money to the capitalist, the largest profits to the adventurer, and the best wages to the labourer; and the agency of their respective services is naturally attracted by these advantages towards those particular channels.

In a community, city, province, or nation, that produces abundantly, and adds every moment to the sum of its products, almost all the branches of commerce, manufacture, and generally of industry, yield handsome profits, because the demand is great, and because there is always a large quantity of produce in the market, ready to bid for new productive services. And, *vice versa*, wherever, by reason of the blunders of the nation or its government, production is stationary, or does not keep pace with consumption, the demand gradually declines; the value of the products is less than the charges of their production; no productive exertion is properly rewarded; profits and wages decrease; the employment of capital becomes less advantageous and more hazardous; it is consumed piecemeal, not through extravagance, but through necessity, and because the sources of profit are dried up. The labouring classes experience a want of work; families before in tolerable circumstances, are more cramped and confined; and those before in difficulties, are left altogether destitute. Depopulation, misery, and returning barbarism, occupy the place of abundance and happiness.

Such are the concomitants of declining production, which are only to be remedied by frugality, intelligence, activity, and freedom.

Chapter XVI. Of the Benefits Resulting from the Brisk Circulation of Money and Commodities

It is common to hear people descant upon the benefits of an active circulation; that is to say, of numerous and rapid sales. It is material to appreciate them correctly.

The values engaged in actual production can not be realised and employed in production again, until arrived at the last stage of completion, and sold to the consumer. The sooner a product is finished off and sold, the sooner also can the portion of capital vested in it be applied to the business of fresh production. The capital being engaged a shorter time, there is less interest payable to the capitalist; there is a saving in the charges of production; it is, therefore, an advantage, that the successive operations performed in the course of production should be rapidly executed.

By way of illustrating the effects of this activity of circulation, let us trace them in the instance of a piece of printed calico.

A Lisbon trader imports the cotton from Brazil. It is his interest, that his factors in America be expeditious in making purchases and remitting cargoes, and likewise, that he meet no delay in selling his cotton to a French merchant; because he thereby gets his returns the sooner, and can sooner recommence a new and equally lucrative operation. So far, it is Portugal that benefits by the increased activity of circulation; the subsequent advantage is on the side of France. If the French merchant keep the Brazil cotton but a short time in his warehouse, before he sells it to the cotton spinner, if the spinner after spinning sell it immediately to the weaver, if the weaver dispose of it forthwith to the calico printer, and he in his turn sell it without much delay to the retail dealer, from whom it quickly passes to the consumer, this rapid circulation will have occupied for a shorter period the capital embarked by these respective producers; less interest of capital will have been incurred; consequently, the prime cost of the article will be lower, and the capital will have been the sooner disengaged and applicable to fresh operations.

All these different purchases and sales with many others that, for brevity's sake, I have not noticed, were indispensable before the Brazil cotton could be worn in the shape of printed calicoes. They are so many productive fashions given to this product; and the more rapidly they may have been given, the more benefit will have been derived from the production. But, if the same commodity be merely sold several times over in a year in the same place without undergoing any fresh modification, this circulation would be a loss instead of a gain, and would increase, instead of reducing the prime cost to the consumer. A capital must be employed in buying and re-selling, and interest paid for its use, to say nothing of the probable wear and tear of the commodity.

Thus, jobbing in merchandise necessarily causes a loss, either to the jobber, if the price be not raised by transaction, or to the consumer, if it be raised.

The activity of circulation is at the utmost pitch to which it can be carried with advantage, when the product passes into the hands of a new productive agent the instant it is fit to receive a new modification, and is ultimately handed over to the consumer, the instant it has received the last finish. All kind of activity and bustle not tending to this end, far from giving additional activity to circulation, is an impediment to the course of production,—an obstacle to circulation by all means to be avoided.

With respect to the rapidity of production arising from the more skilful direction of industry, it is an increase of rapidity, not in circulation, but in productive energy. The advantage is analogous; it abridges the occupation of capital.

I have made no distinction between the circulation of goods and of money, because there really is none. While a sum of money lies idle in a merchant's coffers, it is an inactive portion of his capital, precisely of the same nature, as that part of his capital which is lying in his warehouse in the shape of goods ready for sale.

The best stimulus of useful circulation is, the natural wish of all classes, especially the producers themselves, to incur the least possible amount of interest upon the capital embarked in their respective undertakings. Circulation is much more apt to be interrupted by the obstacles thrown in its way, than by the want of proper encouragement. Its greatest obstructions are, wars, embargoes, oppressive duties, the dangers and difficulties of transport. It flags in times of alarm and uncertainty, when social order is threatened, and all undertakings are hazardous. It flags too, under the general dread of arbitrary exactions, when every one tries to conceal the extent of his ability. Finally, it flags in times of of jobbing and speculation, when the sudden fluctuations caused by gambling in produce make people look for a profit from every variation of mere relative price: goods are then held back in expectation of a rise, and money in the prospect of a fall; and, in the interim, both these capitals remain inactive and useless to production. Under such circumstances, there is no circulation, but of such produce as can not be kept without danger of deterioration; as fruits, vegetables, grain, and all articles that spoil in the keeping. With regard to them, it is thought wiser to incur the loss of present sale, whatever it be, than to risk considerable or total loss. If the national money be deteriorated, it becomes an object to get rid of it in any way, and exchange it for commodities. This was one of the causes of the prodigious circulation that took place during the progressive depreciation of the French *assignats*. Every body was anxious to find some employment for a paper currency, whose value was hourly evaporating; it was only taken to be re-invested immediately, and one might have supposed it burnt the fingers it passed through. On that occasion, men plunged into commerce, of which they were utterly ignorant; manufactures were established, houses repaired and furnished, no expense was spared even in pleasure; until at length all the value each individual possessed in *assignâts* was finally consumed, invested, or lost altogether.

Chapter XVII. Of the Effect of Government Regulations Intended to Influence Production

Strictly speaking, there is no act of government but what has some influence upon production. I shall confine myself in this chapter to such as are avowedly aimed at the exertion of such influence; reserving the effects of the monetary system, of loans, and of taxes, to be treated of in distinct chapters.

The object of governments, in their attempts to influence production, is, either to prescribe the raising of particular kinds of produce, which they judge more advantageous than others, or to prescribe methods of production, which they imagine preferable to other methods. The effects of this two-fold attempt upon national wealth will be investigated in the two first sections of this chapter: in the remaining two, I shall apply the same principles to the particular cases of privileged companies, and of the corn-trade, both on account of their vast importance, and for the purpose of further explaining and illustrating the principles. We shall see by the way, what reasons and circumstances will require or justify a deviation from general principles. The grand mischiefs of authoritative interference proceed not from occasional exceptions to established maxims, but from false ideas of the nature of things, and the false maxims built upon them. It is then that mischief is done by wholesaie, and evil pursued upon system: for it is well to beware, that no set of men are more bigoted to system, than those who boast that they go upon none.

SECTION I. EFFECT OF REGULATIONS PRESCRIBING THE NATURE OF PRODUCTS

The natural wants of society, and its circumstances for the time being, occasion a more or less lively demand for particular kinds of produce. Consequently, in these branches of production, productive services are somewhat better paid than in the rest; that is to say, the profits upon land, capital, and labour, devoted to those branches of production, are somewhat larger. This additional profit naturally attracts producers, and thus the nature of the products is always regulated by the wants of society. We have seen, in a preceding chapter (xv.), that these wants are more ample in proportion to the sum of gross production, and that society in the aggregate is a larger purchaser, in proportion to its means of purchasing.

When authority throws itself in the way of this natural course of things, and says, the product you are about to create, that which yields the greatest profit, and is consequently the most in request, is by no means the most suitable to your circumstances; you must undertake some other; it evidently directs part of the productive energies of the nation towards an object of less desire, at the expense of another object of more urgent desire.

In France, about the year 1794, there were some persons persecuted, and even brought to the scaffold, for having converted corn-land into pasturage. Yet, the moment these unhappy people found it more profitable to feed cattle than to grow corn, one might have been sure, that society stood more in need of cattle than of grain, and that greater value could be produced in one way than in the other.

But, said the public authorities, the value produced is of less importance than the nature of the product, and we would rather have you raise 50 *fr.* worth of grain than 100 of butcher's meat. In this they betrayed their ignorance of this simple truth, that the greatest product is always the best; and that an estate, which should produce in butcher's meat wherewith to purchase twice as much wheat as could have been raised upon it, produces, in reality, twice as much wheat as if it had been sowed with grain; since wheat to twice the amount is to be got for its produce. This way of getting wheat, they will tell you, does not increase its total quantity. True, unless it be introduced from abroad; but nevertheless, this article must at the time be relatively more plentiful than butcher's meat, because the produce of two acres of wheat is given for that of one acre of pasture. And, if wheat be sufficiently scarce, and in sufficient request to make tillage more profitable than grazing, legislative interference is superfluous altogether; for self-interest will make the producer turn his attention to the former.

The only question then is, which is the most likely to know what kind of cultivation yields the largest returns, the cultivator or the government; and we may fairly take it for granted, that the cultivator, residing on the spot, making it the object of constant study and inquiry, and more interested in success than any body, is better informed in this respect than the government.

Should it be insisted upon in argument, that the cultivator knows only the price-current of the day, and does not, like the government, provide for the future wants of the people, it may be answered, that one of the talents of a producer, and a talent his own interest obliges him assiduously to cultivate, is not the mere knowledge, but the fore-knowledge of human wants.

An evil of the same description was occasioned, when, at another period the proprietors were compelled to cultivate beet-root, or woad, in lieu of grain: indeed, we may observe, *en passant*, that it is always a bad speculation to attempt raising the products of the torrid, under the sun of the temperate latitudes. The saccharine and colouring juices, raised on the European soils with all the forcing in the world, are very inferior in quantity and quality to those that grow in profusion in other climates: while, on the other hand, those soils yield abundance of grain and fruits too bulky and heavy to be imported from a distance. In condemning our lands to the growth of products ill-suited to them, instead of those they are better calculated for, and, consequently, buying very dear what we might have cheap enough, if we would consent to receive them from places where they are produced with advantage, we are ourselves the victims of our own absurdity. It is the very *acmé* of skill, to turn the powers of nature to the best account, and the height of madness to content against them; which is in fact wasting part of our strength, in destroying those powers she designed for our aid.

Again, it is laid down as a maxim, that it is better to buy produce dear, when the price remains in the country, than to get it cheap from foreign growers. On this point I must refer my readers to that analysis of production which we have just gone through. It will there be seen, that products are not to be obtained without some sacrifice,—without the consumption of substances and productive agency in some ratio or other, the value of which is in this way as completely lost to the community, as if it were to be exported.

I can hardly suppose any government will be bold enough to object, that it is indifferent about the profit, which might be derived from a more advantageous production, because it would fall to the lot of individuals. The worst governments, those which set up their own interest in the most direct opposition to that of their subjects, have by this time learnt, that the revenues of individuals are the regenerating source of public revenue; and that, even under despotic and military sway, where taxation is mere organized spoliation, the subjects can pay only what they have themselves acquired.

The maxims we have been applying to agriculture accord equally with manufacture. Sometimes a government entertains a notion, that the manufacture of a native raw material is better for the national industry, than the manufacture of a foreign raw material. It is in conformity to this notion, that we have seen instances of preference given to the woollen and linen above the cotton manufacture. By this conduct we contrive, as far as in us lies, to limit the bounty of nature, who pours forth in different climates a variety of materials adapted to our innumerable wants. Whenever human efforts succeed in attaching to these gifts of nature a value, that is to say, a degree of utility, whether by their import, or by any modification we may subject them to, an useful act is performed, and an item added to national wealth. The sacrifice we make to foreigners in procuring the raw material is not a whit more to be regretted, than the sacrifice of advances and consumption, that must be made in every branch of production, before we can get a new product. Personal interest is, in all cases, the best judge of the extent of the sacrifice, and of the indemnity we may expect for it; and, although this guide may sometimes mislead us, it is the safest in the long run, as well as the least costly.

But personal interest is no longer a safe criterion, if individual interests are not left to counteract and control each other. If one individual, or one class, can call in the aid of authority to ward off the effects of competition, it acquires a privilege to the prejudice and at the cost of the whole community; it can then make sure of profits not altogether due to the productive services rendered, but composed in part of an actual tax upon consumers for its private profit; which tax it commonly shares with the authority, that thus unjustly lends its support.

The legislative body has great difficulty in resisting the importunate demands for this kind of privileges; the applicants are the producers that are to benefit thereby, who can represent, with much plausibility, that their own gains are a gain to the industrious classes, and to the nation at large, their workmen and themselves being members of the industrious classes, and of the nation.

When the cotton manufacture was first introduced in France, all the merchants of Amiens, Rheims, Beauvais, &c. joined in loud remonstrances, and represented, that the industry of these towns was annihilated. Yet they do not appear less industrious or rich than they were fifty years ago; while the opulence of Rouen and all Normandy has been wonderfully increased by the new fabric.

The outcry was infinitely greater, when printed calicoes first came into fashion; all the chambers of commerce were up in arms; meetings, debates, were every where held; memorials and deputations poured in from every quarter, and great sums were spent in the opposition. Rouen now stood forward to represent the misery about to assail her, and painted, in moving colours, "old men, women, and children, rendered destitute; the best cultivated lands in the kingdom lying waste, and the whole of a rich and beautiful province depopulated." The city of Tours urged the lamentations of the deputies of the whole kingdom, and foretold "a commotion that would shake the frame of social order itself." Lyons could not view in silence a project "which filled all her manufactories with alarm." Never on so important an occasion had Paris presented itself at the foot of a throne, "watered with the tears of commerce." Amiens viewed the introduction of printed calicoes as the gulf, that must inevitably swallow up all the manufactures of the kingdom. The memorial of that city, drawn up at a joint meeting of the three corporations, and signed unanimously, ended in these terms: 'To conclude, it is enough for the eternal prohibition of the use of printed calicoes, that the whole kingdom is chilled with horror at the news of their proposed toleration. *Vox populi, vox dei.*'

Hear what Roland de la Platiére, who had the presentation of these remonstrances in quality of inspector-general of manufactures, says on this subject, 'Is there a single individual at the present moment, who is mad enough to deny, that the fabric of printed calicoes employs an immense number of hands, what with the dressing of cotton, the spinning, weaving, bleaching, and printing? This article has improved the art of dyeing in a few years, more than all the other manufactures together have done in a century.'

I must beg my readers to pause a moment, and reflect, what firmness and extensive information respecting the sources of public prosperity were necessary to uphold an administration against so general a clamour, supported, amongst the principal agents of authority, by other motives, besides that of public utility.

Though governments have too often presumed upon their power to benefit the general wealth, by prescribing to agriculture and manufacture the raising of particular products, they have interfered much more particularly in the concerns of commerce, especially of external commerce. These bad consequences have resulted from a general system, distinguished by the name of the *exclusive* or *commercial system*, which attributes the profits of a nation to what is technically called, *a favourable balance of trade*. Before we enter upon the investigation of the real effect of regulations, intended to secure to a nation this balance in its favour, it may be as well to form some notion what it really is, and what is its professed object; which I shall attempt in the following digression upon what is called the balance of trade.

Book II. Of the Distribution of Wealth

Chapter V. Of the Manner in Which Revenue Is Distributed Amongst Society

The causes, which determine the value of things, and which operate in the way described in the preceding chapters, apply without exception to all things possessed of value, however perishable; amongst others, therefore, to the productive service yielded by industry, capital, and land, in a state of productive activity. Those, who have at their disposal any one of these three sources of production, are the venders of what we shall here denominate productive agency; and the consumers of its product are the purchasers. Its relative value, like that of every other commodity, rises in direct ratio to the demand, and inverse ratio to the supply.

The wholesale employers of industry, or adventurers, as they have been called, are but a kind of brokers between the venders and the purchasers, who engage a quantum of productive agency upon a particular product, proportionate to the demand for that product. The farmer, the manufacturer, the merchant, is constantly occupied in comparing the price, which the consumer of a given product will and can give for it, with the necessary charges of its production; if that comparison determine him to produce it, he is the organ of a demand for all the productive agency applicable to this object, and thus furnishes one of the bases of the value of that agency.

On the other hand, the agents of production, animate and inanimate, land, capital, and human labour, are supplied in larger or smaller quantity, according to the action of the various motives, that will be detailed in the succeeding chapters; thus forming the other basis of the value at which their agency is rated.

Every product, when completed, repays by its value the whole amount of productive agency employed in its completion. A great part of this agency has been paid for before the entire completion of the product, and must have been advanced by somebody; other part has been remunerated on its completion; but the whole is always paid for ultimately out of the value of the product.

By way of exemplifying the mode, in which the value of a product is distributed amongst all that have concurred in its production, let us take a watch, and trace from the commencement, the manner in which its smallest parts have been procured, and in which their value has been paid to every one of the infinite number of concurring producers.

In the first place we find, that the gold, copper, and steel, used in its construction, have been purchased of the miner, who has received in exchange for these products, the wages of labour, interest of capital, and rent paid to the landed proprietor.

The dealers in metal, who buy of the original producer, resell to those engaged in watch-making, and are thus reimbursed their advance, and paid the profits of their business into the bargain.

The respective mechanics, who fashion the different parts whereof a watch is composed, sell them to the watchmaker, who, in paying them, refunds the advance of their previous value, together with the interest upon that advance; and pays, besides, the wages of labour hitherto incurred. This very complex operation of payment may be effected by a single sum, equal to the aggregate of those united values. In the same way, the watchmaker deals with the mechanics that furnish the dial plate, the glass, &c., and such ornaments as he may think fit to add,—diamonds, enamel, or any thing he pleases.

Last of all, the individual purchaser of the watch for his own use refunds to the watchmaker the whole of his advances, together with interest on each part respectively, and pays him besides, a profit upon his personal skill and industry.

We find, then, that the total value of the watch has been shared amongst all its producers, perhaps long before it was finished; and those producers are much more numerous than I have described, or than is generally imagined. Among them, probably, may be found the unconscious purchaser himself, who has bought the watch, and wears it in his fob. For who knows but he may have advanced his own capital to a mining adventurer, or a dealer in metal; or to the director of a large factory; or to an individual who acts himself in none of these capacities, but has underlent to one or more such persons a part of the funds he has borrowed at interest from the identical consumer of the watch?

It has been observed, that it is by no means necessary for a product to be perfected for use, before the majority of its concurring producers can have been reimbursed that portion of value they have contributed to its completion; in a great many cases, these producers have even consumed their equivalent long before the product has arrived at perfection. Each successive producer makes the advance to his precursor of the then value of the product, including the labour already expended upon it. His successor in the order of production, reimburses him in turn, with the addition of such value as the product may have received in passing through his hands. Finally, the last producer, who is generally the retail dealer, is compensated by the consumer for the aggregate of all these advances, *plus* the concluding operation performed by himself upon the product.

The whole revenues of the community are distributed in one and the same manner.

That portion of the value produced, which accrues in this manner to the landed proprietor, is called the *profit of land;* which is sometimes transferred to the farmer, in consideration of a fixed rent.

The portion assigned to the capitalist, or person making the advances, however minute and for however short a period of time, is called the *profit of capital;* which capital is sometimes lent, and the profit relinquished on condition of a stipulated interest.

The portion assigned to the mere mechanic or labourer is called the *profit of labour;* which is sometimes relinquished for a fixed salary.

Thus, each class receives its respective share of the total value produced; and this share composes its revenue. Some classes receive their share piecemeal, and consume as fast as they receive it; and these are the most numerous, for they comprise most of the labouring classes. The land-holder and the capitalist, who do not themselves turn their means to account, receive their revenue periodically, once or twice, or perhaps four times a year, according to the terms of the contract with the transferee. But, in whatever manner a revenue may be derived, it is always analogous in its nature, and must originate in actual value produced. Whatever value an individual receives in satisfaction of his wants, without having either directly or indirectly concurred in production of some kind or other, must be wholly either a gratuitous gift or a spoliation; there is no other alternative.

It is in this way, that the total value of products is distributed amongst the members of the community; I say, the *total* value, because such part of the whole value produced, as does not go to one of the concurring producers, is received by the rest. The clothier buys wool of the farmer, pays his workmen in every department, and sells the cloth, the result of their united exertion, at a price that reimburses all his advances, and affords himself a profit. He never reckons as profit, or as the revenue of his own industry, any thing more than the *net* surplus, after deducting all charges and outgoings; but those outgoings are merely an advance of their respective revenues to the previous producers, which are refunded by the *gross* value of the cloth. The price paid to the farmer for his wool is the compound of the several revenues of the cultivator, the shepherd, and the landlord. Although the farmer reckons as *net* produce only the surplus remaining after payment of his landlord and his servants in husbandry, yet to them these payments are items of revenue,—rent to the one and wages to the other; to the one, the revenue of his land, to the other, the revenue of his industry. The aggregate of all these is defrayed out of the value of the cloth, the whole of which forms the revenue of some one or other, and is entirely absorbed in that way.

When it appears, that the term *net* produce applies only to the individual revenue of each separate producer or adventurer in industry; but that the aggregate of an individual revenue, the total revenue of the community, is equal to the *gross* produce of its land, capital, and industry. Which entirely subverts the system of the economists of the last century, who considered nothing but the net produce of the land as forming revenue, and therefore concluded, that this net produce was all that the community had to consume; instead of admitting the obvious inference, that the whole of what has been created, may also be consumed by mankind.

If national revenue consisted of the mere excess of value produced above value consumed, this most absurd consequence would be inevitable; viz. that, where a nation consumes in the year the total of its annual product, it will have no revenue whatever. Is a man possessed of an income of 10,000 *fr.* a year to be said to have no revenue, because he may think proper to spend the whole of it?

The whole amount of profit derived by an individual from his land, capital, and industry, within the year, is called his *annual revenue.* The aggregate of the revenues of all the individuals, whereof a nation consists, is its national revenue. Its sum is the *gross* value of the national product, *minus* the portion exported; for the relation of one nation, is like that of one individual to another. The profits of an individual are limited to the excess of his income above his expenditure, which expenditure, indeed, form the revenue of other persons, but, if those other persons be foreigners, must be reckoned in the estimate of the revenue of the respective nations they may belong to. Thus, for instance, when a consignment of ribbons is made to Brazil to the amount of 10,000 *fr.* and the returns received in cotton, in estimating the resulting product to France from this act of dealing, the export made to Brazil in payment of the cotton must be deducted. Supposing the investment of ribbons to procure, say 40 bales of cotton, which, when they reach France, will fetch 12,000 *fr.,* 2,000 *fr.* only of that sum will go to the revenue of France, and the residue to that of Brazil.

Did all mankind form but one vast nation or community, it would be equally true in respect to mankind at large, as to the internal product of each insulated nation, that the whole gross value of the product would be revenue. But so long as it shall be necessary to consider the human race as split into distinct communities, taking each an independent interest, this circumstance must be taken into the account. Wherefore, a nation, whose imports exceed its exports in value, gains in revenue to the extent of the excess; which excess constitutes the profit of its external commerce. A nation that should export to the value of 100,000 *fr.* and import to the value of 120,000 *fr.* wholly in goods, without any money passing on either side, would make a profit of 20,000 *fr.,* in direct contradiction to the theory of the partisans of the balance of trade.

The voluminous head of perishable products consumed within the year, nay, often at the very moment of production, as in the case of all immaterial products, is nevertheless an item of national revenue. For what are they but so many values produced and consumed in the satisfaction of human wants, which are the sole characteristics of revenue?

The estimation of individual and of national revenue is made in the same way, as that of every collection of values, under whatever varieties of form; as of the estate of a deceased person. Each product is successively valued in money or coin. For instance, the revenues of France are said to amount to 8,000,000,000 *fr.;* which by no means implies, that the commerce of France produces a return of that amount in specie. Probably a very small amount of specie, or none at all, may have been imported. All that is meant by the assertion is, that the aggregate annual products of the nation, valued separately and successively in silver coin, make the total value above stated. The only reason of making the estimate in money is, the greater facility acquired by habit of forming an idea of the unchangeable value of a specific amount of money, than of other commodities. Were it not for that facility, it would be quite as well to make the estimate in corn; and to say, that the revenues of France amounted to 400,000,000 *hectolitres* of wheat, which, at 20 *fr.* the *hectolitre*, would make precisely the same amount.

Money facilitates the circulation from hand to hand of the values composing both revenue and capital; but is itself not an item of annual revenue, not being an annual product, but a product of previous commerce or metallurgy, of a date more or less remote. The same coin has effected the circulation of the former year, possibly of the former century, and has all the while remained the same in amount; nay, if the value of its material have declined in the interim, the nation will even have lost upon its capital existing under the form of money; just in the same way as a merchant would lose upon the fall of price of the goods in his warehouses.

Thus, although the greater part of revenue, that is to say, of value produced, is momentarily resolved into money, the money, the quantity of silver coin itself, is not what constitutes revenue; revenue is value produced, wherewith that quantity of silver coin has been bought; and, as that value assumes the form of money but for a moment, the same identical pieces of money are made use of many times in the course of a year, for the purpose of paying or receiving specific portions of revenue. Indeed, some portions of revenue never assume the form of money at all. The manufacturer, that boards his workmen himself, pays part of their wages in food; so that this far greater portion of the mechanic's revenue is paid, received, and consumed, without having once taken the shape of money, even for an instant. In the United States of America, and in countries similarly circumstanced, it is not uncommon for the colonist to derive from the produce of his own estate, food, lodging, and raiment for the whole of his establishment; receiving and consuming his whole revenue in kind, without any intervention of money whatsoever.

I think I have said enough to warn the reader against confounding the money, into which revenue may be converted, with revenue itself; and to establish a conviction that the revenue of an individual, or of a nation, is not composed of the money received in lieu of the products of his or their creation, but is the actual product or its value, which, by a process of exchange, may undoubtedly arrive at its destination in the shape of a bag of crown pieces, or in any other shape whatsoever.

No value, whether received in the shape of money or otherwise, can form a portion of annual revenue; unless it be the product, or the price of a product, created within the year: all else is capital,—is property passing from one hand to another, either in exchange, as a gift, or by inheritance. For an item of capital, or one of revenue, may be transferred or paid any how, whether in the shape of personal or real, of moveable or immoveable property, or of money. But, no matter what shape it assume, revenue differs from capital essentially in this, that it is the result or product of a pre-existing source, whether land, capital, or industry.

It has with some been a matter of doubt, whether the same value, which has already been received by one individual as the profit or revenue of his land, capital, or industry, can constitute the revenue of a second. For instance, a man receives 100 crowns in part of his personal revenue, and lays it out in books; can this item of revenue, thus converted into books, and in that shape destined to his consumption, further contribute to form the revenue of the printer, bookseller, and all the other concurring agents in the production of the books, and be by them consumed a second time? The difficulty may be solved thus. The value forming the revenue of the first individual, derived from his land, capital, or industry, and by him consumed in the shape of books, was not originally produced in that form. There has been a double production: 1. of corn perhaps by the land and the industry of the farmer, which has been converted into crown pieces, and paid as rent to the proprietor: 2. of books by the capital and industry of the bookseller. The two products have been subsequently interchanged one for the other, and consumed, each by the producer of the other; having arrived at the particular form adapted to their respective wants.

So likewise of immaterial products. The opinion of the lawyer, the advice of the physician, is the product of their respective talents and knowledge, which are their peculiar productive means. If the merchant have occasion to purchase their assistance he gives for it a commercial product of his own converted into money. Each of them ultimately consumes his own revenue respectively, transformed into the object best adapted to his peculiar occasions.

Chapter VII. Of the Revenue of Industry

SECTION II. OF THE PROFITS OF THE MAN OF SCIENCE

The philosopher, the man who makes it his study to direct the laws of nature to the greatest possible benefit of mankind, receives a very small proportion of the products of that industry, which derives such prodigious advantage from the knowledge, whereof he is at the same time the depositary and the promoter. The cause of his disproportionate payment seems to be, that, to speak technically, he throws into circulation, in a moment, an immense stock of his product, which is one that suffers very little by wear; so that it is long before operative industry is obliged to resort to him for a fresh supply.

The scientific acquirements, without which abundance of manufacturing processes could never have been executed, are probably the result of long study, intense reflection and a course of experiments equally ingenious and delicate, that are the joint occupation of the highest degree of chemical, medical and mathematical skill. But the knowledge, acquired with so much difficulty, is probably transmissible in a few pages; and, through the channel of public lectures, or of the press, is circulated in much greater abundance, than is required for consumption; or rather, it spreads of itself, and, being imperishable, there is never any necessity to recur to those, from whom it originally emanated.

Thus, according to the natural laws, whereby the price of things is determined, this superior class of knowledge will be very ill paid: that is to say, it will receive a very inadequate portion of the value of the product, to which it has contributed. It is from a sense of this injustice, that every nation, sufficiently enlightened to conceive the immense benefit of scientific pursuits, has endeavoured, by special favours and flattering distinctions, to indemnify the man of science, for the very trifling profit derivable from his professional occupations, and from the exertion of his natural or acquired faculties.

Sometimes a manufacturer discovers a process, calculated either to introduce a new product, to increase the beauty of an old one, or to produce with greater economy; and, by observance of strict secrecy, may make for many years, for his whole life perhaps, or even bequeath to his children, profits exceeding the ordinary ratio of his calling. In this particular case the manufacturer combines two different operations of industry; that of the man of science, whose profit he engrosses himself, and that of the adventurer too. But few such discoveries can long remain secret; which is a fortunate circumstance for the public, because this secrecy keeps the price of the particular product it applies to above, and the number of consumers enabled to enjoy it below, the natural level.

It is obvious, that I am speaking only of the revenue a man of science derives from his calling. There is nothing to prevent his being at the same time a landed proprietor, capitalist, or adventurer, and possessed of other revenue in these different capacities.

SECTION III. OF THE PROFITS OF THE MASTER-AGENT, OR ADVENTURER, IN INDUSTRY

We shall, in this section, consider only that portion of the profits of the master-agent, or adventurer, which may be considered as the recompense of that peculiar character. If a master-manufacturer have a share of the capital embarked in his concern, he must be ranked *pro tanto* in the class of capitalists, and the benefits thence derived be set down as part of the profits of the capital so embarked.

It very seldom happens, that the party engaged in the management of any undertaking, is not at the same time in the receipt of interest upon some capital of his own. The manager of a concern rarely borrows from strangers the whole of the capital employed. If he have but purchased some of the implements with his own capital, or made advances from his own funds, he will then be entitled to one portion of his revenue in quality of manager, and another in that of capitalist. Mankind are so little inclined to sacrifice any particle of their self-interest, that even those, who have never analyzed these respective rights, know well enough how to enforce them to their full extent in practice.

Our present concern is, to distinguish the portion of revenue, which the adventurer receives as adventurer. We shall see by-and-by, what he, or somebody else, derives in the character of capitalist.

It may be remembered, that the occupation of adventurer is comprised in the second class of operations specified as necessary for the setting in motion of every class of industry whatever; that is to say, the application of acquired knowledge to the creation of a product for human consumption. It will likewise be recollected, that such application is equally necessary in agricultural, manufacturing, and commercial industry; that the labour of the farmer or cultivator on his own account, of the master-manufacturer and of the merchant, all come under this description; they are the adventurers in each department of industry respectively. The nature of the profits of these three classes of men, is what we are now about to consider.

The price of their labour is regulated, like that of all other objects, by the ratio of the supply, or quantity of that labour thrown into circulation, to the demand or desire for it. There are two principal causes operating to limit the supply, which, consequently, maintain at a high rate the price of this superior kind of labour.

It is commonly requisite for the adventurer himself to provide the necessary funds. Not that he must be already rich; for he may work upon borrowed capital; but he must at least be solvent, and have the reputation of intelligence, prudence, probity, and regularity; and must be able, by the nature of his connexions, to procure the loan of capital he may happen himself not to possess. These requisites shut out a great many competitors.

In the second place, this kind of labour requires a combination of moral qualities, that are not often found together. Judgment, perseverance, and a knowledge of the world, as well as of business. He is called upon to estimate, with tolerable accuracy, the importance of the specific product, the probable amount of the demand, and the means of its production: at one time he must employ a great number of hands; at another, buy or order the raw material, collect labourers, find consumers and give at all times a rigid attention to order and economy; in a word, he must possess the art of superintendence and administration. He must have a ready knack of calculation, to compare the charges of production with the probable value of the product when completed and brought to market. In the course of such complex operations, there are abundance of obstacles to be surmounted, of anxieties to be repressed, of misfortunes to be repaired, and of expedients to be devised. Those who are not possessed of a combination of these necessary qualities, are unsuccessful in their undertakings; their concerns soon fall to the ground, and their labour is quickly withdrawn from the stock in circulation; leaving such only, as is successfully, that is to say, skilfully directed. Thus, the requisite capacity and talent limits the number of competitors for the business of adventurers. Nor is this all: there is always a degree of risk attending such undertakings; however well they may be conducted, there is a chance of failure; the adventurer may, without any fault of his own, sink his fortune, and in some measure his character; which is another check to the number of competitors, that also tends to make their agency so much the dearer.

All branches of industry do not require an equal degree of capacity and knowledge. A farmer, who adventures in tillage, is not expected to have such extensive knowledge as a merchant, who adventures in trade with distant countries. The farmer may do well enough with a knowledge of the ordinary routine of two or three kinds of cultivation. But the science necessary for conducting a commerce with long returns is of a much higher order. It is necessary to be well versed, not only in the nature and quality of the merchandise in which the adventure is made, but likewise to have some notion of the extent of demand, and of the markets whither it is consigned for sale. For this purpose, the trader must be constantly informed of the price-current of every commodity in different parts of the world. To form a correct estimate of these prices, he must be acquainted with the different national currencies, and their relative value, or, as it is termed, the rate of exchange. He must know the means of transport, its risk and expense, the custom and laws of the people he corresponds with; in addition to all which, he must possess sufficient knowledge of mankind to preserve him from the dangers of misplaced confidence in his agents, correspondents, and connexions. If the science requisite to make a good farm is more common than that which can make a good merchant, it is not surprising, that the labour of the former is but poorly paid, in comparison with that of the latter.

It is not meant by this to be understood, that commercial industry, in every branch, requires a combination of rarer qualifications than agricultural. The retail dealers for the most part pursue the routine of their business quite as mechanically as the generality of farmers; and, in some kinds of cultivation, very uncommon care and sagacity are requisite. It is for the reader to make the application: the business of the teacher is, firmly to establish general principles; whence it will be easy to draw a multitude of inferences, varied and modified by circumstances, which are themselves the consequences of other principles laid down in other parts of the subject. Thus, in astronomy, when we are told, that all the planets describe equal areas in the same space of time, there is an implied reservation of such derangements, as arise from the proximity of other planets, whose atractive powers depend on another law of natural philosophy; and this must be attended to in the examination of the phenomena of each in particular. It is for him, who would apply general laws to particular and isolated cases, to make allowance for the influence of each of those laws or principles, whose existence is already recognised.

In reviewing presently the profits of mere manual labour, we shall see the peculiar advantage, which his character of master gives to the adventurer over the labourer; but it may be useful to observe by the way the other advantages within reach of an intelligent superior. He is the link of communication, as well between the various classes of producers, one with another, as between the producer and the consumer. He directs the business of production, and is the centre of many bearings and relations; he profits by the knowledge and by the ignorance of other people. and by every accidental advantage of production.

Thus, it is this class of producers, which accumulates the larges fortunes, whenever productive exertion is crowned by unusual success.

PART II

THE MALTHUSIAN CONTROVERSY

1. Benjamin Franklin: (*a*) "Observations concerning the Increase of Mankind and the Peopling of Countries."
   (*b*) "Reflections on the Augmentation of Wages which will be Occasioned in Europe by the American Revolution."

2. William Godwin: (*a*) "Political Justice."
   (*b*) "Population."

3. Thomas Robert Malthus: (*a*) "Essay on Population" (First Edition).
   (*b*) "Essay on Population" (Sixth Edition).
   (*c*) "Principles of Political Economy."
   (*d*) "Definitions in Political Economy."

BENJAMIN FRANKLIN

(1706–1790)

The life of Benjamin Franklin is familiar to all American students. Excellent biographies and complete collections of his works are easily accessible. The best collection of Frankliniana, including most of his original manuscripts, is that of the American Philosophical Society at Philadelphia.

It isinteresting to note that Franklin's fame as a statesman and as a man of letters has overshadowed his reputation as a scientist. Again, within the field of science, his discoveries in the physical sciences have obscured his important contributions to the social sciences. Nevertheless, Benjamin Franklin was the first American economist, as well as the pioneer in many other fields of intellectual and political endeavor. The mark of genius on his broad brow makes us ashamed to quibble about the distinction between pure and applied economics.

Franklin was the intimate friend of various important thinkers among the physiocrats, including Quesnay, Turgot, and many others. Again, he had met, conversed with, and corresponded with equally important figures in the intellectual and political life of Great Britain, including Adam Smith, David Hume, Edmund Burke, and many others. It is interesting to the student of the history of economic thought to note that Franklin anticipated Turgot and Smith in some of their discussions of interest. Even more familiar is Franklin's famous prior statement of the Malthusian law, which, by a curious trick of history, bears the name of the English clergyman rather than that of the American skeptic.

The chief economic works of Franklin were as follows: "A Modest Enquiry into the Nature and Necessity of a Paper Currency" (1729); "Observations concerning the Increase of Mankind and the Peopling of Countries" (1751); "The Interest of Great Britain Considered with regard to Colonies and the Acquisition of Canada and Guadaloupe" (1760); "Remarks and Facts relative to the American Paper Money" (1765); "Comparison of Great Britain and the United States in regard to the bases of Credit in the two Countries" (1777); "On the Paper Money of the United States" (1781); "Reflections on the Augmentation of Wages which will be occasioned in Europe by the American Revolution" (1783); "Internal State of America, being a true description of the Interest and Policy of that vast Continent" (1784); and "Information to those who would Remove to America" (1784).

Credit for the discovery of a law of population, like that for most discoveries, belongs not to one individual but to several. The history of thought is a maze of slow evolution, in which many minds seem to be moving toward the same point from different angles. In this particular case it is interesting to observe that both Franklin (1751) and Malthus (1798) were preceded by the famous French writer, Montesquieu, who stated in his "Spirit of the Laws" (1748) conjectures and observations foreshadowing the famous Malthusian law of population. It is also important to note that Malthus probably had not seen Franklin's small paper on population when his first essay on the same subject was published anonymously in 1798. References to Franklin first appeared in the second edition of Malthus's "Essay on Population," which appeared in 1803, and which differed greatly from the first edition.

In addition to selections from Franklin's "Observations concerning the Increase of Mankind and the Peopling of Countries," selections have been included from his essay entitled "Reflections on the Augmentation of Wages which will be Occasioned in Europe by the American Revolution." Here we see the many sided Franklin, not only as a diplomat and an internationalist, but also as the advocate of the great American gospel of high wages for the workers.

BENJAMIN FRANKLIN

SELECTIONS FROM "OBSERVATIONS CONCERNING THE INCREASE OF MANKIND AND THE PEOPLING OF COUNTRIES"

1. Tables of the proportion of marriages to births, of deaths to births, of marriages to the number of inhabitants, &c., formed on observations made upon the bills of mortality, christenings, &c. of populous cities, will not suit countries; nor will tables formed on observations made on full-settled old countries as Europe, suit new countries as America.

2. For people increase in proportion to the number of marriages, and that is greater in proportion to the ease and convenience of supporting a family. When families can be easily supported, more persons marry, and earlier in life.

3. In cities, where all trades, occupations, and offices are full, many delay marrying till they can see how to bear the charges of a family; which charges are greater in cities, as luxury is more common; many live single during life and continue servants to families, journeymen to trades; hence cities do not, by natural generation, supply themselves with inhabitants; the deaths are more than the births.

4. In countries full settled the case must be nearly the same; all lands being occupied and improved to the height, those who cannot get land must labor for others that have it; when laborers are plenty their wages will be low; by low wages a family is supported with difficulty; this difficulty deters many from marriage, who therefore long continue servants and single. Only as the cities take supplies of people from the country, and thereby make a little more room in the country, marriage is a little more encouraged there, and the births exceed the deaths.

5. Europe is generally full settled with husbandmen, manufacturers, &c., and therefore cannot now much increase in people. America is chiefly occupied by Indians, who subsist mostly by hunting. The hunter, of all men, requires the greatest quantity of land from whence to draw his subsistence (the husbandman subsisting on much less, the gardener on still less, and the manufacturer requiring least of all). The Europeans found America as fully settled as it well could be by hunters; yet these, having large tracts, were easily prevailed on to part with portions of territory to the new comers, who did not much interfere with the natives in hunting, and furnished them with many things they wanted.

6. Land being thus plenty in America, and so cheap as that a laboring man that understands husbandry can in a short time save money enough

to purchase a piece of new land sufficient for a plantation, whereon he may subsist a family, such are not afraid to marry; for, if they even look far enough forward to consider how their children, when grown up, are to be provided for, they see that more land is to be had at rates equally easy, all circumstances considered.

7. Hence, marriages in America are more general, and more generally early than in Europe. And if it is reckoned there that there is but one marriage per annum among one hundred persons, perhaps we may here reckon two; and if in Europe they have but four births to a marriage (many of their marriages being late), we may here reckon eight, of which, if one half grow up, and our marriages are made, reckoning one with another, at twenty years of age, our people must at least be doubled every twenty years.

8. But, notwithstanding this increase, so vast is the territory of North America, that it will require many ages to settle it fully, and, till it is fully settled, labor will never be cheap here, where no man continues long a laborer for others, but gets a plantation of his own; no man continues long a journeyman to a trade, but goes among those new settlers and sets up for himself, &c. Hence labor is no cheaper now in Pennsylvania than it was thirty years ago, though so many thousand laboring people have been imported.

9. The danger, therefore, of these colonies interfering with their mother country in trades that depend on labor, manufactures, &c., is too remote to require the attention of Great Britain.

10. But in proportion to the increase of the colonies, a vast demand is growing for British manufactures, a glorious market wholly in the power of Britain, in which foreigners cannot interfere, which will increase in a short time even beyond her power of supplying, though her whole trade should be to her colonies; therefore, Britain should not too much restrain manufactures in her colonies. A wise and good mother will not do it. To distress is to weaken, and weakening the children weakens the whole family.

11. Besides, if the manufactures of Britain (by reason of the American demands) should rise too high in price, foreigners who can sell cheaper will drive her merchants out of foreign markets; foreign manufactures will thereby be encouraged and increased, and consequently foreign nations, perhaps her rivals in power, grow more populous and more powerful; while her own colonies, kept too low, are unable to assist her, or add to her strength.

12. It is an ill-grounded opinion that, by the labor of slaves, America may possibly vie in cheapness of manufactures with Britain. The labor of slaves can never be so cheap here as the labor of workingmen is in Britain. Any one may compute it. Interest of money is in the colonies from six to ten per cent. Slaves, one with another, cost thirty pounds sterling per

head. Reckon then the interest of the first purchase of a slave, the insurance or risk on his life, his clothing and diet, expenses in his sickness and loss of time, loss by his neglect of business (neglect is natural to the man who is not to be benefited by his own care or diligence), expense of a driver to keep him at work, and his pilfering from time to time, almost every slave being by nature a thief, and compare the whole amount with the wages of a manufacturer of iron or wool in England, you will see that labor is much cheaper there than it ever can be by negroes here. Why, then will Americans purchase slaves? Because slaves may be kept as long as a man pleases, or has occasion for their labor; while hired men are continually leaving their masters (often in the midst of his business) and setting up for themselves (sec. 8).

*   *   *   *   *

22. There is, in short, no bound to the prolific nature of plants or animals, but what is made by their crowding and interfering with each other's means of subsistence. Were the face of the earth vacant of other plants, it might be gradually sowed and overspread with one kind only, as, for instance, it might in a few ages be replenished from one nation only, as for instance, with Englishmen. Thus, there are supposed to be now upwards of one million English souls in North America (though it is thought scarce eighty thousand has been brought over sea), and yet perhaps there is not one the fewer in Britain, but rather many more, on account of the employment the colonies afford to manufacturers at home. This million doubling, suppose but once in twenty-five years, will in another century be more than the people of England, and the greatest number of Englishmen will be on this side of the water. What an accession of power to the British empire by sea as well as land! What increase of trade and navigation! What numbers of ships and seamen! We have been here but little more than one hundred years, and yet the force of our privateers in the late war, united, was greater, both in men and guns, than that of the whole British navy in Queen Elizabeth's time. How important an affair then to Britain is the present treaty for settling the bounds between her colonies and the French, and how careful should she be to secure room enough, since on the room depends so much the increase of her people.

23. In fine, a nation well regulated is like a polypus. Take away a limb, its place is soon supplied; cut it in two, and each deficient part shall speedily grow out of the part remaining. Thus, if you have room and substance enough, as you may by dividing make ten polypuses out of one, you may of one make ten nations, equally populous and powerful, or rather increase a nation ten fold in numbers and strength.

And since detachments of English from Britain, sent to America, will have their places at home so soon supplied and increase so largely here, why should the Palatine boors be suffered to swarm into our settlements, and, by herding together, establish their language and manners, to the exclusion of ours? Why should Pennsylvania, founded by the English, become a colony of aliens, who will shortly be so numerous as to Germanize us, instead of our Anglifying them and will never adopt our language or customs any more than they can acquire our complexion?

24. Which leads me to add one remark, that the number of purely white people in the world is proportionably very small. All Africa is black or tawny; Asia chiefly tawny; America (exclusive of the new comers) wholly so. And in Europe, the Spaniards, Italians, French, Russians, and Swedes are generally of what we call a swarthy complexion; as are the Germans also, the Saxons only excepted, who, with the English, make the principal body of white people on the face of the earth. I could wish their numbers were increased. And while we are, as I may call it, scouring our planet, by clearing America of woods, and so making this side of our globe reflect a brighter light to the eyes of inhabitants in Mars or Venus, why should we, in the sight of superior beings, darken its people? Why increase the sons of Africa by planting them in America, where we have so fair an opportunity, by excluding all blacks and tawnys, of increasing the lovely white and red? But perhaps I am partial to the complexion of my country, for such kind of partiality is natural to mankind.

BENJAMIN FRANKLIN

SELECTIONS FROM "REFLECTIONS ON THE AUGMENTATION OF WAGES WHICH WILL BE OCCASIONED IN EUROPE BY THE AMERICAN REVOLUTION"

The independence and prosperity of the United States of America will raise the price of wages in Europe, an advantage of which I believe no one has yet spoken.

The low rate of wages is one of the greatest defects in the political associations of Europe, or rather of the old world.

If the term *wages* be taken in its widest signification, it will be found that almost all the citizens of a large State receive and pay wages. I shall confine my remarks, however, to one description of wages, the only one with which government should inter-meddle, or which requires its care. I mean the wages of the lowest class, those men without property, without capital, who live solely by the labor of their hands. This is always the most numerous class in a state; and consequently, that cannot be pronounced happy in which, from the lowness and insufficiency of wages, the laboring class procure so scanty a subsistence that, barely able to provide for their own necessities, they have not the means of marrying and rearing a family, and are reduced to beggary whenever employment fails them or age and sickness oblige them to give up work.

Further, the wages under consideration ought not to be estimated by their amount in money, but by the quantity of provisions, clothing, and other commodities which the laborer can procure for the money which he receives.

Unhappily, in all the political states of the old world, a numerous class of citizens have nothing to live upon but their wages, and these are inadequate to their support. This is the real cause of the misery of so many day laborers who work in the fields, or in manufactories in towns; of pauperism, an evil which is spreading every day, more and more, because governments attempt to check it by feeble remedies only; of depravity of morals; and of almost every crime. The policy of tyranny and of commerce has overlooked and disguised these truths. The horrible maxim that the people must be poor, in order that they may remain in subjection, is still held by many persons of hard hearts and perverted understanding, with whom it were useless to contend. Others, again, think that the people should be poor, from a regard of the supposed interests of commerce. They believe that to increase the rate of wages would raise the price of the productions of the soil, and especially of industry, which are sold to foreign nations, and thus that exportation and the profits arising from it would be diminished. But this motive is at once cruel and ill founded.

It is cruel; for, whatever may be the advantages of foreign commerce, if in order to possess them, half the nation must languish in misery, we cannot without crime endeavor to obtain them, and it becomes the duty of a government to relinquish them. To desire to keep down the rate of wages, with the view of favoring the exportation of merchandise, is to seek to render the citizens of a state miserable, in order that foreigners may purchase its productions at a cheaper rate; it is, at the most, attempting to enrich a few merchants by impoverishing the body of the nation; it is taking the part of the stronger in that contest, already so unequal, between the man who can pay wages, and him who is under the necessity of receiving them; it is, in one word, to forget that the object of every political society ought to be the happiness of the largest number.

This motive is, moreover, ill founded; for, in order to secure to a nation a profitable export for the products of its agriculture and manufactures, it is not necessary that the rate of wages should be reduced so extremely low as we find it in almost all the countries of Europe. It is not the wages of the workman, but the price of the merchandise, that should be lowered, in order that this merchandise may be sold to foreign nations. But men have always neglected to make this distinction. The wages of the laborer are the price of his day's work. The price of merchandise is the sum it costs to gather the produce of the soil, or prepare any product of industry. The price of this production may be very moderate, while the laborer may receive good wages—that is, the means of procuring a comfortable subsistence. The labor necessary to gather or prepare the article to be sold may be cheap, and the wages of the workman good. Although the workmen of Manchester and Norwich, and those of Amiens and Abbeville, are employed in the same kind of labor, the former receive considerably higher wages than the latter; and yet the woollen fabrics of Manchester and Norwich, of the same quality, are not so dear as those of Amiens and Abbeville.

It would occupy too much time fully to develop this principle. I will only observe here, that it results in a great measure from the fact that the price of labor in the arts, and even in agriculture, is wonderfully diminished by the perfection of the machinery employed in them, by the intelligence and activity of the workmen, and by the judicious division of labor. Now these methods of reducing the price of manufactured articles have nothing to do with the low wages of the workman. In a large manufactory, where animals are employed instead of men, and machinery instead of animal power, and where that judicious division of labor is made which doubles, nay, increases tenfold, both power and time, the article can be manufactured and sold at a much lower rate than in those establishments which do not enjoy the same advantages;

and yet the workmen in the former may receive twice as much as in the latter.

It is, undoubtedly, an advantage for a manufactory to obtain workmen at a moderate price; and excessively high wages are an obstacle to the foundation of large manufacturing establishments. This high price of wages, as I shall presently explain, is one reason for the opinion which is entertained, that it will be many years before the manufactures of the United States of America can rival those of Europe. But we must not conclude from this, that manufactures cannot prosper, unless the wages of the workmen are reduced as low as we find them in Europe. And, moreover, the insufficiency of wages occasions the decline of a manufactory, as its prosperity is promoted by a high rate of wages.

High wages attract the most skilful and most industrious workmen. Thus the article is better made; it sells better; and, in this way, the employer makes a greater profit than he could do by diminishing the pay of the workmen. A good workman spoils fewer tools, wastes less material, and works faster than one of inferior skill; and thus the profits of the manufacturer are increased still more.

The perfection of machinery in all the arts is owing, in a great degree, to the workmen. There is no important manufacture in which they have not invented some useful process, which saves time and materials, or improves the workmanship. If common articles of manufacture, the only ones worthy to interest the statesman, if woollen, cotton, and even silk stuffs, articles made of iron, steel, copper, skins, leather, and various other things, are generally of better quality, at the same price, in England than in other countries, it is because workmen are there better paid.

The low rate of wages, then, is not the real cause of the advantages of commerce between one nation and another; but it is one of the greatest evils of political communities.

Let us now inquire what is the situation of the United States in this respect. The condition of the day laborer, in these States, is infinitely better than in the wealthiest countries in the old world, and particularly England, where, however, wages are higher than in any other part of Europe.

* * * * *

It remains for me to show how the high rate of wages in America will increase their rate in Europe.

Two distinct causes will unite in producing this effect. The first is the greater quantity of labor that Europe will have to perform in consequence of the existence of another great nation in the commercial world, and of its continual increase; and the second, the emigration of European workmen, or the mere possibility of their emigrating, in order to go to America, where labor is better paid.

It is certain that the amount of labor in the various branches of agriculture, manufactures, commerce, and navigation must be augmented in Europe by the addition of several millions of men to the commercial world. Now the amount of manual labor being increased, labor will be somewhat better paid, and the rate of daily wages received by the workmen will be raised by this concurrence of circumstances. For example, if the additional supply of one hundred thousand pieces of cloth, twenty thousand casks of wine, and ten thousand casks of brandy, is to be furnished to the Americans, not only will the persons necessarily employed in the production or manufacture of these commodities receive higher wages, but the price of all other kinds of labor will be augmented.

The rate of wages in Europe will be raised by yet another circumstance with which it is important to be acquainted. I have already said that the value of wages ought not to be estimated solely by the amount of money, nor even by the quantity of subsistence which the workman receives per day, but also by the number of days in which he is employed; for it is by such a calculation alone that we can find out what he has for each day. Is it not evident that he who should be paid at the rate of forty pence a day, and should fail of obtaining work half the year, would really have but twenty pence to subsist upon, and that he would be less advantageously situated than the man, who receiving but thirty pence, could yet be supplied with work every day? Thus the Americans, occasioning in Europe an increased demand and necessity for labor, would also necessarily cause there an augmentation of wages, even supposing the price of the day's work to remain at the same rate.

Perhaps it will be objected to what I have said, that this new nation will contain within itself as many laboring people as it can employ, and that thus, adding nothing to the quantity of work to be performed in Europe, it will be no advantage to the men who perform this work. But I reply that it is impossible but that the United States of America, in their present condition, and much more when their population and wealth shall be doubled, nay quadrupled, should employ the labor of Europeans one way or another. It is impossible, because in this respect the Americans are not differently situated from other nations, who all have need of each other. The fertility of the American soil, the abundance and variety of its productions, the activity and industry of its inhabitants, and the unrestricted commerce, which will sooner or later be established in Europe in consequence of the American independence, secure the relations of America with other countries, because she will furnish to other nations such of her productions as they may require; and as each country possesses some productions peculiar to itself, the demand and advantage will be reciprocal.

The second cause, which I have said must cooperate in producing an augmentation of wages in Europe, is emigration, or the mere possibility of emigrating to America, where labor is better paid. It is easy to conceive that when this difference is generally known, it will draw to the United States many men, who, having no means of subsistence but their labor, will flock to the place where this labor is best recompensed. Since the last peace the Irish have been continually emigrating to America. The reason of this is, that in Ireland wages are much less than in England, and that the lower classes are consequently great sufferers. Germany has also furnished new citizens to the United States; and all these laborers must, by leaving Europe, have raised the price of work for those who remain.

This salutary effect will be produced even without emigration, and will result from the mere possibility of emigrating, at least in those states of Europe whose inhabitants are not compelled to leave their own country by excessive taxation, bad laws, and the intolerance of government.

WILLIAM GODWIN

(1756–1836)

William Godwin was an English idealist who believed firmly in the perfectibility of mankind and in the inherent goodness of human nature. He will be remembered by students of literature as the father-in-law of the great poet Shelley, who imbibed much of his idealism from him.

Godwin believed that the characters of men were determined largely by external circumstances, such as political institutions. As a man of letters, his thesis was the opposite of the Great Man Theory of History, propounded later by Emerson and Carlyle, and it was also in conflict with the modern teachings of biology and psychology. It may be viewed as the product of John Locke's philosophy of *tobula resa* and as a reaction against the Cartesian theory of innate ideas and the Calvinistic doctrine of original sin.

William Godwin is interesting to the student of the history of economic thought because he precipitated the famous Malthusian controversy. Godwin's first book was entitled "Political Justice," or, to be exact, "An Enquiry Concerning Political Justice and Its Influence on General Virtue and Happiness." The first edition appeared in 1793 and the second edition, with material alterations, in 1796. It was followed in 1797 by a collection of essays entitled the "Enquirer." In answer to one of these essays of Godwin, entitled "Avarice and Prodigality," Malthus published anonymously in 1798 the first edition of his famous "Essay on Population." In 1820, after several editions of Malthus had appeared and the authorship of the famous essay was no longer a secret, Godwin published his reply to Malthus in another work entitled "On Population," or, to be exact, "An Enquiry Concerning the Power of Increase in the Number of Mankind, Being an Answer to Mr. Malthus's Essay on that Subject."

The following brief selections are taken from Godwin's works, "Political Justice" and "On Population." The student will observe how Godwin influenced the thinking of Malthus. He will also see how bitterly the Malthusian controversy raged between materialists and idealists, scientists and theologians, naturalists and institutionalists. The ramifications of this argument frequently led their authors into strange and inconsistent positions.

WILLIAM GODWIN

SELECTIONS FROM "AN ENQUIRY CONCERNING POLITICAL JUSTICE AND ITS INFLUENCE ON GENERAL VIRTUE AND HAPPINESS"

VOLUME I

Preface

Few works of literature are held in greater estimation, than those which treat in a methodical and elementary way of the principles of science. But the human mind in every enlightened age is progressive; and the best elementary treatises after a certain time are reduced in their value by the operation of subsequent discoveries. Hence it has always been desired by candid enquirers, that preceding works of this kind should from time to time be superseded, and that other productions including the larger views that have since offered themselves, should be substituted in their place.

It would be strange if something of this kind were not desirable in politics, after the great change that has been produced in men's minds upon this subject, and the light that has been thrown upon it by the recent discussions of America and France. A sense of the value of such a work, if properly executed, was the motive which gave birth to these volumes. Of their execution the reader must judge.

Authors who have formed the design of superseding the works of their predecessors, will be found, if they were in any degree equal to the design, not merely to have collected the scattered information that had been produced upon the subject, but to have increased the science with the fruit of their own meditations. In the following work principles will occasionally be found, which it will not be just to reject without examination, merely because they are new. It was impossible perseveringly to reflect upon so prolific a science, and a science which may be said to be yet in its infancy, without being led into ways of thinking that were in some degree uncommon.

Another argument in favour of the utility of such a work was frequently in the author's mind, and therefore ought to be mentioned. He conceived politics to be the proper vehicle of a liberal morality. That description of ethics deserves to be held in slight estimation, which seeks only to regulate our conduct in articles of particular and personal concern, instead of exciting our attention to the general good of the species. It appeared sufficiently practicable to make of such a treatise, exclusively of its direct political use, an advantageous vehicle of moral improvement. He was accordingly desirous of producing a work, from the perusal of which no man should rise without being strengthened in habits of sincerity, fortitude and justice.

Having stated the considerations in which the work originated, it is proper to mention a few circumstances of the outline of its history. The sentiments it contains are by no means the suggestions of a sudden effervescence of fancy. Political enquiry had long held a foremost place in the writer's attention. It is now twelve year since he became satisfied, that monarchy was a species of government unavoidably corrupt. He owed this conviction to the political writings of Swift and to a perusal of the Latin historians. Nearly at the same time he derived great additional instruction from reading the most considerable French writers upon the nature of man in the following order, *Systeme de la Nature*, Rousseau and Helvetius. Long before he thought of the present work, he had familiarized to his mind the arguments it contains on justice, gratitude, rights of man, promises, oaths and the omnipotence of truth. Political complexity is one of the errors that take strongest hold on the understanding; and it was only by ideas suggested by the French revolution, that he was reconciled to the desirableness of a government of the simplest construction. To the same event he owes the determination of mind which gave existence to this work.

Such was the preparation which encouraged him to undertake the present treatise. The direct execution may be dismissed in a few words. It was projected in the month of May 1791: the composition was begun in the following September, and has therefore occupied a space of sixteen months. This period was devoted to the purpose with unremitted ardour. It were to be wished it had been longer; but it seemed as if no contemptible part of the utility of the work depended upon its early appearance.

The printing of the following treatise, as well as the composition, was influenced by the same principle, a desire to reconcile a certain degree of dispatch with the necessary deliberation. The printing was for that reason commenced, long before the composition was finished. Some disadvantages have arisen from this circumstance. The ideas of the author became more perspicuous and digested, as his enquiries advanced. The longer he considered the subject, the more accurately he seemed to understand it. This circumstance has led him into a few contradictions. The principal of these consists in an occasional inaccuracy of language, particularly in the first book, respecting the word government. He did not enter upon the work, without being aware that government by its very nature counteracts the improvement of individual mind; but he understood the full meaning of this proposition more completely as he proceeded, and saw more distinctly into the nature of the remedy. This, and a few other defects, under a different mode of preparation would have been avoided. The candid reader will make a suitable allowance. The author judges upon a review, that these defects are such as not materially to injure the object of the work, and that more has been gained than lost by the conduct he has pursued.

The period in which the work makes its appearance is singular. The people of England have assiduously been excited to declare their loyalty, and to mark every man as obnoxious who is not ready to sign the Shibboleth of the constitution. Money is raised by voluntary subscription to defray the expence of prosecuting men who shall dare to promulgate heretical opinions, and thus to oppress them at once with the enmity of government and of individuals. This was an accident wholly unforeseen when the work was undertaken; and it will scarcely be supposed that such an accident could produce any alteration in the writer's designs. Every man, if we may believe the voice of rumour, is to be prosecuted who shall appeal to the people by the publication of any unconstitutional paper or pamphlet; and it is added, that men are to be prosecuted for any unguarded words that may be dropped in the warmth of debate. It is now to be tried whether, in addition to these alarming encroachments upon our liberty, a book is to fall under the arm of the civil power, which, beside the advantage of having for one of its express objects the dissuading from all tumult and violence, is by its very nature an appeal to men of study and reflection. It is to be tried whether a project is formed for suppressing the activity of mind, and putting an end to the disquisitions of science. Respecting the event in a personal view the author has formed his resolution. Whatever conduct his countrymen may pursue, they will not be able to shake his tranquillity. The duty he is most bound to discharge is the assisting the progress of truth; and if he suffer in any respect for such a proceeding, there is certainly no vicissitude that can befall him, that can ever bring along with it a more satisfactory consolation.

But, exclusively of this precarious and unimportant consideration, it is the fortune of the present work to appear before a public that is panic struck, and impressed with the most dreadful apprehensions of such doctrines as are here delivered. All the prejudices of the human mind are in arms against it. This circumstance may appear to be of greater advantage than the other. But it is the property of truth to be fearless, and to prove victorious over every adversary. It requires no great degree of fortitude, to look with indifference upon the false fire of the moment, and to forsee the calm period of reason which will succeed.

January 7, 1793.

Book I. Of the Importance of Political Institutions

Chapter VI. Human Inventions Capable of Perpetual Improvement

Perfectibility of Man . . .

If we would form to ourselves a solid estimate of political, or indeed of any other science, we ought not to confine our survey to that narrow portion of things which passes under our own immediate inspection, and rashly pronounce every thing that we have not ourselves seen, to be impossible. There is no characteristic of man, which seems at present at least so eminently to distinguish him, or to be of so much importance in every branch of moral science, as his perfectibility. Let us carry back our minds to man in his original state, a being capable of impressions and knowledge to an unbounded extent, but not having as yet received the one or cultivated the other; and let us contrast this being with all that science and genius have effected: and from hence we may form some idea what it is of which human nature is capable. It is to be remembered, that this being did not as now derive assistance from the communications of his fellows, nor had his feeble and crude conceptions assisted by the experience of successive centuries; but that in the state we are figuring all men were equally ignorant. The field of improvement was before them, but for every step in advance they were to be indebted to their untutored efforts. Nor is it of any consequence whether such was actually the progress of mind, or whether, as others teach, the progress was abridged, and man was immediately advanced half way to the end of his career by the interposition of the author of his nature. In any case it is an allowable and no unimproving speculation, to consider mind as it is in itself, and to enquire what would have been its history, if immediately upon its production, it had been left to be acted upon by those ordinary laws of the universe with whose operation we are acquainted.

*   *   *   *   *

Book VIII. Of Property

Chapter VII. Of the Objection to This System from the Principle of Population

The objection stated.—Remoteness of its operation.—Conjectural ideas respecting the antidote.—Omnipotence of mind.—Illustrations. . . .

An author who has speculated widely upon subjects of government, has recommended equal, or, which was rather his idea, common property, as a complete remedy, to the usurpation and distress which are at present the most powerful enemies of human kind, to the vices which infect education in some instances, and the neglect it encounters in more, to all the turbulence of passion, and all the injustice of selfishness. But, after having exhibited this picture, not less true than delightful, he finds an argument that demolished the whole, and restores him to indifference and despair, in the excessive population that would ensue.

One of the most obvious answers to this objection is, that to reason thus is to foresee difficulties at a great distance. Three fourths of the habitable globe is now uncultivated. The parts already cultivated are capable of immeasurable improvement. Myriads of centuries of still increasing population may probably pass away, and the earth still be found sufficient for the subsistence of its inhabitants. Who can say how long the earth itself will survive the casualties of the planetary system? Who can say what remedies shall suggest themselves for so distant an inconvenience, time enough for practical application, and of which we may yet at this time have not the smallest idea? It would be truly absurd for us to shrink from a scheme of essential benefit to mankind, lest they should be too happy, and by necessary consequence at some distant period too populous.

But, though these remarks may be deemed a sufficient answer to the objection, it may not be amiss to indulge in some speculations to which such an objection obviously leads. The earth may, to speak in the style of one of the writers of the Christian Scriptures, "abide for ever." It may be in danger of becoming too populous. A remedy may then be necessary. If it may, why should we sit down in supine indifference and conclude that we can discover no glimpse of it? The discovery, if made, would add to the firmness and consistency of our prospects; nor is it improbable to conjecture that that which would form the regulating spring of our conduct then, might be the medium of a salutary modification now. What follows must be considered in some degree as a deviation into the land of conjecture. If it be false, it leaves the great system to which it is appended in all found reason as impregnable as ever. If this do not lead us to the true remedy, it does not follow that there is no remedy. The great object of enquiry will still remain open, however defective may be the suggestions that are now to be offered.

Let us here return to the sublime conjecture of Franklin, that "mind will one day become omnipotent over matter." If over all other matter, why not over the matter of our own bodies? If over matter at ever so great a distance, why not over matter which, however ignorant we may be of the tie that connects it with the thinking principle, we always carry about with us, and which is in all cases the medium of communication between that principle and the external universe? In a word, why not man be one day immortal.

The different cases in which thought modifies the external universe are obvious to all. It is modified by our voluntary thoughts or design. We desire to stretch out our hand, and it is stretched out. We perform a thousand operations of the same species every day, and their familiarity annihilates wonder. They are not in themselves less wonderful than any of those modifications which we are least accustomed to conceive. Mind modifies body involuntarily. Emotion excited by some unexpected word, by a letter that is delivered to us, occasions the most extraordinary revolutions in our frame, accelerates the circulation, causes the heart to palpitate, the tongue to refuse its office, and has been known to occasion death by extreme anguish or extreme joy. These symptoms we may either encourage or check. By encouraging them habits are produced of fainting or of rage. To discourage them is one of the principal offices of fortitude. The effort of mind in resisting pain in the stories of Cranmer and Mucius Scaevola is of the same kind. It is reasonable to believe that that effort with a different direction might have cured certain diseases of the system. There is nothing indeed of which physicians themselves are more frequently aware, than the power of the mind in assisting or retarding convalescence.

* * * * *

WILLIAM GODWIN

SELECTIONS FROM "POPULATION—AN ENQUIRY CONCERNING THE POWER OF INCREASE IN THE NUMBERS OF MANKIND, BEING AN ANSWER TO MR. MALTHUS'S ESSAY ON THAT SUBJECT"

PREFACE

It happens to men sometimes, where they had it in their thoughts to set forward and advance some mighty benefit to their fellow creatures, not merely to fail in giving substance and efficacy to the sentiment that animated them, but also to realize and bring on some injury to the party they purposed to serve. Such is my case, if the speculations that have now been current for nearly twenty years, and which have scarcely been heard of before, are to be henceforth admitted, as forming an essential branch of the science of politics.

When I wrote my Enquiry concerning Political Justice, I flattered myself that there was no mean probability that I should render an important service to mankind. I had warmed my mind with all that was great and illustrious in the republics of Greece and Rome, which had been favourite subjects of meditation with me, almost from my infancy. I became further animated by the spectacle of the Revolutions of America and France, the former of which commenced when I was just twenty years of age, (though I never approved of the mode in which the latter was effected, and the excesses which to a certain degree marked its very beginning) and by the speculations, which in England, and other parts of Europe, among learned men and philosophers, precede, and contributed to, and have in some measure attended upon, and accompanied, every step of these events. I thought it was possible to collect whatever existed that was best and most liberal in the science of politics, to condense it, to arrange it more into a system, and to carry it somewhat farther, than had been done by any preceding writer.

The book I produced seemed for some time fully to answer in its effects the most sanguine expectations I had conceived from it. I could not complain that it "fell dead-born from the press," or that it did not awaken a considerable curiosity among my countrymen. I was never weak enough to suppose, that it would immediately sweep away all error before it, like a mighty influx of the waves of the ocean. I hailed the opposition it encountered, direct and indirect, argumentative and scurrilous, as a symptom (we will suppose, not altogether unequivocal) of the result I so earnestly desired. Among other phenomena of the kind, I hailed the attack of Mr. Malthus. I believed, that the Essay on Population, like other erroneous and exaggerated representations of things, would soon find its own level.

In this I have been hitherto disappointed. It would be easy to assign the causes of my disappointment; the degree in which, by the necessity of the case, the theory of this writer flattered the vices and corruption of the rich and great, and the eager patronage it might very naturally be expected to obtain from them: but this makes no part of what it is my purpose to say. Finding therefore, that whatever arguments have been produced against it by others, it still holds on its prosperous career, and has not long since appeared in the impressive array of a Fifth Edition, I cannot be contented to go out of the world, without attempting to put into a permanent form what has occurred to me on the subject. I was sometimes idle enough to suppose, that I had done my part, in producing the book that had given occasion to Mr. Malthus's Essay, and that I might safely leave the comparatively easy task, as it seemed of demolishing the "Principle of Population," to some one of the men who have risen to maturity since I produced my most considerable performance. But I can refrain no longer. "I will also answer my part; I likewise will shew my opinion: for I am full of matter; and the spirit within me constraineth me."

This is a task in which I am the more bound to engage, because, as I have said, if the dogmas which are now afloat on the subject of population are to become permanent, I have, instead of contributing as I desired to the improvement of society, become, very unintentionally, the occasion of placing a bar upon all improvements to come, and bringing into discredit all improvements that are past. If Mr. Malthus's way of reasoning only tended to the overthrow of what many will call "the visionary speculations" of the Enquiry concerning Political Justice, the case would have been different. I might have gone to my grave with the disgrace, to whatever that might amount, of having erected castles in the air, for the benefit, not of myself, but of my species, and of then seeing them battered to pieces before my face. But I cannot consent to close my eyes for ever, with the judgment, as the matter now seems to stand, recorded on my tomb, that, in attempting one further advance in the route of improvement, I should have brought on the destruction of all that Solon, and Plato, and Montesquieu, and Sidney, in ancient times, and in a former age, has seemed to have effected for the redemption and the elevation of mankind.

It is not a little extraordinary, that Mr. Malthus's book should now have been twenty years before the public, without any one, so far as I know, having attempted a refutation of his main principle. It was easy for men of a generous temper to vent their horror at the revolting nature of the conclusions that he drew from his principle; and this is nearly all that has been done. That principle is delivered by him in the most concise and summary manner. He says, that he "considered it as established in the first six pages. The American increase was related (in three lines); and the geometrical ratio was proved." Now, it stands out broadly to the common sense of mankind, that this was proving nothing. Population, and the descent, and increase or otherwise, of one generation of mankind after another, is not a subject of such wonderful simplicity, as to be thus established. It is in reality the complexity and thorniness of the question, that have had the effect of silencing Mr. Malthus's adversaries respecting it. They seem with one consent to have shrunk from a topic, which required so much patient investigation. In the midst of this general desertion of the public interest, I have ventured to place myself in the breach. With what success it is for others to judge.

It may seem strange, that what was so summarily stated, and successfully asserted, by Mr. Malthus, should require so much research and labour to overthrow. The Essay on Population has set up a naked assertion; no more. I might have made a contradictory assertion; and, equitably speaking, the matter was balanced, and what Mr. Malthus has written ought to go for nothing. But this would not have been the case. "Possession," says the old proverb, "is nine points of the law," and the Essay on Population had gotten possession of the public mind. This author entered on a desert land, and, like the first discoveries of countries, set up a symbol of occupation, and without further ceremony said, "It is mine." His task was easy: he gave the word; his vessel was launched, and his voyage completed. Like Cymochles in the Fairy Queen, he could say,

> My wandering ship I row,
> That knows her port, and thither sails by aim;
> Ne care, ne fear I, how the wind do blow;
> Both swift and slow alike do serve my turn.

But the task in which I have engaged has been of a different sort. It was necessary that my advances should be slow, and my forces firm. It was mine, not only to dislodge the usurper from his fastnesses and retreats; but further, by patient exertions, and employing the most solid materials, to build up a Pharos, that the sincere enquirer might no longer wander in the dark, and be liable to be guided by the first daring adventurer that would lead him into the paths of error and destruction.

I beg leave to repeat one passage here from the ensuing volume, as containing a thought very proper to be presented to the reader in the outset of the enquiry. "If America had never been discovered, the geometrical ratio, as applied to the multiplication of mankind, would never have been known. If the British colonies had never been planted, Mr. Malthus would never have written. The human species might have perished of a long old age, a fate to which perhaps all sublunary things are subject at last, without one statesman or one legislator, through myriads of centuries, having suspected this dangerous tendency to increase, 'in comparison with which human institutions, however they may appear to be the causes of much mischief to society, are mere feathers.'"

In the following pages I confine myself strictly to Mr. Malthus's book, and the question which he has brought under consideration. My bitterest enemy will hardly be able to find in this volume the author of the Enquiry concerning Political Justice. I have scarcely allowed myself to recollect the beautiful visions (if they shall turn out to be visions), which enchanted my soul, and animated my pen, while writing that work. I conceived that any distinct reference to what is there treated of, would be foreign to the subject which is now before me. The investigation of the power of increase in the numbers of mankind, must be interesting to every one to whom the human species and human society appear to be matters of serious concern: and I should have thought that I was guilty of a sort of treason against that interest, if I had unnecessarily obtruded into the discussion any thing that could shock the prejudices, or insult the views, of those whose conceptions of political truth might be most different from my own.

I am certainly very sorry that I was not sooner in possession of Mr. Malthus's calculation for peopling the whole visible universe with human beings at the rate of four men to every square yard, contained in his Principles of Political Economy. A considerable portion of my work was printed, before the appearance of that volume. Several passages in these sheets will read comparatively flat and tame, for want of the assistance of this happy *reductio ad absurdum* from the pen of the author.

I cannot close these few pages of Preface, without testifying my obligations to one friend in particular, Mr. David Booth, formerly of Newburgh in the county of Fife, now of London. Without the encouragement and pressing instances of this gentleman my work would never have been begun; and the main argument of the Second Book is one of his suggesting. But indeed the hints and materials for illustration I have derived from his conversation are innumerable; and his mathematical skill assisted my investigations, in points in which my habits for many years, were least favourable to my undertaking. It is further necessary I should add, that Mr. Booth has scarcely in any instance inspected my sheets, and that therefore I only am responsible for any errors they may contain.

The reader will find, annexed to the end of the Second Book, a Dissertation on the Ratios of Increase in Population, and in the Means of Subsistence, which that gentleman had the goodness to supply to me.

This is all that is necessary for me to say in the way of Preface. Except that I feel prompted to make my apology in this place, if I shall appear any where to have been hurried into undue warmth. I know how easily this sin is accustomed to beset all controversial writers. I hold Mr. Malthus in all due respect, at the same time that I willingly plead guilty to the charge of regarding his doctrines with inexpressible abhorrence. I fully admit however the good intentions of the author of the Essay on Population, and cheerfully seize this occasion to testify my belief in his honourable character, and his unblemished manners.

LONDON,
October 21, 1820.

POSTSCRIPT

I think I should be guilty of a certain omission, with which, if my readers could detect it, they would have a right to reproach me, if I did not fairly state some of the discouragements under which my work was undertaken, and has been carried on to its completion. But this I cannot do without making free with the letters of my friends; and, as long as I carefully suppress their names, I hope they will pardon the liberty I take.

The following is an extract of a letter from one of the most intelligent and highly endowed merchants of the city of London.

November 23, 1817.

"You guess rightly, in supposing that I should hear with pleasure of your intending to controvert Mr. Malthus's book on population, especially as I think his opinion both *true* and important. Your work will not fail to draw, not only mine, but the public attention, to the most interesting subject in the whole science of political economy. If you are victorious, you will deserve a civic crown."

A zealous friend from the North writes to me in these terms:

February 24, 1819.

"I have now to report the opinion of a good friend of yours and of mankind, to whom I communicated the great object that at present employs your pen. 'Implore Mr. Godwin,' he exclaimed, 'not to be in a hurry in publishing, and not to dispute with Malthus the prolific principle of population in new countries. The great and conclusive argument against Malthus is the increase of refinement, luxury, dissipation, debauchery, and great cities, in old countries.' (This appears to me to be Mr. Malthus's own statement, and not an argument against him.) I add further, several of your friends here are of the same opinion, and feel considerable solicitude about the view you seem to be taking of the question."

A gentleman of the most eminent literary attainments writes to me thus:

September 9, 1819.

"Though I have a great esteem for Malthus, I shall certainly read your work with the most respectful attention, and I shall open it with the assurance that, if it does not *alter my opinion,* it will exercise and delight my mind."

I will add one more passage from an individual of the most earnest zeal for the welfare of his fellow creatures, and who was peculiarly shocked with the views exhibited in the Essay on Population.

May 10, 1820.

"I wish your work on population success; the views of Mr. Malthus are very dreadful. He seems to have convinced almost all men of their absolute truth, and I am sorry to say that I do not perceive his statements to be false. I shall indeed rejoice, if they are shewn to be so."

To these private communications I will add a few lines from a speech of Mr. Brougham in the House of Commons, delivered December 16, 1819. *See the Morning Chronicle.*

"Mr. Brougham had no hesitation in stating that the excess of population was one of the great causes of the distress which at present afflicted the country. This proposition from the best consideration which he had been able to give the subject, he was fully prepared to maintain. But it was among the most melancholy mal-practices of the low part of the press, to depreciate this which was the soundest principle of political economy. Nay, the worst expedients were used to calumniate the writers by whom that principle was mainly supported, though among those writers were to be found men of the most exalted morals, of the purest views, of the soundest intellect, and even of the most humane feelings. Yet against the writers who sought to guard society against this great evil, the utmost obloquy was directed."

A decision so absolute, at the time that my book was already in the press, might well have startled me. It fell from the lips of one of the most enlightened speakers of the present day, standing in his place in parliament. I cheerfully subscribe to the high endowments and extensive information of Mr. Brougham: and, if I could have bowed to authority merely, on a subject which had for two years occupied my almost undivided attention, I should have suppressed my work. There is certainly a wide difference between the being seduced (as so many men have been) by the specious simplicity of Mr. Malthus's system, and the case of him who is "fully prepared" to maintain its tenets.

Book I. Of the Population of Europe, Asia, Africa, and South America, in Ancient and Modern Times

Chapter I. Introduction

Mr. Malthus has published what he calls an Essay on the Principle of Population, by which he undertakes to annul every thing that had previously been received, respecting the views that it is incumbent upon those who preside over political society to cherish, and the measures that may conduce to the happiness of mankind. His theory is evidently founded upon nothing. He says, that "population, when unchecked, goes on doubling itself every twenty-five years, or increases in a geometrical ratio." If we ask why we are to believe this, he answers that, "in the northern states of America, the population has been found so to double itself for above a century and a half successively." All this he delivers in an oraculous manner. He neither proves nor attempts to prove what he asserts. If Mr. Malthus has taken a right view of the question, it is to be hoped that some author will hereafter arise, who will go into the subject and shew that it is so.

Mr. Malthus having laid down a theory in this dogmatical manner, a sort of proceeding wholly unworthy of a reflecting nation or an enlightened age, it is time in reality that some one should sweep away this house of cards, and endeavour to ascertain whether any thing is certainly known on the subject.

This is the design and the scheme of the present volume. I shall make no dogmatical assertions; or, at least I am sure I will make none respecting the proposition or propositions which form the basis of the subject. I shall call upon my reader for no implicit faith. I shall lay down no positions authoritatively, and leave him to seek for evidence, elsewhere, and as he can, by which they may be established. All that I deliver shall be accompanied by its proofs. My purpose is to engage in a train of patient investigation, and to lay before every one who will go along with me, the facts which satisfy my mind on the subject, and which I am desirous should convey similar satisfaction to the minds of others.

The consequence is, that I, the first, as far as I know, of any English writer in the present century, shall have really gone into the question of population. If what I shall deliver is correct, some foundation will be laid, and the principle will begin to be understood. If what I allege as fact shall be found to be otherwise, or the conclusions I draw from my facts do not truly follow from them, I shall have set before other enquirers evidence that they may scan, and arguments that they may refute. I simply undertake to open the door for the gratification of the curious, or, more properly speaking, of those who feel an interest in the honour and happiness of the human species, which hitherto in this respect has been shut. Conscious how little as yet is known on the subject, I attempt no more than to delineate Outlines of the Doctrine of Population.

The first point then that I have to examine, and which will form the subject of Three of the Six Books into which my treatise is divided, is respecting the Power of Increase in the Numbers of the Human Species, and the Limitations of that Power. This question, precisely speaking, is the topic of the Second Book only: though I have thought proper to prefix in a First Book a view of the numbers of mankind in Europe, Asia, Africa, and South America, in ancient and modern times, where population has generally been supposed not to increase; and in another (the Fourth) to subjoin a view of the United States of North America in this particular, where from some cause or other the population has multiplied exceedingly.

The result of our investigations into the subject of population, I believe, will afford some presumption that there is in the constitution of the human species a power, absolutely speaking, of increasing its numbers. Mr. Malthus says; that the power is equal to the multiplication of mankind by a doubling every twenty-five years, that is, to an increase for ever in a geometrical series, of which the exponent is 2: a multiplication, which it is difficult for human imagination, or (as I should have thought) for human credulity to follow: and therefore his theory must demand the most tremendous checks (their names in the Essay on Population are vice and misery) to keep the power in that state of neutrality, in which it is perhaps in almost all cases to be found in Europe. I think I shall be able to make out that the power of increase in the numbers of the human species is extremely small. But, be that as it may, it must be exceedingly interesting to assign the Causes by which this Power is Restrained from producing any absolute multiplication, from century to century, in those many countries where population appears to be at a stand: and I have accordingly endeavoured to take the question out of the occult and mystical state in which Mr. Malthus has left it. This disquisition forms the subject of my Third Book; as it was necessary to give it precedence over the examination of the population of the United States, that we might be the better enabled to see, how far the causes which keep down population are peculiar to us, and how far they extend their agency to North America.

Such is the outline of the most essential parts of the following work; and here I might perhaps without impropriety have put an end to my labours. But, as Mr. Malthus has taken occasion to deliver many positions respecting subsistence, and various other points of political economy, I have thought it might not be useless to follow him into these topics.

The question of subsistence indeed Mr. Malthus has made an essential member of his system, having stated the power of increase in the numbers of mankind as equal to a doubling every twenty-five years for ever in geometrical series, and the utmost power of increase in the means of subsistence as reaching only to a perpetual addition of its own quantity in similar periods, or a progression in arithmetical series. Thus,

Population 1 2 4 8 16 32 64 128 256
Subsistence 1 2 3 4 5 6 7 8 9

I have therefore devoted my Fifth Book to the consideration of the Means which the Earth Affords for the Subsistence of Man.

The topic I have reserved for my Sixth Book is, at least to my apprehension, in no way less interesting than the question of Subsistence. Dr. Franklin and other writers who have attributed to the human species a power of rapidly multiplying their numbers, have either foreseen no mischief to arise from this germ of multiplication, or none but what was exceedingly remote. It is other wise with Mr. Malthus. The geometrical ratio is everywhere with him a practical principle, and entitled to the most vigilant and unremitted attention of mankind. He has deduced from this consideration several moral and political maxims, which enjoins it upon the governors of the world to attend to. I am persuaded that the elements of our author's theory are unsound, and that therefore his conclusions must follow the fate of the principle on which they are founded. But I should have left my undertaking imperfect, if I did not proceed to expose these maxims; thus, in the first place, setting the system of the Essay on Population and its practical merits in the full light of day; and, in the second, holding up for the instruction of those who may come after, an example of the monstrous errors into which a writer may be expected to fall, who shall allow himself, upon a gratuitous and wholly unproved assumption, to build a system of legislation, and determine the destiny of all his fellow-creatures. An examination of the Moral and Political Maxims Inculcated in the Essay on Population therefore constitutes the subject of my Sixth Book.

I might indeed have written a treatise in which I should have endeavoured to trace the outlines of the subject of population, without adverting to Mr. Malthus. But, in the first place it was gratifying to me to name an author, who, however false and groundless his theories appear to me, has had the merit of successfully drawing the attention of the public to the subject. I think it but fair, so far as depends upon me, that his name should be preserved, whatever becomes of the volumes he has written. If any benefit shall arise from the discussion of the Doctrine of Population, there is a propriety in recollecting the person by whose writings the question has been set afloat, though he has not been discussed. And, in the second place, I know that the attention of the majority of readers is best secured by the appearance of a contention. If I had delivered the speculations of the following pages in a form severely scientific, and still more if I had written my book without Mr. Malthus's going before me, I should have appeared to multitudes to be elaborately explaining what was too clear for an argument, and could not have expected to excite an interest, to which under the present circumstances, if I have done any thing effectually on the subject, I may be thought reasonably entitled.

Chapter II. Survey of the Creation from Natural History

Previously to our entering directly on the subject before us, it will probably be found not wholly unworthy of attention to recollect, in how different a way the multiplication of the human species has ordinarily been regarded, by writers whose purpose it was to survey the various classes of existence that form the subject of natural history, and who were satisfied to discover "the wisdom of God in the works of creation," from the ideas expressed by Mr. Malthus. The following is the manner in which the subject is stated by Goldsmith, one of the latest of the number, in his History of the Earth and Animated Nature.

"We may observe, that that generation is the most complete, in which the fewest animals are produced: Nature, by attending to the production of one at a time, seems to exert all her efforts in bringing it to perfection: but, where this attention is divided, the animals so produced come into the world with partial advantages. In this manner twins are never, at least while infants, so large or strong as those that come singly into the world; each having, in some measure, robbed the other of its right; as that support which Nature meant for one, has been prodigally divided.

"In this manner, as those animals are the best that are produced singly, so we find that the noblest animals are ever the least fruitful. These are seen usually to bring forth but one at a time, and to place all their attention upon that alone. On the other hand, all the oviparous kinds produce in amazing plenty; and even the lower tribes of the viviparous animals increase in a seeming proportion to their minuteness and imperfection. Nature seems lavish of life in the lower orders of creation; and, as if she meant them entirely for the use of the nobler races, she appears to have bestowed greater pains in multiplying the number, than in completing the kind. In this manner, while the elephant and the horse bring forth but one at a time, the spider and the beetle are seen to produce a thousand: and even among the smaller quadrupeds, all the inferior kinds are extremely fertile; any one of these being found, in a very few months, to become the parent of a numerous progeny.

"In this manner therefore the smallest animals multiply in the greatest proportion; and we have reason to thank Providence, that the most formidable animals are the least fruitful. Had the lion and the tiger the same degree of fecundity with the rabbit or the rat, all the arts of man would be unable to oppose these fierce invaders, and we should soon perceive them become the tyrants of those who claim lordship of the creation. But Heaven, in this respect, has wisely consulted the advantage of all. It has opposed to man only such enemies, as he has art and strength to conquer, and as large animals require proportional supplies, nature was unwilling to give new life, where it in some measure denied the necessary means of subsistence.

"In consequence of this pre-established order, the animals that are endowed with the most perfect methods of generation, and bring forth but one at a time, seldom begin to procreate, till they have almost acquired their full growth. On the other hand, those which bring forth many, engender before they have arrived at half their natural size. The horse and the bull come almost to perfection before they begin to generate; the hog and the rabbit scarcely leave the teat before they become parents themselves. In whatever light therefore we consider this subject, we shall find that all creatures approach most to perfection, whose generation most nearly resembles that of man. The reptile produced from cutting, is but one degree above the vegetable. The animal produced from the egg, is a step higher in the scale of existence: that class of animals which are brought forth alive, are still more exalted. Of these, such as bring forth one at a time are the most complete; and foremost of these stands man, *the great master of all*, who seems to have united the perfections of all the rest in his formation."

Chapter III. General Views as to the Alleged Increase of Mankind

To take a just view of any subject, one rule that is extremely worthy of our attention is, that we should get to a proper distance from it. The stranger to whom we would convey an adequate image of the city of London, we immediately lead to the top of St. Paul's Church. And, if I may introduce an allusion to the records of the Christian religion, the devil took our Saviour "up into an exceeding high mountain," when he would "shew him all the kingdoms of the world, and the glory of them."

Mr. Malthus has taken his stand upon the reports of Dr. Franklin and Dr. Ezra Styles. He repairs with them to the northern parts of the United States of America, and there he sees, or thinks he sees, "the population doubling itself, for above a century and a half successively, in less than twenty-five years," and that "from procreation only." He does not discover an ample population even in this, his favourite county. Far from it. The reason why the population goes on so rapidly in North America is, according to him, because there is "ample room and verge enough" for almost all the population that can be poured into it. He sees, in his prophetic conception, that country, some centuries hence, full of human inhabitants, even to overflowing, and groaning under the multitude of the tribes that shall dwell in it.

Would it not have been fairer to have taken before him the globe of earth at one view, and from thence to have deduced the true "Principle of Population," and the policy that ought to direct the measures of those who govern the world?

How long the race of man has subsisted, unless we derive our opinions on the subject from the light of revelation, no man knows. The Chinese, and the people of Indostan, carry back their chronology through millions of years. Even if we refer to the Bible, the Hebrew text, and the Samaritan which is perhaps of equal authority, differ most considerably and fundamentally from each other. But Mr. Malthus is of opinion, that, in reasoning on subjects of political economy, we are bound to regulate our ideas by statistical reports, and tables that have been scientifically formed by proficients in that study, and has accordingly confined himself to these.

But, though we know not how long the human race has existed, nor how extensive a period it has had to multiply itself in, we are able to form some rude notions respecting its present state. It has by some persons been made an objection to the Christian religion, that it has not become universal. It would perhaps be fairer, to make it an objection to the "Principle of Population," as laid down by Mr. Malthus, that the earth is not peopled.

If I were to say that the globe would maintain twenty times its present inhabitants, or, in other words, that for every human creature now called into existence, twenty might exist in a state of greater plenty and happiness than with our small number we do at present, I should find no one timid and saturine enough to contradict me. In fact, he must be a literal and most uninventive speculator, who would attempt to set bounds to the physical powers of the earth to supply the means of human subsistence.

The first thing therefore that would occur to him who should survey "all the kingdoms of the earth," and the state of their population, would be the thinness of their numbers, and the multitude and extent of their waste and desolate places. If his heart abounded with "the milk of human kindness," he would not fail to contrast the present state of the globe with its possible state; he would see his species as a little remnant widely scattered over a fruitful and prolific surface, and would weep to think that the kindly and gracious qualities of our mother earth were turned to so little account. If he were more of a sober and reasoning, than of a tender and passionate temper, perhaps, he would not weep, but I should think he would set himself seriously to enquire, how the populousness of nations might be increased, and the different regions of the globe replenished with a numerous and happy race.

Dr. Paley's observations on this head are peculiarly to the purpose. "The quantity of happiness," he says, "in any given district, although it is possible it may be increased, the number of inhabitants remaining the same, is chiefly and most naturally affected by alteration of the numbers; consequently, *the decay of population is the greatest evil that a state can suffer;* and the improvement of it is the object, which ought in all countries to be aimed at, in preference to every other political purpose whatsoever."

Such has been the doctrine, I believe, of every enlightened politician and legislator since the world began. But Mr. Malthus has placed this subject in a new light. He thinks that there is a possibility that the globe of earth may at some time or other contain more human inhabitants than it can subsist; and he has therefore written a book, the direct tendency of which is to keep down the numbers of mankind. He has no con-

sideration for the millions and millions of men, who might be conceived
as called into existence, and made joint partakers with us in such happiness as a sublunary existence, with liberty and improvement, might
impart; but, for the sake of a future possibility, would shut against them
once for all the door of existence.

He says indeed, "The difficulty, so far from being remote, is imminent
and immediate. At every period during the progress of cultivation, from
the present moment to the time when the whole earth was become like a
garden, the distress for want of food would be constantly pressing on all
mankind." He adds it is true in this place, "if they were equal." But these
words are plainly unnecessary, since it is almost the sole purpose of his
book to shew, that, in all old established countries, "the population is
always pressing hard against the means of subsistence."

This however—I mean the distress that must always accompany us in
every step of our progress—is so palpably untrue, that I am astonished
that any man should have been induced by the love of paradox, and the
desire to divulge something new, to make the assertion. There is no
principle respecting man and society more certain, than that every man
in a civilized state is endowed with the physical power of producing more
than shall suffice for his own subsistence. This principle lies at the foundation of all the history of all mankind. If it were otherwise, we should be
all cultivators of the earth. We should none of us ever know the sweets
of leisure; and all human science would be contained in the knowledge
of seed-time and harvest. But no sooner have men associated in tribes
and nations, than this great truth comes to be perceived, that comparatively a very small portion of labour on the part of the community,
will subsist the whole. Hence it happens that even the farmer and the
husbandman have leisure for their religion, their social pleasures, and their
sports; and hence it happens, which is of infinitely more importance
in the history of the human mind, that, while a minority of the community
are employed in the labours indispensably conducive to the mere subsistence of the whole, the rest can devote themselves to art, to science, to
literature, to contemplation, and even to all the wanton refinements of
sensuality, luxury, and ostentation.

What is it then, we are naturally led to ask, that causes any man to
starve, or prevents him from cultivating the earth, and subsisting upon
its fruits, so long as there is a portion of soil in the country in which he
dwells, that has not been applied to the producing as much of the means
of human subsistence, as it is capable of producing? Mr. Malthus says,
it is "*the Law of Nature.*" "After the public notice which I have proposed,
if any man chose to marry, without a prospect of being able to support a
family, he should have the most perfect liberty to do so. Though to marry,
in this case, is in my opinion clearly an immoral act, yet it is not one which
society can justly take upon itself to prevent or punish. To the *punish-*

ment of Nature therefore he should be left." And elsewhere, "A man who is born into a world already possessed, if he cannot get subsistence from his parents, and if the society do not want his labour, has no claim of right to the smallest portion of food, and in fact has no business to be where he is. At *Nature's mighty feast* there is no vacant cover for him. *She* tells him to be gone, and will quickly execute *her own* orders."

Never surely was there so flagrant an abuse of terms, as in this instance. Mr. Malthus is speaking of England, where there are many thousands of acres wholly uncultivated, and perhaps as many more scarcely employed in any effectual manner to increase the means of human subsistence; for these passages occur in chapters of his Essay where he is treating of our Poor-laws, and the remedies that might be applied to the defects he imputes to them. I grant him then, that it is *Law* which condemns the persons he speaks of to starve. So far we are agreed. This Law Mr. Malthus may affirm to be just, to be wise, to be necessary to the state of things as we find them. All this would be open to fair enquiry. Great and cogent no doubt are the reasons that have given so extensive a reign to this extreme inequality. But it is not *the Law of Nature*. It is *the Law of every artificial life*. It is the Law which "heaps upon some few with vast excess" the means of every wanton expence and every luxury, while others, some of them not less worthy, are condemned to pine in want.

Compare this then with Mr. Malthus's favourite position, in opposition to what he calls "the great error under which Mr. Godwin labours," that "political regulations and the established administration of property are in reality light and superficial causes of mischief to society, in comparison with those which result from the *Laws of Nature*."

But to return, and resume the point with which this chapter commenced. If Mr. Malthus's doctrine is true, why is the globe not peopled? If the human species has so strong a tendency to increase, that, unless the tendency were violently and calamitously counteracted, they would every where "double their numbers in less than twenty-five years," and that for ever, how comes it that the world is a wilderness, a wide and desolate place, where men crawl about in little herds, comfortless, unable from the dangers of free-booters, and the dangers of wild beasts to wander from climate to climate, and without that mutual support and cheerfulness which a populous earth would most naturally afford? The man on the top of St. Paul's would indeed form a conception of innumerable multitudes: but he who should survey "all the kingdoms of the world," would receive a very different impression. On which side then lies the evidence? Do the numbers of mankind actually and in fact increase or decrease? If mankind has so powerful and alarming a tendency to increase, how is it that this tendency no where shews itself in general history? Mr. Malthus and his followers are reduced to confess the broad and glaring fact that mankind do not increase, but he has found out a calculation, a geometrical ratio, to shew that they ought to do so, and then sits down to write three volumes, assigning certain obscure, vague, and undefinable causes, why his theory and the stream of ancient and modern history are completely at variance with each other.

Chapter IV. *General View of the Arguments against the Increase of Mankind*

Mr. Malthus's theory is certainly of a peculiar structure, and it is somewhat difficult to account for the success it has met with.

The subject is population.

It has been agreed among the best philosophers in Europe, especially from the time of Lord Bacon to the present day, that the proper basis of all our knowledge respecting man and nature, respecting what has been in times that are past, and what may be expected in time to come, is experiment. This standard is peculiarly applicable to the subject of population.

Mr. Malthus seems in one respectfully to concur in this way of viewing the subject. There are two methods of approaching the question, the first, by deriving our ideas respecting it from the volumes of sacred writ, and the second, by having recourse to such enumerations, statistical tables, and calculations, as the industry of mere uninspired men has collected; and Mr. Malthus has made his election for the latter. Dr. Robert Wallance, an able writer on these subjects, whose works have lately engaged in a considerable degree the attention of curious enquirers, has taken the opposite road. He begins his Dissertation on the Numbers of Mankind in Ancient and Modern Times, printed in 1753, with the position that the whole human race is descended "from a single pair," and, taking that for the basis of his theory, proceeds to calculate the periods of the multiplication of mankind.

Mr. Malthus, on the contrary reposes throughout his Essay on the pure basis of human experience and unenlightened human reason; and I have undertaken to write a refutation of his theories. He has chosen his ground; and I followed him to the contest. He had made no allusion to Adam and Eve, and has written just as any speculator in political economy might have done, to whom the records of the Bible were unknown. If there is any thing irreverend in this, to Mr. Malthus, and not to me, the blame is to be imputed. He has constructed his arguments upon certain *data*, and I have attempted nothing more than the demolishing of those arguments. If any one shall be of opinion that the whole question is in the jurisdiction of another court, the Treatise I am writing has nothing to . do with this. I design nothing more than an investigation of mere human authorities, and an examination of the theories of the Essay on Population; and I leave the question in all other respects as I have found it. To return.

It will appear, I think, in the course of our discussion, that population is a subject with which mankind as yet are very little acquainted. But let us first recollect what it is that we are supposed to know. And I will first state those things which are admitted by Mr. Malthus, and which appear to make very little for the support of his system.

The globe we inhabit may be divided into the Old World and the New. Our knowledge of the history of Europe and Asia extends backward some thousand years. We know a little of the history of Africa. America was discovered about three hundred years ago, but has not in many of its parts been by any means so long a place of reception for European colonies. Mr. Malthus does not venture to carry his appeal on the subject of population there, farther back than one hundred and fifty years.

Well then, how stands the question of population in the Old World? Mr. Malthus freely and without hesitation admits, that on this side of the globe population is, and has long been, at a stand; he might safely have added that it has not increased as far back as any authentic records of profane history will carry us. He brings forward some memorable examples of a striking depopulation: he might have added many more: he would certainly have found it difficult to produce an example equally unequivocal, of an increase of population, in any quarter of the Old World.

As to South America, and the indigenous inhabitants of North America, it is hardly to be disputed, and Mr. Malthus is very ready to admit, that they have sustained a melancholy diminution since the voyage of Columbus.

Such then is, so far, the foundation of our knowledge, as afforded us by experience, on the subject of population. Mr. Malthus has brought forward an exception to all this, which I shall hereafter take occasion fully to examine, in a certain tract of the globe, now known by the name of the United States of America, and he affirms this exception to spread itself over a period of one hundred and fifty years. The entire foundation of his work lies in one simple sentence: "In the Northern States of America, the population has been found to double itself for above a century and a half successively, in less than twenty-five years."

The pith of Mr. Malthus's book therefore, and a bolder design has seldom entered into the mind of man, is to turn the exception into the rule, and the whole stream of examples in every other case, into exceptions, that are to be accounted for without detracting from the authority of the rule.

The Essay on Population is the most oddly constructed, of any book, pretending to the character of science, that was perhaps ever given to the world.

It consists, in the copy now lying before me, of three volumes.

The first chapter, containing sixteen pages, comprises the whole doctrine upon which the work is founded. He that should read the first chapter, and no more, would be in possession of everything in the book, that is solid and compressed, and bears so much as the air of science.

The next 698 pages, the most considerable portion of the work, are wholly employed in assigning causes why every region of the globe, in every period of its history, part of the United States of America for the last one hundred and fifty years excepted, appears to contradict the positions of Mr. Malthus's theory. This is done by exhibiting certain checks on population, the whole of which, as will more fully appear hereafter, falls under the two heads of vice and misery. The remainder of the work treats of the different systems or expedients which have been proposed or have prevailed, as they affect the evils which arise out of the author's principle of population, and of our future prospects respecting the removal or mitigation of these evils.

Now upon this shewing, I affirm that Mr. Malthus is the most fortunate man that ever lived, Sterne's king of Bohemia himself not being excepted. Notwithstanding this glaring rottenness and fallacy in the first concoction of his work, the author has carried the whole world before him; no other system of thinking on the subject is admitted into the company of the great; hundreds of men who were heretofore earnest champions of the happiness of mankind have become his converts; and though, I believe, from thirty to forty answers have been written to the Essay on Population, not one of them, so far as I know, has undertaken to controvert the main principle and corner-stone of his system.

The strength of Mr. Malthus's writing wholly depends upon his intrenching himself in general statements. If we hope for any victory over him, it must be by drawing him out of his strong hold, and meeting him upon the fair ground of realities.

The hypothesis of the Essay on Population is this. The human species doubles itself in the United States of America every twenty-five years: therefore it must have an inherent tendency so to double itself: therefore it would so double itself in the Old World, were not the increase intercepted by causes which have not yet sufficiently engaged the attention of political enquirers.

To clear up this point let us consider how many children may be allowed to a marriage, upon the supposition that the object is barely to keep the numbers of the human species up to their present standard. In the first place it is clear, that every married pair may be allowed two upon an average, without any increase to the population, nay, with the certainty of diminution if they fall short of this. In the next place it is unquestionable, that every child that is born, does not live to years of maturity, so as to be able to propagate the kind; for this condition is necessary, the children who die in their nonage plainly contributing nothing to the keeping up the numbers of our species. I should have thought therefore, that we might safely allow of three children to every marriage, without danger of overstocking the community. It will hereafter appear that all political economists allow four, it being the result of various censuses and tables of population, that one-half of the born die under years of maturity. To this number of children to be allowed to every marriage upon an average, the purpose being barely to keep up the numbers of our species to the present standard, something must be added in consideration of the known fact, that every man and woman do not marry, and thus put themselves in the road for continuing their species.

When Mr. Malthus therefore requires us to believe in the geometrical ratio, or that the human species has a natural tendency to double itself every twenty-five years, he does nothing less in other words, than require us to believe that every marriage among human creatures produces upon an average, including prolific marriages, those in which the husband or wife die in the vigour of their age or in the early years of their union, those in which the prolific power seems particularly limited, and the marriages that are totally barren, eight children.

All this Mr. Malthus requires us to believe, because he wills it. Let it never again be made one of the reproaches of the present day, that we are fallen upon an age of incredulity. I am sure no false prophet, in the darkest ages of ignorance, could ever boast of a greater number of hoodwinked and implicit disciples, than Mr. Malthus in this enlightened period.

How comes it, that neither this author, nor any one for him, has then looked into this view of the question? There are such things as registers of marriages and births. To these it was natural for Mr. Malthus to have recourse for a correlative argument to support his hypothesis. The writer of the Essay on Population has resorted to certain statements of the population of the United States, and from them has inferred that the number of its citizens have doubled every twenty-five years, and as he adds, "by procreation only:" that is, in other words, as we have shown, that every marriage in America, and by parity of reasoning, in all other parts of the world, produces upon an average eight children. For the difference between the United States and the Old World does not, I presume, lie in the superior fecundity of their women, but that a greater number of children are cut off in the Old World in years of nonage, by vice a nd misery. We double very successfully (if they double) in the first period; but we do not, like them rear our children, to double over again in the second. Naturally therefore he would have produced a strong confirmation of his hypothesis, by shewing from the registers of different parts of the world, or of different countries of Europe, that every marriage does upon an average produce eight children: and if he had done this, I think he would have saved me the trouble of writing this volume. Something however has been done in the way of collating the registers of marriages and births; and of this I shall make full use in my second book.

It may however be objected, that there are two ways in which an increase of population may be intercepted; either by the number of children who shall perish in their nonage, through the powerful agency, as Mr. Malthus informs us, of vice and misery; or by certain circumstances which shall cause a smaller number to be born; it may not therefore be merely by the ravages of an extensive mortality, that population in the Old World is kept down to its level.

Mr. Malthus himself has furnished me with a complete answer to this objection. In the first edition of his book he sets out with what he called "fairly making two *postulata:* first, that food is necessary to the existence of man: secondly, that the passion between the sexes is necessary, and will always remain nearly in its present state."

This indeed is one of the "passages, which the author has expunged in the later editions of his book, that he might not inflict an unnecessary violence upon the feelings of his readers" or, as he himself expresses it, is one of the places, in which he "has endeavoured to soften some of the harshest conclusions of his first Essay—in doing which he hopes he has not violated the principles of just reasoning." But, as Mr. Malthus has retained to the last all the conclusions drawn from these *postulata*, and as his argument respecting the impracticability of a permanent state of equality among human beings, founded upon the parity of these two propositions, stands in the Fifth Edition *verbatim* as it stood in the first, I cannot myself consent to his withdrawing his premises, at the same time that he retains the inferences built upon them.

Again: in compliance with "the feelings of certain readers," Mr. Malthus has added in his subsequent editions, to the two checks upon population, *viz.* vice and misery, as they stood in the first, a third which he calls moral restraint. But then he expressly qualifies this by saying, "the principle of moral restraint has undoubtedly in past ages operated with very inconsiderable force"; subjoining at the same time his protest against "any opinion respecting the probable improvement of society, in which we are not borne out by the experience of the past."

It is clearly therefore Mr. Malthus's doctrine, that population is kept down in the Old World, not by a smaller number of children being born among us, but by the excessive number of children that perish in their nonage through the instrumentality of vice and misery.

Let us then proceed to illustrate this proposition, in its application to our own beloved country of England. We will take its present population at ten millions. Of this population we will suppose five millions to be adults. There must then, according to the statement of Dr. Franklin and other calculators, be ten millions of children, born and to be born from these five millions of adults, to give us a chance of keeping up the race of Englishmen. Of these ten millions five millions must be expected to die in their nonage, according to the constitution and course of nature. Surely this, together with the incessant uninterrupted mortality of the middle-aged, and of the more ancient members of society, may be regarded as sufficiently rendering the globe we inhabit "a universe of death."

But Mr. Malthus demands from us, by virtue of his geometrical ratio, ten millions of children more than our unsuspecting ancestors ever dreamed of, that is, eight children for every pair of adults. I say eight, because, if in countries where they have room and every facility for rearing their children, two perish in their nonage out of the first four, there can be no reason that I can apprehend, why as many should not perish out of the second four. Thus it appears that, for every five millions that grow up to the estate of man and woman, twenty millions of children are born, of which fifteen millions, every where in the Old World, perish in their infancy. The first five millions of those who die in this manner constitute a mortality that we must be contented to witness, since such, it seems, is the condition of our existence. But the next ten millions I should call a sort of superfetation of alternate births and deaths, purely for the benefit of the geometrical ratio.

But where is the record of all this? In most civilized countries some sort of register is kept of births, marriages, and deaths. I believe no trace of these additional births which Mr. Malthus has introduced to our acquaintance, is any where to be found. Were all these children sent out of the world, without so much as the ceremonies of baptism? Were they exposed among the wilds of Mount Taygetus, or cast into the Barathrum, or hurled from the Tarpeian rock, or carelessly thrown forth, as Mr. Malthus says the Chinese infants are in the streets of Pekin? For my own part, I am disposed to require some further evidence on the subject, than merely to be told they must have been born and have died, in defiance of all received evidence on the subject, because such is the inference that follows from the principles of the Essay on Population.

In reality, if I had not taken up the pen with the express purpose of confuting all the errors of Mr. Malthus's book, and of endeavouring to introduce other principles, more cheering, more favourable to the best interests of mankind, and better prepared to resist the inroads of vice and misery, I might close my argument here, and lay down the pen with this brief remark, that, when this author shall have produced from any country, the United States of North America not excepted, a register of marriages and births, from which it shall appear that there are on an average eight births to a marriage, then, and not till then, can I have any just reason to admit his doctrine of the geometrical ratio.

THOMAS ROBERT MALTHUS

(1766–1834)

Thomas Robert Malthus came of an old and rather distinguished English family. He was graduated with honors from Jesus College, Cambridge, after which he took orders in the established church.

In 1798 appeared anonymously the first edition of his "Essay on Population," or, to be exact, "An Essay on the Principles of Population as it affects the Future Improvement of Society, with remarks on the Speculations of Mr. Godwin, M. Condorcet and other Writers." After its publication, Malthus saw fit to travel on the continent of Europe.

The "Essay on Population" attracted so much attention that the modest but scholarly English clergyman was forced to reveal his identity. In 1801, the temporary Peace of Amiens between the Napoleanic wars, enabled Malthus again to visit the continent of Europe, after which travels a second edition of his "Essay on Population" appeared in 1803, under the title, "Essay on the Principles of Population; or a View of its Past and Present Effects on Human Happiness with an Enquiry into our Prospects respecting the Future Removal or Mitigation of the Evils which it Occasions."

The second edition was decidedly different from the first. Numerous other later editions appeared, but the changes were less drastic. The following selections are taken from the first edition of 1798 and the sixth edition of 1826. The student is asked to observe the differences in the two editions, and to see how, if at all, the early views of Malthus were changed.

The student of economics is apt to think of Malthus, not only as the sole discoverer of the Malthusian law, but also merely as the author of the "Essay on Population." Both views are incorrect. Other writers before Malthus had discussed the principle of population. On the other hand, Malthus made numerous other contributions to economics in addition to the principle of population.

Among the other writings of Malthus were: "An Investigation of the Cause of the Present High Price of Provisions" (1800); "Observations on the Effects of the Corn Laws" (1814); and "Nature and Progress of Rent" (1815). The latter states very clearly the principle of diminishing returns from land, on which his famous law of population rests. It also anticipates the Ricardian law of rent. In 1815 also appeared "Ground of an Opinion on the Policy of Restricting the Importation of Foreign Corn." In it Malthus advocated at least temporary protection for the British farmer. In 1817, appeared "The Poor Law."

"Principles of Political Economy" appeared in 1820. This general treatise on economics contained his mature and rather complete statement of economic theory, in which he disagreed with his friend Ricardo on certain points. Malthus believed agricultural improvements did raise rents, and he also refused to consider *mere necessities* as the natural price of labor. In 1823, appeared "Measure of Value," in which Malthus also contended that labor was the true measure of value; and in 1827, "Definitions in Political Economy," a valuable brief statement of Malthusian concepts.

In addition to selections from the first and the sixth edition of his "Essay on Population," there follow selections from Malthus's "Principles of Political Economy" and "Definitions in Political Economy." The student is asked to trace his views carefully and to compare them with those of Ricardo.

THOMAS ROBERT MALTHUS

SELECTIONS FROM "ESSAY ON POPULATION" (FIRST EDITION)

Preface

The following Essay owes its origin to a conversation with a friend, on the subject of Mr. Godwin's Essay, on avarice and profusion, in his Enquirer. The discussion started the general question of the future improvement of society; and the Author at first sat down with an intention of merely stating his thoughts to his friend, upon paper, in a clearer manner than he thought he could do, in conversation. But as the subject opened upon him, some ideas occurred, which he did not recollect to have met with before; and as he conceived, that every, the least light, on a topic so generally interesting, might be received with candour, he determined to put his thoughts in a form for publication.

The Essay might, undoubtedly, have been rendered much more complete by a collection of a greater number of facts in elucidation of the general argument. But a long and almost total interruption, from very particular business, joined to a desire (perhaps imprudent) of not delaying the publication much beyond the time that he originally proposed, prevented the Author from giving to the subject an undivided attention. He presumes, however, that the facts which he has adduced, will be found, to form no inconsiderable evidence for the truth of his opinion respecting the future improvement of mankind. As the Author contemplates this opinion at present, little more appears to him to be necessary than a plain statement, in addition to the most cursory view of society, to establish it.

It is an obvious truth, which has been taken notice of by many writers, that population must always be kept down to the level of the means of subsistence; but no writer, that the Author recollects, has inquired particularly into the means by which this level is effected: and it is a view of these means, which forms, to his mind, the strongest obstacle in the way to any very great future improvement of society. He hopes it will appear, that, in the discussion of this interesting subject, he is actuated solely by a love of truth; and not by any prejudices against any particular set of men, or of opinions. He professes to have read some of the speculations on the future improvement of society, in a temper very different from a wish to find them visionary; but he has not acquired that command over his understanding which would enable him to believe what he wishes, without evidence, or to refuse his assent to what might be unpleasing, when accompanied with evidence.

The view which he has given of human life has a melancholy hue; but he feels conscious, that he has drawn these dark tints, from a conviction that they are really in the picture; and not from a jaundiced eye, or an inherent spleen of disposition. The theory of mind which he has sketched in the two last chapters, accounts to his own understanding, in a satisfactory manner, for the existence of most of the evils of life; but whether it will have the same effect upon others, must be left to the judgment of his readers.

If he should succeed in drawing the attention of more able men, to what he conceives to be the principal difficulty in the way to the improvement of society, and should, in consequence, see this difficulty removed, even in theory, he will gladly retract his present opinions, and rejoice in a conviction of his error.

June 7, 1798.

CHAPTER I

Question stated.—Little prospect of a determination of it, from the enmity of the opposing parties.—The principal argument against the perfectibility of man and of society has never been fairly answered.—Nature of the difficulty arising from population.—Outline of the principal argument of the essay.

The great and unlooked for discoveries that have taken place of late years in natural philosophy; the increasing diffusion of general knowledge from the extension of the art of printing; the ardent and unshackled spirit of inquiry that prevails throughout the lettered, and even unlettered world; the new and extraordinary lights that have been thrown on political subjects, which dazzle, and astonish the understanding; and particularly that tremendous phenomenon in the political horizon the French revolution, which, like a blazing comet, seems destined either to inspire with fresh life and vigour, or to scorch up and destroy the shrinking inhabitants of the earth, have all concurred to lead many able men into the opinion, that we were touching on a period big with the most important changes, changes that would in some measure be decisive of the future fate of mankind.

It has been said, that the great question is now at issue, whether man shall henceforth start forwards with accelerated velocity towards illimitable, and hitherto unconceived improvement; or be condemned to a perpetual oscillation between happiness and misery, and after every effort remain still at an immeasurable distance from the wished-for goal.

Yet, anxiously as every friend of mankind must look forwards to the termination of this painful suspense; and, eagerly as the inquiring mind would hail every ray of light that might assist its view into futurity, it is much to be lamented, that the writers on each side of this momentous question still keep far aloof from each other. Their mutual arguments do not meet with a candid examination. The question is not brought to rest on fewer points; and even in theory scarcely seems to be approaching to a decision.

The advocate for the present order of things, is apt to treat the sect of speculative philosophers, either as a set of artful and designing knaves, who preach up ardent benevolence, and draw captivating pictures of a happier state of society, only the better to enable them to destroy the present establishments, and to forward their own deep-laid schemes of ambition: or, as wild and mad-headed enthusiasts, whose silly speculations, and absurd paradoxes, are not worthy the attention of any reasonable man.

The advocate for the perfectibility of man, and of society, retorts on the defender of establishments a more than equal contempt. He brands him as the slave of the most miserable, and narrow prejudices; or, as the defender of the abuses of civil society, only because he profits by them. He paints him either as a character who prostitutes his understanding to his interest; or as one whose powers of mind are not of a size to grasp any thing great and noble; who cannot see above five yards before him; and who must therefore be utterly unable to take in the views of the enlightened benefactor of mankind.

In this unamicable contest, the cause of truth cannot but suffer. The really good arguments on each side of the question are not allowed to have their proper weight. Each pursues his own theory, little solicitous to correct, or improve it, by an attention to what is advanced by his opponents.

The friend of the present order of things condemns all political speculations in the gross. He will not even condescend to examine the grounds from which the perfectibility of society is inferred. Much less will he give himself the trouble in a fair and candid manner to attempt an exposition of their fallacy.

The speculative philosopher equally offends against the cause of truth. With eyes fixed on a happier state of society, the blessings of which he paints in the most captivating colours, he allows himself to indulge in the most bitter invectives against every present establishment, without applying his talents to consider the best and safest means of removing abuses, and without seeming to be aware of the tremendous obstacles that threaten, even in theory, to oppose the progress of man towards perfection.

It is an acknowledged truth in philosophy, that a just theory will always be confirmed by experiment. Yet so much friction, and so many minute circumstances occur in practice, which it is next to impossible for the most enlarged and penetrating mind to foresee, that on few subjects can any theory be pronounced just, that has not stood the test of experience. But an untried theory cannot fairly be advanced as probable, much less as just, till all the arguments against it, have been maturely weighed, and clearly and consistently refuted.

I have read some of the speculations on the perfectibility of man and of society, with great pleasure. I have been warmed and delighted with the enchanting picture which they hold forth. I ardently wish for such happy improvements. But I see great, and, to my understanding, unconquerable difficulties in the way to them. These difficulties it is my present purpose to state; declaring, at the same time, that so far from exulting in them, as a cause of triumph over the friends of innovation, nothing would give me greater pleasure than to see them completely removed.

The most important argument that I shall adduce is certainly not new. The principles on which it depends have been explained in part by Hume, and more at large by Dr. Adam Smith. It has been advanced and applied to the present subject, though not with its proper weight, or in the most forcible point of view, by Mr. Wallace: and it may probably have been stated by many writers that I have never met with. I should certainly therefore not think of advancing it again, though I mean to place it in a point of view in some degree different from any that I have hitherto seen, if it had ever been fairly and satisfactorily answered.

The cause of this neglect on the part of the advocates for the perfectibility of mankind, is not easily accounted for. I cannot doubt the talents of such men as Godwin and Condorcet. I am unwilling to doubt their candour. To my understanding, and probably to that of most others, the difficulty appears insurmountable. Yet these men of acknowledged ability and penetration, scarcely deign to notice it, and hold on their course in such speculations, with unabated ardour, and undiminished confidence. I have certainly no right to say that they purposely shut their eyes to such arguments. I ought rather to doubt the validity of them, when neglected by such men, however forcibly their truth may strike my own mind. Yet in this respect it must be acknowledged that we are all of us too prone to err. If I saw a glass of wine repeatedly presented to a man, and he took no notice of it, I should be apt to think that he was blind or uncivil. A juster philosophy might teach me rather to think that my eyes deceived me, and that the offer was not really what I conceived it to be.

In entering upon the argument I must premise that I put out of the question, at present, all mere conjectures; that is, all suppositions, the probable realization of which cannot be inferred upon any just philosophical grounds. A writer may tell me that he thinks man will ultimately become an ostrich. I cannot properly contradict him. But before he can expect to bring any reasonable person over to his opinion, he ought to shew, that the necks of mankind have been gradually elongating; that the lips have grown harder, and more prominent; that the legs and feet are daily altering their shape; and that the hair is beginning to change into stubs of feathers. And till the probability of so wonderful a conversion can be shewn, it is surely lost time and lost eloquence to expatiate on the happiness of man in such a state; to describe his powers, both of running and flying; to paint him in a condition where all narrow luxuries would be contemned; where he would be employed only in collecting the necessaries of life; and where, consequently, each man's share of labour would be light, and his portion of leisure ample.

I think I may fairly make two postulata.

First, That food is necessary to the existence of man.

Secondly, That the passion between the sexes is necessary, and will remain nearly in its present state.

These two laws ever since we have had any knowledge of mankind, appear to have been fixed laws of our nature; and, as we have not hitherto seen any alteration in them, we have no right to conclude that they will ever cease to be what they now are, without an immediate act of power in that Being who first arranged the system of the universe; and for the advantage of his creatures, still executes, according to fixed laws, all its various operations.

I do not know that any writer has supposed that on this earth man will ultimately be able to live without food. But Mr. Godwin has conjectured that the passion between the sexes may in time be extinguished. As, however, he calls this part of his work, a deviation into the land of conjecture, I will not dwell longer upon it at present, than to say, that the best arguments for the perfectibility of man, are drawn from a contemplation of the great progress that he has already made from the savage state, and the difficulty of saying where he is to stop. But towards the extinction of the passion between the sexes, no progress whatever has hitherto been made. It appears to exist in as much force at present as it did two thousand, or four thousand years ago. There are individual exceptions now as there always have been. But, as these exceptions do not appear to increase in number, it would surely be a very unphilosophical mode of arguing, to infer merely from the existence of an exception, that the exception would, in time, become the rule, and the rule the exception.

Assuming then, my postulata as granted, I say, that the power of population is indefinitely greater than the power in the earth to produce subsistence for man.

Population, when unchecked, increases in a geometrical ratio. Subsistence increases only in an arithmetical ratio. A slight acquaintance with numbers will shew the immensity of the first power in comparison of the second.

By that law of our nature which makes food necessary to the life of man, the effects of these two unequal powers must be kept equal.

This implies a strong and constantly operating check on population from the difficulty of subsistence. This difficulty must fall some where; and must necessarily be severely felt by a large portion of mankind.

Through the animal and vegetable kingdoms, nature has scattered the seeds of life abroad with the most profuse and liberal hand. She has been comparatively sparing in the room, and the nourishment necessary to rear them. The germs of existence contained in this spot of earth, with ample food, and ample room to expand in, would fill millions of worlds in the course of a few thousand years. Necessity, that imperious all pervading law of nature, restrains them within the prescribed bounds. The race of plants, and the race of animals shrink under this great restrictive law. And the race of man cannot, by any efforts of reason, escape from it. Among plants and animals its effects are waste of seed, sickness, and premature death. Among mankind, misery and vice. The former, misery, is an absolutely necessary consequence of it. Vice is a highly probable consequence, and we therefore see it abundantly prevail; but it ought not, perhaps, to be called an absolutely necessary consequence. The ordeal of virtue is to resist all temptation to evil.

This natural inequality of the two powers of population, and of production in the earth, and that great law of our nature which must constantly keep their effects equal, form the great difficulty that to me appears insurmountable in the way to the perfectibility of society. All other arguments are of slight and subordinate consideration in comparison of this. I see no way by which man can escape from the weight of this law which pervades all animated nature. No fancied equality, no agrarian regulations in their utmost extent, could remove the pressure of it even for a single century. And it appears, therefore, to be decisive against the possible existence of a society, all the members of which, should live in ease, happiness, and comparative leisure; and feel no anxiety about providing the means of subsistence for themselves and families.

Consequently, if the premises are just, the argument is conclusive against the perfectibility of the mass of mankind.

I have thus sketched the general outline of the argument; but I will examine it more particularly; and I think it will be found that experience, the true source and foundation of all knowledge, invariably confirms its truth.

CHAPTER II

The different ratios in which population and food increase.—The necessary effects of these different ratios of increase.—Oscillation produced by them in the condition of the lower classes of society.—Reasons why this oscillation has not been so much observed as might be expected.—Three propositions on which the general argument of the essay depends.—The different states in which mankind have been known to exist proposed to be examined with reference to these three propositions.

I said that population, when unchecked, increased in a geometrical ratio; and subsistence for man in an arithmetical ratio.

Let us examine whether this position be just.

I think it will be allowed, that no state has hitherto existed (at least that we have any account of) where the manners were so pure and simple, and the means of subsistence so abundant, that no check whatever has existed to early marriages; among the lower classes, from a fear of not providing well for their families; or among the higher classes, from a fear of lowering their condition in life. Consequently in no state that we have yet known, has the power of population been left to exert itself with perfect freedom.

Whether the law of marriage be instituted, or not, the dictate of nature and virtue, seems to be an early attachment to one woman. Supposing a liberty of changing in the case of an unfortunate choice, this liberty would not affect population till it arose to a height greatly vicious; and we are now supposing the existence of a society where vice is scarcely known.

In a state therefore of great equality and virtue, where pure and simple manners prevailed, and where the means of subsistence were so abundant, that no part of the society could have any fears about providing amply for a family, the power of population being left to exert itself unchecked, the increase of the human species would evidently be much greater than any increase that has been hitherto known.

In the United States of America, where the means of subsistence have been more ample, the manners of the people more pure, and consequently the checks to early marriages fewer, than in any of the modern states of Europe, the population has been found to double itself in twenty-five years.

This ratio of increase, though short of the utmost power of population, yet as the result of actual experience, we will take as our rule; and say,

That population, when unchecked, goes on doubling itself every twenty-five years, or increases in a geometrical ratio.

*   *   *   *   *

THOMAS ROBERT MALTHUS

SELECTIONS FROM "ESSAY ON POPULATION" (SIXTH EDITION)

Book I

Chapter I

I. STATEMENT OF THE SUBJECT. RATIOS OF THE INCREASE OF POPULATION AND FOOD

In an inquiry concerning the improvement of society the mode of conducting the subject which naturally presents itself is,

1. To investigate the causes that have hitherto impeded the progress of mankind towards happiness; and

2. To examine the probability of the total or partial removal of these causes in the future.

To enter fully into this question and to enumerate all the causes that have hitherto influenced human improvement would be much beyond the power of an individual. The principal object of the present essay is to examine the effects of one great cause intimately united with the very nature of man; which, though it has been constantly and powerfully operating since the commencement of society, has been little noticed by the writers who have treated this subject. The facts which establish the existence of this cause have, indeed, been repeatedly stated and acknowledged; but its natural and necessary effects have been almost totally overlooked; though probably among these effects may be reckoned a very considerable portion of that vice and misery, and of that unequal distribution of the bounties of nature, which it has been the unceasing object of the enlightened philanthropist in all ages to correct.

The cause to which I allude is the constant tendency in all animated life to increase beyond the nourishment prepared for it.

It is observed by Dr. Franklin that there is no bound to the prolific nature of plants or animals but what is made by their crowding and interfering with each other's means of subsistence. Were the face of the earth, he says, vacant of other plants, it might be gradually sowed and overspread with one kind only, as for instance with fennel; and were it empty of other inhabitants, it might in a few ages be replenished from one nation only, as for instance with Englishmen.

This is incontrovertibly true. Through the animal and vegetable kingdoms nature has scattered the seeds of life abroad with the most

137

profuse and liberal hand, but has been comparatively sparing in the room and the nourishment necessary to rear them. The germs of existence contained in this earth, if they could freely develop themselves, would fill millions of worlds in the course of a few thousand years. Necessity, that imperious, all-pervading law of nature, restrains them within the prescribed bounds. The race of plants and the race of animals shrink under this great restrictive law; and man cannot by any efforts of reason escape from it.

In plants and irrational animals the view of the subject is simple. They are all impelled by a powerful instinct to the increase of their species; and this instinct is interrupted by no doubts about providing for their offspring. Wherever therefore there is liberty, the power of increase is exerted; and the superabundant effects are repressed afterwards by want of room and nourishment.

The effects of this check on man are more complicated. Impelled to the increase of his species by an equally powerful instinct, reason interrupts his career, and asks him whether he may not bring beings into the world for whom he cannot provide the means of support. If he attend to this natural suggestion, the restriction too frequently produces vice. If he hear it not, the human race will be constantly endeavoring to increase beyond the means of subsistence. But as, by that law of our nature which makes food necessary to the life of man, population can never actually increase beyond the lowest nourishment capable of supporting it, a strong check on population, from the difficulty of acquiring food, must be constantly in operation. This difficulty must fall somewhere, and must necessarily be severely felt in some or other of the various forms of misery, or the fear of misery, by a large portion of mankind.

That population has this constant tendency to increase beyond the means of subsistence, and that it is kept to its necessary level by these causes will sufficiently appear from a review of the different states of society in which man has existed. But before we proceed to this review the subject will, perhaps, be seen in a clearer light, if we endeavor to ascertain what would be the natural increase of population if left to exert itself with perfect freedom, and what might be expected to be the rate of increase in the productions of the earth under the most favorable circumstances of human industry.

It will be allowed that no country has hitherto been known where the manners were so pure and simple, and the means of subsistence so abundant, that no check whatever has existed to early marriages from the difficulty of providing for a family, and that no waste of the human species has been occasioned by vicious customs, by towns, by unhealthy occupations, or too severe labor. Consequently, in no state that we have yet known has the power of population been left to exert itself with perfect freedom.

Whether the law of marriage be instituted or not, the dictates of nature and virtue seem to be an early attachment to one woman; and where there were no impediments of any kind in the way of an union to which such an attachment would lead, and no causes of depopulation afterwards, the increase of the human species would be evidently much greater than any increase which has hitherto been known.

In the Northern States of America, where the means of subsistence have been more ample, the manners of the people more pure, and the checks to early marriages fewer than in any of the modern states of Europe, the population has been found to double itself, for above a century and a half successively, in less than twenty-five years. Yet, even during these periods, in some of the towns the deaths exceeded the births, a circumstance which clearly proves that, in those parts of the country which supplied this deficiency, the increase must have been much more rapid than the general average.

In the back settlements, where the sole employment is agriculture, and vicious customs and unwholesome occupations are little known, the population has been found to double itself in fifteen years. Even this extraordinary rate of increase is probably short of the utmost power of population. Very severe labor is requisite to clear a fresh country; such situations are not in general considered as particularly healthy; and the inhabitants, probably, are occasionally subject to the incursions of the Indians, which may destroy some lives, or at any rate diminish the fruits of industry.

According to a table of Euler, calculated on a mortality of one to thirty-six, if the births be to the deaths in the proportion of three to one, the period of doubling will be only twelve years and four fifths. And this proportion is not only a possible supposition, but has actually occurred for short periods in more countries than one.

Sir William Petty supposes a doubling possible in so short a time as ten years.

But, to be perfectly sure that we are far within the truth, we will take the slowest of these rates of increase, a rate in which all concurring testimonies agree, and which has been repeatedly ascertained to be from procreation only.

It may safely be pronounced, therefore, that population, when unchecked, goes on doubling itself every twenty-five years, or increases in a geometrical ratio.

The rate according to which the productions of the earth may be supposed to increase it will not be so easy to determine. Of this, however, we may be perfectly certain—that the ratio of their increase in a limited territory must be of a totally different nature from the ratio of the increase of population. A thousand millions are just as easily doubled every twenty-five years by the power of population as a thousand. But the food to support the increase from the greater number will by no means be obtained with the same facility. Man is necessarily confined in room. When acre has been added to acre till all the fertile land is occupied, the yearly increase of food must depend upon the melioration of the land already in possession. This is a fund which, from the nature of all soils, instead of increasing, must be gradually diminishing. But population, could it be supplied with food, would go on with unexhausted vigor; and the increase of one period would furnish the power of a greater increase the next, and this without any limit.

From the accounts we have of China and Japan, it may be fairly doubted whether the best-directed efforts of human industry could double the produce of these countries even once in any number of years. There are many parts of the globe, indeed, hitherto uncultivated and almost unoccupied, but the right of exterminating, or driving into a corner where they must starve, even the inhabitants of these thinly-peopled regions, will be questioned in a moral view. The process of improving their minds and directing their industry would necessarily be slow; and during this time, as population would regularly keep pace with the increasing produce, it would rarely happen that a great degree of knowledge and industry would have to operate at once upon rich unappropriated soil. Even where this might take place, as it does sometimes in new colonies, a geometrical ratio increases with such extraordinary rapidity that the advantage could not last long. If the United States of America continue increasing, which they certainly will do, though not with the same rapidity as formerly, the Indians will be driven further and further back into the country, till the whole race is ultimately exterminated and the territory is incapable of further extension.

These observations are, in a degree, applicable to all the parts of the earth where the soil is imperfectly cultivated. To exterminate the inhabitants of the greatest part of Asia and Africa is a thought that could not be admitted for a moment. To civilize and direct the industry of the various tribes of Tartars and Negroes would certainly be a work of considerable time, and of variable and uncertain success.

Europe is by no means so fully peopled as it might be. In Europe there is the fairest chance that human industry may receive its best direction. The science of agriculture has been much studied in England and Scotland, and there is still a great portion of uncultivated land in these countries. Let us consider at what rate the produce of this island might be supposed to increase under circumstances the most favorable to improvement.

If it be allowed that by the best possible policy, and great encouragement to agriculture, the average produce of the island could be doubled in the first twenty-five years, it will be allowing, probably, a greater increase than could with reason be expected.

In the next twenty-five years it is impossible to suppose that the produce could be quadrupled. It would be countrary to all our knowledge of the properties of land. The improvement of the barren parts would be a work of time and labor; and it must be evident, to those who have the slightest acquaintance with agricultural subjects, that in proportion as cultivation is extended, the additions that could yearly be made to the former average produce must be gradually and regularly diminishing. That we may be the better able to compare the increase of population and food, let us make a supposition which, without pretending to accuracy, is clearly more favorable to the power of production in the earth than any experience we have had of its qualities will warrant.

Let us suppose that the yearly additions which might be made to the former average produce, instead of decreasing, which they certainly would do, were to remain the same; and that the produce of this island might be increased every twenty-five years by a quantity equal to what it at present produces. The most enthusiastic speculator cannot suppose a greater increase than this. In a few centuries it would make every acre of land in the island like a garden.

If this supposition be applied to the whole earth, and if it be allowed that the subsistence for man which the earth affords might be increased every twenty-five years by a quantity equal to what it at present produces, this will be supposing a rate of increase much greater than we can imagine that any possible exertions of mankind could make it.

It may be fairly pronounced, therefore, that considering the present average state of the earth, the means of subsistence, under circumstances the most favorable to human industry, could not possibly be made to increase faster than in an arithmetical ratio.

The necessary effects of these two different rates of increase, when brought together, will be very striking. Let us call the population of this island eleven millions; and suppose the present produce equal to the easy support of such a number. In the first twenty-five years the population would be twenty-two millions, and the food being also doubled, the means of subsistence would be equal to this increase. In the next twenty-five years the population would be forty-four millions, and the means of subsistence only equal to the support of thirty-three millions. In the next period the population would be eighty-eight millions and the means of subsistence just equal to the support of half that number. And at the conclusion of the first century the population would be a hundred and seventy-six millions, and the means of subsistence only equal to the support of fifty-five millions, leaving a population of a hundred and twenty-one millions totally unprovided for.

Taking the whole earth instead of this island, emigration would of course be excluded; and, supposing the present population equal to a thousand millions, the human species would increase as the numbers,

1, 2, 4, 8, 16, 32, 64, 128, 256, and subsistence as 1, 2, 3, 4, 5, 6, 7, 8, 9. In two centuries the population would be to the means of subsistence as 256 to 9; in three centuries, as 4096 to 13; and in two thousand years the difference would be almost incalculable.

In this supposition no limits whatever are placed to the produce of the earth. It may increase forever, and be greater than any assignable quantity; yet still, the power of population being in every period so much superior, the increase of the human species can only be kept down to the level of the means of subsistence by the constant operation of the strong law of necessity, acting as a check upon the greater power.

Chapter II

OF THE GENERAL CHECKS TO POPULATION, AND THE MODE OF THEIR OPERATION

The ultimate check to population appears then to be a want of food arising necessarily from the different ratios according to which population and food increase. But this ultimate check is never the immediate check, except in cases of actual famine.

The immediate check may be stated to consist in all those customs, and all those diseases, which seem to be generated by a scarcity of the means of subsistence; and all those causes, independent of this scarcity, whether of a moral or physical nature, which tend prematurely to weaken and destroy the human frame.

These checks to population, which are constantly operating with more or less force in every society, and keep down the number to the level of the means of subsistence, may be classed under two general heads—the preventive, and the positive checks.

The preventive check, as far as it is voluntary, is peculiar to man, and arises from that distinctive superiority in his reasoning faculties which enables him to calculate distant consequences. The checks to the indefinite increase of plants and irrational animals are all either positive, or, if preventive, involuntary. But man cannot look around him and see the distress which frequently presses upon those who have large families; he cannot contemplate his present possessions or earnings, which he now nearly consumes himself, and calculate the amount of each share, when with very little addition they must be divided, perhaps, among seven or eight, without feeling a doubt whether, if he follow the bent of his inclinations, he may be able to support the offspring which he will probably bring into the world. In a state of equality, if such can exist, this would be the simple question. In the present state of society other considerations occur. Will he not lower his rank in life, and be obliged to give up in great measure his former habits? Does any mode of employment present itself by which he may reasonably hope to maintain a family? Will he not at any rate subject himself to greater difficulties and more severe labor than in his single state? Will he not be unable to transmit to his children the same advantages of education and improvement that he had himself possessed? Does he even feel secure that, should he have a large family, his utmost exertions can save them from rags and squalid poverty, and their consequent degradation in the community? And may he not be reduced to the grating necessity of forfeiting his independence, and of being obliged to the sparing hand of charity for support?

These considerations are calculated to prevent, and certainly do prevent, a great number of persons in all civilized nations from pursuing the dictate of nature in an early attachment to one woman.

If this restraint does not produce vice, it is undoubtedly the least evil that can arise from the principle of population. Considered as a restraint on a strong natural inclination, it must be allowed to produce a certain degree of temporary unhappiness, but evidently slight compared with the evils which result from any of the other checks to population, and merely of the same nature as many other sacrifices of temporary to permanent gratification, which it is the business of a moral agent continually to make.

When this restraint produces vice, the evils which follow are but too conspicuous. A promiscuous intercourse to such a degree as to prevent the birth of children seems to lower, in the most marked manner, the dignity of human nature. It cannot be without its effect on men, and nothing can be more obvious than its tendency to degrade the female character and to destroy all its most amiable and distinguishing characteristics. Add to which, that among those unfortunate females with which all great towns abound more real distress and aggravated misery are, perhaps, to be found, than in any other department of human life.

When a general corruption of morals with regard to the sex pervades all the classes of society, its effects must necessarily be to poison the springs of domestic happiness, to weaken conjugal and parental affection, and to lessen the united exertions and ardor of parents in the care and education of their children—effects which cannot take place without a decided diminution of the general happiness and virtue of the society; particularly as the necessity of art in the accomplishment and conduct of intrigues and in the concealment of their consequences necessarily leads to many other vices.

The positive checks to population are extremely various, and include every cause, whether arising from vice or misery, which in any degree contributes to shorten the natural duration of human life. Under this head, therefore, may be enumerated all unwholesome occupations, severe labor and exposure to the seasons, extreme poverty, bad nursing of children, great towns, excesses of all kinds, the whole train of common diseases and epidemics, wars, plague, and famine.

On examining these obstacles to the increase of population which I have classed under the heads of preventive and positive checks, it will appear that they are all resolvable into moral restraint, vice, and misery.

Of the preventive checks, the restraint from marriage which is not followed by irregular gratifications may properly be termed moral restraint.[1]

Promiscuous intercourse, unnatural passions, violations of the marriage bed, and improper arts to conceal the consequences of irregular connections are preventive checks that clearly come under the head of vice.

Of the positive checks, those which appear to arise unavoidably from the laws of nature may be called exclusively misery, and those which we obviously bring upon ourselves, such as wars, excesses, and many others which it would be in our power to avoid, are of a mixed nature. They are brought upon us by vice, and their consequences are misery.

The sum of all these preventive and positive checks taken together forms the immediate check to population; and it is evident that in every country where the whole of the procreative power cannot be called into action, the preventive and the positive checks must vary inversely as each other; that is, in countries either naturally unhealthy or subject to a great mortality, from whatever cause it may arise, the preventive check will prevail very little. In those countries, on the contrary, which are naturally healthy, and where the preventive check is found to prevail with considerable force, the positive check will prevail very little, or the mortality be very small.

In every country some of these checks are with more or less force in constant operation; yet, notwithstanding their general prevalence, there are few states in which there is not a constant effort in the population to increase beyond the means of subsistence. This constant effort as constantly tends to subject the lower classes of society to distress, and to prevent any great permanent melioration of their condition.

These effects, in the present state of society, seem to be produced in the following manner. We will suppose the means of subsistence in any country just equal to the easy support of its inhabitants. The con-

---

[1] It will be observed that I here use the term *moral* in its most confined sense. By moral restraint I would be understood to mean a restraint from marriage from prudential motives, with a conduct strictly moral during the period of this restraint; and I have never intentionally deviated from this sense. When I have wished to consider the restraint from marriage unconnected with its consequences, I have either called it prudential restraint, or a part of the preventive check, of which indeed it forms the principal branch. In my review of the different stages of society I have been accused of not allowing sufficient weight in the prevention of population to moral restraint; but when the confined sense of the term, which I have here explained, is adverted to, I am fearful that I shall not be found to have erred much in this respect. I should be very glad to believe myself mistaken.

stant effort towards population, which is found to act even in the most vicious societies, increases the number of people before the means of subsistence are increased. The food, therefore, which before supported eleven millions, must now be divided among eleven millions and a half. The poor consequently must live much worse, and many of them be reduced to severe distress. The number of laborers also being above the proportion of work in the market, the price of labor must tend to fall, while the price of provisions would at the same time tend to rise. The laborer, therefore, must do more work to earn the same as he did before. During this season of distress the discouragements to marriage and the difficulty of rearing a family are so great that the progress of population is retarded. In the meantime the cheapness of labor, the plenty of laborers, and the necessity of an increased industry among them encourage cultivators to employ more labor upon their land, to turn up fresh soil, and to manure and improve more completely what is already in tillage, till ultimately the means of subsistence may become in the same proportion to the population as at the period from which we set out. The situation of the laborer being then again tolerably comfortable, the restraints to population are in some degree loosened; and after a short period the same retrograde and progressive movements, with respect to happiness, are repeated.

This sort of oscillation will not probably be obvious to common view; and it may be difficult even for the most attentive observer to calculate its periods. Yet that in the generality of old states some alternation of this kind does exist, though in a much less marked and in a much more irregular manner than I have described it, no reflecting man who considers the subject deeply can well doubt.

One principal reason why this oscillation has been less remarked, and less decidedly confirmed by experience than might naturally be expected, is, that the histories of mankind which we possess are, in general, histories only of the higher classes. We have not many accounts that can be depended upon of the manners and customs of that part of mankind where these retrograde and progressive movements chiefly take place. A satisfactory history of this kind, of one people and of one period, would require the constant and minute attention of many observing minds in local and general remarks on the state of the lower classes of society, and the causes that influenced it; and to draw accurate inferences upon this subject, a succession of such historians for some centuries would be necessary. This branch of statistical knowledge has, of late years, been attended to in some countries, and we may promise our selves a clearer insight into the internal structure of human society from the progress of these inquiries. But the science may be said yet to be in its infancy, and many of the objects, on which it would be desirable to have information, have been either omitted or not stated with sufficient accuracy. Among these, perhaps, may be reckoned the proportion of the number of adults to the number of marriages; the extent to which vicious customs have prevailed in consequence of the restraints upon matrimony; the comparative mortality among the children of the most distressed part of the community and of those who live rather more at their ease; the variations in the real price of labour; the observable differences in the state of the lower classes of society, with respect to ease and happiness, at different times during a certain period; and very accurate registers of births, deaths, and marriages, which are of the utmost importance in this subject.

A faithful history, including such particulars, would tend greatly to elucidate the manner in which the constant check upon population acts; and would probably prove the existence of the retrograde and progressive movements that have been mentioned; though the times of their vibration must necessarily be rendered irregular from the operation of many interrupting causes; such as, the introduction or failure of certain manufactures; a greater or less prevalent spirit of agricultural enterprise; years of plenty or years of scarcity; wars, sickly seasons, poor laws, emigrations, and other causes of a similar nature.

A circumstance which has, perhaps, more than any other, contributed to conceal this oscillation from common view is the difference between the nominal and real price of labour. It very rarely happens that the nominal price of labour universally falls; but we well know that it frequently remains the same while the nominal price of provisions has been gradually rising. This, indeed, will generally be the case if the increase of manufactures and commerce be sufficient to employ the new labourers that are thrown into the market, and to prevent the increased supply from lowering the money-price. But an increased number of labourers receiving the same money-wages will necessarily, by their competition, increase the money-price of corn. This is, in fact, a real fall in the price of labour; and, during this period, the condition of the lower classes of the community must be gradually growing worse. But the farmers and capitalists are growing rich from the real cheapness of labour. Their increasing capitals enable them to employ a greater number of men; and, as the population has probably suffered some check from the greater difficulty of supporting a family, the demand for labour, after a certain period, would be great in proportion to the supply, and its price would of course rise, if left to find its natural level; and thus the wages of labour, and consequently the condition of the lower classes of society, might have progressive and retrograde movements, though the price of labour might never nominally fall.

In savage life, where there is no regular price of labour, it is little to be doubted that similar oscillations took place. When population has increased nearly to the utmost limits of the food, all the preventive and the positive checks will naturally operate with increased force. Vicious habits with respect to the sex will be more general, the exposing of children more frequent, and both the probability and fatality of wars and epidemics will be considerably greater; and these causes will probably continue their operation till the population is sunk below the level of the food; and then the return to comparative plenty will again produce an increase, and, after a certain period, its further progress will again be checked by the same causes.

But without attempting to establish these progressive and retrograde movements in different countries, which would evidently require more minute histories than we possess, and which the progress of civilisation naturally tends to counteract, the following propositions are intended to be proved:—

1. Population is necessarily limited by the means of subsistence.

2. Population invariably increases where the means of subsistence increase, unless prevented by some very powerful and obvious checks.

3. These checks, and the checks which repress the superior power of population, and keep its effects on a level with the means of subsistence, are all resolvable into moral restraint, vices, and misery.

The first of these propositions scarcely needs illustration. The second and third will sufficiently be established by a review of the immediate checks to population in the past and present state of society.

This review will be the subject of the following chapters.

THOMAS ROBERT MALTHUS

SELECTIONS FROM "PRINCIPLES OF POLITICAL ECONOMY"

INTRODUCTION

It has been said, and perhaps with truth, that the conclusions of Political Economy partake more of the certainty of the stricter sciences than those of most of the other branches of human knowledge. Yet we should fall into a serious error if we were to suppose that any propositions, the practical results of which depend upon the agency of so variable a being as man, and the qualities of so variable a compound as the soil, can ever admit of the same kinds of proof, or lead to the same conclusions, as those which relate to figure and number. There are indeed in political economy great general principles, to which exceptions are of the most rare occurrence, and prominent land-marks which may almost always be depended upon as safe guides; but even those, when examined, will be found to resemble, in most particulars, the great general rules in morals and politics founded upon the known passions and propensities of human nature: and whether we advert to the qualities of man, or of the earth he is destined to cultivate, we shall be compelled to acknowledge, that the science of political economy bears a nearer resemblance to the science of morals and politics than to that of mathematics.

* * * * *

The principle cause of error, and of the differences which prevail at present among the scientific writers on political economy, appears to me to be, a precipitate attempt to simplify and generalize; and while their more practical opponents draw too hasty inferences from a frequent appeal to partial facts, these writers run into a contrary extreme, and do not sufficiently try their theories by a reference to that enlarged and comprehensive experience which, on so complicated a subject, can alone establish their truth and utility.

To minds of a certain cast there is nothing so captivating as simplification and generalization. It is indeed the desirable and legitimate object of genuine philosophy, whenever it can be effected consistently with truth; and for this very reason, the natural tendency towards it has, in almost every science with which we are acquainted, led to crude and premature theories.

In political economy the desire to simplify has occasioned an unwillingness to acknowledge the operation of more causes than one in the production of particular effects; and if one cause would account for a considerable portion of a certain class of phenomena, the whole has been ascribed to it without sufficient attention to the facts, which would not admit of being so solved. I have always thought that the late controversy on the bullion question presented a signal instance of this kind of error. Each party being possessed of a theory which would account for an unfavourable exchange, and an excess of the market price above the mint price of bullion, adhered to that single view of the question, which it had been accustomed to consider as correct; and scarcely one writer seemed willing to admit of the operation of both theories, the combination of which, sometimes acting in conjunction and sometimes in opposition, could alone adequately account for the variable and complicated phenomena observable.

It is certain that we cannot too highly respect and venerate that admirable rule of Newton, not to admit more causes than are necessary to the solution of the phenomena we are considering; but the rule itself implies, that those which really are necessary must be admitted. Before the shrine of truth, as discovered by facts and experience, the fairest theories and the most beautiful classifications must fall. The chemist of thirty years ago may be allowed to regret, that new discoveries in the science should disturb and confound his previous systems and arrangements; but he is not entitled to the name of philosopher, if he does not give them up without a struggle, as soon as the experiments which refute them are fully established.

The same tendency to simplify and generalize, produces a still greater disinclination to allow of modifications, limitations, and exceptions to any rule or proposition, than to admit the operation of more causes than one. Nothing indeed is so unsatisfactory, and gives so unscientific and unmasterly an air to a proposition, as to be obliged to make the admissions of this kind; yet there is no truth of which I feel a stronger conviction, than that there are many important propositions in political economy which absolutely require limitations and exceptions, and it may be confidently stated, that the frequent combination of complicated causes, the action and reaction of cause and effect on each other, and the necessity of limitations and exceptions in a considerable number of important propositions, form the main difficulties of the science, and occasions those frequent mistakes which it must be allowed are made in the prediction of results.

* * * * *

The tendency to premature generalization occasions also, in some of the principal writers on political economy, an unwillingness to bring their theories to the test of experience. I should be the last person to lay an undue stress upon isolated facts, or to think that a consistent theory, which would account for the great mass of phenomena observable, was immediately invalidated by a few discordant appearances, the reality and the bearings of which, there might not have been an opportunity of fully examining. But, certainly, no theory can have any pretension to be accepted as correct, which is inconsistent with general experience. Such inconsistency appears to me at once a full and sufficient reason for its rejection. Under such circumstances it must be either radically false, or essentially incomplete; and in either case, it can neither be adopted as a satisfactory solution of existing phenomena, nor acted upon with any degree of safety for the future.

The first business of philosophy is to account for things as they are; and till our theories will do this, they ought not to be the ground of any practical conclusion. I should never have had that steady and unshaken confidence in the theory of population which I have invariably felt, if it had not appeared to me to be confirmed, in the most remarkable manner, by the state of society as it actually exists in every country with which we are acquainted. To this test I appealed in laying it down; and a frequent appeal to this sort of experience is pre-eminently necessary in most of the subjects of political economy, where various and complicated causes are often in operation, the presence of which can be ascertained only in this way. A theory may appear to be correct, and may really be correct under given premises; it may further *appear* that these premises are the same as those under which the theory is about to be applied; but a difference, which might before have been unobserved, may shew itself in the difference of the results from those which were expected; and the theory may justly be considered as failing, whether this failure arise from an original error in its formation, or from its general inapplicability, or specific misapplication, to actual circumstances.

Where unforeseen causes may possibly be in operation, and the causes that are foreseen are liable to great variations in their strength and efficacy, an accurate yet comprehensive attention to facts is necessary, both to prevent the multiplication of erroneous theories, and to confirm and sanction those that are just.

The science of political economy is essentially practical, and applicable to the common business of human life. There are few branches of human knowledge where false views may do more harm, or just views more good. I cannot agree, therefore, with a writer in one of our most popular critical journals, who considers the subjects of population, bullion, and corn laws in the same light as the scholastic questions of the middle ages, and puts marks of admiration to them expressive of his utter astonishment that such perishable stuff should engage any portion of the public attention.

In the very practical science of political economy perhaps it might be difficult to mention three subjects more practical, than those unfortunately selected for a comparison with scholastic questions. But in fact, most of the subjects which belong to it are peculiarly applicable to the common concerns of mankind. What shall we say of all the questions relating to taxation, various and extensive as they are? It will hardly be denied that they come home to the business and bosoms of mankind. What shall we say of the laws which regulate exchangeable value, or every act of purchase and exchange which takes place in our markets? What of the laws which regulate the profits of stock, the interest of money, the rent of land, the value of the precious metals in different countries, the rates of exchange, &c. &c.?

The study of the laws of nature is, in all its branches, interesting. Even those physical laws by which the more distant parts of the universe are governed, and over which, of course, it is impossible for man to have the slightest influence, are yet noble and rational objects of curiosity; but the laws which regulate the movements of human society have an infinitely stronger claim to our attention, both because they relate to objects about which we are daily and hourly conversant, and because their effects are continually modified by human interference.

There are some eminent persons so strongly attached to the received general rules of political economy, that, though they are aware that in practice some exceptions to them may occasionally occur; yet they do not think it wise and politic to notice them, for fear of directing the public attention too much and too frequently to exceptions, and thus weakening the force and utility of the general rules.

It is, for instance, one of the most general rules in political economy, governments should not interfere in the direction of capital and industry, but leave every person, so long as he obeys the laws of justice, to pursue his own interest in his own way, as the best security for the constant and equable supply of the national wants. Though to this rule they allow that exceptions may possibly occur; yet thinking that the danger from the officious meddling of governments is so much greater than any which could arise from the neglect of such exceptions, they would be inclined to make the rule universal.

In this, however, I cannot agree. Though I should most readily allow that altogether more evil is likely to arise from governing too much, than from a tendency to the other extreme; yet, still, if the consequences of not attending to these exceptions were of sufficient magnitude and frequency to be conspicuous to the public, I should be decidedly of opinion, that the cause of general principles was much more likely to lose than to gain by concealment. Nothing can tend so strongly to bring theories and general principles into discredit, as the occurrence of consequences, from particular measures, which have not foreseen. Though in reality such an event forms no just objection to theory, in the general and proper sense of the term; yet it forms a most valid objection to the specific theory in question, as proving it in some way or other wrong; and with the mass of mankind this will pass for an impeachment of general principles, and of the knowledge or good faith of those who are in the habit of inculcating them. It appears to me, I confess, that the most perfect sincerity, together with the greatest degree of accuracy attainable, founded upon the most comprehensive view of all the circumstances of the case, are necessary to give that credit and circulation to general principles which is so desirable. And no views of temporary advantage, nor, what is more likely to operate, the fear of destroying the simplicity of a general rule, should ever tempt us to deviate from the strict line of truth, or to conceal or overlook any circumstances that may interfere with the universality of the principle.

There is another class of persons who set a very high value upon the received general rules of political economy, as of the most extensive practical use. They have seen the errors of the mercantile system refuted and replaced by a more philosophical and correct view of the subject; and having made themselves masters of the question so far, they seem to be satisfied with what they have got, and do not look with a favorable eye on new and further inquiries, particularly if they do not see at once clearly and distinctly to what beneficial effects they lead.

This indisposition to innovation, even in science, may possibly have its use, by tending to check crude and premature theories; but it is obvious that, if carried too far, it strikes at the root of all improvement. It is impossible to observe the great events of the last twenty-five years in their relation to subjects belonging to political economy, and sit down satisfied with what has been already done in the science. But if the science be manifestly incomplete, and yet of the highest importance, it would surely be most unwise to restrain inquiry, conducted upon just principles, even where the immediate practical utility of it was not visible. In mathematics, chemistry, and every branch of natural philosophy, how many are the inquiries necessary to their improvement and completion, which, taken separately, do not appear to lead to any specifically advantageous purpose! How many useful inventions, and how much valuable and improving knowledge would have been lost, if a rational curiosity and a mere love of information had not generally been allowed to be a sufficient motive for the search after truth!

I should not, therefore, consider it as by any means conclusive against further inquiries in political economy, if they would not always bear the rigid application of the test of *cui bono?* But such, in fact, is the nature of the science, so intimately is it connected with the business of mankind, that I really believe more of its propositions will bear this test than those of any other department of human knowledge.

To trace distinctly the operations of that circle of causes and effects in political economy which are acting and re-acting on each other, so as to foresee their results, and lay down general rules accordingly, is, in many cases, a task of very great difficulty. But there is scarcely a single inquiry belonging to these subjects, however abstruse and remote it may at first appear, which in some point or other does not bear directly upon practice. It is unquestionably desirable, therefore, both with a view to the improvement and completion of the science, and the practical advantages which may be expected from it, that such inquiries should be pursued; and no common difficulty or obscurity should be allowed to deter those who have leisure and ability for such researches.

In many cases, indeed, it may not be possible to predict results with certainty, on account of the complication of the causes in action, the different degrees of strength and efficacy with which they may operate, and the number of unforeseen circumstances which are likely to interfere; but it is surely knowledge of the highest importance, to be able to draw a line, with tolerable precision, between those cases where the expected results are certain, and those where they are doubtful; and further to be able satisfactorily to explain, in the latter case, the reasons of such uncertainty.

To know what can be done, and how to do it, is, beyond a doubt, the most valuable species of information. The next to it is, to know what cannot be done, and why we cannot do it. The first enables us to attain a positive good, to increase our powers, and augment our happiness: the second saves us from the evil of fruitless attempts, and the loss and misery occasioned by perpetual failure.

But these inquiries demand more time and application than the practical statesman, whom of all others they most nearly concern, can give to them. In the public measures of every state all are, no doubt, interested; but a peculiar responsibility, as well as interest, must be felt by those who are the principal advisers of them, and have the greatest influence in their enactment; and if they have not leisure for such researches themselves, they should not be unwilling, under the guidance of a sound discretion, to make use of the advantages which may be afforded by the leisure of others. They will not indeed be justified in taking any decided steps, if they do not themselves see, or at least think they see, the way they are going; but they may be fairly expected to make use of all the lights which are best calculated to illuminate their way, and enable them to reach the object which they have in view.

* * * * *

CHAPTER III. OF THE RENT OF LAND

Section 1. *Of the Nature and Causes of Rent*

The rent of land may be defined to be that portion of the value of the whole produce which remains to the owner of the land, after all the outgoings belonging to its cultivation, of whatever kind, have been paid, including the profits of the capital employed, estimated according to the usual and ordinary rate of the profits of agricultural stock at the time being.

It sometimes happens that, from accidental and temporary circumstances, the farmer pays more, or less, than this; but this is the point towards which the actual rents paid are constantly gravitating, and which is therefore always referred to when the term is used in a general sense.

Rent then being the excess of price above what is necessary to pay the wages of the labour and the profits of the capital employed in cultivation, the first object which presents itself for inquiry, is, the cause or causes of this excess of price.

After very careful and repeated revisions of the subject, I do not find myself able to agree entirely in the view taken of it, either by Adam Smith, or the Economists; and still less, by some more modern writers.

Almost all these writers appear to me to consider rent as too nearly resembling, in its nature, and the laws by which it is governed, that excess of price above the costs of production, which is the characteristic of a common monopoly.

Adam Smith, though in some parts of the eleventh chapter of his first book he contemplates rent quite in its true light, and has interspersed through his work, more just observations on the subject than any other writer, has not explained the most essential cause of the high price of raw produce with sufficient distinctness, though he often touches on it; and by applying occasionally the term monopoly to the rent of land, without stopping to mark its more radical peculiarities, he leaves the reader without a definite impression of the real difference between the cause of the high price of the necessaries of life, and of monopolized commodities.

Some of the views which the Economists have taken of the nature of rent appear to me also to be quite just; but they have mixed them with so much error, and have drawn such unwarranted inferences from them, that what is true in their doctrines has produced little effect. Their great practical conclusion, namely, the propriety of taxing exclusively the net rents of the landlords, evidently depends upon their considering these rents as completely disposeable, like that excess of price above the cost of production, which distinguishes a common monopoly.

* * * * *

That there are some circumstances connected with rent, which have a strong affinity to a natural monopoly, will be readily allowed. The extent of the earth itself is limited, and cannot be enlarged by human demand. The inequality of soils occasions, even at an early period of society, a comparative scarcity of the best lands; and this scarcity is undoubtedly one of the causes of rent properly so called. On this account, perhaps the term *partial monopoly* may be fairly applicable to it. But the scarcity of land, thus implied, is by no means alone sufficient to produce the effects observed. And a more accurate investigation of the subject will shew us how different the high price of raw produce is, both in its nature and origin, and the laws by which it is governed, from the high price of a common monopoly.

The causes of the excess of the price of raw produce above the costs of production, may be stated to be three.

First, and mainly, That quality of the earth, by which it can be made to yield a greater portion of the necessaries of life than is required for the maintenance of the persons employed on the land.

2dly, That quality peculiar to the necessaries of life of being able, when properly distributed, to create their own demand, or to raise up a number of demanders in proportion to the quantity of necessaries produced.

And, 3dly, The comparative scarcity of fertile land, either natural or artificial.

The quality of the soil here noticed as the primary cause of the high price of raw produce, is the gift of nature to man. It is quite unconnected with monopoly, and yet is so absolutely essential to the existence of rent, that without it no degree of scarcity or monopoly could have occasioned an excess of the price of raw produce above what was necessary for the payment of wages and profits.

If, for instance, the soil of the earth had been such, that, however well directed might have been the industry of man, he could not have produced from it more than was barely sufficient to maintain those whose labour and attention were necessary to its products; though, in this case, food and raw materials would have been evidently scarcer than at present, and the land might have been in the same manner monopolized by particular owners; yet it is quite clear, that neither rent nor any essential surplus produce of the land in the form of high profits and high wages could have existed.

On the other hand, it will be allowed, that in whatever way the produce of a given portion of land may be actually divided, whether the whole is distributed to the labourers and capitalists, or a part is awarded to a landlord, the *power* of such land to yield rent is exactly proportioned to its fertility, or to the general surplus which it can be made to produce beyond what is strictly necessary to support the labour and keep up the capital employed upon it. If this surplus be as 1, 2, 3, 4, or 5, then its *power* of yielding a rent will be as 1, 2, 3, 4, or 5; and no degree of monopoly—no possible increase of external demand can essentially alter their different *powers*.

But if no rent can exist without this surplus, and if the power of particular soils to pay rent be proportioned to this surplus, it follows that this surplus from the land, arising from its fertility, must evidently be considered as the foundation or main cause of all rent.

Still however, this surplus, necessary and important as it is, would not be sure of possessing a value which would enable it to command a proportionate quantity of labour and other commodities, if it had not a power of raising up a population to consume it, and, by the articles produced in return, of creating an effective demand for it.

It has been sometimes argued, that it is mistaking the principle of population to imagine, that the increase of food or of raw produce alone can occasion a proportionate increase of population. This is no doubt true; but it must be allowed, as has been justly observed by Adam Smith, that "when food is provided, it is comparatively easy to find the necessary clothing and lodging." And it should always be recollected, that land does not produce one commodity alone, but in addition to that most indispensable of all commodities—food, it produces the materials for clothing, lodging, and firing.

It is therefore strictly true, that land produces the necessaries of life—produces the means by which, and by which alone, an increase of people may be brought into being and supported. In this respect it is fundamentally different from every other kind of machine known to man; and it is natural to suppose that the use of it should be attended with some peculiar effects.

* * * * *

In all common monopolies, the price of the produce, and consequently the excess of price above the cost of production, may increase without any definite bounds. In the partial monopoly of the land which produces necessaries, the price of the produce cannot by any possibility exceed the value of the labour which it can maintain; and the excess of its price above the cost of its production is subjected to a limit as impassable. This limit is the surplus of necessaries which the land can be made to yield beyond the lowest wants of the cultivators, and is strictly dependent upon the natural or acquired fertility of the soil. Increase this fertility, the limit will be enlarged, and the land may yield a high rent; diminish it, the limit will be contracted, and a high rent will become impossible; diminish it still further, the limit will coincide with the cost of production, and all rent will disappear.

In short, in the one case, the power of the produce to exceed in price the cost of the production depends mainly upon the degree of the monopoly; in the other, it depends entirely upon the degree of fertility. This is surely a broad and striking distinction.

Is it, then, possible to consider the price of the necessaries of life as regulated upon the principle of a common monopoly? Is it possible, with M. de Sismondi, to regard rent at the sole produce of labour, which has a value purely nominal, and the mere result of that augmentation of price which a seller obtains in consequence of a peculiar privilege: or, with Mr. Buchanan, to consider it as no addition to the national wealth, but merely as a transfer of value, advantageous only to landlords, and proportionably *injurious* to the consumers?

Is it not, on the contrary, a clear indication of a most inestimable quality in the soil, which God has bestowed on man—the quality of being able to maintain more persons than are necessary to work it? Is it not a part, and we shall see farther on that it is an absolutely necessary part, of that surplus produce from the land, which has been justly stated to be the source of all power and enjoyment; and without which, in fact, there would be no cities, no military or naval force, no arts, no learning, none of the finer manufactures, none of the conveniences and luxuries of foreign countries, and none of that cultivated and polished society, which not only elevates and dignifies individuals, but which extends its beneficial influence through the whole mass of the people?

Section 2. On the Necessary Separation of the Rent of Land from the Profits of the Cultivator and the Wages of the Labourer

In the early periods of society, or more remarkably perhaps, when the knowledge and capital of an old society are employed upon fresh and fertile land, the surplus produce of the soil shews itself chiefly in extraordinary high profits, and extraordinary high wages, and appears but little in the shape of rent. While fertile land is in abundance, and may be had by whoever asks for it, nobody of course will pay a rent to a landlord. But it is not consistent with the laws of nature, and the limits and quality of the earth, that this state of things should continue. Diversities of soil and situation must necessarily exist in all countries, All land cannot be the most fertile: all situations cannot be the nearest to navigable rivers and markets. But the accumulation of capital beyond the means of employing it on land of the greatest natural fertility, and the most advantageously situated, must necessarily lower profits; while the tendency of population to increase beyond the means of subsistence must, after a certain time, lower the wages of labour.

The expense of production will thus be diminished; but the value of the produce, that is, the quantity of labour, and of the other products of labour (besides corn) which it can command, instead of diminishing, will be increased. There will be an increasing number of people demanding subsistence, and ready to offer their services in any way in which they can be useful. The exchangeable value of food will therefore be in excess above the cost of production, on all the more fertile lands; and this excess is that portion of the general surplus derived from land which has been peculiarly denominated rent.

The quality of the earth first mentioned, or its power to yield a greater portion of the necessaries of life than is required for the maintenance of the persons employed in cultivation, is obviously the foundation of this rent, and the limit to its possible increase. The second quality noticed, or the tendency of an abundance of food to increase population, is necessary both to give a value to the surplus of necessaries which the cultivators can obtain on the first land cultivated; and also to create a demand for more food than can be procured from the richest lands. And the third cause, or the comparative scarcity of fertile land, which is clearly the natural consequence of the second, is finally to separate a portion of the general surplus from the land, into the specific form of rent to a landlord.

Nor is it possible that rents should permanently remain as parts of the profits of stock, or of the wages of labour. If profits and wages were not to fall, then, without particular improvements in cultivation, none but the very richest lands could be brought into use. The fall of profits and wages which practically takes place, undoubtedly transfers a portion of produce to the landlord, and forms a part, though, as we shall see farther on, only a part of his rent. But if this transfer can be considered as injurious to the consumers, then every increase of capital and population must be considered as injurious; and a country which might maintain well ten millions of inhabitants ought to be kept down to a million. The transfer from profit and wages, and such a price of produce as yields rent, which have been objected to as injurious, and as depriving the consumer of what it gives to the landlord, are absolutely necessary in order to obtain any considerable addition to the wealth and revenue of the first settlers in a new country; and are the natural and unavoidable consequences of that increase of capital and population for which nature has provided in the propensitites of the human race.

When such an accumulation of capital takes place on the lands first chosen, as to render the returns of the additional stock employed less than could be obtained from inferior land, it must evidently answer to cultivate such inferior land. But the cultivators of the richer land, after profits had fallen, if they paid no rent, would cease to be mere farmers, or persons living upon the profits of agricultural stock; they would evidently unite the characters of landlords and farmers—a union by no means uncommon, but which does not alter in any degree the nature of rent, or its essential separation from profits and wages.

If the profits of stock on the inferior land taken into cultivation, were thirty per cent and portions of the old land would yield forty per cent, ten per cent of the forty would obviously be rent by whomsoever received. When capital had further accumulated, and labour fallen on the more eligible lands of a country, other lands, less favourably circumstanced with respect to fertility or situation, might be occupied with advantage. The expenses of cultivation, including profits, having fallen, poorer land, or land more distant from rivers and markets, though yielding at first no rents, might fully repay these expenses, and fully answer to the cultivator. And again, when either the profits of stock, or the wages of labour, or both, have still further fallen, land still poorer or still less favourably situated, might be taken into cultivation. And at every step it is clear, that if the price of produce do not fall, the rent of land must rise. And the price of produce will not fall so long as the industry and ingenuity of the labouring classes, assisted by the capitals of those not employed upon the land, can find something to give in exchange to the cultivators and landlords, which will stimulate them to continue undiminished their agricultural exertions, and maintain their excess of produce.

It may be laid down, therefore, as an incontrovertible truth, that as a nation reaches any considerable degree of wealth, and any considerable fullness of population, the separation of rents, as a kind of fixture upon lands of a certain quality, is a law as invariable as the action of the principle of gravity; and that rents are neither a mere nominal value, nor a value unnecessarily and injuriously transferred from one set of people to another; but a most real and essential part of the whole value of the national property, and placed by the laws of nature where they are, on the land, by whomsoever possessed, whether by few or many, whether by the landlord, the crown, or the actual cultivator.

* * * * *

Section 3. *Of the Causes Which Tend to Raise Rents in the Ordinary Progress of Society*

In tracing more particularly the laws which govern the rise and fall of rents, the main causes which diminish the expenses of cultivation, or reduce the costs of the instruments of production, compared with the price of produce, require to be more specifically enumerated. The principal of these seem to be four—1st, Such an accumulation of capital as will lower the profits of stock; 2dly, such an increase of population as will lower the wages of labour; 3dly, such agricultural improvements, or such increase of exertions, as will diminish the number of labourers necessary to produce a given effect; and 4thly, such an increase in the price of agricultural produce, from increased demand, as, without nominally lowering the expense of production, will increase the difference between this expense and the price of produce.

* * * * *

Section 4. *Of the Causes Which Tend to Lower Rents*

The causes which lead to a fall of rents are, as may be expected, exactly of an opposite description to those which lead to a rise; namely diminished capital, diminished population, a bad system of cultivation, and the low market price of raw produce. They are all indications of poverty and decline, and are necessarily connected with the throwing of inferior land out of cultivation, and the continued deterioration of the land of a superior quality.

* * * * *

It has appeared also, that in the progress of cultivation, and of increasing rents, rent, though greater in positive amount, bears a less and less proportion to the quantity of capital employed upon the land, and the quantity of produce derived from it. According to the same principle, when produce diminishes and rents fall, though the amount of rent will always be less, the proportion which it bears to capital and produce will be greater. And as, in the former case, the diminished proportion of rent was owing to the necessity of yearly taking fresh land of an inferior quality into cultivation, and proceeding in the improvement of old land, when it would return only the common profits of stock, with little or no rent; so, in the latter case, the high proportion of rent is owing to the discouragement of a great expenditure in agriculture, and the necessity of employing the reduced capital of the country in the exclusive cultivation of the richest lands, and leaving the remainder to yield what rent can be got for them in natural pasture, which, though small, will bear a large *proportion* to the labour and capital employed. In proportion therefore, as the relative state of prices is such as to occasion a progressive fall of rents, more and more lands will be gradually thrown out of cultivation, the remainder will be worse cultivated, and the diminution of produce will proceed still faster than the diminution of rents.

If the doctrine here laid down respecting the laws which govern the rise and fall of rents, be near the truth, the doctrine which maintains that, if the produce of agriculture were sold at such a price as to yield less net surplus, agriculture would be equally productive to the general stock, must be very far from the truth. With regard to my own conviction, indeed, I feel no sort of doubt that if, under the impression that the high price of raw produce, which occasions rent, is as injurious to the consumer as it is advantageous to the landlord, a rich and improved nation were determined by law to lower the price of produce, till no surplus in the shape of rent any where remained, it would inevitably throw not only all the poor land, but all except the very best land, out of cultivation, and probably reduce its produce and population to less than one-tenth of their former amount.

Section 5. On the Dependence of the Actual Quantity of Produce Obtained from the Land, upon the Existing Rents and the Existing Prices

From the preceding account of the progress of rent, it follows that the actual state of the natural rent of land is necessary to the actual produce;

and that the price of corn, in every progressive country, must be just about equal to the cost of production on land of the poorest quality actually in use, with the addition of the rent it would yield in its natural state; or to the cost of raising additional produce on old land, which additional produce yields only the usual returns of agricultural stock with little or no rent.

It is quite obvious that the price cannot be less; or such land would not be cultivated, nor such capital employed. Nor can it ever much exceed this price, because it will always answer to the landlord to continue letting poorer and poorer lands, as long as he can get any thing more than they will pay in their natural state; and because it will always answer to any farmer who can command capital, to lay it out on his land, if the additional produce resulting from it will fully repay the profits of his stock, although it yields nothing to his landlord.

It follows then, that the price of corn, in reference to the *whole quantity* raised, is sold at the natural or necessary price, that is, at the price necessary to obtain the actual amount of produce, although by far the largest part is sold at a price very much above that which is necessary to its production; owing to this part being produced at less expense, while its exchangeable value remains undiminished.

The difference between the price of corn and the price of manufactures, with regard to natural or necessary price, is this; that if the price of any manufacture were essentially depressed, the whole manufacture would be entirely destroyed; whereas, if the price of corn were essentially depressed, the *quantity* of it only would be diminished. There would be some machinery in the country still capable of sending the commodity to market at the reduced price.

The earth has been sometimes compared to a vast machine, presented by nature to man for the production of food and raw materials; but, to make the resemblance more just, as far as they admit of comparison, we should consider the soil as a present to man of a great number of machines, all susceptible of continued improvement by the application of capital to them, but yet of very different original qualities and powers.

This great inequality in the powers of the machinery employed in producing raw produce, forms one of the most remarkable features which distinguishes the machinery of the land from the machinery employed in manufactures.

When a machine in manufactures is invented, which will produce more finished work with less labour and capital than before, if there be no patent, or as soon as the patent has expired, a sufficient number of such machines may be made to supply the whole demand, and to supersede entirely the use of all the old machinery. The natural consequence is, that the price is reduced to the price of production from the best machinery, and if the price were to be depressed lower, the whole of the commodity would be withdrawn from the market.

The machines which produce corn and raw materials, on the contrary, are the gifts of nature, not the works of man; and we find, by experience, that these gifts have very different qualities and powers. The most fertile lands of a country, those which, like the best machinery in manufactures, yield the greatest products with the least labour and capital, are never found sufficient, owing to the second main cause of rent before stated, to supply the effective demand of an increasing population. The price of raw produce, therefore, naturally rises till it becomes sufficiently high to pay the cost of raising it with inferior machines, and by a more expensive process; and, as there cannot be two prices for corn of the same quality, all the other machines, the working of which requires less capital compared with the produce, must yield rents in proportion to their goodness.

Every extensive country may thus be considered as possessing a gradation of machines for the production of corn and raw materials, including in this gradation not only all the various qualities of poor land, of which every large territory has generally an abundance, but the inferior machinery which may be said to be employed when good land is further and further forced for additional produce. As the price of raw produce continues to rise, these inferior machines are successively called into action; and as the price of raw produce continues to fall, they are successively thrown out of action. The illustration here used serves to shew at once the necessity of the actual price of corn to the actual produce, in the existing state of most of the countries with which we are acquainted, and the different effect which would attend a great reduction in the price of any particular manufacture, and a great reduction in the price of raw produce.

We must not however draw too large inferences from this gradation of machinery on the land. It is what actually exists in almost all countries, and accounts very clearly for the origin and progress of rent, while land still remains in considerable plenty. But such a gradation is not strictly necessary, either to the original formation, or the subsequent regular rise of rents. All that is necessary to produce these effects, is, the existence of the two first causes of rent formerly mentioned, with the addition of limited territory, or a scarcity of fertile land.

Whatever may be the qualities of any commodity, it is well known that it can have no exchangeable value, if it exists in a great excess above the wants of those who are to use it. But such are the qualities of the necessaries of life that, in a limited territory, and under ordinary circumstances, they cannot be permanently in excess; and if all the land of such a country were precisely equal in quality, and all very rich, there cannot be the slightest doubt, that after the whole of the land had been taken into cultivation, both the profits of stock, and the real wages of labour, would go on diminishing, till profits had been reduced to what were necessary to keep up the actual capital, and the wages to what were necessary to keep up the actual population, while the rents would be high, just in proportion to the fertility of the soil.

Nor would the effect be essentially different, if the quantity of stock which could be employed with advantage upon such fertile soil were extremely limited, so that no further capital were required for it than what was wanted for ploughing and sowing. Still there can be no doubt that capital and population might go on increasing in other employments, till they both came to a stand, and rents had reached the limits prescribed by the powers of the soil, and the habits of the people.

In these cases it is obvious that the rents are not regulated by the gradations of the soil, or the different products of capital on the same land; and that it is too large an inference from the theory of rent to conclude with Mr. Ricardo, that "It is only because land is of different qualities with respect to its productive powers, and because in the progress of population, land of an inferior quality, or less advantageously situated, is called into cultivation, that rent is ever paid for the use of it."

There is another inference which has been drawn from the theory of rent, which involves an error of much greater importance, and should therefore be very carefully guarded against.

In the progress of cultivation, as poorer and poorer land is taken into tillage, the rate of *profits* must be limited in amount by the powers of the soil last cultivated, as will be shewn more fully in a subsequent chapter. It has been inferred from this, that when land is successively thrown out of cultivation, the rate of profits will be high in proportion to the superior natural fertility of the land which will then be the least fertile in cultivation.

If land yielded no rent whatever in its natural state, whether it were poor or fertile, and if the relative prices of capital and produce remained the same, then the whole produce being divided between profits and wages, the inference might be just. But the premises are not such as are here supposed. In a civilized country uncultivated land always yields a rent in proportion to its natural power of feeding cattle or growing wood; and of course, when land has been thrown out of tillage, particularly if this has been occasioned by the importation of cheaper corn from other countries, and consequently without a diminution of population, the last land so thrown out may yield a moderate rent in pasture, though considerably less than before. As was said in the preceding section, rent will diminish, but not so much in proportion either as the capital employed on the land, or the produce derived from it. No landlord will allow his land to be cultivated by a tillage farmer paying little or no rent when by laying it down to pasture, and saving the yearly expenditure of capital upon it, he can obtain a much greater rent. Consequently, as the produce of the worst lands actually cultivated can never be wholly divided between profits and wages, and in the case above supposed, not nearly so, the state of such land or its degree of fertility cannot possibly regulate the rate of profits upon it.

If to this circumstance we add the effect arising from a rise in the value of money, and the probable fall of corn more than of working cattle, it is obvious that permanent difficulties will be thrown in the way of cultivation, and that richer land may not yield superior profits. The higher rent paid for the last land employed in tillage, together with the greater expense of the materials of capital compared with the price of produce, may fully counterbalance, or even more than counterbalance, the difference of natural fertility.

With regard to the capital which the tenant may lay out on his farm in obtaining more produce without paying additional rent for it, the rate of its returns must obviously conform itself to the general rate of profits. If the prices of manufactured and mercantile commodities were to remain the same notwithstanding the fall of labour, profits would certainly be raised; but they would not remain the same, as was shown in the preceding chapter. The new prices of commodities and the new profits of stock would be determined upon principles of competition; and whatever the rate was, as so determined, capital would be taken from the land till this rate was attained. The profits of capital employed in the way just described must always follow, and can never lead or regulate.

It should be added, that in the regular progress of a country towards general cultivation and improvement, and in a natural state of things, it may fairly be presumed, that if the last land taken into cultivation be rich, capital is scarce, and profits will then certainly be high; but if land be thrown out of cultivation on account of means being found of obtaining corn cheaper elsewhere, no such inference is justifiable. On the contrary, capital may be abundant, compared with the demand for corn and commodities, in which case and during the time that such abundance lasts, whatever may be the state of the land, profits must be low.

This is a distinction of the greatest practical importance, which it appears to me has been quite overlooked by Mr. Ricardo.

It will be observed, that the rents paid for what the land will produce in its natural state, though they make a most essential difference in the questions relating to profits and the component parts of price, in no respect invalidate the important doctrine that, in progressive countries in their usual state with gradations of soil, corn is sold at its natural or necessary price, that is, at the price necessary to bring the actual quantity to market. This price must on an average be at the least equal to the costs of its production on the worst land actually cultivated, together with the rent of such land in its natural state: because, if it falls in any degree below this, the cultivator of such land will not be able to pay the landlord so high a rent as he could obtain from the land without cultivation, and consequently the land will be left uncultivated, and the produce will be diminished. The rent of land in its natural state is therefore obviously so necessary a part of the price of all cultivated products, that, if it be not paid they will not come to market, and the real price actually paid for corn is, on an average, absolutely necessary to the production of the same quantity, or, in the words before stated, corn, in reference to the whole quantity produced, is sold at its necessary price.

I hope to be excused for presenting to the reader in various forms the doctrine, that corn, in reference to the quantity actually produced, is sold at its necessary price, like manufactures; because I consider it as a truth of high importance, which has been entirely overlooked by the Economists, by Adam Smith, and all those writers who have represented raw produce as selling always at a monopoly price.

Section 10. General Remarks on the Surplus Produce of the Land

* * * * *

Another most desirable benefit belonging to a fertile soil is, that states so endowed are not obliged to pay much attention to that most distressing and disheartening of all cries to every man of humanity—the cry of the master manufacturers and merchants for low wages, to enable them to find a market for their exports. If a country can only be rich by running a successful race for low wages, I should be disposed to say at once, perish such riches! But, though a nation which purchases the main part of its food from foreigners, is condemned to this hard alternative, it is not so with the possessors of fertile land. The peculiar products of a country, though never probably sufficient to enable it to import a large proportion of its food as well as of its conveniences and luxuries, will generally be sufficient to give full spirit and energy to all its commercial dealings, both at home and abroad; while a small sacrifice of produce, that is, the not pushing cultivation too far, would, with prudential habits among the poor, enable it to maintain the whole of a large population in wealth and plenty. Prudential habits, among the labouring classes of a country mainly depending upon manufactures and commerce, might ruin it. In a country of fertile land, such habits would be the greatest of all conceivable blessings.

* * * * *

CHAPTER IV. OF THE WAGES OF LABOUR

Section 1. Of the Dependence of Wages of Labour upon Supply and Demand

The wages of labour are the remuneration to the labourer for his personal exertions.

They may be divided, like the prices of commodities, into real and nominal.

The real wages of labour consist of their value, estimated in the necessaries, conveniences, and luxuries of life.

The nominal wages of labour consist in their value, estimated in money.

As the value of labour, as well as of commodities, is most frequently compared with money, it will be advisable in general to adopt this mode of comparison, with a frequent reference, however, where it is necessary, to the money's worth, or the real wages of labour.

The money wages of labour are determined by the demand and supply of money, compared with the demand and supply of labour: and, during periods when money may be supposed to maintain nearly the same value, the variations in the wages of labour, may be said to be regulated by the variations in the demand compared with the supply of labour.

The principle of demand and supply is the paramount regulator of the prices of labour as well as of commodities, not only temporarily but permanently; and the costs of production affect these prices only as they are the necessary condition of the permanent supply of labour, or of commodities.

It is as the condition of the supply, that the prices of the necessaries of life have so important an influence on the price of labour. A certain portion of these necessaries is required to enable the labourer to maintain a stationary population, a greater portion to maintain an increasing one; and consequently, whatever may be the prices of the necessaries of life, the money wages of the labourer must be such as to enable him to purchase these portions, or the supply cannot possibly take place in the quantity required.

To shew that what may be called the cost of producing labour only influences wages as it regulates the supply of labour, it is sufficient to turn our attention to those cases, where, under temporary circumstances, the cost of production does not regulate the supply; and here we shall always find that this cost immediately ceases to regulate prices.

When, from a course of abundant seasons, or any cause which does not impair the capitals of the farmers, the price of corn falls for some time together, the cost of producing labour may be said to be diminished, but it is not found that the wages of labour fall; and for this obvious reason, that the reduced cost of production cannot, under sixteen or eighteen years, materially influence the *supply* of labour in the market. On the other hand, when the prices of corn rise from a succession of indifferent seasons, or any cause which leaves the demand for labour nearly the same as before, wages will not rise: because the same number of labourers remain in the market; and though the price of production has risen, the supply is not for some time affected by it. So entirely indeed, does the effect of the cost of production on price depend upon the manner in which it regulates supply, that if in this, or any other country during the last twenty years, the production of labour had cost absolutely nothing, but had still been supplied in exactly the same proportion to the demand, the wages of labour would have been in no respect different. Of the truth of this position, we may be quite assured, by the instance alluded to in a former chapter, of a paper currency so limited in quantity as not to exceed the metallic money, which would otherwise have circulated, in which case, though the cost of the paper is comparatively nothing, yet, as it performs the same function, and is supplied only in the same quantity as the money, it acquires the same value in exchange.

Adam Smith is practically quite correct, when he says, that, "the money price of labour is necessarily regulated by two circumstances; the demand for labour; and the price of the necessaries and conveniences of life." But it is of great importance to a thorough understanding of the subject, to keep constantly under our view the precise mode in which the costs of poduction operate on the price of labour, and to see clearly and distinctly the constant and predominant action of the principle of supply and demand.

* * * * *

Section 2. Of the Causes Which Principally Affect the Habits of the Labouring Classes

Mr. Ricardo has defined the natural price of labour to be "that price which is necessary to enable the labourers one with another to subsist, and to perpetuate their race, without either increase or diminution." This price I should really be disposed to call a most unnatural price; because in a natural state of things, that is, without great impediments to the progress of wealth and population, such a price could not generally occur for hundreds of years. But if this price be really rare, and, in an ordinary state of things, at so great a distance in point of time, it must evidently lead to great errors to consider the market-prices of labour as only temporary deviations above and below that fixed price to which they will very soon return.

The natural or necessary price of labour in any country I should define to be, "that price which, in the actual circumstances of the society, is necessary to occasion an average supply of labourers, sufficient to meet the average demand." And the market price I should define to be, the actual price in the market, which from temporary causes is sometimes above, and sometimes below, what is necessary to supply this average demand.

The condition of the labouring classes of society must evidently depend, partly upon the rate at which the resources of the country and the demand for labour are increasing; and partly, on the habits of the people in respect to their food, clothing and lodging.

If the habits of the people were to remain fixed, the power of marrying early, and of supporting a large family, would depend upon the rate at which the resources of the country and the demand for labour were increasing. And if the resources of the country were to remain fixed, the comforts of the lower classes of society would depend upon their habits, or the amount of those necessaries and conveniences, without which they would not consent to keep up their numbers.

It rarely happens, however, that either of them remain fixed for any great length of time together. The rate at which the resources of a country increase is, we well know, liable, under varying circumstances, to great variation; and the habits of a people though not so liable, or so necessarily subject to change, can scarcely ever be considered as permanent. In general, their tendency is to change together. When the resources of a country are rapidly increasing, and the labourer commands a large portion of necessaries, it is to be expected that if he has the opportunity of exchanging his superfluous food for conveniences and comforts, he will acquire a taste for these conveniences, and his habits will be formed accordingly. On the other hand, it generally happens that, when the resources of a country become nearly stationary, such habits, if they ever have existed, are found to give way; and, before the population comes to a stop, the standard of comfort is essentially lowered.

*   *   *   *   *

CHAPTER VII. ON THE IMMEDIATE CAUSES OF THE PROGRESS OF WEALTH

Section 1. *Statement of the Particular Object of Inquiry*

There is scarcely any inquiry more curious, or from its importance, more worthy of attention, than that which traces the causes which practically check the progress of wealth in different countries, and stop it, or make it proceed very slowly, while the power of production remains comparatively undiminished, or at least would furnish the means of a great and abundant increase of produce and population.

In a former work I endeavoured to trace the causes which practically keep down the population of a country to the level of its actual supplies. It is now by object to shew what are the causes which chiefly influence these supplies, or call the powers of production forth into the shape of increasing wealth.

Among the primary and most important causes which influence the wealth of nations, must unquestionably be placed, those which come under the head of politics and morals. Security of property, without a certain degree of which, there can be no encouragement to individual industry, depends mainly upon the political constitution of a country, the excellence of its laws and the manner in which they are administered. And those habits which are the most favourable to regular exertions as well as to general rectitude of character, and are consequently most favourable to the production and maintenance of wealth, depend chiefly upon the same causes, combined with moral and religious instruction. It is not however my intention at present to enter fully into these causes, important and effective as they are; but to confine myself chiefly to the more immediate and proximate causes of increasing wealth, whether they may have their origin in these political and moral sources, or in any others more specifically and directly within the province of political economy.

It is obviously true that there are many countries, not essentially different either in the degree of security which they afford to property, or in the moral and religious instruction received by the people, which yet, with nearly equal natural capabilities, make a very different progress in wealth. It is the principle object of the present inquiry to explain this: and to furnish some solution of certain phenomena frequently obtruded upon our attention, whenever we take a view of the different states of Europe, or of the world; namely, countries with great powers of production comparatively poor, and countries with small powers of production comparatively rich.

If the actual riches of a country are not subject to repeated violences and a frequent destruction of produce, be not after a certain period in some degree proportioned to its power of producing riches, this deficiency must have arisen from the want of an adequate stimulus to continued production. The practical question then for our consideration is, what are the most immediate and effective stimulants to the continued creation and progress of wealth.

THOMAS ROBERT MALTHUS

SELECTIONS FROM "DEFINITIONS IN POLITICAL ECONOMY"

CHAPTER X. DEFINITIONS IN POLITICAL ECONOMY

Wealth

1. The material objects necessary, useful or agreeable to man, which have required some portion of human exertion to appropriate or produce.

Utility

2. The quality of being serviceable or beneficial to mankind. The utility of an object has generally been considered as proportioned to the necessity and real importance of these services and benefits.

All wealth is necessarily useful; but all that is useful is not necessarily wealth.

Value

3. Has two meanings—value in use, and value in exchange.

Value in Use

4. Is synonymous with Utility. It rarely occurs in political economy, and is never implied by the word value when used alone.

Value, or Value in Exchange

5. The relation of one object to some other, or others in exchange, resulting from the estimation in which each is held. When no second object is specified, the value of a commodity naturally refers to the causes which determine this estimation, and the object which measures it.

Value is distinguished from wealth in that it is not confined to material objects, and is much more dependent upon scarcity and difficulty of production.

Production

6. The creation of objects which constitute wealth.

Product, Produce

7. The portion of wealth created by production.

Sources of Wealth

8. Land, labour, and capital. The two original sources are land and labour; but the aid which labour receives from capital is applied so very early, and is so very necessary in the production of wealth, that it may be considered as a third source.

Land

9. The soil, mines, waters, and fisheries of the habitable globe. It is the main source of raw materials and food.

Labour

10. The exertions of human beings employed with a view to remuneration. If the term be applied to other exertions, they must be particularly specified.

Productive Labour

11. The labour which is so directly productive of wealth as to be capable of estimation in the quantity or value of the products obtained.

Unproductive Labour

12. All labour which is not directly productive of wealth. The terms productive and unproductive are always used by political economists in a restricted and technical sense exclusively applicable to the direct production or non-production of wealth.

Industry

13. The exertion of the human faculties and powers to accomplish some desirable end. No very marked line is drawn in common language, or by political economists, between industry and labour; but the term industry generally implies more superintendence and less bodily exertion than labour.

Stock

14. Accumulated wealth, either reserved by the consumer for his consumption, or kept, or employed with a view to profit.

Capital

15. That portion of the stock of a country which is kept or employed with a view to profit in the production and distribution of wealth.

Fixed Capital

16. That portion of stock employed with a view to profit which yields such profit while it remains in the possession of the owner.

Circulating Capital

17. That portion of stock employed with a view to profit which does not yield such profit till it is parted with.

Revenue

18. That portion of stock or wealth which the possessor may annually consume without injury to his permanent resources. It consists of the rents of land, the wages of labour, and the profits of stock.

Accumulation of Capital

19. The employment of a portion of revenue as capital. Capital may therefore increase without an increase of stock or wealth.

Saving

20. In modern times, implies the accumulation of capital, as few people now lock up their money in a box.

Rent of Land

21. That portion of the produce of land which remains to the owner after all the outgoings belonging to its cultivation are paid, including the ordinary profits of the capital employed.

Money-rent of Land

22. The average rent of land as before defined, estimated in money.

Gross Surplus of the Land

23. That portion of the produce of land which is not actually consumed by the cultivators.

Wages of Labour

24. The remuneration paid to the labourer for his exertions.

Nominal Wages

25. The wages which the labourer receives in the current money of the country.

Real Wages

26. The necessaries, conveniencies, and luxuries of life which the wages of the labourer enable him to command.

The Rate of Wages

27. The ordinary wages paid to the labourer by the day, week, month, or year, according to the custom of the place where he is employed. They are generally estimated in money.

The Price of Labour

28. Has generally been understood to mean the average money-price of common day-labour, and is not therefore different from the rate of wages, except that it more specifically refers to money.

The Amount of Wages

29. The whole earnings of the labourer in a given time, which may be much more or much less than the average rate of wages, or the price of common day-labour.

The Price of Effective Labour

30. The price in money of a given quantity of human exertion of a given strength and character, which may be essentially different from the common price of day-labour, or the whole money-earnings of the labourer in a given time.

Accumulated Labour

31. The labour worked up in the raw materials and tools applied to the production of other commodities.

Profits of Stock

32. When stock is employed as capital in the production and distribution of wealth, its profits consist of the difference between the value of capital advanced, and the value of the commodity when sold or used.

The Rate of Profits

33. The percentage proportion which the value of the profits upon any capital bears to the value of such capital.

The Interest of Money

34. The net profits of a capital in money separated from the risk and trouble of employing it.

The Profits of Industry, Skill, and Enterprise

35. That portion of the gross profits of capital, independent of monopoly which remains after deducting the net profits, or the interest of money.

Monopoly Profits

36. The profits which arise from the employment of capital where the competition is not free.

Conditions of the Supply of Commodities

37. The advance of the quantity of accumulated and immediate labour necessary to their production, with such a percentage upon the whole of

the advances for the time they have been employed as is equivalent to ordinary profits. If there be any other necessary conditions of the supply arising from monopolies of any description, or from taxes, they must be added.

Elementary Costs of Production

38. An expression exactly equivalent to the conditions of the supply.

Measure of the Conditions of the Supply, or of the Elementary Costs of Production

39. The quantity of labour for which the commodity will exchange, when it is in its natural and ordinary state.

The Value, Market Value, or Actual Value, of a Commodity at Any Place or Time

40. The estimation in which it is held at that place and time, determined in all cases by the state of the supply compared with the demand, and ordinarily by the elementary costs of production which regulate that state.

The Natural Value of a Commodity at Any Place and Time

41. The estimation in which it is held when it is in its natural and ordinary state, determined by the elementary costs of its production, or the conditions of its supply.

Measure of the Market or Actual Value of a Commodity at Any Place or Time

42. The quantity of labour which it will command or exchange for at that place and time.

Measure of the Natural Value of a Commodity at Any Place and Time

43. The quantity of labour for which it will exchange at that place and time, when it is in its natural and ordinary state.

The Price, the Market Price, or Actual Price of a Commodity at Any Place and Time

44. The quantity of money for which it exchanges at that place and time, the money referring to the precious metals.

The Natural Price of a Commodity at Any Place and Time

45. The price in money which will pay the elementary costs of its production, or the money conditions of its supply.

Supply of Commodities

46. The quantity offered, or ready to be immediately offered, for sale.

Demand for Commodities

47. Has two distinct meanings: one, in regard to its extent, or the quantity of commodities purchased; and the other, in regard to its intensity, or the sacrifice which the demanders are able and willing to make in order to satisfy their wants.

Demand in Regard to Its Extent

48. The quantity of the commodity purchased, which generally increases with the increase of the supply, and diminishes with the diminution of it. It is often the greatest when commodities are selling below the costs of production.

Demand in Regard to Its Intensity

49. The sacrifice which the demanders are able and willing to make in order to satisfy their wants. It is this species of demand alone which, compared with the supply, determines prices and values.

Effectual Demand, in Regard to Its Extent

50. The quantity of a commodity wanted by those who are able and willing to pay the costs of its production.

Effectual Demand, in Regard to Its Intensity

51. The sacrifice which the demanders must make, in order to effectuate the continued supply of a commodity.

Measure of the Intensity of the Effectual Demand

52. The quantity of labour for which the commodity will exchange, when in its natural and ordinary state.

Excess of the Demand above the Supply

53. The demand for a commodity is said to be in excess above the supply, when, either from the diminution of the supply, or the increase of the effectual demand, the quantity in the market is not sufficient to supply all the effectual demanders. In this case the intensity of the demand increases, and the commodity rises, in proportion to the competition of the demanders, and the sacrifice they are able and willing to make in order to satisfy their wants.

Excess of the Supply above the Demand, or Partial Glut

54. The supply of a commodity is said to be in excess above the demand, or there is a partial glut, when, either from the superabundance of supply, or the diminution of demand, the quantity in the market exceeds the quantity wanted by those who are able and willing to pay the elementary costs of production. It then falls below these costs in propor-

tion to the eagerness of the sellers to sell; and the glut is trifling, or great, accordingly.

General Glut

55. A glut is said to be general, when, either from superabundance of supply or diminution of demand, a considerable mass of commodities falls below the elementary costs of production.

A Given Demand

56. A given demand, in regard to price, is a given quantity of money intended to be laid out in the purchase of certain commodities in a market; and a given demand, in regard to value, is the command of a given quantity of labour intended to be employed in the same way.

Variations of Prices and Values

57. Prices and values vary as the demand directly and the supply inversely. When the demand is given, prices and values vary inversely as the supply; when the supply is given, directly as the demand.

Consumption

58. The destruction wholly or in part of any portions of wealth.

Productive Consumption

59. The consumption or employment of wealth by the capitalist, with a view to future production.

Unproductive Consumption, or Spending

60. The consumption of wealth, as revenue, with a view to the final purpose of all production—subsistence and enjoyment; but not with a view to profit.

PART III

CLASSICISM AND UTILITARIANISM

1. Jeremy Bentham: (*a*) "An Introduction to the Principles of Morals and Legislation."
   (*b*) "Principles of the Civil Code."
   (*c*) "A Manual of Political Economy."
   (*d*) "Anarchical Fallacies."

2. David Ricardo: (*a*) "The High Price of Bullion."
   (*b*) "An Essay on the Influence of a Low Price of Corn on the Profits of Stock."

3. James Mill: "Elements of Political Economy."

4. William Nassau Senior: "An Outline of Political Economy."

5. John Stuart Mill: (*a*) "On Liberty."
   (*b*) "Utilitarianism."

6. John Elliott Cairnes: "Political Economy."

JEREMY BENTHAM

(1748–1832)

Jeremy Bentham was an English philosopher, reformer, economist, student of jurisprudence and man of letters. His complete works, edited by Bowring with an introduction by Burton, fill eleven stout volumes.

Bentham's outstanding contributions were in government and law. His first important work was "Fragment on Government," the first edition of which appeared in 1776. It was followed in 1789 by his equally important but more comprehensive "Introduction to the Principles of Morals and Legislation." Both works are important to students of economics and ethics, as well as of political science, because they contain Bentham's famous statements of the utilitarian principle.

Bentham's first work specifically in the field of economics was his "Defense of Usury" (1787), in which he criticized Adam Smith for failing to carry out his system of *laissez-faire* consistently to the prohibition of, rather than a condonement of, a legal rate of interest. Other important works of Bentham in economics were: "Protest against Law Taxes" (1795); "Observations on the Poor Bill of Mr. Pitt" (1797); and "A Manual of Political Economy" (1798).

Bentham's chief contribution to economics was his analysis of human nature and social institutions. His crude psychology was hedonism, a rational calculus of maximum pleasure and minimum pain. His social ethics were utilitarianism, that is, the greatest happiness for the greatest number.

Bentham's influence was very important on the English classical school, especially so in the case of John Stuart Mill. The Benthamites reared the social philosophy of utilitarianism on the speculative psychology of hedonism. Both were used to buttress Smith's old foundations of *laissez-faire* into Mill's more elaborate edifice of individual liberty.

The following brief selections are taken from "An Introduction to the Principles of Morals and Legislation," "Principles of the Civil Code," "A Manual of Political Economy," and "Anarchical Fallacies." In the first two selections, the student is asked to study Bentham's formulation of utilitarianism and to observe his announcement of the principle of diminishing utility. In the third selection, Bentham states his views of the economic functions of government, which should be compared with those of Smith and Mill, and which should also be remembered in reading his own views on anarchy and his criticisms of the French declaration of rights, in our fourth and last selection.

JEREMY BENTHAM

SELECTIONS FROM "AN INTRODUCTION TO THE PRINCIPLES OF MORALS AND LEGISLATION"

CHAPTER I. OF THE PRINCIPLE OF UTILITY

Nature has placed mankind under the governance of two sovereign masters, *pain* and *pleasure*. It is for them alone to point out what we ought to do, as well as to determine what we shall do. On the other hand the standard of right and wrong, on the other chain of causes and effects, are fastened to their throne. They govern us in all we do, in all we say, in all we think: every effort we can make to throw off our subjection, will serve but to demonstrate and confirm it. In words a man may pretend to abjure their empire: but in reality he will remain subject to it all the while. The *principle of utility* recognises this subjection, and assumes it for the foundation of that system, the object of which is to rear the fabric of felicity by the hands of reason and of law. Systems which attempt to question it, deal in sounds instead of sense, in caprice instead of reason, in darkness instead of light.

But enough of metaphor and declamation: it is not by such means that moral science is to be improved.

II. The principle of utility is the foundation of the present work: it will be proper therefore at the outset to give an explicit and determinate account of what is meant by it. By the principle of utility is meant that principle which approves or disapproves of every action whatsoever, according to the tendency which it appears to have to augment or diminish the happiness of the party whose interest is in question: or, what is the same thing in other words, to promote or to oppose that happiness. I say of every action whatsoever; and therefore not only of every action of a private individual, but of every measure of government.

III. By utility is meant that property in any object, whereby it tends to produce benefit, advantage, pleasure, good, or happiness (all this in the present case comes to the same thing), or (what comes again to the same thing) to prevent the happening of mischief, pain, evil, or unhappiness to the party whose interest is considered: if that party be the community in general, then the happiness of the community: if a particular individual, then the happiness of that individual.

IV. The interest of the community is one of the most general expressions that can occur in the phraseology of morals: no wonder that the meaning of it is often lost. When it has a meaning, it is this. The community is a fictitious *body*, composed of the individual persons who **are** considered as constituting as it were its *members*. The interest of the community then is, what?—the sum of the interests of the several members who compose it.

V. It is in vain to talk of the interest of the community, without understanding what is the interest of the individual. A thing is said to promote the interest, or to be *for* the interest, of an individual, when it tends to add to the sum total of his pleasures: or, what comes to the same thing, to diminish the sum total of his pains.

VI. An action then may be said to be conformable to the principle of utility, or, for shortness sake, to utility (meaning with respect to the community at large), when the tendency it has to augment the happiness of the community is greater than any it has to diminish it.

VII. A measure of government (which is but a particular kind of action, performed by a particular person or persons) may be said to be conformable to or dictated by the principle of utility, when in like manner the tendency which it has to augment the happiness of the community is greater then any which it has to diminish it.

VIII. When an action, or in particular a measure of government, is supposed by a man to be conformable to the principle of utility, it may be convenient, for the purposes of discourse, to imagine a kind of law or dictate, called a law or dictate of utility; and to speak of the action in question, as being conformable to such law or dictate.

IX. A man may be said to be a partizan of the principle of utility, when the approbation or disapprobation he annexes to any action, or to any measure, is determined, by and proportioned to the tendency which he conceives it to have to augment or to diminish the happiness of the community: or in others words, to its conformity or unconformity to the laws or dictates of utility.

X. Of an action that is conformable to the principle of utility, one may always say either that it is one that ought to be done, or at least that it is not one that ought not to be done. One may say also, that it is right it should be done; at least that it is not wrong it should be done: that it is a right action; at least that it is not a wrong action. When thus interpreted, the words *ought*, and *right* and *wrong*, and others of that stamp, have a meaning: when otherwise, they have none.

XI. Has the rectitude of this principle been ever formally contested? It should seem that it had, by those who have not known what they have been meaning. Is it susceptible of any direct proof? It should seem not: for that which is used to prove every thing else, cannot itself be proved: a chain of proofs must have their commencement somewhere. To give such proof is as impossible as it is needless.

XII. Not that there is or ever has been that human creature breathing, however stupid or perverse, who has not on many, perhaps on most occasions of his life, deferred to it. By the natural constitution of the human frame, on most occasions of their lives men in general embrace this principle, without thinking of it: if not for the ordering of their own actions, yet for the trying of their own actions, as well as of those of other men. There have been, at the same time, not many, perhaps, even of the most intelligent, who have been disposed to embrace it purely and without reserve. There are even few who have not taken some occasion or other to quarrel with it, either on account of their not understanding always how to apply it, or on account of some prejudice or other which they were afraid to examine into, or could not bear to part with. For such is the stuff that man is made of: in principle and in practice, in a right track and in a wrong one, the rarest of all human qualities is consistency.

XIII. When a man attempts to combat the principle of utility, it is with reasons drawn, without his being aware of it, from that very principle itself. His arguments, if they prove any thing, prove not that the principle is *wrong*, but that, according to the applications he supposes to be made of it, it is *misapplied*. Is it possible for a man to move the earth? Yes; but he must first find out another earth to stand upon.

XIV. To disprove the propriety of it by arguments is impossible; but, from the causes that have been mentioned, or from some confused or partial view of it, a man may happen to be disposed not to relish it. Where this is the case, if he thinks the settling of his opinions on such a subject worth the trouble, let him take the following steps, and at length, perhaps, he may come to reconcile himself to it.

1. Let him settle with himself, whether he would wish to discard this principle altogether; if so, let him consider what it is that all his reasonings (in matters of politics especially) can amount to?

2. If he would, let him settle with himself, whether he would judge and act without any principle, or whether there is any other he would judge and act by?

3. If there be, let him examine and satisfy himself whether the principle he thinks he has found is really any separate intelligible principle; or whether it be not a mere principle in words, a kind of phase, which at bottom expresses neither more or less than the mere averment of his own unfounded sentiments; that is, what in another person he might be apt to call caprice?

4. If he is inclined to think that his own approbation or disapprobation, annexed to the idea of an act, without any regard to its consequences, is a sufficient foundation for him to judge and act upon, let him ask himself whether his sentiment is to be a standard of right and wrong, with respect to every other man, or whether every man's sentiment has the same privilege of being a standard to itself?

5. In the first case, let him ask himself whether his principle is not despotical, and hostile to all the rest of human race?

6. In the second case, whether it is not anarchial, and whether at this rate there are not as many different standards of right and wrong as there are men? and whether even to the same man, the same thing, which is right to-day, may not (without the least change in its nature) be wrong to-morrow? and whether the same thing is not right and wrong in the same place at the same time? and in either case, whether all argument is not at an end? and whether, when two men have said, "I like this," and "I don't like it," they can (upon such a principle) have any thing more to say.

7. If he should have said to himself, No: for that the sentiment which he proposes as a standard must be grounded on reflection, let him say on what particulars the reflection is to turn? If on particulars having relation to the utility of the act, then let him say whether this is not deserting his own principle, and borrowing assistance from that very one in opposition to which he sets it up: or if not on those particulars on what other particulars?

8. If he should be for compounding the matter, and adopting his own principle in part, and the principle of utility in part, let him say how far he will adopt it?

9. When he has settled with himself where he will stop, then let him ask himself how he justifies to himself the adopting it so far? and why he will not adopt it any farther?

10. Admitting any other principle than the principle of utility to be a right principle, a principle that it is right for a man to pursue; admitting (what is not true) that the word *right* can have a meaning without reference to utility let him say whether there is any such thing as a *motive* that a man can have to pursue the dictates of it: if there is, let him say what that motive is, and how it is to be distinguished from those which enforce the dictates of utility: if not, then lastly let him say what it is this other principle can be good for?

JEREMY BENTHAM

SELECTIONS FROM "PRINCIPLES OF THE CIVIL CODE"

CHAPTER VI. PROPOSITIONS OF PATHOLOGY UPON WHICH THE ADVANTAGE OF EQUALITY IS FOUNDED

1. Each portion of wealth is connected with a corresponding portion of happiness.

2. Of two individuals, possessed of unequal fortunes, he who possesses the greatest wealth will possess the greatest happiness.

3. The excess of happiness on the part of the most wealthy will not be so great as the excess of his wealth.

4. For the same reason, the greater the disproportion between the two masses of wealth, the less the probability that there exists an equally great disproportion between the masses of happiness.

5. The more nearly the actual proportion approaches to equality, the greater will be the total mass of happiness.

* * * * *

JEREMY BENTHAM

SELECTIONS FROM "A MANUAL OF POLITICAL ECONOMY"

CHAPTER I. INTRODUCTION

Political Economy is at once a *science* and an *art*. The value of the science has for its efficient cause and measure, its subserviency to the art.

According to the principle of utility in every branch of the art of legislation, the object or end in view should be the production of the maximum of happiness in a given time in the community in question.

In the instance of this branch of the art, the object or end in view should be the production of that maximum of happiness, in so far as this more general end is promoted by the production of the maximum of wealth and the maximum of population.

The practical questions, therefore, are—How far the measures respectively suggested by these two branches of the common end agree?—how far they differ, and which requires the preference?—how far the end in view is best promoted by individuals acting for themselves? and in what cases these ends may be best promoted by the hands of government?

Those cases in which, and those measures or operations by which, the end is promoted by individuals acting for themselves, and without any special interference exercised with this special view on the part of government, beyond the distribution made and maintained, and the protection afforded by the civil and penal branches of the law, may be said to arise *sponte acta*.

What the legislator and the minister of the interior have it in their power to do towards increase either of wealth or population, is as nothing in comparison with what is done of course, and without thinking of it, by the judge, and his assistant the minister of police.

The cases in which, and the measures by which, the common end may be promoted by the hands of government, may be termed *agenda*.

With the view of causing an increase to take place in the mass of national wealth, or with a view to increase of the means either of subsistence or enjoyment, without some special reason, the general rule is, that nothing ought to be done or attempted by government. The motto, or watchword of government, on these occasions, ought to be—*Be quiet*.

For this quietism there are two main reasons:—1. Generally speaking, any interference for this purpose on the part of government is *needless*.

The wealth of the whole community is composed of the wealth of the several individuals belonging to it taken together. But to increase his particular portion is, generally speaking, among the constant objects of each individual's exertions and care. Generally speaking, there is no one who knows what is for your interest, so well as yourself—no one who is disposed with so much ardour and constancy to pursue it.

2. Generally speaking, it is moreover likely to be pernicious, viz. by being unconducive, or even obstructive, with reference to the attainment of the end in view. Each individual bestowing more time and attention upon the means of preserving and increasing his portion of wealth, than is or can be bestowed by government, is likely to take a more effectual course than what, in his instance and on his behalf, would be taken by government.

It is, moreover, universally and constantly pernicious in another way, by the restraint or constraint imposed on the free agency of the individual. Pain is the general concomitant of the sense of such restraint, wherever it is experienced.

Without being productive of such coercion, and thereby of such pain —in such a way more or less direct—more or less perceptible, with this or any other view, the interposition of government can hardly take place. If the coercion be not applied to the very individual whose conduct is endeavoured to be made immediately subservient to this purpose, it is at any rate applied to others—indeed, to the whole community taken together.

In coercive measures, so called, it is only to the individual that the coercion is applied. In the case of measures of encouragement, the field of coercion is vastly more extensive. Encouragements are grants of money or money's worth, applied in some shape or other to this purpose. But for this, any more than any other purpose, money is not raised but by taxes, and taxes are the produce of coercive laws applied to the most coercive purpose.

This would not be the less true, though the individual pieces of money thus applied happened to come from a source which had not been fed by any such means. In all communities, by far the greatest share of the money disposed of by government being supplied by taxes, whether this or that particular portion of money so applied, be supplied from that particular source, makes no sort of difference.

To estimate the good expected from the application of any particular mass of government money, compare it always with the mischief produced by the extraction of an equal sum of money by the most burthensome species of tax; since, by forbearing to make application of that sum of money, you might forbear levying the amount of that same sum of money by that tax, and thereby forbear imposing the mass of burthen that results from it.

JEREMY BENTHAM

SELECTIONS FROM "ANARCHICAL FALLACIES"

Specimens of a Criticism of the French Declarations of Rights

Article I.—Men (all men) are born and remain free, and equal in respect of rights. Social distinctions cannot be founded, but upon common utility.

In this article are contained, grammatically speaking, two distinct sentences. The first is full of error, the other of ambiguity.

In the first are contained four distinguishable propositions, all of them false—all of them notoriously and undeniably false:—

1. That all men are born free.

2. That all men remain free.

3. That all men are born equal in rights.

4. That all men remain (i.e., remain for ever, for the proposition is indefinite and unlimited) equal in rights.

All men are born free? All men remain free? No, not a single man: not a single man that ever was, or is, or will be. All men, on the contrary, are born in subjection, and the most absolute subjection—the subjection of a helpless child to the parents on whom he depends every moment for his existence. In this subjection every man is born—in this subjection he continues for years—for a great number of years—and the existence of the individual and of the species depends upon his so doing.

What is the state of things to which the supposed existence of these supposed rights is meant to bear reference?—a state of things prior to the existence of government, or a state of things subsequent to the existence of government? If to a state prior to the existence of government, what would the existence of such rights as these be to the purpose, even if it were true, in any country where there is such a thing as government? If to a state of things subsequent to the formation of government—if in a country where there is a government, in what single instance—in the instance of what single government, is it true? Setting aside the case of parent and child, let any man name that single government under which any such equality is recognized.

All men born free? Absurd and miserable nonsense! When the great complaint—a complaint made perhaps by the very same people at the same time, is—that so many men are born slaves. Oh! but when we acknowledge them to be born slaves, we refer to the laws in being; which laws being void, as being contrary to those laws of nature which are the efficient causes of those rights of man that we are declaring, the men in

186

question are free in one sense, though slaves in another;—slaves, and free, at the same time:—free in respect of the laws of nature—slaves in respect of the pretended human laws, which, though called laws, are no laws at all, as being contrary to the laws of nature. For such is the difference—the great and perpetual difference, betwixt the good subject, the rational censor of the laws, and the anarchist—between the moderate man and the man of violence. The rational censor, acknowledging the existence of the law he disapproves, proposes the repeal of it: the anarchist, setting up his will and fancy for a law before which all mankind are called upon to bow down at the first word—the anarchist, trampling on truth and decency, denies the validity of the law in question,—denies the existence of it in the character of a law, and calls upon all mankind to rise up in a mass, and resist the execution of it.

* * * * *

Article II.—The end in view of every political association is the preservation of the natural and imprescriptible rights of man. These rights are liberty, property, security, and resistance to oppression.

Sentence 1. The end in view of every political association, is the preservation of the natural and imprescriptible rights of man.

More confusion—more nonsense,—and the nonsense, as usual, dangerous nonsense. The words can scarcely be said to have a meaning: but if they have, or rather if they had a meaning, these would be the propositions either asserted or implied:—

1. That there are such things as rights anterior to the establishment of governments: for natural, as applied to rights, if it mean anything, is meant to stand in opposition to *legal*—to such rights as are acknowledged to owe their existence to government, and are consequently posterior in their date to the establishment of government.

2. That these rights *can not* be abrogated by government; for *can not* is implied in the form of the word imprescriptible, and the sense it wears when so applied, is the cut-throat sense above explained.

3. That the governments that exist derive their origin from formal associations, or what are now called *conventions*: associations entered into by a partnership contract, with all the members for partners,—entered into at a day prefixed, for a predetermined purpose, the formation of a new government where there was none before (for as to formal meetings holden under the control of an existing government, they are evidently out of question here) in which it seems again to be implied in the way of inference, though a necessary and unavoidable inference, that all governments (that is, self-called governments, knots of persons exercising the power of government) that have had any other origin than an association of the above description, are illegal, that is, no governments at all; resistance to them, and subversion of them, lawful and commendable; and so on.

Such are the notions implied in this first of the article. How stands the truth of things? That there are no such things as natural rights—no such things as rights anterior to the establishment of government—no such things as natural rights opposed to, in contradistinction to, legal; that the expression is merely figurative; that when used, in the moment you attempt to give it a literal meaning, it leads to error, and to that sort of error that leads to mischief—to the extremity of mischief.

We know what it is for men to live without government—and living without government, to live without rights: we know what it is for men to live without government, for we see instances of such a way of life— we see it in many savage nations, or rather races of mankind; for instance, among the savages of New South Wales, whose way of living is so well known to us; no habit of obedience, and thence no government—no government, and thence no laws,—no laws, and thence no such things as rights—no security—no property: liberty, as against regular control, the control of laws and government—perfect but as against all irregular control, the mandates of stronger individuals, none. In this state at a time earlier than the commencement of history—in this same state, judging from analogy, we, the inhabitants of the part of the globe we call Europe, were;—no government, consequently no rights: no rights, consequently no property—no legal security—no legal liberty: security not more than belongs to beasts—forecast and sense of insecurity keener consequently in point of happiness below the level of the brutal race.

In proportion to the want of happiness resulting from the want of rights, a reason exists for wishing that there were such things as rights. But reasons for wishing there were such things as rights, are not rights; —a reason for wishing that a certain right were established, is not that right—want is not supply—hunger is not bread.

That which has not existence cannot be destroyed—that which cannot be destroyed cannot require anything to preserve it from destruction. *Natural rights* is simple nonsense: natural and imprescriptible rights, rhetorical nonsense,—nonsense upon stilts. But this rhetorical nonsense ends in the old strain of mischievous nonsense: for immediately a list of these pretended natural rights is given, and those are so expressed as to present to view legal rights. And of these rights, whatever they are, there is not, it seems, any one of which any government *can*, upon any occasion whatever, abrogate the smallest particle.

So much for terrorist language. What is the language of reason and plain sense upon this same subject? That in proportion as it is *right* or *proper*, *i.e.* advantageous to the society in question, that this or that right—a right to this or that effect—should be established and maintained, in that same proportion it is *wrong* that is should be abrogated: but, that as there is no *right*, which ought not to be maintained so long as it is upon the whole advantageous to society that it should be maintained, so there is no right which, when the abolition of it is advantageous to society, should not be abolished. To know whether it would be more for the advantage of society that this or that right should be maintained or abolished, the time at which the question about maintaining or abolishing is proposed, must be given, and the circumstances under which it is proposed to maintain or abolish it; the right itself must be specifically described, not jumbled with an undistinguishable heap of others, under any such vague general terms as property, liberty, and the like.

One thing, in the midst of all this confusion, is but too plain. They know not of what they are talking under the name of natural rights, and yet they would have the imprescriptible—proof against all the power of the laws—pregnant with occasions summoning the members of the community to rise up in resistance against those laws. What, then, was their object in declaring the existence of imprescriptible rights, and without specifying a single one by any such mark as it could be known by? This, and no other—to excite and keep up a spirit of resistance to all laws—a spirit of insurrection against all governments—against the governments of all other nations instantly,—against the government of their own nation—against the government they themselves were pretending to establish—even that, as soon as their own reign should be at an end. In us is the perfection of virtue and wisdom: in all mankind besides, the extremity of wickedness and folly. Our will shall consequently reign without control, and for ever: reign now, we are living—reign after we are dead.

All nations—all future ages—shall be, for they are predestined to be, our slaves.

Future governments will not have honesty enough to be trusted with the determination of what rights shall be maintained, what abrogated— what laws kept in force, what repealed. Future subjects (I should say future citizens, for French government does not admit of subjects) will not have wit enough to be trusted with the choice whether to submit to the determination of the government of their time, or to resist it. Governments, citizens—all to the end of time—all must be kept in chains.

Such are their maxims—such their premises: for it is by such premises only that the doctrine of imprescriptible rights and unrepealable laws can be supported.

What is the real source of these imprescriptible rights—these unrepealable laws? Power turned blind by looking from its own height: self-conceit and tyranny exalted into insanity. No man was to have any other man for a servant, yet all men were for ever to be *their* slaves. Making laws with imposture in their mouths, under pretence of declaring them—giving for laws any thing that came uppermost, and these unrepealable ones, on pretence of finding them ready made. Made by what? Not by God—they allow of none; but by their goddess, Nature.

The origination of governments from a contract is a pure fiction, or, in other words, a falsehood. It never has been known to be true in any instance; the allegation of it does mischief, by involving the subject in error and confusion, and is neither necessary nor useful to any good purpose.

All governments that we have any account of have been gradually established by habit, after having formed by force; unless in the instance of governments formed by individuals who have been emancipated, or have emancipated themselves from governments already formed, the governments under which they were born—a rare case, and from which nothing follows with regard to the rest. What signifies it how governments are formed? Is it the less proper—the less conducive to the happiness of society—that the happiness of society should be the one object kept in view by the members of the government in all their measures? Is it the less the interest of men to be happy—less to be wished that they may be so—less the moral duty of their governors to make them so, so far as they can, at Magadore than at Philadelphia?

Whence is it, but from government, that contracts derive their binding force? Contracts came from government, not government from contracts. It is from the habit of enforcing contracts, and seeing them enforced, that governments are chiefly indebted for whatever disposition they have to observe them.

DAVID RICARDO

(1772–1823)

David Ricardo was born in England, but his father was a Dutch immigrant and his ancestors were Portuguese Jews. Young David embraced Christianity, and married a Christian, for which he was disowned by his father.

David Ricardo received but little formal education, for he entered business at an early age, following the career of his father, which had been that of a stockbroker. It is interesting to note that he became wealthy at the early age of twenty-five and amassed an enormous fortune before his death.

The later years of Ricardo's life were devoted to economic studies and to political life. In 1819, he was elected to the House of Commons where his advice was much sought, and his opinion on financial matters was accepted with great veneration. He was also a philanthropist and was interested in education.

One of the paradoxes of economics is that David Ricardo, whose background was that of a practical business man, wrote in such an abstract and unreal fashion, whereas Adam Smith, whose background had been an academic one, wrote in such a vigorous and practical manner.

The chief works of Ricardo were as follows: "The High Price of Bullion a Proof of the Depreciation of Bank Notes" (1810); "Reply to Mr. Bosanquet's Practical Observations on the Report of the Bullion Committee" (1811); "An Essay on the Influence of a Low Price of Corn on the Profits of Stock" (1815); "Proposals for an Economical and Secure Currency" (1816); "On the Principles of Political Economy and Taxation" (1817); "The Funding System" (1820); "Protection to Agriculture" (1822); "Plans for the Establishment of a National Bank" (1824, the year following the author's death).

M'Culloch was the literary heir of Ricardo, and his edition of Ricardo's works is probably the best one. The attention of the student is also called to the recently discovered manuscript of Ricardo, giving his notes on Malthus's "Principles of Political Economy," edited by Professors Hollander and Gregory and published by the Johns Hopkins Press in 1928.

Every student of the history of economic thought should have a copy of Ricardo's "Principles of Political Economy and Taxation." Not only is this book most important, but it is easily accessible in inexpensive editions.

The following selections are taken from the important but less familiar works of Ricardo. The first is from "The High Price of Bullion," and the second from "An Essay on the Influence of a Low Price of Corn on the Profits of Stock." In the first selection, the student is asked to examine Ricardo's views on the quantity theory of money and his plan for the restoration of a sound currency. The second selection is interesting because it gives the essence of the Ricardian theory of distribution, and because it takes issue with Malthus on several points.

DAVID RICARDO

SELECTIONS FROM "THE HIGH PRICE OF BULLION, A PROOF OF THE DEPRECIATION OF BANK NOTES"

The precious metals employed for circulating the commodities of the world, previously to the establishment of banks, have been supposed by the most approved writers on political economy to have been divided into certain proportions among the different civilized nations of the earth, according to the state of their commerce and wealth, and therefore according to the number and frequency of the payments which they had to perform. While so divided they preserved every where the same value, and as each country had an equal necessity for the quantity actually in use, there could be no temptation offered to either for their importation or exportation.

Gold and silver, like other commodities, have an intrinsic value, which is not arbitrary, but is dependent on their scarcity, the quantity of labour bestowed in procuring them, and the value of the capital employed in the mines which produce them.

"The quality of utility, beauty, and scarcity," says Dr. Smith, "are the original foundation of the high price of those metals, or of the great quantity of other goods for which they can every where be exchanged. This value was antecedent to, and independent of, their being employed as coin, and was the quality which fitted them for that employment."

If the quantity of gold and silver in the world employed as money were exceedingly small, or abundantly great, it would not in the least affect the proportions in which they would be divided among the different nations—the variation in their quantity would have produced no other effect than to make the commodities for which were exchanged comparatively dear or cheap. The smaller quantity of money would perform the functions of a circulating medium, as well as the larger. Ten millions would be as effectual for that purpose as 100 millions. Dr. Smith observes, "that the most abundant mines of the precious metals would add little to the wealth of the world. A produce of which the value is principally derived from its scarcity is necessarily degraded by its abundance."

If in the progress toward wealth, one nation advanced more rapidly than the others, that nation would require and obtain a greater proportion of the money of the world. Its commerce, its commodities, and its payments, would increase, and the general currency of the world would be divided according to the new proportions. All countries, therefore, would contribute their share to this effectual demand.

In the same manner, if any nation wasted part of its wealth, or lost part of its trade, it could not retain the same quantity of circulating medium which it before possessed. A part would be exported, and divided among the other nations till the usual proportions were re-established.

While the relative situation of countries continued unaltered, they might have abundant commerce with each other, but their exports and imports would on the whole be equal. England might possibly import more goods from, than she would export to, France, but she would in consequence export more to some other country, and France would import more from that country; so that the exports and imports of all countries would balance each other; bills of exchange would make the necessary payments, but no money would pass because it would have the same value in all countries.

If a mine of gold were discovered in either of these countries, the currency of that country would be lowered in value in consequence of the increased quantity of the precious metals brought into circulation, and would therefore no longer be of the same value as that of other countries. Gold and silver, whether in coin or in bullion, obeying the law which regulates all other commodities, would immediately become articles of exportation; they would leave the country where they were cheap, for those countries where they were dear, and would continue to do so, as long as the mine should prove productive, and till the proportion existing between capital and money in each country before the discovery of the mine, were again established, and gold and silver restored every where to one value. In return for the gold exported, commodities would be imported; and though what is usually termed the balance of trade would be against the country exporting money or bullion, it would be evident that she was carrying on a most advantageous trade, exporting that which was no way useful to her, for commodities which might be employed in the extension of her manufactures, and the increase of her wealth.

If instead of a mine being discovered in any country, a bank were established, such as the Bank of England, with the power of issuing its notes for a circulating medium; after a large amount had been issued, either by way of loan to merchants, or by advances to Government, thereby adding considerably to the sum of the currency, the same effect would follow as in the case of the mine. The circulating medium would be lowered in value, and goods would experience a proportionate rise. The equilibrium between that and other nations would only be restored by the exportation of part of the coin.

The establishment of the bank, and the consequent issue of its notes, therefore, as well as the discovery of the mine, operates as an inducement to the exportation either of bullion, or of coin, and are beneficial only in as far as that object may be accomplished. The bank substitutes a currency of no value for one most costly, and enables us to turn the precious metals (which, though a very necessary part of our capital, yield no revenue), into a capital which will yield one. Dr. A. Smith compares the advantages attending the establishment of a bank to those which would be obtained by converting our highways into pastures and corn fields, and procuring a road through the air. The highways, like the coin, are highly useful, but neither yield any revenue. Some people might be alarmed at the specie leaving the country, and might consider that as a disadvantageous trade which required us to part with it; indeed the law so considers it by its enactments against the exportation of specie; but a very little reflection will convince us that it is our choice, and not our necessity, that sends it abroad; and that it is highly beneficial to us to exchange that commodity which is superfluous, for others which may be made productive.

The exportation of the specie may at all times be safely left to the discretion of individuals; it will not be exported more than any other commodity, unless its exportation should be advantageous to the country. If it be advantageous to export it, no laws can effectually prevent its exportation. Happily, in this case, as well as in most others in commerce, where there is free competition, the interests of the individual and that of the community are never at variance.

* * * * *

The Bank might continue to issue their notes, and the specie be exported with advantage to the country, while their notes were payable in specie on demand, because they could never issue more notes than the value of the coin which would have circulated had there been no bank.

If they attempted to exceed this amount, the excess would be immediately returned to them for specie; because our currency, being thereby diminished in value, could be advantageously exported, and could not be retained in our circulation. These are the means, as I have already explained, by which our currency endeavours to equalize itself with the currencies of other countries. As soon as this equality was attained, all advantage arising from exportation would cease; but if the Bank, assuming that because a given quantity of circulating medium had been necessary last year, therefore the same quantity must be necessary this, or for any other reason, continued to re-issue the returned notes, the stimulus which a redundant currency first gave to the exportation of the coin would be again renewed with similar effects; gold would be again demanded, the exchange would become unfavourable, and gold bullion would rise, in a small degree, above its Mint price, because it is legal to export bullion, but illegal to export the coin, and the difference would be about equal to the fair compensation for the risk.

In this manner, if the Bank persisted in returning their notes into circulation, every guinea might be drawn out of their coffers.

* * * * *

The Bank would be obliged, therefore, ultimately to adopt the only remedy in their power to put a stop to the demand for guineas. They would withdraw part of their notes from circulation, till they should have increased the value of the remainder to that of gold bullion, and, consequently, to the value of the currencies of other countries. All advantage from the exportation of gold bullion would then cease, and there would be no temptation to exchange bank notes for guineas.

In this view of the subject, then, it appears that the temptation to export money in exchange for goods, or what is termed an unfavourable balance of trade, never arises but from a redundant currency. But Mr. Thornton, who has considered this subject very much at large, supposes that a very unfavourable balance of trade may be occasioned to this country by a bad harvest, and the consequent importation of corn; and that there may be at the same time an unwillingness in the country to which we are indebted to receive our goods in payment; the balance due to the foreign country must therefore be paid out of that part of our currency consisting of coin, and that hence arises the demand for gold bullion, and its increased price. He considers the Bank as affording considerable accomodation to the merchants, by supplying with their notes the void occasioned by the exportation of the specie.

*   *   *   *   *

It is evident, then, that a depreciation of the circulating medium is the necessary consequence of its redundance; and that in the common state of the national currency this depreciation is counteracted by the exportation of the precious metals.

Such, then appear to me to be the laws that regulate the distribution of the precious metals throughout the world, and which cause and limit their circulation from one country to another, by regulating their value in each. But before I proceed to examine on these principles the main object of my inquiry, it is necessary that I should show what is the standard measure of value in this country, and of which, therefore, our paper currency ought to be the representative, because it can only be by a comparison to this standard that its regularity, or its depreciation, may be estimated.

No permanent measure of value can be said to exist in any nation while the circulating medium consists of two metals, because they are constantly subject to vary in value with respect to each other. However exact the conductors of the Mint may be, in proportioning the relative value of gold to silver in the coins, at the time when they fix the ratio, they cannot prevent one of these metals from rising, while the other remains stationary, or falls in value. Whenever this happens, one of the coins will be melted to be sold for the other. Mr. Locke, Lord Liverpool, and many other writers, have ably considered this subject, and have all agreed, that the only remedy from the evils in the currency proceeding from this source, is the making one of the metals only the standard measure of value. Mr. Locke considered silver as the most proper metal for this purpose, and proposed that gold coins should be left to find their own value, and pass for a greater or lesser number of shillings, as the market price of gold might vary with respect to silver.

Lord Liverpool, on the contrary, maintained that gold was not only the most proper metal for a general measure of value in this country, but that, by the common consent of the people, it had become so, was so considered by foreigners, and that it was best suited to the increased commerce and wealth of England.

* * * * *

While the circulating medium consists, therefore, of coin undebased, or of paper-money immediately exchangeable for undebased coin, the exchange can never be more above, or more below par, than the expenses attending the transportation of the precious metals. But when it consists of a depreciated paper-money, it necessarily will fall according to the degree of the depreciation.

The exchange will, therefore, be a tolerably accurate criterion by which we may judge of the debasement of the currency, proceeding either from a clipped coinage or a depreciated paper-money.

* * * * *

We may, therefore, fairly conclude, that this difference in the relative value, or, in other words, that this depreciation in the actual value of bank notes has been caused by the too abundant quantity which the Bank has sent into circulation. The same cause which has produced a difference of from 15 to 20 per cent in bank notes when compared with gold bullion, may increase it to 50 per cent. There can be no limit to the depreciation which may arise from a constantly increasing quantity of paper. The stimulus which a redundant currency gives to the exportation of the coin has acquired new force, but cannot, as formerly, relieve itself. We have paper-money only in circulation, which is necessarily confined to ourselves. Every increase in its quantity degrades it below the value of gold and silver bullion, below the value of the currencies of other countries.

The effect is the same as that which would have been produced from clipping our coins.

If one-fifth were taken off from every guinea, the market price of gold bullion would rise one-fifth above the Mint price. Forty-four guineas and a half (the number of guineas weighing a pound, and therefore called the Mint price), would no longer weigh a pound, therefore a fifth more than that quantity, or about 56*l.* would be the price of a pound of gold, and the difference between the market and the Mint price, between 56*l.* and 46*l.*14s,6d. would measure the depreciation.

If such debased coin were to continue to be called by the name of guineas, and if the value of gold bullion and all other commodities were rated in the debased coin, a guinea fresh from the Mint would be said to be worth 1*l*.5s., and that sum would be given for it by the illicit trader; but it would not be the value of the new guinea which had increased, but that of the debased guineas which had fallen. This would immediately be evident, if a proclamation were issued, prohibiting the debased guineas from being current but by weight at the Mint price of 3*l*.17s. 10½d.; this would be constituting the new and heavy guineas the standard measure of value, in lieu of the clipped and debased guineas. The latter would then pass at their true value, and be called 17 or 18 shillings-pieces. So if a proclamation to the same effect were now enforced, bank notes would not be less current, but would pass only for the value of the gold bullion which they would purchase. A guinea would then no longer be said to be worth 1*l*.5s., but a pound note would be current only for 16 or 17 shillings. At present gold coin is only a commodity, and bank notes are the standard measure of value, but in that case gold coin would be that measure, and bank notes would be the marketable commodity.

"It is," says Mr. Thornton, "the maintenance of our general exchanges, or, in other words, it is the agreement of the Mint price with the bullion price of gold, which seems to be the true proof that the circulating paper is not depreciated."

*   *   *   *   *

It is contended, that the rate of interest, and not the price of gold or silver bullion, is the criterion by which we may always judge of the abundance of paper money; that if it were too abundant, interest would fall, and if not sufficiently so, interest would rise. It can, I think, be made manifest, that the rate of interest is not regulated by the abundance or scarcity of money, but by the abundance or scarcity of that part of capital not consisting of money.

"Money," observes Dr. A. Smith, "the great wheel of circulation, the great instrument of commerce, like all other instruments of trade, though it makes a part, and a very valuable part of the capital, makes no part of the revenue of the society to which it belongs; and though the metal pieces of which it is composed, in the course of their annual circulation, distribute to every man the revenue which properly belongs to him, they make themselves no part of that revenue.

"When we compute the quantity of industry which the circulating capital of any society can employ, we must always have regard to those parts of it only which consist in provisions, materials, and finished work: the other, which consists in money, and which serves only to circulate those three, must always be deducted. In order to put industry into motion, three things are requisite:—materials to work upon, tools to work with, and the wages or recompense for the sake of which the work is done. Money is neither a material to work upon nor a tool to work with; and though the wages of the workman are commonly paid to him in money, his real revenue, like that of all other men, consists not in money, but in money's worth; not in metal pieces, but what can be got for them."

And in other parts of his work, it is maintained, that the discovery of the mines in America, which so greatly increased the quantity of money, did not lessen the interest for the use of it; the rate of interest being regulated by the profits on the employment of capital, and not by the number or quality of the prices of metal which are used to circulate its produce.

Mr. Hume has supported the same opinion. The value of the circulating medium of every country bears some proportion to the value of the commodities which it circulates. In some countries this proportion is much greater than in others, and varies, on some occasions, in the same country. It depends upon the rapidity of circulation, upon the degree of confidence and credit existing between traders, and, above all, on the judicious operations of banking. In England, so many means of economizing the use of circulating medium have been adopted, that its value, compared with the value of the commodities which it circulates, it probably (during a period of confidence) reduced to as small a proportion as is practical. What that proportion may be has been variously estimated.

No increase or decrease of its quantity, whether consisting of gold, silver, or paper money, can increase or decrease its value above or below this proportion. If the mines cease to supply the annual consumption of the precious metals, money will become more valuable, and a smaller quantity will be employed as a circulating medium. The diminution in the quantity will be proportioned to the increase of its value. In like manner, if new mines be discovered, the value of the precious metals will be reduced, and an increased quantity used in the circulation so that in either case the relative value of money to the commodities which it circulates will continue as before.

If, whilst, the Bank paid their notes on demand in specie, they were to increase their quantity, they would produce little permanent effect on the value of the currency, because nearly an equal quantity of the coin would be withdrawn from circulation and exported.

If the Bank were restricted from paying their notes in specie, and all the coin had been exported, any excess of their notes would depreciate the value of the circulating medium in proportion to the excess. If 20 millions had been the circulation of England before the restriction, and 4 millions were added to it, the 24 millions would be of no more value than the 20 were before, provided commodities had remained the same, and there had been no corresponding exportation of coins; and if the Bank were successively to increase it to 50 or 100 millions, the increased quantity would be all absorbed in the circulation of England, but would be, in all cases, depreciated to the value of the 20 millions.

I do not dispute, that if the Bank were to bring a large additional sum of notes into the market, and offer them on loan, but that they would for a time affect the rate of interest. The same effect would follow from the discovery of a hidden treasure of gold or silver coin. If the amount were large, the Bank, or the owner of the treasure, might not be able to lend the notes or the money at 4, nor perhaps above 3 per cent; but having done so, neither the notes, nor the money, would be retained unemployed by the borrowers; they would be sent into every market, and would everywhere raise the prices of commodities, till they were absorbed in the general circulation. It is only during the interval of the issues of the Bank, and their effect on prices, that we should be sensible of an abundance of money; interest would, during that interval, be under its natural level; but as soon as the additional sum of notes or of money became absorbed in the general circulation, the rate of interest would be as high, and new loans would be demanded with as much eagerness as before the additional issues.

The circulation can never be over full. If it be one of gold and silver, any increase in its quantity will be spread over the world. If it be one of paper, it will diffuse itself only in the country where it is issued. Its effects on prices will then be only local and nominal, as a compensation by means of the exchange will be made to foreign purchasers.

To suppose that any increased issues of the Bank can have the effect of permanently lowering the rate of interest, and satisfying the demands of all borrowers, so that there will be none to apply for new loans, or that a productive gold or silver mine can have such an effect, is to attribute a power to the circulating medium which it can never possess. Banks would, if this were possible, become powerful engines indeed. By creating paper money, and lending it at 3 or 2 per cent under the present market rate of interest, the Bank would reduce the profits on trade in the same proportion; and if they were sufficiently patriotic to lend their notes at an interest no higher than necessary to pay the expenses of their establishment, profits would be still further reduced; no nation, but by similar means, could enter into competition with us, we should engross the trade of the world. To what absurdities would not such a theory lead us! Profits can only be lowered by a competition of capitals not consisting of circulating medium. As the increase of bank notes does not add to this species of capital, as it neither increases our exportable commodities, our machinery, or our raw materials, it cannot add to our profits nor lower interest.

* * * * *

The remedy which I propose for all the evils in our currency, is that the Bank should gradually decrease the amount of their notes in circulation until they shall have rendered the remainder of equal value with the coins which they represent, or, in other words, till the prices of gold and silver bullion shall be brought down to their Mint price. I am well aware that the total failure of paper credit would be attended with the most disastrous consequences to the trade and commerce of the country, and even its sudden limitation would occasion so much ruin and distress, that it would be highly inexpedient to have recourse to it as the means of restoring our currency to its just and equitable value.

If the Bank were possessed of more guineas than they had notes in circulation, they could not, without great injury to the country, pay their notes in specie, while the price of gold bullion continued greatly above the Mint price, and the foreign exchanges unfavourable to us. The excess of our currency would be exchanged for guineas at the Bank, and exported, and would be suddenly withdrawn from circulation. Before, therefore, they can safely pay in specie, the excess of notes must be gradually withdrawn from circulation. If gradually done, little inconvenience would be felt; so that the principle were fairly admitted, it would be for future consideration whether the object should be accomplished in one year or in five. I am fully persuaded that we shall never restore our currency to its equitable state, but by this preliminary step, or by the total overthrow of our paper credit.

If the Bank directors had kept the amount of their notes within reasonable bounds; *if they had acted up to the principle which they have avowed to have been that which regulated their issues when they were obliged to pay their notes in specie, namely, to limit their notes to that amount which should prevent the excess of the market above the Mint price of gold, we should not have been now exposed to all the evils of a depreciated, and perpetually varying currency.*

* * * * *

When the order of council for suspending the cash payments became necessary in 1797, the run upon the Bank was, in my opinion, caused by political alarm alone, and not by a superabundant, or a deficient quantity (as some have supposed) of their notes in circulation.

This is a danger to which the Bank, from the nature of its institution, is at all times liable. No prudence on the part of the directors could perhaps have averted: but if their loans to Government had been more limited; if the same amount of notes had been issued to the public through the medium of discounts; they would have been able, in all probability, to have continued their payments till the alarm had subsided. At any rate, as the debtors to the Bank would have been obliged to discharge their debts in the space of sixty days, that being the longest period for which any bill discounted by the Bank has to run, the directors would in that time, if necessary, have been enabled to redeem every note in circulation. It was then owing to the too intimate connexion between the Bank and Government that the restriction became necessary; it is to that cause, too, that we owe its continuance.

To prevent the evil consequences which may attend the perserverance in this system, we must keep our eyes steadily fixed on the repeal of the restriction bill.

The only legitimate security which the public can possess against the indiscretion of the Bank is to oblige them to pay their notes on demand in specie; and this can only be effected by diminishing the amount of bank notes in circulation till the nominal price of gold be lowered to the Mint price.

Here I will conclude, happy if my feeble efforts should awaken the public attention to a due consideration of the state of our circulating medium. I am well aware that I have not added to the stock of information with which the public has been enlightened by many able writers on the same important subject. I have had no such ambition. My aim has been to introduce a calm and dispassionate inquiry into a question of great importance to the State, and the neglect of which may be attended with consequences which every friend of his country would deplore.

DAVID RICARDO

SELECTIONS FROM "AN ESSAY ON THE INFLUENCE OF A LOW PRICE OF CORN ON THE PROFITS OF STOCK" SHEWING THE INEXPEDIENCY OF RESTRICTIONS ON IMPORTATION WITH REMARKS ON MR. MALTHUS'S TWO LAST PUBLICATIONS: "AN INQUIRY INTO THE NATURE AND PROGRESS OF RENT"; AND "THE GROUNDS OF AN OPINION ON THE POLICY OF RESTRICTING THE IMPORTATION OF FOREIGN CORN"

INTRODUCTION

In treating on the subject of the profits of capital, it is necessary to consider the principles which regulate the rise and fall of rent, as rent and profits, it will be seen, have a very intimate connexion with each other. The principles which regulate rent are briefly stated in the following pages, and differ in a very slight degree from those which have been so fully and so ably developed by Mr. Malthus in his late excellent publication, to which I am very much indebted. The consideration of those principles, together with those which regulate the profit of stock, have convinced me of the policy of leaving the importation of corn unrestricted by law. From the general principle set forth in all Mr. Malthus's publications, I am persuaded that he holds the same opinion, as far as profit and wealth are concerned with the question; but, viewing, as he does, the danger as formidable of depending on foreign supply for a large portion of our food, he considers it wise, on the whole, to restrict importation. Not participating with him in those fears, and perhaps estimating the advantages of a cheap price of corn at a higher value, I have come to a different conclusion. Some of the objections urged in his last publication—"Grounds of an Opinion," &c., I have endeavoured to answer; they appear to me to be unconnected with the political danger he apprehends, and to be inconsistent with the general doctrines of the advantages of a free trade, which he has himself, by his writings, so ably contributed to establish.

Rent, then, is in all cases a portion of the profits previously obtained on the land. It is never a new creation of revenue, but always part of a revenue already created.

Profits of stock fall only, because land equally well adapted to produce food cannot be procured; and the degree of the fall of profits, and the rise of rents, depends wholly on the increased expense of production.

If, therefore, in the progress of countries in wealth and population, new portions of fertile land could be added to such countries, with every increase of capital, profits would never fall, nor rents rise.

If the money price of corn, and the wages of labour, did not vary in price in the least degree, during the progress of the country in wealth and population, still profits would fall and rents would rise; because *more* labourers would be employed on the more distant or less fertile land, in order to obtain the same supply of raw produce; and therefore the cost of production would have increased, whilst the value of the produce continued the same.

But the price of corn, and of all other raw produce, has been invariably observed to rise as a nation became wealthy, and was obliged to have recourse to poorer lands for the production of part of its food; and very little consideration will convince us, that such is the effect which would naturally be expected to take place under such circumstances.

The exchangeable value of all commodities rises as the difficulties of their production increase. If, then, new difficulties occur in the production of corn, from more labour being necessary, whilst no more labour is required to produce gold, silver, cloth, linen, &c., the exchangeable value of corn will necessarily rise, as compared with those things. On the contrary, facilities in the production of corn, or of any other commodity of whatever kind, which shall afford the same produce with less labour, will lower its exchangeable value. Thus we see that improvements in agriculture, or in the implements of husbandry, lower the exchangeable value of corn; improvements in the machinery connected with the manufacture of cotton, lower the exchangeable value of cotton goods; and improvements in mining, or the discovery of new and more abundant mines of the precious metals, lower the value of gold and silver, or, which is the same thing, raise the price of all other commodities. Wherever competition can have its full effect, and the production of the commodity be not limited by nature, as is the case with some wines, the difficulty or facility of their production will ultimately regulate their exchangeable value. The sole effect, then, of the progress of wealth on prices, independently of all improvements, either in agriculture or manufactures, appears to be to raise the price of raw produce and of labour, leaving all other commodities at their original prices, and to lower general profits in consequence of the general rise of wages.

This fact is of more importance than at first sight appears, as it relates to the interest of the landlord, and the other parts of the community. Not only is the situation of the landlord improved (by the increasing difficulty of procuring food, in consequence of accumulation), by obtaining an increased quantity of the produce of the land, but also by the increased exchangeable value of that quantity. If his rent be increased from 14 to 28 quarters, it would be more than doubled, because he would be able to command more than double the quantity of commodities, in exchange for the 28 quarters. As rents are agreed for, and paid in money, he would, under the circumstances supposed, receive more than double of his former money rent.

In like manner, if rent fell, the landlord would suffer two losses; he would be a loser of that portion of the raw produce which constituted his additional rent; and further, he would be a loser by the depreciation in the real or exchangeable value of raw produce in which, or in the value of which, his remaining rent would be paid.

As the revenue of the farmer is realized in raw produce, or in the value of raw produce, he is interested, as well as the landlord, in its high exchangeable value, but a low price of produce may be compensated to him by a great additional quantity.

It follows, then, that the interest of the landlord is always opposed to the interest of every other class in the community. His situation is never so prosperous, as when food is scarce and dear: whereas, all other persons are greatly benefited by procuring food cheap. High rent and low profits, for they invariably accompany each other, ought never to be the subject of complaint, if they are the effect of the natural course of things.

They are the most unequivocal proofs of wealth and prosperity, and of an abundant population, compared with the fertility of the soil. The general profits of stock depend wholly on the profits of the last portion of capital employed on the land; if, therefore, landlords were to relinquish the whole of their rents, they would neither raise the general profits of stock, nor lower the price of corn to the consumer. It would have no other effect, as Mr. Malthus has observed, than to enable those farmers, whose lands now pay a rent, to live like gentlemen, and they would have to expend that portion of the general revenue which now falls to the share of the landlord.

A nation is rich, not according to the abundance of its money, nor to the high money value at which its commodities circulate, but according to the abundance of its commodities, contributing to its comforts and enjoyments. Although this is a proposition, from which few would dissent, many look with the greatest alarm at the prospect of the diminution of their money revenue, though such reduced revenue should have so improved in exchangeable value, as to procure considerably more of all the necessaries and luxuries of life.

If, then, the principles here stated as governing rent and profit be correct, general profits on capital can only be raised by a fall in the exchangeable value of food, and which fall can only arise from three causes:

1st. The fall of the real wages of labour, which shall enable the farmer to bring a greater excess of produce to market.

2d. Improvements in agriculture, or in the implements of husbandry, which shall also increase the excess of produce.

3dly. The discovery of new markets, from whence corn may be imported at a cheaper price than it can be grown for at home.

The first of these causes is more or less permanent, according as the price from which wages fall, is more or less near that remuneration for labour which is necessary to the actual subsistence of the labourer.

The rise or fall of wages is common to all states of society, whether it be the stationary, the advancing, or the retrograde state. In the stationary state, it is regulated wholly by the increase or falling off of the population. In the advancing state, it depends on whether the capital or the population advance, at the more rapid course. In the retrograde state, it depends on whether population or capital decrease with the greater rapidity.

As experience demonstrates that capital and population alternately take the lead, and wages in consequence are liberal or scanty, nothing can be positively laid down, respecting profits, as far as wages are concerned.

But I think it may be most satisfactorily proved, that in every society advancing in wealth and population, independently of the effect produced by liberal or scanty wages, general profits must fall, unless there be improvements in agriculture, or corn can be imported at a cheaper price.

It seems the necessary result of the principles which have been stated to regulate the progress of rent.

This principle will, however, not be readily admitted by those who ascribe to the extension of commerce, and discovery of new markets, where our commodities can be sold dearer, and foreign commodities can be bought cheaper, the progress of profits, without any reference whatever to the state of the land, and the rate of profit obtained on the last portions of capital employed upon it. Nothing is more common than to hear it asserted, that profits on agriculture no more regulate the profits of commerce, than that the profits of commerce regulate the profits on agriculture. It is contended that they alternately take the lead; and, if the profits of commerce rise, which it is said they do, when new markets are discovered, the profits of agriculture will also rise; for it is admitted, that if they did not do so, capital would be withdrawn from the land to be employed in the more profitable trade. But if the principles respecting the progress of rent be correct, it is evident, that, with the same population and capital, whilst none of the agricultural capital is withdrawn from the cultivation of the land; agricultural profits cannot rise, nor can rent fall: either then it must be contended, which is at variance with all the principles of political economy, that the profits on commercial capital will rise considerably, whilst the profits on agricultural capital suffer no alteration, or that, under such circumstances, the profits on commerce will not rise.

It is this latter opinion which I consider as the true one. I do not deny that the first discoverer of a new and better market may, for a time, before competition operates, obtain unusual profits. He may either sell the commodities he exports at a higher price than those who are ignorant of the new market, or he may purchase the commodities imported at a cheaper price. Whilst he, or a few more exclusively follow this trade, their profits will be above the level of general profits. But it is of the general rate of profit that we are speaking, and not of the profits of a few individuals; and I cannot doubt that, in proportion as such trade shall be generally known and followed, there will be such a fall in the price of the foreign commodity in the importing country, in consequence of its increased abundance, and the greater facility with which it is procured, that its sale will afford only the common rate of profits—that so far from the high profits obtained by the few who first engaged in the new trade elevating the general rate of profits—those profits will themselves sink to the ordinary level.

The effects are precisely similar to those which follow from the use of improved machinery at home.

Whilst the use of the machine is confined to one, or a very few manufacturers, they may obtain unusual profits, because they are enabled to sell their commodities at a price much above the cost of production—but as soon as the machine becomes general to the whole trade, the price of the commodities will sink to the actual cost of production, leaving only the usual and ordinary profits.

During the period of capital moving from one employment to another, the profits on that to which capital is flowing will be relatively high, but will continue so no longer than till the requisite capital is obtained.

There are two ways in which a country may be benefited by trade—one by the increase of the general rate of profits, which, according to my opinion, can never take place but in consequence of cheap food, which is beneficial only to those who derive a revenue from the employment of their capital, either as farmers, manufacturers, merchants, or capitalists, lending their money at interest—the other by the abundance of commodities, and by a fall in their exchangeable value, in which the whole community participate. In the first case, the revenue of the country is augmented—in the second, the same revenue becomes efficient in procuring a greater amount of the necessaries and luxuries of life.

It is in this latter mode only that nations are benefited by the extension of commerce, by the division of labour in manufactures, and by the discovery of machinery,—they all augment the amount of commodities, and contribute very much to the ease and happiness of mankind; but they have no effect on the rate of profits, because they do not augment the produce compared with the cost of production on the land, and it is impossible that all other profits should rise whilst the profits on land are either stationary, or retrograde.

Profits, then, depend on the price, or rather on the value of food. Every thing which gives facility to the production of food, however scarce, or however abundant commodities may become, will raise the rate of profits, whilst on the contrary, every thing which shall augment the cost of production without augmenting the quantity of food, will, under every circumstance, lower the general rate of profits. The facilities of obtaining food are beneficial in two ways to the owners of capital; it at the same time raises profits and increases the amount of consumable commodities. The facilities in obtaining all other things only increase the amount of commodities.

If, then, the power of purchasing cheap food be of such great importance, and if the importation of corn will tend to reduce its price, arguments almost unanswerable respecting the danger of dependence on foreign countries for a portion of our food—for in no other view will the question bear an argument—ought to be brought forward to induce us to restrict importation, and thereby forcibly to detain capital in an employment which it would otherwise leave for one much more advantageous.

If the legislature were at once to adopt a decisive policy with regard to the trade in corn—if it were to allow a permanently free trade, and did not, with every variation of price, alternately restrict and encourage importation, we should undoubtedly be a regularly importing country. We should be so in consequence of the superiority of our wealth and population, compared to the fertility of our soil over our neighbours. It is only when a country is comparatively wealthy, when all its fertile land is in a state of high cultivation, and that it is obliged to have recourse to its inferior lands to obtain the food necessary for its population; or when it is originally without the advantages of a fertile soil, that it can become profitable to import corn.

It is, then, the dangers of dependence on foreign supply for any considerable quantity of our food, which can alone be opposed to the many advantages which, circumstanced as we are, would attend the importation of corn.

These dangers do not admit of being very correctly estimated; they are in some degree matters of opinion, and cannot, like the advantages on the other side, be reduced to accurate calculation. They are generally stated to be two—1st, That in the case of war a combination of the Continental powers, or the influence of our principal enemy, might deprive us of our accustomed supply—2dly, That when bad seasons occured abroad, the exporting countries would have, and would exercise, the power of withholding the quantity usually exported to make up for their own deficient supply.

If we became a regularly importing country, and foreigners could confidently rely on the demand of our market, much more land would be cultivated in the corn countries with a view to exportation. When we consider the value of even a few weeks' consumption of corn in England, no interruption could be given to the export trade, if the Continent supplied us with any considerable quantity of corn, without the most extensively ruinous commercial distress—distress which no sovereign, or combination of sovereigns, would be willing to inflict on their people; and, if willing, it would be a measure to which probably no people would submit. It was the endeavour of Buonaparte to prevent the exportation of the raw produce of Russia, more than any other cause, which produced the astonishing efforts of the people of that country against the most powerful force perhaps ever assembled to subjugate a nation.

. The immense capital which would be employed on the land, could not be withdrawn suddenly, and under such circumstances, without immense loss; besides which, the glut of corn in their markets, which would affect their whole supply, and lower its value beyond calculation; the failure of those returns, which are essential in all commercial adventures, would occasion a scene of wide-spreading ruin, which, if a country would patiently endure, would render it unfit to wage war with any prospect of success. We have all witnessed the distress in this country, and we have all heard of the still greater distress in Ireland, from a fall in the price of corn, at a time, too, when it is acknowledged that our own crop has been deficient; when importation has been regulated by price, and when we have not experienced any of the effects of a glut. Of what nature would that distress have been if the price of corn had fallen to a half a quarter, or an eighth part of the present price? For the effects of plenty or scarcity, on the price of corn, are incalculably greater than in proportion to the increase or deficiency of quantity. These, then are the inconveniences which the exporting countries would have to endure.

Ours would not be light. A great diminution in our usual supply, amounting probably to one-eighth of our whole consumption, it must be confessed, would be an evil of considerable magnitude; but we have obtained a supply equal to this, even when the growth of foreign countries, was not regulated by the constant demand of our market. We all know the prodigious effects of a high price in procuring a supply. It cannot, I think, be doubted, that we should obtain a considerable quantity from those countries with which we were not at war; which, with the most economical use of our own produce, and the quantity in store, would enable us to subsist till we had bestowed the necessary capital and labour on our own land, with a view to future production. That this would be a most afflicting change, I certainly allow; but I am fully persuaded that we should not be driven to such an alternative, and that, notwithstanding the war, we should be freely supplied with corn, expressly grown in foreign countries for our consumption. Buonaparte, when he was most hostile to us, permitted the exportation of corn to England by licenses, when our prices were high from a bad harvest, even when all other commerce was prohibited. Such a state of things could not come upon us suddenly; a danger of this nature would be partly foreseen, and due precautions would be taken. Would it be wise, then, to legislate with the view of preventing an evil which might never occur; and, to ward off a most improbable danger, sacrifice annually a revenue of some millions?

In contemplating a trade in corn, unshackled by restrictions on importation, and a consequent supply from France, and other countries, where it can be brought to market at a price not much above half that at which we can ourselves produce it on some of our poorer lands, Mr. Malthus does not sufficiently allow for the greater quantity of corn which would be grown abroad, if importation was to become the settled policy of this country. There cannot be the least doubt that if the corn countries could depend on the markets of England for a regular demand, if they could be perfectly secure that our laws respecting the corn trade would not be repeatedly vacillating between bounties, restrictions, and prohibitions, a much larger supply would be grown, and the danger of a greatly diminished exportation, in consequence of bad seasons, would be less likely to occur. Countries which have never yet supplied us might, if our policy was fixed, afford us a considerable quantity.

It is at such times that it would be particularly the interest of foreign countries to supply our wants, as the exchangeable value of corn does not rise in proportion only to the deficiency of supply, but two, three, four times as much, according to the amount of the deficiency.

If the consumption of England is 10 million quarters, which, in an average year, would sell for 40 millions of money; and, if the supply should be deficient one-fourth, the 7,500,000 quarters would not sell for 40 millions only, but probably for fifty millions or more. Under the circumstances, then, of bad seasons, the exporting country would content itself with the smallest possible quantity necessary for their own consumption, and would take advantage of the high price in England to sell all they could spare, as not only would corn be high, as compared with money, but as compared with all other things; and if the growers of corn adopted any other rule, they would be in a worse situation, as far as regarded wealth, than if they had constantly limited the growth of corn to the wants of their own people.

If 100 millions of capital were employed on the land to obtain the quantity necessary to their own subsistence, and 20 millions more that they might export the produce, they would lose the whole return of the 20 millions in the scarce year, which they would not have done had they not been an exporting country. At whatever price exportation might be restricted by foreign countries, the chance of corn rising to that price would be diminished by the greater quantity produced in consequence of our demand.

With respect to the supply of corn, it has been remarked, in reference to a single country, that if the crops are bad in one district they are generally productive in another; that if the weather is injurious to one soil, or to one situation, it is beneficial to a different soil and different situation; and, by this compensating power, Providence has bountifully secured us from the frequent recurrence of dearths. If this remark be just as applied to one country, how much more strongly may it be applied to all the countries together which compose our world? Will not the deficiency of one country be made up by the plenty of another? and, after the experience which we have had of the power of high prices to procure a supply, can we have any just reason to fear that we shall be exposed to any particular danger from depending on importation for so much corn as may be necessary for a few weeks of our consumption.

From all that I can learn, the price of corn in Holland, which country depends almost wholly on foreign supply, has been remarkably steady, even during the convulsed times which Europe has lately experienced—a convincing proof, notwithstanding the smallness of the country, that the effects of bad seasons are not exclusively borne by importing countries.

That great improvements have been made in agriculture, and that much capital has been expended on the land, it is not attempted to deny; but, with all those improvements, we have not overcome the natural impediments resulting from our increasing wealth and prosperity, which obliges us to cultivate at a disadvantage our poor lands if the importation of corn is restricted or prohibited. If we were left to ourselves, unfettered by legislative enactments, we should gradually withdraw our capital from the cultivation of such lands, and import the produce which is at present raised upon them. The capital withdrawn would be employed in the manufacture of such commodities as would be exported in return for the corn. Such a distribution of part of the capital of the country would be more advantageous or it would not be adopted. This principle is one of the best established in the science of political economy, and by no one is more readily admitted than by Mr. Malthus. It is the foundation of all his arguments, in his comparison of the advantages and disadvantages attending an unrestricted trade in corn, in his "Observations on the Corn Laws."

In his last publication, however, in one part of it, he dwells with much stress on the losses of agricultural capital, which the country would sustain, by allowing an unrestricted importation. He laments the loss of that which by the course of events has become of no use to us, and by the employment of which we actually lose. We might just as fairly have been told, when the steam-engine or Mr. Arkwright's cotton machine was brought to perfection, that it would be wrong to adopt the use of them, because the value of the old clumsy machinery would be lost to us. That the farmers of the poorer lands would be losers, there can be no doubt, but the public would gain many times the amount of their losses; and, after the exchange of capital from land to manufactures had been effected, the farmers themselves, as well as every other class of the community, except the landholders, would very considerably increase their profits.

It might, however, be desirable, that the farmers, during their current leases, should be protected against the losses which they would undoubtedly suffer from the new value of money, which would result from a cheap price of corn, under their existing money engagements with their landlords.

Although the nation would sacrifice much more than the farmers would save even by a temporary high price of corn, it might be just to lay restrictive duties on importation for three or four years, and to declare that, after that period, the trade in corn should be free, and that imported corn should be subject to no other duty than such as we might find it expedient to impose on corn of our own growth.

Mr. Malthus is, no doubt, correct, when he says, "If merely the best modes of cultivation now in use, in some parts of Great Britain, were generally extended, and the whole country was brought to a level, in proportion to its natural advantages, of soil and situation, by the further accumulation and more equable distribution of capital and skill, the quantity of additional produce would be immense, and would afford the means of subsistence to a very great increase of population.

This reflection is true, and is highly pleasing—it shows that we are yet at a great distance from the end of our resources, and that we may contemplate an increase of prosperity and wealth far exceeding that of any country which has preceded us. This may take place under either system, that of importation or restriction, though not with an equally accelerated pace, and is no argument why we should not, at every period of our improvement, avail ourselves of the full extent of the advantages offered to our acceptance—it is no reason why we should not make the very best disposition of our capital, so as to ensure the most abundant return. The land, has as I before said, been compared by Mr. Malthus, to a great number of machines, all susceptible of continued improvement by the application of capital to them, but yet of very different original qualities and powers. Would it be wise at a great expense to use some of the worst of these machines, when at a less expense we could hire the very best from our neighbours.

Mr. Malthus thinks that a low money price of corn would not be favourable to the lower classes of society, because the real exchangeable value of labour, that is, its power of commanding the necessaries, conveniences, and luxuries of life, would not be augmented, but diminished by a low money price. Some of his observations on this subject are certainly of great weight, but he does not sufficiently allow for the effects of a better distribution of the national capital of the situation of the lower classes. It would be beneficial to them, because the same capital would employ more hands; besides, that the greater profits would lead to further accumulation; and thus would a stimulus be given to population by really high wages, which could not fail for a long time to ameliorate the condition of the labouring classes.

The effects on the interests of this class, would be nearly the same as the effects of improved machinery, which, it is now no longer questioned, has a decided tendency to raise the real wages of labour.

Mr. Malthus also observes, "that of the commercial and manufacturing classes, only those who are directly engaged in foreign trade will feel the benefit of the importing system."

If the view which has been taken of rent be correct—if it rise as general profits fall, and fall as general profits rise—and if the effect of importing corn is to lower rent, which has been admitted, and ably exemplified by Mr. Malthus himself—all who are concerned in trade—all capitalists whatever, whether they be farmers, manufacturers, or merchants, will have a great augmentation of profits. A fall in the price of corn, in consequence of improvements in agriculture or of importation, will lower the exchangeable value of corn only—the price of no other commodity will be affected. If, then, the price of labour falls, which it must do when the price of corn is lowered, the real profits of all descriptions must rise; and no person will be so materially benefited as the manufacturing and commercial part of society.

If the demand for home commodities should be diminished, because of the fall of rent on the part of the landlords, it will be increased in a far greater degree by the increased opulence of the commercial classes.

If restrictions on the importation of corn should take place, I do not apprehend that we shall lose any part of our foreign trade; on this point I agree with Mr. Malthus. In the case of a free trade in corn, it would be considerably augmented; but the question is not, whether we can retain the same foreign trade—but, whether, in both cases, it will be equally profitable.

Our commodities would not sell abroad for more or less in consequence of a free trade, and a cheap price of corn; but the cost of production to our manufacturers would be very different if the price of corn was eighty, or was sixty shillings per quarter; and consequently profits would be augmented by all the cost saved in the production of the exported commodities.

Mr. Malthus notices an observation, which was first made by Hume, that a rise of prices has a magic effect on industry; he states the effects of a fall to be proportionally depressing. A rise of prices has been stated to be one of the advantages, to counter-balance the many evils attendant on a depreciation of money, from a real fall in the value of the precious metals, from raising the denomination of the coin, or from the over-issue of paper-money.

It is said to be beneficial, because it betters the situation of the commercial classes at the expense of those enjoying fixed incomes—and that it is chiefly in those classes, that the great accumulations are made, and productive industry encouraged.

A recurrence to a better monetary system, it is said, though highly desirable, tends to give a temporary discouragement to accumulation and industry, by depressing the commercial part of the community, and is the effect of a fall of prices: Mr. Malthus supposes that such an effect will be produced by the fall of the price of corn. If the observation made by Hume were well founded, still it would not apply to the present instance:—for every thing that the manufacturer would have to sell, would be as dear as ever: it is only what he would buy that would be cheap, namely, corn and labour, by which his gains would be increased. I must again observe, that a rise in the value of money lowers all things; whereas a fall in the price of corn, only lowers the wages of labour, and therefore raises profits.

If, then, the prosperity of the commercial classes will most certainly lead to accumulation of capital, and the encouragement of productive industry; these can by no means be so surely obtained as by a fall in the price of corn.

I cannot agree with Mr. Malthus in his approbation of the opinion of Adam Smith, "that no equal quantity of productive labour employed in manufactures, can *ever* occasion so great a re-production as in agriculture." I suppose that he must have overlooked the term ever in this passage, otherwise the opinion is more consistent with the doctrine of the Economist, than with those which he has maintained; as he has stated, and I think correctly that in the first settling of a new country, and in every stage of its improvement, there is a portion of its capital employed on the land, for the profits of stock merely, and which yields no rent whatever. Productive labour employed on such land never does in fact afford so *great* a re-production, as the same productive labour employed in manufactures.

The difference is not indeed great, and is voluntarily relinquished, on account of the security and respectability which attends the employment of capital on land. In the infancy of society, when no rent is paid, is not the re-production of value in the coarse manufactures, and in the implements of husbandry with a given capital, at least as great as the value which the same capital would afford if employed on the land?

This opinion indeed is at variance with all the general doctrines of Mr. Malthus, which he has so ably maintained in this as well as in all his other publications. In the "Inquiry," speaking of what I consider a similar opinion of Adam Smith, he observes, "I cannot, however, agree with him in thinking that all land which yields food must necessarily yield rent. The land which is successively taken into cultivation in improving countries, may only pay profits and labour. A fair profit on the stock employed, including, of course, the payment of labour, will always be a sufficient inducement to cultivate." The same motives will also induce some to manufacture goods, and the profits of both, in the same stages of society, will be nearly the same.

In the course of these observations, I have often had occasion to insist, that rent never falls without the profits of stock rising. If it suit us to-day to import corn rather than grow it, we are solely influenced by the cheaper price. If we import, the portion of capital last employed on the land, and which yielded no rent, will be withdrawn; rent will fall and profits rise, and another portion of capital employed on the land will come under the same description of only yielding the usual profits of stock.

If corn can be imported cheaper than it can be grown on this rather better land, rent will again fall and profits rise, and another and better description of land will now be cultivated, for profits only. In every step of our progress, profits of stock increase and rents fall, and more land is abandoned; besides which, the country saves all the difference between the price at which corn can be grown, and the price at which it can be imported, on the quantity we receive from abroad.

Mr. Malthus has considered, with the greatest ability, the effect of a cheap price of corn on those who contribute to the interest of our enormous debt. I most fully concur in many of his conclusions on this part of the subject. The wealth of England, would, I am persuaded, be considerably augmented by a great reduction in the price of corn, but the whole money value of that wealth would be diminished. It would be diminished by the whole difference of the money value of the corn consumed—it would be augmented by the increased exchangeable value of all those commodities which would be exported in exchange for the corn imported. The latter would, however, be very unequal to the former; therefore the money value of the commodities of England would, undoubtedly, be considerably lowered.

But, though it is true, that the money value of the mass of our commodities would be diminished, it by no means follows that our annual revenue would fall in the same degree. The advocates for importation ground their opinion of the advantages of it on the conviction that the revenue would not so fall. And, as it is from our revenue that taxes are paid, the burthen might not be really augmented.

Suppose the revenue of a country to fall from 10 to 9 millions, whilst the value of money altered in the proportion of 10 to 8, such country would have a larger net revenue, after paying a million from the smaller, then it would have after paying it from the larger sum.

That the stockholder would receive more in real value than what he contracted for, in the loans of the late years, is also true; but, as the stockholders themselves contribute very largely to the public burthens, and therefore to the payment of the interest which they receive, no inconsiderable proportion of the taxes would fall on them; and, if we estimate at its true value the additional profits made by the commercial class, they would still be great gainers, notwithstanding their really augmented contributions.

The landlord would be the only sufferer by paying really more, not only without any adequate compensation, but with lowered rents.

It may, indeed, be urged, on the part of the stockholder, and those who live on fixed incomes, that they have been by far the greatest sufferers by the war. The value of their revenue has been diminished by the rise in the price of corn, and by the depreciation in the value of paper-money, whilst, at the same time, the value of their capital has been very much diminished from the lower price of the funds. They have suffered, too, from the inroads lately made on the sinking fund, and which, it is supposed, will be still further extended—a measure of the greatest injustice, —in direct violation of solemn contracts; for the sinking fund is as much a part of the contract as the dividend, and, as a source of revenue, utterly at variance with all sound principles. It is to the growth of that fund that we ought to look for the means of carrying on future wars, unless we are prepared to relinquish the funding system altogether. To meddle with the sinking fund, is to obtain a little temporary aid at the sacrifice of a great future advantage. It is reversing the whole system of Mr. Pitt, in the creation of that fund: he proceeded on the conviction that, for a small present burthen, an immense future advantage would be obtained; and, after witnessing, as we have done, the benefits which have already resulted from his inflexible determination to leave that fund untouched, even when depressed by the greatest financial distress, when 3 per cents were so low as 48, we cannot, I think, hesitate in pronouncing that he would not have countenanced, had he still lived, the measures which have been adopted.

To recur, however to the subject before me, I shall only further observe, that I shall greatly regret that considerations for any particular class are allowed to check the progress of the wealth and population of the country. If the interests of the landlord be of sufficient consequence, to determine us not to avail ourselves of all the benefits which would follow from importing corn at a cheap price, they should also influence us in rejecting all improvements in agriculture, and in the implements of husbandry; for it is as certain that corn is rendered cheap, rents are lowered, and the ability of the landlord to pay taxes is, for a time at least, as much impaired by such improvements as by the importation of corn. To be consistent, then, let us by the same act arrest improvement, and prohibit importation.

JAMES MILL

(1773–1836)

James Mill is chiefly remembered as the father of the illustrious John Stuart Mill, in whose education he played a very important part, as attested in the famous autobiography of John Stuart Mill. James Mill was a close friend of David Ricardo, whom he induced to publish his great work on "The Principles of Political Economy and Taxation." Nevertheless, James Mill was a fairly important economist in his own right. He represented, perhaps, the quintessence of English classicism.

One of the most famous works of James Mill was in history rather than economics, namely, "The History of India," published in 1818. His works in economics included "An Essay on the Impolicy of a Bounty on the Exportation of Grain and on the Principles which ought to regulate the Commerce of Grain" (1804), and "Commerce Defended" (1807). He also wrote numerous articles for the *Edinburgh Review,* and made numerous contributions to the "Encyclopaedia Britannica."

The chief work of interest to students in the history of economic thought is Jame Mill's "Elements of Political Economy," which appeared in 1819. A second edition appeared in 1824 and a third edition in 1826. The following brief selections have been taken from the third edition of this work.

Students should note the oversimplicity of this text, which was designed to appeal to immature students, and which was based on the current assumption that economics could be reduced to the mere statement of a very few fundamental principles. It will also be observed that James Mill, along with the other classicists, was an advocate of the wage fund theory. In conclusion, the student is asked to observe to what extent John Stuart Mill was indebted to his father.

JAMES MILL

SELECTIONS FROM "ELEMENTS OF POLITICAL ECONOMY"

INTRODUCTION

The Subject—Its Limits—and Division

Political Economy is to the State, what domestic economy is to the family.

The family consumes; and, in order to consume, it must supply.

Domestic economy has, therefore, two grand objects; the consumption and supply of the family. The consumption being a quantity always indefinite, for there is no end to the desire of enjoyment, the grand concern is, to increase the supply.

Those things, which are produced, in sufficient abundance for the satisfaction of all, without the intervention of human labour; as air, the light of the sun, water, and so on; are not the objects of care or providence; and therefore, accurately speaking, do not form part of the subject of domestic economy. The art of him, who manages a family, consists in regulating the supply and consumption of those things, which cannot be obtained but with cost; in other words, with human labour, "the original purchase-money, which is given for everything."

The same is the case with Political Economy. It also has two grand objects, the Consumption of the Community, and the Supply upon which the consumption depends. Those things, which are supplied without the intervention of human labour, as nothing is required in order to obtain them, need not be taken into account. Had every thing, desired for consumption, existed without human labour, there would have been no place for Political Economy. Science is not implied in putting forth the hand, and using. But when labour is to be employed, and the objects of desire can be multiplied only by a preconcerted plan of operations, it becomes an object of importance to ascertain completely the means of that multiplication, and to frame a system of rules for applying them with greatest advantage to the end.

It is not pretended, that writers on Political Economy have always limited their disquisitions to this object. It seems, however, important to detach the science from all considerations not essential to it. The reader is therefore requested to observe that, in the following pages, I have merely in view, to ascertain the laws, according to which the production and

219

consumption are regulated of those commodities, which the intervention of human labour is necessary to procure.

The Science of Political Economy, thus defined, divides itself into two great inquiries; that which relates to Production, and that which relates to Consumption.

But, after things are produced, it is evident, that, before they are consumed, they must be distributed. The laws of distribution, therefore, constitute an intermediate inquiry.

When commodities are produced, and distributed, it is highly convenient, for the sake both of reproduction and consumption, that portions of them would be exchanged for one another. To ascertain, therefore, the laws, according to which commodities are exchanged for one another, is a second inquiry, preceding that which relates to the last great topic of Political Economy, Consumption.

It thus appears, that four inquiries are comprehended in this science.

1st. What are the laws, which regulate the production of commodities.

2dly. What are the laws, according to which the commodities, produced by the labour of the community, are distributed:

3dly. What are the laws, according to which the commodities are exchanged for one another:

4thly. What are the laws, which regulate consumption.

Chapter II. Distribution

Section 2. *Wages*

That the Rate of Wages Depends on the Proportion between Population, and Employment, in Other Words Capital.

We come now to the question as to what determines the share of the labourer, or the proportion in which the commodity, or its worth, is divided between him and the capitalist. Whatever the share of the labourer, such is the rate of wages; and, vice versa, whatever the rate of wages, such is the share of the commodity, or commodities worth, which the labourer receives.

It is very evident, that the share of the two parties is the subject of a bargain between them; and if there is a bargain, it is not difficult to see on what the terms of the bargain must depend. All bargains, when made in freedom, are determined by competition, and the terms alter according to the state of supply and demand.

Let us begin by supposing that there is a certain number of capitalists, with a certain quantity of food, raw material, and instruments, or machinery; that there is also a certain number of labourers; and that the proportion, in which the commodities produced are divided between them, has fixed itself at some particular point.

Let us next suppose, that the labourers have increased in number one half, without an increase in the quantity of capital. There is the same quantity of the requisites for the employment of labour; that is, of foods, tools, and material, as there was before; but for every 100 labourers there are now 150. There will be 50 men, therefore, in danger of being left out of employment. To prevent their being left out of employment they have but one resource; they must endeavour to supplant those who have fore-stalled the employment; that is, they must offer to work for a smaller reward. Wages, therefore, decline.

If we suppose, on the other hand, that the quantity of capital has increased, while the number of labourers remains the same, the effect will be reversed. The capitalists have a greater quantity than before of the means of employment; of capital, in short; from which they wish to derive advantage. To derive this advantage they must have more labourers. To obtain them, they also have but one resource, to offer higher wages. But the masters by whom the labourers are now employed are in the same predicament, and will of course offer higher to induce them to remain. This competition is unavoidable, and the necessary effect of it is a rise of wages.

It thus appears, that, if population increases without an increase of capital, wages fall; and that, if capital increases, without an increase of population, wages rise. It is evident, also, that if both increase, but one faster than the other, the effect will be the same as if the one had not increased at all, and the other had made an increase equal to the difference. Suppose, for example, that population has increased one-eighth, and capital one-eighth; this is the same thing as if they had stood still, with regard to the effect upon labour. But suppose that, in addition to the above statement one-eighth, population had increased another eighth, the effect, in that case, upon wages, would be the same as if the capital had not increased at all, and population had increased one-eighth.

Universally, then, we may affirm, that, other things remaining the same, if the ratio which capital and population bear to one another remains the same, wages will remain the same; if the ratio which capital bears to population increases, wages will rise; if the ratio which population bears to capital increases, wages will fall.

From this law, clearly understood, it is easy to trace the circumstances which, in any country, determine the condition of the great body of the people. If that condition is easy and comfortable, all that is necessary to keep it so, is, to make capital increase as fast as population; or, on the other hand, to prevent population from increasing faster than capital. If that condition is not easy and comfortable, it can only be made so, by one of two methods; either by quickening the rate at which capital increases, or retarding the rate at which population increases; augmenting in short, the ratio which the means of employing the people bear to the number of people.

If it were the natural tendency of capital to increase faster than population, there could be no difficulty in preserving a prosperous condition of the people. If on the other hand, it were the natural tendency of population to increase faster than capital, the difficulty would be very great. There would be a perpetual tendency in wages to fall. The progressive fall of wages would produce a greater and a greater degree of poverty among the people, attended with its inevitable consequences, misery and vice. As poverty, and its consequence misery increased, mortality would also increase. Of a numerous family born, a certain number only, from want of the means of well-being, would be reared. By whatever proportion the population tended to increase faster than capital, such a proportion of those who were born would die: the ratio of increase in capital and population would then remain the same, and the fall of wages would proceed no farther.

That the population has a tendency to increase faster, than, in most places, capital has actually increased, is proved, incontestably, by the condition of the population in most parts of the globe. In almost all countries, the condition of the great body of the people is poor and miserable. This would have been impossible, if capital had increased faster than population. In that case wages must have risen; and high wages would have placed the labourer above miseries of want.

This general misery of mankind is a fact, which can be accounted for, upon one only of two suppositions: either that there is a natural tendency in population to increase faster than capital, or that capital has, by some means, been prevented from increasing so fast as it has a tendency to increase. This, therefore, is an inquiry of the highest importance.

Chapter III. Interchange

Section 2

What Determines the Quantity in which Commodities Exchange for One Another.

When a certain quantity of one commodity is exchanged for a certain quantity of another commodity; a certain quantity of cloth, for example, for a certain quantity of corn; there is something which determines the owner of the cloth to accept for it such and such a quantity of corn; and, in like manner, the owner of the corn to accept such and such a quantity of corn.

This is, evidently, the principle of demand and supply, in the first instance. If a great quantity of corn comes to market to be exchanged for cloth, and only a small quantity of cloth to be exchanged for corn, a great quantity of corn will be given for a small quantity of cloth. If the quantity of cloth, which thus comes to market, is increased, without any increase in the quantity of corn, the quantity of corn which is exchanged for a given quantity of cloth will be proportionally diminished.

This answer, however, does not resolve the whole of the question. The quantity in which commodities exchange for one another depends upon the proportion of supply to demand. It is evidently therefore necessary to ascertain upon what that proportion depends. What are the laws according to which supply is furnished to demand, is one of the most important inquiries in Political Economy.

Demand creates, and the loss of demand annihilates, supply. When an increased demand arises for any commodity, an increase of supply, if the supply is capable of increase, follows, as a regular effect. If the demand for any commodity altogether ceases, the commodity is no longer produced.

The connexion here, of causes and effects, is easily explained. If corn is brought to market, the cost of bringing it has been so much. For the benefit of simplicity, the number of commodities in the market is here supposed to be two: it is of no consequence, with regard to the result, whether they are understood to be few or many.

The cost of bringing the corn to market has been either equal to that of bringing the cloth, or unequal. If it has been equal there is no motive, to those who bring the cloth or the corn, for altering the quantity of either. They cannot obtain more of the commodity which they receive in exchange, by transferring their labour to its production. If the cost has been unequal, there immediately arises a motive for altering the proportions. Suppose that the cost of bringing the whole of the corn has been greater than that of bringing the whole of the cloth; and that the whole of the one is exchanged against the whole of the other, either at once, or in parts; the persons who brought the cloth have in that case possessed themselves of a quantity of corn at less cost than that at which it was brought to market, by those who produced it; those, on the other hand, who brought the corn have possessed themselves of a quantity of cloth, at a greater cost than that at which it can be made and brought to market.

Here motives rise, to diminish the quantity of corn and increase the quantity of cloth; because the men who have been producing corn, and purchasing cloth, can obtain more cloth, by transferring their means of production from the one to the other. As soon, again as no more cloth can be obtained by applying the same amount of means to the production of cloth, than by applying them to corn, and exchanging it for cloth, all motive to alter the quantity of one as compared with that of the other is at an end. Nothing is to be gained by producing corn rather than cloth, or cloth rather than corn. The cost of production on both sides is equal.

It thus appears that the relative value of commodities, or in other words, the quantity of one which exchanges for a given quantity of another, depends upon demand and supply, in the first instance; but upon cost of production, ultimately; and hence, in accurate language, upon cost of production, entirely. An increase or diminution of demand or supply, may temporarily increase or diminish, beyond the point of productive cost, the quantity of one commodity which exchanges for a given quantity of another; but the law of competition, wherever it is not obstructed, tends invariably to bring to that point, and to keep it there.

Cost of production, then, regulates the exchangeable value of commodities.

WILLIAM NASSAU SENIOR

(1790–1864)

William Nassau Senior was an English economist whose career, like that of his contemporary, James Mill, may be said to mark the acme of classical economy. It is interesting to note that he was a professor of political economy at Oxford. This chair, created in 1825, was the first one in economics to be established in England. Senior was also a member of the Royal Commission of 1832 to examine the operation of the poor laws and to report remedies.

Senior's writings of importance were as follows: "An Introductory Lecture on Political Economy (1827); "Three Lectures on the Transmission of the Precious Metals and the Mercantile Theory of Wealth (1828); "Three Lectures on the Cost of Obtaining Money, and of Some Effects of Private and Government Paper Money" (1830); "Two Lectures on Population" (1831); "Three Lectures on the Rate of Wages" (1831); and "Four Introductory Lectures" (1852).

The principal work of Senior was "An Outline of Political Economy" (1836), which first appeared as an article in the "Encyclopaedia Metropolitana." It is from this work that the following selections have been taken. The student will be interested to observe the very brief and precise forms in which the fundamental principles of economics are stated. Indeed, the form is similar to that of propositions in geometry. One of Senior's chief contributions was his treatment of abstinence as a necessary cost of production.

Even the dry subject of political economy has its romances. One of them is the recent discovery of the notes of Ricardo on Malthus's "Principles of Political Economy," referred to in a preceding section. Another startling recent discovery was that by S. L. Levy of an unpublished manuscript of Nassau Senior. Well selected and carefully edited selections from this original manuscript were published in 1928 by Henry Holt & Company in two volumes under the title "Industrial Efficiency and Social Economy."

WILLIAM NASSAU SENIOR

SELECTIONS FROM "AN OUTLINE OF POLITICAL ECONOMY"

INTRODUCTION

Definition of the Science.—We propose in the following Treatise to give an outline of the Science which treats of the Nature, the Production, and the Distribution of Wealth. To that Science we give the name of Political Economy. Our readers must be aware that that term has often been used in a much wider sense. The earlier writers who assumed the name of Political Economists avowedly treated not of Wealth but of Government. Mercier de la Riviere entitled his Work *The Natural and Essential Organization of Society*, and professed to propose an organization "which shall necessarily produce all the happiness that can be enjoyed on earth." Sir James Steuart states, that "the principal object of the Science is to secure a certain fund of subsistence for all the inhabitants, to obviate every circumstance which may render it precarious, and to provide every thing necessary for supplying the wants of the society." The modern continental writers have in general entered into an equally extensive inquiry. "Political Economy," says M. Storch, "is the Science of the natural laws which determine the prosperity of nations, that is to say, their wealth and their civilization." M. Sismondi considers "the physical welfare of man, so far as it can be the work of government, as the object of Political Economy." "Political Economy," says M. Say, "is the economy of society; a Science combining the results of our observations on the nature and functions of the different parts of the social body." The modern writers of the English school have in general professed to limit their attention to the theory of Wealth; but some of the most eminent among them, after having expressed their intention to confine themselves within what appears to us to be their proper province, have invaded that of the general legislator or the statesman. Thus Mr. M'Culloch, after having defined Political Economy to be "the Science of the laws which regulate the production, accumulation, distribution, and consumption of those articles or products that are necessarily useful or agreeable to man, and possess exchangeable value"; or "The Science of Values"; adds, that "its object is to point out the means by which the industry of man may be rendered most productive of wealth, to ascertain the circumstances most favourable to its accumulation, the proportions in which it is divided, and the mode in which it may be most advantageously consumed."

Limits of the Science.—It is impossible to overstate the importance of these inquiries, and it is not easy to state their extent. They involve, as their general premises, the consideration of the whole theory of morals of government, and of civil and criminal legislation; and, for their particular premises, a knowledge of all the facts which affect the social condition of every community whose conduct the Economist proposes to influence. We believe that such inquiries far exceed the bounds of any single Treatise, and indeed the powers of any single mind. We believe that by confining our own and the reader's attention to the Nature, Production, and Distribution of Wealth, we shall produce a more clear, and complete, and instructive work than if we allowed ourselves to wander into the more interesting and more important, but far less definite, fields by which the comparatively narrow path of Political Economy is surrounded. The questions, To what extent and under what circumstances the possession of Wealth is, on the whole, beneficial or injurious to its possessor, or to the society of which he is a member? What distribution of Wealth is most desirable in each different state of society? And What are the means by which any given Country can facilitate such a distribution?—all these are questions of great interest and difficulty, but no more form part of the Science of Political Economy, in the sense in which we use that term, than Navigation forms part of the Science of Astronomy. The principles supplied by Political Economy, are indeed necessary elements in their solution, but they are not the only, or even the most important elements. The writer who pursues such investigations is in fact engaged on the great Science of legislation; a Science which requires a knowledge of the general principles supplied by Political Economy, but differs from it essentially in its subject, its premises, and its conclusions. The subject of legislation is not Wealth, but human Welfare. Its premises are drawn from an infinite variety of phenomena, supported by evidence of every degree of strength, and authorizing conclusions deserving every degree of assent, from perfect confidence to bare suspicion. And its expounder is enabled, and even required, not merely to state general facts, but to urge the adoption or rejection of actual measures or trains of action.

On the other hand, the subject treated by the Political Economist, using that term in the limited sense in which we apply it, is not Happiness, but Wealth; his premises consist of a very few general propositions, the result of observation, or consciousness, and scarcely requiring proof, or even formal statement, which almost every man, as soon as he hears them, admits as familiar to his thoughts, or at least as included in his previous knowledge; and his inferences are nearly as general, and, if he has reasoned correctly, as certain, as his premises. Those which relate to the Nature and the Production of Wealth are universally true; and though those which relate to the Distribution of Wealth are liable to be affected by the peculiar institutions of particular Countries, in the cases for instance of slavery, legal monopolies, or poor laws, the natural state of things can be laid down as the general rule, and the anomalies produced by particular disturbing causes can be afterwards accounted for. But his conclusions, whatever be their generality and their truth, do not authorize him in adding a single syllable of advice. That privilege belongs to the writer or the statesman who has considered all the causes which may promote or impede the general welfare of those whom he addresses, not to the theorist who has considered only one, though among the most important, of those causes. The business of a Political Economist is neither to recommend nor to dissuade, but to state general principles, which it is fatal to neglect, but neither advisable, nor perhaps practicable, to use as the sole, or even the principal, guides in the actual conduct of affairs. In the meantime the duty of each individual writer is clear. Employed as he is upon a Science in which error or even ignorance, may be productive of such intense and such extensive mischief, he is bound, like a juryman, to give deliverance true according to the evidence, and allow neither sympathy with indigence, nor disgust at profusion or at avarice—neither reverence for existing institutions, nor detestation of existing abuses—neither love of popularity, nor of paradox, nor of system, to deter him from stating what he believes to be the facts, or from drawing from those facts what appear to him to be the legitimate conclusions. To decide in each case how far those conclusions are to be acted upon, belongs to the art of government, an art to which Political Economy is only one of many subservient Sciences; which involves the consideration of motives, of which the desire for Wealth is only one among many, and aims at objects to which the possession of Wealth is only a subordinate means.

The confounding Political Economy with the Sciences and Arts to which it is subservient, has been one of the principal obstacles to its improvement. It has acted thus in two different modes:—

First, by exciting, in the public unfavourable prejudices.

And, secondly, by misleading Economists, both with respect to the object of their Science and the means of attaining it.

With respect to the first of these obstacles, it has often been made a matter of grave complaint against Political Economists, that they confine their attention to Wealth, and disregard all consideration of Happiness or Virtue. It is to be wished that this complaint were better founded; but its general existence implies an opinion that it is the business of Political Economists not merely to state propositions, but to recommend actual measures; for on no other supposition could they be blamed for confining their attention to a single subject. No one blames a writer upon tactics for confining his attention to military affairs, or, from his doing so, infers that he recommends perpetual war. It must be admitted that an author who, having stated that a given conduct is productive of Wealth, should, on that account alone, recommend it, or assume that, on that account alone, it ought to be pursued, would be guilty of the absurdity of implying that Happiness and the possession of wealth are identical. But his error would consist not in confining his attention to Wealth, but in confounding Wealth with Happiness. Supposing that error, and it is a very obvious one, to be avoided, the more strictly a writer confines his attention to his own Science, the more likely he is to extend its bounds.

Secondly, The confounding the Science of Political Economy with the Sciences and Arts to which it is subservient, has seduced Economists sometimes to undertake inquiries too vague to lead to any practical results, and sometimes to pursue the legitimate objects of the Science by means unfit for their attainment. To their extended view of the objects of Political Economy is to be attributed the undue importance which many Economists have ascribed to the collection of facts, and their neglect of the far more important process of reasoning accurately from the facts before them. We are constantly told that it is a Science of facts and experiment, a Science *avide de faits*. The practical applications of it, like the practical applications of every other Science, without doubt, require the collection and examination of facts to an almost indefinite extent. The facts collected as materials for the amendment of the poor-laws, and the opening of the trade to China, fill more than twice as many volumes as could be occupied by all the Treatises that have ever been written on Political Economy; but the facts on which the general principles of the Science rest may be stated in a very few sentences, and indeed in a very few words. But that the reasoning from these facts, the drawing from them correct conclusions, is a matter of great difficulty, may be inferred from the imperfect state in which the Science is now found after it has been so long and so intensely studied.

This difficulty arises partly from the extremely complicated nature of the subjects which it investigates, and the consequent abstractness and generality of its terms. A description, if it were possible, of all the different things which are designated by the word "Wealth," or even by the less comprehensive word "Capital," would fill an Encyclopaedia. It arises partly, also, from the circumstances, that the terms which we are forced to use as signs for these abstractions are taken from ordinary language, commonly used in senses too wide or too narrow for scientific purposes. In the case, therefore, both of the writer and of the reader, they are often associated with ideas which are intended to be excluded, or separated from ideas which are meant to be comprehended. Thus, in ordinary language, the word Capital is sometimes used as comprehending every species of Wealth, and sometimes as confined to Money.

If Economists had been aware that the Science depends more on reasoning than on observation, and that its principal difficulty consists not in the ascertainment of its facts, but in the use of its terms, we cannot doubt that their principal efforts would have been directed to the selection and consistent use of an accurate nomenclature. So far is this from having been the case, that it is only within a very short period that serious attention has been given to its nomenclature. *The Wealth of Nations* contains scarcely a definition: most of the modern French writers, and some indeed of our own, have not only neglected definitions, but have expressly reprobated their use; and the English Work which has attracted the most attention during the present century, Mr. Ricardo's *Principles of Political Economy*, is deformed by a use of words so unexplained, and yet so remote from ordinary usage, and from that of other writers on the same subject, and frequently so inconsistent, as to perplex every reader, and not unfrequently to have misled the writer himself. We do not complain of all his innovations in language: such innovations are, for scientific purposes, frequently indispensable, and we shall be forced to make many ourselves. What we do complain of is, that his innovations, such, for instance, as the substitution of the word *Value* for *Cost*, are frequently unnecessary, and are almost always made without any warning to his readers; and that the same words, such, for example, as the adjectives *high* and *low*, when applied to wages, are used by him sometimes in their popular sense, as expressing an amount, and sometimes in a technical sense of his own, as expressing a proportion.

Our object in these remarks has been not only to account for the slow progress which has as yet been made by Political Economy, and to suggest means by which its advancement may be accelerated, but also to warn the reader of the nature of the following Treatise. He will find it consist, in a great degree, of discussions as to the most convenient use of a few familiar words. Such discussions it is impossible to render amusing, but we trust that they will be useful, by directing his attention to the great difficulties of the Science, though he may often disapprove our classification or nomenclature.

Nature of Wealth

Wealth Defined.—Having stated that the Science which we propose to consider, and to which we apply the term Political Economy, is the Science which treats of the Nature, the Production, and the Distribution of Wealth, our first business is to explain the meaning in which we use the word Wealth.

Under that term we comprehend all those things, and those things only, which are transferable, are limited in supply, and are directly or indirectly productive of pleasure or preventive of pain; or, to use an equivalent expression, which are susceptible of *exchange;* (using the word exchange to denote hiring as well as absolute purchase) or, to use a third equivalent expression, which have *Value;* a word which, in a subsequent portion of this Treatise, we shall explain at some length, merely premising at present that we can use it in its popular sense, as denoting the capacity of being given and received in exchange.

Constituents of Wealth

1. *Utility.*—Of the three qualities which render any thing an article of Wealth, or, in other words, give it Value, the most striking is the power, direct or indirect, of producing pleasure, including under that term gratification of every kind, or of preventing pain, including under that term every species of discomfort. Unfortunately, we have no word which precisely expresses this power; *utility*, which comes nearest to it, being generally used to express the quantity of preventing pain or of indirectly producing pleasure, as a means. We shall venture to extend the signification of that word, and consider it as also including all those things which produce pleasure directly. We must admit that this is a considerable innovation in English language. It is, however, sanctioned by Mr. Malthus, (Definitions, p. 234) and has been ventured by M. Say in French, a language less patient of innovation than our own. Feeling the same difficulty, he has solved it in the same way by using the term *utilité* as comprehending every quality that renders any thing an object of desire. Attractiveness and desirableness have both been suggested to us as substitutes, but on the whole they appear to us more objectionable than *utility*, objectionable as we must admit that word to be.

Utility, thus explained, is a necessary constituent of value; no man would give any thing possessing the slightest utility for a thing possessing none; and even an exchange of two useless things would be, on the part of each party to the exchange, an act without a motive. Utility, however, denotes no intrinsic quality in the things which we call useful; it merely expresses their relations to the pains and pleasures of mankind. And, as the susceptibility of pain and pleasure from particular objects is created and modified by causes innumerable, and constantly varying, we find an endless diversity in the relative utility of different objects to different persons, a diversity which is the motive of all exchange.

2. *Limitation in Supply.*—The next constituent of value is *limitation in supply*. It may appear inaccurate to apply this expression to any class of things, as it, in fact, belongs to all; there being nothing which, strictly speaking, is unlimited in supply. But, for the purposes of Political Economy, every thing may be considered as unlimited in supply *in its existing state*, of which a man may have as much as he pleases for the mere trouble of taking it into his possession. Thus the water of the open sea is, in our use of the term, unlimited in supply; any man who chooses to go for it may have as much of it as he pleases: that portion of it which has been brought to London is limited in supply, and is to be obtained not merely by going to the reservoir and taking possession of it, but by giving for it an

equivalent. The copper ores which Sir. John Franklin discovered on the shores of the Arctic Sea may be considered, *in their existing state*, as unlimited in supply, and therefore susceptible of value. Many things are unlimited in supply; any man may have as much of them as he has strength and patience to extract. The extracted portion would be limited in supply, and therefore susceptible of value. Many things are unlimited in supply for some purposes, and limited for others. The water in a river is in general more than sufficient for all the domestic purposes for which it can be required; nobody pays therefore for permission to take a bucket-full: but it is seldom sufficient for all those who may wish to turn their mills with it; they pay, therefore, for that privilege.

It must be further observed that, for economical purposes, the term *limitation in supply* always involves the consideration of the causes by which the existing supply is limited. The supply of some articles of Wealth is limited by insurmountable obstacles. The number of Raphael's pictures, or of Canova's statues, may be diminished, but cannot possibly be increased. There are others of which the supply may be increased to an indefinite extent. Such things may be considered as comparatively limited in supply, in proportion, not to the existing supply of each, but to the force of the obstacles opposed to their respective increase. It is supposed that there is now about forty-five times as much of silver extracted from the mines, and current in Europe, as there is of gold. Human exertion is the only means by which the supply of either can be increased, and they may both be increased by human exertion to an amount of which we do not know the limit. The obstacle, therefore, by which they are each limited in supply is, the amount of human exertion necessary to their respective increase. About sixteen times more exertion is necessary to produce an ounce of gold than an ounce of silver. The obstacle, therefore, which limits the supply of gold is sixteen times more powerful than that which limits the supply of silver. In our sense of the term, therefore, gold is only sixteen times more limited in supply than silver, though the actual weight of silver in Europe is forty-five times as great as that of gold. To take a more familiar example, the number of coats and waistcoats in England is perhaps about equal. The supply of each may be increased by human exertion to an indefinite extent; but it requires about three times as much exertion to produce a coat as to produce a waistcoat. As the obstacle, therefore, which limits the supply of coats is three times as forcible as that which limits the supply of waistcoats, we consider coats three times more limited in supply than waistcoats, though the existing supply of each may perhaps be equal. Whenever, therefore, we apply the words *limited in supply*, as a comparative expression, to those commodities of which the quantity can be increased, we refer to the comparative force of the obstacles which limit the respective supplies of the objects compared.

3. *Transferableness.*—The third and last quality which a thing must possess to constitute it an article of Wealth, or, in other words, to give it value, is *Transferableness*, by which term (we are sorry to say, an unusual one) we mean to express that all or some portion of its powers of giving pleasure, or preventing pain, are capable of being transferred, either absolutely, or for a period. For this purpose it is obvious that is must be capable of appropriation; since no man can give what he cannot refuse. The sources of pleasure and preventives of pain which are absolutely incapable of appropriation are very few. We almost doubt whether there are any, and we are sure that the instances which are usually given are incorrect. "The earth," observes M. Say, *Econ. Pol.* Liv. ii. Ch. ix. "is not the only material agent with productive power, but it is the only one, or nearly so, that can be appropriated. The water of the rivers and of the sea, which supplies us with fish, gives motion to our mills, and supports our vessels, has productive powers. The wind gives us force, and the sun heat, but happily no man can say, 'The wind and the sun belong to me, and I will be paid for their services.'" Now, in fact, air and sunshine are local. This is so obvious that it would be absurd to prove, by serious induction, that some situations have too much wind, and others too little, or that the sun's rays are more powerful productive agents in England than in Melville Island, or in the Tropics than in England. And as the land is every where capable of appropriation, the qualities of climate, which are attributes of that land, must be so too. What gives their principal value to the vineyards of the Côte Rotie, but the warmth of their sun? or to the houses which overlook Hyde Park, but the purity of their air? Rivers and the sea are equally unfortunate illustrations. Many of the rivers of England are not less strictly appropriated, and are far greater sources of wealth, than any equal superficies of land. When M. Say visited Lancashire, he must have found every inch of fall in every stream the subject of lease and purchase. And so far are the services of the sea from being incapable of appropriation, that, during the late war, £60,000 was sometimes paid for a license to make use of it for a single voyage; and the privilege of fishing in particular parts of it has been the subject of wars and treaties.

The things of which the utility is imperfectly transferable may be divided into two great classes. The first comprises all those material objects which are affected by the particular mental associations, or adapted to the peculiar wants, of individuals. A mansion may flatter the pride of its owner as having been the residence of his ancestors, or be endeared to him as the scene of his childhood; or he may have built it in a form which pleases no eye, or laid it out in apartments that suit no habits but his own. Still its substantial powers of affording warmth and shelter will obtain him purchasers or tenants, though they may demand a reduction from the price in consequences of those very qualities which, with him, formed its principal merits. The palace of St. James's is full of comfort and convenience, and would supply a man of large fortune with an excellent residence; but the long suite of apartments within apartments, which is admirably adapted for holding a Court, would be a mere incumbrance to any but a royal personage. Any individual might hire Alnwick or Blenheim and enjoy their mere beauty and magnificence, perhaps, more than their owners who have been long familiarized to them; but he could never feel the particular pleasure which they seem fitted to give to a Percy and a Churchhill. There are many things, such as clothes and furniture, which sink in utility in the estimation of every one but their purchaser, from the mere fact of having changed hands. A hat or a table which has just been sent home does not appear to the purchaser less useful than when he saw it in the shop; but if he attempt to resell either, he will find that with the rest of the world it has sunk into the degraded rank of second-hand.

The second class of things imperfectly transferable includes the greater part, perhaps all, of our personal qualities. This classification, which places talents and accomplishments among the articles of wealth, may appear at first sight strange and inconvenient; it certainly is different from that of most Economists. We will therefore venture to illustrate it more fully.

Health, strength, and knowledge, and the other natural and acquired powers of body and mind, appear to us to be articles of wealth, precisely analogous to a residence having some qualities that are universally useful, and others peculiarly adapted to the tastes of its owner. They are limited in supply, and are causes of pleasure and preventives of pain far more effectual than the possession of Alnwick or of Blenheim. A portion of the advantages which arise from them are inseparably annexed to their possessor, like the associations of an hereditary property: another portion, and often a very large one, is as transferable as the palpable convenience of the mansion, or beauty of the gardens. What cannot be transferred is the temporary pleasure which generally accompanies the exercise of any accomplishment, and the habitual satisfaction arising from the consciousness of possessing it. What can be transferred are the beneficial results which follow from its having been employed during the period for which its services have been hired. If an Erskine or a Sugden undertakes my cause, he transfers to me, for that occasion, the use of all his natural and acquired ability. My defence is as well conducted as if I had myself the knowledge and the eloquence of an accomplished advocate. What he cannot transfer is the pleasure which he feels in the exercise of his dexterity; but how small is his pleasure compared to mine, if he succeeds for me! A passenger may envy the activity and intrepidity of the crew; they cannot actually implant in him their strength, or their insensibility to danger; but so far as these qualities are means towards an end, so far as they enable him to perform his voyage with quickness and safety, he enjoys the use of them as fully as if they belonged to himself. A hunter probably feels somewhat the same sort of pleasure in the chase which Erskine felt in court; and this pleasure cannot be transferred any more than his muscles or his lungs; but, so far as his strength, speed, and bottom are means towards the end of enabling his rider to keep up with the hounds, they can be purchased or hired as effectually as his bridle or saddle. In the greater part of the world a man is as purchasable as a horse. In such Countries the only difference in value between a slave and a brute consists in the degree in which they respectively possess the sale-able qualities that we have been considering. If the question whether personal qualities are articles of wealth had been proposed in classical times, it would have appeared too clear for discussion. In Athens, every one would have replied that they, in fact, constituted the whole value of an εμψιχον οϛγανον. The only differences in this respect between a freeman and a slave are, first, that the freeman sells *himself*, and only for a period, and to a certain extent, the slave may be sold by others, and absolutely; and, secondly, that the personal qualities of the slave are a portion of the wealth of his master; those of the freeman so far as they can be made the subjects of exchange, are a part of his own wealth. They perish indeed by his death, and may be impaired or destroyed by disease, or rendered valueless by any changes in the customs of the Country which shall destroy the demand for his services; but, subject to these contingencies, they are wealth, and wealth of the most valuable kind. The amount of revenue derived from their exercise in England far exceeds the rental of all the lands in Great Britain.

Limitations in Supply the most important.—Of the three conditions of value, utility, transferableness, and limitation in supply, the last is by far the most important. The chief sources of its influence on value are two of the most powerful principles of human nature, the love of variety, and the love of distinction. The mere necessaries of life are few and simple. Potatoes, water, and salt, simple raiment, a blanket, a hut, an iron pot, and the materials of firing, are sufficient to support mere animal existence in this climate: they do in fact, support the existence of the greater part of the inhabitants of Ireland; and in warmer countries much less will suffice. But no man is satisfied with so limited a range of enjoyment. His first object is to vary his food; but this desire, though urgent at first, is more easily satisfied than any other, except perhaps that of dress. Our ances-tors, long after they had indulged in considerable luxury in other respects, seem to have been contented with a very uniform though grossly abun-dant diet. And even now, notwithstanding the common declamation on the luxury of the table, we shall find that most persons, including even those whose appetites are not controlled by frugality, confine their prin-cipal solid food to but a few articles, and their liquids to still fewer.

The next desire is variety of dress; a taste which has this peculiarity, that, though it is one of the first symptoms that a people is emerging from the brutishness of the lowest savage life, it quickly reaches its highest point, and, in the subsequent progress of refinement, in one sex at least, diminishes until even the highest ranks assume an almost quaker-like simplicity.

Last comes the desire to build, to ornament, and to furnish: tastes which are absolutely insatiable where they exist, and seem to increase with every improvement in civilization. The comforts and conveniences which we now expect in an ordinary lodging, are more than were enjoyed by people of opulence a century ago: and even a century ago a respectable tradesman would have been dissatisfied if his bed-room had been no better furnished than that of Henry VIII, which contained, we are told, only a bed, a cupboard of plate, a joint-stool, a pair of andirons, and a small mirror. And yet Henry was among the richest and the most magnificent sovereigns of his times. Our great grand-children perhaps will despise the accomodations of the present Age, and their poverty may, in turn, be pitied by their successors.

It is obvious, however, that our desires do not aim so much at quantity as at diversity. Not only are there limits to the pleasure which commodities of any given class can afford, but the pleasure diminishes in a rapidly increasing ratio long before those limits are reached. Two articles of the same kind will seldom afford twice the pleasure of one, and still less will ten give five times the pleasure of two. In proportion, therefore, as any article is abundant, the number of those who are provided with it, and do not wish, or wish but little, to increase their provision, is likely to be great; and, so far as they are concerned, the additional supply loses all, or nearly all, its utility. And in proportion to its scarcity the number of those who are in want of it, and the degree in which they want it, are likely to be increased; and its utility, or, in other words, the pleasure which the possession of a given quantity of it will afford, increases proportionally.

But strong as is the desire for variety, it is weak compared with the desire for distinction: a feeling which, if we consider its universality and its constancy, that it affects all men and at all times, that it comes with us from the cradle, and never leaves us till we go into the grave, may be pronounced to be the most powerful of human passions.

The most obvious source of distinction is the possession of superior wealth. It is the one which excites most the admiration of the bulk of mankind, and the only one which they feel capable of attaining. To seem more rich, or, to use a common expression, to keep up a better appearance, than those within their own sphere of comparison, is, with almost all men who are placed beyond the fear of actual want, the ruling principle of conduct. For this object they undergo toil which no pain or pleasure addressed to the senses would lead them to encounter; into which no slave could be lashed or bribed. But this object is attained by appearances, and, indeed, cannot be attained by any thing else. All the gold in the Pactolus, even if the Pactolus were as rich as when Midas had just washed in it, would obviously confer no distinction on the man who was unable to exhibit it. The only mode by which wealth can be exhibited is, by the apparent possession of some object of desire which is limited in supply. Mere limitation of supply, indeed, unless there be some other circumstance constituting the article in question as an object of desire, or, in other words, giving it utility, is insufficient. This circumstance must be its having some quality to which some person beside the owner annexes the notion of utility. The original manuscript of every schoolboy's exercise is as limited in supply as any thing can be, but there is nothing to make it an object of desire after it has served its purpose in school. It is merely a blotted manuscript, unique certainly, but valueless. But if the original manuscript of the *Wealth of Nations* could be discovered, it would excite an interest throughout Europe. Curiosity would be eager to trace the first workings of a mind whose influence will be felt as long as civilized society endures. It might, perhaps, be purchased by some ignorant collector only for the purposes of ostentation, but it could not serve even those purposes unless recommended by some circumstance beyond mere singularity.

It is impossible, however, to conceive any thing more trifling or more capricious than the circumstances which may make a thing an object of desire, and therefore, in our extended use of that word, give it utility when its supply is narrowly limited.

The substance which at present is the greatest object of desire, and of which, therefore, a given quantity will exchange for the greatest quantity of all other things, is the diamond. A bracelet belonging to the king of Persia, the stones in which do not weigh two ounces, is said to be worth a million sterling. Now, a million sterling would command the whole labour of about thirty thousand English families for a year. If that labour were employed in producing and reproducing commodities for the purposes of sale, it would probably give for ever a clear annual income equal to the labour of three thousand families, or twelve thousand individuals. It would place at the disposal of its owner all the commodities that could be produced by all the labour of all the inhabitants of a considerable town. And a few pieces of mineral, not weighing two ounces, capable of gratifying no sense but the sight, and which any eye would be tired of looking at for a minute, is invested by our caprice with a value equal to that of the commodities which would give comfortable support to thousands of human beings in an advanced state of civilization. Hardness and brightness must have been the qualities which first attracted notice to the diamond. They enabled it to please the eye and adorn the person, and thus associated with it the notion of utility. But a diamond weighing an ounce is not found once in a century; there are not five such known to exist. The possession of an object of desire so limited in supply soon became one of the most unequivocal proofs of wealth. And, as to appear rich is the ruling passion of the bulk of mankind, diamonds will probably continue the objects of eager competition while the obstacles that limit their supply are undiminished. If a Sinbad should discover a valley of diamonds, or we should succeed in manufacturing them from charcoal, they will probably be used only as ornaments for savages, playthings for children, and as affording tools and raw materials for some of the Arts; and we may send cargoes of diamonds to the coast of Guinea to be bartered for equal quantities of ivory or gum.

VALUE

Value defined.—Our definition of Wealth, as comprehending all those things, and those things only which have *Value*, requires us to explain at some length the signification which we attribute to the word Value; especially as the meaning of that word has been the subject of long and eager controversy. We have already stated that we use the word VALUE in its popular acceptation, as signifying *that quality in any thing which fits it to be given and received in Exchange;* or, in other words, to be lent or sold, hired or purchased.

So defined, Value denotes a relation reciprocally existing between two objects, and the precise relation which it denotes is the quantity of the one which can be obtained in exchange for a given quantity of the other. It is impossible, therefore, to predicate value of any object, without referring, expressly or tacitly, to some other objects in which its value is to be estimated; or, in other words, of which a certain quantity can be obtained in exchange for a certain quantity of the object in question.

We have already observed that the substance which at present is most desired, or, in other words, possesses the highest degree of value, is the diamond. By this we meant to express that there is no substance of which a given quantity will exchange for so large a quantity of every other commodity. When we wished to state the value of the king of Persia's bracelet, we stated first the amount of gold, and afterwards of English labour, which it would command in exchange. If we had attempted to give a perfect account of its value, we could have done so only by enumerating separately the quantity of every other article of wealth which could be obtained in exchange for it. Such an enumeration, if it could have been given, would have been a most instructive commercial lesson, for it would have shown not only the value of the diamond in all other commodities, but the reciprocal value of all other commodities in one another. If we had ascertained that a diamond weighing an ounce would exchange for one million five hundred thousand tons of Hepburn coal, or one hundred thousand tons of Essex wheat, or two thousand five hundred tons of English foolscap paper, we might have inferred that the coal, wheat, and paper would mutually exchange in the same proportions in which they were exchangeable for the diamond, and that a given weight of paper would purchase six hundred times as much coal, and forty times as much wheat.

Demand and Supply.—The causes which determine the reciprocal values of commodities, or, in other words, which determine that a given quantity of one shall exchange for a given quantity of another, must be divided into two sets those which occasion the one to be limited in supply and useful, (using that word to express the power of occasioning pleasure and preventing pain), and those which occasion those attributes to belong to the other. In ordinary language, the *force* of the causes which give utility to a commodity is generally indicated by the word *Demand;* and the *weakness* of the obstacles which limit the quantity of a commodity by the word *Supply.*

Thus the common statement that commodities exchange in proportion to the Demand and Supply of each, means that they exchange in proportion to the force or weakness of the causes which give utility to them respectively, and to the weakness or force of the obstacles by which they are respectively limited in supply.

Unfortunately, however, the words Demand and Supply have not been always so used. Demand is sometimes used as synonymous with consumption, as when an increased production is said to generate an increased demand; sometimes it is used to express not only the desire to obtain a commodity, but the power to give the holder of it something which will induce him to part with it. "A Demand," says Mr. Mill, *Political Economy*, p. 23, 3d edition, "means the will to purchase and the power of purchasing." Mr. Malthus, Definitions in *Political Economy*, p. 244, states that "Demand for commodities has two distinct meanings: one in regard to its extent, or the quantity of commodities purchased; the other in regard to its intensity, or the sacrifice which the demanders are able and willing to make in order to satisfy their wants."

Demand.—Neither of these expressions appears to be consistent with common usage. It must be admitted that the word Demand is used in its ordinary sense when we say that a deficient wheat harvest increases the Demand for oats and barley. But this proposition is not true if we use the word Demand in any other sense than as expressing the increased utility of oats and barley; or, in other words, the increased desire of the community to obtain them. The deficiency of wheat would not give to the consumers of oats and barley any increased power of purchasing them, nor would the quantity purchased or consumed be increased. The mode of consumption would be altered; instead of being applied to the feeding of horses, or to the supply of stimulant liquids, a certain portion of them would be used as human food. And, as the desire to eat is more urgent than the desire to feed horses, or drink beer or spirits, the desire to obtain oats and barley, or, in other words, the pleasure given, or the pain averted, by the possesion of a given quantity of them or, in other words, the utility of a given quantity of them, would increase. A fact, which, in ordinary language, would be expressed by saying, that the demand for them was increased.

But though the vagueness with which the word Demand has been used renders it an objectionable term, it is too useful and concise to be given up; but we shall endeavour never to use it in any other signification than as expressing the utility of a commodity; or, what is the same, for we have seen that all utility is relative, the degree in which its possession is desired.

Supply.—We cannot complain of equal vagueness in the use of the word Supply. In ordinary language, as well as in the writings of Political Economists, it is used to signify the quantity of a commodity actually brought to market. The complaint is, not that the word Supply has been used in this sense, but that, when used in this sense, it has been considered as a cause of value, except in a few cases, or for very short periods. We have shown, in the examples of coats and waistcoats, and gold and silver, that the reciprocal value of any two commodities depends, not on the quantity of each brought to market, but on the comparative force of the obstacles which in each case oppose any increase in that quantity. When, therefore, we represent increase or diminution of supply as affecting value, we must be understood to mean not a mere positive increase or diminution, but an increase or diminution occasioned by a diminution or increase of the obstacles by which the supply is limited.

Intrinsic and Extrinsic Causes of the Value of a Commodity.—To revert to our original proposition, the reciprocal Values of any two commodities must be determined by two sets of causes; those which determine the Demand and Supply of the one, and those which determine the Demand and Supply of the other. The causes which give utility to a commodity and limit it in supply may be called the *intrinsic* causes of its value; those which limit the supply and occasion the utility of the commodities for which it is to be exchanged, may be called the *extrinsic* causes of its value. Gold and silver are now exchanged for one another in Europe in the proportion of one ounce of gold for about sixteen ounces of silver. This proportion must arise partly from the causes which give utility to gold and limit its supply, and partly from those which create the utility and limit the supply of silver. When talking of the value of gold we may consider the first set of causes affect gold only so far as it is said to be exchanged for silver, which may be called one of its specific values; the aggregate of its specific values forming its general value. If while the causes which give utility to silver and limit it in supply were unaltered, those which affect gold should vary; if, for instance, fashion should require every well-dressed man to have all his buttons of pure gold, or the disturbances in South America should permanently stop all the gold works of Brazil and Columbia, and thus (as would be the case) intercept five-sixths of our supplies of gold, the reciprocal values of gold and silver would in time be materially varied. Though silver would be unaltered both as to its utility and as to its limitation in supply, a given quantity of it would exchange for a less quantity of gold, in the proportion perhaps of twenty to one, instead of sixteen to one. As between one another the rise and fall of gold and silver would precisely correspond, silver would fall and gold would rise one-fourth. But the fall of silver would not be general but specific; though fallen as estimated in gold, it would command precisely the same quantities as before of all other commodities. The rise of gold would be more general; a given quantity of it would command one-fourth more not only of silver, but of all other commodities. The holder of a given quantity of silver would be just as rich as before for all purposes except the purchase of gold; the holder of a given quantity of gold would be richer than before for all purposes.

The circumstances by which each different class of commodities is invested with utility and limited in supply are subject to perpetual variation. Sometimes one of the causes alone varies. Sometimes they both vary in the same direction; sometimes in opposite directions. In the last case the opposite variations, wholly or partially neutralize one another.

The effects of an increased Demand concurrent with increased obstacles to Supply, and of diminished Demand concurrent with increased facility of Supply, are well exemplified by hemp. Its average price before the revolutionary war, exclusive of duty, did not exceed £30 per ton. The increased Demand, occasioned by a maritime war, and the natural obstacles to a proportionate increase of Supply, raised it, in the year 1796, to above £50 a ton; at about which price it continued during the next twelve years. But in 1808, the rupture between England and the Baltic powers, the principal source of our supplies, suddenly raised it to £118 a ton, being nearly four times the average price in peace. At the close of the war, both the extraordinary demand and the extraordinary obstacles to the supply ceased together, and the price fell to about its former average.

We have already stated that the utility of a commodity, in our extended sense of the term utility, or, in other words, the demand for it as an object of purchase or hire, is principally dependent on the obstacles which limit its supply. But there are many cases in which, while the existing obstacles remain unaltered, the demand is affected by the slightest suspicion that their force may at a future period be increased or diminished. This occurs with respect to those commodities of which the supply is not susceptible of accurate regulation, but is afforded either in uncertain quantities and at stated periods, between which it cannot be increased or diminished—in the case for instance of the annual products of the earth—or is dependent on our relations with foreign Countries. If a harvest deficient by one-third should occur, that deficiency must last for a whole year, or be supplied from abroad at an extravagant cost. If we should go to war with Russia, the obstacles to the supply of hemp would be increased while the war lasted. In either case the holders of corn or hemp would obtain great profits. In all rich Countries, and particularly in our own, there is a great number of persons who have large masses of wealth capable of being suddenly applied to the purchase of any given objects. The instant such persons suspect that the obstacles to the supply of any article are likely to be increased, they are anxious to become holders of it. They enter the market as new demanders; the price rises, and the mere fact that it has risen is a cause of its rising further. The details of commerce are so numerous, the difficulty of obtaining early and accurate information is so great, and the facts themselves are so constantly changing, that the most cautious merchants are often forced to act upon very doubtful premises; and the imprudent, dazzled by the chance of an enormous gain, which will be their own, and little restrained by the fear of a loss which may principally fall upon their creditors, are often ready to act upon scarcely any premises at all. They see that the price of some article has risen, and they suppose that there must be some good cause for it. They see that if they had purchased a month ago, they would have been gainers now, and conclude that if they purchase now they will be gainers a month hence. So far is this reasoning, if it can be called reasoning, carried, that a rise in the price of any one important commodity is generally found to occasion a rise in the price of many others. "A" (thinks a speculator) "bought hemp before the price had risen, and has resold it at a profit. Cotton has not yet risen, nor do I see clearly why it should rise, any more than I see why hemp should have risen, but it probably will rise like hemp, therefore I will purchase."

When we consider that the supply of large classes of commodities is dependent on our amicable or hostile relations with foreign States, and on the commercial and financial legislation both of those States and of our own Country, and that the supply of still larger classes is dependent not only on those contingencies, but on the accidents of the seasons—and when we consider how the demand is affected not merely by the existing, or the anticipated obstacles to the supply, but often by a spirit of speculation as blind as that of a gambler ignorant of the odds and even of the principles of his game—it is obvious that the general value of all commodities, the quantity of each which will exchange for a given quantity of every other, can never remain the same for a single day. Every day there will be a variation in the demand or the supply of one or more of the innumerable classes of commodities which are the objects of exchange in a commercial Country. A given quantity of the commodity which has varied will consequently exchange for a greater or a less quantity of all other commodities. All other commodities, therefore, will have varied in value as estimated in the first-mentioned commodity. It is as impossible for one commodity to remain perfectly unaltered in value while any other is altered, as it would be for a lighthouse to keep at the same distance from all the ships in a harbour while any one of them should approach it or recede.

Steadiness in Value, on what it depends.—But it may be asked, what do we mean when we say that a commodity has, for a given period, remained *steady* in value?

The question must be answered by referring to the different effects produced on the value of a commodity by an alteration in the intrinsic, or an alteration in the extrinsic, causes on which value depends. If the causes which give utility to a commodity and limit its supply, and which we have called the intrinsic causes of its value, are altered, the rise or fall in its value will be general. A given quantity of it will exchange for a greater or a less quantity than before of every other commodity which has not also varied at the same time, in the same direction, and in the same degree; a coincidence which rarely occurs. Every other commodity must also rise or fall in value as estimated in the first-mentioned commodity, but not generally.

The fluctuations in value to which a commodity is subject by alternations, in what we have called the extrinsic causes of its value, or, in other words, by alterations in the demand or supply of other commodities, have a tendency, like all other extensive combinations of chances, to neutralize one another. It may be said, without impropriety, therefore, to remain steady in value. But the rise or fall in value which a commodity experiences in consequence of an alteration in its utility, or in the obstacles to its supply, is, in fact, entirely uncompensated. It is compensated only with regard to those commodities of which the utility or the supply has also varied at the same time and in the same direction. And as quite as many are likely to experience a similar variation, but in an opposite direction, there is really no compensation. A commodity, therefore, which is strikingly subject to such variations, is properly said to be unsteady in value.

But we may be asked to account for another and not unfrequent statement, that at particular periods *all* commodities have been observed to rise or fall in value. Literally taken, this statement involves a contradiction in terms, since it is impossible that a given quantity of every commodity should exchange for a greater or a less quantity of every other. When those who make this statement have any meaning, they always tacitly exclude some one commodity, and estimate in that the rise or fall of all others. The excluded commodity is, in general, money or labour.

Estimated in labour, all commodities, money included, have fallen in value in England since the XVIth Century. It is scarcely possible to mention one of which a given quantity will not purchase less labour than it did at the close of Elizabeth's reign; estimated in money, almost all commodities, labour included, have fallen in England since the termination of the late war.

The last remark which we shall now make on value is, that, with a very few exceptions, it is strictly local. A ton of coal at the bottom of the pit near Newcastle is perhaps worth 2s.6d., at the pit's mouth it is perhaps worth 5s., at ten miles off 7s., at Hull 10s. By the time the collier has reached the Pool, its cargo is seldom worth less than 16s. a ton; and the inhabitant of Grosvenor Square may perhaps think himself fortunate if he can fill his coal cellars at 25s. a ton. A ton of coal, though physically identical, must be considered, for economical purposes, as a different commodity at the bottom of the pit and at its mouth, in Hull and in Grosvenor Square. At every different stage of its progress it is limited in supply by different obstacles, and consequently exchangeable for different things and in different proportions. Supposing that at Newcastle a ton of the best wheat is now worth about twenty tons of the best coal: the same wheat and coal at the west end of London may probably exchange in the proportions of about four tons of coal for one of wheat. At Odessa, they may perhaps exchange about weight for weight.

Whenever, therefore, we speak of the value of a commodity, it is necessary to state the locality both of the commodity in question, and of the commodity in which its value is estimated. And in most cases we shall find their respective proximity to the places where they are respectively to be made use of one of the principal constituents of their respective values. The purchaser of the distant commodity has to consider the labour of transporting it to the place of consumption, the time for which that labour must be paid in advance, and the taxation, and the risk of injury or loss to which it may be subject in its transit. Nor is this all. He must also consider the danger that its quality may not correspond with the description or sample which guided him in making the purchase. The whole expense and risk attending the transport of a diamond from Edinburgh to London are but trifling; but its value is so dependent on its form and lustre, and those are qualities as to which it is so difficult to satisfy any purchaser who cannot ascertain them by inspection, that it would be difficult to obtain in London a fair price for a diamond in Edinburgh. Again, though a given quantity of coal from a given mine is generally of an ascertained quality, yet the expense, loss of time, risk, and taxation, which must be incurred in its transport from Newcastle to Grosvenor Square, are such, that a ton of coal, when it has reached Grosvenor Square, may be of nearly five times the value which it bore at Newcastle.

OBJECTIONS TO THE DEFINITION OF WEALTH CONSIDERED

The definition of Wealth, as comprehending all those things, and those things only, which have Value, or, in other words, which may be purchased or hired, does not, we believe, precisely agree with that adopted by any Economist except Archbishop Whately.

The principal differences are these: some writers confine the term Wealth to what have been termed material products; some to those things which have been produced or acquired by human labour; and some object to the ideas of value or exchange being introduced into the definition of Wealth.

The question whether the things which have been called immaterial ought to be considered articles of wealth, we shall consider when we treat of production.

Some of the writers who, expressly or impliedly, restrict the term Wealth to the things, the production or appropriation of which has cost human labour, as for instance Mr. Mill, Mr. M'Culloch, Colonel Torrens, Mr. Malthus, and M. Flores-Estrada, appear to suppose that a definition so restricted will comprise every thing that can properly be termed wealth; others, among whom is Mr. Ricardo, admit that there are some things falling within that term which have not been acquired by human exertion, but think them so few or unimportant that it is better to omit them than to disorder the symmetry of the Science by extending it to any thing that is not the result of labour.

* * * * *

Mr. M'Culloch appears to use the word labour as including all voluntary action. And without doubt, if we use the word labour in so extended a sense, it is true that labour is almost necessarily incidental to the *enjoyment* of wealth. If it be an act of industry to gather an apple, it is equally an act of industry to raise it from one's plate; and every guest at a festival earns his food by the labour which he exerts in appropriating his own portion. Such attempts as these to bend the facts and language into accordance with hasty generalization, have thrown on Political Economy a degree of ridicule which is one of the principal obstacles to its progress.

Mr. Malthus, Colonel Torrens, and the other Economists who consider labour, using that word in its popular sense, as a necessary constituent of wealth, appear to have been led to that opinion by observing, first, that some quality besides mere utility is necessary to value; secondly, that all those things which are useful, and are acquired by labour, are valuable; and thirdly, that almost every thing which is valuable *has* required some labour for its acquisition. But the fact that that circumstance is not essential to value will be demonstrated if we can suppose a case in which value could exist without it. If, while carelessly lounging along the sea-shore, I were to pick up a pearl, would it have no value?

Mr. M'Culloch would answer that the value of the pearl was the result of my appropriative industry in stooping to pick it up. Suppose then that I met with it while eating an oyster? Supposing that aerolithes consisted of gold, would they have no value? Or, suppose that meteoric iron were the only form in which that metal were produced, would not the iron supplied from heaven be far more valuable than any existing metal? It is true that, wherever there is utility, the addition of labour necessary to production constitutes value, because, the supply of labour being limited, it follows that the object, to the supply of which it is necessary, is by that very necessity limited in supply. But any other cause limiting supply is just as efficient a cause of value in an article as the necessity of labour to its production. And, in fact, if all the commodities used by man were supplied by nature without any intervention whatever of human labour, but were supplied in precisely the same quantities as they now are, there is no reason to suppose either that they would cease to be valuable, or would exchange in any other than their present proportions.

The reply to Mr. Ricardo is, first, that the articles of wealth which do not owe the principal part of their value to the labour which has been bestowed on their respective actual production, form, in fact, the bulk of wealth, instead of a small and unimportant portion of it; and secondly, that, as limitation of supply is essential to the value of labour itself, to assume labour, and exclude limitation of supply, as the condition on which value depends, is not only to substitute a partial for a general cause, but pointedly to exclude the very cause which gives force to the cause assigned.

We have lastly to consider the objections which have been raised to the definition of wealth as a general name for the things which have value. Those who use the word value as synonymous with *cost*, or as comprehending whatever is useful, of course object to its introduction into the definition of wealth; and so should we do if we used the word value in its popular sense, have objected to that, according to the definition which we have adopted, the same thing will be wealth to one person and not to another. This consequence is evident; and it is evident that even to the same person the same quality may be wealth under some circumstances, and not so under others. The knowledge of English law is profitable in England, that of French law in France; if an English lawyer, with no other property but his knowledge, were to settle in France, or a French lawyer in England, he would find himself instantly reduced from affluence to poverty. The power of telling long stories is a source of profit in Asia, but valueless in Europe. According to our nomenclature, therefore, it would be wealth in Persia, and cease to be so in England. If an actress should embrace a religious sect of which the tenets should be incompatible with the stage, her vocal and dramatic talents would no longer be exchangeable, she would no longer be able to let them out by the evening.

We should say, therefore, that they had ceased to be a part of her wealth. But we are at a loss to conceive how the power of making this distinction is an objection to the language in question. It seems to be its principal convenience.

Again, Colonel Torrens supposes a solitary family, or a nation in which each person should consume only his own productions, or one in which there should be a community of goods, and urges, as a *reductio ab absurdum* that in these cases, though there might be an abundance of commodities, as there would be no exchanges, there would, in our sense of the term, be no wealth. The answer is, that, for the purposes of Political Economy, there would be no wealth; for, in fact, in such a state of things, supposing it possible, the Science of Political Economy would have no application. In such a state of society, Agriculture, Mechanics, or any other of the Arts which are subservient to the production of the commodities which are, with us, the subjects of exchange, might be studied, but the Science of Political Economy would not exist. We may add, that if the common usage which identifies wealth with the things which have value is a convenient one in all the forms which human nature really exhibits, it is no objection to it that it would not be convenient in a state of society of which we have no experience.

STATEMENT OF THE FOUR ELEMENTARY PROPOSITIONS OF THE SCIENCE OF POLITICAL ECONOMY

We have already stated that the general facts on which the Science of Political Economy rests, are comprised in a few general Propositions, the result of observation or consciousness. The Propositions to which we then alluded are these:

1. *That every man desires to obtain additional Wealth with as little sacrifice as possible.*

2. *That the Population of the world, or, in other words, the number of persons inhabiting it, is limited only by moral or physical evil, or by fear of a deficiency of those articles of wealth which the habits of the individuals of each class of its inhabitants lead them to require.*

3. *That the powers of Labour, and of the other instruments which produce wealth, may be indefinitely increased by using their Products as the means of further Production.*

4. *That, agricultural skill remaining the same, additional Labour employed on the land within a given district produces in general a less proportionate return, or, in other words, that though, with every increase of the labour bestowed, the aggregate return is increased, the increase of the return is not in proportion to the increase of the labour.*

The first of these Propositions is a matter of consciousness, the three others are matter of observation. As the first and second involve little use of the peculiar abstractions of Political Economy, except those implied in the term Wealth, and may therefore be explained with little recourse to its peculiar nomenclature, we shall consider them immediately; leaving the third and fourth for discussion in a subsequent part of this Treatise. They are, however, so nearly self-evident, that we will venture in the mean time to assume their truth. No one who reflects on the difference between the unassisted force of man, and the more than gigantic powers of capital and machinery, can doubt the former proposition; and, to convince ourselves of the other, it is necessary only to recollect that, if it were false, no land except the very best could ever be cultivated: since, if the return from a single farm were to increase in full proportion to any amount of increased labour bestowed on it, the produce of that one farm might feed the whole population of England.

PRODUCTION

Development of the Third Elementary Proposition of the Science, namely,—*That the Powers of Labour, and of the other Instruments which produce Wealth, may be indefinitely increased by using their Products as the means of further Production.*

Production.—Having explained the sense in which we use the word Wealth, and given an outline of the doctrine of Population, we now proceed to consider Production, or the means by which wealth is produced. The first terms to be defined are the verb *produce*, and the substantive *product*.

Product.—To *produce*, as far as Political Economy is concerned, *is to occasion an alteration in the condition of the existing particles of matter, for the occasioning of which alteration, or for the things thence resulting, something may be obtained in exchange.* This alteration is a *product*. It is scarcely necessary to remind our readers that matter is susceptible neither of increase nor diminution, and that all which man, or any other agent of which we have experience, can effect, is to alter the condition of its existing particles. But as Political Economy treats only of wealth, and therefore only of these alterations of which wealth is the result, we are forced to exclude all other alterations from the definition of Products. The child who builds a castle with sand on the shore, and the child who kicks it down, each occasions effects the same in kind as the man who builds or pulls down a palace; but as the exertions of the latter entitle him to be paid, he is properly said to produce, and the result of his conduct, whether it be the covering with buildings ground previously unoccupied, or rendering vacant what was previously built over, is properly called a Product.

Products divided into Services and Commodities.—Products have been divided into material and immaterial, or, to express the same distinction in different words, into commodities and services. This distinction appears to have been suggested by Adam Smith's well known division of labour into productive and unproductive. Those who thought the principle of that division convenient, feeling at the same time the difficulty of terming unproductive the labour without which all other labour would be inefficient invented the term services, or immaterial products, to express its results.

It appears to us, however, that the distinctions that have been attempted to be drawn between productive and unproductive labourers, or between the producers of material and immaterial products, or between commodities and services, rest on differences existing not in the things themselves, which are the objects considered, but in the modes in which they attract our attention. In those cases in which our attention is principally called, not to the act of occasioning the alteration, but to the result of that act, to the things altered, Economists have termed the person who occasioned that alteration a productive labourer, or the producer of a *commodity* or material product. Where, on the other hand, our attention is principally called not to the thing altered, but to the act of occasioning that alteration, Economists have termed the person occasioning that alteration an unproductive labourer, and his exertions, *services*, or immaterial products. A shoemaker alters leather, and thread, and wax, into a pair of shoes. A shoeblack alters a dirty pair of shoes into a clean pair. In the first case our attention is called principally to the things as altered. The shoemaker, therefore, is said to *make* or *produce* shoes. In the case of the shoeblack, our attention is called principally to the act as performed. He is not said to make or produce the commodity, clean shoes, but to perform the service of cleaning them. In each case there is, of course, an act and a result; but in the one case our attention is called principally to the act, in the other to the result.

Among the causes which direct our attention principally to the *act*, or principally to the *result*, seem to be, first, the degree of change produced; and secondly, the mode in which the person who benefits by that change generally purchases that benefit.

1. Where the alteration is but slight, especially if the thing that has been subjected to alteration still retains the same name, our attention is directed principally to the act. A cook is not said to *make* roast beef, but to *dress* it; but he is said to make a pudding, or those more elaborate preparations which we call *made* dishes. The change of name is very material: a tailor is said to *make* cloth into a coat; a dyer is not said to *make* undyed cloth into dyed cloth. The change produced by the dyer is perhaps greater than that produced by the tailor, but the cloth in passing through the tailor's hands changes its name; in passing through the dyer's it does not: the dyer has not produced a *new name*, nor, consequently, in our minds, a *new thing*.

The principal circumstance, however, is the mode in which the payment is made. In some cases the producer is accustomed to sell, and we are accustomed to purchase, not his labour, but the subject on which that labour has been employed; as when we purchase a wig or a chest of medicine. In other cases, what we buy is not the thing altered, but the labour of altering it, as when we employ a haircutter or a physician. Our attention in all these cases naturally fixes itself on the thing which we are accustomed to purchase; and according as we are accustomed to buy the labour, or the thing on which that labour has been expended,—as we are, in fact, accustomed to purchase a commodity or a service, we consider a commodity or a service as the thing produced. The ultimate object both of painting and of acting is the pleasure derived from imitation. The means adopted by the painter and the actor are the same in kind. Each exercises his bodily organs, but the painter exercises them to distribute colours over a canvas, the actor to put himself into certain attitudes, and to utter certain sounds. The actor sells his exertions themselves. The painter sells not his exertions, but the picture on which those exertions have been employed. The mode in which their exertions are sold constitutes the only difference between menial servants and the other labouring classes: a servant who carries coal from the celler to the drawing-room performs precisely the same operation as the miner who raises them from the bottom of the pit to its mouth. But the consumer pays for the coals themselves when raised and received into his cellar, and pays the servant for the act of bringing them up. The miner, therefore, is said to produce the material commodity, coals; the servant the immaterial product, or service. Both, in fact, produce the same thing, an alteration in the condition of the existing particles of matter; but our attention is fixed in the one case on the act, in the other on the result of that act. In the ruder states of society almost all manufactures are domestic: the Queens and Princesses of heroic times were habitually employed in overlooking the labours of their maidens. The division of labour has banished from our halls to our manufactories the distaff and the loom; and, if the language to which we have been adverting were correct, the division of labour must be said to have turned spinners and weavers from unproductive into productive labourers; from producers of immaterial services into producers of material commodities.

Service and Commodity discriminated.—But, objecting as we do to a nomenclature which should consider producers as divided, by the nature of their products, into producers of services and producers of commodities, we are ready to admit the convenience of the distinction between services and commodities themselves, and to apply the term *service* to the act of occasioning an alteration in the existing state of things, the term *commodity* to the thing as altered; the term *product* including both commodities and services.

It is to be observed that, in ordinary language, a person is not said to produce a thing unless he has employed himself for that especial purpose. If an English oyster-fisher should meet with an oyster containing a pearl, he would be called not the producer of the pearl, but its casual finder. But a Ceylon oyster-fisher, whose trade is to fish for pearl oysters, is called a producer of pearls. The *mere existence* of the pearls is in both cases owing to the agency of nature; their existence as articles of value is in both cases owing to the agency of the fisher in removing them from a situation in which they were valueless. In the one case he did this intentionally, in the other accidentally. Attention is directed in the one case to *his* agency, and *he* is therefore called the producer of the pearl. In the other case it is directed to the agency of nature, and he is called only the appropriator. But it appears to us the more convenient classification, for scientific purposes, to term him in both cases the producer.

INSTRUMENTS OF PRODUCTION

Having explained the nature of Production and Consumption, we now proceed to consider the Agents by whose intervention Production takes place.

I. *Labour.*—The primary Instruments of Production are Labour, and those Agents of which nature, unaided by man, affords us the assistance.

Labour is the voluntary exertion of bodily or mental faculties for the purpose of Production. It may appear unnecessary to define a term having a meaning so precise and so generally understood. Peculiar notions respecting the causes of value have, however, led some Economists to employ the term labour in senses so different from its common acceptation, that for some time to come it will be dangerous to use the word without explanation. We have already observed that many recent writers have considered value as solely dependent on labour. When pressed to explain how wine in a cellar, or an oak in its progress from a sapling to a tree, could, on this principle, increase in value, they replied that they considered the improvement of the wine and the growth of the tree as so much additional labour bestowed on each. We do not quite understand the meaning of this reply; but we have given a definition of labour, lest we should be supposed to include in it the unassisted operations of nature. It may also be well to remind our readers that this definition excludes all those exertions which are not intended, immediately or through their products, to be made the subjects of exchange. A hired messenger and a person walking for his amusement, a sportsman and a gamekeeper, the ladies at an English ball and a company of Natch girls in India, undergo the same fatigues; but ordinary language does not allow us to consider those as undergoing labour who exert themselves for the mere purpose of amusement.

II. *Natural Agents.*—Under the term "the Agents offered to us by nature," or, to use a shorter expression, "Natural Agents," we include every productive agent so far as it does not derive its powers from the act of man.

The term "Natural Agent" is far from being a convenient designation, but we have adopted it partly because it has been already made use of in this sense by eminent writers, and partly because we have not been able to find one less objectionable. The principal of these agents is the land, with its mines, its rivers, its natural forests with their wild inhabitants, and, in short, all its spontaneous productions. To these must be added the ocean, the atmosphere, light and heat, and even those physical laws, such as gravitation and electricity, by the knowledge of which we are able to vary the combinations of matter. All these productive agents have in general, by what appears to be an inconvenient synecdoche, been designated by the term *land;* partly because the land, as a source of profit, is the most important of those which are susceptible of appropriation, but chiefly because its possession generally carries with it the command over most of the others. And it is to be remembered that, though the powers of nature are necessary to afford a substratum for the other instruments of production to work upon, they are not of themselves, when universally accessible, causes of value. Limitation in supply is, as we have seen, a necessary constituent of value; and what is universally accessible is practically unlimited in supply.

III. *Abstinence.*—But although Human Labour, and the Agency of Nature, independently of that of man, are the primary Productive Powers, they require the concurrence of a Third Productive Principle to give to them complete efficiency. The most laborious population, inhabiting the most fertile territory, if they devoted all their labour to the production of immediate results, and consumed its produce as it arose, would soon find their utmost exertions insufficient to produce even the mere necessaries of existence.

To the Third Principle, or Instrument of Production, without which the two others are inefficient, we shall give the name of *Abstinence:* a term by which we express the conduct of a person who either abstains from the unproductive use of what he can command, or designedly prefers the production of remote to that of immediate results.

It was to the effects of this Third Instrument of Production that we adverted, when we laid down, as the third of our elementary propositions, *that the Powers of Labour and of the other Instruments which produce Wealth, may be indefinitely increased by using their Products as the means of further Production.* All our subsequent remarks on abstinence are a development and illustration, because it can scarcely be said to require formal proof.

The division of the Instruments of Production into three great branches has long been familiar to Economists. Those branches they have generally termed Labour, Land, and Capital. In the principle of this division we agree; though we have substituted different expressions for the second and third branches. We have preferred the term Natural Agents to that of Land, to avoid designating a whole genus by the name of one of its species: a practice which has occasioned the other cognate species to be generally slighted and often forgotten. We have substituted the term Abstinence for that of Capital on different grounds.

The term Capital has been so variously defined that it may be doubtful whether it have any generally received meaning. We think, however, that, in popular acceptation, and in that of Economists themselves, when they are not reminded of their definitions, that word signifies *an article of wealth, the result of human exertion, employed in the production or distribution of wealth*. We say the result of human exertion, in order to exclude those productive instruments to which we have given the name of natural agents, and which afford not profit, in the scientific sense of that word, but rent.

It is evident that Capital, thus defined, is not a simple productive instrument; it is in most cases the result of all the three productive instruments combined. Some natural agent must have afforded the material, some delay of enjoyment must in general have reserved it from unproductive use, and some labour must in general have been employed to prepare and preserve it. *By the word Abstinence, we wish to express that agent, distinct from labour and the agency of nature, the concurrence of which is necessary to the existence of Capital, and which stands in the same relation to Profit as Labour does to Wages*. We are aware that we employ the word Abstinence in a more extensive sense than is warranted by common usage. Attention is usually drawn to abstinence only when it is not united with labour. It is recognized instantly in the conduct of a man who allows a tree or a domestic animal to attain its full growth; but it is less obvious when he plants the sapling or sows the seed corn. The observer's attention is occupied by the labour, and he omits to consider the additional sacrifice made when labour is undergone for a distant object. This additional sacrifice we comprehend under the term Abstinence; not because Abstinence is an unobjectionable expression for it, but because we have not been able to find one to which there are not still greater objections. We once thought of using "providence"; but providence implies no self-denial, and has no necessary connection with profit. To take out an umbrella is provident, but not in the usual sense of the word profitable. We afterwards proposed "frugality," but frugality implies some care and attention, that is to say, some labour; and though in practice Abstinence is almost always accompanied by some degree of labour, it is obviously necessary to keep them separate in an analysis of the instruments of production.

It may be said that pure Abstinence, being a mere negation, cannot produce positive effects; the same remark might as well be applied to intrepidity, or even to liberty; but who ever objected to their being con-

sidered as equivalent to active agents? To abstain from the enjoyment
which is in our power, or to seek distant rather than immediate results,
are among the most painful exertions of the human will. It is true that
such exertions are made, and indeed are frequent in every state of society,
except perhaps in the very lowest, and have been made in the very lowest,
for society could not otherwise have improved; but of all the means by
which man can be raised in the scale of being, abstinence, as it is perhaps
the most effective, is the slowest in its increase, and the least generally
diffused. Among nations, those that are the least civilized, and among the
different classes of the same nation those which are the worst educated,
are always the most improvident, and consequently the least abstinent.

Capital.—We have already defined Capital to be an article of wealth,
the result of human exertion, employed in the production or distribution
of wealth, and we have observed that each individual article of capital
is in general the result of a combination of all the three great instruments
of production—labour, abstinence, and the agency of nature.

DISTRIBUTION OF WEALTH

Of the three great branches of Political Economy, the Nature, the
Production, and the Distribution of Wealth, we have now considered the
two former, and we proceed to treat of the last, namely of the laws according to which all that is produced is *Distributed* among those who become
its ultimate consumers. In that state of society which is presupposed by
the Political Economist, this is principally effected by means of Exchange.
We may indeed conceive a state of human existence admitting of this
distribution without the intervention of Exchanges. But such a situation
of society, if it can be called society, neither deserves nor requires scientific
investigation. Political Economy considers men in that more advanced
state, which may fairly be called their natural state, since it is the state to
which they are impelled by the provisions of nature, in which each individual relies on his fellows for the greater part, in many cases for the whole
of what he consumes, and supplies his own wants principally or wholly by
the Exchanges in which he contributes to theirs.

But we must admit that we use each of the words Production and
Exchange in a sense rather more extensive than is usual. We have already
stated that we apply the word Production to much that would commonly
be called appropriation, and that we include under Exchanges what are
usually termed public burdens. We consider all that is received by the
officers of Government as given in Exchange for Services affording protection, more or less complete, against foreign or domestic violence or
fraud. It is true, as we have already remarked, that this Exchange is
conducted on peculiar principles. In those governments which are not
democratic or representative, the rulers themselves assess the amount
which they are to receive, and generally assess it at the utmost which,

under such circumstances, can be extorted from their subjects. And even under representative or democratic institutions, no individual inhabitant is permitted to refuse his share of the general contribution, though he should disclaim his share in the general protection. But the transaction, though often involuntary, and still more often inequitable, is still an Exchange, and on the whole a beneficial exchange. The worst and most inefficient Government affords to its subjects a cheaper and a more effectual Protection than they could obtain by their individual and unaided exertions.

The laws by which Exchanges are regulated may be divided into two great branches. The one comprises those laws which apply generally to all Exchanges; the other those which apply specifically to the respective kinds of Exchanges in which the owners of the different Productive Instruments exchange specifically with one another the Produce of those Instruments.

In treating of the one, we have to consider the general laws which regulate Exchanges; in treating of the other, the relative proportions in which different classes of the community benefit by those laws. The things exchanged will be the principal subjects of the one discussion, the exchanging parties of the other.

One of the greatest difficulties to which a writer on Political Economy is exposed, arises from the mutual dependence of the different propositions constituting the Science; a dependence which makes it difficult to explain any one without a frequent allusion to many others. And this is particularly the case with respect to distribution. The proportions in which different classes of the community are entitled to the things that are produced, cannot be explained without a constant reference to the general Laws of Exchange; and, on the other hand, those Laws cannot be discussed without a constant reference to the exchanging parties. Admitting, as we are forced to do, that no arrangement can be free from objection, we have thought that the least objectionable mode of presenting the subject of distribution will be to begin by a general classification of the parties among whom the results of the different instruments of production are divided; then to proceed to state the general laws of exchange; and, lastly, to point out the general circumstances which decide in what proportions the different classes of the community share in the general distribution.

Society Divided into Three Classes—Labourers, Capitalists, and Proprietors of Natural Agents

According to the usual language of Political Economists, Labour, Capital, and Land are the three Instruments of Production; Labourers, Capitalists, and Landlords are the three classes of Producers; and the

whole Produce is divided into Wages, Profits, and Rent: the first designating the Labourer's share, the second that of the Capitalist, and the
third that of the Landlord. We approve, on the whole, of the principles
on which this classification is founded, but we have been forced, much
against our will, to make considerable alterations in the language in which
it has been usually expressed; to add some new terms, and to enlarge or
contract the signification of some others.

It appears to us that, to have a nomenclature which should fully and
precisely indicate the facts of the case, not less than *twelve* distinct terms
would be necessary. For each class there ought to be a name for the
Instrument employed or exercised, a name for the *Class of persons* who
employ or exercise it, a name for the *Act* of employing or exercising it, and
a name for the *Share* of the produce by which that act is remunerated.
Of these terms we have not much more than half, as will appear if we
examine each class separately.

Nomenclature applicable to the First Class, the Labourers.—For the
first class we have the terms "to Labour," "a Labourer," and "Wages."
Neither of these terms expresses the instruments of production: the substantive "labour," and the verb "to labour," express merely an act.
"A labourer" is an agent, and wages are a result: but what is the thing
employed? what is it that the labourer exerts? Clearly his mental or bodily
faculties. With the addition of this term the nomenclature of the first
class will be complete. To Labour is to employ strength of body or mind
for the purpose of Production; the person who does so is a Labourer, and
Wages are his remuneration.

Nomenclature applicable to the Second Class, the Capitalists.—In the
second class we have the words Capital, Capitalist, and Profit. These
terms express the instrument, the person who employs or exercises it,
and his remuneration; but there is no familiar term to express the act, the
conduct of which profit is the reward, and which bears the same relation
to profit which labour does to wages. To this conduct we have already
given the name of Abstinence. The addition of this term will complete the
nomenclature of the second class. Capital is an article of wealth, the result
of human exertion, employed in the production or distribution of Wealth.
Abstinence expresses both the act of abstaining from the unproductive
use of capital, and also the similar conduct of the man who devotes his
labour to the production of remote rather than of immediate results. The
person who so acts is a Capitalist, the reward of his conduct is Profit.

*Nomenclature applicable to the Third Class, the Proprietors of Natural
Agents.*—The defectiveness of the established nomenclature is more
striking when we come to the third class. Wages and profits are the creation of man. They are the recompense for the sacrifice made in the one
case, of ease, in the other, of immediate enjoyment. But a considerable
part of the produce of every country is the recompense of no sacrifice

whatever; is received by those who neither labour nor put by, but merely hold out their hands to accept the offerings of the rest of the community.

The powers of nature, as distinguished from those of man, are necessary to afford a field for the exercise of human abstinence and labour. Of these, some from their abundance and the notoriety of the means of employing them, are incapable of appropriation. Being universally accessible, they bear no price notwithstanding their utility; and what has been produced with their assistance has no value beyond that of the labour and abstinence which it has cost. It sells therefore for a price equal to, but not exceeding, the sum of the wages and profits which must be paid if the production is to be continued. The agency of nature is equally essential to the production of timber in the forests of Upper Canada and in England. But the supply of timber in the forests of Upper Canada is practically unlimited. No portion of the price of a Canadian hut is paid for the agency of nature in producing the logs of which it is constructed. The pine while standing was valueless. The purchaser pays only for the labour and abstinence necessary to fell and to fashion it.

But the assistance of an *Appropriated* Natural Agent may render possible the production of a commodity more valuable than the result of equal labour and abstinence without such assistance. Such a commodity sells for a price exceeding the sum of the wages and profits which are sufficient to repay the capitalist and the labourer who have been employed on it. The surplus is taken by the proprietor of the natural agent, and is his reward, not for having laboured or abstained, but simply for not having withheld what he was able to withhold; for having permitted the gifts of nature to be accepted.

If we subtract from the price of an English oak what must be paid for the labour of him who planted the sapling, and for the abstinence of those who allowed it to grow for a century, still something is to be paid for the use of the land by which it was nourished. And that is the price of the agency not of man but of nature.

Of the Agents afforded by nature, the principal is the Land, with its Rivers, Ports, and Mines. In the rare cases in which the quantity of useful land is practically unlimited, a state of things which occurs only in the early stages of colonization, Land is an agent universally accessible, and, as nothing is paid for its use, the whole produce belongs to the cultivators, and is divided, under the names of wages and profit, between the capitalists and the labourers, of whose abstinence and industry it is the result.

But in all old Countries, and even in colonies within a very few years after their foundation, certain Lands, from peculiar advantages of soil or situation, are found to make more than the average return to a given expenditure of capital and industry. The proprietor of such lands, if he cultivate them himself, receives a surplus after having paid the wages of his labourers and deducted the profit to which he is entitled on his capital. He of course receives the same surplus if, instead of cultivating them himself, he lets them out to some other capitalist. The tenant receives the same profit, and the labourers receive the same wages as if they were employed on land possessing merely average natural advantages; the surplus forms the rent of the proprietor, or, as we usually term him, the landlord. The whole produce, instead of two, is divided into three shares —Rent, Profit, and Wages. If the owner is also the capitalist or farmer, he receives two of these shares, both the profit and the rent. If he allow it to be cultivated by the capital of another, he receives only rent. But rent, with or without profit, he necessarily receives. And when the whole of a Country has been appropriated, though it be true, as will be shown hereafter, that some of the produce is raised by the application of additional capital without payment of additional rent, and may therefore be said to be raised rent free, yet it is equally true that a rent is received from every cultivated acre; a rent rising or falling according to the accidents of soil and situation, but the necessary result of limited extent and productive power.

It is obvious, however, as we have already stated, that land, though the principal, is not the only natural agent that can be appropriated. The mere knowledge of the operations of nature, as long as the use of that knowledge can be confined either by secrecy or by law, creates a revenue to its possessor analogous to the rent of land. The knowledge of the effect on the fibres of cotton of rollers moving with different velocities, enabled a village barber to found in a very few years a more than aristocratic fortune. Still greater wealth might probably have been acquired by Dr. Jenner, if he could have borne somewhat to limit the benefits which he has conferred on mankind.

When the author of a useful discovery puts it himself in practice, he is like a proprietor farming his own property; the produce, after paying average wages for the labour, and average profits for the capital, employed, affords a still further revenue, the effect not of that capital or of that labour, but of the discovery, the creation not of man but of nature. If, instead of using it himself, he let out to another the privilege of using it, be obtains a revenue so precisely resembling the rent of land, that it often receives the same name. The payment made by a manufacturer to a patentee for the privilege of using the patent process, is usually termed, in commercial language, a RENT; and under the same head must be ranked all the peculiar advantages of situation or connection, and all extraordinary qualities of body and mind. The surplus revenue which they occasion beyond average wages and profits is a revenue for which no additional sacrifice has been made. The proprietor of these advantages differs from a landlord only in the circumstance that he cannot in general let them out to be used by another, and must consequently either allow them to be useless or turn them to account himself. He is forced, therefore, always to employ on them his own industry, and generally his own capital, and receives not only rent, but wages and profit. If, therefore, the established division is adhered to, and all that is produced is to be divided into rent, profit and wages—and certainly that appears to be the most convenient classification; and if wages and profit are to be considered as the rewards of peculiar sacrifices, the former the remuneration for labour, and the latter for abstinence from immediate enjoyment, it is clear that under the term "rent" must be included all that is obtained without any sacrifice; or, which is the same thing, beyond the remuneration for that sacrifice; all that nature or fortune bestows either without any exertion on the part of the recipient, or in addition to the average remuneration for the exercise of industry or the employment of capital.

But though we see no objection to this extension of the word rent, the terms land and landlord are too precise to admit of being equally extended. It would be too great an innovation to include under the term land every natural agent which is capable of appropriation, or under the term landlord every proprietor of such an agent. For these terms we must substitute those of *natural agent*, and *proprietor of a natural agent*. And the third class will then have a term for the third instrument of production, a term for the owner of that instrument, and a term for the share which he receives of the produce: terms corresponding with the terms faculties of body and mind, labourer, and wages, as applied to the first class, and with capital, capitalist, and profit, as applied to the second. We shall still want a term corresponding with labour and abstinence—a term indicating the *conduct* which enables the proprietor of a natural agent to receive a rent. But as this conduct implies no sacrifice—as it consists merely in not suffering the instrument of which he is the owner to be useless, it perhaps does not require a distinct designation. When a man possesses an estate, we take it for granted that he does not allow it to lie waste, but either uses it himself, or lets it to a tenant. In ordinary language, the receipt of rent is included under the term ownership. There will therefore be little danger of obscurity if we consider the word "possess," when applied to the proprietor of a natural agent, as implying the receipt of the advantages afforded by that agent, or, in other words, of rent. Talents, indeed, often lie idle, but in that case they may be considered for economical purposes as not possessed. In fact, unaccompanied by the will to use them, they are useless.

But though the whole produce may be considered as divided into three shares, one of which is taken by the capitalists, another by the labourers, and another by the proprietors of the natural agents which have concurred in the production, it is very seldom that any given commodity, or the produce of any one productive exertion is thus actually divided. The nearest approach to it takes place in those cases in which producers belonging to different classes become partners, and agree that the produce of their joint exertions shall be sold and the price divided between them. Such a partnership is often formed between a capitalist and his labourers when the success of the enterprise depends much on the zeal of the labourers, and the capitalist is unable to overlook them. Such is the case in the Greenland fishery. The men seldom receive preascertained wages, but, on the termination of the voyage, the blubber is sold, and the price divided between the owners and the crew. The practice is the same in privateering, and probably in many other maritime speculations. Somewhat similar is the mode of letting land called the métayer system. Under that system, which is still common on the Continent of Europe, and probably is always to be found in a certain state of society, the landlord supplies the capital as well as the land, and receives half the crop, the remainder forming the wages of the tenant or head labourer, and of the inferior work-people in his employ. But these are exceptions occasioned by the peculiarities of the adventure, or by the poverty or ignorance of imperfect civilization. The usual practice is to consider one of the parties as entitled to the whole product, paying to the others a price for their co-operation. The person so entitled is uniformly the capitalist: the sums which he pays for wages and rent are the purchase-money for the services of the labourer, and for the use of the natural agent employed.

In most cases a considerable interval elapses between the period at which the natural agent and the labourer are first employed, and the completion of the product. In this climate the harvest is seldom reaped until nearly a year after it has been sown; a still longer time is required for the maturity of oxen; and a longer still for that of a horse; and sixty or seventy years may pass between the commencement of a plantation, and the time at which the timber is saleable. It is obvious that neither the landlord nor the labourer, as such, can wait during all this interval for their remuneration. The doing so would, in fact, be an act of abstinence. It would be the employment of land and labour in order to obtain remote results. This sacrifice is made by the capitalist, and he is repaid for it by his appropriate remuneration, profit. He advances to the landlord and the labourer, and in most cases to some previous capitalist, the price of their respective assistance; or, in other words, the hire of the land and capital belonging to one, and of the mental and bodily powers of another, and becomes solely entitled to the whole of the product. The success of his operations depends on the proportion which the value of that produce, (or, in commercial language, the value of his returns), bears to the value of his advances, taking into consideration the time for which those advances have been made. If the value of the return is inferior to that of the advance, he is obviously a loser; he is a loser if it be merely equal, as he has incurred abstinence without profit, or, in ordinary language, has lost the interest on his capital. He is a loser even if the value of his returns do not exceed that of his advances by an amount equal to the current rate of profit for the period during which the advance has been made. In any of these cases the product is sold, so far as the capitalist is concerned, for less than the cost of its production. The employment of capital, therefore, is necessarily a speculation; it is the purchase of so much productive power which may or may not occasion a remunerative return.

The common language of Economists, therefore, which describes the landlord, the capitalist, and the labourer as sharers of the produce, is a fiction. Almost all that is produced is in the first instance the property of the capitalist; he has purchased it by having previously paid the rent and wages, and incurred or paid for the abstinence, which were necessary to its production. A portion of it, but generally a small portion, he consumes himself, in the state in which he receives it; the remainder he sells. He may, if he think fit, employ the price of all that he sells in purchases for his own gratification; but he cannot remain a capitalist unless he consent to employ some portion of it in the hire of the land and labour, by the assistance of which the process of production is to be continued or recommenced. He cannot, generally speaking, fully retain his situation as a capitalist unless he employ some portion of it in the hire of the land and labour, by the assistance of which the process of production is to be continued or recommenced. He cannot, generally speaking, fully retain his situation as a capitalist unless he employ enough to hire as much land and labour as before; and if he wish to raise himself in the world, he must, generally speaking, not merely keep up, but increase the sum which he devotes to the purchase of productive force. If, for instance, he has hired the use of a farm for a year for £1000, and has paid £2000 more as wages to his labourers, and has expended £1000 in the purchases, from other capitalists, of agricultural stock, and at the end of the year has sold the produce for £4400, he may if he like, spend on his own gratification the whole of that £4400; or he may so spend only £400, and employ the rest in hiring the farm and the labourers, and purchasing stock for another year; or he may spend on himself only £200, and by employing productively £4200 instead of £4000, hire more land, or more labourers, or purchase more stock and provide for the increase of his capital and his profit. But in whatever way he employ his £4400, he still must pay it to landlords, (using that word to comprise all proprietors of natural agents), capitalists, and labourers.

It has been objected, however, that this nomenclature is incomplete. Rent, profit, and wages, it has been said, designate only those portions of the annual produce which the producers consume for their own gratification. They form the *revenue* of a nation. A further portion, and a very large one, must be employed, not as revenue, but as capital; not in directly supplying the wants or directly ministering to the enjoyments of either landlords, labourers, or capitalists, but merely in keeping up the instruments of production. Thus of the farmer's whole return, which we have supposed to be of the value of £4,400, we may suppose a portion, amounting in value to £200, to have consisted of corn which he returned to the earth as seed, and another portion, amounting to the same value, to have consisted of the forage which he gave to his working cattle. It has been said that neither this seed nor this forage was rent, profit, or wages.

The answer to this objection is, that the seed-corn and forage in question were the result of land, labour, and abstinence; they were entitled, therefore, when produced, to be denominated rent, wages, or profit, and the circumstance that they were employed to produce future instead of immediate gratification, does not vary their character. When produced, they were revenue; their *conversion* into capital was a subsequent accident. No one would object against the expression that such and such a labourer has *saved part of his wages* and employed them in stocking his garden. If the words revenue and income were co-extensive with expenditure, the common statement, that a man is living within his income, would be a contradiction in terms.

Perhaps this may be made clearer if we retrace the history of capital.

The primary instruments of production were labour, and those productive agents which are spontaneously afforded by nature. The first dwellers on the earth had only rent and wages. The savage who, instead of devouring the animals which he had entrapped, reserved them to become the origin of a domesticated flock, and he who reserved, to be employed as seed, some of the grains which he had gathered, laid the foundation of capital. The produce of that flock and of that seed was partly rent, partly wages, and partly profit. And it did not cease to be so, although he refused to employ the whole of it on his immediate gratification.

It must be admitted, however, that the portion of the annual produce which is employed in the production or the support of brute or inanimate capital is not usually termed rent, wages, or profits. It has not, in fact, any specific name. But it appears to us to be the most philosophical arrangement to consider it as rent, wages, or profit, according to the character of its proprietor, without regard to its subsequent destination.

EXCHANGE

Having made this general classification of the parties among whom the results of the different productive instruments are divided, we now proceed to consider the general laws which regulate the proportions in which those results are exchanged for one another. To a certain degree this question was considered when we treated of value; but not having at that time explained the words production, wages, profit, or rent, we were unable to do more than to state and illustrate the following propositions:

First, that all those things, and those things only, are susceptible of exchange, which, being transferable, are limited in supply, and are capable, directly or indirectly, of affording pleasure or preventing pain; a capacity to which we have affixed the name of utility. Secondly, that the reciprocal values of any two things, or, in other words, the quantity of the one which will exchange for a given quantity of the other, depend on two sets of causes; those which occasion the utility and limit the supply of the one, and those which limit the supply and occasion the utility of the other. The causes which occasion the utility and limit the supply of any given commodity or service, we denominate the *intrinsic* causes of its value. Those which limit the supply and occasion the utility of the commodities or services for which it is capable of being exchanged, we denominate the *extrinsic* causes of its value. And, thirdly, that comparative limitation of supply, or, to speak more familiarly, though less philosophically, comparative scarcity, though not sufficient to constitute value, is by far its most important element; utility, or, in other words, demand, being mainly dependent on it. We had not then shown the means by which supply is effected. Having done this, having shown that human Labour and Abstinence, and the spontaneous agency of Nature, are the three instruments of production, we are at liberty to explain what are the obstacles which limit the supply of all that is produced, and the mode in which those obstacles affect the reciprocal values of the different subjects of exchange.

Price.—In the following discussion, however, we shall in general substitute *price* or value in money for general value.

The general value of any commodity, that is, the quantity of all the other subjects of exchange which might be obtained in return for a given quantity of it, is incapable of being ascertained. Its specific value in any other commodity may be ascertained by the experiment of an exchange; the anxiety of each party in the exchange to give as little, and obtain as much as possible, leading him to investigate, as accurately as he can, the intrinsic causes giving value to each of the articles to be exchanged. This is, however, a troublesome operation, and many expedients are used to diminish its frequency. The most obvious one is to consider a single exchange, or the mean of a few exchanges, as a model for subsequent exchanges of a similar nature. By an extension of this expedient it may become a model for exchanges not of a similar nature. If given quantities of two different articles are each found by experience to exchange for a given quantity of a third article, the proportionate value of the two first-mentioned articles may, of course, be inferred. It is *measured* by the third. Hence arise the advantages of selecting, as one of the subjects of every exchange, a single commodity, or, more correctly, a species of commodities constituted of individuals of precisely similar qualities. In the first place, all persons can ascertain, with tolerable accuracy, the intrinsic causes which give value to the selected commodity, so that one half the trouble of an exchange is ready performed. And, secondly, if an exchange is to be effected between any other two commodities, the quantity of each that is usually exchanged for a given quantity of the third commodity is ascertained, and their relative value is inferred. The commodity thus selected as the general instrument of exchange, whatever be its substance, whether salt, as in Abyssinia, cowries, on the Coast of Guinea, or the precious metals, as in Europe, is *money*. When the use of such a commodity, or, in other words, of money, has become established, value in money, or price, is the only value familiarly contemplated. The scarcity and durability of gold and silver (the substances used as money by all civilized nations) make them peculiarly unsusceptible of alteration in value from intrinsic causes. On these accounts we think it better, in the following discussion, to refer rather to *price* than to general value, and to consider the value of money, so far as it depends on intrinsic causes, to be unvarying.

We must preface our explanation of the effect on price of the causes limiting supply, by a remark which may appear self-evident, but which must always be kept in recollection, namely that "*Where the only natural agents employed are those which are universally accessible, and therefore are practically unlimited in supply, the utility of the produce, or, in other words, its power, directly or indirectly, of producing gratification, or preventing pain, must be in proportion to the sacrifices made to produce it, unless the producer has misapplied his exertions; since no man would willingly employ a given amount of labour or abstinence in producing one commodity, if he could obtain more gratification by devoting them to the production of another.*"

We now revert to the causes which limit supply.

There are some commodities the results of agents no longer in existence, or acting at remote and uncertain periods, the supply of which cannot be increased, or cannot be reckoned upon. Antiques and relics belong to the first class, and all the very rare productions of Nature of Art, such as diamonds of extraordinary size, or pictures, or statues of extraordinary beauty, to the second. The values of such commodities are subject to no definite rules, and depend altogether on the wealth and taste of the community. In common language, they are said to bear a fancy price, that is, a price depending principally on the caprice or fashion of the day. The Boccaccio, which a few years ago sold for £2,000, and after a year or two's interval for £700, may, perhaps, fifty years hence, be purchased for a shilling. Relics which, in the ninth century, were thought too valuable to admit of a definite price, would now be thought equally incapable of price in consequence of their utter worthlessness. In the following discussion we shall altogether omit such commodities and confine our attention to those of which the supply is capable of increase, either regular, or sufficiently approaching to regularity, to admit of calculation.

The obstacle to the supply of those commodities which are produced by labour and abstinence, with that assistance only from nature which every one can command, consists solely in the difficulty of finding persons ready to submit to the labour and abstinence necessary to their production. In other words, their supply is limited by the cost of their production.

Cost of Production.—The term "cost of production" must be familiar to those who are acquainted with the writings of modern Economists; but, like most terms in Political Economy, though currently used, it has never been accurately defined; and it appears to us impossible that it should have been defined without the assistance of the term "abstinence," or of some equivalent expression.

Mr. Ricardo, who originally introduced the term "cost of production," uses as an equivalent expression, "the quantity of labour which has been bestowed on the production of a commodity." Mr. Mill (Ch. III., sec. 2) appears to consider cost of production as equivalent to "quantity of labour." Mr. Malthus more elaborately defines it as "the advance of the quantity of accumulated and immediate labour necessary to production, with such a percentage upon the whole of the advances for the time they have been employed as is equivalent to ordinary profits." (*Definitions*, p. 242.)

In a note to the third edition, page 46, Mr. Ricardo admits that profit also forms a part of the cost of production. Mr. Mill, by a stretch of language, in the convenience of which we cannot concur, includes profit under the term labour. The definitions of Mr. Ricardo and Mr. Mill appear, therefore, to coincide. And that adopted by Mr. Malthus only differs from them in referring, not to the labour that *has* been employed, but to that which must be employed if the production must be continued. In this respect the language of Mr. Malthus is undoubtedly the most correct. The sacrifices that *have* been made to produce a given commodity have no effect on its value. All that the purchaser considers is the amount of sacrifice that its production would require at the time of the exchange. If the expense of producing a pair of stockings were suddenly to fall or to rise by one half, a rise or fall in the value of the existing stockings would be the consequence, although the labour that *has* been employed on them is of course unalterable. And when Mr. Ricardo and Mr. Mill speak of the labour which *has* been employed on a commodity as affecting its value, they must be understood as implying that the circumstances of production remain unchanged.

Colonel Torrens considers cost of production as equivalent to "the amount of capital expended on production," and refuses to consider profit as forming one of its elements. His remarks throw so much light on the whole subject, that we will venture to extract them at some length.

* * * * *

Colonel Torrens's remarks are just, so far as they apply to the mere expressions which he is criticising. Profit is certainly not a means but a result. It is true that unless that result were expected, production would not be continued. Neither the farmer nor the manufacturer could be induced by any other motive to abstain from the unproductive enjoyment of his capital; so food would not be produced unless its consumption were necessary or agreeable. But the obtaining a profit is no more a part of the cost of producing a harvest than the gratification of appetite is a part of the cost of producing a dinner, or protection from cold part of the cost of producing a coat.

Want of the term abstinence, or of some equivalent expression has led Mr. Malthus into inaccuracy of language. He seems to have felt that something besides mere labour is essential to production. He felt that simple industry would not convert a naked heath into a valuable wood; that the planter, in addition to the labour of inserting and protecting the saplings, incurred the additional *sacrifice* of directing his labour to the production of remote results; and that the successive generations of proprietors, in suffering the young plantation to become mature, sacrificed their own emolument to that of their successors. He seems to have felt that these sacrifices were part of the cost of producing the wood, and, having no term to express them he denominated them by the name of their reward. When he termed profit a part of the cost of production, he appears to us to have meant not profit, but that conduct which is repaid by profits: an inaccuracy precisely similar to that committed by those who term wages a part of the cost of production; meaning not wages, which are a result, but the labour for which wages are the remuneration.

Colonel Torrens's error is an error of omission. He refuses to consider profit as part of the cost of production, but he does not substitute for it abstinence or any equivalent expression. Although he admits that where equal capitals are employed the value of the products may differ if the one be brought to market sooner than the other, he has not stated the principle on which this difference depends. That principle is that, though in both cases the labour employed is the same, more abstinence is necessary in the one case than in the other.

Cost of Production Defined.—By *Cost of Production*, then, we mean the sum of the labour and abstinence necessary to production. But cost of Production, thus, defined must be divided into the cost of production, on the part of the producer or seller, and the cost of production on the part of the consumer or purchaser. The first is of course the amount of labour and abstinence which must be undergone by him who offers for sale a given class of commodities or services in order to enable him to continue to produce them. The second is, the amount of the labour and abstinence which must be undergone by those to whom a given commodity or service is offered for sale, if, instead of purchasing, they themselves, or some of them on the behalf of themselves and the others, were to produce it. The first is equal to the minimum, the second to the maximum, of price. For, on the one hand, no man would continue to buy what they themselves, or some of them on behalf of themselves and the others, could produce at less expense. With respect to those commodities, or, to speak more accurately, with respect to the value of those parts or attributes of commodities, which are the subjects of equal competition, which may be produced by all persons with equal advantages, the cost of production to the producer and the cost of production to consumer are the same. Their price, therefore, represents the aggregate amount of the labour and abstinence necessary to continue their production. If their price should fall lower, the wages or the profits of those employed in their production must fall below the average remuneration of the labour and abstinence that must be undergone if their production is to be continued. In time, therefore, it is discontinued or diminished, until the value of the product has been raised by the diminution of the supply. If the price should rise beyond the cost of their production, the producers must receive more than an average remuneration for their sacrifices. As soon as this has been discovered, capital and industry flow towards the employment which, by this supposition, offers extraordinary advantages. Those who formerly were purchasers, or persons on their behalf, turn producers themselves, until the increased supply has equalized the price with the cost of production.

Some years ago London depended for water on the New River Company. As the quantity which they can supply is limited, the price rose with the extension of buildings, until it so far exceeded the cost of production as to induce some of the consumers to become producers. Three new Water Companies were established, and the price fell as the supply increased, until the shares in the New River Company fell to nearly one-fourth of their former value; from £15,000 to £4,000. If the metropolis should continue to increase, these transactions will recur. The price of water will increase and exceed the cost at which it could be afforded. New Companies will arise, and, unless the additional supply is checked by greater natural obstacles than those which the existing Companies have to surmount, the price will again fall to its present level.

But though, under free competition, cost of production is the regulator of price, its influence is subject to much occasional interruption. Its operation can be supposed to be perfect only if we suppose that there are no disturbing causes, that capital and labour can be at once transferred, and without loss, from one employment to another, and that every producer has full information of the profit to be derived from every mode of production. But it is obvious that these suppositions have no resemblance to the truth. A large portion of the capital essential to production consists of buildings, machinery, and other implements, the results of much time and labour, and of little service for any except their existing purposes. A still larger portion consists of knowledge and of intellectual and bodily dexterity, applicable only to the processes in which those qualities were originally acquired. Again, the advantage derived from any given business depends so much upon the dexterity and the judgment with which it is managed, that few capitalists can estimate, except upon an average of some years, the amount of their own profits, and still fewer can estimate those of their neighbours. Established businesses, therefore, may survive the causes in which they originated, and become gradually extinguished as their comparative unprofitableness is discovered, and the labourers and capital engaged in them wear away without being replaced; and, on the other hand, other employments are inadequately supplied with the capital and industry which they could profitably absorb. During the interval, the products of the one sell for less, and those of the others for more, than their cost of production. Political Economy does not deal with particular facts but with general tendencies, and when we assign to cost of production the power of regulating price in cases of equal competition, we mean to describe it not as a point to which price is attached, but as a centre of oscillation which it is always endeavouring to approach.

We have seen that, under circumstances of equal competition, or, in other words, where all persons can become producers, and that with equal advantages, the cost of production on the part of the producer or seller, and the cost production on the part of the consumer or purchaser, are the same, and that the commodity thus produced sells for its cost of production; or, in other words, at a price equal to the sum of the labour and abstinence which its production requires; or, to use a more familiar expression, at a price equal to the amount of the wages and profits which must be paid to induce the producers to continue their exertions. It has lately been a general opinion that the bulk of commodities is produced under circumstances of equal competition. "By far the greater part of those goods," says Mr. Ricardo, (*Principles*, &c. p. 3) "Which are the objects of desire, are produced by labour, and may be multiplied almost without any assignable limit, if we are disposed to bestow the labour necessary to obtain them. In speaking then of commodities, of their exchangeable value, and of the laws which regulate their relative prices, we always mean such commodities only as can be increased in quantity by the exertion of human industry, and in the production of which competition operates without restraint."

Now it is clear that the production in which no appropriated natural agent has concurred, is the only production which has been made under circumstances of perfectly equal competition. And how few are the commodities of which the production has in no stage been assisted by peculiar advantages of soil, or situation, or by extraordinary talent of body or mind, or by processes generally unknown, or protected by law from imitation. Where the assistance of these agents, to which we have given the general name of natural agents, has been obtained, the result is more valuable than the result of equal labour and abstinence unassisted by similar aids. A commodity thus produced is called the subject of a *monopoly;* and the person who has appropriated such a natural agent, a *monopolist.*

JOHN STUART MILL

(1806–1873)

John Stuart Mill was born in London in 1806, the son of the illustrious James Mill. He was a most precocious child, who had the benefit of his father's personal attention. John Stuart Mill's education is well described in his famous autobiography. The method should be carefully studied by all students of education and social science. Jeremy Bentham also had an important influence on the life of John Stuart Mill. Mill's own wife was a great inspiration and a help to him in the preparation of his manuscripts.

John Stuart Mill is an important figure not merely as an economist, but also as a philosopher, a student of jurisprudence, and a man of letters. He was an independent member of Parliament from 1858 to 1868, a strong liberal, advocating suffrage for women, improved conditions for the laboring classes, and numerous Irish reforms, especially those directed against rack rent.

Mill began publication in 1822 at the early age of sixteen in the form of contributions to newspapers. He continued throughout his life to be the prolific author of short articles, many of which appeared in the *Westminster Review*, *The London Review*, and *The Fortnightly Review*.

Among the important works of Mill was his "System of Logic" (1843), which was one of the best treatises in its field, and which subsequently passed through numerous revisions. A collection of "Essays on Some Unsettled Questions of Political Economy" was published the following year in 1844. It is interesting to note that this manuscript had been previously declined by the publishers, but the success of his book on logic insured the success of this publication venture in economics.

"Principles of Political Economy" appeared in 1848, a date as easy to remember as that of the publication of "Wealth of Nations" in 1776. "Principles of Political Economy" is another masterpiece which should be in the possession of every student of the history of economic thought. Although Ashley's edition is perhaps the best, there are numerous, excellent and inexpensive editions. Mill's "Principles of Political Economy" was the authoritative text in economics for one or two generations of English speaking students.

The other important works of Mill were chiefly essays, many of which have been collected and bound together into one or more volumes. They include the following: "On Liberty," "Considerations on Representative Government"; "Utilitarianism"; "Examination of Sir William Hamiliton's Philosophy"; and "Subjection of Women."

The following selections have been taken from Mill's famous essay "On Liberty" and his essay "Utilitarianism." His logic is excellent and his method of expression remarkably lucid.

JOHN STUART MILL

SELECTIONS FROM "ON LIBERTY"

CHAPTER I. INTRODUCTORY

* * * * *

The object of this Essay is to assert one very simple principle, as entitled to govern absolutely the dealings of society with the individual in the way of compulsion and control, whether the means used be physical force in the form of legal penalties, or the moral coercion of public opinion. That principle is, that the sole end for which mankind are warranted, individually or collectively, in interfering with the liberty of action of any of their number, is self-protection. That the only purpose for which power can be rightfully exercised over any member of a civilised community, against his will, is to prevent harm to others. His own good, either physical or moral, is not a sufficient warrant. He cannot rightfully be compelled to do or forbear because it will be better for him to do so, because it will make him happier, because, in the opinions of others, to do so would be wise, or even right. These are good reasons for remonstrating with him, or reasoning with him, or persuading him, or entreating him, but not for compelling him, or visiting him with any evil in case he do otherwise. To justify that, the conduct from which it is desired to deter him must be calculated to produce evil to some one else. The only part of the conduct of any one, for which he is amenable to society, is that which concerns others. In the part which merely concerns himself, his independence is, of right, absolute. Over himself, over his own body and mind, the individual is sovereign.

* * * * *

It is proper to state that I forego any advantage which could be derived to my argument from the idea of abstract right, as a thing independent of utility. I regard utility as the ultimate appeal on all ethical questions; but it must be utility in the largest sense, grounded on the permanent interests of a man as a progressive being. Those interests, I contend, authorise the subjection of individual spontaneity to external control, only in respect to those actions of each, which concern the interest of other people. If any one does an act hurtful to others, there is a *prima facie* case for punishing him, by law, or, where legal penalties are not safely applicable, by general disapprobation. There are also many positive acts for the benefit of others, which he may rightfully be compelled to perform; such as to give evidence in a court of justice; to bear his fair share in the common defence, or in any other joint work necessary to the interest of the society of which he enjoys the protection; and to perform certain acts of individual beneficence, such as saving a fellow-creature's life, or interposing to protect the defenceless against ill-usage, things which whenever it is obviously a man's duty to do, he may rightfully be made responsible to society for not doing. A person may cause evil to others not only by his actions but by his inaction, and in either case he is justly accountable to them for the injury. The latter case, it is true, requires a much more cautious exercise of compulsion than the former. To make any one answerable for doing evil to others is the rule; to make him answerable for not preventing evil is, comparatively speaking, the exception. Yet there are many cases clear enough and grave enough to justify that exception. In all things which regard the external relations of the individual, he is *de jure* amenable to those whose interests are concerned, and, if need be, to society as their protector. There are often good reasons for not holding him to the responsibility; but these reasons must arise from the special expediencies of the case: either because it is a kind of case in which he is on the whole likely to act better, when left to his own discretion, than when controlled in any way in which society have it in their power to control him; or because the attempt to exercise control would produce other evils, greater than those which it would prevent. When such reasons as these preclude the enforcement of responsibility, the conscience of the agent himself should step into the vacant judgment seat, and protect those interests of others which have no external protection; judging himself all the more rigidly, because the case does not admit of his being made accountable to the judgment of his fellow-creatures.

But there is a sphere of action in which society, as distinguished from the individual, has, if any, only an indirect interest; comprehending all that portion of a person's life and conduct which affects only himself, or if it also affects others, only with their free, voluntary, and undeceived consent and participation. When I say only himself, I mean directly, and in the first instance; for whatever affects himself, may affect others through himself; and the objection which may be grounded on this contingency, will receive consideration in the sequel. This, then, is the appropriate region of human liberty. It comprises, first, the inward domain of consciousness; demanding liberty of conscience in the most comprehensive sense; liberty of thought and feeling; absolute freedom of opinion and sentiment on all subjects, practical or speculative, scientific, moral, or theological. The liberty of expressing and publishing opinions may seem to fall under a different principle, since it belongs to that part of the conduct of an individual which concerns other people; but, being almost of as much importance as the liberty of thought itself, and resting in great part on the same reasons, is practically inseparable from it. Secondly, the principle requires liberty of tastes and pursuits; of framing the plan of our life to suit our own character; of doing as we like, subject to such consequences as may follow: without impediment from our fellow-creatures, so long as what we do does not harm them, even though they should think our conduct foolish, perverse, or wrong. Thirdly, from this liberty of each individual, follows the liberty, within the same limits, of combination among individuals; freedom to unite, for any purpose not involving harm to others: the persons combining being supposed to be of full age, and not forced or deceived.

No society in which these liberties are not, on the whole, respected, is free, whatever may be its form of government; and none is completely free in which they do not exist absolute and unqualified. The only freedom which deserves the name, is that of pursuing our own good in our own way, so long as we do not attempt to deprive others of theirs, or impede their efforts to obtain it. Each is the proper guardian of his own health, whether bodily, *or* mental and spiritual. Mankind are greater gainers by suffering each other to live as seems good to themselves, than by compelling each to live as seems good to the rest.

*   *   *   *   *

Chapter IV. Of the Limits to the Authority of Society over the Individual

What, then, is the rightful limit to the sovereignty of the individual over himself? Where does the authority of society begin? How much of human life should be assigned to individuality, and how much to society?

Each will receive its proper share, if each has that which more particularly concerns it. To individuality should belong the part of life in which it is chiefly the individual that is interested; to society, the part which chiefly interests society.

Though society is not founded on a contract, and though no good purpose is answered by inventing a contract in order to deduce social obligations from it, every one who receives the protection of society owes a return for the benefit, and the fact of living in society renders it indispensable that each should be bound to observe a certain line of conduct towards the rest. This conduct consists, first, in not injuring the interests of one another; or rather certain interests, which, either by express legal provision or by tacit understanding, ought to be considered as rights; and secondly, in each person's bearing his share (to be fixed on some equitable principle) of the labours and sacrifices incurred for defending the society or its members from injury and molestation. These conditions society is justified in enforcing, at all costs to those who endeavour to withhold fulfilment. Nor is this all that society may do. The acts of an individual may be hurtful to others, or wanting in due consideration for their welfare, without going to the length of violating any of their constituted rights. The offender may then be justly punished by opinion, though not by law. As soon as any part of a person's conduct affects prejudically the interests of others, society has jurisdiction over it, and the question whether the general welfare will or will not be promoted by interfering with it, becomes open to discussion. But there is no room for entertaining any such question when a person's conduct affects the interests of no persons besides himself, or needs not affect them unless they like (all the persons concerned being of full age, and the ordinary amount of understanding). In all such cases, there should be perfect freedom, legal and social, to do the action and stand the consequences.

It would be a great misunderstanding of this doctrine, to suppose that it is one of selfish indifference, which pretends that human beings have no business with each other's conduct in life, and that they should not concern themselves about the well-doing or well-being of one another, unless their own interest is involved. Instead of any diminution, there is need of a great increase of distinterested exertion to promote the good of others. But disinterested benevolence can find other instruments to persuade people to their good, than whips and scourges, either of the literal or the metaphorical sort. I am the last person to undervalue the self-regarding virtues; they are only second in importance, if even second, to the social. It is equally the business of education to cultivate both. But even education works by conviction and persuasion as well as by compulsion, and it is by the former only that, when the period of education is past, the self-regarding virtues should be inculcated. Human beings owe to each other help to distinguish the better from the worse, and encouragement to choose the former and avoid the latter. They should be forever stimulating each other to increased exercise of their higher faculties, and increased direction of their feelings and aims towards wise instead of foolish, elevating instead of degrading, objects and contemplations. But neither one person, nor any number of persons, is warranted in saying to another human creature of ripe years, that he shall not do with his life for his own benefit what he chooses to do with it. He is the person most interested in his own well-being: the interest which any other person, except in cases of strong personal attachment, can have in it, is trifling, compared with that which he himself has; the interest which society has in him individually (except as to his conduct to others) is fractional, and altogether indirect: while, with respect to his own feelings and circumstances, the most ordinary man or woman has means of knowledge immeasurably surpassing those that can be possessed by any one else. The interference of society to over-rule his judgment and purposes in what only regards himself must be grounded on general presumptions; which may be altogether wrong, and even if right, are as likely as not to be misapplied to individual cases, by persons no better acquainted with the circumstances of such cases than those are who look at them merely from without. In this department, therefore, of human affairs, individuality has its proper field of action. In the conduct of human beings towards one another, it is necessary that general rules should for the most part be observed, in order that people may know what they have to expect; but in each person's own concerns, his individual spontaneity is entitled to free exercise. Considerations to aid his judgment, exhortations to strengthen his will, may be offered to him, by others; but he, himself, is the final judge. All errors which he is likely to commit against advice and warning are far outweighed by the evil of allowing others to constrain him to what they deem his good.

*   *   *   *   *

What I contend for is, that the inconveniences which are strictly inseparable from the unfavorable judgment of others are the only ones to which a person should ever be subjected for that portion of his conduct and character which concerns his own good, but which does not affect the interests of others in their relations with him. Acts injurious to others require a totally different treatment.

*   *   *   *   *

But with regard to the merely contingent, or, as it may be called, constructive injury which a person causes to society, by conduct which neither violates any specific duty to the public, nor occasions perceptible hurt to any assignable individual except himself; the inconvenience is one which society can afford to bear, for the sake of the greater good of human freedom. If grown persons are to be punished for not taking proper care of themselves, I would rather it were for their own sake, than under pretence of preventing them from impairing their capacity of rendering to society benefits which society does not pretend it has a right to exact. But I cannot consent to argue the point as if society had no means of bringing its weaker members up to its ordinary standard of rational conduct, except waiting till they do something irrational, and then punishing them, legally or morally, for it. Society has had absolute power over them during all the early portion of their existence: it has had the whole period of childhood and nonage in which to try whether it could make them capable of rational conduct in life. The existing generation is master both of the training and the entire circumstances of the generation to come; it cannot indeed make them perfectly wise and good, because it is itself so lamentably deficient in goodness and wisdom; and its best efforts are not always, in individual cases, its most successful ones; but it is perfectly well able to make the rising generation, as a whole, as good as, and a little better than, itself. If society lets any considerable number of its members grow up mere children, incapable of being acted on by rational consideration of distant motives, society has itself to blame for the consequences.

* * * * *

But the strongest of all the arguments against the interference of the public with purely personal conduct, is that when it does interfere, the odds are that it interferes wrongly, and in the wrong place. On questions of social morality, of duty to others, the opinion of the public, that is, of an overruling majority, though often wrong, is likely to be still oftener right; because on such questions they are only required to judge of their own interests; of the manner in which some mode of conduct, if allowed to be practised, would affect themselves. But the opinion of a similar majority, imposed as a law on the minority, on questons of self-regarding conduct, is quite as likely to be wrong as right; for in these cases public opinion means, at best, some people's opinion of what is good or bad for other people; while very often it does not even mean that; the public, with the most perfect indifference, passing over the pleasure or convenience of those whose conduct they censure, and considering only their own preference.

* * * * *

A recent writer, in some respects of considerable merit, proposes (to use his own words) not a crusade, but a *civilizade*, against this polygamous community, to put an end to what seems to him a retrograde step in civilization. It also appears so to me, but I am not aware that any community has a right to force another to be civilized. So long as the sufferers by the bad law do not invoke assistance from other communities, I cannot admit that persons entirely unconnected with them ought to step in and require that a condition of things with which all who are directly interested appear to be satisfied, should be put an end to because it is a scandal to persons some thousands of miles distant, who have no part or concern in it. Let them send missionaries, if they please, to preach against it; and let them, by any fair means (of which silencing the teachers is not one), oppose the progress of similar doctrines among their own people. If civilisation has got the better of barbarism when barbarism had the world to itself, it is too much to profess to be afraid lest barbarism, after having been fairly got under, should revive and conquer civilisation. A civilisation that can thus succumb to its vanquished enemy, must first have become so degenerate, that neither its appointed priests and teachers, nor anybody else, has the capacity, or will take the trouble, to stand up for it. If this be so, the sooner such a civilisation receives notice to quit the better. It can only go on from bad to worse, until destroyed and regenerated (like the Western Empire) by energetic barbarians.

Chapter V. Applications

The principles asserted in these pages must be more generally admitted as the basis for discussion of details, before a consistent application of them to all the various departments of government and morals can be attempted with any prospect of advantage. The few observations I propose to make on questions of detail are designed to illustrate the principles, rather than to follow them out to their consequences. I offer, not so much applications, as specimens of application; which may serve to bring into greater clearness the meaning and limits of the two maxims which together form the entire doctrine of this Essay, and to assist the judgment in holding the balance between them, in the cases where it appears doubtful which of them is applicable to the case.

The maxims are, first, that the individual is not accountable to society for his actions, in so far as these concern the interests of no person but himself. Advice, instruction, persuasion, and avoidance by other people if thought necessary by them for their own good, are the only measures by which society can justifiably express its dislike or disapprobation of his conduct. Secondly, that for such actions as are prejudicial to the interests of others, the individual is accountable, and may be subjected either to social or to legal punishment, if society is of opinion that the one or the other is requisite for its protection.

In the first place, it must by no means be supposed, because damage, or probability of damage, to the interests of others, can alone justify the interference of society, that therefore it always does justify such interference. In many cases, an individual, in pursuing a legitimate object, necessarily and therefore legitimately causes pain or loss to others, or intercepts a good which they had a reasonable hope of obtaining. Such oppositions of interest between individuals often arise from bad social institutions, but are unavoidable while those institutions last; and some would be unavoidable under any institutions. Whoever succeeds in an overcrowded profession, or in a competitive examination; whoever is preferred to another in any contest for an object which both desire, reaps benefit from the loss of others, from their wasted exertion and their disappointment. But it is, by common admission, better for the general interest of mankind, that persons should pursue their objects undeterred by this sort of consequences. In other words, society admits no right, either legal or moral, in the disappointed competitors to immunity from this kind of suffering; and feels called on to interfere, only when means of success have been employed which it is contrary to the general interest to permit—namely, fraud or treachery, and force.

Again, trade is a social act. Whoever undertakes to sell any description of goods to the public, does what affects the interest of other persons, and of society in general; and thus his conduct, in principle, comes within the jurisdiction of society: accordingly, it was once held to be the duty of governments, in all cases which were considered of importance, to fix prices, and regulate the processes of manufacture. But it is now recognised, though not till after a long struggle, that both the cheapness and the good quality of commodities are most effectually provided for by leaving the producers and sellers perfectly free, under the sole check of equal freedom to the buyers for supplying themselves elsewhere. This is the so-called doctrine of Free Trade, which rests on grounds different from, though equally solid with, the principle of individual liberty asserted in this Essay. Restrictions on trade, or on production for purposes of trade, are indeed restraints; and all restraint, *quâ* restraint, is an evil: but the restraints in question affect only that part of conduct which society is competent to restrain, and are wrong solely because they do not really produce the results which it is desired to produce by them. As the principle of individual liberty is not involved in the doctrine of Free Trade, so neither is it in most of the questions which arise respecting the limits of that doctrine; as, for example, what amount of public control is admissible for the prevention of fraud by adulteration; how far sanitary precautions, or arrangements to protect workpeople employed in dangerous occupations, should be enforced on employers. Such questions involve considerations of liberty, only in so far as leaving people to themselves is always better, *caeteris paribus*, than controlling them: but that they may be legitimately controlled for these ends is in principle undeniable. On the other hand, there are questions relating to interference with trade which are essentially questions of liberty; such as the Maine Law, already touched upon; the prohibition of the importation of opium into China; the restriction of the sale of poisons; all cases, in short, where the object of the interference is to make it impossible or difficult to obtain a particular commodity. These interferences are objectionable, not as infringements on the liberty of the producer or seller, but on that of the buyer.

* * * * *

The objections to government interference, when it is not such as to involve infringement of liberty, may be of three kinds.

The first is, when the thing to be done is likely to be better done by individuals than by the government. Speaking generally, there is no one so fit to conduct any business, or to determine how or by whom it shall be conducted, as those who are personally interested in it. This principle condemns the interferences, once so common, of the legislature, or the officers of government, with the ordinary progresses of industry. But this part of the subject has been sufficiently enlarged upon by political economists, and is not particularly related to the principles of this Essay.

The second objection is more nearly allied to our subject. In many cases, though individuals may not do the particular thing so well, on the average, as the officers of government, it is nevertheless desirable that it should be done by them, rather than by the government, as a means to their own mental education—a mode of strengthening their active faculties, exercising their judgment, and giving them a familiar knowledge of the subjects with which they are thus left to deal. This is a principal, though not the sole, recommendation of jury trial (in cases not political); of free and popular local and municipal institutions; of the conduct of industrial and philanthropic enterprises by voluntary associations. These are not questions of liberty, and are connected with that subject only by remote tendencies; but they are questions of development. It belongs to a different occasion from the present to dwell on these things as parts of national education; as being, in truth, the peculiar training of a citizen, the practical part of the political education of a free people, taking them out of the narrow circle of personal and family selfishness, and accustoming them to the comprehension of joint interests, the management of joint concerns—habituating them to act from public or semi-public motives, and guide their conduct by aims which unite instead of isolating them from one another. Without these habits and powers, a free constitution can neither be worked nor preserved; as is exemplified by the too-often transitory nature of political freedom in countries where it does not rest upon a sufficient basis of local liberties. The management of purely local business by the localities, and of the great enterprises of industry by the union of those who voluntarily supply the pecuniary means, is further recommended by all the advantages which have been set forth in this Essay as belonging to individuality of development, and diversity of modes of action. Government operations tend to be everywhere alike. With individuals and voluntary associations, on the contrary, there are varied experiments, and endless diversity of experience. What the State can usefully do is to make itself a central depository, and active circulator and diffuser, of the experience resulting from many trials. Its business is to enable each experimentalist to benefit by the experiments of others; instead of tolerating no experiments but its own.

The third and most cogent reason for restricting the interference of government is the great evil of adding unnecessarily to its power. Every function superadded to those already exercised by the government causes its influence over hopes and fears to be more widely diffused, and converts, more and more, the active and ambitious part of the public into hangers-on of the government, or of some party which aims at becoming the government. If the roads, the railways, the banks, the insurance offices, the great joint-stock companies, the universities, and the public charities, were all of them branches of the government; if, in addition, the municipal corporations and local boards, with all that now devolves on them, became departments of the central administration; if the employes of all these different enterprises were appointed and paid by the government, and looked to the government for every rise in life; not all the freedom of the press and popular constitution of the legislature would make this or any other country free otherwise than in name. And the evil would be greater, the more efficiently and scientifically the administrative machinery was constructed—the more skilful the arrangements for obtaining the best qualified hands and heads with which to work it. In England it has of late been proposed that all the members of the civil service of government should be selected by competitive examination, to obtain for these employments the most intelligent and instructed persons procurable; and much has been said and written for and against this proposal. One of the arguments most insisted on by its opponents is that the occupation of a permanent official servant of the State does not hold out sufficient prospects of emolument and importance to attract the highest talents, which will always be able to find a more inviting career in the professions, or in the service of companies and other public bodies. One would not have been surprised if this argument had been used by the friends of the proposition, as an answer to its principal difficulty. Coming from the opponents it is strange enough. What is urged as an objection is the safety-valve of the proposed system. If indeed all the high talent of the country *could* be drawn into the service of the government, a proposal tending to bring about that result might well inspire uneasiness. If every part of the business of society which required organized concert, or large and comprehensive views, were in the hands of the government, and if government offices were universally filled by the ablest men, all the enlarged culture and practised intelligence in the country, except the purely speculative, would be concentrated in a numerous bureaucracy, to whom alone the rest of the community would look for all things: the multitude for direction and dictation in all they had to do; the able and aspiring for personal advancement. To be admitted into the ranks of this bureaucracy, and when admitted, to rise therein, would be the sole objects of ambition. Under this *régime*, not only is the outside public ill-qualified, for want of practical experience, to criticise or check the mode of operation of the bureaucracy, but even if the accidents of despotic or the natural working of popular institutions occasionally raise to the summit a ruler or rulers of reforming inclinations, no reform can be effected which is contrary to the interest of the bureaucracy. Such is the melancholy condition of the Russian empire, as shown in the accounts of those who have had sufficient opportunity of observation. The Czar himself is powerless against the bureaucratic body; he can send any one of them to Siberia, but he cannot govern without them, or against their will. On every decree of his they have a tacit veto, by merely refraining from carrying it into effect. In countries of more advanced civilisation and of a more insurrectionary spirit, the public, accustomed to expect everything to be done for them by the State, or at least to do nothing for themselves without asking from the State not only leave to do it, but even how it is to be done, naturally hold the State responsible for all evil which befalls them, and when the evil exceeds their amount of patience, they rise against the government, and make what is called a revolution; whereupon somebody else, with or without legitimate authority from the nation, vaults into the seat, issues his orders to the bureaucracy, and everything goes on much as it did before; the bureaucracy being unchanged, and nobody else being capable of taking their place.

* * * * *

It is not, also, to be forgotten, that the absorption of all the principal ability of the country into the governing body is fatal, sooner or later, to the mental activity and progressiveness of the body itself. Banded together as they are—working a system which, like all systems, necessarily proceeds in a great measure by fixed rules—the official body are under the constant temptation of sinking into indolent routine, or, if they now and then desert that mill-horse round, of rushing into some half-examined crudity which has struck the fancy of some leading member of the corps; and the sole check to these closely allied, though seemingly opposite, tendencies, the only stimulus which can keep the ability of the body itself up to a high standard, is liability to the watchful criticism of equal ability outside the body. It is indispensable, therefore, that the means should exist, independently of the government, of forming such ability, and furnishing it with the opportunities and experience necessary for a correct judgment of great practical affairs. If we would possess permanently a skilful and efficient body of functionaries—above all, a body able to originate and willing to adopt improvements; if we would not have our bureaucracy degenerate into a pedantocracy, this body must not engross all the occupations which form and cultivate the faculties required for the government of mankind.

* * * * *

JOHN STUART MILL

SELECTIONS FROM "UTILITARIANISM"

CHAPTER II. WHAT UTILITARIANISM IS

A passing remark is all that needs be given to the ignorant blunder of supposing that those who stand up for utility as the test of right and wrong, use the term in that restricted and merely colloquial sense in which utility is opposed to pleasure. An apology is due to the philosophical opponents of utilitarianism, for even the momentary appearance of confounding them with any one capable of so absurd a misconception; which is the more extraordinary, inasmuch as the contrary accusation, of referring everything to pleasure, and that too in its grossest form, is another of the common charges against utilitarianism: and, as has been pointedly remarked by an able writer, the same sort of persons, and often the very same persons, denounce the theory "as impracticably dry when the word utility precedes the word pleasure, and as too practicably voluptuous when the word pleasure precedes the word utility." Those who know anything about the matter are aware that every writer, from Epicurus to Bentham, who maintained the theory of utility, meant by it, not something to be contradistinguished from pleasure, but pleasure itself, together with exemption from pain; and instead of opposing the useful to the aggreeable or the ornamental, have always declared that the useful means these, among other things. Yet the common herd, including the herd of writers, not only in newspapers and periodicals, but in books of weight and pretension, are perpetually falling into this shallow mistake. Having caught up the word utilitarian, while knowing nothing whatever about it but its sound, they habitually express by it the rejection, or the neglect, of pleasure in some of its forms; of beauty, of ornament, or of amusement. Nor is the term thus ignorantly misapplied solely in disparagement, but occasionally in compliment; as though it implied superiority to frivolity and the mere pleasures of the moment. And this perverted use is the only one in which the word is popularly known, and the one from which the new generation are acquiring their sole notion of its meaning, Those who introduced the word, but who had for many years discontinued it as a distinctive appellation, may well feel themselves called upon to resume it, if by doing so they can hope to contribute anything towards rescuing it from this utter degradation.

The creed which accepts as the foundation of morals, Utility, or the Greatest Happiness Principle, holds that actions are right in proportion as they tend to promote happiness, wrong as they tend to produce the reverse of happiness. By happiness is intended pleasure, and the absence of pain; by unhappiness, pain, and the privation of pleasure. To give a clear view of the moral standard set up by the theory, much more requires to be said; in particular, what things it includes in the ideas of pain and pleasure; and to what extent this is left an open question. But these supplementary explanations do not affect the theory of life on which this theory of morality is grounded—namely, that pleasure, and freedom from pain, are the only things desirable as ends; and that all desirable things (which are as numerous in the utilitarian as in any other scheme) are desirable either for the pleasure inherent in themselves, or as means to the promotion of pleasure and the prevention of pain.

Now, such a theory of life excites in many minds, and among them in some of the most estimable in feeling and purpose, inveterate dislike. To suppose that life has (as they express it) no higher end than pleasure— no better and nobler object of desire and pursuit—they designate as utterly mean and groveling; as a doctrine worthy only of swine, to whom the followers of Epicurus were, at a very early period, contemptuously likened; and modern holders of the doctrine are occasionally made the subject of equally polite comparisons by its German, French, and English assailants.

When thus attacked, the Epicureans have always answered, that it is not they, but their accusers, who represent human nature in a degrading light; since the accusation supposes human beings to be capable of no pleasures except those of which swine are capable. If this supposition were true, the charge could not be gainsaid, but would then be no longer an imputation; for if the sources of pleasure were precisely the same to human beings and to swine, the rule of life which is good enough for the one would be good enough for the other. The comparison of the Epicurean life to that of beasts is felt as degrading, precisely because a beast's pleasures do not satisfy a human being's conceptions of happiness. Human beings have faculties more elevated than the animal appetites, and when once made conscious of them, do not regard anything as happiness which does not include their gratification. I do not, indeed, consider the Epicureans to have been by any means faultless in drawing out their scheme of consequences from the utilitarian principle. To do this in any sufficient manner, many Stoic, as well as Christian elements require to be included. But there is no known Epicurean theory of life which does not assign to the pleasures of the intellect, of the feelings and imagination, and of the moral sentiments, a much higher value as pleasures than to those of mere sensation. It must be admitted, however, that utilitarian writers in general have placed the superiority of mental over bodily pleasures chiefly in the greater permanency, safety, uncostliness, etc., of the former—that is, in their circumstantial advantages rather than in their intrinsic nature. And on all these points utilitarians have fully proved their case; but they might have taken the other, and, as it may be called, higher ground, with entire consistency. It is quite compatible with the principle of utility to recognise the fact, that some *kinds* of pleasure are more desirable and more valuable than others. It would be absurd that while, in estimating all other things, quality is considered as well as quantity, the estimation of pleasures should be supposed to depend on quantity alone.

* * * * *

According to the Greatest Happiness Principle, as above explained, the ultimate end, with reference to and for the sake of which all other things are desirable (whether we are considering our own good or that of other people), is an existence exempt as far as possible from pain, and as rich as possible in enjoyments, both in point of quantity and quality; the test of quality, and the rule for measuring it against quantity, being the preference felt by those who in their opportunities of experience, to which must be added their habits of self-consciousness and self-observation, are best furnished with the means of comparison. This, being, according to the utilitarian opinion, the end of human action, is necessarily also the standard of morality; which may accordingly be defined, the rules and precepts for human conduct, by the observance of which an existence such as has been described might be, to the greatest extent possible, secured to all mankind; and not to them only, but, so far as the nature of things admits, to the whole sentient creation.

Against this doctrine, however, arises another class of objectors, who say that happiness, in any form, cannot be the rational purpose of human life and action; because, in the first place, it is unattainable: and they contemptuously ask, what right hast thou to be happy? a question which Mr. Carlyle clenches by the addition, What right, a short time ago, hadst thou even *to be?* Next, they say, that men can do *without* happiness; that all noble human beings have felt this, and could not have become noble but by learning the lesson of Entsagen, or renunciation; which lesson, thoroughly learnt and submitted to, they affirm to be the beginning and necessary condition of all virtue.

The first of these objections would go to the root of the matter were it well founded; for if no happiness is to be had at all by human beings, the attainment of it cannot be the end of morality, or of any rational conduct. Though, even in that case, something might still be said for the utilitarian theory; since utility includes not solely the pursuit of happiness, but the prevention or mitigation of unhappiness; and if the former aim be chimerical, there will be all the greater scope and more imperative need for the latter, so long at least as mankind think fit to live, and do not take refuge in the simultaneous act of suicide recommended under certain conditions by Novalis. When, however, it is thus positively asserted to be impossible that human life should be happy, the assertion, if not something like a verbal quibble, is at least an exaggeration. If by happiness be meant a continuity of highly pleasurable excitement, it is evident enough that this is impossible. A state of exalted pleasure lasts only moments, or in some cases, and with some intermissions, hours or days, and is the occasional brilliant flash of enjoyment, not its permanent and steady flame. Of this the philosophers who have taught that happiness is the end of life were as fully aware as those who taunt them. The happiness which they meant was not a life of rapture; but moments of such, in an existence made up of few and transitory pains, many and various pleasures, with a decided predominance of the active over the passive, and having as the foundation of the whole, not to expect more from life than it is capable of bestowing. A life thus composed, to those who have been fortunate enough to obtain it, has always appeared worthy of the name of happiness. And such an existence is even now the lot of many, during some considerable portion of their lives The present wretched education, and wretched social arrangements, are the only real hindrance to its being attainable by almost all.

The objectors perhaps may doubt whether human beings, if taught to consider happiness as the end of life, would be satisfied with such a moderate share of it. But great numbers of mankind have been satisfied with much less. The main constituents of a satisfied life appear to be two, either of which by itself is often found sufficient for the purpose: tranquillity, and excitement. With much tranquillity, many find that they can be content with very little pleasure: with much excitement, many can reconcile themselves to a considerable quantity of pain. There is assuredly no inherent impossibility in enabling even the mass of mankind to unite both; since the two are so far from being incompatible that they are in natural alliance, the prolongation of either being a preparation for, and exciting a wish for, the other. It is only those in whom indolence amounts to a vice, that do not desire excitement after an interval of repose: it is only those in whom the need of excitement is a disease, that feel the tranquillity which follows excitement dull and insipid, instead of pleasurable in direct proportion to the excitement which preceded it. When people who are tolerably fortunate in their outward lot do not find in life sufficient enjoyment to make it valuable to them, the cause generally is, caring for nobody but themselves. To those who have neither public nor private affections, the excitements of life are much curtailed, and in any case dwindle in value as the time approaches when all selfish interests must be terminated by death: while those who leave after them objects of personal affection, and especially those who have also cultivated a fellow-feeling with the collective interests of mankind, retain as lively an interest in life on the eve of death as in the vigour of youth and health. Next to selfishness, the principal causes which makes life unsatisfactory is want of mental cultivation. A cultivated mind—I do not mean that of a philosopher, but any mind to which the fountains of knowledge have been opened, and which has been taught, in any tolerable degree, to exercise its faculties—finds sources of inexhaustible interest in all that surrounds it; in the objects of nature, the achievements of art, the imaginations of poetry, the incidents of history, the ways of mankind, past and present, and their prospects in the future. It is possible, indeed, to become indifferent to all this, and that too without having exhausted a thousandth part of it; but only when one has had from the beginning no moral or human interest in these things, and has sought in them only the gratification of curiosity.

Now there is absolutely no reason in the nature of things why an amount of mental culture sufficient to give an intelligent interest in these objects of contemplation, should not be the inheritance of every one born in a civilised country. As little is there an inherent necessity that any human being should be a selfish egotist, devoid of every feeling or care but those which centre in his own miserable individuality. Something far superior to this is sufficiently common even now, to give ample earnest of what the human species may be made. Genuine private affections, and a sincere interest in the public good, are possible, though in unequal degrees, to every rightly brought up human being. In a world in which there is so much to interest, so much to enjoy, and so much also to correct and improve, every one who has this moderate amount of moral and intellectual requisites is capable of an existence which may be called enviable; and unless such a person, through bad laws, or subjection to the will of others, is denied the liberty to use the sources of happiness within his reach, he will not fail to find this enviable existence, if he escape the positive evils of life, the great sources of physical and mental suffering—such as indigence, disease, and the unkindness, worthlessness, or premature loss of objects of affection. The main stress of the problem lies, therefore, in the contest with these calamities, from which it is a rare good fortune entirely to escape; which, as things now are, cannot be obviated, and often cannot be in any material degree mitigated. Yet no one whose opinion deserves a moment's consideration can doubt that most of the great positive evils of the world are in themselves removable, and will, if human affairs continue to improve, be in the end reduced within narrow limits. Poverty, in any sense implying suffering, may be completely extinguished by the wisdom of society, combined with the good sense and providence of individuals. Even that most intractable of enemies, disease, may be indefinitely reduced in dimensions by good physical and moral education, and proper control of noxious influences; while the progress of science holds out a promise for the future of still more direct conquests over this detestable foe. And every advance in that direction relieves us from some, not only of the chances which cut short our own lives but, what concerns us still more, which deprive us of those in whom our happiness is wrapt up. As for vicissitudes of fortune, and other disappointments connected with worldly circumstances, these are principally the effect either of gross imprudence, of ill-regulated desires, or of bad or imperfect social institutions. All the grand sources, in short, of human suffering are in a great degree, many of them almost entirely, conquerable by human care and effort; and though their removal is grievously slow—though a long succession of generations will perish in the breach before the conquest is completed, and this world becomes all that, if will and knowledge were not wanting, it might easily be made— yet every mind sufficiently intelligent and generous to bear a part, how- ever small and unconspicuous, in the endeavour, will draw a noble enjoy- ment from the contest itself, which he would not for any bribe in the form of selfish indulgence consent to be without.

And this leads to the true estimation of what is said by the objectors concerning the possibility, and the obligation, of learning to do without happiness. Unquestionably it is possible to do without happiness; it is done involuntarily by nineteen-twentieths of mankind, even in those parts of our present world which are least deep in barbarism; and it often has to be done voluntarily by the hero or the martyr, for the sake of something which he prizes more than his individual happiness. But this something, what is it, unless the happiness of others, or some of the requisites of happiness? It is noble to be capable of resigning entirely one's own portion of happiness, or chances of it: but, after all, this self-sacrifice must be for some end; it is not its own end; and if we are told that its end is not happiness, but virtue, which is better than happiness, I ask, would the sacrifice be made if the hero or martyr did not believe that it would earn for others immunity from similar sacrifices? Would it be made if he thought that his renunciation of happiness for himself would produce no fruit for any of his fellow creatures, but to make their lot like his, and place them also in the condition of persons who have renounced happi- ness? All honour to those who can abnegate for themselves the personal enjoyment of life, when by such renunciation they contribute worthily to increase the amount of happiness in the world; but he who does it, or professes to do it, for any other purpose, is no more deserving of admiration than the ascetic mounted on his pillar. He may be an inspirit- ing proof of what men *can* do, but assuredly not an example of what they *should*.

Though it is only in a very imperfect state of the world's arrangements that any one can best serve the happiness of others by the absolute sacrifice of his own, yet so long as the world is in that imperfect state, I fully acknowledge that the readiness to make such a sacrifice is the highest virtue which can be found in man. I will add, that in this condition of the world, paradoxical as the assertion may be, the conscious ability to do without happiness gives the best prospect of realising such happiness as is attainable. For nothing except that consciousness can raise a person above the chances of life, by making him feel that, let fate and fortune do their worst, they have not power to subdue him: which, once felt, frees him from excess of anxiety concerning the evils of life, and enables him, like many a Stoic in the worst times of the Roman Empire, to cultivate in tranquillity the sources of satisfaction accessible to him, without concerning himself about the uncertainty of their duration, any more than about their inevitable end.

Meanwhile, let utilitarians never cease to claim the morality of self devotion as a possession which belongs by as good a right to them, as either to the Stoic or to the Transcendentalist. The utilitarian morality does recognise in human beings the power of sacrificing their own greatest good for the good of others. It only refuses to admit that the sacrifice is itself a good. A sacrifice which does not increase, or tend to increase, the sum total of happiness, it considers as wasted. The only self-renunciation which it applauds, is devotion to the happiness, or to some of the means of happiness, of others; either of mankind collectively, or of individuals within the limits imposed by the collective interests of mankind.

I must again repeat, what the assailants of utilitarianism seldom have the justice to acknowledge, that the happiness which forms the utilitarian standard of what is right in conduct, is not the agent's own happiness, but that of all concerned. As between his own happiness and that of others, utilitarianism requires him to be as strictly impartial as a disinterested and benevolent spectator. In the golden rule of Jesus of Nazareth, we read the complete spirit of the ethics of utility. To do as you would be done by, and to love your neighbour as yourself, constitute the ideal perfection of utilitarian morality. As the means of making the nearest approach to this ideal, utility would enjoin, first, that laws and social arrangements should place the happiness, or (as speaking practically it may be called) the interest, of every individual, as nearly as possible in harmony with the interest of the whole; and secondly, that education and opinion, which have so vast a power over human character, should so use that power as to establish in the mind of every individual an indissoluble association between his own happiness and the good of the whole; especially between his own happiness and the practice of such modes of conduct, negative and positive, as regard for the universal happiness prescribes; so that not only he may be unable to conceive the possibility of happiness to himself, consistently with conduct opposed to the general good, but also that a direct impulse to promote the general good may be in every individual one of the habitual motives of action, and the sentiments connected therewith may fill a large and prominent place in every human being's sentient existence. If the impugners of the utilitarian morality represented it to their own minds in this its true character, I know not what recommendation possessed by any other morality they could possibly affirm to be wanting to it; what more beautiful or more exalted developments of human nature any other ethical system can be supposed to foster, or what springs of action, not accessible to the utilitarian, such systems rely on for giving effect to their mandates.

* * * * *

Chapter V. On the Connection between Justice and Utility

In all ages of speculation, one of the strongest obstacles to the reception of the doctrine that Utility or Happiness is the criterion of right and wrong, has been drawn from the idea of Justice. The powerful sentiment, and apparently clear perception, which that word recalls with a rapidity and certainty resembling an instinct, have seemed to the majority of thinkers to point to an inherent quality in things; to show that the Just must have an existence in Nature as something absolute, generically distinct from every variety of the Expedient, and, in idea, opposed to it, though (as is commonly acknowledged) never, in the long run, disjoined from it in fact.

In the case of this, as of our other moral sentiments, there is no necessary connection between the question of its origin, and that of its binding force. That a feeling is bestowed on us by Nature, does not necessarily legitimate all its promptings. The feeling of justice might be a peculiar instinct, and might yet require, like our other instincts, to be controlled and enlightened by a higher reason. If we have intellectual instincts, leading us to judge in a particular way, as well as animal instincts that prompt us to act in a particular way, there is no necessity that the former should be more infallible in their sphere than the latter in theirs: it may as well happen that wrong judgments are occasionally suggested by those, as wrong actions by these. But though it is one thing to believe that we have natural feelings of justice, and another to acknowledge them as an ultimate criterion of conduct, these two opinions are very closely connected in point of fact. Mankind are always predisposed to believe that any subjective feeling, not otherwise accounted for, is a revelation of some objective reality. Our present object is to determine whether the reality, to which the feeling of justice corresponds, is one which needs any such special revelation; whether the justice or injustice of an action is a thing intrinsically peculiar, and distinct from all its other qualities, or only a combination of certain of those qualities, presented under a peculiar aspect. For the purpose of this inquiry it is practically important to consider whether the feeling itself, of justice and injustice, is *sui generis* like our sensations of colour and taste, or a derivative feeling, formed by a combination of others. And this it is the more essential to examine, as people are in general willing enough to allow, that objectively the dictates of Justice coincide with a part of the field of General Expediency; but inasmuch as the subjective mental feeling of Justice is different from that which commonly attaches to simple expediency, and, except in the extreme cases of the latter, is far more imperative in its demands, people find it difficult to see, in Justice, only a particular kind or branch of general utility, and think that its superior binding force requires a totally different origin.

To throw light upon this question, it is necessary to attempt to ascertain what is the distinguishing character of justice, or of injustice: what is the quality, or whether there is any quality, attributed in common to all modes of conduct designated as unjust (for justice, like many other moral attributes, is best defined by its opposite), and distinguishing them from such modes of conduct as are disapproved, but without having that particular epithet of disapprobation applied to them. If in everything which men are accustomed to characterise as just or unjust, some one common attribute or collection of attributes is always present, we may judge whether this particular attribute or combination of attributes would be capable of gathering round it a sentiment of that peculiar character and intensity by virtue of the general laws of our emotional constitution, or whether the sentiment is inexplicable, and requires to be regarded as a special provision of Nature. If we find the former to be the case, we shall, in resolving this question, have resolved also the main problem: if the latter, we shall have to seek for some other mode of investigating it.

To find the common attributes of a variety of objects, it is necessary to begin by surveying the objects themselves in the concrete. Let us therefore advert successively to the various modes of action, and arrangements of human affairs, which are classed, by universal or widely spread opinion, as Just or as Unjust. The things well known to excite the sentiments associated with those names are of a very multifarious character. I shall pass them rapidly in review, without studying any particular arrangement.

In the first place, it is mostly considered unjust to deprive any one of his personal liberty, his property, or any other thing which belongs to him by law. Here, therefore, is one instance of the application of the terms just and unjust in a perfectly definite sense, namely, that it is just to respect, unjust to violate, the *legal rights* of any one. But this judgment admits of several exceptions, arising from the other forms in which the notions of justice and injustice present themselves. For example, the person who suffers the deprivation may (as the phrase is) have *forfeited* the rights which he is so deprived of: a case to which we shall return presently. But also,

Secondly; the legal rights of which he is deprived, may be rights which *ought* not to have belonged to him; in other words, the law which confers on him these rights, may be a bad law. When it is so, or when (which is the same thing for our purpose) it is supposed to be so, opinions will differ as to the justice or injustice of infringing it. Some maintain that no law, however bad, ought to be disobeyed by an individual citizen; that his opposition to it, if shown at all, should only be shown in endeavouring to get it altered by competent authority. This opinion (which condemns many of the most illustrious benefactors of mankind, and would often protect pernicious institutions against the only weapons which, in the state of things existing at the time, have any chance of succeeding against them) is defended, by those who hold it, on grounds of expediency; principally on that of the importance, to the common interest of mankind, of maintaining inviolate the sentiment of submission to law. Other persons, again, hold the directly contrary opinion, that any law, judged to be bad, may blamelessly be disobeyed, even though it be not judged to be unjust, but only inexpedient; while others would confine the licence of disobedience to the case of unjust laws: but again, some say, that all laws which are inexpedient are unjust; since every law imposes some restriction on the natural liberty of mankind, which restriction is an injustice, unless legitimated by tending to their good. Among these diversities of opinion, it seems to be universally admitted that there may be unjust laws, and that law, consequently, is not the ultimate criterion of justice, but may give to one person a benefit, or impose on another an evil, which justice condemns. When, however, a law is thought to be unjust, it seems always to be regarded as being so in the same way in which a breach of law is unjust, namely, by infringing somebody's right; which, as it cannot in this case be a legal right, receives a different appellation, and is called a moral right. We may say, therefore, that a second case of injustice consists in taking or withholding from any person that to which he has a *moral right.*

Thirdly, it is universally considered just that each person should obtain that (whether good or evil) which he *deserves;* and unjust that he should obtain a good, or be made to undergo an evil, which he does not deserve. That is, perhaps, the clearest and most emphatic form in which the idea of justice is conceived by the general mind. As it involves the notion of desert, the question arises, what constitutes desert? Speaking in a general way, a person is understood to deserve good if he does right, evil if he does wrong; and in a more particular sense, to deserve good from those to whom he does or has done good, and evil from those to whom he does or has done evil. The precept of returning good for evil has never been regarded as a case of the fulfilment of justice, but as one in which the claims of justice are waived, in obedience to other considerations.

Fourthly, it is confessedly unjust to *break faith* with any one: to violate an engagement, either express or implied, or disappoint expectations raised by our own conduct, at least if we have raised those expectations knowingly and voluntarily. Like the other obligations of justice already spoken of, this one is not regarded as absolute, but as capable of being overruled by a stronger obligation of justice on the other side; or by such conduct on the part of the person concerned as is deemed to absolve us from our obligation to him, and to constitute a *forfeiture* of the benefit which he has been led to expect.

Fifthly, it is, by universal admission, inconsistent with justice to be *partial;* to show favour or preference to one person over another, in matters to which favour and perference do not properly apply. Impartiality, however, does not seem to be regarded as a duty in itself, but rather as instrumental to some other duty; for it is admitted that favour and preference are not always censurable, and indeed the cases in which they are condemned are rather the exception than the rule. A person would be more likely to be blamed than applauded for giving his family or friends no superiority in good offices over strangers, when he could do so without violating any other duty; and no one thinks it unjust to seek one person in preference to another as a friend, connection, or companion. Impartiality where rights are concerned is of course obligatory, but this is involved in the more general obligation of giving to every one his right. A tribunal, for example, must be impartial, because it is bound to award, without regard to any other consideration, a disputed object to the one of two parties who has the right to it. There are other cases in which impartiality means, being solely influenced by desert; as with those who, in the capacity of judges, preceptors, or parents, administer reward and punishment as such. There are cases, again, in which it means, being solely influenced by consideration for the public interest; as in making a selection among candidates for a government employment. Impartiality, in short, as an obligation of justice, may be said to mean, being exclusively influenced by the considerations which it is supposed ought to influence the particular case in hand; and resisting the solicitation of any motives which prompt to conduct different from what those considerations would dictate.

Nearly allied to the idea of impartiality is that of *equality;* which often enters as a component part both into the conception of justice and into the practice of it, and, in the eyes of many persons, constitutes its essence. But in this, still more than in any other case, the notion of justice varies in different persons, and always conforms in its variations to their notion of utility. Each person maintains that equality is the dictate of justice, except where he thinks that expediency requires inequality. The justice of giving equal protection to the rights of all, is maintained by those who support the most outrageous inequality in the rights themselves. Even in slave countries it is theoretically admitted that the rights of the slave, such as they are, ought to be as sacred as those of the master; and that a tribunal which fails to enforce them with equal strictness is wanting in justice; while, at the same time, institutions which leave to the slave scarcely any rights to enforce, are not deemed unjust, because they are not deemed inexpedient. Those who think that utility requires distinctions of rank, do not consider it unjust that riches and social privileges should be unequally dispensed; but those who think this inequality inexpedient, think it unjust also. Whoever thinks that government is necessary, sees no injustice in as much inequality as is constituted by giving to the magistrate powers not granted to other people. Even among those who hold levelling doctrines, there are as many questions of justice as there are differences of opinion about expediency. Some Communists consider it unjust that the produce of the labour of the community should be shared on any other principle than that of exact equality; others think it just that those should receive most whose wants are greatest; while others hold that those who work harder, or who produce more, or whose services are more valuable to the community, may justly claim a larger quota in the division of the produce. And the sense of natural justice may be plausibly appealed to in behalf of every one of these opinions.

Among so many diverse applications of the term Justice, which yet is not regarded as ambiguous, it is a matter of some difficulty to seize the mental link which holds them together, and on which the moral sentiment adhering to the term essentially depends. Perhaps, in this embarrassment, some help may be derived from the history of the word, as indicated by its etymology.

*   *   *   *   *

To recapitulate: the idea of justice supposes two things; a rule of conduct, and a sentiment which sanctions the rule. The first must be supposed common to all mankind, and intended for their good. The other (the sentiment) is a desire that punishment may be suffered by those who infringe the rule. There is involved, in addition, the conception of some definite person who suffers by the infringement; whose rights (to use the expression appropriated to the case) are violated by it. And the sentiment of justice appears to me to be, the animal desire to repel or retaliate a hurt or damage to oneself, or to those with whom one sympathises, widened so as to include all persons, by the human capacity of enlarged sympathy, and the human conception of intelligent self-interest. From the latter elements, the feeling derives its morality; from the former, its peculiar impressiveness, and energy of self-assertion.

I have, throughout, treated the idea of a *right* residing in the injured person, and violated by the injury, not as a separate element in the composition of the idea and sentiment, but as one of the forms in which the other two elements clothe themselves. These elements are, a hurt to some assignable person or persons on the one hand, and a demand for punishment on the other. An examination of our own minds, I think, will show. that these two things include all that we mean when we speak of violation of a right. When we call anything a person's right, we mean that he has a valid claim on society to protect him in the possession of it, either by the force of law, or by that of education and opinion. If he has what we consider a sufficient claim, on whatever account, to have something guaranteed to him by society, we say that he has a right to it. If we desire to prove that anything does not belong to him by right, we think this done as soon as it is admitted that society ought not to take measures for securing it to him, but should leave him to chance, or to his own exertions. Thus, a person is said to have a right to what he can earn in fair professional competition; because society ought not to allow any other person to hinder him from endeavouring to earn in that manner as much as he can. But he has not a right to three hundred a-year, though he may happen to be earning it; because society is not called on to provide that he shall earn that sum. On the contrary, if he owns ten thousand pounds three per cent. stock, he *has* a right to three hundred a-year; because society has come under an obligation to provide him with an income of that amount.

To have a right, then, is, I conceive, to have something which society ought to defend me in the possession of. If the objector goes on to ask, why it ought? I can give him no other reason than general utility. If that expression does not seem to convey a sufficient feeling of the strength of the obligation, nor to account for the peculiar energy of the feeling, it is because there goes to the composition of the sentiment, not a rational only, but also an animal element, the thirst for retaliation; and this thirst derives its intensity, as well as its moral justification, from the extraordinarily important and impressive kind of utility which is concerned. The interest involved is that of security, to every one's feelings the most vital of all interests. All other earthly benefits are needed by one person, not needed by another; and many of them can, if necessary, be cheerfully foregone, or replaced by something else; but security no human being can possibly do without; on it we depend for all our immunity from evil, and for the whole value of all and every good, beyond the passing moment; since nothing but the gratification of the instant could be of any worth to us, if we could be deprived of anything the next instant by whoever was momentarily stronger than ourselves. Now this most indispensable of all necessaries, after physical nutriment, cannot be had, unless the machinery for providing it is kept unintermittedly in active play. Our notion, therefore, of the claim we have on our fellow-creatures to join in making safe for us the very groundwork of our existence, gathers feelings around it so much more intense than those concerned in any of the more common cases of utility, that the difference in degree (as is often the case in psychology) becomes a real difference in kind. The claim assumes that character of absoluteness, that apparent infinity, and incommensurability with all other considerations, which constitute the distinction between the feeling of right and wrong and that of ordinary expediency and inexpediency. The feelings concerned are so powerful, and we count so positively on finding a responsive feeling in others (all being alike interested), that *ought* and *should* grow into *must*, and recognised indispensability becomes a moral necessity, analogous to physical, and often not inferior to it in binding force.

* * * * *

JOHN ELLIOTT CAIRNES

(1824–1875)

John Elliott Cairnes was an Irish economist and a member of the bar. He was graduated from Trinity College, Dublin, and spent a considerable part of his life teaching political economy in various Irish and English institutions.

The more important works of Cairnes were "Character and Logical Method of Political Economy," a series of lectures previously delivered (published in 1857, revised in 1875); "The Slave Power," an interesting economic interpretation of history and a powerful defense of the Northern cause at a very critical time in American history (1862, revised in 1863); and "Essays in Political Economy Theoretical and Applied" (1873). The chief work of Cairnes was "Political Economy" or "Some Leading Principles of Political Economy Newly Expounded" (1874), from which work the following selections have been taken.

Cairnes may be classified as the last of the classicists. Although the subtitle of his principal work contains the adjective "newly expounded," he was a defender of the old rather than an expounder of the new. The chief mission of Cairnes was that of a stanch defender of the faith. Even after his great master, John Stuart Mill, had recanted the wage fund theory, Cairnes continued its defense and sought its resurrection. Failing to see the new approach of his contemporary Jevons, Cairnes continued along the path of average costs of production and ignored marginal utility. To Cairnes, values were costs of production and costs were labor pains. In pushing his analysis of the failure of monetary expenses to be proportionate to human sacrifice, Cairnes made his great discovery of noncompeting groups.

JOHN ELLIOTT CAIRNES

SELECTIONS FROM "POLITICAL ECONOMY"

CHAPTER II. SUPPLY AND DEMAND

Section 6

I have so far spoken of Demand and Supply as general facts, as related not to particular commodities or services, but to commodities and services in general. I proceed now to consider them as they stand related to particular commodities and services. And here we must in the first place note that that fundamental identity and mutual interdependence which have been found to characterize the phenomena in the light in which we have hitherto regarded them, are no longer observable when they are considered with reference to particular commodities. Thus, as I have shown, it is impossible for the general demand of a community to increase or diminish save through a corresponding increase or diminution of the general supply of commodities in that community; but it is perfectly possible that the demand for a particular commodity or service should increase or diminish, the supply undergoing no corresponding change; and, as every one will recognize, such failure of correspondence between Supply and Demand is the most common of all occurrences. In truth, it but rarely happens that the supply of any commodity remains for any length of time in perfect accordance with the demand for it. What we find is a pretty constant state of fluctuation, the demand sometimes in excess of the supply; the supply sometimes in excess of the demand; and the alterations in the relation indicated by parallel alterations in the prices of the commodity so affected.

I have spoken of supply corresponding with, or being greater or less than, demand in the case of a given commodity. There is no expression in more frequent use in commercial and economic discussion; and it is probable that most people will think that it stands in need of no elucidation. But the slightest reflection will show that its meaning is by no means so clear as it might at first sight be considered. What is meant by the supply of a given commodity being equal to the demand for it? The demand varies with the price; and so does the supply. It is evident, therefore, that, to give meaning to our assertion, it must be understood as made with reference to some assumed price; but what price? This is a point which is not at once apparent.

Again, supposing this difficulty got over, and that we have settled at what price Demand and Supply are to be taken, demand at a given price may be measured either by the quantity of purchasing power offered, or by the quantity of the commodity demanded. Which standard are we to adopt? I have already stated my view as to the proper sense of "demand"; nor do I see any necessity for departing in this context from the meaning I have contended for. According to that view, as Supply would be measured by the quantity of the commodity offered; and the "correspondence" (which I think would be a better word than "equality") of Supply with Demand at a given price would mean such a state of Demand and Supppy as would result, on the one hand, in the absorption of the purchasing power forth-coming at this price by the supply at the same price; and, on the other hand, in the absorption of the supply by the purchasing power; while the non-correspondence of Supply and Demand would mean the existence of an unsatisfied residuum on either side. This, I confess, is the sense of the phrase which I should myself, on scientific grounds, prefer. I have admitted, however, that there are occasions in which "demand" may conveniently be employed in other senses; and this perhaps is one of them. At all events it is certain that, understanding Demand in this context as measured by the quantity demanded, the result will not be affected by the change of standard. When Supply corresponds with Demand in the one sense, it will correspond with it in the other; and as the latter, that is to say Demand as measured by quantity demanded, is perhaps the more familiar conception where the problem has to do with particular commodities, it will on the whole, perhaps, be more convenient to adopt this sense for the purposes of this particular discussion. I shall therefore understand equality or correspondence of Demand and Supply at a given price, when particular commodities are in question, as meaning equality or correspondence of quantity demanded with quantity supplied at that price.

But we have got to determine what is the price assumed or contemplated in statements regarding the equality or inequality of Supply and Demand. To resolve this point, two sorts of such statements must be considered. We may assert the equality or inequality of Demand and Supply either with reference to a particular occasion, or with reference to a continuing state of things. We may say, for example, that the demand for wheat exceeded the supply in a particular market; or we may say that the demand for meat has from some time exceeded, and is likely for some time longer to exceed, the supply of that article. In the former case, it seems to be, the price assumed, so far as people speak with distinct meaning, would always be the price current in the particular market; and the statement would mean that there were people in that market who at the current price would have purchased more wheat had it been at that price obtainable. I am aware that, in assuming the possibility of such an occurrence as a market price which does not equalize Supply and Demand, I am putting myself in conflict with a celebrated theory.

I hope, however, afterward to justify this boldness. For the moment I assume that the price current in the particular market is the price with reference to which statements of the kind we are considering are made; and common language certainly presupposes the possibility of a divergence of Demand and Supply at this price. But how with regard to assertions of the other kind indicated, where we declare that, as a continuing state of things, the demand for a commodity is in excess of the supply of it—shall we say, following the analogy of the explanation just given, that the price here assumed is the price current during the period to which the remark applies; and that the meaning is that the demand at that price has been and is likely to be in excess of the supply? If we attempt to deal with any actual case we shall find that this explanation will not serve us. For example, most persons acquainted with the present state of the iron trade would say that the demand for iron at the present time—meaning, not in this or that market, but in the country generally and over a period of some duration—is greatly in excess of the supply, and would point to the advance in price as evidence of this. Now it is certain that, in the opinion of those most competent to form an opinion, in the opinion of dealers and speculators in the article, the demand for iron in the country at the present time is not in excess of the supply of it *at existing prices;* for did they think so, they would at once by purchases raise the price beyond its present level. In truth, the precise function which such persons perform is that of adapting demand to supply by acting on price; and, however the adaptation may fail in particular markets, it is impossible that, as a phenomenon of some duration, the demand at existing prices should remain, and be known to be, in excess of the supply. How, then, are we to deal with the assertion which undoubtedly would be made by those very persons? It is perhaps not improbable that most of those who make it have not very clearly defined their meaning. Still it would be unreasonable to assume that, where so many people, experts in the matter in hand, concur in making the same statement, their assertion is absolutely without meaning. I shall certainly not presume to find a meaning for any one, but I venture to lay down this proposition, that, in order to render such statements as those of which I have given examples at once significant and true, demand must be understood as existing at some price other than that actually prevailing in the markets; and if I am asked to say what that price is, I answer, the "normal price"—the price which, in the absence of disturbing causes, people consider would be the price of the commodity. Accordingly, the sense in which I understand statements of the kind under consideration, which apply not to particular markets but to a state of things for some time in existence, is as expressing the result of a comparison between demand taken *as it would exist* at the normal price, and supply either such as it would be at that same price, or such as it actually is.

Thus understood, such statements become significant; and, if founded on knowledge of the facts in question, convey information of a really important kind. The result, then, of this verbal but necessary discussion may be thus summed up:

1st. Supply and Demand, when spoken of with reference to particular commodities, must, if our statements are to be significant, be understood to mean Supply and Demand at a given price; the comparison of Supply and Demand at the price, being made by comparing the quantity of the commodity supplied with the amount of purchasing power offered, or with the quantity of the commodity demanded. For considerations of practical convenience, the latter measure of Demand is employed in this particular discussion.

2d. Where statements respecting the supply and demand of particular commodities have reference to particular markets, the price assumed as that at which Demand and Supply are compared is the price current in that market.

3d. Where such statements have reference to the country at large and to a continuing state of things, then the price assumed is that at which Demand is measured either at this or at the actual price. The comparison instituted is thus between Demand at the normal price, and Supply either at the normal or at actual prices.

Section 7

The meaning of this part of our phraseology being thus ascertained, I proceed to lay down what seems to me the fundamental law of Demand and Supply considered in connection with particular commodities. It is as follows: The supply of a commodity always tends to adapt itself to the demand at the normal price. I may here say briefly, that by the normal price of a commodity I mean that price which suffices, and no more than suffices, to yield to the producers what is considered to be the average and usual remuneration on such sacrifices as they undergo; and the statement is that the supply of each commodity tends to adapt itself to the demand at this price. That it does so is the direct consequence of the motives which induce people to engage in productive industry, and which attract them so far as circumstances permit, toward those occupations which offer the largest rewards in proportion to the sacrifices undergone. It follows from this that, where the price of a commodity is above the normal level, and where consequently the producers are reaping more than average rewards, more producers will be drawn to that employment, and the supply of the commodity will be increased. But the increase of supply, by the competition for sales, will tend to lower price, and thus to bring it down toward the normal level. If the increase of supply is not sufficient to reduce the market price quite to the normal level, then, under the influence of the same industrial motives, supply will be further increased; and the process will go on till this result is accomplished. On the other hand, if the stimulus to production carry the movement too far and price fall below the normal level, motives of the opposite kind will at once come into play to curtail production, and the price will rise till the normal level be once more reached. Such is the law of Supply and Demand in relation to particular commodities: it is described by Adam Smith under the figure of a gravitation of market toward natural price; but, however described, it is fundamental in this part of our subject, and is the constant assumption running through all reasonings which have to do with value and price. It is not, however, necessary to advert to its bearings further at present; these will sufficiently appear in the course of the following discussions.

I recapitulate briefly the results of the present chapter:

I. Demand and Supply, considered as general facts, are not independent phenomena, but essentially the same phenomena regarded from different points of view; consequently general Demand can not increase or diminish, except in constant relation with general Supply. All notions and doctrines therefore that proceed upon the contrary assumption are unfounded and fallacious.

II. Demand and Supply, considered with reference to particular commodities, may increase or diminish (in the sense explained) in relation to each other; but in all their mutations they obey this law: Supply always tends to adapt itself to Demand at the normal price of the commodity.

Chapter III. Normal Value

Section 5

It seems to me that a sufficient case has now been made out to justify an attempt at a fresh exposition of the doctrine of Cost of Production. I therefore proceed to submit to the reader that view of it which such reflection as I have been able to give to the subject has led me to form.

And here I must, in the first place, insist that cost means sacrifice, and can not, without risk of hopelessly confusing ideas, be identified with anything that is not sacrifice. It represents what man parts with in the barter between him and nature, which must be kept eternally distinct from the return made by nature on that payment. This is the essential nature of cost; and the problem of cost of production as bearing on the theory of value is to ascertain how far and in what way the payment thus made by man to nature in productive industry determines or otherwise influences the exchange value of the products which result. To find an answer to this question we need not go beyond that fundamental principle of conduct which leads men to seek their ends by the easiest and shortest means. The end of engaging in industry is the acquisition of

wealth; and the means, self-denial, toil, forethought, vigilance. The
problem of industry, is therefore, to attain wealth at the least expenditure
of those bodily and mental exertions—or, as we may say, at the least
sacrifice or cost. And the law of cost of production as governing value, is
merely the practical consequence and outcome of the pursuit of wealth
under this condition.

In order to perceive this, it is only necessary to keep steadily in view
the following facts: First, that under the influence of the motive just
indicated, men, in selecting their occupations, whether as laborers or as
capitalists, will, *so far as they have the power of choice*, select those which,
in return for a given sacrifice, yield, or promise to yield, the largest
rewards; and secondly, the fact that, under a system of separation of
employments, industrial rewards consist for each producer, or, more
properly, for each group of producers, employed on a given work in the
value of the commodities which result from their exertions. I say in the
value of the commodities, not in the commodities themselves; for it is
not always that the man who is engaged in industry needs the particular
commodity on which his own exertions are bestowed, and it is seldom that
he needs more than at most an insignificant quantity of what he produces; consequently his remuneration must come, not from the direct but
from the indirect results of his labors—from those things, whatever they
are, which the commodity he produces enables him by sale and purchase
to command—in other words, from its value. Given the productiveness
of a man's industry, this alone will not enable us to determine the amount
of his remuneration. In order to do this, we must further know the proportions in which what he produces will exchange for what he wants—that
is to say, for the articles of his consumption. The value of the product
resulting from industry forms thus the source from which, under the
actual state of things, industry is remunerated. Nor is this conclusion
invalidated by the fact that, under the industrial organization prevailing in
this and other civilized countries, the laborer commonly receives his reward
in the form of wages advanced by the capitalist before the product is completed; since what he receives is subsequently recouped to the capitalist,
the sum being drawn from *the value of the product* from which the remuneration of all concerned in the creation of that product ultimately comes.
Wages and profits in each branch of industry are thus derived from the
value of the commodities proceeding from that branch of industry, and,
as (with the exception of the case where rent is also an element in the
value of commodities—a case which, those acquainted with the economic
theory of rent will perceive, does not affect the general argument) wages
and profits also absorb the whole of that value, it follows that, other
things being the same, the aggregate of wages and profits received by
any given group of producers will always vary with the value of the
aggregate of commodities which they produce. Where wages and profits,

therefore, in different occupations are in proportion to the sacrifices undergone, the value of the commodities proceeding from those occupations will also be in proportion to the same sacrifices, that is to say, the commodities will exchange in proportion to their costs of production. Now wages and profits will be in proportion to the sacrifices undergone wherever, and only so far as, competition prevails among producers—wherever, and so far only as, laborers and capitalists have an effective choice in selecting among the various occupations presented to them in the industrial field. Give them this effective choice, and the correspondence of remuneration to sacrifice, not indeed in the every act of production, but as a permanent and continuing state of things, is secured by the most active and constant of human motives. Each competitor, aiming at the largest reward in return for his sacrifices, will be drawn toward the occupations which happen at the time to be the best remunerated; while he will equally be repelled from those in which the remuneration is below the average level. The supply of products proceeding from the better paid employments will thus be increased, and that from the less remunerative reduced, until supply, acting on price corrects the inequality, and brings remuneration into proportion with the sacrifices undergone. Competition, therefore, is at once the security for the correspondence of industrial remuneration with sacrifice, and also, and because it is so, the security for the correspondence of the values of commodities with the costs of their production.

The indispensable condition to the action of cost of production as the regulator of normal values is thus the existence of an effective competition among those engaged in industrial pursuits; and the point to which we have now to turn our attention is the extent to which such effective competition is actually realized in industrial communities. Confining our attention for the present to England, we find competition here active and widely prevalent. In trade, as distinguished from industry, I mean in the buying and selling of commodities as distinguished from their production, it may be said to be universal and unlimited. Every one is at liberty, and not only at liberty, but in general has the practical power, to sell his commodity. whatever it may be, in any market in the country. Again, every one, speaking broadly, is free, so far as the law is concerned, to engage in any industrial pursuit he pleases, from hedging and ditching up to the learned professions. But for the present purpose something more than this is necessary. Not only must there be for dealers the right and power of selling the commodity where they please, and for workmen the legal right of admission to whatever occupation each prefers, but there must be for laborers and capitalists respectively, the practical power of employing their labor and capital in whatever direction each may please—in a word, an effective choice in deciding on the destination of the instrument of which they have each to dispose. It matters not what the obstacle may be to the effectiveness of the choice, whether law, ignorance, or poverty—if there be an obstacle, if the producer can not pass freely from the less to the more lucrative occupation, competition is defeated, so far as regards the requirements of the law of cost, since there can be no security under such circumstance that remuneration shall be brought into correspondence with sacrifice. This is the sort of competition through which cost of production, as a regulator of value, works; and the question is, How far does competition in this sense prevail in this and other industrial communities?

There is a school of reasoners who will not hesitate to answer this question by flatly denying the existence of competition at all in the sense defined. I shall be told that the assumption so readily made by economists, that capital and labor may be shifted about from one occupation to another in search of the highest remuneration, is a mere figment of the economical brain, without foundation or fact. Once embodied in a form suited to actual work, capital, it will be urged, is for the most part incapable of being turned to other uses. The buildings, plant, and material required for one kind of manufacture can rarely be adapted to any other, and even where the conversion is possible, the process will only be accomplished at great expense and loss. The difficulty of transferring labor, it will be contended, is even greater, since we are here in contact with mental as well as physical obstacles. Industrial skill is not a thing to be acquired in a moment, and that which a man possesses is the result, in general, of considerable time and outlay devoted to its acquisition. Is it likely that, having spent his time and money in acquiring this skill and fitting himself for a particular occupation, a workman will desert the line of life he has chosen on the first sign of an advance in remuneration elsewhere? We are reminded how long the hand-loom weavers persisted in their unprofitable labors after power-looms were in general use; and we can imagine how extreme the case would be which would cause a carpenter to become a smith, or a smith a carpenter, still more, which would cause either to take to hair-dressing or tailoring. On such grounds, it has been contended that competition, such as I have defined it as necessary to the action of the principle of cost, has no real existence, and that consequently all theories assuming its existence fall to the ground. Alike with regard to capital and labor, it is held that either, once embarked in a particular employment, is practically committed to that employment, and may therefore be regarded as taken out of the field of competition with agents of the same kind engaged in other branches of industy. I am anxious to do the fullest justice to the quantum of truth contained in this argument, and I admit at once that the facts alleged are substantially true. But I think it will not be difficult to show that they by no means sustain the practical conclusion they are adduced to support, and that, taking account of other conditions of the case which the argument overlooks, they are perfectly compatible with the existence of an effective industrial competition.

In the first place, it may be remarked that, in order to secure an effective industrial competition—such a competition as shall bring rewards into correspondence with sacrifices—it is not necessary that every portion of capital, or that every laborer, should be at all times capable of being turned to any selected occupation. It is enough that a certain quantity of each agent—varying according to circumstances—should be thus disposable. Suppose some branch of industry to be especially flourishing and to be realizing exceptional gains, there is no need that the whole industry of the country should be disturbed to correct the inequality. A small diversion of capital and labor—small, I mean, in comparison with the aggregate embarked in any important industry—will in general suffice for the purpose. Even on extraordinary occasions, when unlooked-for events in the political or commercial world disturb ordinary calculations and give an enormous advantage to particular industries—such occasions, for example, as occurred in the early years of railway enterprise, or again in the linen trade on the breaking out of the American civil war—even on such occasions, the equilibrium of remuneration and cost can always be restored, not indeed in a moment, but after no long delay, through the action of labor and capital still uncommitted to actual industrial employment, and without any sensible encroachment on the stock already actively employed. All that is necessary, therefore, with a view to an effective industrial competition, is the presence in a community of a certain quantity of those instruments of production existing in disposable form, ready to be turned toward the more lucrative pursuits, and sufficiently large to correct inequalities as they arise. Now, it will not be difficult to show that this condition is fulfilled in many industrial communities, completely in the case of capital, and less perfectly, but still within certain limits really and effectually, in the case of labor also.

The existence of a large amount of capital in commercial countries in disposable form—or, to speak less equivocally, in the form of money or other purchasing power, capable of being turned to any purpose required is a patent and undeniable fact. Nor is it less certain that this capital is constantly seeking the best investments, and rapidly moves toward any branch of industry that happens at the moment to offer special attractions. It is plain, too, that the capital thus disposable is sufficient for the purpose we have here in view, namely, to render competition effective among the various industries; since we find a portion of it constantly moving abroad for foreign investment—a destination it would scarcely receive while there was a prospect of reaping exceptionally high returns from investment within the country. We have, therefore, in the existence of this fund all that is required for a practically effective competition, so far as *one* instrument of production is concerned, and this without necessitating any serious encroachment on the capital actually engaged in productive operations. But is the corresponding condition satisfied in the case of labor? A little consideration will show that, within certain limits and subject to certain qualifications, it is fulfilled in this as well.

For here also we have a disposable fund, capable of being turned, as remuneration may tempt, in various directions. Granted that labor, once engaged in a particular occupation, is practically committed to that species of occupation; all labor is not thus engaged and committed. A young generation is constantly coming forward, whose capabilities may be regarded as still in disposable form, fulfilling the same function in relation to the general labor force of the country which capital, while yet existing as purchasing power, discharges in relation to its general capital. The young persons composing this body, or others interested in their welfare, are eagerly watching the prospects of industry in its several branches, and will not be slow to turn toward the pursuits that promise the largest rewards. Individual tastes, no doubt, will go for something in the decision, but varieties of tastes, taken over a large area, may be assumed pretty well to balance each other; and there will remain a steady gravitation of disposable labor toward the more remunerative callings. On the other hand, while fresh labor is coming on the scene, worn-out labor is passing off; and the departments of industry, in which remuneration has from any cause fallen below the average level, ceasing to be recruited, the numbers of those employed in them will quickly decline, until supply is brought within the limits of demand, and remuneration is restored to its just proportions. In this way, then, in the case of labor as in that of capital, the conditions for an effective competition exist, notwithstanding the practical difficulties in the way of transferring labor, once trained to a particular occupation, to new pursuits. But, as I have already intimated, the conditions are in this case realized only in an imperfect manner, and this involves, as a consequence, certain limitations on the action of competition in the labor market, and certain corresponding effects on the values of commodities. What the nature of those limitations are I shall now proceed to point out.

I remarked just now that the youthful labor constantly coming forward to recruit the labor market might be compared to the capital still existing in the form of purchasing power, and ready to be applied to any occupation, according as the prospect of profit might determine. In one important respect, however, the analogy fails. Of the capital existing in this disposable form any portion may be applied to any industrial purpose. But of the disposable labor each element—that is to say, each individual laborer—can only choose his employment within certain tolerably well-defined limits. These limits are the limits set by the qualifications required for each branch of trade and the amount of preparation necessary for their acquisition. Take an individual workman whose occupation is still undetermined, he will, according to circumstances, have a narrower or wider field of choice; but in no case will this be co-extensive with the entire range of domestic industry. If he belongs to the class of agricultural laborers, all forms of mere unskilled labor are open to him, but beyond this he is practically shut out from competition. The barrier is his social position and circumstances, which render his education defective, while his means are too narrow to allow of his repairing the defect, or of deferring the return upon his industry till he has qualified himself for a skilled occupation. Mounting a step higher in the industrial scale—to the artisan class, including with them the class of small dealers whose pecuniary position is much upon a par with artisans, here also within certain limits there is complete freedom of choice, but beyond a certain range practical exclusion. The man who is brought up to be an ordinary carpenter, mason, or smith, may go to any of these callings, or a hundred more, according as his taste prompts, or the prospect of remuneration attracts him; but practically he has no power to compete in those higher departments of skilled labor for which a more elaborate education and larger training are necessary, for example, mechanical engineering. Ascend a step higher still, and we find ourselves again in presence of similar limitations: we encounter persons competent to take part in any of the higher skilled industries, but practically excluded from the professions. It is true, indeed, that in none of these cases is the exclusion absolute. The limits imposed are not such as may not be overcome by extraordinary energy, self-denial, and enterprise; and by virtue of these qualities individuals in all classes are escaping every day from the bounds of their original position, and forcing their way into the ranks of those who stand above them. All this, no doubt, is true. But such exceptional phenomena do not affect the substantial truth of our position. What we find, in effect, is, not a whole population competing indiscriminately for all occupations, but a series of industrial layers, superposed on one another, within each of which the various candidates for employment possess a real and effective power of selection, while those occupying the several strata are, for all purposes of effective competition, practically isolated from each other. We may perhaps venture to arrange them in some such order as this: first, at the bottom of the scale there would be the large group of unskilled or nearly unskilled laborers, comprising agricultural laborers, laborers engaged in miscellaneous occupations in towns, or acting in attendance on skilled labor. Secondly, there would be the artisan group, comprising skilled laborers of the secondary order—carpenters, joiners, smiths, masons, shoe-makers, tailors, hatters, etc., etc., with whom might be included the very large class of small retail dealers, whose means and position place them within the reach of the same industrial opportunities as the class of artisans. The third layer would contain producers and dealers of a higher order, whose work would demand qualifications only

obtainable by persons of substantial means and fair educational opportunities—for example, civil and mechanical engineers, chemists, opticians,
watch-makers, and others of the same industrial grade, in which might
also find a place the superior class of retail tradesmen; while above these
there would be a fourth, comprising persons still more favorably circumstanced, whose ampler means would give them a still wider choice. This
last group would contain members of the learned professions, as well as
persons engaged in the various careers of science and art, and in the
higher branches of mercantile business. The reader will not understand
me as offering here an exhaustive classification of the industrial population.
I attempt nothing of the kind; but merely seek to exhibit in rough outline
the form which industrial organization, under the actual conditions of
modern life, tends to assume; my object being, by putting the fact in a
concrete shape, to furnish help toward a more distinct apprehension of the
limitations imposed by social circumstances on the free competition of
labor than would be obtained from more general statements. As I have
already said, I am far from contending for the existence of any hard lines
of demarcation between any categories of persons in this country. No
doubt the various ranks and classes fade into each other by imperceptible
gradations, and individuals from all classes are constantly passing up or
dropping down; but while this is so, it is nevertheless true that the average
workman, from whatever rank he be taken, finds his power of competition
limited for practical purposes to a certain range of occupations, so that,
however high the rates of remuneration in those which lie beyond may
rise, he is excluded from sharing them. We are thus compelled to recognize
the existence of non-competing industrial groups as a feature of our social
economy; and this is the fact which I desire here to insist upon. It remains
to be considered how this organization of industry is calculated to modify
the action of the principle of cost of production.

The reader will remember that there are two distinct sacrifices undergone in the business of production—the sacrifice of the capitalist, and the
sacrifice of the laborer. As regards the former, the competition of capital
being, as we have seen, effective over the entire industry of each commercial country, it follows that so much of the value of commodities as
goes to remunerate the capitalist's sacrifice, and which may be regarded
as the "profit fund," will correspond throughout the range of domestic
industry with that portion of the cost which falls to the capitalist. The
defalcation from the principle of cost occurs not here, but in that other and
larger element in the value of commodities which goes to remunerate the
laborer. The nature of the failure may be thus described: The exchange of
all commodities produced by laborers belonging to the same industrial
group, or competing circle, will be governed by the principle of cost—this
results necessarily from the fact that competition is effective within such
groups or circles; but the exchange of commodities produced by laborers

belonging to different groups or competing circles, will, for the opposite reason, not be governed by this principle. Thus all the products of unskilled labor will exchange for each other in proportion to their costs; as will also all the products of ordinary artisan labor *as among themselves.* But the latter products will not exchange against the former in proportion to their costs, nor will the products of artisan labor, or of unskilled labor, exchange in proportion to their costs against those of the higher industrial groups. The price of a deal table and the price of a common lock will be found to correspond to the sacrifices actually undergone by their producers; or again, the price of a barometer and the price of a watch will be found to correspond to the same conditions; but if we compare the price of either of the latter commodities with that of the former, we shall find that the correspondence fails; the prices of the barometer and of the watch will bear a far larger proportion to their respective costs than those of the deal table, or of the common lock, to theirs. If any one questions the fact, the evidence is to be found in the relative remuneration of the producers of the several articles. That remuneration, as I have shown, comes from the price of the commodity in each case; but, while it is in proportion to the relative sacrifices of production in the case of the workmen who are in competition with each other, it is not in proportion to those sacrifices where the workmen are excluded from mutual competition. The result, then, is that the principle of cost of production controls exchange value in the transactions taking place within certain limited industrial areas; while, in the reciprocal dealings of those several areas with one another, its operation fails.

This is the principal modification suffered by cost of production in consequence of the circumstance we are considering. In reality, however, the effects of that state of things are a good deal more complex than would appear from the statement just made; for in that statement account was not taken of the fact that the same commodity is very frequently the product of labor belonging to different industrial circles. For example, a house is mainly produced by masons, brick-layers, carpenters, plasterers, and others, who would all rank in the class of artisans; but a considerable quantity of purely unskilled labor is also employed in attendance upon these, as labor of a higher degree of skill than that of the ordinary artisan is employed in the finishing and decoration of the house. Now suppose a commodity of this kind, the joint production of workmen of different orders, to be exchanged against one produced by workmen belonging to some one industrial group, or to several groups, but in proportions different from those obtaining in the other case, what principle would here govern exchange value, or—to express the conception in a more familiar form—the relative prices of the commodities? Manifestly more than one principle will be engaged in determining the result. So far as the two commodities are the products of workmen in competition with each other, their values will be governed by cost of production, but so far as they proceed from workmen not in mutual competition, they will be governed by that other principle, yet to be ascertained, which governs normal value in the absence of competition. Supposing the commodity with which a house is compared were produced exclusively by the artisan class, the cost principle would be mainly operative in determining the exchange relation; but it would not be entirely so, since a portion, though a small portion, of the house has been produced by workmen not in competition with the producers of the other article. On the other hand, if the comparison were made between a house and a commodity produced either wholly by unskilled labor, or wholly by labor of a degree of skill superior to that of ordinary artisan labor, the relative values would follow, but in a slight degree, the rule of cost of production, being mainly controlled by the principle prevailing in the absence of the conditions which secure the action of cost. This example will serve to show the great complication that arises in the relative values of commodities under the actual conditions of their production. And if we bear in mind that all manufactured commodities are produced from raw materials which are very frequently the product of workmen not in competition with those who perform the manufacturing process, we shall see how widely the range of this sort of complication extends. Still we must not exaggerate its importance. What mainly happens is, that the bulk of the value of each commodity follows one law—say the law of cost, or what we shall afterward find to be the law of reciprocal demand, while a small remaining element is governed by a different principle. Thus, reverting for a moment to a previous illustration, a barometer and a watch are in very large proportion the products of workmen of a high order of skill, and in industrial competition with each other; in a very insignificant degree, of workmen of an inferior order: as, on the other hand, a deal table and a common lock are mainly the products of ordinary artisan labor, though, it may be in some small degree, also of labor not in competition with the labor of artisans. In so far, however, as any portion of the labor employed on the barometer is out of competition with some portion of that employed on the watch, and in so far as the same is true of the labor employed on the other compared articles, to that extent we were not justified in asserting that the commodities in question exchanged, either pair of them, in proportion to their costs of production. Nevertheless, it is certain that our statement was substantially true, since the chief portion, and so much the chief portion as to be nearly the whole, of the labor employed on each pair fulfilled the required condition; and this would govern a corresponding proportion of their values. A similar qualification would be needed in the case of most assertions of a like nature. In strictness, we can seldom say that the values of two commodities are in their whole extent governed by their costs of production: we can only say that they are so mainly, and in their chief elements. In effect the point in question is of little more than theoretic importance. As a point of theory it is proper to notice it, but the circumstance it deals with has little sensible effect upon the facts of exchange.

The mode in which the cost of producing commodities operates in regulating their values has now, I trust, been made tolerably clear. It will probably have been observed, that as I have departed from the current doctrine in my view of the elements of cost, so also have I departed from it in my manner of representing the operation of the law. That law is ordinarily regarded as a principle governing value *universally* wherever it affects value at all—governing, that is to say, the value of certain classes of commodities *in all exchanges;* so that, the conditions of their production being known, the law of their value is supposed to be known, whatever may be the nature or the conditions of production of the commodities against which they are exchanged. For example, the price of calico would commonly be said to be governed by its cost of production, and this would be laid down without any limitation as to the article which might form the other member in the exchange. If, however, the exposition contained in the foregoing pages be sound, this conception of the law can not be correct. For what has there appeared is a tendency in commodities to exchange in proportion to their costs of production *only so far as there exists free competition among their producers.* The exchange, therefore, in proportion to cost would only take place within the limits of the field of free competition; and a commodity produced within this field, but exchanged against one produced by workmen from beyond it, would not in such case exchange in proportion to its cost of production. Supposing, for example, A,B,C,D,E,F, to be commodities, the producers of which are all in free competition with each other, such commodities would exchange among themselves in proportion to their costs. Again, supposing, X,Y,Z, to be commodities produced by workmen also in free competition with each other, but excluded from competing with those who had produced A, B,C,D, etc.; here again the values of X,Y,Z, in the exchanges of these commodities against each other would be governed by the principle of cost. But now suppose the exchange to be made of a commodity belonging to the former category against one belonging to the latter—value would in this case be no longer governed by cost of production, inasmuch as there was no longer free competition among those who had produced the commodities exchanged. Now if the reader will recall the description that has been given of the various non-competing groups of which our industrial system is made up, he will perceive that the case last supposed represents no inconsiderable proportion of all the exchanges which take place within such a country as this; and that, therefore, the action of cost of production in regulating value is by no means as extensively prevalent, even within the limits of the same country, as the current theory would lead us to suppose. The same commodity follows the law of cost of production in some exchanges and does not follow it in others; nor is it true that the value of any commodity conforms to the principle of cost in all exchanges. In order that this should happen, effective competition should be established among producers over the entire field of industry—a condition which, I need hardly say, is very far yet from being anywhere fulfilled. The true conception of the law of cost is thus, not of a law governing universally the values of any class of commodities, but that of one governing the values of certain commodities in certain exchanges.

Section 6

In what has gone before, cost of production has been discussed without more than a passing reference to the nature of the elements which compose it. There was no need to discriminate those elements with particularity while we were occupied in establishing the general principle, but the evidence for that principle having now been set forth, it will be desirable to attempt some analysis and characterization of the constituents of cost.

*   *   *   *

Our analysis, then, of cost of production resolves it into three principal elements, which, I may remark, are also *ultimate* elements—Labor, Abstinence, and Risk; the first, under the prevailing industrial arrangements of this and other civilized countries, borne by the laborer, in that enlarged sense of the term in which "laborer" includes all who take a personal part in the business of production; the second by the capitalist; the third falling upon laborer and capitalist alike. A few remarks on each of these elements will suffice for my present purpose.

Considering labor as an element of cost of production, the principal remark that seems called for is that, in estimating it in this character, three circumstances, and three circumstances only, must be taken account of—namely, the duration of the exertion, the degree of its severity or irksomeness, and the risk or liability to injury of any kind attending it.

*   *   *   *

The true relation between skill and value may be expressed in the following propositions:

First, skill, as skill, produces no direct effect upon value; in other words, commodities do not under any circumstances exchange for each other in proportion to the degree of skill bestowed upon them. Secondly, skill, though in itself inoperative on value, nevertheless affects it indirectly in two distinct ways: first, where competition is effective among producers, through the cost which must be undergone in acquiring the skill—in such cases the value of skilled products will, *caeteris paribus*, exceed that of unskilled by the amount of the normal returns upon this cost; and, secondly, in the absence of effective competition, through the principle of monopoly, by limiting the number of competitors in skilled occupations, and so acting on the supply of skilled products. In either of these ways skill may raise value; but, as skill, that is to say, in the virtue of its own excellence, whether measured by the standard of utility or of artistic merit, it is powerless for this result.

* * * * *

The term "abstinence" is the name given to the sacrifice involved in the advance of capital. As to the nature of this sacrifice, it is mainly of a negative kind; consisting chiefly in the deprivation or postponement of enjoyment, implied in the fact of parting with our wealth so far at least as concerns our present power of commanding it. The term, indeed, would imply that the sacrifice is wholly negative; but I am inclined to include in it a certain small positive element, namely, that low degree of risk which is never absent from the advance of capital. That some degree of risk always accompanies the act in question is evident from the nature of the case, since it implies either the trusting of one's wealth to other persons, or, where it is employed by the owner himself in productive industry, the putting of it, with a view to future results, into forms not capable of being directly converted to his uses. It will be more convenient, I think to consider this slight and inevitable risk, which is always present where abstinence is exercised for economic ends, as an incident of that sacrifice, than as a substantive element of cost to be associated with "risk" as I have defined it in that character. I shall, therefore, so understand it, and shall accordingly define "abstinence" as the act of abstaining from the personal use of wealth with a view to employing it in productive industry, combined with that low degree of risk inevitably attaching to every such act.

* * * * *

Another possible ambiguity it may be well to clear up. As was intimated just now, the sacrifice involved in a given act of abstinence is very different in the case of different persons. A rich man abstains from the consumption of his superfluous wealth, and is scarcely conscious, perhaps quite unconscious, of having suffered any deprivation whatever: his surplus income goes to his capital account, which continues to grow, while his expenditure remains precisely as before. On the other hand, the same or a much smaller amount of wealth reserved from personal consumption by an artisan or a small tradesman will frequently demand the most rigorous self-denial. The same individual, too, feels very differently the pains of abstinence at different stages of his career—in the struggling outset and at the successful close. And it is similar with labor. The laborious effort fitted to produce a given result does not represent the same sacrifice for different people: it is one thing for the strong, another for the weak: one for the trained workman, another for the raw beginner. This being so, the question arises—How are such differences to be dealt with in computing the cost of production? Are we to take account of what is personal and peculiar to the actual producers, and regard the cost of the commodity as higher or lower according as it has been produced by a weak or strong workman, or by capital the result of painful or of painless saving? The answer must be in the negative. The sacrifices to be taken account of, and which govern exchange value, are, not those undergone by A,B, or C, but the average sacrifices undergone by the class of laborers or capitalists to which the producers of the commodity belong. A few remarks will enable us to make this clear.

What at bottom maintains the connection between value and cost of production is, it must always be remembered, the power of choice residing in laborers and capitalists to decide between different occupations. Now what is it determines the choice? No doubt the prospects of the pursuit, the remuneration being compared with the sacrifice. But what sacrifice? Plainly the sacrifice about to be undergone by the particular workman or capitalist who has to make the choice. Each takes account of the incidents of the course proposed as it bears upon himself, and considers how it stands in the comparison with others equally open to him. The conclusion he arrives at on this point determines his decision. Through a process of this kind every laborer and capitalist, either personally himself, or vicariously through a parent or other adviser, passes. Carried on over any given field of industrial competition, it is evident the result of this proceeding must be not to bring the remuneration of each of the individuals comprised within it into conformity with the sacrifice which each undergoes, but to establish this conformity among the aggregates of those engaged in the several competing occupations; so that the total remuneration falling to each branch of industry shall bear the same proportion to the total sacrifices undergone in that branch as the total remuneration falling to any other within the same field bears to the sacrifices undergone in that other. The total remuneration falling to any branch of industry, however, consists of the total value of the commodities proceeding from it. This value, therefore, will bear the same proportion to the sacrifices undergone in producing it, as the value proceeding from any other industry within the same field of competition bears to the sacrifices of which it is the result. It follows that the relation which competition establishes between cost and value is one, not between the value of particular commodities and the sacrifices of the individual or individuals who have produced each such commodity, but one between commodities taken as sorts and their cost of production. We can not, for example, assert that a particular pair of shoes will exchange against a particular coat in proportion to the sacrifices undergone respectively by the shoe-maker and the tailor in the actual case; but we may assert that, within a given field of competition, shoes, as one sort of commodity, will exchange against coats as another in this

proportion. The costs, therefore, to which the values of particular commodities correspond are not the particular sacrifices undergone in producing each commodity, but the average sacrifice undergone in producing
each sort of commodity. We may, therefore, state broadly, that difference in the sacrifices incident to production, whether of labor or of
abstinence, which are due to peculiarities either in the physical, mental,
or social circumstances of individuals, are to be excluded from consideration in estimating cost of production. What we have to do with is, not
individual sacrifice, but the average sacrifice of each industrial class.

This point being cleared up, we can have no difficulty in seeing how
cost in its principal elements is to be computed. In the case of labor, the
cost of producing a given commodity will be represented by the number
of average laborers employed in its production—regard at the same time
being had to the severity of the work and the degree of risk it involves—
multiplied by the duration of their labors. In that of abstinence, the principle is analogous: the sacrifice will be measured by the quantity of wealth
abstained from, taken in connection with the risk incurred, and multiplied
by the duration of the abstinence.

Section 7

We have now treated the subject of normal value, so far as it is regulated by the principle of cost of production. But, as I stated in the opening
of this chapter, the phenomenon in question is by no means confined to
cases in which the conditions necessary to the action of cost of production exist. The essence of normal value, as I then remarked, is a tendency
in the exchanging proportions of commodities to gravitate toward a central point, and this tendency is observable in departments of exchange
where effective competition among exchanging producers has no place.
The most important example of this kind is furnished by international
trade. As between the producers in different nations, whether laborers
or capitalists, there is no effective competition, nothing, therefore, to
secure that industrial rewards in different countries shall be brought into
correspondence with industrial sacrifices; nor, consequently, that international values shall correspond with cost of production. Nevertheless
international values, or, let us say, the relative prices of the products of
different nations, do not vary at random irrespective of rule or measure,
but exhibit precisely the same tendency to gravitate toward a central
point as is manifested in those exchanges which are governed by cost of
production. A less striking and hitherto, so far as I know, unnoticed,
example of the same kind meets us in domestic trade. As I have pointed
out, cost of production does not control value universally even within
the limits of a single country: in respect to a considerable class of exchanges—all those, namely, which take place between what I have called
non-competing industrial groups—its action fails. Yet not the less **we**

observe here, as in international trade, the phenomenon of normal value. The exchanges between the non-competing groups—or, let us say, the relative prices of the products of such non-competing groups—though unamenable to the law of cost, are not without a controlling force which restrains their fluctuations and guides them toward a normal result. This is the phenomenon with which we have now to deal; and the question to be considered is the nature of the force or forces which, in such cases, come into play.

Fortunately the problem has already, in principle at least, been solved for us by Mr. Mill. Mr. Mill has not, indeed, carried his solution beyond the case of international values; but his doctrine is manifestly applicable to all cases in which groups of producers, excluded from reciprocal industrial competition, exchange their products. Such cases, as I have shown, occur in domestic trade in the exchanges between those non-competing industrial groups of which I have spoken. The principle, therefore, which operates in international trade must operate here; and little more needs to be done, to complete the theory of this part of our subject, than to point the application of Mr. Mill's doctrine to this strictly parallel case.

That doctrine may be thus briefly stated: International values are governed by the reciprocal demand of commercial countries for each other's productions, or, more precisely, by the demand of each country for the productions of all other countries as against the demand of all other countries for what it produces; the result of this play of forces being that, on the whole, the export of each country discharge its liabilities (of which the principal are on account of its imports) toward all other countries. Whatever be the exchanging proportions—or, let us say, whatever be the state of relative prices—in different countries which is requisite to secure this result, those exchanging proportions, that state of relative prices, will become normal—will furnish the central point toward which the fluctuations of international prices will gravitate, the rule to which in the long run they will conform. Such is the law governing international values, called by Mr. Mill "the Equation of International Demand." What we have now to consider is the mode in which this principle operates in the case of the non-competing groups of domestic trade.

And first, in what sense are we to understand "reciprocal demand" as applied to non-competing industrial groups? Manifestly, in conformity with the analogy of the international case, as the demand of each group for the products of all other groups compared with the demand of all other groups for what this group produces. How, again, are we to measure such demand? Again I say, in conformity with the same analogy, by the quantity of the products of each group available for the purchase of the products of other groups; while the products of other groups available for the purchase of the products of any given group will measure their demand for the products of that group. Lastly, how are we to understand the "Equation of Demand," as applied to non-competing groups? Still following the international analogy, I reply, as such a state of exchanging proportions among the products of the various groups—or, let us say, as such a state of relative prices among such products as shall enable that portion of the products of each group which is applied to the purchase of the products of all other groups, to discharge its liabilities toward those other groups. The two cases thus run strictly on all-fours, and the play of the forces in action is in all respects the same. As in international trade an increased demand for the products of other countries will, other things being equal, affect international values—or, let us say, affect the relative prices of the products of different countries—unfavorably for the country whose demand is increased; and as, again, the converse of this condition, an increased demand by other countries for the products of a given country, will operate in the contrary direction; so it will be in the exchanges which take place between non-competing domestic groups. Whatever increases the demand of a given group for the products of outside, that is to say non-competing industries, or (what comes to the same thing) whatever increases the supply of its products available for the purchase of the products of such industries, will, other things being the same, depress the prices of its products in relation to the prices of the products of the industries against which they are exchanged, and *vice versa;* while whatever increases the demand of the outside industries for the products of a given group will have the contrary effect, and will raise the level of its prices in relation to those of the non-competing groups with which it trades, and *vice versa*. The relative position, commercially considered, of each group may thus be affected either by an increase or diminution of its own products not consumed within the group, or by an increase or diminution of the products of other groups, so far as those products are disposable for the purchase of the products of the group in question. Such is the nature of "reciprocal demand," and of its mode of action as between the non-competing groups of domestic industry. As the reader will observe, it is simply "supply and demand" taken twice over, first in the sale and then in the purchase, or, rather, we may describe it as Supply and Demand contemplated at once from both sides of a completed exchange.

But it may not be at once apparent how a principle of this character is fitted to accomplish the result ascribed to it—that of determining *normal*, as distinguished from temporary or market, value. As I have remarked, Reciprocal Demand is merely duplicate Supply and Demand regarded in its full significance; but Supply and Demand, as we are most familiar with their action, are, in their relation to prices, merely proximate agencies, governing indeed the fluctuations of the market, but themselves controlled by forces lying deeper in the economy of production. How then does it happen that, in the cases under consideration, those agencies are capable of doing more than this—capable of determining, not simply the fluctuations of the market, but the rule to which, in the long run, the fluctuations of the market conform?

The answer to this question is to be found in the circumstances which give stability to Reciprocal Demand in the class of exchanges we are now considering. Reciprocal Demand, or, if the reader prefers it, Supply and Demand, in relation to a particular commodity, or even to a considerable number of commodities, may, as we know, vary in almost any conceivable degree, and with great rapidity. But when we consider them as affecting aggregates of transactions carried on between limited bodies of producers —for example, between independent nations, or between non-competing industrial groups—the case is very different; and the limits within which variation is possible are in fact pretty strictly determined; for in this case the measure of the aggregate demand of each trading body will be the total of its productions, and the measure of its demand for the productions of the bodies with which it trades will be the proportion of its total production which it desires to apply to the purchase of the productions of those bodies. Now, in the absence of any great changes in the conditions of productive industry, and of legislation specially contrived for this purpose, neither the aggregate production of a community nor the proportion of its means employed in interchanges with other communities can easily undergo on a sudden serious variation. The total production will depend on the nature and extent of its resources; and the proportion employed in external trading on the comparative character of those resources as they stand related to those of the communities with which it trades. These, indeed, are not circumstances which can be regarded as absolutely fixed. On the contrary, the conditions of productive industry over the best portion of the industrial world are and have for long been pretty steadily progressive. But the progress, though steady, has in general been slow. Sudden changes, at least on a scale large enough to effect great aggregates of transactions, but rarely occur; and further, what is pertinent to our purpose, where important improvements in productive industry do happen, they are seldom confined to a single community, but, after an interval more or less brief, are in general shared by other communities, so that the relative positions of the various trading bodies are in the end but slightly affected. It follows that the demand of such bodies, however it may vary in respect to particular commodities, can not easily as an aggregate undergo any great or sudden change; while their reciprocal demand for each other's productions, which expresses their relative industrial condition, will be still less liable to serious or abrupt disturbance. Here, then, we find the conditions fitted to produce that stability of exchanging relations which is implied in the term "normal value." While the prices of particular commodities may fluctuate indefinitely in international as in other trade, the same possibility does not exist for the prices of aggregates of commodities exchanged by definite groups of producers, such as independent nations, or the non-competing sections in domestic industry. The limits to such fluctuations are set in the limited purchasing power, incident to the limited productive power, at any given time possessed by such trading groups. It is in this way that a normal relation arises in the terms of the transactions carried on, and that a central point is furnished toward which the fluctuations of the market gravitate, performing in such trade the same function discharged under a *regime* of competition by the principle of cost.

Cost of Productions and Reciprocal Demand in the sense explained, it thus appears, perform in certain circumstances similar economic offices. It remains now to point out an important difference in their modes of action and in the character of the results which flow from them. They each, as I have said, furnish a centre about which market values gravitate; but there is this difference between the two cases: The centre furnished by Cost of Productions stands related to the fluctuations of the individual commodity; that supplied by Reciprocal Demand to the average fluctuations of considerable aggregates of commodities. A reduction in the cost of producing a hat will lower its price, but will have no tendency to affect the price of any other thing. But an alteration in the reciprocal demand of two trading nations will act upon the price, not of any commodity in particular, but of every commodity which enters into the trade. What such an alteration necessitates is a change in the *average* terms on which the trade is carried on: but it decides nothing as to the details by which the required average shall be attained and maintained. This is determined, not by international demand, but by those circumstances in the internal industries of each country which regulate in each the relative prices of its products. And similarly in the interchange of non-competing domestic groups, what the reciprocal demand of the groups determines is the average relative level of prices within each group; the distribution of price among the individual products being regulated by the cause which governs value within it, namely cost of productions.

The net result would seem to be this: Reciprocal International Demand determines the average level of prices throughout the entire trade of each commercial country in relation to that prevailing in other countries in commercial connection with it. Reciprocal Domestic Demand determines certain minor relative averages extending over classes of articles, the products of non-competing industrial groups; while Cost of Production acts upon particular commodities, and, in each case, within the range of industrial competition, determines their relative prices. The actual price, therefore, of any given commodity will, it is evident be the composite result of the combined action of these several agencies.

Another distinction needs to be noticed between Reciprocal Demand and Cost of Production in their operation upon normal value. The former is, on the whole, far more steady and equable in its action than the latter. The reason is plain. Changes in cost of production depend mainly on the progress of the industrial arts, and this has for some time been and, we may perhaps assume, is likely for a long time to continue to be, remarkably rapid. Thus we find in the course of the present century an immense reduction in the costs of producing a large number of articles of general consumption, accompanied by a corresponding reduction in their value. On the other hand, changes in reciprocal demand are chiefly due to moral, social, and political causes, operating on a scale large enough to affect the relative positions of considerable bodies of men. Such changes are necessarily of slow accomplishment; and consequently the variations in value which result from them are rarely of a striking character, and in general proceed so slowly that they can seldom be perceived unless the comparison be made between prices taken at periods separated by considerable intervals of time. Still such changes do occur, and international values, as well as the corresponding class of values in domestic trade, respond to them. For example, I think we may assume that the adoption of free trade by England has improved her international position in the trade of the world. I do not refer to the extension of her trade, which, as all the world knows, has been enormous, but to the terms on which it is carried on. A given exertion of English industry will now command in the exchange with foreign countries the product of a larger exertion of foreign industry than formerly. In the domestic sphere, probably the most potent agency affecting reciprocal demand is the progress of popular education. Supposing, for example, that the system of primary education now being established in this country proves as successful as the friends of education desire; and supposing again, and more particularly, that effective provision is made in it for facilitating the ascent of promising boys from the lower to the higher educational levels, I think we may with some confidence predict that the movement will issue in a considerable change in the relative prices of certain classes of commodities in this country; nor can we have much difficulty in perceiving what will be the general direction of the change. Plainly the effect will be to augment the number of skilled workmen in relation to the unskilled, and of highly skilled workmen in relation to workmen possessing skill of the more common sorts. The social wall of partition which now divides the non-competing groups will to a large extent be broken down, and many of those occupying the lower levels will take advantage of the breach to press into those above them. The result will be a change in the reciprocal demand of the several groups. The demand of the groups representing the higher sorts of industrial skill will increase relatively to that of the groups representing the lower; or, to put the same point in a different form, the supply of the products of the former groups will increase relatively to that of the products of the latter. The inevitable consequence must be a change in relative prices unfavorable to the higher, and in a corresponding degree favorable to the lower sorts, of skilled industry. In a word, the qualified monopolies resting upon social conditions which now exist will be still further qualified: the range of competition will be enlarged; and, just in proportion as these results are attained, relative prices, and with them relative wages, will be made to approximate, more closely than at present, to the rule of cost. We may illustrate the case by the state of things in new colonies. There, owing to causes precisely similar to those which the educational movement is tending to develop here—owing, that is to say, to the great equality of conditions prevailing among the industrial population—the coarser kinds of labor and the lower sorts of skill are not merely positively, but comparatively, in relation to the finer and higher sorts, far more highly remunerated than any are at present with us. The explanation is that which has just been given: competition has there a wider range; and wherever this is so, prices and remuneration will represent more truly the actual sacrifices undergone by producers.

PART IV
RISE OF MARGINALISM

WILLIAM STANLEY JEVONS

(1835–1882)

William Stanley Jevons was born in Liverpool, England. He attended the University College, London, after which he assumed the position of Assayer of the Mint at Sidney, Australia. On his return to England, he became professor of political economy at Owens College and later at University College. He met an untimely death by drowning at the early age of forty-seven.

Jevons was not only an economist, but also a mathematician and logician. Like John Stuart Mill, he was the author of a text on logic. His most famous work in economics was "Theory of Political Economy," published in 1871, which went through numerous editions. It is from the third edition of this work published in 1888 that the following selections have been taken. Other writings of Jevons were: "The Coal Question" (1865); "Money and the Mechanism of Exchange" (1875); and "The State in Relation to Labor" (1882). After his death were published "Methods of Social Reform" and "Investigations in Currency and Finance,"as well as his famous "Logic."

Not only did Jevons revolutionize deductive economic theory, but also he made a number of special inductive studies of specific problems. Indeed, he may be regarded as one of the founders of the modern statistical method. Naturally, the approach of Jevons to the study of economic theory was mathematical in character. His work abounds in geometrical diagrams and algebraic expressions of economic principles.

Jevons is important to the student of economic theory because of his stress on consumption. Again, he succeeded in stating clearly the principle of diminishing utility and in showing its great influence on value. It must be remembered, however, that Jevons was not the discoverer of this principle which can easily be traced back to Bentham. Finally, Jevons is important for his concepts of marginalism, that is, he showed the significance of marginal utility and marginal disutility as determinants of value. His distinction between total utility and marginal utility gave the key to Smith's famous paradox of value.

It will be remembered that Cairnes, the last of the classicists, stressed costs rather than utility, and average costs rather than marginal costs. But Jevons shifted attention from costs and supply to utility and demand. Unfortunately, he failed to expand his utility curve into a demand schedule. Again, his psychology remained that of hedonism.

WILLIAM STANLEY JEVONS

SELECTIONS FROM "THEORY OF POLITICAL ECONOMY"

Chapter I. Introduction

The science of Political Economy rests upon a few notions of an apparently simple character. Utility, wealth, value, commodity, labour, land, capital, are the elements of the subject; and whoever has a thorough comprehension of their nature must possess or be soon able to acquire a knowledge of the whole science. As almost every economic writer has remarked, it is in treating the simple elements that we require the most care and precision, since the least error of conception must vitiate all our deductions. Accordingly, I have devoted the following pages to an investigation of the conditions and relations of the above-named notions.

Repeated reflection and inquiry have led me to the somewhat novel opinion, that *value depends entirely upon utility*. Prevailing opinions make labour rather than utility the origin of value; and there are even those who distinctly assert that labour is the *cause* of value. I show, on the contrary, that we have only to trace out carefully the natural laws of the variation of utility, as depending upon the quantity of commodity in our possession, in order to arrive at a satisfactory theory of exchange, of which the ordinary laws of supply and demand are a necessary consequence. This theory is in harmony with facts; and, whenever there is any apparent reason for the belief that labour is the cause of value, we obtain an explanation of the reason. Labour is found often to determine value, but only in an indirect manner, by varying the degree of utility of the commodity through an increase or limitation of the supply.

These views are not put forward in a hasty or ill-considered manner. All the chief points of the theory were sketched out ten years ago; but they were then published only in the form of a brief paper communicated to the Statistical or Economic Section of the British Association at the Cambridge Meeting, which took place in the year 1862. A still briefer abstract of that paper was inserted in the Report of the Meeting, and the paper itself was not printed until June 1866. Since writing that paper, I have, over and over again, questioned the truth of my own notions, but without ever finding any reason to doubt their substantial correctness.

Mathematical Character of the Science

It is clear that Economics, if it is to be a science at all, must be a mathematical science. There exists much prejudice against attempts to introduce the methods and language of mathematics into any branch of the moral sciences. Many persons seem to think that the physical sciences form the proper sphere of mathematical method, and that the moral sciences demand some other method—I know not what. My theory of Economics, however, is purely mathematical in character. Nay, believing that the quantities with which we deal must be subject to continuous variation, I do not hesitate to use the appropriate branch of mathematical science, involving though it does the fearless consideration of infinitely small quantities. The theory consists in applying the differential calculus to the familiar notions of wealth, utility, value, demand, supply, capital, interest, labour, and all the other quantitative notions belonging to the daily operations of industry. As the complete theory of almost every other science involves the use of that calculus, so we cannot have a true theory of Economics without its aid.

To me it seems that *our science must be mathematical, simply because it deals with quantities.* Wherever the things treated are capable of being *greater or less*, there the laws and relations must be mathematical in nature. The ordinary laws of supply and demand treat entirely of quantities of commodity demanded or supplied, and express the manner in which the quantities vary in connection with the price. In consequence of this fact the laws *are* mathematical. Economists cannot alter their nature by denying them the name; they might as well try to alter red light by calling it blue. Whether the mathematical laws of Economics are stated in words, or in the usual symbols, x, y, z, p, q, etc., is an accident, or a matter of mere convenience. If we had no regard to trouble and prolixity, the most complicated mathematical problems might be stated in ordinary language, and their solution might be traced out by words. In fact, some distinguished mathematicians have shown a liking for getting rid of their symbols, and expressing their arguments and results in language as nearly as possible approximating to that in common use. In his *Système du Monde*, Laplace attempted to describe the truths of physical astronomy in common language; and Thomson and Tait interweave their great *Treatise on Natural Philosophy* with an interpretation in ordinary words, supposed to be within the comprehension of general readers.

These attempts, however distinguished and ingenious their authors, soon disclose the inherent defects of the grammar and dictionary for expressing complicated relations. The symbols of mathematical books are not different in nature from language; they form a perfected system of language, adapted to the notions and relations which we need to express. They do not constitute the mode of reasoning they embody; they merely facilitate its exhibition and comprehension. If, then, in Economics, we have to deal with quantities and complicated relations of quantities, we must reason mathematically; we do not render the science less mathematical by avoiding the symbols of algebra—we merely refuse to employ, in a very imperfect science, much needing every kind of assistance, that apparatus of appropriate signs which is found indispensable in other sciences.

Confusion between Mathematical and Exact Sciences

Many persons entertain a prejudice against mathematical language, arising out of a confusion between the ideas of a mathematical science and an exact science. They think that we must not pretend to calculate unless we have the precise data which will enable us to obtain a precise answer to our calculations; but, in reality, there is no such thing as an exact science, except in a comparative sense. Astronomy is more exact than other sciences, because the position of a planet or star admits of close measurement; but, if we examine the methods of physical astronomy, we find that they are all approximate. Every solution involves hypotheses which are not really true: as, for instance, that the earth is a smooth, homogeneous spheroid. Even the apparently simpler problems in statics or dynamics are only hypothetical approximations to the truth.

We can calculate the effect of a crowbar, provided it be perfectly inflexible and have a perfectly hard fulcrum—which is never the case. The data are almost wholly deficient for the complete solution of any one problem in natural science. Had physicists waited until their data were perfectly precise before they brought in the aid of mathematics, we should have still been in the age of science which terminated at the time of Galileo.

When we examine the less precise physical sciences, we find that physicists are, of all men, most bold in developing their mathematical theories in advance of their data. Let any one who doubts this examine Airy's "Theory of the Tides," as given in the *Encyclopaedia Metropolitana;* he will there find a wonderfully complex mathematical theory which is confessed by its author to be incapable of exact or even approximate application, because the results of the various and often unknown contours of the seas do not admit of numerical verification. In this and many other cases we have mathematical theory without the data requisite for precise calculation.

The greater or less accuracy attainable in a mathematical science is a matter of accident, and does not affect the fundamental character of the science. There can be but two classes of sciences—those which are *simply logical*, and *those which, besides being logical, are also mathematical*. If there be any science which determines merely whether a thing be or be not— whether an event will happen, or will not happen—it must be a purely logical science; but if the thing may be greater or less, or the event may happen sooner or later, nearer or farther, then quantitative notions enter, and the science must be mathematical in nature, by whatever name we call it.

Capability of Exact Measurement

Many will object, no doubt, that the notions which we treat in this science are incapable of any measurement. We cannot weigh, nor gauge, nor test the feelings of the mind; there is no unit of labour, or suffering, or enjoyment. It might thus seem as if a mathematical theory of Economics would be necessarily deprived for ever of numerical data.

I answer, in the first place, that nothing is less warranted in science than an uninquiring and unhoping spirit. In matters of this kind, those who despair are almost invariably those who have never tried to succeed. A man might be despondent had he spent a lifetime on a difficult task without a gleam of encouragement; but the popular opinions on the extension of mathematical theory tend to deter any man from attempting tasks which, however difficult, ought, some day, to be achieved.

* * * * *

Measurement of Feeling and Motives

Many readers may, even after reading the preceding remarks, consider it quite impossible to create such a calculus as is here contemplated, because we have no means of defining and measuring quantities of feeling, like we can measure a mile, or a right angle; or any other physical quantity. I have granted that we can hardly form the conception of a unit of pleasure or pain, so that the numerical expression of quantities of feeling seems to be out of the question. But we only employ units of measurement in other things to facilitate the comparison of quantities; and if we can compare the quantities directly, we do not need the units.

* * * * *

Logical Method of Economics

* * * * *

To return, however, to the topic of the present work, the theory here given may be described as *the mechanics of utility and self-interest*. Oversights may have been committed in tracing out its details, but in its main features this theory must be the true one. Its method is as sure and demonstrative as that of kinematics or statics, nay, almost as self-evident as are the elements of Euclid, when the real meaning of the formulae is fully seized.

I do not hesitate to say, too, that Economics might be gradually erected into an exact science, if only commercial statistics were far more complete and accurate than they are at present, so that the formulae could be endowed with exact meaning by the aid of numerical data. These data would consist chiefly in accurate accounts of the quantities of goods possessed and consumed by the community, and the prices at which they are exchanged. There is no reason whatever why we should not have those statistics, except the cost and trouble of collecting them, and the unwillingness of persons to afford information. The quantities themselves to be measured and registered are most concrete and precise. In a few cases we already have information approximating to completeness, as when a commodity like tea, sugar, coffee, or tobacco is wholly imported. But when articles are untaxed, and partly produced within the country, we have yet the vaguest notions of the quantities consumed. Some slight success is now, at last, attending the efforts to gather agricultural statistics; and the great need felt by men engaged in the cotton and other trades to obtain accurate accounts of stocks, imports, and consumption, will probably lead to the publication of far more complete information than we have hitherto enjoyed.

The deductive science of Economics must be verified and rendered useful by the purely empirical science of Statistics. Theory must be invested with the reality and life of fact. But the difficulties of this union are immensely great, and I appreciate them quite as much as does Cairnes in his admirable lectures "On the Character and Logical Method of Political Economy." I make hardly any attempt to employ statistics in this work, and thus I do not pretend to any numerical precision. But, before we attempt any investigation of facts, we must have correct theoretical notions; and of what are here presented, I would say, in the words of Hume, in his *Essay on Commerce*, "If false, let them be rejected: but no one has a right to entertain a prejudice against them merely because they are out of the common road."

Relation of Economics to Ethics

I wish to say a few words, in this place, upon the relation of Economics to Moral Science. The theory which follows is entirely based on a calculus of pleasure and pain; and the object of Economics is to maximise happiness by purchasing pleasure, as it were, at the lowest cost of pain. The language employed may be open to misapprehension, and it may seem as if pleasures and pains of a gross kind were treated as the all-sufficient motives to guide the mind of man. I have no hesitation in accepting the Utilitarian theory of morals which does uphold the effect upon the happiness of mankind as the criterion of what is right and wrong. But I have never felt that there is anything in that theory to prevent our putting the widest and highest interpretation upon the terms used.

Jeremy Bentham put forward the Utilitarian theory in the most uncompromising manner. According to him, whatever is of interest or importance to us must be the cause of pleasure or of pain; and when the terms are used with a sufficiently wide meaning, pleasure and pain include all the forces which drive us to action. They are explicitly or implicitly the matter of all our calculations, and form the ultimate quantities to be treated in all the moral sciences. The words of Bentham on this subject may require some explanation and qualification, but they are too grand and too full of truth to be omitted. "Nature," he says, "has placed mankind under the governance of two sovereign masters—*pain* and *pleasure*. It is for them alone to point out what we ought to do, as well as to determine what we shall do. On the one hand the standard of right and wrong, on the other the chain of causes and effects, are fastened to their throne. They govern us in all we do, in all we say, in all we think: every effort we can make to throw off our subjection will serve but to demonstrate and confirm it. In words a man may pretend to abjure their empire; but, in reality, he will remain subject to it all the while. The *principle of utility* recognises this subjection, and assumes it for the foundation of that system, the object of which is to rear the fabric of felicity by the hands of reason and of law. Systems which attempt to question it deal in sounds instead of sense, in caprice instead of reason, in darkness instead of light."

* * * * *

CHAPTER III. THE THEORY OF UTILITY

Utility Is Not an Intrinsic Quality

My principal work now lies in tracing out the exact nature and conditions of utility. It seems strange indeed that economists have not bestowed more minute attention on a subject which doubtless furnishes the true key to the problem of economics.

In the first place, utility, though a quality of things, is *no inherent quality*. It is better described as *a circumstance of things* arising out of their relation to man's requirements. As Senior most accurately says, "Utility denotes no intrinsic quality in the things which we call useful; it merely expresses their relations to the pains and pleasures of mankind." We can never, therefore, say absolutely that some objects have utility and others have not. The ore lying in the mine, the diamond escaping the eye of the searcher, the wheat lying unreaped, the fruit ungathered for want of consumers, have no utility at all. The most wholesome and necessary kinds of food are useless unless there are hands to collect and mouths to eat them sooner or later. Nor, when we consider the matter closely, can we say that all portions of the same commodity possess equal utility. Water, for instance, may be roughly described as the most useful of all substances. A quart of water per day has the high utility of saving a person from dying in a most distressing manner. Several gallons a day may possess much utility for such purposes as cooking and washing; but after an adequate supply is secured for these uses, any additional quantity is a matter of comparative indifference. All that we can say, then, is that water, up to a certain quantity, is indispensable; that further quantities will have various degrees of utility; but that beyond a certain quantity the utility sinks gradually to zero; it may even become negative, that is to say, further supplies of the same substance may become inconvenient and hurtful.

Exactly the same considerations apply more or less clearly to every other article. A pound of bread per day supplied to a person saves him from starvation, and has the highest conceivable utility. A second pound per day has also no slight utility; it keeps him in a state of comparative plenty, though it be not altogether indispensable. A third pound would begin to be superfluous. It is clear, then, that *utility is not proportional to commodity:* the very same articles vary in utility according as we already possess more or less of the same article. The like may be said of other things. One suit of clothes per annum is necessary, a second convenient, a third desirable, a fourth not unacceptable, but we sooner or later reach a point at which further supplies are not desired with any perceptible force unless it be for subsequent use.

Law of the Variation of Utility

Let us now investigate this subject a little more closely. Utility must be considered as measured by, or even as actually identical with, the addition made to a person's happiness. It is a convenient name for

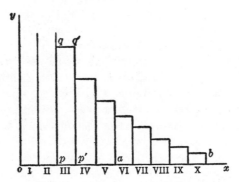

the aggregate of the favorable balance of feeling produced,—the sum of the pleasure created and the pain prevented. We must now carefully discriminate between the *total utility* arising from any commodity and the utility attaching to any particular portion of it. Thus the total utility of the food we eat consists in maintaining life, and may be considered as infinitely great; but if we were to subtract a tenth part from what we eat daily, our loss would be but slight. We should certainly not lose a tenth part of the whole utility of food to us. It might be doubtful whether we should suffer any harm at all.

Let us imagine the whole quantity of food which a person consumes on an average during twenty-four hours to be divided into ten equal parts. If his food be reduced by the last part, he will suffer but little; if a second tenth part be deficient, he will feel the want distinctly; the subtraction of the third tenth part will be decidedly injurious; with every subsequent subtraction of a tenth part his sufferings will be more and more serious, until at length he will be upon the verge of starvation. Now, if we call each of the tenth parts *an increment*, the meaning of these facts is, that each increment of food is less necessary, or possesses less utility, than the previous one. To explain this variation of utility we may make use of space representations, which I have found convenient in illustrating the laws of economics in my college lectures during fifteen years past.

Let the line *ox* be used as a measure of the quantity of food, and let it be divided into ten equal parts to correspond to the ten portions of food mentioned above. Upon these equal lines are constructed rectangles and the area of each rectangle may be assumed to represent the utility of the increment of food corresponding to its base. Thus the utility of the last increment is small, being proportional to the small rectangle on *x*. As we approach towards *o*, each increment bears a larger rectangle, that standing upon III being the largest complete rectangle. The utility of the next increment, II, is undefined, as also that of I, since these portions of food would be indispensable to life, and their utility, therefore, infinitely great.

We can now form a clear notion of the utility of the whole food, or of any part of it, for we have only to add together the proper rectangles. The utility of the first half of the food will be the sum of the rectangles standing on the line *oa*; that of the second half will be represented by the sum of the smaller rectangles between *a* and *b*. The total utility of the food will be the whole sum of the rectangles, and will be infinitely great.

The comparative utility of the several portions is, however, the most important. Utility may be treated as *a quantity of two dimensions*, one dimension consisting in the quantity of the commodity, and another in the intensity of the effect produced upon the consumer. Now the quantity of the commodity is measured on the horizontal line *ox*, and the intensity of utility will be measured by the length of the upright lines, or *ordinates*. The intensity of utility of the third increment is measured either by *pq*, or *p'q'*, and its utility is the product of the units in *pp'* multiplied by those in *pq*.

But the division of the food into ten equal parts is an arbitrary supposition. If we had taken twenty or a hundred or more equal parts, the same general principle would hold true, namely, that each small portion would be less useful and necessary than the last. The law may be considered to hold true theoretically, however small the increments are made; and in this way we shall at last reach a figure which is undistinguishable from a continuous curve. The notion of infinitely small quantities of food may seem absurd as regards the consumption of one individual; but when we consider the consumption of a nation as a whole, the consumption may well be conceived to increase or diminish by quantities which are, practically speaking, infinitely small compared with the whole consumption. The laws which we are about to trace out are to be conceived as theoretically true of the individual; they can only be practically verified as regards the aggregate transactions, productions, and consumptions of a large body of people. But the laws of the aggregate depend of course upon the laws applying to individual cases.

The law of the variation of the degree of utility of food may thus be represented by a continuous curve *pbq*, and the perpendicular height of each point at the curve above the line *ox* represents the degree of utility of the commodity when a certain amount has been consumed. (See following chart.)

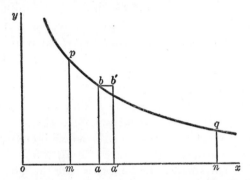

Thus, when the quantity *oa* has been consumed, the degree of utility corresponds to the length of the line *ab*; for if we take a very little more food, *aa'*, its utility will be the product of *aa'* and *ab* very nearly, and more nearly the less is the magnitude of *aa'*. The degree of utility is thus properly measured by the height of a very narrow rectangle corresponding to a very small quantity of food, which theoretically ought to be infinitely small.

Total Utility and Degree of Utility

We are now in a position to appreciate perfectly the difference between the *total utility* of any commodity and the *degree of utility* of the commodity at any point. These are, in fact, quantities of altogether different kinds, the first being represented by an area, and the second by a line. We must consider how we may express these notions in appropriate mathematical language.

Let *x* signify, as is usual in mathematical books, the quantity which varies independently—in this case the quantity of commodity. Let *u* denote the *whole utility* proceeding from the consumption of *x*. Then *u* will be, as mathematicians say, *a function of x*; that is, it will vary in some continuous and regular, but probably unknown, manner, when *x* is made to vary. Our great object at present, however, is to express the *degree of utility*.

Mathematicians employ the sign Δ prefixed to a sign of quantity, such as x, to signify that a quantity of the same nature as x, but small in proportion to x, is taken into consideration. Thus Δx means a small portion of x, and $x + \Delta x$ is therefore a quantity a little greater than x. Now when x is a quantity of commodity, the utility of $x + \Delta x$ will be more than that of x as a general rule. Let the whole utility of $x + \Delta x$ be denoted by $u + \Delta u$; then it is obvious that the increment of utility Δu belongs to the increment of commodity Δx; and if, for the sake of argument, we suppose the degree of utility uniform over the whole of Δx, which is nearly true, owing to its smallness, we shall find the corresponding degree of utility by dividing Δu by Δx.

We find these considerations fully illustrated by the last figure, in which oa represents x, and ab is the degree of utility at the point a. Now, if we increase x by the small quantity $a\acute{a}$, or Δx, the utility is increased by the small rectangle $abb'a'$, or Δu; and since a rectangle is the product of its sides, we find that the length of the line ab, the degree of utility, is represented by the fraction $\Delta u/\Delta x$.

As already explained, however, the utility of a commodity may be considered to vary with perfect continuity, so that we commit a small error in assuming it to be uniform over the whole increment Δx. To avoid this, we must imagine Δx to be reduced to an infinitely small size, Δu decreasing with it. The smaller the quantities are the more nearly we shall have a correct expression for ab, the degree of utility at the point a. Thus the *limit* of this fraction $\Delta u/\Delta x$, or, as it is commonly expressed, du/dx, is the degree of utility corresponding to the quantity of commodity x. *The degree of utility is*, in mathematical language, *the differential coefficient of u considered as a function of x*, and will itself be another function of x.

We shall seldom need to consider the degree of utility except as regards the last increment which has been consumed, or, which comes to the same thing, the next increment which is about to be consumed. I shall therefore commonly use the expression *final degree of utility*, as meaning the degree of utility of the last addition, or the next possible addition of a very small, or infinitely small, quantity to the existing stock. In ordinary circumstances, too, the final degree of utility will not be great compared with what it might be. Only in famine or other extreme circumstances do we approach the higher degrees of utility. Accordingly we can often treat the lower portions of the curves of variation (pbq) which concern ordinary commercial transactions, while we leave out of sight the portions beyond p or q. It is also evident that we may know the degree of utility at any point while ignorant of the total utility, that is, the area of the whole curve. To be able to estimate the total enjoyment of a person would be an interesting thing, but it would not be really so important as to be able to estimate the additions and subtractions to his enjoyment which circumstances occasion. In the same way a very wealthy person may be quite unable to form any accurate statement of his aggregate wealth, but he may nevertheless have exact accounts of income and expenditure, that is, of additions and subtractions.

Variation of the Final Degree of Utility

The final degree of utility is that function upon which the theory of economics will be found to turn. Economists, generally speaking, have failed to discriminate between this function and the total utility, and from this confusion has arisen much perplexity. Many commodities which are most useful to us are esteemed and desired but little. We cannot live without water, and yet in ordinary circumstances we set no value on it. Why is this? Simply because we usually have so much of it that its final degree of utility is reduced nearly to zero. We enjoy every day the almost infinite utility of water, but then we do not need to consume more than we have. Let the supply run short by drought, and we begin to feel the higher degrees of utility, of which we think but little at other times.

The variation of the function expressing the final degree of utility is the all-important point in economic problems. We may state, as a general law, that *the degree of utility varies with the quantity of commodity, and ultimately decreases as that quantity increases.* No commodity can be named which we continue to desire with the same force, whatever be the quantity already in use or possession. All our appetites are capable of *satisfaction* or *satiety* sooner or later, in fact, both these words mean, etymologically, that we have had *enough*, so that more is of no use to us. It does not follow, indeed, that the degree of utility will always sink to zero. This may be the case with some things, especially the simple animal requirements, such as food, water, air, etc. But the more refined and intellectual our needs become, the less are they capable of satiety. To the desire for articles of taste, science, or curiosity, when once excited, there is hardly a limit.

* * * * *

Disutility and Discommodity

A few words will suffice to suggest that as utility corresponds to the production of pleasure, or, at least, a favorable alteration in the balance of pleasure and pain, so negative utility will consist in the production of pain, or the unfavorable alteration of the balance. In reality we must be almost as often concerned with the one as with the other; nevertheless, economists have not employed any distinct technical terms to express that production of pain which accompanies so many actions of life. They have fixed their attention on the more agreeable aspect of the matter. It will be allowable, however, to appropriate the good English word *dis-commodity*, to signify any substance or action which is the opposite of *commodity*, that is to say, *anything which we desire to get rid of*, like ashes or sewage. Discommodity is, indeed, properly an abstract form signifying inconvenience, or disadvantage; but as the noun *commodities* has been used in the English language for four hundred years at least as a concrete term, so we may now convert discommodity into a concrete term, and speak of *discommodities* as substances or things which possess the quality of causing inconvenience or harm. For the abstract notion, the opposite or negative of utility, we may invent the term *disutility*, which will mean something different from inutility, or the absence of utility. It is obvious that utility passes through inutility before changing into disutility, these notions being related as $+$, 0, and $-$.

Distribution of Commodity in Different Uses

The principles of utility may be illustrated by considering the mode in which we distribute a commodity when it is capable of several uses. There are articles which may be employed for many distinct purposes: thus, barley may be used either to make beer, spirits, bread, or to feed cattle; sugar may be used to eat, or for producing alcohol; timber may be used in construction, or as fuel; iron and other metals may be applied to many different purposes. Imagine, then, a community in the possession of a certain stock of barley; what principles will regulate their mode of consuming it? Or, as we have not yet reached the subject of exchange, imagine an isolated family, or even an individual, possessing an adequate stock, and using some in one way and some in another. The theory of utility gives, theoretically speaking, a complete solution of the question.

Let s be the whole stock of some commodity, and let it be capable of two distinct uses. Then we may represent the two quantities appropriated to these uses by x_1 and y_1, it being a condition that $x_1 + y_1 = s$. The person may be conceived as successively expending small quantities of the commodity; now it is the inevitable tendency of human nature to choose that course which appears to offer the greatest advantage at the moment. Hence, when the person remains satisfied with the distribution he has made, it follows that no alteration would yield him more pleasure, which amounts to saying that an increment of commodity would yield exactly as much utility in one use as in another. Let Δu_1, Δu_2 be the increments of utility which might arise respectively from consuming an increment of commodity in the two different ways. When the distribution is completed, we ought to have $\Delta u_1 = \Delta u_2$; or at the limit we have the equation

$$\frac{du_1}{dx} = \frac{du_2}{dy},$$

which is true when x, y are respectively equal to x_1, y_1. We must, in other words, have the *final degrees of utility* in the two uses equal.

The same reasoning which applies to uses of the same commodity will evidently apply to any two uses, and hence to all uses simultaneously, so that we obtain a series of equations less numerous by a unit than the number of ways of using the commodity. The general result is that commodity, if consumed by a perfectly wise being, must be consumed with a maximum production of utility.

We should often find these equations to fail. Even when x is equal to $99/100$ of the stock, its degree of utility might still exceed the utility attaching to the remaining $1/100$ part in either of the other uses. This would mean that it was preferable to give the whole commodity to the first use. Such a case might perhaps be said to be not the exception but the rule; for whenever a commodity is capable of only one use, the circumstance is theoretically represented by saying that the final degree of utility in this employment always exceeds that in any other employment.

Under peculiar circumstances great changes may take place in the consumption of a commodity. In a time of scarcity the utility of barley as food might rise so high as to exceed altogether its utility, even as regards the smallest quantity, in producing alcoholic liquors; its consumption in the latter way would then cease. In a beseiged town the employment of articles becomes revolutionized. Things of great utility in other respects are ruthlessly applied to strange purposes. In Paris a vast stock of horses was eaten, not so much because they were useless in other ways, as because they were needed more strongly as food. A certain stock of horses had, indeed, to be retained as a necessary aid to locomotion, so that the equation of the degrees of utility never wholly failed.

Chapter IV. Theory of Exchange

Popular Use of the Term Value

In the popular use of the word value no less than three distinct though connected meanings seem to be confused together. These may be described as

(1) Value in use;
(2) Esteem, or urgency of desire;
(3) Ratio of exchange.

Adam Smith, in the familiar passage already referred to distinguished between the first and the third meanings. He said,[1] "The word value, it is to be observed, has two different meanings, and sometimes expresses the power of purchasing other goods which the possession of that object conveys. The one may be called 'value in use'; the other 'value in exchange.' The things which have the greatest value in use have frequently little or no value in exchange; and, on the contrary those which have the greatest value in exchange have frequently little or no value in use. Nothing is more useful than water: but it will purchase scarce anything; scarce anything can be had in exchange for it. A diamond, on the con-

[1] *Wealth of Nations*, book i., chap. iv., near the end.

trary, has scarce any value in use; but a very great quantity of other goods may frequently be had in exchange for it."

It is sufficiently plain that, when Smith speaks of water as being highly useful and yet devoid of purchasing power, he means *water in abundance*, that is to say, water so abundantly supplied that it has exerted its full useful effect, or its *total utility*. Water, when it becomes very scarce, as in a dry desert, acquires exceedingly great purchasing power. Thus Smith evidently means by value in use, *the total utility of a substance of which the degree of utility has sunk very low, because the want of such substance has been well nigh satisfied.* By purchasing power he clearly means the ratio of exchange for other commodities. But here he fails to point out that the quantity of goods received in exchange depends just as much upon the nature of the goods received, as on the nature of those given for them. In exchange for a diamond we can get a great quantity of iron, or corn, or paving-stones, or other commodity of which there is abundance; but we can get very few rubies, sapphires, or other precious stones. Silver is of high purchasing power compared with zinc, or lead, or iron, but of small purchasing power compared with gold, platinum, or iridium. Yet we might well say in any case that diamond and silver are things of high value. Thus I am led to think that the word value is often used in reality to mean *intensity of desire or esteem for a thing.* A silver ornament is a beautiful object apart from all ideas of traffic; it may thus be valued or esteemed simply because it suits the taste and fancy of its owner, and is the only one possessed. Even Robinson Crusoe must have looked upon each of his possessions with varying esteem and desire for more, although he was incapable of exchanging with any other person. Now, in this sense value seems to be identical with the final degree of utility of a commodity, as defined in a previous page; it is measured by the intensity of the pleasure or benefit which would be obtained from a new increment of the same commodity. No doubt there is a close connection between value in this meaning, and value as ratio of exchange. Nothing can have a high purchasing power unless it be highly esteemed in itself; but it may be highly esteemed apart from all comparison with other things; and, though highly esteemed, it may have a low purchasing power, because those things against which it is measured are still more esteemed.

Thus I come to the conclusion that, in the use of the word value, three distinct meanings are habitually confused together, and require to be thus distinguished—

(1) Value in use = total utility;

(2) Esteem = final degree of utility;

(3) Purchasing power = ratio of exchange.

It is not to be expected that we could profitably discuss such matters as economic doctrines, while the fundamental ideas of the subject are thus jumbled up together in one ambiguous word. The only thorough remedy consists in substituting for the dangerous name *value* that one of the three stated meanings which is intended in each case. In this work, therefore, I shall discontinue the use of the word value altogether, and when, as will be most often the case in the remainder of the book, I need to refer to the third meaning, often called by economists *exchange* or *exchangeable value*, I shall substitute the wholly unequivocal expression *Ratio of Exchange*, specifying at the same time what are the *two articles* exchanged. When we speak of the ratio of exchange of pig-iron and gold, there can be no possible doubt that we intend to refer to the ratio of the number of units of the one commodity to the number of units of the other commodity for which it exchanges, the units being arbitrary concrete magnitudes, but the ratio an abstract number.

When I proposed, in the first edition of this book, to use Ratio of Exchange instead of the word value, the expression had been so little, if at all, employed by English economists, that it amounted to an innovation. J. S. Mill, indeed, in his chapters on Value, speaks once and again of things exchanging for each other "in the ratio of their cost of production"; but he always omits to say distinctly that exchange value is itself a matter of ratio. As to Ricardo, Malthus, Adam Smith, and other great English economists, although they usually discourse at some length upon the meanings of the word value, I am not aware that they ever explicitly apply the name *ratio* to exchange or exchangeable value. Yet ratio is unquestionably the correct scientific term, and the only term which is strictly and entirely correct.

It is interesting, therefore, to find that, although overlooked by English economists, the expression had been used by two or more of the truly scientific French economists, namely, Le Trosne and Condillac Le Trosne carefully defines value in the following terms: "La valeur consiste dans le rapport d'échange qui se trouve entre telle chose et telle autre, entre telle mesure d'une production et telle mesure des autres." Condillac apparently adopts the words of Le Trosne, saying of value: "Qu'elle consiste dans le rapport d'échange entre telle chose et telle autre." Such economical works as those of Baudeau, Le Trosne, and Condillac were almost wholly unknown to English readers until attention was drawn to them by Mr. H. D. Macleod and Professor Adamson; but I shall endeavour for the future to make proper use of them.

Dimension of Value

There is no difficulty in seeing that, when we use the word Value in the sense of ratio of exchange, its dimension will be simply zero. Value will be expressed, like angular magnitude and other ratios in general, by abstract number. Angular magnitude is measured by the ratio of a line to a line, the ratio of the arc subtended by the angle to the radius of the circle. So value in this sense is a ratio of the quantity of one commodity to the quantity of some other commodity exchanged for it. If we compare the commodities simply as physical quantities, we have the dimensions M divided by M, or MM^{-1}, or M^0. Exactly the same result would be obtained if, instead of taking the mere physical quantities, we were to compare their utilities, for we should then have MU divided by MU or M^0U^0, which, as it really means *unity*, is identical in meaning with M^0.

When we use the word value in the sense of esteem, or urgency of desire, the feeling with which Oliver Twist must have regarded a few more mouthfuls when he "asked for more," the meaning of the word, as already explained, is identical with *degree of utility*, of which the dimension is U. Lastly, the *value in use* of Adam Smith, or the *total utility*, is the integral of $U.dM$, and has the dimensions MU. We may thus tabulate our results concerning the ambiguous uses of the word *value*—

Popular Expression of Meaning	Scientific Expression	Dimensions
(1) Value in use	Total Utility..........	MU
(2) Esteem, or Urgency of Desire for more	Final Degree of Utility	U
(3) Purchasing Power	Ratio of Exchange.....	M^0

The Law of Indifference

When a commodity is perfectly uniform or homogeneous in quality, any portion may be indifferently used in place of an equal portion: hence, in the same market, and at the same moment, all portions must be exchanged at the same ratio. There can be no reason why a person should treat exactly similar things differently, and the slightest excess in what is demanded for one over the other will cause him to take the latter instead of the former. In nicely balanced exchanges it is a very minute scruple which turns the scale and governs the choice. A minute difference of quality in a commodity may thus give rise to preference, and cause the ratio of exchange to differ. But where no difference exists at all, or where no difference is known to exist, there can be no ground for preference whatever. If, in selling a quantity of perfectly equal and uniform barrels of flour, a merchant arbitrarily fixed different prices on them, a purchaser would of course select the cheaper ones; and where there was absolutely no difference in the thing purchased, even an excess of a penny in the price of a thing worth a thousand pounds would be a valid ground of choice. Hence follows what is undoubtedly true, with proper explanations, that *in the same open market, at any one moment, there cannot be two prices for the same kind of article*. Such differences as may practically occur arise from extraneous circumstances, such as the defective credit of the purchasers, their imperfect knowledge of the market, and so on.

The principle above expressed is a general law of the utmost importance in Economics, and I propose to call it *The Law of Indifference*, meaning that, when two objects or commodities are subject to no important difference as regards the purpose in view, they will either of them be taken instead of the other with perfect indifference by a purchaser. Every such act of indifferent choice gives rise to an equation of degrees of utility, so that in this principle of indifference we have one of the central pivots of the theory.

Though the price of the same commodity must be uniform at any one moment, it may vary from moment to moment, and must be conceived as in a state of continual change. Theoretically speaking, it would not usually be possible to buy two portions of the same commodity *successively* at the same ratio of exchange, because, no sooner would the first portion have been bought than the conditions of utility would be altered. When exchanges are made on a large scale, this result will be verified in practice. If a wealthy person invested £100,000 in the funds in the morning, it is hardly likely that the operation could be repeated in the afternoon at the same price. In any market, if a person goes on buying largely, he will ultimately raise the price against himself. Thus it is apparent that extensive purchases would best be made gradually, so as to secure the advantage of a lower price upon the earlier portions. In theory this effect of exchange upon the ratio of exchange must be conceived to exist in some degree, however small may be the purchases made. Strictly speaking, the ratio of exchange at any moment is that of dy to dx, of an infinitely small quantity of one commodity to the infinitely small quantity of another which is given for it. The ratio of exchange is really a differential coefficient. The quantity of any article purchased is a function of the price at which it is purchased, and the ratio of exchange expresses the rate at which the quantity of the article increases compared with what is given for it.

We must carefully distinguish, at the same time, between the Statics and Dynamics of this subject. The real condition of industry is one of perpetual motion and change. Commodities are being continually manufactured and exchanged and consumed. If we wished to have a complete solution of the problem in all its natural complexity, we should have to treat it as a problem of motion—a problem of dynamics. But it would surely be absurd to attempt the more difficult question when the more easy one is yet so imperfectly within our power. It is only as a purely statical problem that I can venture to treat the action of exchange. Holders of commodities will be regarded not as continuously passing on these commodities in streams of trade, but as possessing certain fixed amounts which they exchange until they come to equilibrium.

It is much more easy to determine the point at which a pendulum will come to rest than to calculate the velocity at which it will move when displaced from that point of rest. Just so, it is a far more easy task to lay down the conditions under which trade is completed and interchange ceases, than to attempt to ascertain at what rate trade will go on when equilibrium is not attained.

The difference will present itself in this form: dynamically we could not treat the ratio of exchange otherwise than as the ratio of dy and dx, infinitesimal quantities of commodity. Our equations would then be regarded as differential equations, which would have to be integrated. But in the statical view of the question we can substitute the ratio of the finite quantities y and x. Thus, from the self-evident principle, stated earlier, that there cannot, in the same market, at the same moment, be two different prices for the same uniform commodity, it follows that *the last increments in an act of exchange must be exchanged in the same ratio as the whole quantities exchanged.* Suppose that two commodities are bartered in the ratio of x for y; then every m^{th} part of x is given for the mth part of y, and it does not matter for which of the mth parts. No part of the commodity can be treated differently from any other part. We may carry this division to an indefinite extent by imagining m to be constantly increased, so that, at the limit, even an infinitely small part of x must be exchanged for an infinitely small part of y, in the same ratio as the whole quantities. This result we may express by stating that the increments concerned in the process of exchange must obey the equation.

$$\frac{dy}{dx} = \frac{y}{x}.$$

The use which we shall make of this equation will be seen in the next section.

The Theory of Exchange

The keystone of the whole Theory of Exchange, and of the principal problems of Economics, lies in this proposition—*The ratio of exchange of any two commodities will be the reciprocal of the ratio of the final degrees of utility of the quantities of commodity available for consumption after the exchange is completed.* When the reader has reflected a little upon the meaning of this proposition, he will see, I think, that it is necessarily true, if the principles of human nature have been correctly represented in previous pages.

Imagine that there is one trading body possessing only corn, and another possessing only beef. It is certain that, under these circumstances, a portion of the corn may be given in exchange for a portion of the beef with a considerable increase of utility. How are we to determine at what point the exchange will cease to be beneficial? This question must involve both the ratio of exchange and the degrees of utility. Suppose, for a moment, that the ratio of exchange is approximately that of ten pounds of corn for one pound of beef: then if, to the trading body which possesses corn, ten pounds of corn are less useful than one of beef, that body will desire to carry the exchange further. Should the other body possessing beef find one pound less useful than ten pounds of corn, this body will also be desirous to continue the exchange. Exchange will thus go on until each party has obtained all the benefit that is possible, and loss of utility would result if more were exchanged. Both parties, then, rest in satisfaction and equilibrium, and the degrees of utility have come to their level, as it were.

This point of equilibrium will be known by the criterion, that an infinitely small amount of commodity exchanged in addition, at the same rate, will bring neither gain nor loss of utility. In other words, if increments of commodities be exchanged at the established ratio, their utilities will be equal for both parties. Thus, if ten pounds of corn were of exactly the same utility as one pound of beef, there would be neither harm nor good in further exchange at this ratio.

It is hardly possible to represent this theory completely by means of a diagram, but the accompanying figure may, perhaps, render it clearer. Suppose the line *pqr* to be a small portion of the curve of utility of one commodity, while the broken line *p'qr'* is the like curve of another com-

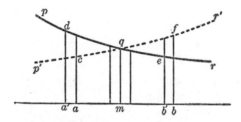

modity which has been reversed and superposed on the other. Owing to this reversal, the quantities of the first commodity are measured along the base line from *a* towards *b*, whereas those of the second must be measured in the opposite direction. Let units of both commodities be represented by equal lengths: then the little line of *a'a* indicates an increase of the first commodity, and a decrease of the second. Assume the ratio of exchange to be that of unit for unit, or 1 to 1: then, by receiving the commodity *a'a* the person will gain the utility *ad*, and lose the utility *a'c*; or he will make a net gain of the utility corresponding to the mixtilinear figure *cd*. He will, therefore, wish to extend the exchange. If he were to go up to the point *b'*, and were still proceeding, he would, by the next small exchange, receive the utility *be*, and part with *b'f*; or he would have a net loss of *ef*. He would, therefore, have gone too far; and it is pretty obvious that the point of intersection, *q*, defines the place where he would stop with the greatest advantage. It is there that a net gain is converted into a net loss, or rather where, for an infinitely small quantity, there is neither gain nor loss. To represent an infinitely small quantity, or even an exceedingly small quantity, on a diagram is, of course, impossible; but on either side of the line *mq* I have represented the utilities of a small quantity of commodity more or less, and it is apparent that the net gain or loss upon the exchange of these quantities would be trifling.

Symbolic Statement of the Theory

To represent this process of reasoning in symbols, let Δx denote a small increment of corn, and Δy a small increment of beef exchanged for it. Now our Law of Indifference comes into play. As both the corn and the beef are homogeneous commodities, no parts can be exchanged at a different ratio from other parts in the same market: hence, if x be the whole quantity of corn given for y the whole quantity of beef received, Δy must have the same ratio to Δx as y to x; we have then,

$$\frac{\Delta y}{\Delta x} = \frac{y}{x}, \text{ or } \Delta y = \frac{y}{x}\Delta x.$$

In a state of equilibrium, the utilities of these increments must be equal in the case of each party, in order that neither more nor less exchange would be desirable. Now the increment of beef, Δy, is $\frac{y}{x}$ times as great as the increment of corn, Δx, so that, in order that their utilities shall be equal, the degree of utility of beef must be $\frac{x}{y}$ times as great as the degree of utility of corn. Thus we arrive at the principle that *the degrees of utility of commodities exchanged will be in the inverse proportion of the magnitudes of the increments exchanged.*

Let us now suppose that the first body, A, originally possessed the quantity a of corn, and that the second body, B, possessed the quantity b of beef. As the exchange consists in giving x of corn for y of beef, the state of things after exchange will be as follows:—

A holds $a - x$ of corn, and y of beef,
B holds x of corn, and $b - y$ of beef.

Let $\phi_1(a - x)$ denote the final degree of utility of corn to A, and $\phi_2 x$ the corresponding function for B. Also let $\psi_1 y$ denote A's final degree of utility for beef, and $\psi_2(b - y)$ B's similar function. Then, as explained previously A will not be satisfied unless the following equation holds true:—

$$\phi_1(a - x) \cdot dx = \psi_1 y \cdot dy;$$
$$\text{or } \frac{\phi_1(a - x)}{\psi_1 y} = \frac{dy}{dx}.$$

Hence, substituting for the second member by the equation given previously we have

$$\frac{\phi_1(a - x)}{\psi_1 y} = \frac{y}{x}.$$

What holds true of A will also hold true of B, *mutatis mutandis*. He must also derive exactly equal utility from the final increments, otherwise it will be for his interest to exchange either more or less, and he will disturb the conditions of exchange. Accordingly the following equation must hold true:

$$\psi_2(b - y) \cdot dy = \phi_2 x \cdot dx;$$

or, substituting as before,

$$\frac{\phi_2 x}{\psi_2(b - y)} = \frac{y}{x}.$$

We arrive, then, at the conclusion, that whenever two commodities are exchanged for each other, and *more or less can be given or received in infinitely small quantities*, the quantities exchanged satisfy two equations, which may be thus stated in a concise form—

$$\frac{\phi_1(a - x)}{\psi_1 y} = \frac{y}{x} = \frac{\phi_2 x}{\psi_2(b - y)}.$$

The two equations are sufficient to determine the results of exchange; for there are only two unknown quantities concerned, namely, x and y, the quantities given and received.

A vague notion has existed in the minds of economical writers, that the conditions of exchange may be expressed in the form of an equation. Thus, J. S. Mill has said:[1] "The idea of a *ratio*, as between demand and supply, is out of place, and has no concern in the matter: the proper mathematical analogy is that of an *equation*. Demand and supply, the quantity demanded and the quantity supplied, will be made equal." Mill here speaks of an equation as only a proper mathematical *analogy*. But if Economics is to be a real science at all, it must not deal merely with analogies; it must reason by real equations, like all the other sciences which have reached at all a systematic character. Mill's equation, indeed, is not explicitly the same as any at which we have arrived above. His equation states that the quantity of a commodity given by A is equal to the quantity received by B. This seems at first sight to be a mere truism, for this equality must necessarily exist if any exchange takes place at all. The theory of value, as expounded by Mill, fails to reach the root of the matter, and show how the amount of demand or supply is caused to vary. And Mill does not perceive that, as there must be two parties and two quantities to every exchange, there must be two equations.

Nevertheless, our theory is perfectly consistent with the laws of supply and demand; and if we had the functions of utility determined, it would be possible to throw them into a form clearly expressing the equivalence of supply and demand. We may regard x as the quantity demanded on one side and supplied on the other; similarly, y is the quantity supplied on the one side and demanded on the other. Now, when we hold the two equations to be simultaneously true, we assume that the

[1] *Principles of Political Economy*, book iii., chap. ii., sec. 4.

x and y of one equation equal those of the other. The laws of supply and demand are thus a result of what seems to me the true theory of value or exchange.

The Origin of Value

The preceding pages contain, if I am not mistaken, an explanation of the nature of value which will, for the most part, harmonise with previous views upon the subject. Ricardo has stated, like most other economists, that utility is absolutely essential to value; but that "possessing utility, commodities derive their exchangeable value from two sources: from their scarcity, and from the quantity of labour required to obtain them."[1] Senior, again, has admirably defined wealth, or objects possessing value, as "those things, and those things only, which are transferable, are limited in supply, and are directly or indirectly productive of pleasure or preventive of pain." Speaking only of things which are transferable, or capable of being passed from hand to hand, we find that two of the clearest definitions of value recognise *utility* and *scarcity* as the essential qualities. But the moment that we distinguish between the total utility of a mass of commodity and the degree of utility of different portions, we may say that it is scarcity which prevents the fall in the final degree of utility. Bread has the almost infinite utility of maintaining life, and when it becomes a question of life or death, a small quantity of food exceeds in value all other things. But when we enjoy our ordinary supplies of food, a loaf of bread has little value, because the utility of an additional loaf is small, our appetites being satiated by our customary meals.

I have pointed out the excessive ambiguity of the word Value, and the apparent impossibility of using it safely. When intended to express the mere fact of certain articles exchanging in a particular ratio, I have proposed to substitute the unequivocal expression—*ratio of exchange*. But I am inclined to believe that a ratio is not the meaning which most persons attach to the word Value. There is a certain sense of esteem or desirableness, which we may have with regard to a thing apart from any distinct consciousness of the ratio in which it would exchange for other things. I may suggest that this distinct feeling of value is probably identical with the final degree of utility. While Adam Smith's often-quoted *value in use* is the total utility of a commodity to us, the *value in exchange* is defined by the *terminal utility*, the remaining desire which we or others have for possessing more.

There remains the question of labour as an element of value. Economists have not been wanting who put forward labour as the *cause of value*, asserting that all objects derive their value from the fact that labour has been expended on them; and it is thus implied, if not stated, that value will

---

[1] *Principles of Political Economy and Taxation*, 3rd ed., p. 2.

be proportional to labour. This is a doctrine which cannot stand for a moment, being directly opposed to facts. Ricardo disposes of such an opinion when he says:[1] "There are some commodities, the value of which is determined by their scarcity alone. No labour can increase the quantity of such goods, and therefore their value cannot be lowered by an increased supply. Some rare statues and pictures, scarce books and coins, wines of a peculiar quality, which can be made only from grapes grown on a particular soil, of which there is a very limited quantity, are all of this description. Their value is wholly independent of the quantity of labour origically necessary to produce them, and varies with the varying wealth and inclinations of those who are desirous to possess them."

The mere fact that there are many things, such as rare ancient books, coins, antiquities, etc., which have high values, and which are absolutely incapable of production now, disperses the notion that value depends on labour. Even those things which are producible in any quantity by labour seldom exchange exactly at the corresponding values. The market price of corn, cotton, iron, and most other things is, in the prevalent theories of value, allowed to fluctuate above or below its natural or cost value. There may, again, be any discrepancy between the quantity of labour spent upon an object and the value ultimately attaching to it. A great undertaking like the Great Western Railway, or the Thames Tunnel, may embody a vast amount of labour, but its value depends entirely upon the number of persons who find it useful. If no use could be found for the *Great Eastern* steamship, its value would be *nil*, except for the utility of some of its materials. On the other hand, a successful undertaking, which happens to possess great utility, may have a value, for a time at least, far exceeding what has been spent upon it, as in the case of the [first] Atlantic Cable. The fact is, that *labour once spent has no influence on the future value of any article:* it is gone and lost for ever. In commerce bygones are for ever bygones; and we are always starting clear at each moment, judging the values of things with a view to future utility. Industry is essentially prospective, not retrospective; and seldom does the result of any undertaking exactly coincide with the first intentions of its promoters.

But though labour is never the cause of value, it is in a large proportion of cases the determining circumstance, and in the following way:— *Value depends solely on the final degree of utility. How can we vary this degree of utility?—By having more or less of the commodity to consume. And how shall we get more or less of it?—By spending more or less labour in obtaining a supply.* According to this view, then, there are two steps between labour and value. Labour affects supply, and supply affects the degree of utility, which governs value, or the ratio of exchange. In order that there may be no possible mistake about this all-important series of relations, I will re-state it in a tabular form, as follows:—

[1] *On the Principles of Political Economy and Taxation,* 3rd ed., 1821, p. 2.

Cost of production determines supply;
Supply determines final degree of utility;
Final degree of utility determines value.

But it is easy to go too far in considering labour as the regulator of value; it is equally to be remembered that labour is itself of unequal value. Ricardo, by a violent assumption, founded his theory of value on quantities of labour considered as one uniform thing. He was aware that labour differs infinitely in quality and efficiency, so that each kind is more or less scarce, and is consequently paid at a higher or lower rate of wages. He regarded these differences as disturbing circumstances which would have to be allowed for; but his theory rests on the assumed equality of labour. This theory rests on a wholly different ground. I hold labour to be *essentially variable*, so that *its value must be determined by the value of the produce, not the value of the produce by that of the labour*. I hold it to be impossible to compare *à priori* the productive powers of a navvy, a carpenter, an iron-puddler, a schoolmaster, and a barrister. Accordingly, it will be found that not one of my equations represents a comparison between one man's labour and another's. The equation, if there is one at all, is between the same person in two or more different occupations. The subject is one in which complicated action and reaction takes place, and which we must defer until after we have described, in the next chapter, the Theory of Labour.

Chapter V. Theory of Labour

Definition of Labour

Adam Smith said, "The real price of everything, what everything really costs to the man who wants to acquire it, is the toil and trouble of acquiring it . . . Labour was the first price, the original purchase-money, that was paid for all things."[1] If subjected to a very searching analysis, this celebrated passage might not prove to be so entirely true as it would at first sight seem to most readers to be. Yet it is substantially true, and luminously expresses the fact that labour is the beginning of the processes treated by economists, as consumption is the end and purpose. Labour is the painful exertion which we undergo to ward off pains of greater amount, or to procure pleasures which leave a balance in our favour. Courcelle-Seneuil and Hearn have stated the problem of Economics with the utmost truth and brevity in saying, that it is *to satisfy our wants with the least possible sum of labour*.

In defining *labour* for the purposes of the economist we have a choice between two courses. In the first place, we may, if we like, include in it *all exertion of body or mind*. A game of cricket would, in this case, be labour; but if it be undertaken solely for the sake of the enjoyment

[1] *Wealth of Nations*, book i., chap. v.

attaching to it, the question arises whether we need take it under our notice. All exertion not directed to a distant and distinct end must be repaid simultaneously. There is no account of good or evil to be balanced at a future time. We are not prevented in any way from including such cases in our Theory of Economics; in fact, our Theory of Labour will, of necessity, apply to them. But we need not occupy our attention by cases which demand no calculus. When we exert ourselves for the sole amusement of the moment, there is but one rule needed, namely, to stop when we feel inclined—when the pleasure no longer equals the pain.

It will probably be better, therefore, to take the second course and concentrate our attention on such exertion as is not completely repaid by the immediate result. This would give us a definition nearly the same as that of Say, who defined labour as *"Action suivée, dirigée vers un but."* Labour, I should say, is *any painful exertion of mind or body undergone partly or wholly with a view to future good*. It is true that labour may be both agreeable at the time and conducive to future good; but it is only agreeable in a limited amount, and most men are compelled by their wants to exert themselves longer and more severely than they would otherwise do. When a labourer is inclined to stop, he clearly feels something that is irksome, and our theory will only involve the point where the exertion has become so painful as to nearly balance all other considerations. Whatever there is that is wholesome or agreeable about labour before it reaches this point may be taken as a net profit of good to the labourer; but it does not enter into the problem.

* * * * *

Quantitative Notions of Labour

Let us endeavour to form a clear notion of what we mean by amount of labour. It is plain that duration will be one element of it; for a person labouring *uniformly* during two months must be allowed to labour twice as much as during one month. But labour may vary also in intensity. In the same time a man may walk a greater or less distance; may saw a greater or less amount of timber; may pump a greater or less quantity of water; in short, may exert more or less muscular and nervous force. Hence amount of labour will be a quantity of two dimensions, the product of intensity and time when the intensity is uniform, or the sum represented by the area of a curve when the intensity is variable.

But intensity of labour may have more than one meaning; it may mean the quantity of work done, or the painfulness of the effort of doing it. These two things must be carefully distinguished, and both are of great importance for the theory. The one is the reward, the other the penalty, of labour. Or rather, as the produce is only of interest to us so far as it possesses utility, we may say that there are three quantities involved in the theory of labour—the amount of painful exertion, the amount of produce, and the amount of utility gained. The variation of utility, as depending on the quantity of commodity possessed, has already been considered; the variation of the amount of produce will be treated in the next chapter; we will here give attention to the variation of the painfulness of labour.

Experience shows that as labour is prolonged the effort becomes as a general rule more and more painful. A few hours' work per day may be considered agreeable rather than otherwise; but so soon as the overflowing energy of the body is drained off, it becomes irksome to remain at work. As exhaustion approaches, continued effort becomes more and more intolerable. Jennings has so clearly stated this law of the variation of labour, that I must quote his words. " Between these two points, the point of incipient effort and the point of painful suffering, it is quite evident that the degree of toilsome sensations endured does not vary directly as the quantity of work performed, but increases much more rapidly, like the resistance offered by an opposing medium to the velocity of a moving body."[1]

* * * * *

There can be no question of the general truth of the above statement, although we may not have the data for assigning the exact law of the

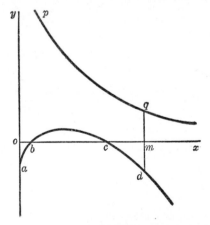

variation. We may imagine the painfulness of labour in proportion to produce to be represented by some such curve as *abcd* (see figure above). In this diagram the height of points above the line *ox* denotes pleasure, and depths below it pain. At the moment of commencing labour it is usually more irksome than when the mind and body are well bent to the work. Thus, at first, the pain is measured by *oa*. At *b* there is neither pain nor pleasure. Between *b* and *c* an excess of pleasure is represented as due to

[1] *"Natural Elements of Political Economy,"* p. 119.

the exertion itself. But after *c* the energy begins to be rapidly exhausted, and the resulting pain is shown by the downward tendency of the line *cd*.

We may at the same time represent the degree of utility of the produce by some such curve as *pq*, the amount of produce being measured along the line *ox*. Agreeably to the theory of utility, already given, the curve shows that, the larger the wages earned, the less is the pleasure derived from a further increment. There will, of necessity, be some point *m* such that *qm = dm*, that is to say, such that the pleasure gained is exactly equal to the labour endured. Now, if we pass the least beyond this point, a balance of pain will result: there will be an ever-decreasing motive in favour of labour, and an ever-increasing motive against it. The labourer will evidently cease, then, at the point *m*. It would be inconsistent with human nature for a man to work when the pain of work exceeds the desire of possession, including all the motives for exertion.

We must consider the duration of labour as measured by the number of hours' work per day. The alternation of day and night on the earth has rendered man essentially periodic in his habits and actions. In a natural and wholesome condition a man should return each twenty-four hours to exactly the same state; at any rate, the cycle should be closed within the seven days of the week. Thus the labourer must not be supposed to be either increasing or diminishing his normal strength. But the theory might also be made to apply to cases where special exertion is undergone for many days or weeks in succession, in order to complete work, as in collecting the harvest. Adequate motives may lead to and warrant overwork, but, if long continued, excessive labour reduces the strength and becomes insupportable; and the longer it continues the worse it is, the law being somewhat similar to that of periodic labour.

EUGEN VON BÖHM-BAWERK

(1851–1914)

Eugen von Böhm-Bawerk was an Austrian economist and statesman. After his graduation from the School of Law of the University of Vienna, he entered the governmental service of the former empire of Austria-Hungary. In 1881, he was appointed professor of economics at the University of Innsbruck, but he was recalled to the ministry of finance in 1889. He was in no small part responsible for the taxation reforms of 1896 and many others which followed. Upon his resignation from the ministry in 1904, he devoted the last decade of his life to teaching economics at the University of Vienna.

Böhm-Bawerk's chief work of interest to students of economic theory was "Capital and Interest." This consisted of two companion volumes, each of which was a complete unit. The first volume "History and Critique of Theories of Interest," commonly known as "Capital and Interest," appeared in 1884 and it went through several editions and translations. The second work, "The Positive Theory of Capital," appeared first in 1889 and, likewise, went through subsequent editions and translations. The following selections have been taken from "Positive Theory of Capital." In general the translation of the first edition by William A. Smart (1891) has been followed.

Böhm-Bawerk was one of the first students to comprehend the significance of the work of Karl Menger. He sought to develop a subjective theory of value, and, if possible, to reconcile it with the previous objective treatment. Marginalism is as important in the work of Böhm-Bawerk as in that of Jevons. Böhm-Bawerk applied his elaborate analysis of value to the factors in production for the development of his elaborate system of distribution. Not merely labor pains, but opportunity costs, are brought into account. Böhm-Bawerk has given us one of the best descriptions of capitalistic or roundabout production.

EUGEN VON BÖHM-BAWERK

SELECTIONS FROM "THE POSITIVE THEORY OF CAPITAL',

BOOK I. THE NATURE AND CONCEPT OF CAPITAL

Chapter II. The Nature of Capital

The end and aim of all production is the making of things with which to satisfy our wants; that is to say, the making of goods for immediate consumption, or Consumption Goods. The method of their production we have already looked at in a general way. We combine our own natural powers and natural powers of the external world in such a way that, under natural law, the desired material good must come into existence. But this is a very general description indeed of the matter, and looking at it closer there comes in sight an important distinction which we have not as yet considered. It has reference to the distance which lies between the expenditure of human labour in the combined production and the appearance of the desired good. We either put forth our labour just before the goal is reached, or we, intentionally, take a roundabout way. That is to say, we may put forth our labour in such a way that it at once completes the circle of conditions necessary for the emergence of the desired good, and thus the existence of the good *immediately* follows the expenditure of the labour; or we may associate our labour first with the more remote causes of the good, with the object of obtaining, not the desired good itself, but aproximate cause of the good; which cause, again, must be associated with other suitable materials and powers, till, finally—perhaps through a considerable number of intermediate members—the finished good, the instrument of human satisfaction, is obtained.

The nature and importance of this distinction will be best seen from a few examples; and, as these will, to a considerable extent, form a demonstration of what is really one of the most fundamental propositions in our theory, I must risk being tedious.

A peasant requires drinking water. The spring is some distance from his house. There are various ways in which he may supply his daily wants. First, he may go to the spring each time he is thirsty, and drink out of his hollowed hand. This is the most direct way; satisfaction follows immediately on exertion. But it is an inconvenient way, for our peasant has to take his way to the well as often as he is thirsty. And it is an insufficient way, for he can never collect and store any great quantity such as he requires for various other purposes. Second, he may take a log of wood, hollow it out into a kind of pail, and carry his day's supply from the spring to his cottage. The advantage is obvious, but it necessitates a roundabout way of considerable length. The man must spend, perhaps, a day in cutting out the pail; before doing so he must have felled a tree in the forest; to do this, again, he must have made an axe, and so on. But there is still a third way; instead of felling one tree he fells a number of trees, splits and hollows them, lays them end for end, and so constructs a runnel or rhone which brings a full head of water to his cottage. Here, obviously, between the expenditure of the labour and the obtaining of the water we have a very roundabout way, but, then, the result is ever so much greater. Our peasant needs no longer take his weary way from house to well with the heavy pail on his shoulder, and yet he has a constant and full supply of the freshest water at his very door.

Another example. I require stone for building a house. There is a rich vein of excellent sandstone in a neighbouring hill. How is it to be obtained? First, I may work the loose stones back and forward with my bare fingers, and break off what can be broken off. This is the most direct, but also the least productive way. Second, I may take a piece of iron, make a hammer and chisel out of it, and use them on the hard stone—a roundabout way, which, of course, leads to a very much better result than the former. Third method—Having a hammer and chisel I use them to drill a hole in the rock; next I turn my attention to procuring charcoal, sulphur, and nitre, and mixing them in a powder, then I pour the powder into the hole, and the explosion that follows splits the stone into convenient pieces—still more of a roundabout way, but one which, as experience shows, is as much superior to the second way in result as the second was to the first.

Yet another example. I am short-sighted, and wish to have a pair of spectacles. For this I require ground and polished glasses, and a steel framework. But all that nature offers towards that end is silicious earth and iron ore. How am I to transform these into spectacles? Work as I may, it is as impossible for me to make spectacles directly out of silicious earth as it would be to make the steel frames out of iron ore. Here there is no immediate or direct method of production. There is nothing for it but to take the roundabout way, and, indeed, a very roundabout way. I must take silicious earth and fuel, and build furnaces for smelting the glass from the silicious earth; the glass thus obtained has to be carefully purified, worked, and cooled by a series of processes; finally, the glass thus prepared—again by means of ingenious instruments carefully constructed beforehand—is ground and polished into the lens fit for short-sighted eyes. Similarly, I must smelt the ore in the blast furnace, change the raw iron into steel, and make the frame therefrom—processes which cannot be carried through without a long series of tools and buildings that, on their part again, require great amounts of previous labour. Thus, by an exceedingly roundabout way, the end is attained.

The lesson to be drawn from all these examples alike is obvious. It is that a greater result is obtained by producing goods in roundabout ways than by producing them directly. Where a good can be produced in either way, we have the fact that, by the indirect way, a greater product can be got with equal labour, or the same product with less labour. But, beyond this, the superiority of the indirect way manifests itself in being the only way in which certain goods can be obtained, if I might say so, it is so much the better that it is often the only way!

That roundabout methods lead to greater results than direct methods is one of the most important and fundamental propositions in the whole theory of production. It must be emphatically stated that the only basis of this proposition is the experience of practical life. Economic theory does not and cannot show *a priori* that it must be so; but the unanimous experience of all the technique of production says that it is so. And this is sufficient; all the more that the facts of experience which tell us this are commonplace and familiar to everybody. But *why* is it so? The economist might quite well decline to answer this question. For the fact that a greater product is obtained by methods of production that begin far back is essentially a purely technical fact, and to explain questions of technique does not fall within the economist's sphere. For instance, that tropical lands are more fruitful than the polar zone; that the alloy of which coins is made stands more wear and tear than pure metal; that a railroad is better for transport than an ordinary turnpike road;—all these are matters of fact with which the economist reckons, but which his science does not call on him to explain. But this is exactly one of those cases where, in the economist's own interest—the interest he has in limiting and defining his own task—it is exceedingly desirable to go beyond the specific economic sphere. If the sober physical truth is once made clear, political economy cannot indulge in any fancies or fictions about it; and, in such questions, political economy has never been behind in the desire and the attempt to substitute its own imaginings! Although, then, this law is already sufficiently accredited by experience, I attach particular value to explaining its cause, and, after what has been said as to the nature of production, this should not be very difficult.

In the last resort all our productive efforts amount to shiftings and combinations of matter. We must know how to bring together the right forms of matter at the right moment, in order that from those associated forces the desired result, the product wanted, may follow. But, as we saw, the natural forms of matter are often so infinitely large, often so infinitely fine, that human hands are too weak or too coarse to control them. We are as powerless to overcome the cohesion of the wall of rock when we want building stone as we are, from carbon, nitrogen, hydrogen, oxygen, phosphor, potash, etc., to put together a single grain of wheat. But there are other powers which can easily do what is denied to us, and these are the powers of nature. There are natural powers which far exceed the possibilities of human power in greatness, and there are other natural powers in the microscopic world which can make combinations that put our clumsy fingers to shame. If we can succeed in making those forces our allies in the work of production, the limits of human possibility will be infinitely extended. And this we have done.

The condition of our success is, that we are able to control the materials on which the power that helps us depends, more easily than the materials which are to be transformed into the desired good. Happily this condition can be very often complied with. Our weak yielding hand cannot overcome the cohesion of the rock, but the hard wedge of iron can; the wedge and the hammer to drive it we can happily master with little trouble. We cannot gather the atoms of phosphorus and potash out of the ground, and the atoms of carbon and oxygen out of the atmospheric air, and put them together in the shape of the corn or wheat; but the organic chemical powers of the seed can put this magical process in motion, while we on our part can very easily bury the seed in the place of its secret working, the bosom of the earth. Often, of course, we are not able directly to master the form of matter on which the friendly power depends, but in the same way as we would like it to help us, do we help ourselves against it; we try to secure the alliance of a second natural power which brings the form of matter that bears the first power under our control. We wish to bring the well water into the house. Wooden rhones would force it to obey our will, and take the path we prescribe, but our hands have not the power to make the forest trees into rhones. We have not far to look, however, for an expedient. We ask the help of a second ally in the axe and the gouge; their assistance gives us the rhones; then the rhones bring us the water. And what in this illustration is done through the mediation of two or three members may be done, with equal or greater result, through five, ten, or twenty members. Just as we control and guide the immediate matter of which the good is composed by one friendly power, and that power by a second, so can we control and guide the second by a third, the third by a fourth, this, again, by a fifth, and so on,—always going back to more remote causes of the final result—till in the series we come at last to one cause which we can control conveniently by our own natural powers. This is the true importance which attaches to our entering on roundabout ways of production, and this is the reason of the result associated with them: every roundabout way means the enlisting in our service of a power which is stronger or more cunning than the human hand; every extension of the roundabout way means an addition to the powers which enter into the service of man, and the shifting of some portion of the burden of production from the scarce and costly labour of human beings to the prodigal powers of nature.

And now we may put into words an idea which has long waited for expression, and must certainly have occurred to the reader; the kind of production which works in these wise circuitous methods is nothing else than what economists call Capitalist Production, as opposed to that production which goes directly at its object, as the Germans say, "*mit der nackten Faust.*" And Capital is nothing but the complex of intermediate products which appear on the several stages of the roundabout journey.

* * * * *

Chapter IV. The True Concept of Capital

* * * * *

The leading principles we have to observe seem to me to be as follows. First, and chiefly, it is quite clear that our definition of the concept must be logically unassailable; that is to say, it must not contradict itself, and it must apply to the object which it proposes to define. Then, we must not be spendthrift in our terminology; that is to say, we must not attach the name capital to, and make it synonymous with, a conception that already has a name, while other suggestive conceptions, to which naturally the word would equally well apply, have to do without any name. Thirdly, the conception we adopt must be scientifically important and scientifically useful. Lastly, and not least, unless an alteration be urgently demanded on some grounds of logic or appropriateness, the name of capital must be left to that conception for which it has been longest and most generally used. Or, to put it in a more roundabout way: as things are at present, everybody treats of the most weighty theoretical and social problems under the general name of "problems of capital"; that being so, the word capital, wherever possible, should be so used as to spare us the aggravated difficulties that will attend the great controverted questions of the day if we rebaptize their terms.

In view of these rules I would suggest the following as the most adequate solution of the controversy.

Capital in general we shall call a group of Products which serve as means to the Acquisition of Goods. Under this general conception we shall put that of Social Capital as narrower conception. Social Capital we shall call a group of products, which serve as a means to the socio-economical Acquisition of Goods; or, as this acquisition is only possible through production, we shall call it a group of products destined to serve towards further production; or, briefly, a group of Intermediate Products. Synonymous with the wider of the two conceptions, the term Acquisitive Capital may be very suitably used, or, less suitably but more in accordance with usage, the term Private Capital. Social Capital again, the narrower of the two conceptions, may be well and concisely called Productive Capital.

* * * * *

BOOK II. CAPITAL AS INSTRUMENTAL OF PRODUCTION

Chapter II. Capitalistic Production

*   *   *   *   *

To construct goods for human consumption out of these productive elements man may take one of two ways. He may combine the economical productive powers with one another—or with activities of free natural powers—in such a way that the desired good immediately emerges as result of the combination; as when he gathers shellfish on the shore. Or he may take a roundabout way, and, with the element at his command, may make, first, another good, and then, with its assistance, the good he wishes; as, for instance, when he makes a boat and net and takes to fishing systematically. We already know that the former method is identical with what the Germans call *kapitallos* production, the latter with capitalist production; and that the intermediate products, which come into existence in the course of the indirect methods, represent economic social capital.

The adoption of capitalist methods of production is followed by two consequences, equally characteristic and significant. One is an advantage, the other a disadvantage. The advantage we have already looked at; it consists in the greater technical productiveness of those methods. With an equal expenditure of primary productive powers (that is to say, labour and valuable natural powers) more or better goods can be produced by a wisely chosen capitalist process than could be by direct unassisted production. This proposition, which is quite convincingly accredited by daily experience, we illustrated and tried to explain in the second chapter of Book I by a number of examples. We found the explanation to be that, when roundabout methods are skilfully chosen, new allies are obtained from the immense stores of natural powers, and their activity is enlisted in the work of production. It is this well-known fact that is usually indicated by the term "productivity of capital." This name, however, carries into the facts a particular interpretation, the correctness of which has yet to be examined in the next chapter.

The disadvantage connected with the capitalist method of production is its sacrifice of time. The roundabout ways of capital are fruitful but long; they procure us more or better consumption goods, but only at a later period of time. This proposition, no less than the former, is one of the ground pillars of the theory of capital. We shall see later on that the very function of capital, as a means of appropriation or source of interest, to a great extent rests upon it. I must, therefore, guard it against any misunderstanding by the two following remarks.

*   *   *   *   *

Again—though this scarcely needs pointing out—when we speak of capitalist production taking time, it is not relevant to raise the objection that, with a piece of concrete capital *once made*, say a tool, a definite product can be made more quickly than it could be without the assistance of capital; that, for instance, a tailor takes three days to sew a coat by hand, and one day to do it with a sewing-machine. For it is clear that the machine sewing forms only one part, and indeed the smaller part, of the capitalist process; the principal part falls to the making of the sewing-machine, and the total process lasts considerably longer than three days.

Thus far we have considered capitalist production as an undivided whole, and have contrasted it with production carried on entirely without capital. But here we are reminded of a fact that has to be reckoned with, viz. that in capitalist production there are stages and degrees; to speak accurately, there are innumerable degrees of "Capitalism." In the making of a consumption good the possible roundabout methods are of very varying length. We may make intermediate products from which the final good will be obtained in a month, or a year, or ten years, or a hundred years. The question now is, what influence such differences of degree have on product.

On the whole it may be said that not only are the first steps more productive, but that every lengthening of the roundabout process is accompanied by a further increase in the technical result; as the process, however, is lengthened the amount of product, as a rule, increases in a smaller proportion.

* * * * *

Chapter IV. The Theory of the Formation of Capital

In our science there are three views in acceptation as to the formation of capital. One finds its origin in saving, a second in production, and a third in both together. Of these the third enjoys the widest acceptance, and it is also the correct one. But the formula will have to be amplified to some extent, and presented in a way that is, at once, clearer and more true to life than has usually been the case.

* * * * *

Chapter V. Formation of Capital in a Community

* * * * *

Every capital is, by its nature, composed of a mass of intermediate products, and the common goal of all these products is to ripen into consumption goods or means of enjoyment. They reach this goal through the continuation of that production process in the course of which they themselves have come into existence. They are all, as it were, on the way towards the goal of human consumption. But the length of the road which they have had to travel is different. This is partly because the various branches of production adopt roundabout ways of various length: mining, for instance, or railway building, takes a much more roundabout and lengthy method than wood-cutting. But it is partly, also, because those goods which constitute the community's capital at the moment are at various points on their respective roads. Many an intermediate product has just entered on a very lengthy roundabout road, as, for instance, a boring machine, whose life-work it will be to drive a gallery in a mine. Some are midway. Others, again, like clothing stuffs ready for making into coats and mantles, are near the end of the journey their particular production process has to take. Now the inventory of capital lays a kind of cross-section through the production processes, thus unlike in length and unlike in stage of progress, and intersects them, of course, at the most different points, just as a national census lays a section through the paths of life, and encounters and registers the individual members of the nation at the most different stages of life.

Considered with reference to the varying distances at which intermediate products lie from the goal of consumption, the total mass of capital divides itself into a number of annual classes or stages of maturity, which may be very appropriately pictured by a diagram of concentric annual circles. The outmost circle (Fig. 1) embraces those goods which will be transformed into goods ready for consumption within the coming year; the second circle represents those goods which will ripen into consumption goods in the year after; the third circle, those which will be ready the year after that, and so on. In a community where production is not yet strongly capitalistic, the inner circles will rapidly contract (Fig. 2), because, in such a community, very lengthy roundabout ways of production, such as turn out their finished goods only after many years, will be rare. In rich and well-developed communities, again, there will be a considerable number of comprehensive circles, and of these the inner ones will have a content that, although relatively smaller, is not inconsiderable.

This representation of the stages of maturity by concentric circles is peculiarly appropriate on this account that it also gives a very happy expression to the quantitative relations of these stages. Exactly as the outmost of the concentric circles possesses the greatest area, while the inner circles possess a gradually decreasing one, does the first of these classes—that nearest to the completion of the process—always, by its very nature, embrace the largest quota of the total mass of capital, while a decreasingly smaller quota falls to the more remote classes. There are two reasons for this. The first is that the various branches of production generally adopt processes of different lengths—lengths varying with the technical circumstances of each branch. Many complete the entire work of production, from the preliminary processes to the turning out of the finished product, within a year; many require two, three, and five years; only a few have a production period extending over ten, twenty, and

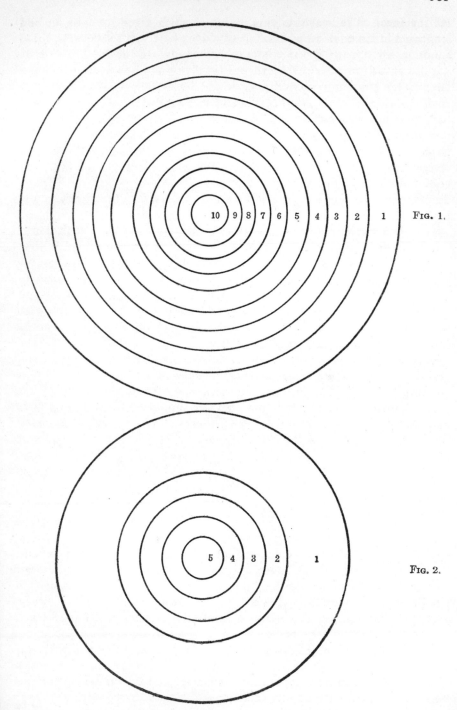

Fig. 1.

Fig. 2.

thirty years. The result is that in the highest classes—those farthest removed in time from the finished product—only a few branches of production are found; intermediate products, for instance, in the tenth circle can only be provided by those branches of production which have at least a ten years' production period. But the lower circles are filled, not only by those last named branches of production (for the intermediate products of these very long processes must pass circle by circle towards maturity), but also by those branches of production which have shorter periods. Thus the quantity of intermediate products grows larger and larger up to the first class, and to this first class every branch of production, without exception, sends its representative.

But there is still another circumstance that works in the same direction. The ripening of intermediate products into consumption goods demands a steady addition of current productive powers. At each stage of the production process new labour is added to the intermediate products which have been passed on to it from the previous stage, and they pass ͗ to the following stage in a more advanced state. In one stage the ͏ntermediate product wool is changed, by the addition of labour, into the ͏ntermediate product yarn; that again in a following stage, by the addition of labour, into the intermediate product cloth, and so on. This has the natural result that, within each branch of production, the amount of ͏nvested capital increases with each advancing stage of the production, or, what is the same thing, at every change into a lower circle. Consequently not only are the lower circles, as has been shown, supplied from more branches of production, but they are supplied with relatively larger amounts of capital, and this gives the lower classes a twofold numerical superiority over the higher ones.

* * * * *

Book III. Value

Chapter I. The Two Concepts of Capital

* * * * *

But, first of all, it is important that we give right names to those things which tradition has handed down to us under the inadequate designations of Use Value and Exchange Value. The two groups of phenomena, to both of which popular usage has given the ambiguous name "Value," we shall distinguish as value in the Subjective and value in the Objective sense.

Value in the Subjective sense is the importance which a good, or a complex of goods, possesses with regard to the wellbeing of a subject. In this sense I should say of any particular good that it was valuable to me, if I recognised that my wellbeing was so associated with it that the possession of it satisfied some want, secured me a gratification or a feeling of pleasure which I should not have had without it, or saved me from a pain which, otherwise, I should have had to endure. In this case the existence of the good means my gain, the absence of it my loss, in wellbeing: to me it is a matter of importance, for me it has value.

By Objective value, on the other hand, is meant the Power or Capacity of a good to procure some one objective result. In this sense there are as many kinds of value as there are external results with which man may be connected. There is a nutritive value of food, a heating value of wood and coal, a fertilising value of manures, a blasting value of explosives, and so on. In any expressions of this kind all reference to the wellbeing or illbeing of a subject is excluded from the conception of value. If we affirm that beech has a superior heating value over pine, we only express the purely objective and, as it were, mechanical fact that with a definite weight of beech a greater amount of heat can be raised than with the same weight of pine. In the above connections, then, instead of the word "Value" we use, as entirely synonymous with it, the expressions "Power" or "Capacity"—expressions which themselves suggest a purely objective relation. Instead of "nutritive value," "heat value," "explosive value," we use "nutritive power" or "nutritive capacity," "heating power," "explosive power," and so on, as meaning exactly the same thing.

The varieties of Objective value just mentioned by way of illustration do not, however, belong to economical but to purely technical relations; and, however frequently they are referred to in economics text-books, they do not properly belong to political economy at all. It does not fall within the province of our science to expound the heating value of wood, nor, in explaining other economical phenomena, has it occasion to lay stress on this heating value any more than it does on any other physical or technical fact. I have given these illustrations purely as illustrations, with the intention of putting in clearer relief the very intimately related nature with the above of that branch of objective values which, of course, has the greatest possible importance for political economy, namely, the objective *Exchange* value of goods. By this expression I mean the objective worth of goods in exchange; or, in other words, the possibility of obtaining in exchange for them a quantity of other economical goods, this possibility being looked upon as a power or a property of the former goods. In this sense we say that a horse is worth £50, or a house worth £1,000, if, in exchange for these, we can obtain, respectively, £50 or £1,000.

Here, again, it must be noted that, as in the kindred expressions heating value and the like, we say nothing at all as to the influence which goods may exert on the wellbeing of any subject whatever; we simply indicate the objective relation that for a particular good a certain amount of other goods may be had in exchange. In this case also the characteristic phenomenon recurs, that the word "Value" can be, quite adequately, replaced by the word "Power," and is, indeed, so replaced in popular speech. Besides the expression "value in exchange" English economists use, quite indifferently, the expression "purchasing power," and we Germans are beginning in the same way to put in general use the term *Tauschkraft*.

The economic theory of value has, then, the double task of interpreting, on the one hand, the laws of Subjective Value, and, on the other, the laws of Objective Exchange Value, as from the economic point of view by far the most important branch of objective value. The first part of this task we shall take up in the present book, the second in the following book dealing with the theory of Price. It is true that the two conceptions, "Price" and "Exchange Value," are by no means identical. Exchange Value is the capacity of a good to obtain in exchange a quantity of other goods. Price is that other quantity of goods. But the laws of these two coincide. So far as the law of price explains that a good actually obtains such and such a price, and why it obtains it, it affords at the same time the explanation that the good is *capable*, and why it is capable, of obtaining a definite price. The law of Price, in fact, contains the law of Exchange Value.

Chapter IV. The Marginal Utility

Turning now to the second question suggested in the last chapter we ask, of several or many wants, which one is it that actually depends on a particular good?

This question would not be put at all if the circumstances of economic life were so simple that single wants always stood over against single goods. If a good were adapted to satisfy a single concrete want, and if it were at the same time the only one of its kind, or, at least, the only one of its kind available, it would be quite clear without further consideration that the satisfaction of the single want depended on our command over the single good. But in practical life the matter is scarcely ever so simple as this; on the contrary, it is usually complicated simultaneously from two sides. First, one and the same good is usually adapted to satisfy various concrete wants, which wants again possess various degrees of importance; and second, several goods of one and the same kind are frequently available, thus leaving it to caprice which good will be used for the satisfaction of an important, and which for an unimportant want. To give the simplest possible example. I have been shooting for a few days on the mountains, and by some accident I miss my companions. I am far from any house or village, and the only food I have for myself and my dog is two entirely similar baker's rolls. It is clear that the satisfaction of my hunger is of infinitely more importance to me than the satisfaction of the dog's hunger and it is just as clear that it lies with me which of the two rolls I shall consume and which I shall give to the dog. And now the question arises, Which of the two wants here is dependent on the bread?

One is tempted to answer, That want to which the bread was actually devoted. But it is evident at once that this is an erroneous conclusion. It would amount to saying that the two rolls, devoted as they are to the satisfaction of wants of different importance, must possess different values; while it does not admit of question that two similar goods, available under similar conditions, must be entirely equal in value.

Here, again, an easy casuistical consideration gives the proper solution. The problem is: Which, among several wants, is dependent on a commodity? This resolves itself very simply when it is known which want it is that would *fail of its satisfaction* if that commodity were not present: that want is evidently the dependent one. And now it is easy to show that the want which failed of its satisfaction would not be that want which the particular commodity was, accidentally and capriciously, selected to satisfy, but would always be the *least important* among all the wants in question; that is to say, among all those wants which would formerly have been provided for out of the total stock of this class of goods.

Consideration for one's own convenience, as obvious as it is imperative, induces every reasonable man who acts economically to maintain a certain fixed order in the satisfaction of his wants. No one would be so foolish as to exhaust the resources at his command in satisfying trifling wants, or wants that could be easily ignored, and thus to deprive himself of the means of satisfying necessary wants. On the contrary, every one would take care to use the resources at his command, in the first instance, to provide for his most important wants; then for wants that come after these in importance; then for those of the third rank, and so on;—always arranging in such a way that the lesser wants were only provided for when all the higher wants had been supplied, and there still remained some means of satisfaction to spare. We act according to the same obvious and reasonable principles when our stock undergoes a change by the loss of one member of that stock. Naturally this will alter the plan according to which we have been employing our resources. Not all the wants we had arranged to satisy can now be provided for, and some abatement in the totality of satisfaction is unavoidable. But, of course, the wise man will try to lay the burden on the least sensitive spot; that is to say, if the loss chances to be in a commodity which was destined to a more important use, he will not give up the satisfaction of this more important want, and, by holding on obstinately to his old plan, provide satisfaction for the less important wants. We may be sure that he will satisfy the more important wants, and will do so by withdrawing provision from that want, among all the wants hitherto marked out for provision, on the satisfaction of which *least* depends. To put it in terms of our former illustration: if our sportsman loses the roll which he has meant for himself, he will scarcely feed his dog with the one that remains, and expose himself to the danger of starving. He will suddenly change his plan, elevate the roll that remains into fulfilling its more important function only, and shift the loss to the least important function, the feeding of the dog.

The case, then, stands as follows. Wants which are more important than this "last" want will not be affected by the loss of the good, for their satisfaction is, as before, guaranteed in case of need by the replacement of substitutes. Nor will those wants be affected which are less important than this "marginal want," for they go unsatisfied whether the good is there or not. The only want affected is the last of those that otherwise would be satisfied: it will be satisfied if the good is there; it will not be satisfied if it is not there. It is thus the dependent want we were seeking.

Here then we have reached the goal of the present inquiry, and may formulate it thus: the value of a good is measured by the importance of that concrete want, or partial want, which is *least urgent* among the wants that are met from the available stock of similar goods. What determines the value of a good, then, is not its greatest utility, not its average utility, but the least utility which it, or one like it, might be reasonably employed in providing under the concrete economical conditions. To save ourselves the repetition of this circumstantial description—which, all the same, had to be somewhat circumstantial to be quite correct—we shall follow Wieser in calling this least utility—the utility that stands on the margin of the economically permissible—the economic Marginal Utility of the good. The law which governs amount of value, then, may be put in the following very simple formula: The value of a good is determined by the amount of its Marginal Utility.

This proposition is the key-stone of our theory of value. But it is more. In my opinion it is the master-key to the action of practical economic men with regard to goods. In the simplest cases, as in all the tangle and complication which our present varied economic life has created, we find men valuing the goods with which they have to deal by the marginal utility of these goods, and dealing with them according to the result of this valuation. And to this extent the doctrine of marginal utility is not only the key-stone of the theory of value, but, as affording the explanation of all economical transactions, it is the key-stone of all economic theory. Those who have observed practical life closely will, I think, be convinced that this claim is not exaggerated. Rightly to observe and rightly to interpret what has been observed, however, is an art not always easy; and in what follows accordingly we shall make use of the value theory to guide us in observing and interpreting what falls within its sphere. We begin, then, with an illustration of the greatest conceivable simplicity.

A colonial farmer, whose log-hut stands by itself in the primeval forest, far away from the busy haunts of men, has just harvested five sacks of grain. These must serve him till the next autumn. Being a thrifty soul he lays his plans for the employment of these sacks over the year. One sack he absolutely requires for the sustenance of his life till the next harvest. A second he requires to supplement this bare living to the extent of keeping himself hale and vigorous. More grain than this, in the shape of bread and farinaceous food generally, he has no desire for. On the other hand, it would be very desirable to have some animal food, and he sets aside, therefore, a third sack to feed poultry. A fourth sack he destines for the making of coarse spirits. Suppose, now, that his various personal wants have been fully provided for by this apportionment of the four sacks, and that he cannot think of anything better to do with the fifth sack than feed a number of parrots, whose antics amuse him. Naturally these various methods of employing the corn are not equal in importance. If, to express this shortly in figures, we make out a scale of ten degrees of importance, our farmer will, naturally, give the highest figure 10 to the sustenance of his life; to the maintenance of his health he will give, say, the figure 8: then, going down the scale, he might give the figure 6 to the improvement of his fare by the addition of meat, the figure 4 to the enjoyment he gets from the liquor, and, finally, to the keeping of parrots, as expressing the least degree of importance, he will give the lowest possible figure 1. And now, putting ourselves in imagination at the standpoint of the farmer, we ask, What in these circumstances will be the importance, as regards his wellbeing, of *one* sack of grain?

This, as we know, will be most simply tested by inquiring, How much utility will he lose if a sack of grain gets lost? Suppose we carry out this in detail. Evidently our farmer would not be very wise if he thought of deducting the lost sack from his own consumption, and imperilled his health and life while using the corn as before to make brandy and feed parrots. On consideration we must see that only one course is conceivable: with the four sacks that remain our farmer will provide for the four most urgent groups of wants, and give up only the satisfaction of the last and least important, the marginal utility—in this case, the keeping of parrots. The only difference, then, that his having or not having the fifth sack of corn makes to his wellbeing is that, in the one case, he may allow himself the pleasure of keeping parrots, in the other he may not; and he will rightly value a *single* sack of his stock according to this unimportant utility. And not only one sack, but *every* single sack; for, if the sacks are equal to one another, it will be all the same to our farmer whether he lose sack A or sack B, so long as, behind the one lost, there are still four other sacks for the satisfying of his more urgent wants.

To vary the illustration, assume that our farmer's wants remain the same, and that he has only three sacks of grain. What now is the value of one sack to him? The test again is quite easily applied. If he has three sacks he can and will provide for the three most important groups of wants. If he has only two sacks, he will be obliged to limit himself to the satisfying of the two most important groups and give up the satisfying of the third, that of animal food. The possession of the third sack—and the third sack, be it remembered, is not a definite sack but any of the three sacks, so long as there are two more behind it—directly carries with it, therefore, the satisfaction of his third most important want; that is, the last or least of those wants covered by the three sacks which constitute his total stock. Any estimate other than that according to the marginal utility would, in this case also, obviously run counter to facts, and would be quite incorrect.

Finally, suppose that our farmer's wants remain as before, and that he only possesses one single sack of corn. In this case it is perfectly clear that all less important methods of using the grain are out of question, and that it will be devoted to and spent in sustaining the farmer's life—a function for which it just suffices. And it is as clear that if this single sack fails the farmer will no longer be able to support himself in life. His possession of the sack, therefore, means life; his loss of it means death; the single sack of corn has the greatest conceivable importance for the wellbeing of the farmer. And all this is still in conformity with our principle of marginal utility. The greatest utility—the preservation of life—is here the sole, as well as the last or marginal utility.

These estimates according to marginal utility are not merely "academic." No one will doubt that our farmer on due occasion—say, on an offer made him for the corn—would act practically according to the same estimates. Any one of us, placed in his position, would undoubtedly be inclined to let one of the five sacks go pretty cheap in consideration of and in correspondence with its small marginal utility. He would charge considerably more for one of the three sacks. And he would not let the irreplaceable *single* sack, with its enormous marginal utility, go for any price whatever.

Transfer, now, the field of illustration from the solitary in the primeval forest to the bustle of a highly organised economic community. Here we encounter, in an altogether dominating position, the empirical proposition that quantity of goods stands in inverse ratio to value of goods. The more goods of one kind there are in the market, the smaller, *ceteris paribus*, is the value of the single commodity, and *vice versa*. Every one knows that economic theory has made use of this empirical proposition—the most elementary proposition in the doctrine of price—to establish the law of "Supply and Demand." But this proposition maintains its validity quite apart from exchange and price. For instance, how much more value does a collector put upon the single specimen, which represents a class in his collection, than upon one of a dozen of such specimens? It is easy to show that well-authenticated facts of experience like these follow, as a natural consequence, from our theory of marginal utility. The more individual goods there are available in any class, the more completely can the wants to which they relate be satisfied, and the less important are the wants which are last satisfied—those whose satisfaction is imperilled by the failure of one of the goods. In other words, the more individual goods there are available in any class, the smaller is the marginal utility which determines the value. If, again, there are available so many individual goods of one class that, after all the wants to which they are relative are completely satisfied, there still remains a number of goods for which no further useful employment can be found, then the marginal utility is equal to zero, and a commodity of that particular class is valueless.

Here, then, we have an entirely natural explanation of the phenomenon which originally struck us as so surprising, that comparatively "useless" things, such as pearls and diamonds, have so high a value, while infinitely more "useful" things, like bread and iron, have a far less value, and water and air no value at all. Pearls and diamonds are to be had in such small quantities that the relative want is only satisfied to a trifling extent, and the point of marginal utility which the satisfaction reaches stands relatively high. Happily for us, on the other hand, bread and iron, water and light, are, as a rule, to be had in such quantities that the satisfaction of all the more important wants which depend on them is assured. Only very trifling concrete wants, or no wants at all, are dependent, for instance, on the command over a piece of bread or a glass of water. It is, of course, true that in abnormal circumstances—as, for instance, in besieged towns, or in desert journeys, where water and food are scarce, and small stores only suffice to meet the most urgent concrete wants of meat and drink—the marginal utility flies up. According to our principles the value of those goods, otherwise of so little account, must rise also, and the inference finds ample empirical confirmation in the enormous prices paid in such circumstances for the most wretched means of subsistence. Thus those very facts which, at first sight, seemed to contradict our theory that the amount of value is dependent on the amount of utility conditioned, on closer examination afford a striking confirmation of it.

Chapter X. The Value of Productive Goods. Value and Costs

* * * * *

From what has been said we may deduce the following general principles as regards the value of means of production. First, since on one and the same utility depend all the groups of means of production which successively pass into one another, the value of all these groups must be substantially the same. Second, the amount of this, their common value, is regulated for all, in the last resort, by the amount of the marginal utility of their finished product. I emphasize "in the last resort." For, thirdly, the value of each group has its immediate measure in the value of its product, the succeeding group. In the *first* instance, the utility and service of the means of production consist and exhaust themselves in the making of their product, and, naturally, the more important and more valuable the product is for us when made, the higher will be the estimate put on the importance of this utility, and of that which provides it. Substantially the third proposition is fully covered by the second, for, in the value of the goods of higher rank, the marginal utility of the final product is mirrored. From this marginal utility value is conducted to all the groups of means of production, but the conduction is done, as it were, by stages. First, and immediately, the amount of the marginal utility stamps itself on the value of the final product. This then forms the measure of the value of the group of foods from which this product comes. This again measures the value of the third group; and the third group, finally, the value of the last group, the goods of fourth rank. From stage to stage the name of the determining element changes, but, under the different names, it is always the same thing that acts—the marginal utility of the final product.

*   *   *   *   *

This leads to several important consequences. First of all, in this way the value of goods which have a higher individual marginal utility is put on a level with the value of the "marginal product"—as we shall call that product which has the least marginal utility—and thus with the value of the means of production, from which both in common come; the theoretical identity of Value and Costs, therefore, holds in this case also. But it is well worthy of notice that here the agreement between value and costs is brought about in a way essentially different from the agreement between costs and marginal product. In the latter case the identity was brought about by the value of means of production adapting itself to the value of the product; the value of the product was the determining, that of the means of production the determined. In the present case, on the contrary, it is the value of the product that must adapt itself. In the *last* resort, of course, it adapts itself only to the value of another product, the marginal product of the cognate production; but, in the *first* instance, it accommodates itself also to the value of the means of production from which it comes, and which are mediated by the substitutionary connection with the marginal product. Here the conduction of value describes, as it were, a broken line. First it goes from the marginal product to the means of production and fixes their value; then it goes in the opposite direction, from the means of production to the other products which may be made from them. In the end, therefore, products of higher immediate marginal utility get their value from the side of their means of production. To translate this from the abstract formula into practice. If we are considering what a good B or C (generally speaking, a product of higher immediate marginal utility) is worth for us, we must say first of all: It is worth exactly as much as the means of production from which we could replace it at any moment. Then if we examine further how much the means of production themselves are worth, we come to the marginal utility of the marginal product A. But very often, indeed, we may save ourselves this further inquiry, as we already know the value of the goods that make up the cost without having to begin at the foundation and follow it from case to case; and in all such cases we measure the value of the products in an abbreviated form, both accurate and convenient—that is to say, simply by their costs.

Here, then, we have the whole truth about the celebrated Law of Costs. As a fact people are right when they say that costs regulate value. Only they must always be conscious of the limits within which this "law" holds, and the source from which it gets its strength. It is, first, only a particular law. It holds only in so far as it is possible to obtain, at will and at the right time, substitutes through production. If there is no opportunity of substitution the value of every product has to be measured by the immediate marginal utility of its own kind, and its agreement with the value of the marginal product, and with the intermediate means of production, is disturbed. Hence the well-known empirical proposition that the law of costs holds only as regards goods "reproducible at will," or "freely produced," and that it is simply an approximate law which does not bind the value of the goods that come under it with slavish exactitude to the level of costs, but—according as production for the moment comes short of demand or runs beyond it—permits of fluctuations now on one side, now on the other.

But it is still more important to emphasise, in the second place, that, even where the law of costs holds, costs are not the final but only the intermediate cause of value. In the last resort they do not *give* it to their products, but receive it from them. In the case of productive goods which have only a single employment this is perfectly clear. That Tokay is not valuable because there are Tokay vineyards, but that the Tokay vineyards are valuable because Tokay has a high value, no one will be inclined to deny, any more than that the value of a quicksilver mine depends on the value of quicksilver, the wheat field on the value of wheat, the brick kiln on that of bricks, and not the other way about. It is only this many-sided character of most cost goods—their capacity of being employed in many different uses—that gives the appearance of the contrary, and a little consideration shows this to be an appearance and nothing more. As the moon reflects the sun's rays on to the earth, so the many-sided costs reflect the value, which they receive from their marginal product, on to their other products. The principle of value is never in them, but outside them, in the marginal utility of the products. The law of costs is not an independent law of value: it only forms an incidental case inside the true universal law of marginal utility. It is simply the great counterpart to the law of Complementary Goods. As the latter disentangles and explains those relations of value which result from the temporary and causal *collocation*—the simultaneous co-operation of several goods to a common useful end; so does the Law of Costs for the value relations of those goods which act in temporary and causal *sequence*—the working of goods after one another and through one another to the same final goal. If we think of the value relations of goods that work into one another as a much-tangled net, we might say that the former law disentangles the meshes in their length and breadth, while the latter disentangles them in their depth; but both fall under the all-embracing law of Marginal Utility, and are nothing but special applications of that law to special problems.

BOOK IV. PRICE

Chapter V. The Law of Supply and Demand

The zone within the limits of which the struggle of competition forces the formation of price is, as we have seen, characterised as lying between the subjective valuations of the marginal pairs, and on this characteristic feature we have formulated our law of price. But this zone has a second characteristic feature: it is that in which exactly as many commodities are offered for sale as are wanted to purchase; or, to use the common expressions, in which supply and demand are quantitatively in equilibrium. In our scheme, at a price which did not rise to £21 more horses were demanded than were offered; at a price which rose above £21: 10s. more horses were offered than were demanded; while in the zone indicated by our law of marginal pairs—that between £21 and £21: 10s.—the position requisite to end the competition was reached, and at that price exactly as many horses were asked as were offered.

Now, if it should be thought preferable, the formulation of the law of price may be based on this second characteristic feature, and it will then take the following shape: The market price is found in that zone in which supply and demand quantitatively balance each other. This formula is as correct as the other. It indicates the same zone in another way. But it is less expressive (1) in so far as it only points to the level of the determining zone in a roundabout way, while, by our formula, the limits of this zone are directly and positively indicated; (2) as it has to contend to some extent with the difficulty of having to use the expressions Supply and Demand,— for the protean ambiguity of these terms is sure to bring innumerable errors and misconceptions in their train, just as it has brought the terms themselves into thoroughly bad repute with many. Still, these drawbacks may very well be overcome by critical attention; and there is no objection, in my opinion, to treat the theory of price under the good old catchwords Supply and Demand, if care is only taken to avoid the errors and misunderstandings which so plentifully surround them, and to inform the old forms and formulas with new and clear knowledge.

* * * * *

Chapter VII. The Law of Costs

* * * * *

The formation of value and price takes its start from the subjective valuations put upon finished products by their consumers. These valuations determine the demand for those products. As supply, over against this demand, stand, in the first instance, the stocks of finished commodities held by producers. The point of intersection of the two-sided valuations, the valuation of the marginal pairs, determines, as we know, the price, and, of course, determines the price of each kind of product separately. Thus, for instance, the price of iron rails is determined by the relation of supply and demand for rails; the price of nails, by the relation of supply and demand for nails; and, similarly, the price of every other product made out of the productive good iron—such as spades, ploughshares, hammers, sheet-iron, boilers, machines, etc.—is determined by the relation between the supply and demand which obtains for these special kinds of products. To make this perfectly clear, let us assume that the relations between requirements and stocks of the various iron products—and, accordingly, their prices to begin with—are very various; that the price of a quantum of commodity which can be made out of one and the same unit of productive material—for instance, from a cwt. of iron—varies from 2s. for the cheapest to 20s. for the dearest class of products. These prices are the result of the position of the market at the moment, and we have first assumed that the stocks of products (the supply) are a given quantity. But they are only for the moment a given quantity. As time goes on, they are always getting supplemented from production, and this makes them a variable quantity. Let us follow the circumstances of this production. For the manufacture of iron fabrics producers, of course, require iron. Under the system of division of labour they must buy this in the iron market. The manufacturers represent this demand for iron. As regards the *extent* of the demand, it is clear that every producer will buy as much iron as he requires to produce that amount of the commodity which he may expect to sell among his customers. But how will it be as regards the *intensity* of the demand? Obviously no producer will give more for the cwt. of iron than he can get for it from his own customers in the shape of price; but, up to this point, even in the worst case, he can and will compete rather than let his production come to a standstill for want of raw material. The manufacturer, therefore, who can profitably employ the cwt. of iron if he gets 20s. from his customers will be a buyer in the iron market up to the price of 20s. as maximum; he who can profitably employ the cwt. of iron at 16s. will, naturally, not buy at a price over 16s., and so on. In this way the market price which each producer of iron wares gets for his particular wares (or the share of the market price which falls to iron according to the law of complementary goods) furnishes him with the concrete valuation which he has in his mind when joining in the demand for iron.

The supply, which stands over against this demand, consists of the stocks of iron held by the mine-owners and ironmasters. These stocks will pass, in methods familiar to us, into the possession of the most capable buyers, and at a price which, approximately, corresponds to the valuation of the last buyer. Suppose the stocks of iron are sufficient to meet the demand of all those buyers who value iron from 20s. down to 6s. per cwt., the valuation of the last buyer, and thus the market price of the iron, will stand at 6s.

And now we have to consider the causal connection which has ended in this price. It runs, in the clearest possible way, in an unbroken chain from value and price of products to value and price of *costs*—from iron wares to raw iron, and not conversely. The links in the chain are these. The valuation which consumers subjectively put upon iron products forms the first link. This helps, next, to determine the figures of the valuation—the money price at which consumers can take part in the demand for iron products. These prices, then, determine, in methods with which we are now familiar, the resultant price of iron products in the market for such products. This resultant price, again, indicates to the *producers* the (exchange) valuation which they in turn may attach to the productive material iron, and thus the figure at which they may enter the market as buyers of iron. From their figures, finally, results the market price of iron.

But still another and very important connection may be gathered from all this. It is that here we have simply the great law of marginal utility fulfilling itself. According to that law the available stock of goods is, successively, conducted into the most remunerative employments— put to the most advantageous uses—and the last use to which the goods are put determines their value. In any individual economy the most remunerative uses are seen to be those which express the most urgent subjective wants, and the value which emerges, as result of these individual relations, is purely personal subjective value. In the more extended sphere of a market, on the other hand, everything is referred, no longer directly to subjective wants, but to those wants as mediated by money— money being, as it were, the neutral common denomination for wants and feelings of various subjects which are not immediately commensurable. Here emerge, as the most remunerative employments, not those which express the wants absolutely most urgent, but those which are represented by the highest money valuation; that is, the *best paying* employments; and the value which results is objective exchange value. Thus it is, first of all, with iron products. In their respective markets they pass to the best paying buyers, and the price which expresses the valuation of the last buyer determines their market value and price. But so it is also, in the second place, in a slightly roundabout way, with the "cost good," iron, itself. In the iron market it goes to the best paying producers, and the valuation of the last of these determines its price. But here the producers are simply mediators. In their conducting of the iron to the best paying consumers, the stock of iron really passes successively to the most re-munerative forms of consumption, and the last of *these* forms provided for determines—through the valuation named by the last producer who enters the market as buyer—the market price of the cost good, iron. It is not this cost good, then, that dictates its fixed price to the products that proceed from it; on the contrary, it receives its own price by the medium of the price of its products, in conformity with the great law of marginal utility, according to which the available stock is forced into the most remunerative employments, and receives its price from the money valua-tions of the last of these.

But connected with this is a series of subsequent phenomena, which, obviously, have given rise to the opinion that costs exert a causal influence on the price of products. So long as the price of various products made from iron varies between 20s. and 2s., while the price of the unit of iron stands at 6s., it is an evidence that the economical principle which should guide the stocks of iron into the most remunerative employments is not fully carried out. Iron is being used in employments where the products fetch only 2s. or 3s. where, accordingly, the use is less than the "last" economically permissible; and, on the other hand, there are still numerous employments unprovided for, where the products would obtain a greater value than 6s. If, for instance, the market price of an iron product stands at 20s., it is a proof that only those consumers of that product who value it at 20s. and upwards are actually purchasing, while other consumers, whose valuations range from 18s. down to 6s., are not supplied in the market. Similarly with products whose market price stands at 16s.; there will be an unsatisfied layer of demand, with a use for the product corre-sponding to the prices 14s. down to 6s., and so on. Now this must be corrected—and the initiation of enterprisers will usually not be long in supplying the needed correction. The production of those iron wares, the price of which still stands above 6s., will, under the inducement of the premium offered by the difference between price and cost, be increased till all those employments where the utility is greater than the amount of 6s. are supplied. Of course this increase of supply has the effect of always reducing the level in which the "last" buyer is found, and thus the market price sinks, till such time as the money valuation of the last buyer, and with it the market price, comes to the normal level of 6s. Conversely, where iron has been put to employments whose products fetch less than 6s., the loss that ensues will prevent more iron being thus employed. This will be brought about by a temporary suspension or limitation of the production of those iron wares, the market price of which is under 6s.

This limitation of supply will soon have the effect of raising the price to 6s., and now, as the state of the case demands, the commodity, iron, will only be attainable by those buyers who can use it to make products that will fetch at least 6s. Thus, from above and from below, all iron products come together at the price of 6s., the amount of their costs; but, quite evidently, the cause of this is not that the cost good, iron, can force its own arbitrary fixed price on its products, but that all the products involved, including the cost good, iron, conform to the law of marginal utility, find their way successively into the most remunerative employments, and together receive their price as regulated by the last of these.

* * * * *

Production may be compared to a giant pump. Every branch of want has its separate pipe sunk down to the great reservoir of the original productive powers, and competes with all the other branches of want in trying to draw its supply by suction from that reservoir. Every branch has a different power of suction, the power increasing with the number and the remunerativeness (that is to say, in the case of organised exchange, the money value) of the employments it embraces. In the nature of the suction pipes, too, there is a difference. Many are quite simple: others have independent intermediate lengths, that convey the pressure that comes from the want, as it were, by stages; and, in correspondence with that, the productive powers which supply the want are raised by stages.

The simile extends still further. Such wants as demand personal services for their satisfaction, attract labour quite directly, according to the payment which they can and will give for them. Such wants, again, as demand material goods for their satisfaction, get these supplied, first, by payment of a market price which is remunerative in itself, and then the remunerative price of the products must attract the productive powers to their manufacture. Sometimes this is done through one or two, sometimes through twenty or thirty, members. In our illustration, human demand asked and paid for iron wares: the market price of iron wares attracted people to the purchase of iron: the price of iron, finally, attracted the original productive powers to the production of iron. In the case of other consumption goods, the number of intermediate members, or, to keep to the terms of our comparison, the number of intermediate lengths in the suction pipe, may be double or twenty times as great. But the principle of the movement, and what chiefly interests us, the result, is always the same. Whether there are many or few intermediate members may hasten or hinder the result, but it cannot weaken or strengthen it; in the end every want, according to the power expressed by its money valuation, draws to itself, mediately or immediately, the productive powers required for its supply. To supply the wants of the rich innumerable productive powers are always active, even if, simultaneously, at other points of the economy, there is want both of men and goods. The reason of this is that the high figures, which the rich are able to offer for the satisfaction of their wants, never fail to exert and continue their attractive force through all the stages of production, right down to the reservoir of the original productive powers.

Thus all human wants exert, as it were, a suction power indicated by the figures of their valuation. Now, that layer of wants which is willing and able to pay, say, 20s. and upwards, for the day's work devoted (mediately or immediately) to its satisfaction, is soon entirely provided for. After it those layers, in succession, draw supply to themselves which can and will pay the day's labour with 18s., 16s., 14s., and 12s., even down to 10s., 8s., 6s., and 4s. If, at the limit of 4s., the entire stock of original powers is required and is taken, this decides two things:—All wants which will not, or cannot, pay the day's labour devoted to their service at 4s., remain unsupplied; and the market price of the day's labour will stand at the figure of the last buyer, namely, 4s. But if, as we may rather assume, the available quantity of labour is greater than this, the wants of still lower levels may be supplied. The last needs—mediate or immediate—which are supplied may be those that pay the day's labour at 2s. only; and, in conformity, the market price of labour also will be fixed at this lower figure of 2s. And, indeed, this market price will be a general one: the uppermost layer will not be paid 20s., and the lowest layer 2s., for the same work or the same commodity: the market price will be the same for all buyers.

And now we come in sight of the answer to the doubt suggested by our former illustration. Suppose that the price of the day's labour is 2s., and the price of a cwt. of iron, which takes three days to produce, is 6s. Suppose now that, all of a sudden, new and productive mines are opened, or some great improvement in process discovered, which makes it possible to produce the cwt. of iron in two days' labour. What is the consequence? So long as the iron and its products maintain the old price of 6s., only those wants in the department of iron wares are supplied which are able and willing to pay 6s. for two days' work; that is, to pay the day's labour at the rate of 3s., while all round, in all other departments of want and branches of production, that layer of want is supplied which pays only 2s. for the day's labour. On economic principles—which are willingly carried out by industrial enterprisers, who are always ready to seize the chance of a profit when offered them—those opportunities of employment which pay the day's work at more than 2s., and have hitherto been unsupplied, will now be supplied: more original productive powers will, accordingly, be invested in the production of iron; and the supply of iron and iron products will be increased till such time as, here as elsewhere, that level of wants which is willing to pay the day's labour at 2s. is satisfied, and therefore the cwt. of iron, which costs two days' labour, fetches 4s. Parallel with this, of course, the price of iron and iron products goes down to the level of 4s. And all this is not in opposition to, but in real fulfillment of our law of Marginal Utility, of which the law of costs, rightly understood, is only a special expression suitable to a special group of phenomena.

* * * * *

PART V

NATIONALISTS AND OPTIMISTS

1. Friedrich List: "National System of Political Economy."

2. Frederic Bastiat: (*a*) "Harmonies of Political Economy."
   (*b*) "Economic Sophisms."
   (*c*) "Essays on Political Economy."

3. Henry Charles Carey: (*a*) "Principles of Social Science."
   (*b*) Kate McKean's "Manual of Carey's Social Science."

4. Robert Ellis Thompson: "Political Economy for High Schools and Academies."

FRIEDRICH LIST

(1789–1846)

Friedrich List was born in Reutlingen, Würtemberg. He entered the civil service in 1818, but was later professor of political economy at the University of Tübingen. Friedrich List was a liberal, using the term in its broad, political sense, rather than in its narrow economic sense. He attacked the German bureaucracy and absolutism. For his radicalism in the Würtemberg parliament, he was expelled. After a short period of imprisonment, List fled to America. He made his home in Pennsylvania, at first on a farm near Harrisburg, and later in Reading, where he published *The National Zeitung*. List returned to Leipzig as United States Consul in 1832, after which he did not again return to America. The later years of his life were devoted to literary labors.

Although List was the author of numerous articles and treatises on economics, his chief work of interest to the student of economic theory was his famous "National System of Political Economy" published in 1841. Its theoretical objective was the shattering of Smith's gospel of free trade. Its practical purpose was the overthrow of the commercial supremacy of England. The two great themes of List were the political force of nationalism and the economic desirability of a protective tariff. List's observations in his native country of Germany and in his adopted land of the United States developed in him a firm conviction along these lines. Indeed, List's influence played no small part in the formation of the famous German Zollverein, which paved the way for the later political unity of the German empire.

The following selections have been taken from List's "National System of Political Economy." The translation used is that by G. A. Matile, published in 1856 by J. B. Lippincott Company of Philadelphia with a preliminary essay and notes by Stephen Colwell.

The student will note List's vivid presentation of his twin themes of nationalism and protection. He is asked to compare this violent reaction with the classical position, but he is also asked to remember that Smith's "Wealth of Nations" was in a similar sense a propagandist volume. Smith was seeking to develop the opposite theory of free trade in an age of mercantilism. Finally, the student is asked to observe the historical method of List and his realistic approach to the subject.

FRIEDRICH LIST

SELECTIONS FROM "NATIONAL SYSTEM OF POLITICAL ECONOMY"

Book II. Theory

Chapter I. Political Economy and Cosmopolite Economy

Before Quesnay and the French economists, there had been only a practical political economy, as shown in national administration. States-men and writers who treated administrative questions, applied them-selves exclusively to the agriculture, manufactures, commerce, and navigation of the country to which they belonged, without analyzing the causes of wealth, and without ascending to the study of the interests of humanity.

Quesnay, who first conceived the idea of universal free trade, extended his view to the whole of mankind, confining himself to no single nation. The title of his work is: *Physiocratie ou du gouvernement le plus avan-tageuse au genre humain.* His starting point is that *the merchants of all countries must be considered as constituting a single commercial republic.* It is obvious that Quesnay treats of the *cosmopolitical* economy; the science which teaches how men may attain to a state of well-being, whilst political economy merely teaches how a nation, in certain circumstances, may attain, by means of agriculture, manufacturing industry, and com-merce, to prosperity or civilization and power.

Adam Smith gave the same extension to his doctrine by endeavouring to establish the cosmopolitical idea of absolute free trade, although he could not but see the gross offences of the Physiocrats against the nature of things, and against logic. Adam Smith did not propose any more than Quesnay to treat of the objects of political economy, or of the policy which each country has to pursue in improving its economical conditions. The title of his work is, "The Nature and Causes of the Wealth of Nations"; that is, of all the nations of the world. He devoted a portion of his work to the various systems of political economy, but only with the view of showing of what little value they were, and of proving that political or *national* economy ought to yield to *universal* economy. If he sometimes speaks of war, it is merely in passing. The idea of *perpetual peace* is the basis of all his arguments. According to the significant remark of Dugald Stewart, his biographer, he has taken as the point of departure for his researches the maxim, "that for the most part the measures of governments for the promotion of public prosperity are useless; and that to raise a State from the lowest degree of barbarism to the highest state of opulence, three things only are necessary, moderate taxation, a good administration of justice, and peace." Adam Smith could only have had in his mind the perpetual peace of the Abbé de St. Pierre.

J. B. Say admits that the idea of free trade depends upon the conception of an universal republic. This writer, who, after all, has merely constructed a scientific building out of the materials furnished by Adam Smith, says, in so many words, in his *Practical Political Economy*, "We may blend in our consideration the family and the head which provides for its wants. The principles, the observations, which concern them, constitute private economy; public economy embraces the observations and the principles which refer to the interests of a particular nation, as susceptible of being opposed to the interests of another nation. Political economy has in view the interest of all nations, or of society in general."

It should be noticed here, that Say acknowledges, under the name of public economy, the existence of a national or political economy, not considered in his works, that he gives the name of political economy to a doctrine evidently cosmopolitical in its nature, and in that doctrine treats only of that economy which embraces the collective interest of human kind, without considering the separate interest of each nation.

This confusion of terms would have disappeared, if, after developing what he calls political economy, which is only cosmopolitical economy, or the economy of mankind, Say had also initiated us in the principles of the doctrine which he calls *public economy*, which is merely the economy of particular nations, or political economy. In the definition or exposition of that science, he could scarcely have refrained from dropping the idea of a nation, and from showing what necessary changes the economy of mankind is to undergo on account of its being divided into distinct nationalities, forming a number of powers and interests, occupying their respective positions of national liberty as between themselves. But by giving to this economy of *the whole* of the human family the name of *political* economy, he saved himself from such an exposition; by a confusion of terms he has produced a confusion of ideas, and masked a series of very grave theoretical errors.

All the later writers have participated in that error. Sismondi calls political economy, "*the science which treats of human happiness.*" Thus Adam Smith and his disciples have, after all, taught nothing else but what Quesnay and his school had taught before them; the articles in the *Revue Methodique* concerning the Physiocrats, employing nearly the same expression, says that the *happiness of individuals depends in general upon that of the whole human family.* The very Coryphaeus of American free trade in the sense of Adam Smith, Thomas Cooper, President of Columbia College, does not hesitate to deny the existence of nationality; a nation, he says, is "merely a grammatical invention, designed to spare periphrases, a nonentity, a thing that has no existence except in the brains of political men." Cooper is, in this, perfectly consistent; much more so than his predecessors and masters; for as soon as the existence of nations in their separate conditions and individual interests is acknowledged, the economy of human society must be modified conformably with these separate interests; if then it is attempted to stigmatize these modifications as errors, it is skilful to deny at once the existence of nations.

For our part, we are far from rejecting the theory of *cosmopolitical* or universal economy as elaborated by the Say school; we only think that political economy, or what Say calls public economy, should also be elaborated scientifically, and that it is always better to designate things by their right names, than to give them denominations contrary to the meaning of words.

If we would remain faithful to logic and to the nature of things, social economy must be distinguished from private economy; and in the latter, political or national, must be distinguished from cosmopolite economy; the one taking its point of departure from the idea of separate nationality, shows how a particular nation in the actual condition of the world, regard being had to its special circumstances, may preserve and improve its economical condition; the other being a system based upon the hypothesis that all the nations of the world form but one society, living in a perpetual peace.

If we assume with this school an universal association or federation of all nations as a guarantee of perpetual peace, the principle of free trade among nations would be fully established. The less an individual is restricted in the pursuit of well-being, the richer and more numerous those with whom he is in relations, the wider is the scope of his activity, the easier and more effective will be the employment of the faculties with which nature has endowed him in the improvement of his condition, and the more available to the same end will be his acquired knowledge and talents, and all other powers which may be at his disposal. As with individuals, so with districts and provinces. It would be folly to maintain that commercial union is less advantageous than interior custom-houses would be to the United States of North America, to the provinces of France, and to those of the German confederation.

The United Kingdoms of Great Britain and Ireland present a striking and decisive example of the immense results of free trade between associated nations.

Suppose a similar association among all the nations of the world, and the liveliest imagination could not fancy the sum of human well-being and enjoyments which it would procure for the human family.

The idea of a confederation of all nations, and of a perpetual peace, are both clearly taught by reason and religion. If duels between individuals are unreasonable, how much more duels between nations! The proofs which social economy draws from the history of civilization in favor of some general association of men under one system of law, are sufficiently striking to influence men of sound understanding.

History teaches us that in a state of war human welfare is at its lowest degree, and that it rises in proportion as the associations of society increase. In a primitive state of the human race, we find only families; afterwards some cities, then confederations of cities, then the union of a whole country, and finally, the association of many States under one constitution. If the nature of things has been strong enough to extend to hundreds of millions the association which commenced with families only, we may imagine that its energy might suffice to effect the union of all nations. If the human mind has been able to appreciate the benefits of society upon such a large scale, we may regard it as capable of comprehending the advantage of an association embracing the whole of humanity. A multitude of symptoms reveal this tendency. It may suffice to recall the progress made in science, art, industry, and social organization. We can now predict, with certainty, that, in some ten years, owing to improved means of communication, civilized nations will be as closely united in their relations, both material and moral, and even more so, than the different counties of England were a century since. The governments of continental nations already possess, in the telegraph, the means of conferring together almost as readily as if they were upon the same spot. Powerful forces hitherto unknown have already elevated industry to a development beyond all expectation, and others still more powerful are giving tokens of their appearance. But as industry advances, and becomes diffused throughout different countries, war is rendered very improbable, if not impossible. Two nations equally advanced in industry can mutually inflict greater injuries in one week than they can repair in the space of a generation. Consider also, that these new powers, hitherto specially devoted to production, will not refuse their energies to the work of destruction, and that they may be used for the purpose of defence generally; but especially are they at the service of the continental nations of Europe, even to the threatened result of depriving Great Britain of the defensive advantages arising from her insular position. In the Congress of its great powers, Europe possesses already the embryo of a future Congress of Nations. Henceforward, the tendency to adjust public differences by means of protocols, must prevail over that of extorting justice by force of arms. More correct ideas on the subject of wealth and industry are now prevalent, and the best minds throughout the world are convinced that the civilization of barbarous and half-barbarous people, the restoring nations which have retrograded, and the foundation of colonies, offers to the more advanced nations a field for the development of their productive power, far more promising and satisfactory than war or hostile commercial regulations. In proportion as this conviction becomes established, and as the means of communication shall open between civilized and uncivilized nations, the former will more fully comprehend that the civilization of barbarous people and nations rent by long-continued anarchy or oppressed by bad governments, is a mission worthy of great national efforts, a mission which belongs to all, and which can only be accomplished by associated efforts.

It seems to be an unalterable law of our nature, an instinct of humanity which prompts or stimulates civilized nations, to extend their power over people of less culture: hence we may infer that the civilization of all nations and the culture of all the world and its inhabitants is the true mission of national power and intelligence. On all sides we observe population, intellectual power, and material capital, increasing under the influence of civilization to the point of being forced forward upon other less civilized countries. When the soil can no longer feed its population nor give employment to those who dwell upon its surface, the unemployed must go to distant countries, seeking more fruitful fields; when talents and industrial capacity no longer obtain a sufficient compensation by reason of an over-supply, they emigrate, seeking homes where their services may be in demand; when, from the accumulation of material capital, the rate of interest falls so low that small capitalists can no longer live, they, too, must emigrate to poorer countries for more profitable investments.

The system of Say or his school rests, therefore, upon a true idea, an idea that science, if faithful to its vocation of aiding the practical, must admit and elaborate; an idea that practice cannot disregard without going astray. This School has, however, neglected to take into account separate nationalities, their interests, their particular condition, and to reconcile them to the idea of universal union and perpetual peace.

The School has admitted as realized a state of things to come. It presupposes the existence of universal association and perpetual peace, and from it infers the great benefit of free trade. It confounds thus the effect and the cause. A perpetual peace exists among provinces and states already associated; it is from that association that their commercial union is derived: they owe to perpetual peace in the place they occupy, the benefits which it has procured them. History proves that political union always precedes commercial union. It does not furnish an instance where the latter has had the precedence. In the actual state of the world, free trade, would bring forth, instead of a community of nations, the universal subjection of nations to the supremacy of the greater powers in manufactures, commerce, and navigation. The reasons for this opinion are not only strong, but in our view beyond all dispute.

An universal republic, as it was understood by Henry IV, and by the Abbé de St. Pierre, that is, an association in which all nations should mutually acknowledge the same legal authority and renounce the right of enforcing justice, as between themselves, is realizable only so far as a certain number shall have reached the same, or nearly the same degree of industry, civilization, political education, and power. Free trade can be extended only by the gradual progress of such an union; it is only by it that nations can obtain the great benefits of which associated states and provinces offer us in our time such an example. The protective system is the only means by which nations less advanced can be raised to the level of that nation which enjoys a supremacy in manufacturing industry—a monopoly not conferred by nature, but seized by being first on the ground; the protective system, regarded from this point of view, will be the most effective promoter of universal association among nations, and consequently free trade. And from this point of view, political economy is a science which regards existing interests and the special condition of nations, shows how each one may arrive at that degree of economical development, to which association with nations of equal culture and advantages, free trade included, may by any possibility carry a nation.

But the School has confounded the two doctrines; it commits the grand error of applying to the condition of different countries principles strictly cosmopolite, and at the same time of disregarding, from political considerations, the cosmopolite tendency of productive power.

It is from having overlooked the cosmopolite tendency of productive power that Malthus has fallen into the error of wishing to restrain the increase of population; that more recently Chalmers and Torrens have conceived the strange idea that the augmentation of capital and of production, without bounds, were evils to which the public interest demands a limit; that Sismondi has declared manufactures to be injurious to society. This theory may be compared to Saturn: it devours its own children; in the development of population, capital, and machinery, it finds the division of labor, and explains by that law the progress of society, and then begins to regard population, capital, machinery, as monsters threatening the prosperity of nations; for regarding in this case only the actual condition of a particular nation, it loses sight of the state of the world and the future progress of mankind.

It is not true that population increases with more rapidity than subsistence; at least it is folly to admit that disproportion, and to attempt the proof by means of intricate calculations and mere sophisms, so long as the earth offers an amount of unemployed forces great enough to feed ten, perhaps an hundred fold more inhabitants than now occupy it.

It is but a narrow view of the subject to assume the actual capacity of productive power as the measure for the number of men who may find subsistence upon a given space. The savage, the hunter, and the fisherman, could not, in their mode of calculation, find room sufficient upon the whole earth for more than a million of men, the shepherd for more than ten millions, the unskilled farmer for more than a hundred millions; and yet Europe alone, in our day, feeds a population of two hundred millions of inhabitants. The cultivation of potatoes and plants, suited for the food of cattle, with other recent improvements in agriculture, have increased ten-fold the power of men for the production of food. In England, during the Middle Ages, an acre of land yielded in wheat four for one; now it yields from ten to twenty for one, and five times more land has been brought under cultivation. In several European countries, the natural fertility of which is the same as that of England, the actual product does not exceed four for one. Who can assign limits to the discoveries, inventions, and progress of mankind? Agricultural chemistry is still in its infancy. Who can say if to-morrow shall not bring forth a new discovery or some new process, which may quadruple, if not decuple the fecundity of the soil? Artesian wells have already furnished the means of transforming thirsty solitudes into fertile fields. How many new elements may yet be buried in the bowels of the earth!

Suppose that some new discovery should enable men to produce heat at pleasure, and at a very low cost, without recourse to any fuel actually known, how much land would not that discovery bring into culture, and in what an incalculable proportion would not the productive power of any given space be increased? If the theory of Malthus appears narrow in its tendencies, it is also in its means contrary to nature, destructive to moral energy—in one word, horrible! It destroys a motive employed by nature to stimulate men to effort of body and mind, to awaken and to exalt their noblest feelings, a motive to which the human race owes the most of its progress. It enacts into law the harshest egotism, it asks us to shut our hearts and our hands against the hungry, for in giving them food and drink, we may be the cause, perhaps, that thirty years hence another may be famished. It substitutes calculation for pity. Such a doctrine would change the hearts of men into stones. And what should we expect from a people with hearts of stone, but the complete ruin of morals, and consequently, the destruction of productive power, the loss of capital, civilization, and the political power of the country?

If the population of a country exceed the production of subsistence, if capital increases so as no longer to find employment, if the use of machinery deprives multitudes of work, if, finally, manufactured products encumber the store-houses, it is a proof that nature intends not industry, civilization, riches, and power, to be the exclusive portion of any single people, so long as a large portion of the surface of the earth suitable for tillage shall be inhabited by savage animals, and the greatest part of the human race shall be plunged in barbarism, ignorance, and misery.

We have just exhibited the errors into which this school of economists has fallen, by considering, from a political point of view, the productive power of man. Let us now point out those which it has committed by regarding the particular interest of nations, from a point of view wholly cosmopolite.

If there existed such a confederation of nations as that of the United States of North America, the surplus of population, talents, industry, power, and material capital, would flow from England toward and over the continent, just as it now flows from the Eastern States of the American Union to and over the Western States, only upon the condition, however, that the countries of the continent could offer the same security to persons and property, the same constitution, the same general laws, and that the English government could be subjected to the collective authority of a general confederation. In such an hypothesis, there could be no better means of elevating those countries to the degree of wealth and civilization which England has attained, than free trade; such is the argument of the School. But in the actual state of the world, what would be the effect of such a free trade?

The English nation, as an independent and isolated nation, should take its own interest as the governing rule of its policy; Englishmen, attached to their bank, to their laws, to their institutions and habits, should, as much as possible, employ their means and capital in the industry of their own country; free trade, by opening all the countries of the world to the products of English manufactures, would encourage their policy; they would not, in such case, be apt to entertain the idea of establishing manufactures in France or in Germany. Any surplus of capital would be of course applied in England to the promotion of external commerce. If obliged to emigrate with the view of investing capital abroad, as is the case in our day, they would prefer to the continental nations of their vicinity, remoter countries, where they would find their own language, their laws, and their institutions. England would thus become one immense central manufacturing city. Asia, Africa, and Australia, would be civilized by her, and be covered with new States after her own image. In the course of time, under the presidency of the mother country, would come forth a world of English states, in which the nations of the European continent would be lost as insignificant and sterile races. France would share with Spain and Portugal the mission of supplying the English world with the best wines, and of drinking themselves the worst; at the most, she might retain the manufacture of a few articles for the world of fashion. Germany would have nothing to furnish this English world but toys for children, wooden clocks, philological writings, and, now and then, a body of auxiliaries, destined to be killed or consumed in some desert of Asia or Africa, in a struggle to extend the manufacturing and commercial supremacy, the literature and the language of England. Not many centuries hence in that English world, the Germans and the French may be spoken of with altogether as much respect as we speak now of Asiatic nations.

But political science teaches that this development by the help of free trade, is contrary to nature. If in the time of the Hanseatic League, so it argues, free trade had been established, German, instead of English nationality, would have taken the start of all others in commerce and in manufactures. It would be supremely unjust to attribute to the English, from cosmopolitical considerations, all the wealth and all the power of the globe, solely because they first developed their own commercial system, and beyond any other people have disregarded the cosmopolite principle. To the end that free trade may operate naturally, it is necessary that the nations less advanced than England, should be raised by artificial means to the same degree of development at which England has arrived artificially. Through fear that in virtue of this cosmopolite tendency of productive power, upon which we have just remarked, distant countries should be sooner improved than the nations of continental Europe, those nations which are certain, that from their moral, intellectual, social, and political state, they can become manufacturing communities, should at once have recourse to the protective system as to the only means of attaining this end. The effects of the protective system are displayed in two ways: first, by excluding, gradually, foreign products from our own markets, we produce in other countries a surplus of labour, of industrial power and capital, which must look abroad for employment; secondly, by premiums offered for the emigration of laborers, industrial skill and capital, we attract to our own country that surplus of productive power, which would otherwise retreat to distant regions of colonies.

Public economy sends us to history for the proof, and asks if England has not drawn to her shores in that manner an immense amount of productive power from Germany, Italy, Holland, Belgium, France, and Portugal. It asks why the cosmopolite school, in comparing the inconveniences and the advantages of the protective system, entirely overlooks that great result.

Chapter II. The Theory of Productive Forces and the Theory of Values

The celebrated work of Adam Smith is entitled: *The Nature and Causes of the Wealth of Nations*. The founder of the reigning school has thus indicated with exactness the double point of view under which the economy of nations, as well as that of individuals, is to be considered. The causes of wealth are quite a different thing from wealth itself. An individual may possess wealth, that is, exchangeable values; but if he is not able to produce more values than he consumes, he will be impoverished. An individual may be poor, but if he can produce more than he consumes, he may grow rich.

The power of creating wealth is then vastly more important than wealth itself; it secures not only the possession and the increase of property already acquired, but even the replacing of that which is lost. If this be so with mere individuals, how much more is it true with nations, which cannot live upon their own income! Germany has been in every age wasted by pestilence, famine, or civil and foreign war, but has always preserved the greater part of her productive power, and thus has always quickly recovered her prosperity; whilst Spain, rich and powerful, but trampled upon by despots and priests, Spain, in full possession of internal peace, has sunk into constantly increasing poverty and misery. The same sun still shines upon the Spaniards, they possess still the same soil, their wines are as rich as ever, they are still the same people as before the discovery of America, and before the establishment of the Inquisition; but Spain has lost by degrees her productive power, and has thus become a poor and miserable country. The war of emancipation cost the Colonies of North America hundreds of millions, but their independence increased so immensely their productive power, that a few years of peace added to their wealth greater possessions than they before enjoyed. Compare the state of France in 1809, with that of 1839: what a difference! And yet France, since 1809, has lost a considerable part of the European continent, has undergone two devastating invasions, and paid millions upon millions for the expenditures of war.

A penetrating mind like that of Adam Smith, could not entirely overlook the difference between wealth and its causes; nor the decisive influence of these causes upon the condition of nations. In his introduction, he distinctly announces that: "Labor is the fund which originally supplies a nation with its wealth; and the abundance or scantiness of the annual supply must depend principally upon the actual state of the skill, dexterity and judgment, with which labor is applied, the productive power of labor, and upon the proportion between the number of those who are annually employed in a useful labor and those who are not so employed." It is easy to see that Adam Smith perfectly understood that the welfare of nations depends chiefly on the amount of their *productive power*.

But, it appears not to be in the order of nature that a science shall come forth complete from the head of any single philosopher. It is but too evident that the cosmopolite idea of the Physiocrats, *universal free trade*, and that really great discovery of the *division of labor*, preoccupied him too much to allow the pursuit of the idea of productive power. However great the obligations of science to him in other respects, the discovery of the division of labor was in his own eyes the strongest of his titles to public favor. It was to make the reputation of his work, and the celebrity of his name. Too shrewd not to understand, that he who is about to sell a precious stone of great value does not carry the jewel to market in a sack of wheat, however useful that grain may be in its place, he knew better how to exhibit his commodity; having too much experience to be ignorant that a debutant (and he was a debutant in political economy when he published his work), who is fortunate enough to make a strong impression in the first act, obtains easily all needed indulgence in the following acts, if he but keeps himself above mediocrity, he wisely commenced his work with the doctrine of the division of labor. Smith was not mistaken in his calculation; his first chapter made the fortune of his book, and established his authority.

We believe ourselves safe in affirming, indeed, that it was the desire of bringing into favorable light the important discovery of the division of labor which hindered Adam Smith from pursuing the idea of productive power announced in his introduction, and so often reproduced by the way, it is true, in the rest of his book; which prevented him from giving to his whole book a more perfect form. The high estimate placed by him upon his idea of the division of labor, led him to represent labor as the basis of the wealth of nations, though he had seen clearly, and though he declares that the productiveness of labor depends on the degree of skill and intelligence with which it is directed. We ask, then, is it reasoning scientifically, to offer as the cause of a phenomenon that which is merely the result of a multitude of more profound causes?

It is beyond all doubt, that riches can only be acquired by the means of the mind and of the body, or of work; but that is not assigning a cause from which useful deductions may be drawn; for history shows that nations have sunk into poverty and misery despite the labor and economy of their citizens. He who wishes to learn how one nation may have risen from poverty and barbarism to opulence and civilization, and how another has fallen from wealth and prosperity into poverty and misery, simply from the doctrine, that labor is the cause of wealth, and idleness is the parent of poverty, (a remark made by Solomon, before Adam Smith), will not fail to put this new question, What, then, is the cause of labor, and what that of idleness? The head, the hands, and the feet of men might be given with more accuracy as causes of wealth. At least, this would be much nearer the truth; the point of the questions would then be to know why these heads, hands and feet applied themselves to the work of production, and why their efforts were successful. What is it but the mind which animates individuals? What is it but social order which makes their activity fruitful, and their natural powers efficient? The better a man comprehends what he owes to the future, the more his ideas and feelings lead him to secure a favorable position in life for those nearest to him, and to make them happy; the more he is accustomed from childhood to reflections and activity, the more his generous instincts have been cultivated, and his body and mind exercised—the more advantage he had in early life of fine examples, the more occasion he had to employ his intellectual and physical powers for the amelioration of his lot, the less is he checked in his proper sphere of activity, the happier are his efforts, and the more assured are the results; the more order and activity give him a title to respect and public consideration, the less is his mind a prey to prejudices, superstition, error and ignorance; finally, the more he applied his mind and members to production, the more will he be able to produce, and the more assuredly will he reap the reward of his labor. In all these respects the principal thing is the condition of society in which the individual has been brought up, and in which he moves. It is important to know if science and art flourish in them; if institutions and laws favor religious sentiment, morality and intelligence, security for person and property, liberty and justice; if in the country all the elements of material prosperity, agriculture, manufacturing, industry, and commerce, are equally and harmoniously developed; if national power is strong enough to secure to individuals the transmission of material and moral progress from one generation to another, and to enable them, not only to employ the whole national power of a country, but also, by means of external commerce and colonies, to employ the national power of foreign countries.

Adam Smith has so little understood the nature of those powers in general that he does not even consider as productive the intellectual efforts of those who are engaged in administering justice, and preserving order, giving instruction, upholding religion, or cultivating science and art. His researches are limited to that activity of men which produces material values. He acknowledges that the productive power of that activity depends on the skill and intelligence with which it is applied; but his investigations as to the causes of that skill and intelligence do not lead him beyond the division of labor, which he explains only by exchange, by increase of material capital, and by the extension of markets. Thus his doctrine becomes more and more materialistic, special and individual. Had he pursued the idea of productive power without suffering himself to be controlled by that of value, *exchangeable value*, he would have comprehended that at the side of a theory of values there is required an independent theory of productive power to explain economical phenomena. But he went so far astray as to explain the moral powers by purely material circumstances, and from this error springs all the absurdities, all the contradictions, of which his school has been guilty down to this day, as will be seen, and which are the chief reasons why the teachings of political economy have found so little favor with the best minds. Smith's school teaches little else but the theory of value; he draws from this idea of exchangeable value, that which serves as the basis of his doctrine, and the very definition which he gives of the science.

According to J. B. Say, this science teaches how riches or exchangeable values are produced, distributed, and consumed. It is evidently not the science which explains how productive power or forces are awakened and maintained, and how they are repressed or annihilated. McCulloch calls it expressly the science of values, and recent English authors designate it by the name of the science of exchange.

Examples drawn from private economy will bring into full light the difference between the theory of productive power and the theory of values. If of two fathers of families, both proprietors of land, each saving yearly the sum of one thousand dollars, and each having five sons, the one invests his savings in keeping his sons at manual labor, whilst the other employs his savings in making two of his sons intelligent agriculturists, and in preparing the three others for professional life, conformably to their several aptitudes, the first acts according to the theory of values, and the second according to that of productive powers. At the time of his death the former will be richer than the latter in exchangeable values, but as to the productive power the contrary will be the case. The estates of the one will be divided into two parts, each being skilfully worked will give a net product equal to the whole before at the same time the three other sons would have in their talents ample means of living. The estate of the other would be divided into five parts, each of which would continue to be as badly cultivated as the whole had been before. In one family a great amount of moral power would have been developed, and many talents destined to increase from generation to generation, each succeeding generation possessing larger resources for the acquisition of wealth than the one preceding. In the other family, on the contrary, stupidity and poverty would increase in proportion as the estate became more and more divided. It is in this way the planter increases, by means of his slaves, the quantity of his exchangeable values, but ruins the productive power of succeeding generations. Every expense for the instruction of youth, for the maintenance of justice, for the defence of the country, is a destruction of values for the benefit of productive power. The greatest part of the consumption of a country has for its object the education of the coming generation, the care of the future productive power.

Christianity, monogamy, the abolition of slavery, and qualified servitude, hereditary thrones, the invention of printing, of posts, of coinage, of weights and measures, of calendaring, of watches, the police, the enfranchisement of lands, and the vastly improved means of transportation, are rich sources of productive power. To be convinced of it we need only compare Europe with Asia. To have a just idea of the influence of liberty of thought and liberty of conscience upon the productive power of a nation, we need only read successively the History of England and the History of Scotland. Publicity of judicial decisions, trial by jury, enactment of laws by a parliament, a government subject to public control, the local administration of towns and corporations by themselves, the liberty of the press, freedom of association for purposes of general utility, all these impart, in constitutional states to the citizens as well as to the government, an energy and power which could scarcely be acquired by any other means. No law or public institution can be imagined but must have more or less influence upon the increase or the decrease of productive power.

If bodily labor be designated as the only producer of riches, how can it be explained that modern nations are incomparably richer, more populous, more powerful and prosperous than the nations of antiquity? Among the ancients, there was relatively to the whole population many more laborers employed. The labor was much harder, land was cultivated in larger parcels, and yet the mass of citizens was worse fed, worse clad, than in modern times. This is explained by the progress of past ages in science and art, in what concerns the family and the nation, in intellectual culture, and in productive capacity. The actual conditions of nations is the result of an accumulation of discoveries, inventions, improvements, the efforts of all previous generations; it is that which constitutes the intellectual capital of the living race of men, and a nation is productive only in proportion as it is able to assimilate or digest these conquests of anterior generations, and to increase them by its own acquisitions. This productiveness will be modified, of course, by natural resources, by the extent and geographical position of territory, the number of inhabitants, and their political power; by capacity for improving within national limits, in a superior and harmonious manner, every branch of labor, and extending moral, intellectual, industrial, commercial, and political influence over less advanced nations and over the world in general.

The School would persuade us that politics and the government of the State have nothing in common with political economy. In so far as it limits its researches to values and to exchange, this may be right; it may be possible to define value, capital, profits, wages, and rent, and to analyze and ascertain their elements, to examine the causes which determine their variations without taking into account political circumstances. But there is obviously an element of private or individual economy in this economy of nations. It suffices to read the history of Venice, of the Hanse Towns, of Portugal, Holland, and England, to understand how far individual wealth and political power act and react upon each other. Wherever that reciprocity of action is manifested, the School falls into the strangest contradictions. We shall confine ourselves to a remark upon Adam Smith's singular opinion of the English Navigation Act.

Not perceiving the true nature of productive power, and not embracing the various kinds of civilization, the School overlooks in particular the importance of a parallel development of agriculture, manufacturing industry, and commerce, public power, and national wealth, and above all, of an independent manufacturing industry, developed in all its branches. It commits the error of classifying manufacturing industry with agriculture, and of speaking in general terms of labor, natural power, capital, etc., without taking into consideration the differences which exist between them. It does not perceive that between a country merely agricultural and a country manufacturing and agricultural, the difference is much greater than between a pastoral people and an agricultural people. Where mere agriculture is the exclusive employment of the people, we find despotism or arbitrary rule and servitude, superstition and ignorance, the want of civilization, trade, and means of transportation. In a country wholly agricultural, a very small portion only of the intellectual and corporeal powers of the people is evoked and developed, the smallest part of its natural powers is brought into exercise, and there is none, or very little increase or accumulation of capital. Compare Poland with England; both countries were formerly in the same stage of culture; but what a difference at present! Manufactures and manufactories are the mothers and the daughters of civil liberty, of intelligence, of arts and sciences, of external and internal trade, of shipping and improved means of transport, of navigation and political power. They are the chief means of emancipating agriculture, of raising it to the rank of an industry, of an art or a science, of increasing the rent of land, agricultural profits, the wages of laborers and the value of land. The School has attributed the chief civilizing power to external trade, and has thus mistaken an intermediate step for a cause. They are foreign manufacturers who furnish to foreign commerce the goods it brings to us, and which consume the agricultural products and raw materials which we deliver in exchange. If dealings with distant manufacturers have such a beneficial influence upon agriculture, how much more profitable and advantageous must be an exchange with manufacturers united in bonds of intimacy at once local, commercial, and political, who purchase from us not merely a small part, but almost all the food and raw materials they consume—products not enhanced in price to either party by expenses of distant transportation. Manufacturers, whose relations with us are not liable to be interrupted by the opening of new markets in foreign countries, nor by war, nor by commercial regulations of countries not under our control.

We see now into what errors, into what strange contradictions the School has fallen from having confined its researches to material riches or to exchangeable values, and from considering bodily labor as the only productive power.

According to it, he who raises swine is accounted a productive member of society; he who raises men is unproductive; he who manufactures for sale bag-pipes or jews-harps, is a producer; the greatest musicians are not, because what they play cannot be exhibited in market. The physician who serves his patient, does not belong to the productive class, but the druggist's boy belongs to it, though the exchangeable values or the pills which he makes have but a few minutes of existence before they are destroyed. A Newton, a Watt, a Kepler, are not as productive as an ass, a horse, or an ox, laborers whom McCulloch has recently placed in the rank of productive members of human society.

Think not that J. B. Say, by his fiction of immaterial products, has corrected this error of Adam Smith; he only masks the absurdity of its consequences, but has not rescued the doctrine from the materialism with which it is imbued. In his view, intellectual or immaterial producers are only productive because they are remunerated by exchangeable values, and because their knowledge has been acquired at the price of such values, but not because they are producers of productive power. In his view, they are nothing but accumulated capital. McCulloch goes farther: he says that man is a product of labor as much as the machine which he produces, and it seems to him that in all economical researches man must be regarded in this point of view. Smith, he says, assented to the correctness of this principle, but omitted to draw from it the legitimate conclusion. One of the consequences which he deduces himself is, that to eat and to drink are productive occupations. Thomas Cooper values a good American lawyer at three thousand dollars, about three times as much as an ablebodied slave.

The errors and contradictions of the School, to which I have just adverted, can be readily rectified when regarded from the point of productive force. Those who raise pigs, and those who manufacture bagpipes or pills, are indeed productive; but the instructors of youth and of manhood, musicians, virtuosos, physicians, judges, and statesmen, are productive in a much higher degree. The former produce exchangeable values; the latter, productive power; of the latter, some prepare future generations for production; others develop in the actual generation the moral and religious sense; others apply themselves to strengthen and to elevate the mind, others restore the productive power of the sick or disabled; others act as legal guardians; others maintain social order; finally, others, by their various arts, and by the enjoyment they afford, encourage and stimulate the production of exchangeable values. In the doctrine of values these producers of productive power cannot be taken into account, except so far as their services are remunerated in exchangeable values: and this mode of considering their functions may have in some cases its practical utility; for instance, taxes must be paid in exchangeable values; but when the inquiry concerns international relations, or the entire interests of a country, this point of view is deceptive, and leads to a series of mistakes, and to a train of narrow ideas.

The property of a nation does not depend, as Say thinks, on the quantity of riches and of exchangeable values it possesses, but upon the degree in which the productive power is developed. If laws and institutions do not produce values directly they produce at least productive power; and Say is mistaken when he asserts that people have grown rich under all forms of government, and that laws cannot create riches.

The external trade of a nation must not be appreciated as that of a merchant, exclusively according to the theory of values, that is to say, upon the sole consideration of the material profits of the moment: the nation must in one view embrace the whole of the interests on which its existence or welfare, its property, its power, present and future, depends.

A nation ought to make the sacrifice and bear the privation of material riches, to acquire intellectual or social power; it must sacrifice present advantages to secure future benefits. We think it has been historically proved, that manufacturing industry, developed in all its branches, is the characteristic of a high degree of civilization, material prosperity, and political power; if it is true, as we believe can be demonstrated, that in the actual state of the world, an infant industry, deprived of protection, is not able to sustain the competition of an industry long established, of an industry protected upon its own territory; how, with arguments borrowed from the theory of values, can any one undertake to prove that a nation, like an individual, must buy the goods it wants in the cheapest market; that they must be insane who manufacture what can be purchased elsewhere at a lower price; that the industry of a country must be left to the unaided and unsupported intelligence and enterprise of private individuals, that protecting duties are monopolies granted to manufacturers at the expense of the people at large?

It is true that protective duties enhance at first the price of manufactured products; but it is equally true, as is admitted by the School itself, that in course of time, in a nation capable of large industrial development, such articles can be produced at a cheaper rate than they can be imported from abroad. If then, protecting duties at first involve some sacrifice of values, this sacrifice is amply compensated by the acquisition of a productive power, which ensures not only a larger product of wealth in future, but also a greater industrial independence in case of war or adverse commercial regulations. With industrial independence and the prosperity which flows from it, a nation acquires the means of carrying on external trade and of extending its navigation; it elevates its civilization, improves its institutions at home, and increases its power abroad.

A nation which has a vocation for manufacturing, pursues, in resorting to protective duties, the same policy as the individual who builds a factory, or plants an orchard, or prepares a farm that his children may reap the benefit and have their living from that which is in the first instance a sacrifice on the part of the kind parent.

The opinion of J. B. Say upon premiums given for the purpose of encouraging the export trade, shows how far the School has been misled in appreciating, by the theory of values, relations which must be chiefly regarded and considered under the light of the theory of productive power; he maintains that such premiums are gifts made by the country from which the goods are exported to the country by which the goods are imported. Suppose then that France considers a duty of twenty-five per cent adequate to protect her manufactures, still in their infancy, but that England allows premiums of export equal to thirty per cent, what would be the effect of such a gift to France? For a few years French consumers might purchase at a cheaper rate than formerly the manufactured articles which they required, but the French manufacturers would be ruined, millions of men would be reduced to beggary or be compelled either to emigrate or devote themselves to agriculture. In the most favorable hypothesis the consumers dependent hitherto on French farmers would become their competitors, agricultural production would increase at the very time when consumption was diminishing. Hence an inevitable depreciation of agricultural products and property in France, the country itself becoming more feeble and impoverished in proportion. England's gift in value would be dearly paid for in productive power; it would be equivalent to the gift which the Sultan makes to his Pashas when he sends them a silken cord with which to hang themselves.

Since the time when the Trojans received the present of a wooden horse from the Greeks, it should be deemed a delicate affair for one nation to receive gifts from another. England has presented the continent with gifts of enormous value, under the form of subsidies; the continental nations have paid dearly for them in the loss of power. These subsidies have operated as premiums of export in favor of English manufactures, to the detriment of German manufactures. If England were willing to supply Germany gratuitously for several years with all the manufactured articles the people need, we should not advise the acceptance of such an offer. Suppose that England has become able by new inventions to manufacture linen forty per cent. cheaper than Germany by the old process, and that she is in advance of Germany several years in these new processes; one of the most important and the most ancient branches of industry in that country would be ruined for want of a protective duty; it would be just as if Germany had lost one of her members. But who would console himself for the loss of an arm, by the fact that he could purchase his shirt forty per cent. cheaper?

The English often appear in the attitude of making gifts to foreigners; the mode varies, and it even happens not unfrequently that they are unwillingly generous; those for whom these bounties are intended, ought, however, to ask themselves whether they are likely to be safe or advantageous. Possessing the manufacturing and commercial monopoly of the world, their manufactures are often in the condition which is designated by the term *glut*, the result of over-production or over-trading. This surplus, so injurious to the home market, is promptly committed to the holds of steamers for foreign shores; in a week, these goods reach Hamburg, Berlin, and Frankfort; in two weeks, they are at New York, offered to foreign consumers at perhaps fifty per cent. below their value. English manufacturers suffer by this temporarily, but their productive power is saved, and they find opportunities of indemnifying themselves afterwards by better prices. German and American manufacturers suffer by the faults or are ruined for the benefit of those of England. English people see the flash, hear the report, but the explosion and the disaster are elsewhere, and when those upon whom the evil has fallen complain of their injuries, the mischief is declared by merchants to have been caused by a conjuncture or revulsion of trade. When we recall to mind how often by such conjunctures the entire interest of manufacturing industry, the credit system, agriculture itself, in a word, the whole economy of nations admitting free competition with England, has been disturbed and shaken to its foundations; when we recollect that afterwards these same nations have largely remunerated the English manufacturers by paying them higher prices, may we not doubt whether this theory of values and these cosmopolite maxims should serve as rules of international commerce? The School has not deemed it expedient to explain the causes and the effects of these crises or commercial conjunctures.

The great statesmen of modern times have almost without exception comprehended the vast influence of manufactures upon the wealth, civilization, and power of nations, and the necessity of protecting them; Edward III and Elizabeth, Frederick the Great, and Joseph II, Washington and Napoleon. Without sounding the depths of theory, their intelligent glance revealed to them the importance of manufacturing industry; and they decided wisely. It was reserved for the physiocrats, astray in their premises and reasoning, to arrive at a different conclusion. The fantastic edifice of that School has vanished; the present School supplanted its predecessor without escaping, however, its fundamental errors, deviating, in fact, but slightly from its mistaken doctrines. Having made no distinction between productive power and exchangeable value, and having made the former subordinate to the latter instead of studying them separately, it could not understand the difference between agricultural productive power and manufacturing productive power. It failed to discover that manufacturing industry on being established in an agricultural country employs and makes available a mass of the power of mind and of body, of natural mechanical forces, or Capital, in the terminology of the School, hitherto inactive, and which without that industry, would never have been productive. The School imagines that the introduction of manufacturing industry is an abstraction of power from agriculture to give it to manufactures, whilst, in fact, a power almost entirely new has been created, a power which, very far from having been acquired at the expense of agriculture, becomes its chief support and promotes its highest success.

Chapter V. Nationality and the Economy of a Nation

The system of the School, as we have shown in the preceding chapters, presents three essential defects; firstly, a chimerical *cosmopolitism*, which does not comprehend nationality, and which has no regard for national interests; secondly, a dead materialism, which regards everywhere the exchangeable value of things, taking account neither of the moral nor of the political interests of the present nor of the future, nor of the productive power of the nation; thirdly, a *separatism*, a disorganizing *individualism;* which disregarding the nature of social labor and the working of associative power towards its highest results, merely describes or depicts individual industry, as it would develop itself if unrestrained in society, that is with the whole human family, were it not separated into different nations.

But between the individual and the whole human race there is the nation with its special language and literature, with its own origin and history, with its manners and habits, its laws and institutions; with its claims to existence, its independence, its progress, its duration, and with its distinct territory; an association having not only an entirely separate existence, but having an intelligence and interest peculiarly its own, a whole existing for itself, acknowledging within itself the authority of the law, but claiming and enjoying full exemption from the control of other similar associations, and consequently in the actual state of the world, able to maintain its independence only by its own strength and proper resources. As an individual acquires chiefly by the aid of the nation and in the bosom of the nation, intellectual culture, productive power, security, and well-being, human civilization can only be conceived as possible by means of the civilization and development of nations.

There are, moreover, enormous differences between nations; we find among them giants and dwarfs, well-constituted bodies and abortions, civilized, half-civilized, and barbarous nations. But all these, as well as all individuals, have received from nature an instinct of preservation, and a desire of progress. It is the mission of political institutions to civilize barbarian nationalities, to enlarge those which are too small, to strengthen those which are weak, and, above all, to secure their existence and their duration. The mission of political economy is to furnish the economical education of the nation, and to prepare it to take its proper place in the universal association of the future.

A normal nation possesses a language and a literature of its own, a territory of considerable extent, proper proportions, and numerous resources; a large population, an agriculture, a manufacturing industry, a commerce and navigation harmoniously developed; the arts and sciences, the means of instruction and general culture, being at the level of the material production. Its political constitution, its laws and institutions, assure its citizens a high degree of security and liberty; its religious sentiments being maintained, morality and comfort soon prevail among the whole population. Such a nation possesses power, by land and sea, sufficient to maintain its independence, and to protect its external trade. It exercises an influence on the development of nations in a less degree of advancement, and with the surplus of its population and capital, both intellectual and material, it plants colonies, and founds new nations.

A nation, the territory of which is not limited by seas, nor by chains of mountains, is exposed to attacks from without, and can only, by great sacrifices, and at best in a very imperfect manner, establish a system of impost duties.

Territorial imperfections are corrected, either by the blending of thrones, as in the case of England and Scotland, or by purchase, as in that of Florida and Louisiana; or, finally, by conquest, as in that of Ireland by Great Britain.

Recently recourse has been had to another means of consolidating territory in a way more conformable to justice, as well as to national welfare, and not depending upon the chance of a blended succession; that is, by association of the interests of States under treaties mutually arranged.

It is by their Customs-Union that the German nations now enjoy one of the most important attributes of nationality. That institution, how-ever, must not be treated as perfect, so long as it does not extend to the whole sea-coast, from the mouth of the Rhine to the frontiers of Poland, including Holland and Denmark. A natural consequence of that union is the admission of these two countries into the German confederation, and of course, into the German nationality, which would thus obtain all its wants at present; that is, fisheries, naval power, with maritime and colo-nial commerce. These two nations belong, besides, by their origin and by their whole history, to the German nationality. The debt which so greatly oppresses them, is the result of a series of excessive exertions to maintain their independence, and it is in the nature of things that the evil should reach a point where it may be intolerable, and when their incorporation into a greater nationality will appear as acceptable as it will be necessary.

Belgium needs to be associated with a more powerful neighbor as a remedy for the inconveniences of her small territory and population. The American Union and Canada, in proportion as their population increase, will be drawn to each other, and England will soon be powerless to prevent their union.

In reference to political economy, nations have to pass through the following stages of development: The savage state, the pastoral state, the merely agricultural state, and the state at once agricultural, manu-facturing, and commercial. The history of industry in England exhibits more clearly than any other the transition from the savage to the pastoral state, from the rearing of cattle to agriculture, and from agriculture to the first attempts in manufacture and navigation; it shows also, that this transition is favored and expedited by free trade with free cities and more advanced nations; and that a prosperous manufacturing industry, a considerable marine, and a vast external commerce, can only be acquired by the intervention and aid of government.

The less agriculture has advanced, the more external trade has had to do in exchanging the surplus of agricultural products and raw materials of the country for articles manufactured abroad; the deeper a nation is plunged into barbarism, the more it requires the regimen of absolute monarchy, the more free trade, that is, the export of agricultural products and the import of manufactured products, concurs in its prosperity and civilization.

On the contrary, when agriculture and other useful arts have been well developed among a people, and when their social and political condition have been improved, less advantage can be derived from the exchange of agricultural products and raw materials for foreign manufactured articles; and competition with more advanced manufacturing nations will prove injurious.

It is only in similar nations, that is, in those possessing all the qualities, all the moral and material resources required to establish a home manufacturing industry, and to reach thus the highest degree of civilization, prosperity, political power, subject, however, to injury from competition with foreign industry, already well advanced, that commercial restrictions for the purpose of creating and sustaining a manufacturing industry, can be legitimate and successful; they are so only until that industry becomes strong enough not any longer to fear foreign competition; and they are legitimate within that interval, only in the necessary degree to protect that industry in its foundations.

The protective system would be contrary to cosmopolite economy, and also to the admitted interest of the nation, if it should completely and suddenly exclude foreign competition, and thus isolate the nation from the rest of the world.

When manufacturing industry is still in the first stage of its development, protective duties should be very moderate; they should be raised by degrees in proportion as intellectual and material capital, skill in the arts, and the spirit of enterprise, increase in the country. But it is not necessary that all branches of industry be equally protected. The most important, those of which the development requires large capital, fixed and circulating, much machinery, consequently, great knowledge, much dexterity and experience, and a vast body of laborers, whose products are to be classed among the chief necessaries of life, having as such, of course, considerable importance, not only in reference to their total value, but in reference to the independence of the country, as the manufactures of wool, cotton, and flax, such only should have the privilege of special protection. When these are suitably appreciated and developed, other branches of less importance grow up round them, even with less protection. Where wages are high and population not considerable, relatively to the extent of territory, as in the case of the United States, the interest of the nation demands less protection for manufactures not using much machinery, than for such as employ machinery in the greatest part of their work, provided that the states from which they receive their manufactured articles take freely in return their agricultural products.

The School mistakes completely the nature of economical relations between nations, in supposing that the exchange of agricultural products for manufactured products is just as useful to the civilization, prosperity, and generally to the social progress of such nations, as the establishment in their own territory of manufacturing industry.

A purely agricultural nation cannot develop to a high degree its home and foreign trade; its communications, its shipping; it cannot increase its prosperity as its population increases; it cannot make sensible progress in its moral, intellectual, social, and political culture; it cannot acquire great political power; it cannot exercise any important influence over the civilization and progress of less advanced nations; nor can it found colonies; a purely agricultural state is very far, in point of national advancement, behind a nation at once agricultural and manufacturing. Economically and politically, the former is always dependent more or less upon those foreign nations which receive its agricultural products in exchange for manufactured articles. It cannot determine of itself the extent of its production that depends upon the wants of the purchasers abroad. Buyers may come from nations both agricultural and manufacturing, in which immense quantities of raw materials and food are produced, and they purchase and import from abroad only the amount of their accidental deficiencies. Thus there is dependence upon the results of foreign harvests, and upon contingencies of crops more or less abundant in agricultural and manufacturing nations; moreover, this is competition with other agricultural nations, so that a market already very uncertain becomes still more unreliable. Finally, trade with manufacturing nations is subject to interruption by war or commercial regulations, and then comes the double inconvenience of finding no buyers for an agricultural surplus, and deprivation of manufactured articles in common use. A purely agricultural nation, as we have said above, is like an individual who, wanting an *arm*, employs the arm of another, the use of which, however, he is not always sure of obtaining; a nation, both agricultural and manufacturing, is like an individual in full possession and use of his own *two* arms.

A fundamental error of the School is its regarding the protective system as a spurious conception of speculative politicians. History attests that this policy of protection had its origin either in the natural struggle of people towards prosperity, independence, and power; in war, or in the hostile measures of powerful manufacturing nations.

The idea of independence and power grows with the nation; the School takes no account of this fact; the object of its researches being, not the economy of nations, but the economy of society at large; that is, of the whole human family. If we imagine an universal confederacy of nations, we no longer find sufficient motive for exertion to promote the independence and power of each of them. The guarantee of their independence rests in the legal constitution of universal society, just as, for instance, the guarantee of the independence of the States of Rhode Island and Delaware, resides in the Union of the American States. From the origin of that Union, those little States never thought of increasing their political power, nor even regarded their independence as less than that of the large States with which they are united.

However conformable to reason this idea of an universal confederacy of nations, it would be folly in a country to shape its policy with a view to realize such an association, and a perpetual peace, as if such facts were possible. Would not every prudent man denounce as insane the rulers who, trusting in the blessings of perpetual peace, should disband their armies, destroy their navies, and raze to the ground their fortresses? Rulers doing so would, however, merely comply with the claims which the School makes upon all nations by inviting them, on the faith of the advantages of free trade, to renounce the benefits of protection.

War has a destructive effect upon the trade between nation and nation. War violently separates the agriculturists of one nation from the manufacturers of another; whilst the latter, especially if inhabiting a navigating and commercial country of great power and resources, readily obtain their supplies from the farmers of their own country, or from those of other countries, to which the sea gives them access. The inhabitants of an agricultural country suffer doubly by this disturbance of commercial relations. They lose the market for their special productions, and consequently the means of paying for the manufactured articles which commerce has made a necessity of life. They are thus restricted, both in their production, and in their consumption.

When an agricultural nation, restrained by war in its production and consumption, has already a considerable population, with a civilization and an agriculture sufficiently developed, the interruption of trade thus produced gives birth, at once, to manufacturing industry. War operates like a system of prohibition.

A nation thus situated learns at once the immense advantage of manufacturing industry, and acknowledges that an interruption of trade makes that advantage greater, instead of inflicting a loss. It seizes immediately upon the idea of passing from the condition of a merely agricultural to that of an agricultural and manufacturing state, and of thus attaining the highest degree of prosperity, civilization, and power.

But when, after great progress has been made in its new career by such a nation, peace is re-established, and other nations are willing to resume former relations, it is soon perceived by all that war has given birth to new interests, which the resumption of free trade would entirely destroy. The agricultural nation finds that, to re-open foreign markets for its agricultural products, it must sacrifice the manufacturing industry which has arisen, and the home market it has afforded in the mean time; the manufacturing nation perceives that the increased agricultural production which has been developed within it during the war, must be in like manner sacrificed, if free trade is re-established. Both find it their interest, in these circumstances, to resort to protective or prohibitory duties. Such is the history of commercial policy during the last fifty years.

War has mainly been the origin of modern systems for protection, and we do not hesitate to say that it would have been the interest of manufacturing powers of the second and third rank to maintain and complete these systems, even if, after the return of peace, England had not committed the enormous mistake of restraining the importation of food and raw materials, and of keeping alive, consequently, and active, all the inducements to protection, even during peace.

As a primitive nation, the agriculture of which is in a very imperfect state, can only advance by trade with a manufacturing and civilized people, so the nation that has reached a higher degree of culture can only increase its prosperity, civilization, and power, by the aid of manufacturing industry. A war which facilitates the transition from a merely agricultural state to that of an agricultural and manufacturing people, may be regarded as a blessing to a country. The war of independence in North America, despite its enormous sacrifices, resulted in a real benefit to all future generations. On the other hand, a peace which thrusts back into the purely agricultural condition a people already embarked in manufactures, is a misfortune and an evil incomparably more injurious than war.

Happily for the manufacturing powers of the second and third rank, England, after the re-establishment of the general peace, of her own accord relaxed her efforts to grasp the manufacturing monopoly of the world, by limiting the importation of food and raw materials. Moreover, if the English agriculturists who, during the war, possessed exclusively the internal market, had been injuriously affected at first by foreign competition, afterwards, as will be fully explained in another place, they would have been largely indemnified for their losses by the manufacturing monopoly, which their country would thus have obtained.

Some of these manufacturing nations of the second and third rank, of which the industry has been stimulated into life by twenty-five years of war, and afterwards strongly consolidated by twenty-five years of inter-diction from the English market for their agricultural products, would have required perhaps not more than ten or fifteen years of efficient protection to be able to encounter free trade with England. It would have been most unreasonable, we repeat, for such nations, after the sacrifices of half a century, to renounce the immense advantages of manufacturing industry, the high degree of culture, prosperity, and independence, enjoyed by agricultural and manufacturing countries, to descend to the inferior rank of dependent agricultural nations, and for the single reason that it pleased England then to acknowledge her error, and to entertain a presentiment of the approaching elevation of the continental nations to a state of rivalry with her.

Even if the manufacturing interest of England should obtain sufficient influence to compel concessions as to the importation of agricultural products, the House of Lords being composed entirely of proprietors of large estates, and the House of Commons also embracing a majority of landowners, who could say, that after a few years a new tory ministry in other circumstances would not restore to life and vigor the old corn-laws? Who could answer for it that a new maritime war, or a new continental system, might not again separate the agriculturists of the continent from the Island manufacturers, and oblige the nations of Europe to return to manufacturers, and to exert anew all their powers to overcome the diffi-culties of beginning another, of which the whole would be again sacrificed on the return of peace?

The School would thus condemn the nations of the continent to roll upward for ever the stone of Sispyhus; to be constantly building manu-factories during war, only to let them go to ruin at the return of peace.

The School has not been able to escape these absurd results, because, in spite of the name given to the science, it has altogether excluded politics from its domain, by entirely disregarding nationality, and taking no account of the effects of war upon the foreign trade of nations.

Very different are the relations between the agriculturist and the manufacturer, when both are living in the same country, and in the mutual enjoyment of *perpetual* peace. Every extension, every improvement of a manufacture already existing, increases the demand for agricultural products. This is no uncertain demand; it depends not on laws, nor upon commercial fluctuations at home or abroad, nor upon political agitations, nor wars, nor invention, nor progress, nor finally, upon the crops of dis-tant countries; the agriculturist of the country does not share it with others abroad, but is sure of it every year as his own market. Whatever may be the state of the harvest in other countries, whatever the excite-ments of the political world, he is certain of the sale of his products, and of his supply of manufactured goods at satisfactory and regular prices. On the other hand, every improvement in the agriculture of a country, every new product or process, is a new stimulus to the manufacturers; for every increase of the agricultural product carries with it a corresponding increase of manufactures. This reciprocal action of these two great industries, ensures the permanent progress of the nation.

Political power not only guarantees a nation the increase of its prosperity by means of external commerce and colonies, but it secures the continuance of prosperity and of national existence, facts of much greater moment than the increase of material wealth. By her Navigation Act England obtained political power, and by the aid of that power she extended her manufacturing supremacy throughout the world. Poland has been razed from the list of nations for want of a strong middle class, which manufacturing industry could alone have called into existence.

The School cannot deny that the internal trade of a nation is tenfold greater than its foreign trade, even where the latter has reached its highest degree of importance, but it has failed to draw from that fact the important but natural conclusion that it is tenfold more needful to preserve and improve its own home market than to seek wealth from without, and that external commerce can only be important as a means of wealth where national industry has attained a high degree of development.

The School has considered markets only in the cosmopolite aspect, and not at all in a political point of view. The largest portion of the sea-coasts of Europe are within the natural circle of supply from the London, Liverpool, or Manchester manufacturers; the manufacturers of other countries can, for the most part, only compete with them in their own maritime cities. Larger capital, more extensive markets wholly their own, and which admit of manufactures upon a larger scale, and consequently at a lower price, improved methods, and lastly, cheap maritime freights, secure at present to English manufacturers, over those of other countries, advantages which long and persevering protection and improvement of the means of communication can alone procure for others. Now the market of the sea-coast is of vast importance to a nation, as well in reference to interior markets as to the exterior, and a nation of which the sea-coast is devoted to foreign more than to the home trade, is both economically and politically divided. Nay, shall I not rather say, there can be no more unfavorable condition for a nation in both respects, than to find its maritime places sympathizing more actively with the interests of people of other nations than with those of their own.

Science should never bring in question nationality, nor be ignorant of it, nor misrepresent it, to sustain any cosmopolite theory. Its true end can be realized only by conforming to nature, and by endeavoring to elevate the different peoples according to its own laws. How little success these lessons of the School have hitherto obtained in practice! This is less the fault of practical men, who certainly understand something of national interests, than of theories contradicted by experience, to adopt which, practical men must hesitate. Have these theorists prevented nations so little advanced as those of South America from adopting the protective system? Have they prevented protection from being extended to the production of food and raw materials—products so little requiring protection, and upon which any restriction can only injure both the nation imposing it, and the nation against which it is directed? Have they prevented the nicest and most costly manufactured articles, objects of luxury, from being included among those which require protection, however evident it may be that such articles might be given up to competition without the slightest danger to the prosperity of a country? No: theory has hitherto accomplished no capital reform, and will not, as long as it stands in opposition to the nature of things. Let theory build upon nature and experience, and it may yet accomplish great good.

It would render, indeed, a special service to the world if it would establish that restrictions upon trade in natural products and raw materials greatly injure the nation that employs them, and that the protective system is legitimate only so far as it has in view the *industrial education* of the country. By establishing upon wise principles the protective system applied to manufactures, it may induce nations still retaining the prohibitive system, France for instance, to renounce it by degrees. Manufacturers will not oppose that change when they shall be assured that the theorists, far from seeking their ruin, assume the maintenance and the development of existing manufactures as the basis of a sound commercial policy.

If theory teaches the Germans that they can advantageously encourage their manufacturing industry only by a gradual elevation, then afterwards by a diminution also gradual of their protective duties, and that foreign competition to a certain degree cannot but aid the progress of their manufacture, it will render to free trade positively a greater service than by any co-operation in the ruin of German industry.

Theory must not require from the United States that they give up to free competition with foreign countries the branches of manufacture in which foreigners are assisted by cheap labor, the low price of raw materials and food, as well as by a greater use of machinery; but it can meet with no objection if it maintains that the United States, whilst wages remain there so much higher than in countries of older culture, will work efficaciously toward the development of their productive power, their civilization, and their political power, by granting easy access to manufactured articles, in the price of which, labor constitutes the principal element, upon condition, however, that other countries admit their agricultural products and their raw materials upon similar terms.

The theory of free trade would then be welcome in Spain, Portugal, and Naples, in Turkey, Egypt, in all countries more or less deficient in civilization, and in all warm climates. Countries in the stage of civilization in which these now are can scarcely be supposed to entertain the extravagant idea of creating a manufacturing industry by means of protective duties.

England must then cease to believe that she has been called to the manufacturing monopoly of the world. She will no longer insist that France, Germany, and the United States shall have to sacrifice their manufactures for the small advantage of having their agricultural products and their raw materials admitted into Great Britain. She will acknowledge the legitimacy of the protective system in those countries, while she finds free trade to be the policy which best promotes her own interests; for theory will demonstrate to her that a nation having reached a manufacturing supremacy can keep her manufacturers and tradesmen from inaction, recoil, and idleness, only by the free importation of food and raw materials, and by the competition of foreign industry.

England will take a course quite contrary to that she has heretofore pursued; instead of soliciting other nations to adopt free trade, whilst she maintains at home her rigorous prohibitive system; she will open to the world her own markets, without troubling herself with the protective system of others; she will postpone her hopes for the advent of free trade, until the time when other nations shall no longer fear the destruction of their manufactures as a result of free competition. In the meanwhile, until that day arrive, England will indemnify herself for her diminished exportation of articles manufactured for general consumption caused by the protective systems of others by exporting freely the finer kinds of goods, and by finding and opening up new markets.

She will endeavor to restore quiet in Spain, in the East, and in the States of Central and South America; she will use her influence in all the barbarous or half-civilized countries of that part of the world as well as of Asia and Africa, to establish stronger and more enlightened governments for the greater security of goods and persons, for the construction of roads and canals, for the promotion of education and knowledge, for the encouragement of morality and industry, for the repression of fanaticism, superstition and indolence. If, at the same time, she removes her restrictions upon the introduction of food and raw materials, her exports of manufactured goods will increase in an enormous proportion, and much more safely than if she should continue to speculate upon the ruin of the continental manufacturers.

But to crown her civilizing efforts among the more or less barbarous nations, England must not be exclusive; she must not attempt by means of commercial privileges, such as were obtained from Brazil, to monopolize markets and to exclude other nations from them.

Such conduct always excites national jealousies and provokes opposition to the efforts of England. This selfish policy explains, obviously, why the influence of civilized nations has been so small hitherto on the civilization of those countries. England should therefore introduce into the law of nations the principle of equality for the commerce of all manufacturing countries in every part of the world; not only would she find the concurrence of all the enlightened powers in her civilizing efforts, but further, without injuring her own trade she might allow other manufacturing people to undertake similar enterprises. Her superiority in all departments would secure for her at all times the largest share in the supply of those markets.

The continual intrigues of the English against foreign manufacturers might perhaps be justified, if the monopoly of the world was indispensable for the prosperity of England, if it were not demonstrable by evidence that other nations besides England, who aim at great manufacturing power, may actually attain their object without any reduction of her power or wealth; that England need not become poorer because other nations grow richer, and that nature offers resources ample enough to permit an industry equal to that of England to be developed in Germany, France, and North America, without injuring her prosperity.

In this respect it is to be first noticed, that a nation which has secured its own internal market and manufacturing industry gains, in the course of time, in production and consumption of manufactured articles, much more than the nation which heretofore supplied it loses, in consequence of its exclusion under the operation of the domestic system; for the nation thus manufacturing for itself and completing its economical development must become incomparably richer and more populous, and by consequence more able to purchase and consume manufactured goods than if it had remained dependent upon foreign producers.

In regard, moreover, to exports of manufactured goods, the countries of the temperate zone, destined and fitted by nature particularly for manufacturing industry, should seek their principal markets in the countries of the torrid zone, which supply them with tropical products in exchange. But the consumption of manufactured goods by tropical countries is limited, on the one hand, by their ability to produce a surplus of articles peculiar to their climate, and on the other, by the activity of the demand for their products in the countries of the temperate zone.

The possibility of the continental nations increasing in that proportion their consumption of tropical products, is demonstrated by the increase of such consumption in England, during the last fifty years; but we must not forget that that increase would have been probably very much greater but for the enormous duties to which these tropical products were subjected.

That it is possible to increase the products of the torrid zone, Holland has furnished us, during the past five years, irrefusable proofs, in Sumatra, and Java; and England, in the East Indies. From 1835 to 1839, England quadrupled her importation of sugar from the East Indies; her importation of coffee from the same country has increased in a proportion still more considerable, and the import of cotton has also notably augmented. English journals of late dates (February, 1840), proudly announce that the productive power of the East Indies for such articles is unbounded, and that the time is not distant when England will become independent as to these products of America and the West Indies.

On the other hand, Holland, overloaded with her colonial productions, is unremittingly in search of new markets. Let us not forget, besides, that the States of North America continue to increase their product of cotton —that Texas has recently become a nation, destined, undoubtedly to conquer the whole of Mexico, and make that fertile country what the Southern States of the American Union are at this time. Let us trust that the reign of order and law, labor and intelligence, may by degrees be extended over all South America, from Panama to Cape Horn; then over all the surface of Asia and Africa; augmenting everywhere, not only production, but a surplus of products. It is easy to comprehend that there is here a field open to the sale of manufactured goods for more than one nation. If we calculate the surface of the world now devoted to the production of tropical products, and if we compare it with the quantity which nature has fitted for that culture, we shall find that hardly the fiftieth part has been occupied.

How could England appropriate to herself the exclusive privilege of supplying manufactured goods for all those countries which produce tropical commodities, when the quantity exported from the West Indies would suffice for the supply of her whole demand for such products? How could England obtain a market for her manufactures in countries of which she cannot take the commodities in exchange? And how can a vast demand for tropical commodities arise upon the European continent, if the continent by its manufactured productions is not enabled to purchase and consume them?

It is obvious then that the repression of the continental manufactures may impede the progress of continental industry without augmenting the wealth of England.

It is very evident that during our times, and for a long future, the torrid zone offers sufficient elements of exchange for all the manufacturing nations.

It is obvious, finally, that a manufacturing monopoly, such as would now result from the free admission of English manufactured products into the continental nations of Europe and into the States of North America, is in no respect more advantageous to mankind than the protective system which tends to the development of manufacturing industry throughout the whole temperate zone, for the benefit of the entire agriculture of the whole torrid zone.

The start which England has taken in manufactures, shipping, and commerce should not deter any of the nations prepared for manufacturing industry, by their territory, their power, or their intelligence, from entering the list of nations holding the sceptre of industry. Manufactures, trade, and shipping have a future which will transcend the present, as much as the present transcends the past. It only needs courage to believe in a great national destiny, and to advance in that faith. But before all, it is necessary to have sufficient national mind to plant now and to prop the tree which will furnish its most abundant fruits to future generations. Each country should at once take possession of its own markets for its own industry, at least, as to the objects of general consumption, and make due exertions to import the products of the torrid zone in exchange for manufactured goods. Such is the special problem which the German association has yet to solve, if Germany would not remain far behind France, North America, or even Russia.

Chapter VI. The Economy of the People and the Economy of the State. Political Economy and National Economy

What refers to the collection, to the use and administration of the material means of a government, or the *financial economy of the state*, should never be confounded with the institutions, the regulations, the laws, and the circumstances which govern the economical condition of the citizens, that is, with the economy of the people. That distinction is to be observed with regard to all societies, great or small, to a whole nation as well as to fragments of a nation.

In a federative State, the financial economy is divided into an economy of the particular states, and into the economy of the union.

The economy of the people becomes a *national economy* when the state or the confederation embraces the whole nation, to which its population, its extent of territory, its political institutions, its civilization, its wealth, and its power, promise independence, duration, and political importance. In this case the economy of the people and national economy are one and the same thing. They constitute, with the financial economy of the state, the political economy of the nation.

In the States, on the contrary, the population and the territory of which consist of only the fraction of a nation, or of a national territory, and which neither by immediate political bond, nor by federative bond, form a whole with other fractions, there can only be an economy of the people, in opposition, as it were, to individual economy, or the financial economy of the State. In such an imperfect condition, the objects and the wants of a great nationality cannot be taken into consideration; the economy of the people cannot be regulated with any view of administering a nation complete in itself, and of securing its independence, duration and power. In this case, politics must of course be excluded from economy;

here men have to consider only the natural laws of social economy in general, as they would exhibit themselves if there were no such thing in existence as a compact and powerful nationality, or a national economy.

It is from this point of view that there has been developed in Germany the science which was called, at first, Economy of the State, afterwards Political Economy, then Economy of the People, without discovery, however, of the fundamental error of the systems thus designated.

The notion of a national economy could not be comprehended, for no such system had been exemplified; and because, for the particular and determinate idea of a nation, the general and vague idea of *association* had been substituted; an idea applicable to the whole of mankind, to a small country, or to a single city, as well as to a nation.

FREDERIC BASTIAT

(1801–1850)

The French economist Bastiat was born in Bayonne. He had expected to become a merchant, but inherited a small estate at the age of twenty-five, after which he affected the life of a gentleman farmer. His later years were spent in study and writing.

Bastiat was also a man of affairs and an important figure in his contemporary political life. He served as a justice of the peace, a member of his department council, and a member of the Constitutional and Legisative Assemblies during the Revolution of 1848. Most of his political activity was devoted to attacks upon protectionists on the one hand and socialists on the other.

Bastiat was naturally very much influenced by his predecessor Jean Baptiste Say. Naturally, his writings breathed optimism and harmony, and were colored by the gospel of *laissez-faire*.

The chief work of Bastiat was "Economic Harmonies." Unfortunately death cut short this ambitious attempt after the first volume had been completed. Indeed, even this did not appear until 1850, a few months after the author's death. Even so, however, its date of publication was several years before Carey's "Principles of Social Science," although over a decade after Carey's first works on economics.

Bastiat was the author of numerous addresses and short articles for current periodicals. After his death many of them were collected and published in book form under the titles "Economic Sophisms" and "Essays on Political Economy."

The following selections have been taken from "Harmonies of Political Economy," "Economic Sophisms," and "Essays on Political Economy." In general, Sterlings translations have been followed.

The student is asked to observe the great similarities between the theoretical system of Carey and that of Bastiat. In fact, so similar are they that allegations of literary plagiarism have been made. On the other hand, the essays of Bastiat were in opposition to a protective tariff, which was the fetish of the American Carey.

FREDERIC BASTIAT

SELECTIONS FROM "HARMONIES OF POLITICAL ECONOMY"

CHAPTER II. WANTS, EFFORTS, SATISFACTIONS

What a profoundly afflicting spectacle France presents to us!

It would be difficult to say if anarchy has passed from ideas to facts, or from facts to ideas, but it is certain that it pervades all, and abounds everywhere.

The poor rise up against the rich, men without fortune or profession against property; the populace against the bourgeoisie; labour against capital; agriculture against manufactures; the country against the town; the provinces against the metropolis; the denizen against the stranger.

And theorists step in, and form a system of this antagonism. "It is the *inevitable* result, they say, of the nature of things, that is to say, of Liberty. Man is endued with *self-love*, and hence comes all the evil; for since he is endued with self-love, he seeks to better his own condition, and he can only do so by entailing misery on his brethren. Let us hinder him, then, from following his inclinations; let us stifle his liberty, change the human heart, substitute other motives for those which God has placed there; let us invent and constitute an artificial society!"

When they have got this length, an unlimited career opens itself to their reason or imagination. If they are possessed of a disputatious turn and a peevish temper, they enter with eagerness into an analysis of Evil. They dissect it, they put it in the crucible, they interrogate it, they remount to its causes, they pursue it to its consequences; and, as by reason of our native imperfection there is nothing in which Evil is not present, they asperse and disparage everything. They exhibit to us Property, Family, Capital, Labour Competition, Liberty, Personal Interest, only in one of their aspects, and always on the dark side, the side which injures or destroys. Their lectures on the natural history of man are, if I may use the expression, clinical lectures—the subject is always on his deathbed. They impiously defy God to reconcile what is said of his infinite goodness with the existence of evil. They stain and sully everything; and yet they obtain only a melancholy and dangerous success with those classes whom suffering disposes but too much to despair.

If, on the other hand, such theorists have a heart open to benevolence, a mind which is pleased with illusions, they rush to the region of chimeras. They dream of an Oceana, an Atlantis, a Salente, a Spensonie, an Icarie,

415

a Utopia, and they people these imaginary regions with a docile, loving, devoted race who always avoid setting themselves up against the fancies of the dreamer. He instals himself complacently in the seat of Providence. He arranges, he disposes, he moulds men after his own fancy. Nothing stops him. He never encounters deceit. He resembles the Roman preacher, who, after having transformed his square cap into Rousseau, refuted warmly the Contrat social, and triumphantly reduced his adversary to silence. It is thus that our Reformers dazzle those who suffer by means of seductive pictures of ideal felicity, well fitted to disgust them with the hard necessities of real life.

The theorist, however, rarely confines himself to such innocent chimeras. The moment he aims at leading mankind, he finds the people impatient of attempted transformations. Men resist—they get angry. In order to gain them over, he harangues them not only on the happiness they reject, but more especially on the evils from which he professes to deliver them. He finds it impossible to make too striking a picture. He is continually charging his palette and deepening his colours. He hunts out the evils of existing society with as much zeal as another employs in discovering the good. He sees nothing but sufferings, rags, leanness, starvation, pain, oppression. He is enraged that society has not a deeper sense of its misery. He neglects no means of making it throw off its insensibility, and, having begun with benevolence, he ends with misanthropy.

God forbid that I should call in question the sincerity of any one. But, in truth, I cannot explain to myself how these writers, who see a radical antagonism in the natural order of things, can ever taste a moment's calm or repose. Discouragement and despair would seem to be their unhappy portion. For, to sum up all, if nature is mistaken in making *personal interest* the mainspring of human society (and the mistake is manifest if it be admitted that the interests of society are fatally antagonistic), how do they not perceive that the evil is without remedy? Being men ourselves, and being able to have recourse only to men, where can be our *point d'appui* for changing the tendencies of human nature? Shall we invoke the Police, the Magistracy, the State, the Legislature? That would only be to invoke men, that is to say, beings subject to the common infirmity. Shall we address ourselves to Universal Suffrage? That would be to give the freest course to the universal tendency.

Only one expedient remains to these gentlemen. It is to hold themselves out as discoverers, as prophets, made of different clay from their follow-men and deriving their inspiration from a different source. This is the reason, no doubt, why we find them so frequently enveloping their systems and their counsels in a mystic phraseology. But if they are ambassadors of God, let them exhibit their credentials. In effect, what they demand is sovereign power, despotism the most absolute that ever existed. They not only wish to govern our acts, but to revolutionize our thoughts. Do they hope that mankind will believe them on their word, when they are not able to agree among themselves?

But before even examining their projects of artificial societies, is there not one point upon which it is necessary to assure ourselves, namely, whether they are not mistaken in the very foundation of their argument? Is it quite certain that *men's interests are naturally antagonistic;* that an irremediable cause of inequality is fatally developed in the natural order of human society under the influence of personal interest, and that Providence is manifestly in error in ordaining that the progress of man should be towards ease and competency?

This is what I propose to inquire into.

Taking man as it has pleased God to constitute him, capable of foresight and experience, perfectible, endued with self-love, it is true—but self-love qualified by the sympathetic principle, and at all events restrained and balanced by encountering an analogous sentiment universally prevailing in the medium in which it acts—I proceed to inquire what social order must necessarily result from the combination and free play of such elements.

If we find that this result is nothing else than a progressive march towards prosperity, improvement, and equality—a sustained approximation of all classes towards the same physical, intellectual, and moral level, accompanied by a constant elevation of that level, the way of God to man will be vindicated. We shall learn with delight that there is no gap, no blank, in creation, and that the social order, like everything else, attests the existence of those *harmonic laws* before which Newton bowed his head, and which elicited from the Psalmist the exclamation, *"the heavens declare the glory of God."*

Rousseau has said, "If I were a prince or a legislator, I should not lose my time in pointing out what was necessary to be done—I should do it, or hold my tongue."

I am not a *prince*, but the confidence of my fellow-citizens has made me a *legislator*. Perhaps they will tell me that this is the time for me to act and not to write.

Let them pardon me. Whether it be truth itself which urges me on, or that I am the dupe of an illusion, I have never ceased to feel the want of concentrating those ideas which have hitherto failed to find acceptance when presented in detached portions. I think I discover in the play of the natural laws of society sublime and consoling *harmonies*. What I see, or think I see, ought I not to try to exhibit to others, in order to rally round a sentiment of concord and fraternity many unsettled minds, many embittered hearts? If, when the much-loved vessel of the state is beat by the tempest, I sometimes appear to absent myself from my post, in order to collect my scattered thoughts, it is because I feel my feeble hands unfitted for the work. Is it, besides, to betray my mission, to reflect upon the causes of the tempest itself, and endeavour to act upon these causes? And then, what I find I cannot do to-day, who knows but it may be given me to accomplish to-morrow?

I shall begin by establishing some Economical ideas. Availing myself of the works of my predecessors, I shall endeavour to sum up the science in one principle—true, simple, and prolific—of which we have had a glimpse from the beginning, to which we are constantly drawing nearer and nearer, and of which, perhaps, the time is now come to fix the formula. By the light thus afforded, I shall afterwards essay the solution of some yet disputed problems—Competition, Machinery, Foreign trade, Luxury, Capital, Rent, &c. I shall note some of the relations, or, I should rather say, the harmonies of Political Economy with the other moral and social sciences, glancing at the important subjects indicated by the terms—Personal Interest, Property, Community, Liberty, Equality, Responsibility, Solidarity, Fraternity, Unity. Last of all, I shall invite attention to the artificial obstacles which the pacific, regular, and progressive development of human society encounters. From these two ideas—Natural harmonic Laws—Artificial disturbing Causes—will be deduced the solution of the Social Problem.

It is easy to see that there are two rocks ahead upon which this undertaking may founder. In the middle of the vortex in which we are carried along, if this work is abstruse, it will not be read; if it obtains readers, the questions of which it treats will be but glanced at. How are we to reconcile the exactions of the reader with the requirements of science? To satisfy all conditions both in form and substance, each word would require to be weighed, and have its proper place assigned to it. It is thus that the crystal is formed drop by drop in silence and obscurity. Retirement, quiet, time, freedom from care—all are wanting to me—and I am forced to trust to the sagacity of the public, and throw myself on its indulgence.

The subject of Political Economy is Man.

But it does not embrace the whole range of human affairs. The science of morals has appropriated all that comes within the attractive regions of Sympathy—the religious sentiment, paternal and maternal tenderness, filial piety, love, friendship, patriotism, charity, politeness. To Political Economy is left only the cold domain of Personal interest. This is unjustly forgotten when Economical science is reproached with wanting the charm and unction of morals. How can it be otherwise? Dispute its right to existence as a science, but don't force it to counterfeit what it is not, and cannot be. If human transactions which have wealth for their object are vast enough, complicated enough, to afford materials for a special science, leave to it its own attractions, such as they are, and don't force it to speak of men's Interests in the language of Sentiment. For my own part, I believe that little good has been effected of late in exacting from writers on Political Economy a tone of enthusiastic sentimentality which in their mouth can only be declamation. Of what do they treat? Of transactions which take place between people who know nothing of each other, who owe each other nothing but common Justice, who seek to defend or advance certain interests. It has to do with claims and pretensions which limit and restrain each other, and with which disinterestedness and devotion have nothing to do. Take a lyre, and chant such themes! As well might Lamartine sing his odes with the aid of the logarithm tables.

Not that Political Economy is without its poetry. There is poetry wherever order and harmony exist. But it is in the results, not in the demonstrations. It is brought out, not created. Keppler did not give himself out as a poet, and yet the laws which he discovered are the true poetry of mind.

Thus, Political Economy regards man only in one aspect, and our first care must be to study man in that point of view. This is the reason why we cannot avoid going back to the primary phenomena of human Sensibility and Activity. Start not, gentle reader! We shall not detain you long in those cloudy regions of metaphysics, and we shall borrow from that science only such notions as are clear, simple, and, if possible, incontestable.

The soul, or (to get rid of the spiritual question) man, is endued with *Sensibility*. Let this sensibility be either in the soul or in the body, man, as a passive being, always experiences sensations either painful or agreeable. As an active being, he makes an effort to drive away the one set of sensations and to multiply the other. The result, which affects him again as a passive being, may be called *Satisfaction*.

The general idea of *Sensibility* springs from other ideas which are more precise: pain, want, desire, taste, appetite, on one side; and, on the other, pleasure, enjoyment, competence.

Between these two extremes a middle term is interposed, and from the general idea of *Activity* spring the more precise ideas of pain, effort, fatigue, labour, production.

In analyzing *Sensibility* and *Activity* we encounter a word common to both; the word *Pain*. To experience certain sensations is a *pain*, and we cannot put an end to it but by an effort, which is also a *pain*. We *feel pains;* we *take pains*. This advertises us that here below we have only a choice of evils.

In the aggregate of these phenomena all is personal, as well the Sensation which precedes the effort, as the Satisfaction which follows it.

We cannot doubt, then, that *Personal interest* is the great mainspring of human nature. It must be perfectly understood, however, that this term is here employed as the expression of a universal fact, incontestable, and resulting from the organization of man—and not of a critical judgment on his conduct and actions, as if, instead of it, we should employ the word *egotism*. Moral science would be rendered impossible, if we were to pervert beforehand the terms of which it is compelled to make use.

Human effort does not always come necessarily to place itself between the sensation and the satisfaction. Sometimes the satisfaction comes of its own accord. More frequently the effort is exercised upon *materials*, by the intervention of *forces* which nature has placed gratuitously at our disposal.

If we give the name of *Utility* to all which effects the satisfaction of wants, there are, then, utilities of two kinds: one, vouchsafed to us gratuitously by Providence; the other (if I may use the expression), requiring to be purchased by an *Effort*.

Thus the complete evolution embraces, or may embrace, these four ideas:

$$\text{Wants} \left\{ \begin{array}{l} \text{Gratuitous Utility} \\ \text{Onerous Utility} \end{array} \right\} \text{Satisfaction}$$

Man is endued with progressive faculties. He compares, he foresees, he learns, he reforms himself, by experience. If want is a pain, effort is a pain also, and there is therefore no reason why he should not seek to diminish the latter, when he can do so without diminishing the satisfaction, which is his ultimate object. This is the reason of his success when he comes to replace *onerous* by *gratuitous Utility*, which is the perpetual object of his search.

It follows from the *interested* nature of the human heart, that we constantly seek to increase the proportion which our Satisfactions bear to our Efforts; and it results from the intelligent nature of our mind that we manage at each step to augment the proportion which gratuitous bears to onerous Utility.

Every time a success of this nature is achieved, a part of our efforts is, so to speak, rendered disposable, and we have the option of either indulging ourselves with longer repose, or of working for the satisfaction of new desires, if these are strong enough to stimulate our activity.

Such is the principle of all economic progress; and it is easy to see that it is the principle also of all deception; for progress and error have both their root in that marvellous gift of God to man—*Free will*.

We are endued with the faculty of comparing, of judging, of choosing, and of acting in consequence; which implies that we may form a right or a wrong judgment, and make a good or a bad choice. It is never useless to remind men of this when they talk of Liberty.

We never deceive ourselves, it is true, regarding the particular nature of our sensations, and we discern with an infallible instinct whether they are painful or agreeable. But how many various forms may our errors take! We may be labouring under a mistake as to the cause, and pursue with ardour, as likely to afford us enjoyment, what can only inflict pain upon us; or we may be mistaken as to the chain of consequences, and be ignorant that an immediate satisfaction will be followed by greater ulterior pain; or, again, we may mistake the relative importance of our wants and our desires.

Not only may we thus give a false direction to our efforts through ignorance, but also through a perverse will. "Man," says M. Bonald, "is an intelligence served by organs." What! is there nothing else in us? Have we no passions?

When we speak of harmony, then, we must not be understood to mean that the natural arrangement of the social world is such that error and vice have been excluded from it. To maintain that thesis in the face of plain facts would be to carry the love of system to madness. To have harmony without dissonance man must either be devoid of free will or he must be infallible. All we say is this, that the great social tendencies are harmonious, inasmuch as—all error leading to deception and all vice to chastisement—the dissonances have a continual tendency to disappear.

A first and vague notion of property may be deduced from these premises. Since it is the individual who experiences the sensation, the desire, the want—since it is he who makes the Effort—the satisfaction must necessarily redound to him, for otherwise the effort would be without cause or reason.

The same may be said of *Inheritance*. No theory, no declamation, is required in order to make fathers love their children. People who sit down to manufacture imaginary societies may think it strange, but it is so; a father makes as many *Efforts* for the *satisfaction* of his children as for his own. Perhaps he makes more. If, then, an unnatural law should interdict the transmission of property, not only would that law violate property by the very act, but it would hinder its formation by abandoning to inaction one-half at least of our *Efforts*.

We shall have occasion to return to the subjects of Personal interest, Property, and Inheritance. Let us, in the first instance, mark out the limits of the science with which we have more immediately to do.

I am not one of those who think that a science, as such, has natural and unalterable boundaries. In the domain of ideas, as in that of facts, all things are bound up and linked together; truths run into one another; and there is no science which, in order to be complete, might not be made to include all. It has been said with reason that to an infinite intelligence there is but a single verity. It is, then, our weakness which obliges us to study separately a certain order of phenomena, and the classifications which result from it cannot escape a certain degree of arbitrariness.

The true merit is to explain accurately the facts, their causes, and their consequences. It is also a merit, although a much less and purely relative one, to determine, not rigorously—for that is impossible—but rationally, the order of the facts which we propose to study.

I say this in order that it may not be supposed that I intend to criticise my predecessors in giving to Political Economy limits somewhat different from those which they have assigned to that science.

Economists have of late been reproached with addicting themselves too much to the study of *Wealth*. It has been wished that they had found a place in their science for all that, directly or indirectly, contributes to the happiness or sufferings of humanity. They have even been supposed to deny everything which they did not profess to teach—for example, the phenomena of sympathy, which is as natural to the heart of man as the principle of self-interest. It is as if they accused the mineralogist of denying the existence of the animal kingdom. What! Wealth, the laws of its production, of its distribution, of its consumption, is not this a subject vast enough, and important enough, to be made the object of a special science? If the conclusions of the Economist were at variance with those of morals and politics, I could conceive ground for the accusation. One might say to him, "In limiting your science you are mistaken, for it is not possible for two verities to run counter to each other." Perhaps one result of the work which I now submit to the public may be, that the Science of Wealth will be found to be in perfect harmony with all the other sciences.

Of the three terms comprehended in the human destinies—Sensation, Effort, Satisfaction—the first and the last are always and necessarily confounded in the same individuality. It is impossible to imagine them separated. We can conceive a sensation unsatisfied, a want unappeased, but it is quite impossible to suppose the want to be in one man and the *satisfaction* to be in another.

If the same observation applied to the middle term, *Effort*, man would be a being completely solitary. The Economic phenomena would then manifest themselves in an isolated individual. There might be a juxtaposition of persons, but there could be no society; there might be a Personal, but not a Political, Economy.

But it is not so. It is very possible, and very often happens, that the *wants* of one owe their *satisfaction* to the *efforts* of another. This is a fact. If any one of us were to pass in review all the satisfactions he enjoys, he would acknowledge that he owes them chiefly to effort which he has not himself made; and in the same way, the labour which we undergo, each in his own profession, goes almost always to satisfy the desires of others.

This tells us, that it is neither in the wants nor in the satisfactions (phenomena essentially personal and intransmissible), but in the nature of the mean term, *human Efforts*, that we must search for the social principle —the origin of Political Economy.

It is in fact to this faculty, given to men, and to men alone, among all creatures, to *work the one for the other;* it is this transmission of efforts, this exchange of services, with all the infinite and involved combinations to which it gives rise, through time and through space, it is this precisely which constitutes Economic Science, points out its origin, and determines its limits.

I, say, then:

Every effort, capable of satisfying, on condition of a return, the wants of a person other than the man who makes the effort, and consequently the wants and satisfactions relative to this species of effort, constitute the domain of Political Economy.

Thus, to give an example: The act of breathing, although it includes the three terms which constitute the Economic phenomenon, does not pertain to that science, and we see the reason. What we have here to do with is a series of facts, of which not only the two extremes—want and satisfaction—are incapable of transmission (they are always so); but the mean term, *Effort*, is also incapable of transmission. To enable us to respire we invoke the assistance of no one; in that there is neither a service to be received nor a service to render. The fact is in its nature individual, not *social*, and consequently cannot enter into a science which is essentially one of relation, as its very name indicates.

But if, in peculiar circumstances, people were to render each other assistance to enable them to breathe, as when a workman descends in a diving-bell, when a physician treats a patient for pulmonary complaints, or when the police take measures for purifying the air, in such cases there is a want satisfied by a person other than the person who experiences the want; there is a service rendered; and respiration itself, as far at least as concerns assistance and remuneration, is brought within the sphere of Political Economy.

It is not necessary that the transaction should be completed, it is sufficient that it is possible, in order to impart to the *labour* employed an *economic* character. The labourer who raises corn for his own use accomplishes an economic fact in this respect that the corn is capable of being exchanged.

To make an effort in order to satisfy another's wants is to render him a *service*. If a service is stipulated in return, there is an exchange of *services;* and as this is the most ordinary case, Political Economy may be defined the *theory of Exchange.*

Whatever may be for one of the contracting parties the urgency of the want, or for the other the intensity of the effort, if the exchanged is free, the two services exchanged are *worth each other*. Value, then consists in the comparative appreciation of reciprocal *services*, and Political Economy again may be defined *the theory of Value.*

I have just defined political Economy, and marked out its domain, without mentioning an essential element, *gratuitous Utility.*

All authors have remarked that we derive a multitude of satisfactions from this source. They denominate these utilities, such as air, water, the light of the sun, &c., *natural wealth,* in contradistinction to *social wealth,* and having done so, they take no more notice of them; and in fact it would seem that, as they give rise to no effort, to no exchange, to no service, as (being destitute of value) they figure in no inventory of goods, they should not be admitted into the domain of Political Economy.

This exclusion would be rational if *gratuitous* utility were a fixed invariable quantity, always separated from *onerous* utility; but they are constantly mixed up, and in inverse proportions. Man's constant endeavour is to substitute the one for the other, that is to say, to arrive, by means of natural and gratuitous agents, at the same results as by efforts. He accomplishes by the wind, by gravitation, by heat, by the elasticity of the air, what he accomplished at first only by muscular exertion.

Now what happens? Although the effect is equally useful, the effort is less. Less effort implies less service, and less service implies less value. Each step of progress, then, annihilates value; but how? Not by suppressing the useful effect, but by substituting gratuitous for onerous utility, natural for social wealth. In one sense the portion of value thus annihilated is excluded from the domain of Political Economy, just as it is excluded from our inventories. It is no longer exchanged, bought, or sold, and mankind enjoy it without effort and almost without consciousness. It is no longer accounted relative wealth, but is ranked among the gifts of God.

But, on the other hand, if science takes it no longer into account, the error is assuredly committed of losing sight of what under all circumstances is the main, the essential thing—the result, the *useful effect.* In that case we overlook the strongest tendencies towards community and equality, and discover much less of harmony in the social order. If this book is destined to advance Political Economy a single step, it will be by keeping constantly before the eyes of the reader that portion of *value* which is successively annihilated, and recovered, under the form of *gratuitous utility,* by mankind at large.

I shall here make an observation which will prove how frequently the sciences unite and nearly run into each other.

I have just defined *service.* It is the *effort* in one man, while the *want* and *satisfaction* are in another. Sometimes the service is rendered gratuitously without remuneration, without any service being exacted in return. It proceeds, then, from the principle of sympathy rather than from the principle of self-interest. It constitutes gift, not exchange. Consequently it would seem to appertain not to Political Economy (which is the theory of exchange), but to morals. In fact, acts of that nature, by reason of their motive, are rather moral than economical. We shall see, however, that, by reason of their effects, they concern the science which now engages us. On the other hand, services rendered for an onerous consideration, on condition of a return, and, by reason of that motive (essentially economic), do not on that account remain excluded from the domain of morals, in so far as their effects are concerned.

Thus these two branches of knowledge have an infinite number of points of contact; and as two truths cannot be antagonistic, when the economist ascribes to a phenomenon injurious consequences, and the moralist ascribes to it beneficial effects, we may affirm that one or other of them is mistaken. It is thus that the sciences verify and fortify one another.

Concluding Observations

In the first part of this work—alas! too hastily written—I have endeavoured to keep the reader's attention fixed upon the line of demarcation, always flexible, but always marked, which separated the two regions of the economic world—natural co-operation, and human labour—the bounty of God, and the work of man—the gratuitous, and the onerous—that which in exchange is remunerated, and that which is transferred without remuneration—aggregate utility, and the fractional and supplementary utility which constitutes value—absolute wealth, and relative wealth—the cooperation of chemical or mechanical forces, constrained to aid production by the instruments which render them available, and the just recompense of the labour which has created these instruments themselves—Community, and Property.

It is not enough to mark these two orders of phenomena which are so essentially different, it is necessary also to describe their relations, and, if I may so express myself, their harmonious evolutions. I have essayed to explain how the business of Property consists in conquering utility for the human race, and, casting it into the domain of Community, to move on to new conquests—so that each given effort, and consequently the aggregate of efforts, should continually be delivering over to mankind satisfactions which are always increasing. Human services exchanged, while preserving their relative value, become the vehicle of an always increasing proportion of utility which is gratuitous, and, therefore, common; and in this consists progress. The possessors of value, then, whatever form it assumes, far from usurping and monopolizing the gifts of God, multiply these gifts, without causing them to lose the character which Providence has affixed to them, of being—Gratuitous.

In proportion as the satisfactions which are handed over by progress to the charge of nature fall by that very fact into the domain of Community, they become equal—it being impossible for us even to conceive inequality except in the domain of human services, which are compared, appreciated, and estimated with a view to an exchange; whence it follows that Equality among men is necessarily progressive. It is so, likewise, in another respect, the action of Competition having for its inevitable result to level and equalize the services themselves, and to bring their recompense more and more into proportion with their merit.

Let us now throw a glance back on the ground over which we have passed.

By the light of the theory, the foundation of which has been laid in the present volume, we shall have to investigate:

The relations of man with the Economic phenomena, in his capacity of producer, and in his character of consumer;

The law of Rent;

That of Wages;

That of Credit;

That of Taxation, which, introducing us into the domain of Politics, properly so called, will lead us to compare those services which are private and voluntary with those which are public and compulsory;

The law of Population.

We shall then be in a situation to solve some practical problems which are still disputed—Free-trade, Machinery, Luxury, Leisure, Association, Organization of Labour, &c.

I hesitate not to say, that the result of this exposition may be expressed beforehand in these terms: *The constant approximation of all men towards a level which is always rising*—in other terms: *Improvement and Equalization* in a single word, HARMONY.

Such is the definitive result of the arrangements of Providence—of the great laws of nature—when they act without impediment, when we regard them as they are in themselves, and apart from any disturbance of their action by error and violence. On beholding this Harmony, the Economist may well exclaim, like the astronomer who regards the planetary movements, or the physiologist who contemplates the structure and arrangement of the human organs—*Digitus Dei est Hic!*

But man is a free agent, and consequently fallible. He is subject to ignorance and to passion. His will, which is liable to err, enters as an element into the play of the economic laws. He may misunderstand them, forget them, divert them from their purpose. As the physiologist, after admiring the infinite wisdom displayed in the structure and relations of our organs and viscera, studies these organs likewise in their abnormal state when sickly and diseased, we shall have to penetrate into a new world—the world of social Disturbances.

We shall pave the way for this new study by some considerations on man himself. It would be impossible for us to give an account of *social evil*, of its origin, its effects, its design—of the limits, always more and more contracted, within which it is shut up by its own action (which constitutes what I might almost venture to call a harmonic dissonance), did we not extend our investigation to the necessary consequences of

Free-will, to the errors of Self-Interest, which are constantly corrected, and to the great laws of human Responsibility and Solidarity.

We have seen the germ of all the *social Harmonies* included in these two principles—PROPERTY, LIBERTY. We shall see that all *social Dissonances* are only the development of these two antagonistic principles—SPOLIATION, OPPRESSION.

The words Property and Liberty, in fact, express only two aspects of the same idea. In an economical point of view, Liberty is allied to the act of production—Property to the things produced. And since Value has its foundation in the human act, we may conclude that Liberty implies and includes Property. The same relation exists between Oppression and Spoliation.

Liberty! here at length we have the principle of harmony. Oppression! here we have the principle of dissonance. The struggle of these two powers fills the annals of the human race.

And as the design of Oppression is to effect an unjust appropriation, as it resolves itself into and is summed up in spoliation, it is Spoliation that must form the subject of our inquiry.

Man comes into this world bound to the yoke of Want, which is pain.

He cannot escape from it but by subjecting himself to the yoke of Labour, which is pain also.

He has, then, only a choice of pains, and he detests pain.

This is the reason why he looks around him, and if he sees that his fellow-man has accumulated wealth, he conceives the thought of appropriating it. Hence comes false property, or Spoliation.

Spoliation! here we have a new element in the economy of society.

From the day when it first made its appearance in the world down to the day when it shall have completely disappeared, if that day ever come, this element has affected and will affect profoundly the whole social mechanism; it will disturb, and to the extent of rendering them no longer recognisable, those laws of social harmony which we have endeavoured to discover and describe.

Our duty, then, will not have been accomplished until we have completed the monography of Spoliation.

It may be imagined that we have here to do with an accidental and exceptional fact, a transient derangement unworthy of the investigation of science.

But in truth it is not so. On the contrary, Spoliation, in the traditions of families, in the history of nations, in the occupations of individuals, in the physical and intellectual energies of classes, in the schemes and designs of governments, occupies nearly as prominent a place as Property itself.

No; Spoliation is not an ephemeral scourge, affecting accidentally the social mechanism, and which economical science may disregard as exceptional.

The sentence pronounced upon man in the beginning was, *In the sweat of thy brow shalt thou eat bread.* Whence it appears that effort and satisfaction are indissolubly united, and that the one must be always the recompense of the other. But on all sides we find man revolting against this law, and saying to his brother, Thine be the labour, and mine the fruit of that labour.

Repair to the hut of the savage hunter, or to the tent of the nomad shepherd, and what spectacle meets your eyes? The wife, lank, pale, disfigured, affrighted, prematurely old, bears the whole burden of the household cares, while the man lounges in idleness. What idea can we form of family Harmonies? The idea has disappeared, for Strength here throws upon Feebleness the weight of labour. And how many ages of civilizing effort will be needed to raise the wife from this state of frightful degradation?

Spoliation, in its most brutal form, armed with torch and sword, fills the annals of the world. Of what names is history made up? Cyrus, Sesostris, Alexander, Scipio, Caesar, Attila, Tamerlane, Mahomet, Pizarro, William the Conqueror—pure Spoliation from beginning to end in the shape of Conquest. Hers are the laurels, the monuments, the statutes, the triumphal arches, the song of the poet, the intoxicating enthusiasm of the fair!

The Conqueror soon finds that he can turn his victories to more profitable account than by putting to death the vanquished; and Slavery covers the earth. Down to our own times, all over the world this has been the form in which societies have existed, bringing with it hates, resistance, internal struggles, and revolutions. And what is Slavery but organized oppression—organized for the purpose of Spoliation?

But Spoliation not only arms Force against Feebleness—she turns Intelligence against Credulity. What hard-working people in the world has escaped being sweated by sacerdotal theocracies, Egyptian priests, Greek oracles, Roman auguries, Gallic druids, Indian brahmins, muftis, ulemas, bonzes, monks, ministers, mountebanks, sorcerers, soothsayers,— spoliators of all garbs and of all denominations. Assuming this guise, Spoliation places the fulcrum of her lever in heaven, and sacrilegiously prides herself on the complicity of the gods! She enslaves not men's limbs only, but their souls. She knows how to impress the iron of slavery as well upon the conscience of Seide as upon the forehead of Spartacus— realizing what would seem impossible—Mental Slavery.

Mental Slavery! what a frightful association of words! O Liberty! we have seen thee hunted from country to country, crushed by conquest, groaning under slavery, insulted in courts, banished from the schools, laughed at in saloons, misunderstood in workshops, denounced in churches. It seems thou shouldst find in thought an inviolable refuge. But if thou art to surrender in this thy last asylum, what becomes of the hopes of ages, and the boasted courage of the human race?

At length, however, the progressive nature of man causes Spoliation to develop, in the society in which it exists, resistance which paralyzes its force, and knowledge which unveils its impostures. But Spoliation does not confess herself conquered for all that; she only becomes more crafty, and, enveloping herself in the forms of government and in a system of checks and counterpoises, she gives birth to Politics, long a prolific resource. We then see her usurping the liberty of citizens, the better to get hold of their wealth, and draining away their wealth to possess herself more surely of their liberty. Private activity passes into the domain of public activity. Everything is transacted through functionaries, and an unintelligent and meddling bureaucracy overspreads the land. The public treasury becomes a vast reservoir into which labourers pour their savings, to be immediately distributed among placement. Transactions are no longer regulated by free bargaining and discussion, and the *mutuality of services* disappears.

In this state of things the true notion of Property is extinguished, and every one appeals to the Law to give his services a fictitious value.

We enter then upon the era of privileges. Spoliation, ever improving in subtility, fortifies herself in Monopoly, and takes refuge behind Restrictions. She displaces the natural current of exchanges, and sends capital into artificial channels, and with capital, labour—and with labour,—population. She gets painfully produced in the North what is produced with facility in the South; creates precarious classes and branches of industry; substitutes for the gratuitous forces of nature the onerous fatigues of labour; cherishes establishments which can sustain no rivalry, and invokes against competitors the employment of force; provokes international jealousies; flatters patriotic arrogance; and invents ingenious theories, which make auxiliaries of her own dupes. She constantly renders imminent industrial crises and bankruptcies, shakes to its foundation all confidence in the future, all faith in liberty, all consciousness of what is just. At length, when science exposes her misdeeds, she stirs up against science her own victims, by proclaiming a Utopia! and ignores not only the science which places obstacles in her path, but the very idea of any possible science, by this crowning sentence of scepticism—There are no principles!

Under the pressure of suffering, at length the masses rise, and overturn everything which is above them. Government, taxes, legislation, everything is at their mercy, and you imagine perhaps that there is now an end to the reign of Spoliation; that the mutuality of services is about to be established on the only possible, or even imaginable basis—Liberty. Undeceive yourself. The fatal idea, alas! has permeated the masses, that Property has no other origin, no other sanction, no other legitimacy, no other foundation, than Law; and then the masses set to work legislatively to rob one another. Suffering from the wounds which have been inflicted upon them, they undertake to cure each of their members by conceding to him the right to oppress his neighbour, and call this Solidarity and Fraternity. "You have produced—I have not produced—we are *solidaries* —let us divide." "You have something—I have nothing—we are brethren —let us share." It will be our duty then to examine the improper use which has been made in these latter days of the terms association, organization, labour, *gratuité du crédit*, &c. We shall have to subject them to this test—Do they imply Liberty or Oppression? In other words, are they in unison with the great Economical laws, or are they disturbances of those laws?

Spoliation is a phenomenon too universal, too persistent, to permit us to attribute to it a character purely accidental. In this, as in many other matters, we cannot separate the study of natural laws from the study of their Perturbations.

But, it may be said, if spoliation enters necessarily into the play of the social mechanism as a *dissonance*, how can you venture to assert the Harmony of the Economic laws?

I must repeat here what I have said in another place, namely, that in all which concerns man, a being who is only *perfectible* because he is *imperfect*, Harmony consists, not in the absolute absence of *evil*, but in its gradual diminution. The social body, like the human body, is provided with a curative force, a *vis medicatrix*, the laws and infallible power of which it is impossible to study without again exclaiming, *Digitus Dei est hic.*

FREDERIC BASTIAT

SELECTIONS FROM "ECONOMIC SOPHISMS"

EQUALIZING OF THE FACILITIES OF PRODUCTION

* * * * *

Here, as elsewhere, we find the theorists who favor protection taking part with the producer. Let us consider the case of the unfortunate consumer, who seems to have entirely escaped their attention. They compare the field of production to the *turf*. But on the turf the race is at once a *means and an end*. The public has no interest in the struggle independent of the struggle itself. When your horses are started in the course with the single object of determining which is the best runner, nothing is more natural than that their burdens should be equalized. But if your object were to send an important and critical piece of intelligence, could you without incongruity place obstacles to the speed of that one whose fleetness would secure the best means of attaining your end? And yet this is your course in relation to industry. You forget the end aimed at, which is the well-being of the community.

But since we cannot lead our opponents to look at things from our point of view, let us now take theirs; let us examine the question as producers.

I will seek to prove

1. That equalizing the facilities of production is to attack the foundations of all trade.

2. That it is not true that the labor of one country can be crushed by the competition of more favored climates.

3. That, even were this the case, protective duties cannot equalize the facilities of production.

4. That freedom of trade equalizes these conditions as much as possible; and

5. That the countries which are the least favored by nature are those which profit most by freedom of trade.

* * * * *

I invoke the patience of the reader, and beg him to believe that I have not lost sight of free trade: I entreat him only to remember the conclusion at which I have arrived: *Remuneration is not proportioned to the usefulness of the articles brought by the producer into the market, but to the labor.*

I have so far taken my examples from human inventions, but will now go on to speak of natural advantages.

431

In every article of production nature and man must concur. But the portion of nature is always gratuitous. Only so much of the usefulness of an article as is the result of human labor becomes the object of mutual exchange, and consequently of remuneration. The remuneration varies much, no doubt, in proportion to the intensity of the labor, of the skill which it requires, of its being apropos to the demand of the day, of the need which exists for it, of the momentary absence of competition, etc. But it is not the less true in principle, that the assistance received from natural laws, which belongs to all, counts for nothing in the price.

We do not pay for the air we breathe, although so useful to us that we could not live two minutes without it. We do not pay for it, because nature furnishes it without the intervention of man's labor. But if we wish to separate one of the gases which compose it, for instance to fill a balloon, we must take some trouble and labor; or if another takes it for us, we must give him an equivalent in something which will have cost us the trouble of production. From which we see that the exchange is between troubles, efforts, labors. It is certainly not for hydrogen gas that I pay, for this is everywhere at my disposal, but for the work that it has been necessary to accomplish in order to disengage it; work which I have been spared, and which I must refund. If I am told that there are other things to pay for—as expense, materials, apparatus—I answer that still in these things it is the work that I pay for. The price of the coal employed is only the representation of the labor necessary to dig and transport it.

We do not pay for the light of the sun, because nature alone gives it to us. But we pay for the light of gas, tallow, oil, wax, because here is labor to be remunerated; and remark, that it is so entirely labor and not utility to which remuneration is proportioned, that it may well happen that one of these means of lighting, while it may be much more effective than another, may still cost less. To cause this, it is only necessary that less human labour should be required to furnish it.

When the water carrier comes to supply my house, were I to pay him in proportion to the *absolute utility* of the water, my whole fortune would not be sufficient. But I pay him only for the trouble he has taken. If he requires more, I can get others to furnish it, or finally go and get it myself. The water itself is not the subject of our bargain, but the labor taken to get the water. This point of view is so important, and the consequences that I am going to draw from it so clear, as regards the freedom of international exchanges, that I will still elucidate my idea by a few more examples.

* * * * *

Thus natural advantages, like improvements in the process of production, are, or have a constant tendency to become, under the law of competition, the common and *gratuitous* patrimony of consumers, of society, of mankind. Countries therefore which do not enjoy these advantages must gain by commerce with those which do; because the exchanges of commerce are between *labor* and *labor;* subtraction being made of all the natural advantages which are combined with these labors; and it is evidently the most favored countries which can incorporate into a given labor the largest proportion of these *natural advantages.* Their produce representing less labor receives less recompense; in other words, is *cheaper.* If then all the liberality of nature results in cheapness, it is evidently not the producing but the consuming country which profits by her benefits.

Hence we may see the enormous absurdity of the consuming country which rejects produce precisely because it is cheap. It is as though we should say: "We will have nothing of that which nature gives you. You ask of us an effort equal to two, in order to furnish ourselves with articles only attainable at home by an effort equal to four. You can do it because with you nature does half the work. But we will have nothing to do with it; we will wait till your climate, becoming more inclement, forces you to ask of us a labor equal to four, and then we can treat with you *upon an equal footing.*"

A is a favored country; B is maltreated by nature. Mutual traffic then is advantageous to both, but principally to B, because the exchange is not between *utility* and *utility,* but between *value* and *value.* Now A furnishes a greater *utility in a similar value,* because the *utility* of any article includes at once what nature and what labor have done; whereas the *value* of it corresponds only to the portion accomplished by labor. B then makes an entirely advantageous bargain; for by simply paying the producer from A for his labor, it receives in return not only the results of that labor, but in addition there is thrown in whatever may have accrued from the superior bounty of nature.

We will lay down the general rule.

Traffic is an exchange of *values;* and as value is reduced by competition to the simple representation of labor, traffic is the exchange of equal labors. Whatever nature has done towards the production of the articles exchanged, is given on both sides *gratuitously;* from whence it necessarily follows, that the most advantageous commerce is transacted with those countries which are the most favored by nature.

PETITION FROM THE MANUFACTURERS OF CANDLES, WAX LIGHTS, LAMPS, CHANDELIERS, REFLECTORS, SNUFFERS, EXTINGUISHERS; AND FROM THE PRODUCERS OF TALLOW, OIL, RESIN, ALCOHOL, AND GENERALLY OF EVERYTHING USED FOR LIGHTS

To the Honorable the Members of the Chamber of Deputies:

GENTLEMEN—You are in the right way: you reject abstract theories; abundance, cheapness, concerns you little. You are entirely occupied with the interest of the producer, whom you are anxious to free from foreign competition. In a word, you wish to secure the *national market* to *national labor*.

We come now to offer you an admirable opportunity for the application of your—what shall we say? your theory? no, nothing is more deceiving than theory—your doctrine? your system? your principle? But you do not like doctrines; you hold systems in horror; and, as for principles, you declare that there are no such things in political economy. We will say, then, your practice; your practice without theory, and without principle.

We are subjected to the intolerable competition of a foreign rival, who enjoys, it would seem, such superior facilities for the production of light, that he is enabled to *inundate* our *national market* at so exceedingly reduced a price, that, the moment he makes his appearance, he draws off all custom for us; and thus an important branch of French industry, with all its innumerable ramifications, is suddenly reduced to a state of complete stagnation. This rival, who is no other than the sun, carries on so bitter a war against us, that we have every reason to believe that he has been excited to this course by our perfidious neighbor England. (Good diplomacy this, for the present time!) In this belief we are confirmed by the fact that in all his transactions with that proud island, he is much more moderate and careful than with us.

Our petition is, that it would please your honorable body to pass a law whereby shall be directed the shutting up of windows, dormers, skylights, shutters, curtains, *vasistas*, *oeil-de-boeufs*, in a word, all openings, holes, chinks, and fissures through which the light of the sun is used to penetrate into our dwellings, to the prejudice of the profitable manufactures which we flatter ourselves we have been enabled to bestow upon the country; which country cannot, therefore, without ingratitude, leave us now to struggle unprotected through so unequal a contest.

We pray your honorable body not to mistake our petition for a satire, nor to repulse us without at least hearing the reasons which we have to advance in its favor.

And first, if, by shutting out as much as possible all access to natural light, you thus create the necessity for artificial light, is there in France an industrial pursuit which will not, through some connection with this important object, be benefited by it?

If more tallow be consumed, there will arise a necessity for an increase of cattle and sheep. Thus artificial meadows must be in greater demand; and meat, wool, leather, and, above all, manure, this basis of agricultural riches, must become more abundant.

If more oil be consumed, it will cause an increase in the cultivation of the olive tree. This plant, luxuriant and exhausting to the soil, will come in good time to profit by the increased fertility which the raising of cattle will have communicated to our fields.

Our heaths will become covered with resinous trees. Numerous swarms of bees will gather upon our mountains the perfumed treasures which are now cast upon the winds, useless as the blossoms from which they emanate. There is, in short, no branch of agriculture which would not be greatly developed by the granting of our petition.

Navigation would equally profit. Thousands of vessels would soon be employed in the whale fisheries, and hence would arise a navy capable of sustaining the honor of France, and of responding to the patriotic sentiments of the undersigned petitioners, candle merchants, etc.

But what words can express the magnificence which Paris will then exhibit! Cast an eye upon the future and behold the gildings, the bronzes, the magnificent crystal chandeliers, lamps, reflectors, and candelabra, which will glitter in the spacious stores, compared with which the splendor of the present day will appear trifling and insignificant.

There is none, not even the poor manufacturer of resin in the midst of his pine forest, nor the miserable miner in his dark dwelling, but who would enjoy an increase of salary and of comforts.

Gentlemen, if you will be pleased to reflect, you cannot fail to be convinced that there is perhaps not one Frenchman, from the opulent stockholder of Anzin down to the poorest vender of matches, who is not interested in the success of our petition.

We foresee your objections, gentlemen; but there is not one that you can oppose to us which you will not be obliged to gather from the works of the partisans of free trade. We dare challenge you to pronounce one word against our petition, which is not equally opposed to your own practice and the principle which guides your policy.

Do you tell us, that if we gain by this protection, France will not gain, because the consumer must pay the price of it?

We answer you:

You have no longer any right to cite the interest of the consumer. For whenever this has been found to compete with that of the producer, you have invariably sacrified the first. You have done this to *encourage labor*, to *increase the demand for labor*. The same reason should now induce you to act in the same manner.

You have yourselves already answered the objection. When you were told, The consumer is interested in the free introduction of coal, iron, corn, wheat, cloths, etc., your answer was, Yes, but the producer is interested in their exclusion. Thus, also, if the consumer is interested in the admission of light, we, the producers, pray for its interdiction.

You have also said, the producer and the consumer are one. If the manufacturer gains by protection, he will cause the agriculturist to gain also; if agriculture prospers, it opens a market for manufactured goods. Thus we, if you confer upon us the monopoly of furnishing light during the day, will as a first consequence buy large quantities of tallow, coals, oil, resin, wax, alcohol, silver, iron, bronze, crystal, for the supply of our business; and then we and our numerous contractors having become rich, our consumption will be great, and will become a means of contributing to the comfort and competency of the workers in every branch of national labor.

Will you say that the light of the sun is a gratuituous gift, and that to repulse gratuitous gifts is to repulse riches under pretense of encouraging the means of obtaining them?

Take care—you carry the death blow to your own policy. Remember that hitherto you have always repulsed foreign produce *because* it was an approach to a gratuitous gift, and *the more in proportion* as this approach was more close. You have, in obeying the wishes of other monopolists, acted only from a *half-motive;* to grant our petition there is a much *fuller inducement.* To repulse us, precisely for the reason that our case is a more complete one than any which have preceded it, would be to lay down the following equation: $+ \times + = -$; in other words, it would be to accumulate absurdity upon absurdity.

Labor and nature concur in different proportions, according to country and climate, in every article of production. The portion of nature is always gratuitous; that of labor alone regulates the price.

If a Lisbon orange can be sold at half the price of a Parisian one, it is because a natural and gratuitous heat does for the one what the other only obtains from an artificial and consequently expensive one.

When, therefore, we purchase a Portuguese orange, we may say that we obtain it half gratuitously and half by the right of labor; in other words, at *half price* compared with those of Paris.

Now it is precisely on account of this *demi-gratuity* (excuse the word) that you argue in favor of exclusion. How, you say, could national labor sustain the competiton of foreign labor, when the first has everything to do, and the last is rid of half the trouble, the sun taking the rest of the business upon himself? If then the *demi-gratuity* can determine you to check competition, on what principle can the *entire gratuity* be alleged as a reason for admitting it? You are no logicians if, refusing the demi-gratuity as hurtful to human labor, you do not *a fortiori,* and with double zeal, reject the full gratuity.

Again, when any article, as coal, iron, cheese, or cloth, comes to us from foreign countries with less labor than if we produced it ourselves, the difference in price is a *gratuitous gift* conferred upon us; and the gift is more or less considerable, according as the difference is greater or less. It is the quarter, the half, or the three quarters of the value of the produce, in proportion as the foreign merchant requires the three quarters, the half, or the quarter of the price. It is as complete as possible when the producer offers, as the sun does with light, the whole in free gift. The question is, and we put it formally, whether you wish for France the benefit of gratuitous consumption, or the supposed advantages of laborious production. Choose, but be consistent. And does it not argue the greatest inconsistency to check as you do the importation of coal, iron, cheese, and goods of foreign manufacture, merely because and even in proportion as their price approaches *zero*, while at the same time you freely admit, and without limitation, the light of the sun, whose price is during the whole day at *zero*?

FREDERIC BASTIAT

SELECTIONS FROM ESSAYS ON POLITICAL ECONOMY

THE SEEN AND THE UNSEEN

In the department of economy, an act, a habit, an institution, a law, gives birth not only to an effect, but to a series of effects. Of these effects the first one is immediate; it manifests itself simultaneously with its cause—*it is seen*. The others unfold in succession—*they are not seen;* it is well for us, if they are *foreseen*. Between a good and a bad economist this constitutes the whole difference—the one takes account of the *visible* effect; the other takes account both of the effects which are *seen*, and also of those which it is necessary to *foresee*. Now this difference is enormous, for it almost always happens that when the immediate consequence is favorable the ultimate consequences are fatal, *and the converse*. Hence it follows that the bad economist pursues a small present good which will be followed by a great evil to come, while the true economist pursues a great good to come, at the risk of a small present evil.

In fact it is the same in the science of health, arts, and in that of morals. It often happens that the sweeter the first fruit of a habit is, the more bitter are the consequences. Take, for example, debauchery, idleness, prodigality. When, therefore, a man, absorbed in the effect which *is seen*, has not yet learned to discern those which are *not seen*, he gives way to fatal habits, not only by inclination, but by calculation.

This explains the fatally grievous condition of mankind. Ignorance surrounds its cradle; then its actions are determined by their first consequences, the only ones which, in its first stage, it can see. It is only in the long run that it learns to take account of the others. It has to learn this lesson from two very different masters—experience and foresight. Experience teaches effectually, but brutally. It makes us acquainted with all the effects of an action by causing us to feel them; and we cannot fail to finish by knowing that fire burns if we have burned ourselves. For this rough teacher, I should like, if possible, to substitute a more gentle one. I mean foresight. For this purpose I shall examine the consequences of certain economical phenomena, by placing in opposition to each other those *which are seen*, and those *which are not seen*.

The Broken Window

Have you ever witnessed the anger of the good shopkeeper, James B., when his careless son happened to break a square of glass? If you have been

438

present at such a scene you will most assuredly bear witness to the fact that every one of the spectators, were there even thirty of them, by common consent apparently, offered the unfortunate owner this invariable consolation: "It is an ill wind that blows nobody good. Everybody must live, and what would become of the glaziers if panes of glass were never broken?"

Now this form of condolence contains an entire theory, which it will be well to show up in this simple case, seeing that it is precisely the same as that which, unhappily, regulates the greater part of our economical institutions.

Suppose it cost six francs to repair the damage, and you say that the accident brings six francs to the glazier's trade—that it encourages that trade to the amount of six francs—I grant it; I have not a word to say against it; you reason justly. The glazier comes, performs his task, receives his six francs, rubs his hands, and, in his heart, blesses the careless child. All this is *that which is seen.*

But if, on the other hand, you come to the conclusion, as is too often the case, that it is a good thing to break windows, that it causes money to circulate, and that the encouragement of industry in general will be the result of it, you will oblige me to call out, "Stop there! your theory is confined to that *which is seen;* it takes no account of that *which is not seen.*"

It is not seen that as our shopkeeper has spent six francs upon one thing, he cannot spend them upon another. *It is not seen* that if he had not had a window to replace, he would, perhaps, have replaced his old shoes, or added another book to his library. In short, he would have employed his six francs in some way which this accident has prevented.

Let us take a view of industry in general, as affected by this circumstance. The window being broken, the glazier's trade is encouraged to the amount of six francs; *this is that which is seen.*

If the window had not been broken, the shoemaker's trade (or some other) would have been encouraged to the amount of six francs; *this is that which is not seen.*

And if *that which is not seen* is taken into consideration, because it is a negative fact, as well as that which is seen, because it is a positive fact, it will be understood that neither industry *in general,* nor the sum total of *national labor* is affected, whether windows are broken or not.

Now let us consider James B. himself. In the former supposition, that of the window being broken, he spends six francs, and has neither more nor less than he had before—the enjoyment of a window.

In the second, where we suppose the window not to have been broken, he would have spent six francs in shoes, and would have had at the same time the enjoyment of a pair of shoes and a window.

Now as James B. forms a part of society, we must come to the conclusion that, taking it altogether, and making an estimate of its enjoyments and its labors, it has lost the value of the broken window.

Whence we arrive at this unexpected conclusion, "Society loses the value of things which are uselessly destroyed"; and we must assent to a maxim which will make the hair of protectionists stand on end—To break, to spoil, to waste, is not to encourage national labor; or, more briefly, "destruction is not profit."

What will you say, *Moniteur Industriel*—what will you say, disciples of good Mr. Chamans, who has calculated with so much precision how much trade would gain by the burning of Paris, from the number of houses it would be necessary to rebuild?

I am sorry to disturb these ingenious calculations, as far as their spirit has been introduced into our legislation; but I beg him to begin them again by taking into the account *that which is not seen*, and placing it alongside of *that which is seen*.

The reader must take care to remember that there are not two persons only, but three, concerned in the little scene which I have submitted to his attention. One of them, James B., represents the consumer, reduced by an act of destruction to one enjoyment instead of two. Another, under the title of the glazier, shows the producer, whose trade is encouraged by the accident. The third is the shoemaker (or some other tradesman), whose labor suffers proportionably by the same cause. It is this third person who is always kept in the shade, and who, personating *that which is not seen*, is a necessary element of the problem. It is he who shows us how absurd it is to think we see a profit in an act of destruction. It is he who will soon teach us that it is not less absurd to see a profit in a restriction, which is, after all, nothing else than a partial destruction. Therefore, if you will only go to the root of all the arguments which are adduced in its favor, all you will find will be the paraphrase of this vulgar saying, *What would become of the glaziers if nobody ever broke windows?*

Public Works

Nothing is more natural than that a nation, after having assured itself that an enterprise will benefit a community, should have it executed by means of a general assessment. But I lose patience, I confess, when I hear this economic blunder advanced in support of such a project— "Besides it will be a means of creating labor for the workmen."

The State opens a road, builds a palace, straightens a street, cuts a canal; and so gives work to certain workmen—*this is what is seen;* but it deprives certain other workmen of work, and this is what *is not seen.*

The road is begun. A thousand workmen come every morning, leave every evening, and take their wages; this is certain. If the road had not been decreed, if the supplies had not been voted, these good people would have had neither work nor salary there; this also is certain.

But is this all? Does not the operation, as a whole, contain something else? At the moment when Mr. Dupin announces the emphatic words,

"The Assembly has adopted," do the millions descend miraculously on a moonbeam into the coffers of Messrs. Fould and Bineau? In order that the operation may be complete, as it is said, must not the State organize the receipts as well as the expenditure? Must it not set its tax-gatherers and taxpayers to work, the former to gather, and the latter to pay?

Study the question now in both its elements. While you state the destination given by the State to the millions voted, do not neglect to state also the destination which the taxpayer would have given, but cannot now give, to the same. Then you will understand that a public enterprise is a coin with two sides. Upon one is engraved a laborer out of work, with the device, *that which is not seen.*

The sophism which this work is intended to refute is the more dangerous when applied to public works, inasmuch as it serves to justify the most wanton enterprises and extravagance. When a railroad or a bridge are of real utility, it is sufficient to mention this utility. But if it does not exist, what do they do? Recourse is had to this mystification, "We must find work for the workmen."

Accordingly, orders are given that the drains in the Champ-de-Mars be made and unmade. The great Napoleon, it is said, thought he was doing a very philanthropic work by causing ditches to be made and then filled up. He said, therefore: "What signifies the result? All we want is to see wealth spread among the laboring classes."

But let us go to the root of the matter. We are deceived by money. To demand the coöperation of all the citizens in a common work, in the form of money, is in reality to demand a concurrence in kind; for every one procures, by his own labor, the sum which he is taxed. Now if all the citizens were to be called together, and made to execute, in conjunction, a work useful to all, this would be easily understood; their reward would be found in the results of the work itself.

But after having called them together, if you force them to make roads which no one will pass through, palaces which no one will inhabit, and this under the pretext of finding them work, it would be absurd, and they would have a right to argue, "With this labor we will have nothing to do; we prefer working on our own account."

A proceeding which consists in making the citizens coöperate in giving money but not labor, does not, in any way, alter the general results. The only thing is, that the loss would react upon all parties. By the former, those whom the State employs escape their part of the loss by adding it to that which their fellow-citizens have already suffered.

There is an article in our constitution which says: "Society favors and encourages the development of labor—by the establishment of public works, by the State, the departments, and the parishes, as a means of employing persons who are in want of work."

As a temporary measure, on any emergency, during a hard winter, this interference with the taxpayers may have its use. It acts in the same way as securities. It adds nothing either to labor or to wages, but it takes labor and wages from ordinary times to give them, at a loss it is true, to times of difficulty.

As a permanent, general, systematic measure, it is nothing else than a ruinous mystification, an impossibility, which shows a little excited labor *which is seen*, and hides a great deal of prevented labor *which is not seen*.

Frugality and Luxury

It is not only in the public expenditure that *what is seen* eclipses *what is not seen*. Setting aside what relates to political economy, this phenomenon leads to false reasoning. It causes nations to consider their moral and their material interests as contradictory to each other. What can be more discouraging or more dismal?

For instance, there is not a father of a family who does not think it his duty to teach his children order, system, the habits of carefulness, of economy, and of moderation in spending money.

There is no religion which does not thunder against pomp and luxury. This is as it should be; but, on the other hand, how frequently do we hear the following remarks:

"To hoard is to drain the veins of the people."

"The luxury of the great is the comfort of the little."

"Prodigals ruin themselves, but they enrich the State."

"It is the superfluity of the rich which makes the bread of the poor."

Here, certainly, is a striking contradiction between the moral and the social idea. How many eminent spirits, after having made the assertion, repose in peace. It is a thing I could never understand, for it seems to me that nothing can be more distressing than to discover two opposite tendencies in mankind. Why, it comes to degradation at each of the extremes; economy brings it to misery; prodigality plunges it into moral degradation. Happily these vulgar maxims exhibit economy and luxury in a false light, taking account, as they do, of those immediate consequences *which are seen*, and not of the remote ones, *which are not seen*. Let us see if we can rectify this incomplete view of the case.

Mondor and his brother Aristus, after dividing the paternal inheritance, have each an income of fifty thousand francs. Mondor practices the fashionable philanthropy. He is what is called a squanderer of money. He renews his furniture several times a year; changes his equipages every month. People talk of his ingenious contrivances to bring them sooner to an end; in short, he surpasses the fast livers of Balzac and Alexandre Dumas.

Thus everybody is singing his praises. It is: "Tell us about Mondor! Mondor forever! He is the benefactor of the workman; a blessing to the people. It is true, he revels in dissipation; he splashes the passers-by; his own dignity and that of human nature are lowered a little; but what of that? He does good with his fortune, if not with himself. He causes money to circulate; he always sends the tradespeople away satisfied. Is not money made round that it may roll?"

Aristus has adopted a very different plan of life. If he is not an egotist, he is, at any rate, an *individualist*, for he considers expense, seeks only moderate and reasonable enjoyments, thinks of his children's prospects, and, in fact, he economizes.

And what do people say of him? "What is the good of a rich fellow like him? He is a skinflint. There is something imposing, perhaps, in the simplicity of his life; and he is humane, too, and benevolent, and generous, but he *calculates*. He does not spend his income; his house is neither brilliant nor bustling. What good does he do to the paper hangers, the carriage makers, the horse dealers, and the confectioners?"

These opinions, which are fatal to morality, are founded upon what strikes the eye—the expenditure of the prodigal; and another, which is out of sight, the equal and even superior expenditure of the economist.

But things have been so admirably arranged by the Divine Inventor of social order, that in this, as in everything else, political economy and morality, far from clashing, agree; and the wisdom of Aristus is not only more dignified, but still more profitable, than the folly of Mondor. And when I say profitable, I do not mean only profitable to Aristus, or even to society in general, but more profitable to the workmen themselves—to the trade of the time.

To prove it, it is only necessary to turn the mind's eye to those hidden consequences of human actions which the bodily eye does not see.

Yes, the prodigality of Mondor has visible effects in every point of view. Everybody can see his landaus, his phaetons, his berlins, the delicate paintings on his ceilings, his rich carpets, the brilliant effects of his house. Every one knows that his horses run upon the turf. The dinners which he gives at the Hôtel de Paris attract the attention of the crowds upon the boulevards; and it is said, "That is a generous man; far from saving his income, he is very likely breaking into his capital." This is *what is seen*.

It is not so easy to see, with regard to the interest of workers, what becomes of the income of Aristus. If we were to trace it carefully, however, we should see that the whole of it, down to the last farthing, affords work to the laborers as certainly as the fortune of Mondor. Only there is this difference: the wanton extravagance of Mondor is doomed to be constantly decreasing, and to come to an end without fail; while the wise expenditure of Aristus will go on increasing from year to year. And if this is the case, then most assuredly the public interest will be in unison with morality.

* * * * *

HENRY CHARLES CAREY

(1793–1879)

Henry Carey was born in Philadelphia in 1793 of Irish parentage. He followed the footsteps of his father in the publishing business, from which he cleared a small fortune. Later he retired to devote himself to literary pursuits.

Carey's writings included: "An Essay on the Rate of Wages with an Examination of Causes of the Difference in the Condition of the Labouring Population throughout the World," (1835); "Principles of Political Economy," in three volumes (published between 1837 and 1840), which was really an enlargement of his first work; "The Credit System of France, Great Britain and the United States" (1838); "An Answer to the Questions: What Constitutes Currency? What are the Causes of its Unsteadiness and What is the Remedy?" (1840); "The Past, the Present and the Future" (1848); "The Harmony of Interests, Agricultural, Manufacturing and Commercial" (1851); and "The Slave Trade, Domestic and Foreign" (1853). His writings also included "Some Letters on International Copyright."

As is easily seen, Carey was a most prolific writer. His chief contribution, however, was "Principles of Social Science," published in three volumes in the years 1857 to 1860, in which he has given us his complete economic system. This work was condensed into one volume by Kate McKean, and published with the author's approval in 1864.

Carey was the first American economist and sociologist. Although our present interest in him is chiefly historical, Carey exerted a powerful influence in his day. The Preface to the condensation of his work by Kate McKean is included here in order that the student may see in what veneration Carey was held by his contemporaries and followers. Robert Ellis Thompson, from whose works a brief selection will also be included, was another important figure who delighted to honor his great master, Carey. Our selections from Carey have been taken from his voluminous work entitled "Social Science."

Both Carey and Bastiat were optimists. The student is asked to note Carey's futile criticism of the principle of diminishing returns and his almost puerile attacks upon the Malthusian law. Although he constantly insisted on rigid logic and on a scientific approach, Carey's work cannot be tested by his own standards. Perhaps it is not too severe a criticism to say that Carey's chief contribution lay in his glaring errors, which succeeded not in shattering the orthodox economic theories, but in producing improved, more exact, and better qualified restatements of them.

Like another great American economist, Simon N. Patten, Carey was impressed by the bounty of nature, rather than by its niggardliness. His approach was theological and he spoke of the beneficence of Providence which made unthinkable the Malthusian law. Carey's historical law of rent was the opposite of that of Ricardo. Progress was not from good land to poor land, but from poor land to good land. It is futile to argue whether Ricardo or Carey was correct, for perhaps there has been no universal tendency in either direction. Each man described accurately what he saw in his own day and country.

HENRY CHARLES CAREY

SELECTIONS FROM "PRINCIPLES OF SOCIAL SCIENCE"

VOLUME I

CHAPTER II. OF MAN—THE SUBJECT OF SOCIAL SCIENCE

Section 1

Man, the molecule of society, is the subject of social science. In common with all other animals he requires to eat, drink, and sleep, but his greatest need is that of ASSOCIATION with his fellow-men. Born the weakest and most dependent of animals, he requires the largest care in infancy, and must be clothed by others, whereas to birds and beasts clothing is supplied by nature. Capable of acquiring the highest degree of knowledge, he appears in the world destitute even of that instinct which teaches the bee and the spider, the bird and the beaver, to construct their habitations, and to supply themselves with food. Dependent upon the experience of himself and others for all his knowledge, he requires language to enable him either to record the results of his own observation, or to profit by those of others; and of language there can be none without association. Created in the image of his Maker, he should participate in his intelligence; but it is only by means of ideas that he can avail himself of the faculties with which he has been endowed, and without language there can be no ideas—no power of thought. Without language, therefore, he must remain in ignorance of the existence of powers granted to him in lieu of the strength of the ox and the horse, the speed of the hare, and the sagacity of the elephant, and must remain below the level of the brute creation. To have language there must be association and combination of men with their fellow-men, and it is on this condition only that man can be man; on this alone that we can conceive of the being to which we attach the idea of man. "It is not good," said God, "That man should live alone," nor do we ever find him doing so; the earliest records of the world exhibiting to us beings living together in society, and using words for the expression of their ideas. Whence came those words? Whence came language? With the same propriety might we ask—Why does fire burn? Why does man see, feel, hear, or walk? Language escapes from him at the touch of nature herself, and the power of using words is his essential faculty, enabling him to maintain commerce with his fellow men, and fitting him for that association without which language cannot exist. The words society and language convey to the mind separate and distinct ideas, and yet by no effort of the mind can we conceive of the existence of the one without the other.

The subject of social science then is man—the being to whom have been given reason and the faculty of individualizing sounds so as to give expression to every variety of idea—and who has been placed in a position to exercise that faculty. Isolate him, and with the loss of the power of speech, he loses the power to reason, and with it the distinctive quality of man. Restore him to society, and with the return of the power of speech he becomes again the reasoning man.

We have here the great law of molecular gravitation as the *indispensable* condition of the existence of the being known as man. The particles of matter having each an independent existence, the atom of oxygen or of hydrogen is as perfect and complete as it could be were it in connection with millions of others like itself. The grain of sand is perfect whether flying alone before the wind or resting with its fellow on the shores of the broad Atlantic. The tree and the shrub, brought from distant lands and standing alone in the conservatory, produce the same fruits and yield the same odors as when they stood in the groves from which they had been transplanted. The individual dog, cat, and rabbit possess all their powers in a state of entire isolation. Such, however, is not the case with man. The wild man, wherever found, has always proved to be not only destitute of the reasoning faculty, but destitute also of the instinct that in other animals takes the place of reason—and therefore the most helpless of beings.

Man tends of necessity to gravitate towards his fellow-men. Of all animals he is the most gregarious, and the greater the number collected in a given space the greater is the attractive force there exerted, as is seen to have been the case with the great cities of the ancient world, Nineveh and Babylon, Athens and Rome, and as is now seen in regard to Paris and London, Vienna and Naples, Philadelphia, New York, and Boston. Gravitation is here, as everywhere else in the material world, in the direct ratio of the mass, and in the inverse one of the distance.

Such being the case, why is it that all the members of the human family do not tend to come together on a single spot of earth? Because of the existence of the same simple and universal law by means of which is maintained the beautiful order of the system of which our planet forms a part. We are surrounded by bodies of various sizes, and some of these are themselves provided with satellites, each having its local centre of attraction, by means of which its parts are held together. Were it possible that that attractive power could be annihilated, the rings of Saturn, the moons of our earth and of Jupiter, would crumble to pieces and fall inward upon the bodies they now attend, a mass of ruins. So, too, with the planets themselves. Small as are the asteroids, each has within itself a local centre of attraction enabling it to preserve its form and substance, despite the superior attraction of the larger bodies by which it is everywhere surrounded.

* * * * *

Chapter III. Of Increase in the Numbers of Mankind

Section 3

* * * * *

That the power of association among men may increase, there must be a constantly increasing interchange—motion—between the earth and the atmosphere, and that there cannot be in any country where there is no diversity of employment; and in which, consequently, the place of consumption being remote from that of production, the farmer is limited to the cultivation of such commodities only as will bear transportation to distant countries. Hence it is that we should see a great decline in the productive powers of the land in those countries of the eastern continent in which there are few or no manufactures—Ireland, Portugal, Turkey, India, and others. Hence, too, it is that with declining population and diminished motion in society, we see the difficulty of obtaining food increasing with diminution of the numbers requiring to be fed. Famines are now more frequent in India than they were a century since when the population was far more numerous, and when combination of action existed throughout that country. Looking to past ages, we see everywhere facts of a similar kind. The valley of the Euphrates once exhibited millions of well-fed men; but as they passed away motion ceased, and its few straggling occupants now obtain with difficulty the means of supporting life. When the African province was well peopled, its people were well fed, but the few who now remain perish for want of food. So has it been in Attica and in Greece generally, in Asia Minor, in Egypt, everywhere in fact. Association, combination of action, is required to enable man to obtain control over the various forces existing in nature—and that combination can never take place except when the loom and the spindle take their natural places by the side of the plough and the harrow. The consumer must take his place by the side of the producer, to enable man to comply with the condition upon which he obtains loans from the great bank of mother Earth—the simple condition that when he has done with the capital furnished to him he will return it to the place from which it had been taken.

* * * * *

Section 5

The view thus presented, differs totally from that now most commonly received, and known as the Malthusian law of population, which may be briefly given in the following words:

Population tends to increase in a geometrical ratio, while the supplies of food can increase in an arithmetical one only. The former is, therefore, perpetually outstripping the later, and hence it is, that there is everywhere seen to arise the disease of overpopulation, with its accompaniments, poverty, wretchedness, and death—a disease requiring for its remedy wars, pestilences, and famines on the one hand, or, on the other, the exercise of that "moral restraint," which shall induce men and women to refrain from matrimony, and thus avoid the danger resulting from further addition to the numbers requiring to be fed. Reduced to distinct propositions, the theory may now be given as follows:

1. Matter tends to take upon itself higher forms, passing from the simple ones of inorganic life to the complex and beautiful ones of vegetable and animal life, and finally terminating in man.

2. This tendency exists in a small degree as relates to the lower forms of life—matter tending to take upon itself the forms of potatoes, turnips, and cabbages, herrings, and oysters, in an arithmetical ratio only.

3. When, however, we reach the highest of all the forms of which matter is capable, we find the tendency to assume that form augmenting in a geometrical ratio; as a consequence of which, while man tends to increase as 1, 2, 4, 8, 16, and 32—the potatoes and cabbages, the peas and turnips, the herrings and the oysters, increase as 1, 2, 3 and 4 only—producing the result that the highest form is perpetually outstripping the lower ones, and causing the disease of over-population.

Were such things asserted in regard to anything else than man, they would be deemed in the highest degree absurd, and those by whom they were asserted, would be required to explain why it was that an universal law had here been set aside. Everywhere else, the increase in number is in the inverse ratio of development. The little coral insects are required, in quantity innumerable, to build up islands, for animals and men that count by thousands, or by millions. Of the *clio borealis*, thousands are required to furnish a mouthful for the mighty whale. The progeny of a pair of carp would, in a single decade, as we are told, amount to millions. The countless ferns prepare the soil for the single oak; and the progeny of a pair of rabbits would, in twenty years, count by millions—whereas, that of a pair of elephants, would not amount to dozens. When, however, we reach the highest condition of which matter is capable, we learn the existence of a new and greater law, in virtue of which man increases in a geometrical ratio, while the increase of herrings, rabbits, oysters, potatoes, turnips, and all other commodities required for his use, is limited to the arithmetical one! Such is the extraordinary law propounded by Mr. Malthus, as existing in reference to the only being on whom has been impressed the desire for association, as necessary for compliance with the sole condition of his existence; the only one, to whom has been given an infinite variety of capacities fitting him for association with his fellow

men, and requiring it for their development; and the only one, too, that—
having been gifted with the power to distinguish right from wrong, and
thus been made responsible for his actions—might with reason have
required, that he should be exempt from any law requiring him to make
his election between abstinence from that association which, of all others
tends most to the improvement of his head and heart, on one hand, and
starvation on the other. Such, however, according to the generally received doctrines of modern political economy, is the law of population
instituted by an all-wise, all-powerful, and all-benevolent Creator, in
reference to the being made in his own likeness, and gifted with power to
control and direct all the forces of nature to his use—and, strange as it
appears, no proposition ever offered for consideration has exercised, or is
now exercising, upon the fortunes of the human race a greater amount of
influence. That such should have been the case had, in part, resulted from
the fact that it has been buttressed up by another one, in virtue of which
man is supposed everywhere to have commenced the work of cultivation
on rich soils—necessarily those of swamps and river bottoms—with large
return to labor; and to have found himself compelled, with the growth of
population and of wealth, to have recourse to poorer ones, with constant
decline in the return to all his efforts—a theory that, if true, would fully
establish the correctness of that of Mr. Malthus. What are its claims to
being received as true, will now be shown.

Chapter IV. Of the Occupation of the Earth

Section 2

Forty years have now elapsed since Mr. Ricardo communicated to the
world his discovery of the nature and causes of rent, and of the laws of its
progress, and during nearly all that time it has been received by a large
portion of the economists of Europe and America, as being so unquestionably true, that doubt of its truth could be regarded only as evidence
of incapacity to comprehend it. Furnishing, as it did, a simple and easy
explanation of the poverty existing in the world—and by help of a law
emanating from an all-wise, all-powerful, and all-beneficent Creator—it
relieved the governing classes from all responsibility for the wretchedness
with which they were surrounded, and was therefore at once adopted.
From that time to the present it has been the established doctrine of a
considerable portion of the schools of this country and of Europe; and
yet no two of its teachers have ever quite agreed as to what it was that
their master had really meant to teach. Having studied the works of the
most eminent among them, and having found an almost universal disagree-
ment, the student turns, in despair, to Mr. Ricardo himself, and there he
finds in his celebrated chapter on rent, contradictions that cannot be
reconciled, and a series of complications such as scarcely ever before was

found in the same number of lines. The more he studies the greater is his difficulty, and the more readily does he account for the variety of doctrines taught by men who profess to belong to the same school; and who all agree, if in little else, in regarding the new theory of rent as the great discovery of the age.

Looking around, he sees that all the recognized laws of nature are characterized by the most perfect simplicity, and the greatest breadth—that they are of universal application—and that those by whom they are taught are freed from any necessity for resorting to narrow exceptions to account for particular facts. The simplicity of Kepler's law of "equal areas in equal times" is perfect. Its truth is, consequently, universal, and all to whom it is explained feel assured not only that it *is* true, but that it must continue to be so in relation to all the planets that may be discovered, numerous though they may be, and however distant from the sun and from us. A child may comprehend it, and the merest novice may so fully master it as to fit himself for teaching it to others. It needs no commentary, no modification, and therein it differs greatly from that to which the reader's attention now is called. Whatever else may be the merits of the latter, it cannot be charged with either simplicity or universality.

At first sight it looks, however, to be exceedingly simple. Rent is said to be paid for land of the first quality, yielding a hundred quarters in return to a given quantity of labor, when it becomes necessary, with the increase of population, to cultivate land of the second quality, capable of yielding but ninety quarters in return to the same quantity of labor; and the amount of rent then paid for No. 1 is equal to the difference between their respective products. No proposition could be calculated to command more universal assent. Every man who hears it sees around him land that pays rent, and sees, too, that that which yields forty bushels to the acre pays more rent than that which yields but thirty; and that the difference is nearly equal to the difference of product. He becomes at once a disciple of Mr. Ricardo, admitting that the reason why prices are paid for the use of land is that soils are different in their qualities; when he would certainly regard it as in the highest degree absurd if any one were to undertake to prove that prices are paid for oxen because one ox is heavier than another—that rents are paid for houses because some will accommodate twenty persons and others only ten—or that all ships command freights because some ships differ from others in their capacity.

The whole system is based, as the reader will perceive, upon the assertion of the existence of the fact, that, in the commencement of cultivation, when population is small and land consequently abundant, the richest soils—those whose qualities fit them for yielding the largest return to any given quantity of labor—alone are cultivated. This fact exists or it does not. If it has no existence, the system falls to the ground.

That it has none, and that it is contrary to the nature of things that it should have had, or can ever have it, it is proposed now to show.

The picture presented by Mr. Ricardo differs totally from that which has above been presented for the consideration of the reader. The former, placing the settler on the lands of highest fertility, requires that his children and his children's children should, each in regular succession to the others, find themselves driven, by sad necessity, to the occupation of those capable of yielding smaller returns to labor—and that they should thus become, from generation to generation, more and more the slaves of nature. The latter, placing the early settler on the poorer soils, exhibits his successors exercising constantly increasing power to pass the cultivation of the richer soils—and becoming, from generation to generation, more and more the masters of nature, compelling her to do their work, and pressing steadily onward from triumph to triumph, with constant increase in the power of association, in the development of individuality, in the feeling of responsibility, and in the power of further progress. Which of these pictures is the true one, is to be settled by the determination of the fact, what it is that men in times past have done, and what it is they are now doing, in regard to the occupation of the earth. If it can be shown that, in every country and at every age, the order of events has been in direct opposition to that it is supposed by Mr. Ricardo to have been, then must this theory be abandoned as wholly destitute of foundation. That it has been so, and that everywhere, in both ancient and modern times, cultivation has commenced on the poorer soils—and that it has been with the growth of population and wealth alone that man has been enabled to subdue to cultivation the richer ones, will now be shown by a brief examination of the facts as presented in the history of the world.

That examination will be commenced with the United States; and for the reason that, their settlement having been recent, and being, indeed, still in progress, the course to which the settler has been and is prompted, can readily be traced. If we find him invariably commencing on the high and thin lands, requiring little clearing and no drainage—those capable of yielding but small return to labor—and as invariably passing from the higher to the lower ones, requiring both clearing and drainage, then will the view presented to the reader as the true one be confirmed by practice —at least by the practice of America. If, however, we can then follow the settler into Mexico, and through Brazil, Peru, and Chili—into Britain, and through France, Germany, Italy, Greece, and Egypt, into Asia and Australia—and show that such has been his invariable course of action, then may it be believed that when population is small, and land consequently abundant, the work of cultivation is, and always must be, commenced upon the poorer soils—that with the growth of population and wealth, the richer ones are always brought into activity, with constantly increasing return to the efforts of the laborer—and that, with the progress of population and wealth, there is a steady diminution in the proportion of those efforts required for obtaining the necessaries of life, with constant increase in the proportion that may be applied to adding to its comforts, conveniences, luxuries, and enjoyments.

Chapter VI. Of Value

Section 3

The house and the axe, the capital that had been accumulated, fell in value, when, by the aid of improved implements, labour had been rendered more productive—the necessary consequence of an increased facility of accumulation. With every step in this direction, the laborer finds an increase in the reward for bodily or mental exertion, as is seen in the fact that the clothing which, half a century since, would have purchased the labor of weeks, could not now command that of as many days. Half a century since, a steam-engine would have required the labor of a life to pay for it, but at present it could be exchanged for that of very few years of a common workman of the United States. In fact, like the house first built by the settler, so great would be found its inferiority to those now produced, that a purchaser at any price whatsoever could with difficulty be found.

The value of commodities or machinery at the time of production is measured by the quantity and quality of labor required to produce them. Every improvement in the mode of production tends to increase the power of labor, and to diminish the quantity required for the reproduction of similar articles. With every such improvement there is a diminution in the quantity that can be obtained in exchange for those previously existing; and because no commodity can be exchanged for more labor than is required for its reproduction. In every community in which population and wealth increase, such changes are taking place, and each is seen to be but preparatory to new and greater ones, with constantly increasing tendency to decline in the labor value of existing commodities, or machines, that have been accumulated. The longer, therefore, that any one, in the mode of producing which improvements have been made, has been in existence—even where there has been no change in its powers from use— the smaller is the proportion which its present value bears to that which it originally possessed.

The silver produced in the fourteenth century was exchanged for labor at the rate of sevenpence halfpenny for that of a week. Since that time it has steadily diminished in its power of commanding the services of men, until, at the present time, twelve or fifteen shillings are required to obtain as much of them as, five centuries, since could be had for 7½d. The various persons through whose hands has passed the silver that existed in the fourteenth century, have thus experienced a constant depreciation in the quantity of labor that their capital would command. An axe made fifty years since, of equal quality with the best of the present time—and which had remained unused—would not now exchange for half as much as it would have done on the day of its production.

Section 4

Diminution in the value of capital is attended by a diminution in the proportion of the product of labor given for its use by those who, unable to purchase, desire to hire it. Had the first axe been the exclusive property of one of our colonists, he would have demanded more than half of the wood that could be cut, in return for granting the loan of it. Although it had cost him a vast amount of labor, it would do but little work; and large as was the *proportion* of its product he was thus enabled to demand, the *quantity* that he would receive would still be very small. His neighbor, on the other hand, would find it far more to his advantage to give three-fourths of the product of his labor for the use of the axe, than to continue to depend on his hands alone; as with it he could fell more trees in a day than without it he could do in a month. The arrival of the ship having given them better axes at smaller cost, neither would now give for their use so large a proportion as he would before have done. The man who, fifty years since, desired the use of such an instrument for a year, would have given the labor of far more days, than he would now, when by that of a single day he might become the owner of one of greatly superior power. When A possessed the only house in the settlement, he could have demanded of B, for permission to use it for any given time, a much larger number of days' labor than B would be willing to give, when the possession of an axe enabled him to construct a similar one in a month. At the time that a week's labor would command only 7½d. of silver, the owner of a pound of that metal could demand a much larger proportion in return for its use, than can now be done, when the laborer obtained that quantity by the exertions of little more than a fortnight. Every improvement by which production is aided, is attended not only by a reduction in the labor value of previously existing machinery; but, also, by a diminution in the proportion of the product of labor that can be demanded in return for granting the use of it.

The more perfect the power of association, and the greater the motion of society, the greater must be the tendency towards the development of individuality, the more rapid the increase of production, the greater the facility of accumulation, the greater the tendency to decline in the value of all existing accumulations—and the smaller the *proportion* of the products of labor that can be claimed in return for their use. In order that association may increase, there must, as the reader has seen, be difference;

and that results from diversity of employments. The greater that diversity, the more rapid must be the growth of the power of accumulation, the greater the tendency to decline in the *rate* of rent, profit, or interest. In all the purely agricultural countries of the world, *the rate* of these is high; and it tends to increase because of diminution in the power of accumulation, consequent upon exhaustion of the soil—being precisely the reverse of what is observed in all those countries in which diversity of employment is increasing and individuality is becoming more and more developed.

Value is the measure of the resistance to be overcome in obtaining those commodities or things required for our purposes—of the power of nature over man.—The great object of MAN, in this world, is to acquire dominion over NATURE—compelling her to do this work; and with every step in that direction labor becomes less severe—while increasing in its reward. With each, the accumulations of the past become less valuable—with constant decline in their power to command the services of the laborers of the present. With each, the power of association grows—with constant increase in the tendency to the development of the various faculties of the individual man, and equally constant increase in the power of further progress; and thus it is, that while combination of action enables man to overcome the resistance of nature, each successive triumph is attended by increased facility for further combinations, to be followed by new and greater triumphs.

Section 9

Robinson Crusoe was surrounded by objects capable of being rendered useful to him either as food or clothing, or as machinery by help of which he might procure the various commodities required for the satisfaction of his wants; but in his then condition he was unable to command their aid. The bird on the wing, and the squirrel that jumped from tree to tree, were as fully competent to satisfy his appetite for food as those he had caught in his trap; but they had for him no UTILITY. The water abounded in fish, but he had no hook with which to take them. It would float a canoe, but—having no knife, or axe, with which to fell a tree or hollow it out—its supporting power was to him as useless as if it had not existed. It was capable of producing steam that could be made to do the work of thousands of laborers, but he possessed none of the machinery by help of which he might command its services. The air abounded in electricity, susceptible of being rendered useful; but its uses were to him unknown. He being weak and nature being strong, the resistance offered by her, to the gratification of his desires, was too great to be overcome by his unassisted powers.

With time, however, we find him calling to his aid the various qualities of wood—its elasticity. hardness, and weight; next, obtaining a cutting instrument by which other forces are made to contribute to his purposes; again, hollowing out a tree and reducing to his service the supporting power of the water; and thus gradually *utilizing* the various forces existing in nature and awaiting demand for their services.

The capability of being rendered useful to man belongs to every atom of matter of which the earth is composed—existing as much in the coal that lies thousands of feet below the surface, as in that which now burns in the grate; and as much in the ore while remaining in the mine, as in that which has been converted into stoves, grates, or railroad bars. To render them useful requires in most cases a considerable amount of physical and intellectual effort; and it is because of the necessity for that effort that man is led to attach the idea of value to the commodities and things that have been so obtained.

Being in some cases supplied to him in abundance, in the precise form, and at the precise place at which they are required—as in the case with the air we breathe—they are then wholly without value. In others, they are furnished by nature in the form in which they are used, as in the case of water and electricity; but even these require change of place, and have, therefore, a value in our estimation equal to the effort required for overcoming the resistance to their attainment. In a third—and the most numerous class of cases—they require to be changed in place and in form; and have then a much higher value, because of the increased resistance to be overcome.

That man may be enabled to effect these changes, he must first utilize those faculties by which he is distinguished from the brute. In the isolated man they are latent, association being needed for stimulating them into the motion required from the production of force. Had Bacon, Newton, Leibnitz, or Des Cartes, been placed alone upon an island, their capacity for being useful to their fellow-men would have been just the same that we see it to have been; but their faculties would have lain dormant, and without utility. As it was—being enabled to associate with others like and unlike themselves—their various idiosyncrasies were stimulated to activity, and individuality became more and more developed—with constant increase in the knowledge accumulated, and in the power of further accumulation.

That "knowledge is power," we are every day assured; and if we desire evidence of the fact, we need only to observe, on the one hand, how great are the poverty and weakness of various communities of the earth, occupying lands abounding in all the qualities required for enabling their owners to become rich and strong—which yet remain unimproved for want of that power of combination so indispensable to the development of the intellectual faculties; and, on the other hand, how great are the wealth and strength of others, whose lands appear to be deficient in almost all the qualities required for the production of either wealth or strength. Few countries offer to their inhabitants a poorer soil for cultivation than is found in our Eastern States—and they have little coal, while altogether deficient as regards most of the metallic products of the earth; and yet New England occupied a high position among the communities of the world, because among her people the habit of association is found existing to an extraordinary extent—with corresponding activity of their faculties. Turning our eyes to Brazil, we find a picture directly the reverse—nature there furnishing a soil rich for all the purposes of cultivation, and abounding in the most valuable minerals and metals—all of which remain almost altogether useless, for want of that activity of mind which results necessarily from the association of man with his fellow-men.

The capacity for obtaining command over the various powers of nature, is a force existing in man—latent, while he is compelled to live and work alone, but more and more stimulated into activity as he is more and more enabled to work in combination with his fellow-men.

The capability of being useful to man exists, as has already been said, in all matter; but, in order that it may have utility, man must have the power required for overcoming the resisting force of nature—and that he cannot have in a state of isolation. Place him in the midst of a large community where employment is infinitely diversified, and his faculties become developed. With individuality comes the power of association, always accompanied with that rapid motion of the intellect whence results power over nature; and every step in that direction is but the preparation for a new and greater one. A century since, he was surrounded everywhere by electricity, capable of being rendered useful to him; but he was totally deficient in the knowledge required for compelling it to do his work. Franklin made one step in identifying lightning with what had before been known as electricity; and since then, Arago, Ampere, Biot, Henry, Morse, and many others, have been engaged in the effort to obtain the knowledge of its qualities required for controlling its movements and utilizing its powers. That having been acquired, instead of looking upon the aurora, and upon the lightning, as mere objects of stupid wonder, we now regard them but as manifestation of the existence of a great force that can be made to carry our messages, plate our knives and forks, and propel our ships.

The utility of things is *the measure of man's power over nature*—and this grows with the power of combination among men. Their value, on the other hand, is *the measure of nature's power over man*—and this declines with the growth of the power of combination. The two thus move in opposite directions, and are always found existing in the inverse ratio of each other.

* * * * *

Chapter VII. Of Wealth

Section 1

* * * * *

Wealth consists *in the power to command the always gratuitous services of nature*—whether rendered by the brain of man, or by the matter by which he is surrounded, and upon which it is required to operate. The greater the *power* of association—the greater the diversity of the demands upon the human intellect—the greater, as we have seen, must be the development of the peculiar faculties—or individuality—of each member of the society; and the greater the capacity for association. With the latter comes increase of power over nature and over himself; and the more perfect his capacity for self-government, the more rapid must be the motion of society—the greater the tendency towards further progress—and the more rapid the growth of wealth.

The supply of power waiting the demands of man is, as has been said, unlimited. To the world at large, it is what the accumulations in the robbers' cave were to Ali Baba, who needed but the magic word to make the doors fly open, and thus to become master of their wealth. To enable man to do the same, and thus to do, in his case, all that the genii, in the other, had power to do, he has only to qualify himself for crying "open sesame," by combining his efforts with those of his fellow-men.

Chapter X. Of Changes of Matter in Place

Section 4

The first and heaviest tax to be paid by land and labor is that of transportation; and it is the only one to which the claims of the state itself are forced to yield precedence. It increases in geometrical proportion, as the distance from market increases arithmetically; and therefore it is, that agreeably to tables recently published, corn that would produce at market $24.75 per ton, is worth nothing at a distance of only a hundred and sixty miles, when the communication is by means of the ordinary wagon road—the cost of transportation being equal to the selling price. By railroad, under ordinary circumstances, that cost is but $2.40—leaving to the farmer $22.35, as the amount of tax saved to him by the construction of the road; and if we now take the product of an acre of land as averaging a ton, the saving is equal to interest, at six per cent, on $370 an acre. Assuming the product of an acre of wheat to be twenty bushels, the saving is equal to the interest on $200; but, if we take the more bulky products—hay, potatoes, and turnips—it will be found to amount to thrice that sum. Hence it is that an acre of land near London sells for thousands of dollars, while one of exactly equal quality may be purchased in Iowa, or Wisconsin, for little more than a single dollar. The owner of the first enjoys the vast advantage of the endless motion of its products—taking from it several crops in the year, and returning to it, at once, a quantity of manure equal to all that he had abstracted; and thus improving his land from year to year. He is *making* a machine; whereas, his western competitor, forced to lose the manure, is *destroying* one. Having no transportation to pay, the former can raise those things of which the earth yields largely—as potatoes, carrots, or turnips—or those whose delicate character forbids that they should be carried to distant markets; and thus does he obtain a large reward for that continuous application of his faculties, and of his land, which results from the power of combination with his fellow-men.

In the case of the latter, all is widely different. Having heavy transportation to pay, he cannot raise potatoes, turnips, or hay, because of them the earth yields by tons; as a consequence of which they would be almost, even when not wholly, absorbed on the road to market. He may raise wheat, of which the earth yields by bushels; or cotton, of which it yields by pounds; but if he raises even Indian corn, he must manufacture it into pork before the cost of transportation can be so far diminished as to enable him to obtain a proper reward for labor. Rotation of crops being, therefore, a thing unknown to him, there can be no continuity of motion in either himself or his land. His corn occupied the latter but a part of the year, while the necessity for renovating the soil, by means of fallows, causes a large portion of his farm to remain altogether idle, although the cost of maintaining roads and fences is precisely the same as if it were all fully employed.

His time, too, being required only for certain portions of the year, much of it is altogether lost—as is that of his wagon and horses—the consumption of which latter is just as great as if they were always at work. He, and they, are in the condition of steam-engines, constantly fed with fuel, while the engineer as regularly wastes the steam that is produced—a proceeding involving heavy loss of capital. Further stoppages in the motion of himself and his land, resulting from changes in the weather, are consequent upon this limitation in the variety of things that may be cultivated. His crop, perhaps, requires rain that does not come, and his corn, or cotton, perishes of drought. Once grown, it requires light and heat, but in their place come clouds and rain; and it and he are nearly ruined. The farmer near London, or Paris, is in the condition of an underwriter who has a thousand risks, some of which are maturing every day; whereas, the distant one is in that of a man who has risked his whole fortune on a single ship. Having made the voyage, she arrives at the entrance of her destined port, when, striking on a rock, she is lost, and her owner is ruined. Precisely such is the condition of the farmer who— having his all at risk on his single crop—sees it destroyed by blight, or mildew, almost at the moment when he had expected to make his harvest. With isolated men, all pursuits are extra-hazardous; but as they are enabled to approach each other, and combine their efforts, the risks diminish, until they almost altogether disappear. Combination of action thus makes of society a general insurance office, by help of which each and all of its members are enabled to secure themselves against almost every imaginable risk.

Great, however, as are these differences, they sink almost into insignificance, compared with that which exists in reference to the maintenance of the powers of the land. The farmer distant from market is always selling the soil, which constitutes his capital; whereas, the one near London not only returns to his land the refuse of its products, but adds thereto the manure resulting from the consumption of the vast amount of wheat brought from Russia and America—of cotton brought from Carolina and India—of sugar, coffee, rice and other commodities, yielded by the tropics—of lumber and of wool, the products of Canada and Australia—not only maintaining the motion of his land, but increasing it from year to year.

VOLUME III

CHAPTER XL. OF CIRCULATION

Section 9

The road to civilization lies in the direction of the approximation of the prices of raw materials and finished products—that being always accompanied by a rise in the prices of labor and land—an increase in the proportion borne by fixed to floating capital—and an increase in the rapidity of circulation. Such being the case, a policy based upon cheapening the raw materials of manufactures—food, wool, and labor—*should* tend towards barbarism and slavery: that it does so, the reader will be satisfied in an examination of the following diagram:

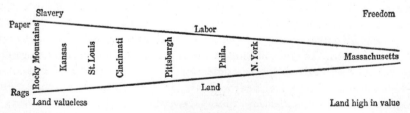

Passing from left to right, we find a steady rise in the prices of land and labor—a diminished necessity for the services of the trader—a diminished proportion of the products of labor assigned him in return for his services—an extension of cultivation over the richer soils—an incessant activity of circulation—and an increase in the power of man—the free proprietor taking the place that first was occupied by the wretched being who was slave to both nature and his fellow-man. This is the *forward*

motion of the being made in the image of his Creator, and endowed with the distinctive faculties of MAN.

Passing now from right to left, we obtain the reverse of this—land declining in value—the trader taking an increased proportion—the land becoming consolidated—circulation declining—and man becoming more and more enslaved—the free population gradually disappearing, as fixed property declines in the proportion borne by it, to that floating capital with which the trader works. This is the *backward* motion of the human animal treated of by the Ricardo-Malthusian schools; the one that must be fed—that will procreate—and that needs the whip of the tax-gatherer, to stimulate him to the proper exercise of the faculties with which he has been endowed.

The first represents the course of all communities, ancient and modern, as the circulation has become more rapid, and as they have increased in civilization, wealth, and real power. The last, that of all which have declined—that in which land has become consolidated—in which circulation has become more sluggish—and in which man has become enslaved.

Looking round us at the present time, we find in the countries whose policy is in harmony with that of Colbert, and which, therefore, follow in the lead of France, all the phenomena first above described—land becoming divided—fixed property increasing in its proportion—the circulation becoming more rapid—and man becoming more free. Turning thence towards Ireland, India, Jamaica, Portugal, and Turkey—the countries following in the direction indicated by the economists of England, we find the reverse phenomena—the land there losing value— fixed property there declining in its proportion—circulation becoming more sluggish—and man becoming from day to day less free. In the first, man grows in individuality, and the communities grow in strength and power. In the last, the human mind is becoming dwarfed, and the communities grow in strength and power. In the last, the human mind is becoming dwarfed, and the communities become weaker, and more helpless, with each succeeding year.

Seeing all these facts, we are led, and that, too, irresistibly, to the conclusion that the advance of communities towards wealth, strength, and power, and that of their members in morals, intellect, and happiness, *is in the inverse ratio of the proportion borne by the land they occupy, to the people by whom it is occupied*—the tendency towards civilization being in the direct ratio of the power of association and combination. Such was the conclusion at which thoughtful men had been generally led to arrive, a century since. Until then, growth in wealth and strength had been regarded as being inseparably connected with increase of numbers—all Europe then uniting with Adam Smith in the belief that "the most decisive mark of the prosperity of any country" was to be found "in the increase of the number of its inhabitants." Dr. Smith, therefore, believed in the advantage to a country resulting from "the liberal reward of labor"—while throughout his work, denouncing the system based upon the idea of cheapening the raw products of the earth, and thus enslaving the man to whose labor they were due.

Holding agriculture in high esteem, and regarding it, as it is, in the light of the most ennobling of human pursuits, he in no manner sympathised with those of his contemporaries who sought to build up trade, by means of measures involving a sacrifice of the interests of both the artisan and the man who held the plough. Seeking for an emphatic denunciation of all the modern British doctrines in regard to land and labor, we must turn to the Wealth of Nations—a great work, whose essential errors have been carefully adopted by the Ricardo-Malthusian school, while rejecting all its truths.

CHAPTER XLI. OF DISTRIBUTION

Section 3

Little as was the work that could be done with the help of an axe of stone, its service to the owner had been very great. It was, therefore, clear to him, that the man to whom he lent it should pay him largely for its use. He could, too, as we readily see, well afford to do so. Cutting, with it, more wood in a day than, without it, he could cut in a month, he would profit by its help, were he allowed but a tenth of his labor's products. Being permitted to retain a fourth, he finds his wages much increased, notwithstanding the large proportion claimed, as profit, by his neighbor capitalist.

The bronze-axe being next obtained, and proving far more useful, its owner—being asked to grant its use—is now, however, required to recollect, that not only had the productiveness of labor greatly increased, but the quantity required to be given to the production of an axe had also greatly decreased—capital thus declining in its power over labor, as labor increased in its power for the *reproduction* of capital. He therefore, limits himself to demanding two-thirds of the price of the more potent instrument—saying to the wood-cutter: "You can do twice as much work with this, as you now do with our neighbor's stone-axe; and if I permit you to retain a third of the wood that is cut, your wages will still be doubled." This arrangement being made, the comparative effects of the earlier and later distributions are as follows:

	Total product	Laborer's share	Capitalist's share
First............................	4	1	3
Second........................	8	2.66	5.33

The reward of labor has more than doubled, as a consequence of the receipt of an *increased proportion* of an increased quantity. The capitalist's share has not quite doubled—he receiving a *diminished proportion* of the same increased quantity. The position of the laborer, which had, at first, stood as only one to three, is now as one to two; with great increase of power to accumulate, and thus to become himself a capitalist. With the substitution of mental for merely physical power, the tendency to equality becomes more and more developed.

The axe of iron next coming, a new distribution is required—the cost of reproduction having again diminished, while labor has again increased in its proportions, as compared with capital. The new instrument cuts twice as much as had been cut by the one of bronze; and yet its owner finds himself compelled to be content with claiming half the product—the following figures now presenting a comparative view of the several modes of distribution:

	Total	Laborer	Capitalist
First	4	1	3
Second	8	2.66	5.33
Third	16	8	8

The axe of iron and steel now coming, the product is again doubled, with further diminution in the cost of reproduction; and now the capitalist is obliged to content himself with a less proportion—the distribution being as follows:

Fourth	32	19.20	12.80

The laborer's share has increased; and—the total product having largely increased—the augmentation of his quantity is very great. That of the capitalist has diminished in proportion; but—the product having so much increased—this reduction of proportion has been accompanied by a large increase of quantity. Both thus profit greatly by the improvements that have been effected. With every further movement in the same direction, the same results continue to be obtained—the proportion of the laborer increasing with every increase in the productiveness of effort— the proportion of the capitalist as steadily diminishing, with constant increase of quantity, and equally constant tendency towards equality among the various portions of which society is composed. The more rapid the progress, the greater is the tendency of mind to acquire power over matter—the value of man rising as compared with capital, and that of capital declining as compared with man. In the natural course of things, the laborers of the present tend, therefore, to acquire power at the cost of the accumulations of the past—that tendency existing, everywhere, in the direct ratio of the rapidity of the circulation, and consequent growth of the power of accumulation.

Such is the great law governing the distribution of labor's products. Of all recorded in the book of science, it is perhaps the most beautiful—

being, as it is, that one, in virtue of which there is established a perfect harmony of real and true interests among the various classes of mankind. Still further, it establishes the fact, that, however great may have been the oppressions of the many at the hands of the few—however large the accumulations resulting from the exercise of the power of appropriation—however striking the existing distinctions among men—all that is required for establishing, everywhere, perfect equality before the law, and for promoting equality in social condition generally, is the pursuit of a system tending to establish in the highest degree the power of association and the development of individuality—that system being found in the observance of perfect respect for the rights of others—thus securing the maintenance of peace, and promoting the growth of wealth and population, both abroad and at home. The more rapid the increase of man's control over nature, the greater must be the tendency towards the establishment of power to direct himself—wealth and power travelling, thus, together.

Section 4

That the law here given, as regards the return to capital invested in axes, is equally true in reference to all other descriptions of capital, will be obvious to the reader upon slight reflection. The house in which he lives, long since produced, cost much more labor than, with the help of the planing, brickmaking, and various other labor-saving instruments, would now be required for producing one superior, both in appearance and convenience; and, with that change, there has been so great a decline in the value of previously existing houses, that it might not exchange for half the labor it had cost. Being asked to pay a rent for it, he would not now be willing to give more than half as much as had at first been paid; and yet, by reason of his increased power over nature, his own physical, or mental, powers would command twice the compensation that had, before, been willingly accepted. This decline in the value of old houses, is constantly being proved by the fact, that they are being everywhere condemned as wholly worthless, and no longer worthy to cumber the ground.

So, too, with money. Brutus charged almost fifty per cent. interest for its use; and, in the days of Henry VIII, the proportion allotted by law to the lender was ten. Since then, it has steadily declined—four per cent. having become so much the established rate, in England, that property is uniformly estimated at twenty-five years' purchase of the rent; so large, nevertheless, having been the increase in the powers of man, that the present receiver of a twenty-fifth can command an amount of convenience, and of comfort, twice greater than could have been obtained by his predecessors who received a tenth. In this decline in the proportion charged for the use of capital, we find the highest proof of man's improved condition. It is evidence that the labors of the present are becoming daily more productive—that the value of all commodities, as measured by labor, is steadily declining—that the laborer is rising, as compared with the capitalist, with constantly increasing facility for becoming himself a capitalist—and that the MAN is becoming more and more developed.

The proportion charged, as interest, in purely agricultural countries, is always high—money, there tending always outwards. The few who can command the services of this most powerful instrument—the one whose possession enables its owner to select at will from among the commodities in the market—will not part with that power, except in consideration of having it returned with large increase. The trader, too, must have large profits—being compelled to forego the high interest he might receive from lending out his money; even when not, himself, compelled to pay such interest. Large, however, as are the proportions, the quantities received are very small—the capital to be lent being trivial in amount, and the quantity of commodities that can be sold, being very small indeed. With the increase of population and wealth, the *proportion* declines—the interest falling to five or six per cent.; but the trader finds his business so much increased, that, whereas, he could scarcely live when he had fifty per cent., he now grows rich upon ten per cent.; while his neighbor, transacting business on a larger scale, accumulates a fortune by means of charges not exceeding one per cent.—all thus obtaining a constantly *increasing quantity*, by means of the retention of a constantly *diminishing proportion* of the property passing through their hands.

So, too, in manufactures. The lonely weaver, with his single loom, must have half the product of his labor, or he could not live. With the growth of wealth, and the increased facility of combination, thousands of looms are brought together, to be driven by the force of steam—labor being thus rendered so much more productive, that a tenth, or even a twentieth part gives large return for the capital so employed.

The canoe carrying but little, the man who manages it must have a large proportion for his labor. The ship carrying many thousands of barrels, the power of association is here strongly exhibited, in the facility with which a dozen men are enabled to do the work that would have required thousands obliged to use canoes—the necessary consequence being, that the owner of a ship is better paid with a twentieth of the cargo, than would have been the owners of the canoes, had they retained the whole of the commodities they carried. Railroad owners grow rich on one per cent. of the commodities carried; whereas the wagoner barely lives on ten per cent. The owner of the machines first used for pounding grain, required to retain a large proportion of the produce of his labor; whereas the owner of the great flour-mill grows rich on portions that would be wasted, were it not for the facility with which production and consumption follow each other at that period of society when mills like his are needed. The more rapid the circulation, the smaller must always be the capitalist's proportion—the greater being then the tendency towards diminution in the cost of reproducing the machinery in which his capital is invested. The larger, however, must then be his quantity—labor becoming daily more productive, with constant diminution in the cost of the finished commodities he needs.

KATE McKEAN

SELECTION FROM "MANUAL OF SOCIAL SCIENCE" BEING A CONDENSATION OF THE "PRINCIPLES OF SOCIAL SCIENCE" OF H. C. CAREY, LL.D.

PREFACE

Why do misery and crime exist? Why, when so large a portion of the earth is yet unoccupied, arc human beings suffering for food, and crowded together in unwholesome dens, to the sacrifice of comfort, decency, and health? Why does one nation export food of which its own members are in need, while another sends its manufactures throughout the world although hundreds of thousands at home are scarcely clothed? Why are nations or individuals seen elbowing each other, so to speak, for room to live? Why are we called to witness everywhere an uneasy jealousy among communities, each watching with an unfriendly eye the expansion of the other—the strong ever encroaching on the rights of the weak? Why should the chief of European nations wage a ceaseless "warfare" against the industry and prosperity of the world at large? In short, what is the cause of the measureless woe that exists in this fair world which its Creator pronounced to be "very good"?

Who that has ever reflected on human affairs has not asked himself these questions, has not at some period of his life sought to solve these problems? It is not, however, in this hitherto favored land that such subjects press with their full weight on heart and mind, adding a heavy item to individual cares and troubles: it is in Europe, especially in the British Isles—that portion of the earth in which man's power over nature seems to be most complete—that immense mass of human suffering, the breadth and depth of which no imagination can measure, most bewitches the understanding while sickening the very soul.

Is there, then no law regulating human affairs? When every portion of this vast universe is ordered by unerring wisdom, are the concerns of God's highest work alone left to the blindest chance? Is there any principle, broad, simple, comprehensive, which can account for all this confusion, and reconcile these contradictions? If so, where is it to be found, to whom has it been revealed? While Physical Science has had its Newton, Physiology its Harvey, Philosophical Anatomy its Geoffroy Saint Hilaire, Palaeontology its Cuvier, Chemistry its Lavoisier—has the Newton of Social Science not yet appeared?

An answer to this question will be vainly sought in European literature. The greatest of English economists, Adam Smith, while setting forth much of valuable truth, failed to reach the fundamental principle, and erred on many important points. England, however, has since his day far retrograded both in theory and practice; and in the monstrous doctrines of the Ricardo-Malthusian school, which attribute human suffering to error of an all-wise Creator, has initiated that which she herself so fitly terms "the dismal science," the "philosophy of despair"; while her literature for well nigh half a century bears constant witness to the existence of a need which it cannot supply, each writer testifying of evils the cause and remedy of which none appear to see. Nor have the writers of the continent been more successful, none of them having attained to any really fundamental truth.

The editor of the following volume having, like so many others, long vainly so sought light on this most interesting subject, first found it in the "Past, Present, and Future" of H. C. Carey. The principles there contained are enlarged, expanded, and corrected by the test of subsequent events in his "Principles of Social Science"; a work which, it is believed, no one capable of understanding it can carefully study without feeling that the Newton of Social Science has indeed appeared.

It may, however, be asked: If this be so, if the truth on this highest of sciences has indeed been discovered, how is it that mankind have not hailed it with a burst of enthusiastic welcome? that when it has been now for seven years before the world, it is as yet so little known? What, however, is the reception ever accorded to a great and fundamental truth? Is it not, that it is at first simply neglected because unrecognized? A few earnest minds, indeed, perceive and embrace it heartily; but the majority brush past it, so to speak, unconscious of its presence. When by degrees it makes way and gains for itself a hearing, it is met by a storm of opposition. Some minds simply dislike what is new; others hate to be disturbed in their ordinary modes of thought; the self-love of some is wounded by finding that they know nearly nothing of what has been their life-long study, and they are unwilling to submit to become learners where they have so long been teachers; while others again find their interests or their influence imperilled by the new idea. In the darker ages of the world's history, persecution, imprisonment, or death, was commonly the reward of the discoverer; now it is simply opposition or misrepresentation, when not even calumny. When at length its opposers are unable to resist the evidence presented of its truth, they next turn round and say: Well, granted that it is so, this is not new; it is to be found in the pages of such or such an author, ancient or modern. And true it is, that those who now in the full light of a truth look back to earlier ages to search for it, will often detect its first faint glimmerings in the works of those who were themselves utterly unconscious of the scope of the idea that had for a moment flashed across their minds, as quickly disappearing, and leaving the darkness as complete as it had been before. At length, however, the time arrives when the new truth finds its place in the intelligence of the age; it is discussed in philosophical works, set forth in elementary treatises, and finally is adopted as the basis of public instruction. Does its discoverer at length meet with the honor due? Rarely even then. Few know the source whence the idea had been derived. Ask them and they will answer: "I never thought otherwise; I learned the theory at college; or I derived it from such or such a work."

It is under the impression that the most certain mode of spreading a knowledge of truths which lie at the root of all national progress, is by making them a part of the instruction of the young, that the editor has ventured, encouraged by the approbation of the author, to undertake a work more suited to a masculine than to a feminine intellect. This *Manual of Social Science*, it will be perceived, is little more than a selection from the great work above referred to, the words of which have been as far as possible preserved, although the vast variety of facts and illustrations which give to it such a living interest have necessarily been sacrificed to brevity. The object in view will account for the free use of italics, which, though perhaps an offence against taste, every experienced teacher knows to be useful in awakening the attention and understanding of the youthful student.

In the years that have now elapsed since Mr. Carey's work was written, and since his first volume was given to the world, there have been many changes, and most especially in the facts presented by these United States, but the editor has deemed it best to give them here as they had been there presented, believing that the careful student may find in them the causes of those greater changes which are now in course of progress.

That this volume may be of some use in impressing upon the rising generation that the true principles of Social Science are in perfect accordance with the great precepts of Christianity, and may thus help to hasten the reign of universal peace and justice upon earth, is the earnest wish and prayer of the Editor,

KATE McKEAN.

Cumberland, Md.,
August 20th, 1864.

ROBERT ELLIS THOMPSON

(1844–1924)

Robert Ellis Thompson was born in Ireland in 1844, but he came to this country as a boy. Nearly his entire life, like that of his great master, Henry C. Carey, was spent in Philadelphia. He was graduated from the Central High School of Philadelphia and took several degrees from the University of Pennsylvania, in both of which institutions he later taught and held administrative positions. Although he was a Presbyterian clergyman, Dr. Thompson's career was chiefly that of an educator, writer, and public lecturer.

A course of instruction under the title of social science was first offered at the University of Pennsylvania during the academic year 1869 to 1870, and in 1874, a professorship of social science was established there. Thus, Robert Ellis Thompson was the pioneer professor of social science in America, and the University of Pennsylvania was the first institution of higher learning in the United States to inaugurate a course in social science and to create a professorship in that subject. As was often the case in that day, sociology and economics were not separated. Moreover, like other economists of the past, Dr. Thompson taught not only social science, but also moral philosophy and the humanities, including mathematics, history, and literature, in the first decade of his teaching career at the University of Pennsylvania.

With the creation, in 1881, of the Wharton School, the oldest collegiate school of business in the United States, Dr. Thompson became its first dean. However, he was retired the following year to the position of librarian of the University. The next year he became the John Welsh Centennial Professor of History and English Literature, resigning then the deanship of the Wharton School.

In 1892, Dr. Thompson resigned from the faculty of the University of Pennsylvania to accept the position of president of the Central High School of Philadelphia, which he retained until his retirement a few years before his death in 1924. During this long period of time he continued to lecture to the senior classes on ethics and political economy. His ardent defense of the protective tariff fell upon the receptive ears of a generation or more of young Philadelphians.

Dr. Thompson was the author of numerous sermons, lectures and pamphlets on social, economic, moral, educational, and literary topics. His chief works of interest to the student of the history of economic

470

thought were: "Social Science and National Economy" (1875); "Political Economy with Special Reference to the Industrial History of Nations" (1875); "Protection to Home Industry" (1886); "Political Economy for High Schools" (1895); "Hand of God in American History" (1902); and "History of the Dwelling House and Its Future" (1914).

Dr. Thompson was a scholar of the old school, whose range of interests was enormous and whose acquisition of information was encyclopaedic. As an economist he is to be classified as a disciple of Carey, showing the same theological bias, the same historical approach, the same merging of economics and sociology, and the same advocacy of protection.

The following brief selection from his high school textbook gives a summary of his defense of the protective tariff. It also reveals his dogmatic sincerity and his keeness in debate.

An excellent brief account of "Robert Ellis Thompson-Pioneer Professor of Social Science," by James H. S. Bossard, can be found in the *American Journal of Sociology* for September, 1929.

ROBERT ELLIS THOMPSON

SELECTION FROM "POLITICAL ECONOMY FOR HIGH SCHOOLS AND ACADEMIES"

CHAPTER XI. FREE TRADE AND PROTECTION

1. For two centuries past people have been divided in opinion between the policy which regards government as having the right and duty to oversee the industrial development of the Nation, and that which would confine it to the maintenance of public order. The latter is called Free Trade, and its friends contend that "no legislation should be of a tendency to divert capital or labor into a channel into which they would not flow without it. When every man is left free to do what he will with his own, he will do what is most beneficial to society as well as to himself. Society is so constituted that it always is profitable for some one to do anything it needs to have done. When government interferes with this natural movement of self-interest, it is sure to do more harm than good. When all men are left to their natural liberty of action, the best results will be obtained, for the natural laws of supply and demand work more evenly and more wisely than any human law, which attempts to interfere with their operation."

2. The Free Traders also say that "there is no need of legislation to foster the growth of manufactures or any other industry. All such industries come as a matter of course, as soon as the country is ready for them. When it has more people than can well live by farming alone, and has acquired a surplus of capital for other industries, then there will be a natural diversion of labor and capital into industries the country needs. To attempt to force the growth of such industries before the time, can result only in a hot-house growth of sickly character, which constantly demands increasing Protection from foreign competition. Such an attempt also requires the diversion of capital and labor from channels of profitable employment into those which are less so, to the disadvantage of the whole people."

3. The Free Trader describes the Protectionist policy as a miserly one in regard to foreign commerce. "Each country," he says, "has its own advantages for the production of some article which it can supply to the rest more cheaply than they can produce it for themselves. There is thus a natural division of labor among the various countries, as well as within the bounds of each. To refuse to recognize this is as though we refused to recognize the differences of climate, and undertook to raise tropical fruits

under glass, instead of importing them. And just as our refusal to buy pine-apples and bananas from the West Indies would result in the reduction of our exports to them, as they could not pay us for our flour if we took no fruit in exchange, so restrictions on other imports work in the same way. Commodities are paid for with commodities. The country that will not import cannot export."

4. The Free Trader also objects to restrictions on the trade between nations as tending to "dearness of the necessaries and comforts of existence. It is legislation, therefore, in the interests of a class, and against the general interests of society, as the producers are a class and the consumers are everybody. The interest of the consumer is simply in cheapness, and whatever puts up prices is adverse to his interest."

5. It is also said that "Protection introduces into government a principle of *paternalism*, which tends to Socialism. It teaches men to lean upon the government, when they ought to rely upon their own thrift, energy and enterprise. It thus prepares them for the Socialism in which the individual is nothing and the State is everything."

These arguments are put into many shapes, but they cover the case for Free Trade as an economic policy.

6. Protectionists do not deny that in most cases, as society is constituted, the man who is left free to do what he will with his own, will do what society needs to have done; and also that in most cases where there is a social need, it will be profitable for some one to supply it. They do not insist on Protection as a universal principle, as the other party does with Free Trade. They only say that there are exceptional cases in which the principle of free competition does not work satisfactorily, and that in these the collective action of society is needed.

Even the Free Trader admits these exceptions in practice, while denying them in theory. (1) He does not leave education to free competition, as that has been tried and does not work well. (2) He does not propose to leave the carriage of letters to free competition. He supports the Post Office, knowing that if we had none, we should see very bad and costly service in the poorer parts of the country. (3) He does not leave Money to free competition. Not only does the Nation coin all the bullion money, but it lays severe restrictions upon the issue of paper money. We once tried Free Trade in paper money, and the results were very bad. (4) He has to admit that our leaving farmers and lumberers to do what they will with their own in the matter of our forests, has not resulted in their doing what was best for society. By clearing the country too completely they have injured the fertility and disturbed the rainfall, so that droughts follow floods, and floods follow droughts. (5) While the Free Trader holds that government should do nothing for manufactures, he is quite ready to have it do a great deal for trade, in constructing and dredging out harbors, blasting rocks, digging canals, promoting railroads, and the like. The English Free Trader goes a little farther, and besides spending many millions of public money on docks, he pays heavy subsidies out of the public Treasury to steamship lines, so as to reduce the cost of carrying the goods of British manufacturers to every part of the world. (6) The Protectionist merely adds one more exception to this list, and insists that a country may be in great need of manufactures, and yet that it may not be profitable for individuals to establish them without help from the community in the shape of bounties, or protective duties, or any other means that may be thought better than these.

7. It is argued that we will get all we need if we will wait long enough, as industries grow up naturally, whenever the growth of population and of capital favors them. It is quite true that they would grow up naturally, if there were no interference from without. But the richer and more advanced countries, being already in possession of what they regard as the more profitable industries, spare no pains to prevent their growth elsewhere. It is shown in reports to the British Parliament that their capitalists even make great sacrifices to prevent the growth of rival industries in other countries, by putting prices so low that the new manufactures cannot compete with them. If all the world were equal in the command of capital and the growth of industrial power, Protection would not be needed. But we must take the world as it is, and it is a world of gross inequalities.

The situation in Ireland shows how the growth of manufactures may be retarded, even when the population is too dense to live by farming alone, and there is surplus capital for the other industries. The Irish have made many trials to start manufactures, but they always have been foiled by foreign competition.

8. That protected industries are not hot-house plants is shown by history. The three greatest of English industries, woolens, iron and steel, and cottons, owe their very existence to Protection, and are now firmly established. The same is true of every great European industry which is now fighting for the world's markets.

9. While Protection does divert capital and labor into channels into which they would not flow otherwise, it does not usually divert them out of any other channel in which they are flowing. No country can have more industry than it has capital and labor; but most countries have a great deal less. The Connecticut towns, for instance, which have become manufacturing centres during the last half-a-century, have not done it by taking capital or labor from farming or anything else. These new industries have found work for idle hands, idle savings and unused credit. No country has so much of these idle things as one which cannot give its people any employment but farming.

10. That there is a natural division of labor among the Nations, and that foreign commerce enables each country to profit by the advantages of the rest, is the belief of the Protectionists equally with the Free Traders. They differ only in that Protectionists believe it is wasteful and spendthrift for a country to buy of another what it can just as well make for itself. Nor do they think that the fact that some countries can at this moment make an article cheaper than we can, is a reason for not trying to make it, if we have the means and the skill.

John Stuart Mill says, "The superiority of one country over another in a branch of industry often arises only from it having begun it sooner. A country which has this skill and experience to acquire may in other respects be better adapted to the production than those earlier in the field; and besides, it is a just remark that nothing has a greater tendency to produce improvement in any branch of production than its trial under a new set of conditions. But it cannot be expected that individuals should at their own risk, or rather to their certain loss, introduce a new manufacture and bear the burden of carrying it on until producers have been educated up to the level of those with whom the processes have become traditional. A protecting duty continued for a reasonable time will sometimes be the least inconvenient mode by which a country can tax itself for the support of such an experiment." Mr. Mill was a Free Trader, but he said once, "I do not say that if I were an American, I should not be a Protectionist."

Prof. Thorold Rogers, another English Free Trader, says that "the circumstances in which" the United States and the British Colonies "are situated exactly square with the hypothesis of Mr. Mill. The countries are young and rising—industries, as yet nascent, are thoroughly suited to the natural capacity of the region and of the people . . . There is no reason, apparently, except that of priority in the market, why the industry of the old country should not be transplanted to the new."

11. That commodities should be paid for with commodities in international trade, is just what the Protectionist asserts. That they always are so, history disproves. We have exported hundreds of millions of much-needed Gold to Europe to pay our balances. Japan has lost all her Gold in the same way. Portugal lost both her Gold and her Silver in the same fashion during the last century. Russia was losing all hers when she went back to Protection in 1823. It is no answer to say that Gold when exported is "merely a commodity like any other." The common sense of the whole business world regards the export as a national loss, because it cannot be afforded.

Protectionists desire the freest of trade in whatever the country cannot produce for itself. They remove the duties from tea, coffee and spices for that reason, while Free Trade countries tax these heavily. But they believe that a Nation which spends more than it makes, or exports more than it imports, is a spendthrift, and will come to grief.

12. That the interest of society is in mere cheapness, whether the producing classes prosper or the reverse, Protectionists do not believe. If that were true, then *hard times* would be the best of times, for they are the times of greatest cheapness. In fact it is impossible to sunder the interests of the producers from those of the consumers, especially in a country like ours, where every one is a producer of some sort. To do so is to act like the man who refused to take quinine for the chills, because the chills were in his back and not in his stomach, where the quinine would go. We are all one body, and if one member suffer, all the members suffer with it. Better therefore than a low price for a thing is a fair price, at which the producer can live comfortably. If we pay less, his loss is likely to come back to us in some shape.

13. The Free Trade argument fixes attention exclusively on the price of what we buy. But no man prospers simply by the cheapness of what he buys. His interest is in the ratio of the price of what he buys to that of what he sells, whether it be clothing he has made, or wheat he has grown, or brain-power he has put at the service of his fellow-men. And this ratio is most favorable when all kinds of industry are associated, when most power is spent in producing and least in transportation, and when there is least idleness of capital and of labor. In this respect Ireland furnishes the contrast to America. In Ireland everything is done for the consumer, and little or nothing for the producer. Everything is cheap in Ireland, and her people fly from this cheapness as from a blight, to find employment for muscle and brain in other lands. An Irish immigrant in America was grumbling that he "could buy as much for a shilling in Ireland as for a dollar in America." "Why did you not stay there?" he was asked. "Because I could not get the shilling!"

14. It is of no advantage to the farmer to be able to buy clothing and hardware cheap, if he has no home market in which to sell his produce. He can sell some things indeed to the foreign artisan who supplies him, but even of these not a quarter so much as the same artisan would consume if he were working in America. If the farmer had to exchange his wheat directly for plows, ox-chains, dress-goods, and the like, he would find how great his advantage is in dealing with the home manufacturer. It is the fact that money is used as the medium, which conceals this advantage.

15. The price of raw materials and of manufactured goods approach each other most nearly where the one is converted into the other. If all our paper-mills were on the Hudson and the Delaware, the price of rags and of paper would be nearer to each other there than anywhere else. As one went westward he would find rags fall and paper rise in price. This is true of all raw material as compared with manufactured goods; and

food is but one general form of raw material, needed for all manufactures equally. It is therefore the interest of the producers of raw materials and of food, that they should be in the neighborhood of those who effect the conversion we call manufacture. There they get the largest share of the manufactured article in exchange for the raw material.

As already shown this interest is opposed to our railroad policy as well as to Free Trade.

16. The workingman finds his interest in Protection because (1) whatever tends to increase the variety of employment in the country increases the demand for labor of all kinds. Merely farming countries are full of idlers, who live off the earnings of those who have work. (2) Variety of employment creates a competition for labor. In its absence, employers, being all of one trade, come to an understanding to keep wages down. Hence, even in the same country, as in Belgium and in England, wages of labor are much higher in districts where there is manufacturing, than in those where there is only farming. (3) Every country has its own kind of public opinion as to the style in which its working classes ought to be able to live. This demands in America a much higher standard of comfort than in Europe. But if the products of European labor and capital came in free of duty, it would not be possible to maintain this higher standard. Our workingmen would be dragged down to the level of the laborers of monarchical and aristocratic societies. Under the Protective Tariffs of 1860–1892, the American standard rose faster and higher than in any part of the world, as was shown by the inflow of European labor to secure the benefits and the (alleged) disadvantages of Protection. Whether it was better to admit or to exclude it, is not here the question. The fact was that it came.

17. The Constitution of the United States says that government is established to "promote the general welfare." In all countries it is held responsible for this. Parties have been driven from power in our own country because business distress prevailed under their administration. In Europe violent revolutions are almost always associated with popular distress and scarcity. To insist that the government shall abstain from all management of industry, is to refuse it the power to discharge this responsibility. It is to limit its powers as the nations in fact never have agreed to have them limited. Now Protection makes no more interference with the movement of industry than is sufficient for its purpose. It does not do anything for individuals, or confer personal advantages of any kind on them. It merely creates a new industrial condition, which every one is equally free to take advantage of. By enlarging the number of employments it also enlarges the range of individual liberty, as it gives greater choice of fields of labor. It thus helps to develop that individuality in the working classes which Socialism seeks to destroy. It leads away from Socialism, not toward it.

In this connection it is well to remember that we do not have Protection because we have manufactures but manufactures because we have had Protection.

18. Protection and Free Trade are in controversy. The former is unfairly charged with artificiality, hostility to freedom, class legislation and paternalism. It has the sanction of even Free Traders in their wiser moments, and can be defended as a benefit to all classes.

PART VI

BRITISH HISTORICAL SCHOOL

1. John Kells Ingram: "The Present Position and Prospects of Political Economy."

2. Thomas Edward Cliffe Leslie: "Essays in Political and Moral Philosophy."

3. Walter Bagehot: "Economic Studies."

4. Arnold Toynbee: "The Industrial Revolution."

JOHN KELLS INGRAM

(1824–1907)

John Kells Ingram was an Irish economist from Trinity College, Dublin. He was an important member of the British historical school, whose views were very similar to those of Cliffe Leslie.

The chief works of Ingram were "The Present Position and Prospects of Political Economy" (1878), and "A History of Political Economy," originally published as an article on Political Economy in the "Encyclopaedia Britannica."

Ingram's "History of Political Economy" appeared in book form in 1888. It passed through several editions and was the standard work in its field for a generation. As late as 1915 a new and enlarged edition was put out with a supplementary chapter by William A. Scott and an introduction by Richard T. Ely.

The following selection is from Ingram's "The Present Position and Prospects of Political Economy," which was first delivered as a presidential address before the British Association for the Advancement of Science in 1878. The student is asked to note the specific indictments which Ingram brought against the economic theory of his day. It raises the still discussed questions of what is a science; is economics a science; if not, can economics ever become a science; and if so, how?

JOHN KELLS INGRAM

"THE PRESENT POSITION AND PROSPECTS OF POLITICAL ECONOMY" THE ADDRESS OF THE PRESIDENT OF SECTION F—ECONOMIC SCIENCE AND STATISTICS—OF THE BRITISH ASSOCIATION FOR THE ADVANCEMENT OF SCIENCE ON AUG. 15, 1878

Had I been called upon at any other time to preside over this Section, I should have followed the example of most of my predecessors, in selecting as the subject of the discourse which it is usual to deliver from this chair, some one of the special economic questions of the day, which my knowledge might have enabled me most adequately, or, let me rather say, least inadequately to treat. But I have felt that the matter with which I should deal has been practically determined for me beforehand. An important crisis in the history of our Section has taken place. Its claim to form a part of the British Association has been disputed. Some of the cultivators of the older branches of research but half recognize the right of Political Economy and Statistics to citizenship in the commonwealth of science; and it is not obscurely intimated on their part that these studies would do well to relinquish pretensions which cannot be sustained, and proceed, with or without shame, to take the lower room to which alone they are entitled.

How far this sentiment is entertained by those who would be recognized as the best representatives of the mathematical, physico-chemical and biological sciences, I am unable to say. But it is natural to suppose that no one clothed with an official character in the association could have assumed towards us such an attitude as I have described, unless supported by a considerable weight of opinion amongst those within the body who are regarded as competent judges. Still more—and this is what lends a peculiar gravity to the incident—such a step could scarcely have been taken if the general mass of the intelligent public entertained strong convictions as to the genuinely scientific character of political economy, as it is usually professed and understood amongst us. It is, in fact, well known that there is a good deal of scepticism current on this question. There may be seen in various quarters evidences sometimes of contemptuous rejection of its claims, sometimes of uneasy distrust as to their validity. And even amongst those who admit its services in the past, there is a disposition to regard it as essentially effete, and as having no scientific or practical future before it.

When some of our leading economists met not long ago to celebrate the centenary of the publication of the "Wealth of Nations," it was plain from the tone of most of the speakers that the present position of their studies, as regards their general acceptance and public influence, was considered to be far from satisfactory.

"To those who are interested in economic science," says a recent writer in "Mind," "few things are more noticeable than the small hold which it has upon the thoughts of our generation. Legislation has been directly influenced by it in the past, and the results of the application of its doctrines are manifest in every department of our laws; yet in spite of its triumph in this region, we find a widespread tendency to look on its teaching with suspicion.

"I seem to observe," said Professor Cairnes in 1870, "in the literature and social discussions of the day, signs of belief that political economy has ceased to be a fruitful speculation; nay, I fear I must go further and admit that it is regarded by some energetic minds in this country as even worse than unfruitful—as obstructive—a positive hindrance in the path of useful reform . . . It is not denied that the science has done some good; only it is thought that its task is pretty well fulfilled."

The attitude which the working classes generally take up with respect to political economy may be seen from Mr. Howell's candid and instructive book on the Conflicts of Capital and Labour.

Professor Jevons has recognized quite recently the state of facts indicated by these testimonies, though he has no misgiving as to any grounds for it in the current methods or doctrines of political economy; if the public do not like the science, so much the worse, he thinks, for the public—"the fact is," he says, "that just as physical science was formerly hated, so now there is a kind of ignorant dislike and impatience of political economy."

It is plain, therefore, that the low estimate of the studies of our Section which is entertained by some members of the Association, is no isolated phenomenon, but is related to a mass of opinion outside the body—that, in fact, the crisis which, as I have said, has shown itself in the Association with respect to our Section, is only the counterpart, in a more limited sphere, of a crisis in the history of economic science, which is apparent on the face of English—and, as I shall point out by and by, not of English only, but of European—thought. It is important to understand the origin and significance of this state of things; and to that subject, accordingly, I purpose to direct your attention.

We must take care to distinguish, at the outset, between two views which are sometimes confounded—namely, between the opinion that economic facts do not admit of scientific investigation, and the quite different opinion that the hitherto prevailing mode of studying those facts is unsatisfactory, and many of the current generalizations respecting them unsound. That economic phenomena are capable of scientific treatment is a proposition which I do not intend to spend time in demonstrating. It is comprehended in the more general question of the possibility of a scientific Sociology; and any one who disputes it will have enough to do in combating the arguments by which Comte, and Mill, and Herbert Spencer have established that possibility. Nor do I intend to waste words in showing that, if there be a science of society, no other branch of investigation can compete with it in importance or in dignity. It has the most momentous influence of all on human welfare. It receives contributions from all other departments of research—whether in the ascertainment of results to be used for its purposes, or in the elaboration of methods to be applied in its inquiries. It presides, in fact, over the whole intellectual system—an office which some, mistaking the foundation for the crown of the ediface, have claimed for Mathematics. It is the most difficult of all the sciences, because it is that in which the phenomena dealt with are most complex and dependent on the greatest variety of conditions, and in which, accordingly, appearances are most deceitful, and error takes the most plausible forms. That the professors of the more stably—because earlier—constituted branches of knowledge should ignore the claims of this great department of inquiry would be doubly disastrous—first, by leaving the scientific system without its necessary completion in a true theory of the highest and most important class of phenomena accessible to our researches; and secondly, by tending, so far as prejudice and misconception can temporarily produce such an effect, to hand over to minds of insufficient power, and destitute of the necessary preparation, studies which, more than any others, require a strong intelligence, disciplined in the methods and furnished with the results of the sciences of inorganic and organic nature. There is, in my judgment, no duty more incumbent in our day on the professors of these last, than that of recognizing the claims of Sociology, whilst at the same time enforcing on its cultivators the necessity of conforming to the genuine scientific type. Yet it is now sought to expel from this Association, which ought to represent the harmonious union of all positive research, the very limited and inadequate portion of the science of society which has ever found recognition in its scheme.

I assume, then, that economic phenomena are proper subjects for scientific treatment. This I imagine the public at large are not disposed to doubt, though they may not repose much confidence in the methods actually followed. But strangely enough, a professor of political economy has recently disputed the possibility, or at least the utility, of a scientific handling of economic questions. Professor Bonamy Price, of the University of Oxford, who has published a volume in which several of those questions are handled with much ability and freshness of treatment, not only repudiates a scientific character for his own inquiries, but alleges the scientific method to be a mistake. According to him, ordinary people are right in believing that they can arrive at truth on these questions by the aid of their natural lights, by their untrained sagacity,—that they can take a shorter and far clearer path through their own observations, than through what he calls "the tangled jungle of scientific refinements." In plain terms, he is in favour of relegating the study of economic phenomena to the domain of empiricism—to what is called the common sense of practical men.

A more fatal suggestion could not, in my judgment, be made. I shall have to express the opinion, that the prevalent methods of economic research and exposition are open to grave criticism; but how can this be remedied by throwing ourselves on the undisciplined and random inspirations of so-called common sense? It was "common sense" that long upheld the mercantile system; and indeed there is scarcely any error that it has not at different times, accepted and propagated. What security can there be in this as in other branches of inquiry against endless aberrations and confusions, but systematic observation and analysis of the phenomena, resulting in a body of ascertained and reasoned truth; and what is this but science? I am forced to say that Professor Price seems to me to labour under radical misconception as to the nature and conditions of science. Because the facts of the production and distribution of wealth have always gone on spontaneously amongst mankind, and definite modes of social action with respect to them have progressively established themselves, economic investigation, he argues, adding nothing to what men have with or more or less sagacity and intelligence always practiced, cannot be regarded as having the nature of a science. But it might be similarly shown that there is no science of human nature, for the intellectual processes, the feelings, and the practical tendencies of man have always been similar; they have not waited for science to develop themselves and pass into action; rather their long continued spontaneous action was the necessary condition of the science that studies them. So, too, with respect to all human action on external nature—practice always must precede theory; art, more or less intelligent, must precede science. Science is simply the ascertainment and co-ordination of laws; a law is the statement of a general fact; we explain a particular fact by showing that is is a case of a more general fact. Now, from the beginning to the end of his own book, Professor Price is endeavouring to ascertain such general facts, and to explain particular facts by means of them—in other words, he is busied upon science without knowing it. He rests much of the importance of economic studies, which he regards as essentially practical, on their efficacy for uprooting the evil weed of false theory; but theory of some sort will always be necessary. *On ne detruit que ce qu'on remplace;* and the only way of extinguishing false theory is to establish the true.

I therefore repudiate the doctrine of Professor Price, and I hold by the truth, which has indeed now become a philosophic commonplace, that social phenomena generally, and amongst them the economic phenomena of society, do admit of scientific treatment. But I believe, though on different grounds from his, that the mode in which the study of these phenomena has been conceived and prosecuted in the hitherto reigning school, is open to serious objections; and the decline in the credit and influence of political economy, of which I have spoken, appears to me to be in a large measure due to the vicious methods followed by its teachers. The distrust of its doctrines manifested by the working classes is no doubt in a great degree owing to the not altogether unfounded belief, that it has tended to justify too absolutely existing social arrangements, and that its study is often recommended with the real, though disguised, object of repressing popular aspirations after a better order of things. And it is doubtless true that some of the opposition which political economy encounters, is founded on the hostility of selfish interests, marshalled against the principles of free-trade, of which it is regarded as the representative. But it is not with manifestations of this kind, which belong to politics rather than philosophy, that I am now chiefly concerned. It is more appropriate to this place to point to the growing coldness or distrust exhibited by the higher intellects towards political economy—a fact which lies on the surface of things, and shows itself everywhere in contemporary literature. The egoistic spirit in which it is steeped may explain the continued protest which Carlyle and Ruskin have, mainly as moral preachers, maintained against it—though that very spirit is, as I shall show, closely connected with vicious method. But what are we to say of Miss Martineau's final judgment? Speaking in her "Autobiography" of that part of her career in which, as Professor Jevons says, "she successfully popularized the truths of political economy in her admirable tales," she tells us that what she then took to be the science of political economy as elaborated by the economists of our time, she had come to regard as being no science at all, strictly speaking. "So many of its parts," she adds, "must undergo essential change, that it may be a question whether future generations will owe much more to it than the benefit (incalculable to be sure) of establishing the grand truth, that social affairs proceed according to great general laws, no less than natural phenomena of every kind." Here is a conclusion resting essentially on intellectual, not moral, grounds; and I presume Professor Jevons will not explain it as a result of ignorant impatience.

But it is no longer necessary to consider scattered indications of the feeling of eminent individualities on this matter, for of late years the growing dissatisfaction has risen to the dimensions of a European revolt, whose organs have appeared not in the ranks of general literature, but within the sphere of economic investigation itself. It is a characteristic result of the narrowness and spirit of routine which have too much prevailed in the dominant English school of economists, that they are either unacquainted with, or have chosen to ignore, this remarkable movement.

The largest and most combined manifestation of the revolt has been in Germany, all of whose ablest economic writers are in opposition to the methods and doctrines of the school of Ricardo. Roscher, Knies, Hildebrand, Nasse, Brentano, Held, Schmoller, Schaffle, Schonberg, Samter, and others, have taken up this attitude. In Italy a group of distinguished writers, amongst whom are named Luzzatti, Forti, and Lampertico, follow the same direction, and have a special organ in which they advocate their views. In Denmark a similar scientific evolution is in progress, chiefly under the leading of Frederiksen. The eminent Belgian publicist, M. de Laveleye, has done much to call attention to these new tendencies of economic doctrine, in which he himself participates. In England a corresponding movement, by no means imitative, but on the contrary, highly original in character, is represented by Mr. Cliffe Leslie, whom I mention with pride as an alumnus of this University. In France, the new direction is not so marked in the economic world, strictly so called, though in that country it really first appeared. For the vices of the old school, which have led to the development of the new, were powerfully stated more than forty years ago by a French thinker, who is too little studied by the mass of his countrymen, Auguste Comte, the greatest master who has ever treated of sociological method. How far the Germans may have been led by national prejudice to ignore his influence in the formation of their views, I will not undertake to say; but there is no doubt of the fact that the tendencies they have sought to impress on economic studies are largely in accordance with the teaching on that subject contained in his "Philosophie Positive."

In the admirable chapters of that work, in which he described the normal conditions and method of social science, whilst paying a warm tribute to the merits of Adam Smith, he criticized what he considered the aberrations of later political economists. The late Professor Cairnes, of whom, as a member of this University, we are justly proud, and whom, even when I differ from him, I name with all the respect due to an able and earnest searcher after truth, attempted an answer to some of these strictures of Comte, which again elicited a reply from Mr. Frederic Harrison. Considering the criticisms of the great Frenchman to have been perfectly just when he wrote them, and only requiring a certain correction now in view of the healthier tendencies apparent in several quarters since his work was published, I shall dwell at some length on the several grounds of his censures, stating and illustrating them in my own way, which will differ considerably from the mode of treatment which they received in the controversy to which I have referred. Those grounds, though nowhere by him formally enumerated, are essentially reducible to four, having relation—first, to the attempt to isolate the study of the facts of wealth from that of the other social phenomena; secondly, to the metaphysical or viciously abstract character of many of the conceptions of the economists; thirdly, to the abusive preponderance of deduction in their processes of research; and fourthly, to the too absolute way in which their conclusions are conceived and enunciated. It will be found that these heads cannot be kept strictly apart, but run into each other at several points. The separation of them will, however, serve to give distinctness and order to the discussion.

I. The first objection is, as I have stated, to the pretension of the economists to isolate the special phenomena they study, the economic phenomena of society, from all the rest—its material aspect from its intellectual, moral, and political aspects, and to constitute an independent science, dealing with the former alone, to the exclusion of the latter. This question as to the relation of economic studies to the general body of human knowledge, is really the most radical and vital that can be raised respecting them, and on it more than on any other depends, in my opinion, the future of these studies.

It is sometimes sought to get rid of this question in a very summary manner, and to represent those who raise it either as weakly sentimental persons, who shrink from studying the conditions of wealth apart, because there are better and higher things than wealth; or as persons of confused intellect, who wish to mix together things which are essentially different in their nature. On the former of these imputations it is unnecessary to dwell. I am far from undervaluing sentiment in its proper sphere; but I take up no sentimental ground on the present question. In denying the propriety of isolating economic investigation, I appeal to considerations derived from the philosophy of science. The second allegation is, therefore, the only one with which I am now concerned.

In a recent elementary treatise on political economy, by a well-known writer, it is argued: "We must do one thing at a time; we cannot learn the social sciences all at the same time. No one objects to astronomy that it treats only of the stars, or to mathematics that it treats only of numbers and quantities . . . There must be many physical sciences, and there must be also many social sciences, and each of these sciences must treat of its own proper subject, and not of things in general."

But a little consideration will show that these remarks touch only the outside of the question. Of course we must do only one thing at a time. Only one out of several branches of a subject can be considered at a time; but they are yet branches of a single subject, and the relations of the branches may be precisely the most important thing to be kept in view respecting them. It might be said, "It is important, no doubt, that plant life and animal life should be understood; but zoology and botany are different sciences; let them be studied apart; let a separate class of *savants* be appropriated to each, and every essential end is secured." But what says Professor Huxley, in unison with all the most competent opinion on the subject? "The study of living bodies is really one discipline, which is divided into zoology and botany simply as a matter of convenience." They are, in fact, branches from the common stem of Biology, and neither can be rightly conceived without bearing this in mind. Now I maintain that for still stronger reasons the several branches of social science must be kept in the closest relation.

Another biological analogy will place these reasons in the clearest light. When we pass from the study of the inorganic world to that of the organic, which presupposes and succeeds to the former, we come upon the new idea of a living whole, with definite structures appropriated to special actions, but all influencing one another, and co-operating to one result—the healthy life of the organism. Here, then, it is plain that we cannot isolate the study of one organ from that of the rest, or of the whole. We cannot break up the study of the human body into a number of different sciences, dealing respectively with the different organs and functions, and, instead of a human anatomy and physiology, construct a cardiology, a hepatology, an enterology. It is not of course meant that special studies of particular organs and functions may not be undertaken—that they may not be temporarily and provisionally separated from each other in our researches; but the fact insisted on is, that it is essential to keep in view their relations and interactions, and that therefore they must be treated as forming part of the subject-matter of one and the same science. And what is thus true of theory is also true of practice—the physician who had studied only one organ and its function would be very untrustworthy even in the therapeutics of that organ. He who treats every disease as purely local, without regard to the general constitution, is a quack; and he who ignores the mutual action of the *physique* and the *moral* in disease, is not properly a physician, but a veterinary.

These considerations are just as applicable, *mutatis mutandis*, to the study of society, which is in so many respects kindred to biology. The most characteristic fact about what is well called the social system is the consensus of its different functions; and the treatment of these functions as independent is sure to land us in theoretic and practical error. There is one great science of Sociology; its several chapters study the several faces of social existence. One of these faces is that of the material well-being of society, its industrial constitution and development. The study of these phenomena is one chapter of Sociology, a chapter which must be kept in close relation with the rest.

The justice of this view is clearly seen when we consider the two-fold aspect of Sociology as statical and dynamical—that is, as dealing on the one hand with laws of coexistence, and on the other with laws of succession. As in biology we have, alongside of the theory of the constitution and actions of an organism, the further theory of its development in time; so in Sociology we have, beside the doctrine of the constitution and actions of society, the doctrine of its evolution from a primitive to a higher condition. Now nothing is plainer than that in the course of the human evolution the several social elements did not follow separate and independent processes of growth. The present economic state, for example, of the nations of western Europe, as a group, or of any individual one amongst them, is the result of a great variety of conditions, many of them not in their own nature economical at all. Scientific, moral, religious, political ideas and institutions have all concurred in determining it. But if they worked in this manner in the past, it follows that they are working so in the present. It is therefore impossible rationally to conceive or explain the industrial economy of society without taking into account the other coexisting social factors.

In nothing is the eminent superiority of Adam Smith more clearly seen than in his tendency to comprehend and combine in his investigations all the different aspects of social phenomena. Before the term "social science" had been spoken or written, it could not be expected that he should have conceived adequately the nature and conditions of that branch of inquiry, much less founded it on definitive bases—a task which was to be achieved more than fifty years later by the genius of Comte. But he proceeded as far in this direction as it was possible to do under the intellectual conditions of his time. In his "Theory of Moral Sentiments" he promises to give in another discourse "an account of the general principles of law and government, and of the different revolutions they have undergone in the different ages and periods of society, not only in what concerns justice, but in what concerns police, revenue, and arms and whatever else is the subject of law." Here is no separation of politics, jurisprudence, and political economy, but rather an anticipation, wonderful for his period, of general sociology, both statical and dynamical—an anticipation which becomes more extraordinary still, when we learn from his literary executors that he had formed the plan of a connected history of the liberal sciences and elegant arts, which would have supplied, in addition to the social aspects already mentioned, a view of the intellectual progress of society. Of this last undertaking there remains to us only the remarkable essay on the history of astronomy, which is evidence at once of his thorough acquaintance with that branch of science, and of his profound philosophical conceptions on the nature of scientific inquiry in general. The other project too was never fully carried out; it may well be though because it was essentially premature. The "Wealth of Nations" is in fact a part of that larger design; and though in this work he has for his main subject the economic phenomena of society, he has incorporated into it so much that relates to the other social aspects that he has on this very ground been censured by some of the later economists. Mill, however, who of all his English successors was the most large-minded and the best equipped in respect of general culture, has recognised it as the great characteristic excellence of Smith that "in his applications of political economy, he perpetually appeals to other and often far larger considerations than pure political economy affords." In consequence of this admirable breadth of view, the study of the work of Adam Smith is, I believe, more fitted than that of the writings of any other economist, to cultivate in theorists a philosophic, and in practical men a statesman-like, habit of mind.

In striking contrast with this spirit of the master is the affectation, habitual in his followers, of ignoring all considerations except the strictly economic, though in doing so they often pass over agencies which have important effects on material well-being. Thus, when Senior is led to make some observations of the utmost importance and interest, on the very doubtful advantage to a labouring family of the employment of the mother and the children in non-domestic work, he thinks it necessary to apologise for having introduced such remarks, as not perhaps, strictly within the province of political economy. And when he finds himself similarly induced to observe on the evils of severe and incessant labour, and the benefits of a certain degree of leisure—subjects so momentous to working men, and closely connected with their material as well as moral condition—he pauses and corrects himself, admitting that he should not only be justified in omitting, but perhaps was bound to omit, all considerations which have no influence on wealth. This is the very pedantry of purism; and the purism is not merely exaggerated, it is really altogether out of place. Mill, though, as I believe, he did not occupy firm ground in relation to the constitution of social science, is free from any such narrowness as this: "For practical purposes," he says, "political economy is inseparably intertwined with many other branches of social philosophy. Except on matter of mere detail, there are perhaps no practical questions, even among those which approach nearest to the character of purely economical questions, which admit of being decided on economical promises alone." This is true; but it is only part of the truth. For purposes of theory as well as of practice, the several branches of social inquiry are inseparably intertwined; and this larger proposition Mill in another place has stated with all the desirable fulness of enunciation, declaring that "we can never understand in theory or command in practice the condition of a society in any one respect, without taking into consideration its conditions in all other respects."

Yet, notwithstanding this ample admission, he appears to exhibit some uncertainty of view with respect to the relation of economic studies to general sociology; at least after repeated careful examination of all that he has written on the subject, I confess myself unable to understand exactly the position he occupies. Sometimes he speaks of political economy as being a department "carved" (to use his own expression) "out of the general body of the science of society"; and again he speaks of it as belonging to a subordinate order of speculation to that with which the science of society is conversant—proposing to itself a quite different sort of question, and supplying only a sort of knowledge sufficient for the more common exigencies of daily political practice. The latter view is apparently reflected in the title of his economical treatise, which is called "Principles of Political Economy, with some of their Applications to Social Philosophy," a phrase which seems to imply that political economy is not a part of social philosophy at all, but is preparatory and ancillary to it. And it is interesting to observe that it was from this point of view of the study, as preliminary only and intended to prepare the way and provide materials for a true science of society, that Comte, in his correspondence with Mill, encouraged the latter in his project of a special treatise on political economy.

The ground which the economists commonly take up in justifying their one-sided attitude, is this: they announce that their treatment of every question is partial and incomplete, and that for a real solution all the other elements involved must be taken into account. Political economy, Professor Cairnes tells us, is absolutely neutral as between all particular schemes and systems of social or industrial life. It furnishes, he tells us, certain data that go towards the formation of a sound opinion, but can never determine our final judgment on any social question. Now this systematic indifferentism amounts to an entire paralysis of political economy as a social power capable of producing or confirming in the mass of the community just convictions on the most important of all subjects. How, it may well be asked, are sufficiently fixed and convergent opinions on such matters to be generated in the public mind? How are the scattered lights, supplied by the several partial and one-sided studies of human affairs, to be combined, so as to convey social truth to the understanding, and impress its practical consequences on men's consciences? These queries bring into the clearest light the doctrine I wish to commend to your attention—namely, that what is wanted for this purpose is a study of social questions from all the points of view that really belong to them, so as to attain definite and matured conclusions respecting them—in other words, a scientific sociology, comprehending true economic doctrine, but comprehending also a great deal more.

Even on the special subjects in which purely economic considerations go for most, it will not do to take into account those considerations only. Professor Fawcett, in his recent timely and useful treatise on Free-trade and Protection, finds that he cannot restrict himself, in the treatment of that question, to the economic point of view. "As complaints," he says, "are constantly made by protectionists that their opponents persistently ignore all the results of protection which are not economic, I will be careful to consider those results." And he goes on to maintain the proposition, in which I entirely concur, that protection may produce social and political consequences even far more mischievous than the economic loss it causes to a country. I believe that the most effective weapons against this and other economic errors will often be found in reasons not based on material interests, but derived from a consideration of the higher ends of society, and the ideal of the collective life of the race. And, *à fortiori*, when we have to deal with the larger economic subjects, now rapidly increasing in urgency, which are more immediately in contact with moral conceptions, these questions of the ultimate ends of the social union cannot be left out of sight. This was recognized by Mill, who was open to all noble ideas, and saw that the practical life of mankind cannot be governed by material egoism. In discussing the claims of Communism, he says: "Assuming all the success which is claimed for this state of society by its partisans, it remains to be considered how much would be really gained for mankind, and whether the form that would be given to life, and the character which would be impressed on human nature, can satisfy any but a very low estimate of the capabilities of the species." Here, you observe, is raised the entire question of the ends of social life; and economic progress is subordinated, as it ought to be, to the intellectual and moral development of humanity.

Mr. Lowe, at the Adam Smith celebration, declared himself not to be sanguine as to the future of political economy; he believes that its great work, which he justly remarks has been rather a negative than a constructive one, has been already accomplished, and that not much more remains to be achieved. Such, indeed, as we have seen, Professor Cairnes declared to be the prevalent idea of the great majority of educated people —that political economy has fulfilled its task by removing impediments to industry; and that it cannot help us—is rather likely to be an obstruction—in the social work which now lies before us. I will not use language so strong; but it does appear to me that either as a fruitful branch of speculation, or as an important source of practical guidance, it will cease to command, or rather will fail to regain attention, unless it be linked in close connection with the general science of society—unless it be, in fact, subsumed under and absorbed into Sociology.

II. The second common error of the political economists since the time of Adam Smith consists in this, that, mainly by the influence of Ricardo, they have been led to conceive and present, in a viciously abstract way, the conceptions with which they deal.

Abstraction is, indeed, necessary to all science, being implied in the search after unity amidst variety. The criterion of true or false science lies precisely in the right or wrong institution of the relation between the abstract and the concrete. Now, in matters of human life especially, we have only to carry abstraction far enough in order to lose all hold on realities, and present things quite other than they in fact are; and, if we use these abstractions in the premises of our reasonings, we shall arrive at conclusions, either positively false, or useless for any practical purpose. As Comte remarked, the most fundamental economic notions have been subtilized in the ordinary treatise, till the discussions about them often wander away from any relation to fact, and lose themselves in a region of nebulous metaphysics; so that exact thinkers have felt themselves obliged to abandon the use of some of the most necessary terms, such as *value, utility, production,* and to express the ideas they attach to them by circuitous phrases. I am far from condemning the effort after accuracy of language and well-defined terms; but the endless fluctuations of economists in the use of words (of which numerous examples are given in Senior's Appendix to Whately's "Logic," and in Professor Price's recent work) certainly indicate a very general failure to apprehend and keep steadily in view the corresponding realities.

A vicious abstraction meets us on the very threshold of political economy. The entire body of its doctrines, as usually taught, rests on the hypothesis that the sole human passion or motive which has economic effects, is the desire of wealth. "It aims," says Mill, "at showing what is the course of action into which mankind living in a state of society would be impelled if that motive"—except so far as it is checked by aversion to labour, and desire of present indulgence—"were absolute master of all their actions." "So strictly is this its object," he adds, "that even the introduction of the principle of population interferes with the strictness of scientific arrangement." But what is the desire of wealth? It is as Mr. Leslie says in an article in "Hermathena," in which he urges the necessity for a new method in political economy—it is the general name for a great variety of wants, desires, and sentiments, widely differing in their economic character and effect, and undergoing fundamental changes in some respects in the successive periods of society. As moralists, viewing the same abstraction, not as a condition of well-being, but as the root of all evil, "have denounced under the common name of love of wealth, not only sensuality, avarice, and vanity, but the love of life, health, cleanliness, decency, and art, so all the needs, appetites, tastes, aims and ideas which the various things comprehended in the word "wealth" satisfy, are lumped together in political economy as a principle of human nature, which is the source of industry, and the moving principle of the economic world." The motives summed up in the phrase vary in different individuals, different classes, different nations, different sexes, and especially in different states of society; in these last, indeed, the several desires comprehended under the general name follow definite laws of succession. The point Mr. Leslie here insists on is, be it observed, not merely—though that is also true—that the phrase *desire of wealth* represents a coarse and crude generalization in the natural history of man; but that the several impulses comprised under the name assume altered forms and vary in their relative strength, and so produce different economic consequences, in different states of society; and therefore that the abstraction embodied in the phrase is too vague and unreal for use in economic investigations of a really scientific character. The special desire for accumulation, apart from the immediate or particular uses of wealth, is no doubt a principle of social growth which must not be overlooked; but this, too, takes different directions and works to different ends in different stages of social development. All these economic motors require to be made the subjects of careful and extensive observation; and their several forms, instead of being rudely massed together under a common name, should be discriminated as they in fact exist. The consumption, or more correctly the use, of wealth, until lately neglected by economists, and declared by Mill to have no place in their science, must, as Professor Jevons and others now see, be systematically studied in its relations to production and to the general material well-being of communities. And none of these things can be really understood without correct views of the structure and evolution of society in all its aspects; in other words, we are led back to the conclusions, that they cannot be fruitfully treated apart from general sociology. I have not been able to do more than indicate the leading features of a criticism which I recommend all who are interested in the subject to pursue in its full development in Mr. Leslie's admirable essay.

There is a common economic abstraction, which, by the unsympathetic colour it has given to political economy, has tended, perhaps more than anything else, to repel the working classes from its study. By habitually regarding labour from the abstract point of view, and overlooking the personality of the labourer, economists are led to leave out of account some of the considerations which most seriously affect the condition of the working man. He comes to be regarded exclusively as an agent—I might almost say, an instrument of production. It is too often forgotten that he is before all things a man and a member of society —that he is usually the head of a household, and that the conditions of his life should be such as to admit his maintaining due relations with his family—that he is also a citizen, and requires for the intelligent appreciation of the social and political system to which he belongs a certain amount of leisure and opportunity for mental culture. Even when a higher education is now sought for him, it is often conceived as exclusively designed to adapt him for the effective exercise of his functions as a producer, and so is reduced to technical instruction; whereas moral and social ideas are for him, as for all of us, by far the most important, because most directly related to conduct. Labour, again, is viewed as a commodity for sale, like any other commodity; though it is plain that, even if it could be properly so called at all, yet in some particulars, as in the difficulty of local transfer (a family having to be considered), and in the frequent impossibility of waiting for a market, it is quite exceptional amongst commodities. By a further abstraction, the difference of the social vocations of the sexes is made to disappear, in economic as in political reasoning, by means of the simple expedient of substituting for *man* in every proposition *persons* or *human being;* and so, by little else than a trick of phraseology, self-support is made as much an obligation of the woman as of the man. It is true that ungenerous sentiment has much to do with the prevalence of these modes of thought; but what it is most suitable to insist on here, is that the science on which they rest, or in which they find justification, is false science. By merely keeping close to facts and not hiding realities under lax generalizations, we shall be led to more humane, as well as truer, conceptions of the proper conditions of industrial life.

It is a characteristic feature of the metaphysical habit of mind (using that phrase in the sense with which Comte has familiarized us) to mistake creations of the speculative imagination for objective realities. Examples of this tendency have not been wanting in the dominant system of political economy. The most remarkable is perhaps furnished by the "Theory of the Wages Fund." The history of that doctrine is instructive, but I cannot here enlarge upon it; it may suffice to say that though the so-called wages fund is simply a scientific figment, the only legitimate use of which would be to facilitate the expression of certain relations, it has been habitually regarded as an actual entity, possessing a determinate magnitude at any assigned instant. It is true that Mill gave up this theory, when Mr. Thornton had convinced him of its unsubstantial nature; but, strange to say, even when relinquished by the master, some of the disciples continued to cling to it. Professor Cairnes in his latest work insisted that Mill was mistaken in abandoning it, and it is still taught in some of the elementary manuals—not, I am glad to observe, in that of Professor Jevons, who indeed never adopted it. There are, in my opinion, other quite as illusory economic conceptions which have met with a good deal of acceptance, and have even obtained the sanction of distinguished names. If I do not now enter on an examination of them, it is because I am unwilling that the general views I am desirous of presenting should be lost in a series of special discussions, for which a more suitable opportunity can easily be found.

III. The third prevailing error of the economists—and, with the exception of the isolation of their study, this is the most serious of all—is that of exaggerating immensely the office of deduction in their investigations.

Deduction has indisputably a real and not inconsiderable place in Sociology. We can sometimes follow the method which Mill calls the direct deductive, that is, we can, from what we know of the nature of man and the laws of the external world, see beforehand what social phenomena will result from their joint action. But, though the economist of the so-called orthodox school recognize no other method, we cannot really proceed far in this way, which is available only in simple cases. Social phenomena are in general too complex, and depend on too manifold conditions, to be capable of such *à priori* determination. In so far as the method can be used, the vital condition of its legitimate employment is the ascertainment of the consilience of the results of deduction with those of observation; and yet such verification from fact of the conclusions of theory, though essential to the admissibility of this process of inquiry, is too often entirely overlooked.

Much more commonly the function of deduction is different from what has just been described, and its relation to observation is inverted. The laws of the economic constitution and movement of society are first obtained by observation, whether directed to contemporary life or to the history of the past. The office of deduction is then to verify and control the inductions which have been arrived at, using for this purpose considerations founded on the qualities of human nature and the external conditions to which society is subjected. Results which could not have been elicited by *à priori* reasoning from the latter data, may, when inductively obtained, be in this way checked and rationalized. The pretension of the economists, formally set forth in Senior's treatise, to deduce all the phenomena of the industrial life of communities from four propositions, is one that cannot be sustained. But conclusions derived from observation may be placed in relation with the laws of the world and of human nature, so far at least as to show that they contradict nothing we know respecting those laws. This method, in which inductive research preponderates, and deduction takes a secondary place as means of verification, is the really normal and fruitful method of sociological inquiry.

But the method of Sociology must be not only inductive, but historical; and by the latter name it may best be characterised. By this is meant, not merely that it finds the materials for its studies in the general field of human history; we mean further that it institutes a comparison of the successive states of society in order to discover the laws of social filiation—a process similar in principle to the biological comparison of organisms of different degrees of development. If we followed exclusively the *à priori* method, in (for example) economic research, and sought to infer the economic facts of life from the nature of the world and man, we could arrive only at one determinate order of things, whilst we know that in reality the economic organization and functions of society vary in time according to definite laws of succession. Mr. Lowe, indeed, will have it that "political economy is founded on the attributes of the human mind, and nothing can change it"; which means, I suppose, that its formulas must always correspond with the phenomena. But how can this view be reconciled with the now ascertained fact, that society has passed through states in which the modern economic constitution was so far from existing, that property did not belong to the individual, but to the community? The *à priori* method, in fact, overlooks what is the main agency in the social movement—namely, the accumulated influence of anterior on subsequent generations of mankind; an influence too complex to be estimated deductively. Every department of social life, and amongst the rest the industrial system, undergoes transformation—not arbitrarily indeed, but in accordance with law; and if we wish to understand any of those departments, we must study its transformations, considering each successive form in relation to all the preceding and contemporary conditions.

There is, indeed, no more important philosophical theorem than this: that the nature of a social fact of any degree of complexity cannot be understood apart from its history. "Only when its genesis has been traced," says Mr. Herbert Spencer, "only when its antecedents of all orders have been observed in their co-operation, generation after generation, through past social states is there reached that interpretation of a fact which makes it a part of sociological science." To understand, for example, the true meaning of the trade societies of modern times, so important an object of economic study, "we must" he says, "go back to the older periods when analogous causes produced analogous results." And facts of this order, he adds, "must be studied not merely in their own successive forms, but in relation to the other phenomena of their time—the political institutions, the class distinctions, the family arrangements, the modes of distribution and degree of intercourse between localities, the amounts of knowledge, the religious beliefs, the morals, the sentiments, the customs." These considerations all point to the historical method, and, I may add, they all confirm what I have already urged, that the economic phenomena of society cannot be isolated from its other aspects. When our object is not the explanation of any past or present fact, but the prevision (within possible limits) of the future, and the adoption of a policy in relation to that future, our guide must still be the historic method, conceived as indicating, from the comparison of successive states, the general tendency of society with respect to the phenomenon considered, and the agencies which are in course of modifying existing systems. "Legislative action of no kind," again says Mr. Spencer, "can be taken that is not either in agreement with or at variance with the processes of national growth and development as naturally going on." We can by judicious action modify in their special mode of accomplishment or in the rate of their development, but we cannot alter in their fundamental nature, the changes which result from the spontaneous tendencies of humanity. An attempt to introduce any social factor which is not essentially conformable to the contemporary civilization will result, if not in serious disturbance, at least in a mere waste of effort. Any proposal of social action, therefore, should repose on a previous analysis of those spontaneous tendencies, and this is possible only by the historic method. Let me give an example from an economic subject which happens just at present to offer a special interest. Attention has been called by Sir Henry Maine to the general law that property in land originally belongs, not to individuals, nor even to families in the modern sense, but to larger societies, and that in the progress of mankind there is a natural movement from common to separate ownership. This historical result has been elaborated by a number of independent inquirers; and M. de Laveleye in a work of great research has brought together a vast mass of evidence, both establishing the main fact, and exhibiting the varied features which the common evolution has assumed in different countries. There is much that is attractive in particular sides of this early organization of territorial property, and M. de Laveleye has yielded to the charm, so far as to regret its disappearance in the developed communities of the West, though he stops short of recommending what others have suggested—namely, a return to the primitive constitution, by replacing the commune in the possession of the soil. Indeed, he himself, by establishing the progressive spontaneous tendency of society towards individual property, shows such a project to be a dream, and banishes it from the field of practical economic policy. From the general appearance of this collective ownership in an early stage of society, it is sometimes argued that it is a *natural* system; but the historic method shows that it is just as natural that it should disappear at a more advanced stage. Serving useful ends in the former period, it becomes in the latter an obstruction to progress by stereotyping agricultural art, and impeding that individual initiative which is an indispensable condition of social improvement. The safe prediction is that the Swiss *Allmend*, the Russian *Mir*, and other forms of collective ownership will disappear, and that personal appropriation will become the universal rule. The social destination of property in land, as of every species of wealth, will be increasingly acknowledged and realized in the future; but that result will be brought about, not through legal institutions, but by the establishment and diffusion of moral convictions.

There have been great differences of opinion as to the method of economic inquiry pursued by Adam Smith. Mr. Lowe insists that his method was deductive—that he had the unique merit of having raised the study of a branch of human transactions to the dignity of a deductive science. At the same celebration at which this opinion was put forward, Professor Thorold Rogers expressed his surprise that anyone should entertain such a view. It seemed to him clear that Adam Smith was pre-eminently an inductive philosopher. Mr. Rogers has edited the "Wealth of Nations," and in doing so has verified all the references; and what strikes him is the extraordinary wideness of the reading from which Smith drew his inferences. The work, he says, is full of facts. It is interesting to observe that David Hume made just the same remark on the book at the time of its publication:—"It has depth," he said, "and solidity, and acuteness, and so much illustrated with curious facts, that it must take the public attention."

Of the two views thus advanced by Mr. Lowe and Mr. Rogers, the latter seems to me much the more correct. That the master tendency of Smith's intellect was the deductive, or that it is at the deductive point of view that he habitually places himself, seems to me plainly at variance with fact. Open his book anywhere, and read a few pages; then do the same with Ricardo's principal work, and observe the difference of the impression produced. Under the guidance of Ricardo you are constantly, not without misgiving, following certain abstract assumptions to their logical results. In Smith you feel yourself in contact with real life, observing human acts and their consequences by the light of experience. Of course deduction is not wanting; but it is in the way of explanation; the facts are *interpreted* from the nature and circumstances of men in general, or particular groups of men. Sagacious observation and shrewd comment go hand in hand.

Adam Smith, besides giving generally a large place to induction, opened several lines of interesting historical investigation, as notably in his Third Book, which contains a view of the economic progress of modern Europe as shaped by political causes. But historic inquiry was neglected by his successors, with a partial exception in the case of Malthus, and the *à priori* method became dominant chiefly by the influence of Ricardo. Professor Price objects to this method as too scientific; but, as Mr. Leslie has said, what ought to be alleged respecting it is that it is unscientific, because ill adapted for the successful investigation of the class of phenomena with which it deals. Setting out from propositions involving the loose abstractions of which I have spoken, it arrives at conclusions which are seldom corrected by the consideration of conditions which were at first, for simplicity, omitted in the premises. And these conclusions can in general not be directly confronted with experience for the purpose of verification, for they are hypothetical only; they give us, not the resultant phenomenon, but only a tendency of a certain character, which will be one component of the resultant.

I am not concerned nor disposed to deny that useful general indications have been gathered by inference of this kind. But it is evidently a very unsafe process, even in purely economic matters, especially when consequences are pushed into any degree of detail. Careful thinkers have a profound distrust of lengthened deductions in economic inquiries. When it is argued that A must lead to B, and B again to C, and so on through a long chain or results, they assume in self-defence a sceptical attitude of mind, and often feel more than half convinced that what is going on is a feat of logical sleight of hand. And this suspiciousness is, I think reasonable; for we are not here on the same ground as in mathematics, where protracted deductions are always safe, because we can be sure that we have before us at every step all the determining data, and each proposition successively used is universally true. But as the most that the economist can affirm is a set of tendencies, the certainty of his conclusions is plainly weakened in a rapidly increasing ratio by the multiplication of links, there being always a possibility that the theorems applied in the course of the demonstration may be subject to special counteractions or limitations in the case we are considering.

I observed before that Mill betrayed some uncertainty of view as to the precise relation of economic inquiries to general sociology. As to the proper method of the social science also, he appears to me not strictly consistent with himself. That method he declares, in so many words, to be the direct deductive. Yet elsewhere he as plainly agrees with Comte, that in the general science of society, as distinguished from its separate departments, nothing of a scientific character is possible except by the inverse deductive—as he chooses to call the historical-method. In one place he seems to assert that the general course of economic evolution could be predicted from the single consideration of the desire of wealth. Yet again he admits that no one could determine *à priori* from the principles of human nature and the general circumstances of the race the order in which human development takes place. Now this involves the conclusion, that the laws of economic progress—like all dynamic laws of Sociology—must be ascertained by observation on the large scale, and only verified by appeal to the laws of the external world and human nature; in other words, that the right method for their study is the historical.

I hope it is not inconsistent with a profound respect for the eminent powers and high aims of Mill, to say that he appears to me never to have extricated himself completely from the vicious habits in regard to sociological method impressed on him by his education. His father had the principal part in the formation of his mind in his early years. Now whatever were the intellectual merits of James Mill, his mode of thinking on social subjects was essentially metaphysical, as opposed to positive. Through him, as well as directly, John Mill came under the influence of Bentham, of whom, whilst fully recognizing his services, we may truly say that he was one of the most unhistorical of writers, building most, I mean, on assumed *à priori* principles, and sympathizing least with the social past, in which he saw little except errors and abuses. It is strong evidence of the natural force of Mill's intellect that he more and more, as he advanced toward maturity, shook himself loose of the prejudices of his early *entourage*. On every side, not even excluding the aesthetic, he grew in comprehensiveness, and his social and historic ideas in particu lar become wider and more sympathetic. The publication of the letters addressed to him by Auguste Comte has revealed more fully, what could already be gathered from his writings, that the study of that eminent thinker's first gieat work happily concurred with and aided his spontaneous tendencies. Hence in his economic studies he broke away in many respects from the narrow traditions of the reigning English school, and by opening larger horizons and discrediting rigid formulas, did much to prepare the public mind for a more complete as well as truly scientific handling of these subjects. But though the interval between his father and himself represents an immense advance, yet never in regard to method did he, in my opinion, attain a perfectly normal attitude. Whilst in his "Logic" he criticized with just severity what he, not very happily, calls the geometrical mode of philosophizing practiced by the Benthamites in political research, he approves what is essentially the same course of proceeding in economic inquiry; and, whilst protesting against the attempt to construct a special science of the political phenomena of society apart from the general sociology, he yet, with whatever restrictions and qualifications, accepts the separate construction of a science of its industrial phenomena. His ambition in his work on political economy was, as may be seen from the preface, to replace the "Wealth of Nations" by a treatise which, whilst more uniformly correct on points of detail, should be in harmony with contemporary social speculation in the widest sense. Admitting fully the great merits of the book, I yet must hold that, chiefly from the absence of any systematic application of the historic method, he has not succeeded in attaining his end. The presentation of what is solid and permanent in the work of the economists, in relation with the largest and truest views of general sociology, is, in my judgment, a task which still remains to be accomplished.

The tendencies of the new school with respect to method are sufficiently indicated by the names of the Realistic and the Historical by which it designates itself. It declares, in the words of Brentano, the description of political economy by the so-called orthodox writers as a hypothetic science, to be only a device to cloak its dissonance with reality; and affirms that much of the current doctrine is made up of hasty generalizations from insufficient and arbitrary premises. It sets out, says Held, from observed facts, and not from definitions, which often serve only to mask foregone conclusions. It aims at describing objectively existing economic relations, not as immutable necessities, but as products of a gradual historical development in the past, and susceptible of gradual modification in the future. "Its philosophical method," says Mr. Leslie, "must be historical, and must trace the connection between the economical and the other phases of national history." In these tendencies the rising school seems to me to be in harmony with all that is best in the spirit of the most advanced contemporary thought.

IV. Lastly has to be noticed the too absolute character of the theoretic and practical conclusions of the political economists. It follows (as I have already indicated) from their *à priori* and unhistoric method that they arrive at results which purport to apply equally to all states of society. Neglecting the study of the social development, they tend too much to conceive the economic structure of society as fixed in type, instead of as undergoing a regular modification in process of time, in relation to the other changing elements of human condition. Similar consequences arose in other branches of sociological inquiry from the prevalence of unhistoric methods. But reforms have been largely carried into effect from the increasing recognition of the principle, that the treatment of any particular aspect of society must be dominated by the consideration of the general contemporary state of civilization. Thus, in jurisprudence there is a marked tendency to substitute for the *à priori* method of the Benthamites a historical method, the leading idea of which is to connect the whole juristic system of any epoch with the corresponding state of society; and this new method has already borne admirable fruits, especially in the hands of Sir Henry Maine. Again, the old search after the best government, which used to be the main element of political inquiry, is now seen to have been radically irrational, because the form of government must be essentially related to the stage of social development and to historic antecedents, and the question, what is best? admits of no absolute answer.

Mill admits that there can be no separate science of government; in other words, that the study of the political phenomena of society cannot be conducted apart, but must, in his own words, stand part of the general science of society, not of any separate branch of it. And Why? Because those phenomena are so closely mixed up, both as cause and effect, with the qualities of the particular people, or of the particular age. Particular age must here mean the state of general social development. But are not economic phenomena very closely bound up with the particular state of development of the society which is under consideration? Mr. Bagehot, indeed, took up the ground that political economy is "restricted to a single kind of society, a society of competitive commerce, such as we have in England." And Mill himself, whilst stating that only through the principle of competition, as the exclusive regulator of economic phenomena, has political economy any claim to the character of a science, admits that competition has, only at a comparatively modern period, become in any considerable degree the governing principle of contracts; that in early periods transactions and engagements were regulated by custom, and that to this day in several countries of Europe, in large departments of human transactions, custom, not competition, is the arbiter.

The truth is, that in most enunciations of economic theorems by the English school, the practice is tacitly to presuppose the state of social development, and the general history of social conditions, to be similar to that of modern England; and when this supposition is not realised, those theorems will often be found to fail.

The absolute character of the current political economy is shown, not only by this neglect of the influence of the general social state, but in the much too unlimited and unconditional form which is given to most of its conclusions. Mr. Fawcett has, in his latest publication, animadverted on this practice; thus, he points to the allegation often met with, that the introduction of machines must improve the position of the workman, the element of time being left out of account; and the assertion that the abolition of protection in the United States could not injure the American manufacturer. But this lax habit cannot, I believe, be really corrected apart from a thorough change of economic method. As long as conclusions are deduced from abstract assumptions, such as the perfectly free flow of labour and capital from one employment to another, propositions which only affirm tendencies will be taken to represent facts, and theorems which would hold under certain conditions will be announced as universally true.

The most marked example the economists have afforded of a too absolute conception and presentation of principle, both theoretical and practical, is found in the doctrine of *laissez faire*. It might be interesting, if time permitted, to follow its history in detail. First inspired by *à priori* optimistic prepossessions, it long served a useful purpose as an instrument of combat against the systematic restrictions with which a mistaken policy had everywhere fettered European industry. But, from the absolute manner in which it was understood and expressed, it tended more and more to annul all governmental intervention in the industrial world, even when intended not to alter the spontaneous course of industry, but only to prevent or remedy the social injustices and other mischiefs arising from the uncontrolled play of private interests. Experience and reflection, however, gradually surmounted the exaggerations of theory. The community at large became impatient of *laissez faire* as an impediment and a nuisance; statesmen pushed it aside, and the economists, after long repeating it as a sacred formula, themselves at last revolted against it. So far has the reaction proceeded, that Professor Cairns has declared the doctrine implied in the phrase—namely, that the economic phenomena of society will always spontaneously arrange themselves in the way which is most for the common good—to be a pretentious sophism, destitute of scientific authority, and having no foundation in nature or fact.

Let me now recapitulate the philosophical conclusions which I have been endeavouring to enforce. They are the following:

(1) That the study of the economic phenomena of society ought to be systematically combined with that of the other aspects of social existence;

(2) That the excessive tendency to abstraction and to unreal simplifications should be checked; (3) That the *à priori* deductive method should be changed for the historical; and (4) That economic laws and the practical prescriptions founded on those laws should be conceived and expressed in less absolute form. These are, in my opinion, the great reforms which are required both in the conduct of economic research, and in the exposition of its conclusions.

I am far from thinking that the results arrived at by the hitherto dominant economic school ought to be thrown away as valueless. They have shed important partial lights on human affairs, and afforded salutary partial guidance in public action. The task incumbent on sociologists in general, or such of them as specially devote themselves to economic inquiries, is to incorporate the truths already elicited into a more satisfactory body of doctrine, in which they will be brought into relation with the general theory of social existence—to recast the first draughts of theory, which, however, incomplete, in most cases indicate real elements of the question considered—and to utilize the valuable materials of all kinds which their predecessors have accumulated. Viewed as provisional and preparatory, the current political economy deserves an approbation and an acceptance to which I think it is not entitled, if regarded as a final systematization of the industrial laws of society.

Returning now from our examination of the condition and prospects of economic study in the general field of human knowledge to the consideration of its position in this Association, what seems to follow from all I have been saying? I do not take into account at all the suggestion that that study should be removed from what professes to be a confederation of the sciences. As has been well said, the omission from the objects of this body of the whole subject of the life of man in communities, although there is a scientific order traceable in that life, would be a degradation of the Association. If the proper study of mankind is man, the work of the Association, after the extrusion of our Section, would be like the play with the part of the protagonist left out. What appears to be the reasonable suggestion, is that the field of the Section should be enlarged, so as to comprehend the whole of Sociology. The economic facts of society, as I have endeavoured to show, cannot be scientifically considered apart; and there is no reason why the researches of Sir Henry Maine, or those of Mr. Spencer, should not be as much at home here as those of Mr. Fawcett or Professor Price. Many of the subjects, too, at present included in the artificial assemblage of heterogeneous inquiries known by the name of Anthropology, really connect themselves with the laws of social development; and if our Section bore the title of the Sociological, studies like those of Mr. Tylor and Sir John Lubbock concerning the early history of civilization would find in it their most appropriate place. I prefer the name Sociology to that of Social Science, which has been at once rendered indefinite and vulgarized in common use, and has come to be regarded as denoting a congeries of incoherent details respecting every practical matter bearing directly or remotely on public interest, which happens for the moment to engage attention. There are other Societies in which an opportunity is afforded for discussing such current questions in a comparatively popular arena. But if we are to be associated here with the students of other sciences, it is our duty, as well as our interest, to aim at a genuinely scientific character in our work. Our main object should be to assist in fixing theoretic ideas on the structure, functions, and development of society. Some may regard this view of the subject with impatience, as proposing to us investigations not bearing on the great and real needs of contemporary social life. But that would be a very mistaken notion. Luciferous research, in the words of Bacon, must come before fructiferous. "Effectual practice," says Mr. Spencer, "depends on superiority of ideas; methods that answer are preceded by thoughts that are true." And in human affairs, it is in general impossible to solve special questions correctly without just conceptions of *ensemble*—all particular problems of government, of education, of social action of whatever kind, connect themselves with the largest ideas concerning the fundamental constitution of society, its spontaneous tendencies, and its moral ideal.

I have as yet said nothing of Statistics, with which the name of this Section at first exclusively connected, and which are still recognized as forming one of its objects. But it is plain that though Statistics may be combined with Sociology in the title of the Section, the two cannot occupy a co-ordinate position. For it is impossible to vindicate for Statistics the character of a science; they constitute only one of the aids or adminicula of science. The ascertainment and systematic arrangement of numerical facts is useful in many branches of research, but, till law emerges, there is no science; and the law, when it does emerge, takes its place in the science whose function it is to deal with the particular class of phenomena to which the facts belong. We may arrange meteorological facts in this way as well as sociological; and, if doing so helps us to the discovery of a law, the law belongs to meteorology: and, in the same manner, a law discovered by the aid of statistics would belong to sociology.

But though the character of a science cannot be claimed for Statistics, it is obvious that if the views I have advocated as to the true nature and conditions of economic study should prevail, the importance of statistical inquiries will rise, as the abstract and deductive method declines in estimation. Senior objected to the saying that political economy is *avide de faits*, because, according to him and the school of Ricardo in general, its work was mainly one of inference from a few primary assumptions. But if the latter notion is given up, every form of careful and conscientious search after the realities of the material life of society, in the present as in the past, will regain its normal importance. This search must, of course, be regulated by definite principles, and must not degenerate into a purposeless and fortuitous accumulation of facts; for here, as in every branch of inquiry, it is true that "*Prudens interrogatio est dimidium scientiae.*"

I do not expect that the views I have put forward as to the necessity of a reform of economic studies will be immediately adopted either in this Section or elsewhere. They may, I am aware, whilst probably in some quarters meeting with at least partial sympathy, in others encounter determined hostility. And it is possible that I may be accused of presumption in venturing to criticize methods used in practice, and justified in principle, by many distinguished men. I should scarcely have undertaken such an office, however profoundly convinced of the urgency of a reform, had I not been supported by what seemed to me the unanswered arguments of an illustrious thinker, and by the knowledge that the growing movement of philosophic Europe is in the direction he recommended as the right one. No one can feel more strongly than myself the inadequacy of my treatment of the subject. But my object has not been so much to produce conviction as to awaken attention. Our economists have undeniably been slow in observing the current of European thought. Whilst such foreign writers as echo the doctrines of the so-called orthodox school are read and quoted in England, the names of those who assume a different and more independent attitude are seldom heard, and their works appear to be almost entirely unknown. But the fence of self-satisfied routine within which in these countries we formerly too often entrenched ourselves is being broken down at every point; and no really vital body of opinion can now exist abroad without speedily disturbing our insular tranquillity. The controversy, therefore, as to the methods of economic research and its relations to Sociology as a whole, cannot long be postponed amongst us. It has, in fact, been already opened from different sides by Mr. Leslie and Mr. Harrison, and it is desirable that it should arrive as promptly as possible at a definitive issue. If I have done anything to-day to assist in launching this great question on the field of general English discussion, the purpose I have set before me will have been abundantly fulfilled.

THOMAS EDWARD CLIFFE LESLIE

(1825 ?–1882)

Like Ingram, Cliffe Leslie was an Irish economist who was educated at Trinity College, Dublin, at which institution he came under the inspiring influence of Sir Henry Maine, the author of "Ancient Law."

Leslie's chief works are collected in two volumes of essays: "Land Systems and Industrial Economy of Ireland, England, and Continental Countries" (1870), and "Essays in Political and Moral Philosophy" (1879).

Like other members of the historical school, Leslie's influence was chiefly critical rather than creative. Perhaps such would not have been the verdict of subsequent history had it not been for an unfortunate accident which destroyed one of his most important manuscripts, in which he had attempted to construct a new system of political economy. No doubt the historical approach would have dominated, and social institutions would have supplemented purely abstract principles.

Leslie's theoretical contributions concerned prices and wages. His voice was another one raised in criticism of the current wage fund theory. Among the various practical problems he treated were the distribution of the precious metals and agrarian problems.

Leslie was as much a sociologist and a historian as he was an economist. Indeed, he was a close student of the great philosopher, Comte. His writings on economics have a distinct social flavor and a definite institutional interest. The following brief selection is taken from his "Essays in Political and Moral Philosophy."

THOMAS EDWARD CLIFFE LESLIE

SELECTION FROM "ESSAYS IN POLITICAL AND MORAL PHILOSOPHY"

CHAPTER XXV. ECONOMIC SCIENCE AND STATISTICS[1]

Economic Science was not formally included within the Statistical Section of the British Association until 1856; and even since then, addresses of distinguished Presidents of the Section have turned mainly on its statistical functions, and have been devoted principally to an inquiry into the nature and province of statistics. That the inquiry is neither so superfluous nor so easy as might at first appear, is sufficiently shown by the fact that there are, according to the great German statist, Dr. Engel, no less than 180 definitions of the term to be met with in the works of different authors. These various definitions may, however, be said to group themselves round one or other of three conceptions, of which one follows the popular view of statistics; the etymological and original meaning almost disappearing in the notion merely of tables of figures, or numbers of facts, of which the chief significance lies in their numerical statement. According to another conception, statistics, following etymology and the signification given to Statistik by the famous Göttingen school, should be regarded as equivalent to the science of States, or political science, but nevertheless, as confining itself to the ascertainment and collection of facts indicative of the condition and prospects of society, without inquiring into causes or reasoning on probable effects, and carefully discarding hypothesis, theory, and speculation in its investigations. A third conception is, that statistical science aims at the discovery, not only of the phenomena of society, but also of their laws, and by no means discards either inquiry into causes and effects or theoretical reasoning.

It is curious that some who give to statistics the first of these three meanings, and who regard the numerical statement of facts, and the marshalling of tables of figures, as the proper business of the statistician, nevertheless speak of statistics as a science. But, as the eminent economist, Roscher, has observed, numbering or numerical statement is only an instrument of which any branch of science may avail itself, and can never, in itself, constitute a science. No one, as he says, would dream of making a science of microscopics, or observations made through the microscope. The distinguished English statistician and economist, Mr. Jevons, has

[1] *Athenaenum*, September 27, 1873.

likewise condemned the misconception of statistics and the misuse of the term we refer to in language worth recalling:—"Many persons now use the word statistical as if it were synonymous with numerical; but it is a mere accident of the information with which we deal that it is often expressed in a numerical or tabular form. As other sciences progress, they become more and more a matter of quantity and number, and so does statistical science; but we must not suppose that the occurrence of numerical statement is the mark of statistical information."

The doctrine that the consideration of causes and probable reasoning are excluded from the province of statistics, and that statisticians should confine themselves to the ascertainment of facts, is hardly more satisfactory. No branch of science, no scientific body, confines itself to the observation of phenomena without seeking to interpret them or to ascertain their laws. It is not, indeed, possible, at present, to explain all the phenomena which come within the observation of the statist, or to connect them with any law of causation; and even naked collections of statistical facts may be useful as aids to further inquiry, or as supplying links in the chain of observed effects. But serious error, and even practical mischief, have followed from attention merely to the recurrence of statistical facts without inquiry into their causes. A theory of a decennial recurrence of commercial crises, for example, was based on the occurrence of crises in 1837, 1847, and 1857. Had the causes of commercial crises been examined, it would have been discovered that they are extremely various and uncertain in their occurrence; that a war, a bad harvest, a drain of the precious metals, anything, in short, which produces a panic, may cause a crisis; and as there is no decennial periodicity in the causes, there can be none in the effects.

These considerations lead us to adopt the third conception noticed above, namely, that statistical science investigates the laws of social phenomena, as well as the phenomena themselves; and, if not co-extensive with sociology, or the science of society,—because not going so far back in its researches, and confining itself to the phenomena of modern society, —yet employs all available methods, inquiry into causes, theory, and probable reasoning for the interpretation of the facts it discovers. But it is not easy to give to a word a signification other than the one which long usage has put upon it; and, unfortunately, to the majority of persons the term statistics denotes simply dry figures and tabulated facts. The Statistical Section of the British Association has found a means to escape from the difficulty, in a great measure, by allying itself formally to Economic Science. It thus embraces definitely and expressly the whole economic side of the science of society, including the investigation of laws of causation as well as the observation of facts, and employing all the methods of scientific investigation and reasoning. But if it deals in this manner with economic facts, it can hardly fail to do so likewise with the other classes of social phenomena which it approaches. And thus, however narrow may be the sense in which the term statistics may be elsewhere employed, the Statistical Section of the British Association is free from all trammel, and unfettered by any exclusion of theory or even speculation in its investigation of political and social problems.

The formal incorporation of economic science with statistics has another great advantage: it tends to correct the error to which economists as well as that to which statisticians are specially prone. If the latter have been apt to think only of facts, it has been the besetting sin of the former to neglect facts altogether; if statisticians have often been content to collect phenomena without heed to their laws, economists more often still have jumped to the laws without heed to the phenomena; if statistics have lain chiefly in the region of dry figures and numerical tables, economics have dwelt chiefly in that region of assumption, conjecture, and provisional generalization, which other sciences, indeed—geology to witness,—have not escaped, but from which they are triumphantly emerging by combining the closest observation of phenomena with the boldest use of speculation and scientific hypothesis.

We may thus look for considerable benefit to both political economy and statistics from the combination of the methods to which the followers of each have been specially addicted. The subjects which occupied the principal place in Mr. Forster's address and in the attention of the Section, conspicuously illustrate the importance of combining statistical with economic inquiry, and the characteristic defects of the economic and statistical methods hitherto commonly followed. Take, for example, the question of wages. The relation of capital and labour, and the causes determining the rates of wages, are not to be summed up or disposed of in any brief formula or so-called "economic law." But much might have been done, by the collection of statistics and careful inquiry into facts, towards obtaining much closer approximations to truth than the generalizations which take the name of "the wages fund," "the equality of profits," "the average rate of wages,"—generalization of which the world generally has grown a little doubtful and not a little weary.

Economists have been accustomed to assume that wages on the one hand and profits on the other are, allowing for differences in skill, and so forth, equalized by competition, and that neither wages nor profits can any where rise above "the average rate," without a consequent influx of labour or of capital bringing things to a level. Had economists, however, in place of reasoning from an assumption, examined the facts connected with the rate of wages, they would have found, from authentic statistics, the actual differences so great, even in the same occupation, that they are double in one place what they are in another. Statistics of profits are not, indeed, obtainable like statistics of wages; and the fact that they are not so, that the actual profits are kept a profound secret in some of the most prominent trades, is itself enough to deprive the theory of equal profits of its base. Enough, however, is known or discovered from time to time by the working men in particular trades, to justify them in the conclusion, on the one hand, that profits will bear a reduction, and that wages may consequently receive an augmentation; and, on the other hand, that competition has not produced and will not produce those results. When, therefore, Mr. Forster assumes that the majority of working men are now disposed to admit as fundamental truths of economic science that the remuneration of labour can be raised only in three ways—by the increase of capital, the diminution of the whole labouring population, or the participation of labourers in capital,—we are reminded that not a few working men in certain trades believe there is another mode by which their remuneration might be raised, namely, by a participation in profits, which are enormously high; and that they believe, too, that this participation can be secured only by combination, not by competition. Not quite consistently with his own statement, that one of the methods by which wages may be raised is a diminution of population, Mr. Forster pointed to the increase of the population of England and Wales from 16½ millions in 1831 to 21½ millions in 1871, simultaneously with an increase of general prosperity, as militating against the theory of population advocated by Malthus and Mr. Mill, and the necessity those great writers contended for, of a prudential check to the potential rate of births. An unrestrained potential increase would have doubled the 16½ millions about 1856; at the present time there would, at the same rate, be about 50 millions of people in England and Wales, and, before the end of the century, the population of that part of the United Kingdom would exceed 100 millions. Either, therefore, the prudential check has been firmly opposed by some classes of the population to the potential increase, and has permitted that increase of prosperity which Mr. Forster assumes, or other checks, in the shape of death and infirmity, have acted instead of the prudential check, and demonstrated the urgent necessity for it. Another point, in connexion with wages, on which Mr. Forster's reasoning seems to need some explanation, relates to the agricultural labourers. He seems to throw out an opinion that there is yet another source, besides those which have been named, from which the wages of labour may be raised, namely, rent; but his language on the subject leaves much to be desired, to use a Gallicism, on the head of clearness. He says it is well there is here "a third class, namely, the landlords, who are able to enter into the question, and to act as mediators." But then he adds that a paper might well be devoted in the Section to the question, how far the rent paid for land affects the question of wages? The innuendo would appear to be that an increase of rural wages may be brought about by an abatement of rent; and we fail to see how that prospect places the landlords in a position to qualify them for the position of impartial mediators between farmers and

men. Another important subject discussed in the Section, the treatment of
which was not exhaustive in respect of either the economic or the statistical methods employed, was that of prices, and the rise in the cost of
living. Mr. Levi took the prices of the Metropolitan Meat Market for
his measure with respect to that article, adding, indeed, the expression of
an opinion, that the rise has been greater in the chief towns than in other
parts of the kingdom. The fact is, that the diffusion of steam communication in the last twenty-five years has raised the price of meat in country
places and remote parts of the kingdom much more than in the chief
towns, because it has raised it from a much lower point in the former to
something like the same price as in the latter localities. In many parts of
Ireland and Scotland, where, thirty years ago, the price of butcher's meat
averaged 3d. a pound, it is now not much below the London price; and
this equalization of prices, where the means of communication have been
equalized, is connected with the distribution of money over the world, in a
manner very necessary to be borne in mind in estimates both of past and
probably future changes in the cost of living. The prices of the Metropolitan Meat Market afford, for another reason, insufficient indications
of power of money. The price of mutton per pound in that market has
risen from 6.37, in 1863–7, to 7.62 in 1873. But in the same period the price
of a mutton-chop in a London railway refreshment room has risen from
6d. to 1s.; and, in fact, the rise in retail prices, on which the cost of living
really depends, is more accurately indicated by the latter figures than by
those which Mr. Levi has cited. It is obvious, too, that the rise in wages is
to a very large class, who have to pay servants' wages, an addition and not
a counterpoise to the increased cost of living arising from the rise of commodities. Mr. Levi, we might add, seems to have caused some confusion
of ideas, if he did not fall into it himself, with respect to the effect on the
price of necessaries and ordinary comforts of an increased expenditure on
luxuries. The consumption of better qualities of food and clothing would
naturally tend to raise the cost of the particular articles on which the
increased outlay took place. But an increased expenditure on luxuries,
such as seal-skin jackets, carriages, wine, tobacco, would, *caeteris paribus*,
diminish the outlay on other things, and would tend to a corresponding
fall in the prices of the latter. Had we, however, much fuller statistics than are forthcoming respecting the changes in prices throughout the
United Kingdom, we should still be unable to form a sound judgment
respecting the most important part of the question, namely, the probable
future range of prices, without a mass of additional information respecting
the causes which have acted on the supply of each article, and on the distribution of money as well as on its amount. And we have in this matter
an illustration of the defective character of that kind of statistical inquiry
which confines itself to the collection of a multitude of instances of facts,
without reference to causes. It must be allowed that the principles laid

down by the illustrious Quetelet rather tend to foster the error to which we advert. He assumed that by enlarging the number of instances, we eliminate chance and arrive at general and stable laws of conditions. But a great number of instances does not give us their law, or justify us in any positive conclusion respecting the future. New conditions, for example, have been acting on prices during the last two years, and mere tables of prices for the last twenty or ten years confound years in which those causes were in operation with years in which they were not.

We cannot close these few remarks and suggestions without thanking Mr. Forster, the eminent President of Section F, for the just, but not the less generous tribute which he paid to the great leader of economic science, whom the world has lately lost in Mr. John Stuart Mill.

WALTER BAGEHOT

(1826–1877)

Walter Bagehot was a banker, a student of social science, a journalist, an author, and a prominent man of affairs. His interests ranged from literature to law, and from economics to sociology.

Bagehot's chief economic works were: "International Coinage" (1869); "Lombard Street" (1873); "Depreciation of Silver" (1877); and "Economic Studies," a collection of essays, published in 1880. His other important works, in the fields of sociology and government, included "Physics and Politics"; "The English Constitution"; and "Essays on Parliamentary Reform."

Although Bagehot was influenced by Ricardo, he burst into open revolt against the abstract and absolute character of English classical economy. As an important member of the English historical school, his approach to the subject of economics was chiefly descriptive. He sought also to reconcile economics and sociology by stressing the importance of social institutions to the economist.

Walter Bagehot had a most facile pen. No student of sociology should fail to read "Physics and Politics," and no student of finance should deny himself the pleasure of "Lombard Street." For students of the history of economic thought, his little work entitled "Economic Studies" has most significance. From it have been taken the following selections.

WALTER BAGEHOT

SELECTIONS FROM "ECONOMIC STUDIES"

THE POSTULATES OF ENGLISH POLITICAL ECONOMY

But notwithstanding these triumphs, the position of our Political Economy is not altogether satisfactory. It lies rather dead in the public mind. Not only does it not excite the same interest as formerly, but there is not exactly the same confidence in it. Younger men either do not study it, or do not feel that it comes home to them, and that it matches with their most living ideas. New sciences have come up in the last few years with new modes of investigation, and they want to know what is the relation of economic science, as their fathers held it, to these new thoughts and these new instruments. They ask, often hardly knowing it, will this "science," as it claims to be, harmonise with what we now know to be sciences, or bear to be tried as we now try sciences? And they are not sure of the answer.

Abroad, as is natural, the revolt is more avowed. Indeed, though the Political Economy of Adam Smith penetrated deep into the continent, what has been added in England since has never penetrated equally; though if our "science" is true, the newer work required a greater intellectual effort, and is far more complete as a scientific achievement than anything which Adam Smith did himself. Political Economy, as it was taught by Ricardo, has had in this respect much the same fate as another branch of English thought of the same age, with which it has many analogies—jurisprudence as it was taught by Austin and Bentham; it has remained insular. I do not mean that it was not often read and understood; of course it was so, though it was often misread and misunderstood. But it never at all reigned abroad as it reigns here; never was really fully accepted in other countries as it was here where it arose. And no theory, economic or political, can now be both insular and secure; foreign thoughts come soon and trouble us; there will always be doubt here as to what is only believed here.

There are, no doubt, obvious reasons why English Political Economy should be thus unpopular out of England. It is known everywhere as the theory of "Free-trade," and out of England Free-trade is almost everywhere unpopular. Experience shows that no belief is so difficult to create, and no one so easy to disturb. The protectionist creed rises like a weed in every soil. "Why," M. Thiers was asked, "do you give these bounties to the French sugar refiners?" "I wish," he replied, "the tall chimneys to smoke." Every nation wishes prosperity for some conspicuous industry. At what cost to the consumer, by what hardship to less conspicuous industries, that prosperity is obtained, it does not care. Indeed, it hardly knows, it will never read, it will never apprehend the refined reasons which prove those evils and show how great they are; the visible picture of the smoking chimneys absorbs the whole mind. And, in many cases, the eagerness of England in the Free-trade cause only does that cause harm. Foreigners say: "You English traders are strong and rich; of course you wish to under-sell our traders, who are weak and poor. You have invented this Political Economy to enrich yourselves and ruin us; we will see that you shall not do so."

And that English Political Economy is more opposed to the action of Government in all ways than most such theories, brings it no accession of popularity. All Governments like to interfere; it elevates their position to make out that they can cure the evils of mankind. And all zealots wish they should interfere, for such zealots think they can and may convert the rulers and manipulate the State control; it is a distinct object to convert a definite man, and if he will not be convinced there is always a hope of his successor. But most zealots dislike to appeal to the mass of mankind; they know instinctively that it will be too opaque and impenetrable for them.

Still I do not believe that these are the only reasons why our English Political Economy is not estimated at its value abroad. I believe that this arises from its special characteristic, from that which constitutes its peculiar value, and, paradoxical as it may seem, I also believe that this same characteristic is likewise the reason why it is often not thoroughly understood in England itself. The science of Political Economy as we have it in England may be defined as the science of business, such as business is in large productive and trading communities. It is an analysis of that world so familiar to many Englishmen—the "great commerce" by which England has become rich. It assumes the principal facts which make that commerce possible, and as is the way of an abstract science it isolates and simplifies them; it detaches them from the confusion with which they are mixed in fact. And it deals too with the men who carry on that commerce, and who make it possible. It assumes a sort of human nature such as we see everywhere around us, and again it simplifies that human nature; it looks at one part of it only. Dealing with matters of "business," it assumes that man is actuated only by motives of business. It assumes that every man who makes anything, makes it for money, that he always makes that which brings him in most at least cost, and that he will make it in the way that will produce most and spend least; it assumes that every man who buys, buys with his whole heart, and that he who sells, sells with his whole heart, each wanting to gain all possible advantage. Of course we know that this is not so, that men are not like this; but we assume it for simplicity's sake, as an hypothesis. And this deceives many excellent people, for from deficient education they have very indistinct ideas what an abstract science is.

More competent persons, indeed, have understood that English Political Economists are not speaking of real men, but of imaginary ones; not of men as we see them, but of men as it is convenient to us to suppose they are. But even they often do not understand that the world which our Political Economists treat of, is a very limited and peculiar world also. They often imagine that what they read is applicable to all states of society, and to all equally, whereas it is only true of—and only proved as to—states of society in which commerce has largely developed, and where it has taken the form of development, or something near the form, which it has taken in England.

This explains why abroad the science has not been well understood. Commerce, as we have it in England, is not so full-grown anywhere else as it is here—at any rate, is not so outside the lands populated by the Anglo-Saxon race. Here it is not only a thing definite and observable, but about the most definite thing we have, the thing which it is most difficult to help seeing. But on the continent, though there is much that is like it, and though that much is daily growing more, there is nowhere the same pervading entity—the same patent, pressing, and unmistakable object.

And this brings out too the inherent difficulty of the subject—a difficulty which no other science, I think, presents in equal magnitude. Years ago, I heard Mr. Cobden say at a league meeting that "Political Economy was the highest study of the human mind, for that the physical sciences required by no means so hard an effort." An orator cannot be expected to be exactly precise, and of course Political Economy is in no sense the highest study of the mind—there are others which are much higher, for they are concerned with things much nobler than wealth or money; nor is it true that the effort of mind which Political Economy requires is nearly as great as that required for the abstruser theories of physical science, for the theory of gravitation, or the theory of natural selection; but, nevertheless, what Mr. Cobden meant had—as was usual with his first-hand mind—a great fund of truth. He meant that Political Economy—effectual Political Economy, Political Economy which in complex problems succeeds—is a very difficult thing; something altogether more abstruse and difficult, as well as more conclusive, than that which many of those who rush in upon it have a notion of. It is an abstract science which labours under a special hardship. Those who are conversant with its abstractions are usually without a true contact with its facts; those who are in contact with its facts have usually little sympathy with and little cognisance of its abstractions. Literary men who write about it are constantly using what a great teacher calls "unreal words"—that is, they are using expressions with which they have no complete vivid picture to correspond. They are like physiologists who have never dissected; like astronomers who have never seen the stars; and, in consequence, just when they seem to be reasoning at their best, their knowledge of facts falls short. Their primitive picture fails them, and their deduction altogether misses the mark—sometimes, indeed, goes astray so far that those who live and move among the facts boldly say that they cannot comprehend "how any one can talk such nonsense." Yet on the other hand, these people who live and move among the facts often, or mostly, cannot of themselves put together any precise reasonings about them. Men of business have a solid judgment—a wonderful guessing power of what is going to happen—each in his own trade; but they have never practised themselves in reasoning out their judgments and in supporting their guesses by argument: probably if they did so some of the finer and correcter parts of their anticipations would vanish. They are like the sensible lady to whom Coleridge said: "Madam, I accept your conclusion, but you must let me find the logic for it." Men of business can no more put into words much of what guides their life than they could tell another person how to speak their language. And so the "theory of business" leads a life of obstruction, because theorists do not see the business, and the men of business will not reason out the theories. Far from wondering that such a science is not completely perfect, we should rather wonder that it exists at all.

* * * * *

I have been careful not to use in this discussion of methods the phrase which is oftenest used, *viz.*, the Historical method, because there is an excessive ambiguity in it. Sometimes it seems what I have called the Enumerative, or "all-case" method; sometimes the "single-case" method; a most confusing double meaning, for by the mixture of the two, the mind is prevented from seeing the defects of either. And sometimes it has other meanings, with which, as I shall show, I have no quarrel, but rather much sympathy. Rightly conceived the historical method is no rival to the abstract method rightly conceived. But I shall be able to explain this better and less tediously at the end of these papers than I can at the beginning.

This conclusion is confirmed by a curious circumstance. At the very moment that our Political Economy is objected to in some quarters as too abstract, in others an attempt is made to substitute for it one which is more abstract still. Mr. Stanley Jevons, and M. Walras, of Lausanne, without communication and almost simultaneously, have worked out a "mathematical" theory of Political Economy;—and any one who thinks what is ordinarily taught in England objectionable, because it is too little concrete in its method, and looks too unlike life and business, had better try the new doctrine, which he will find to be much worse on these points than the old.

But I shall be asked, Do you then say that English Political Economy is perfect?—surely it is contrary to reason that so much difficulty should be felt in accepting a real science properly treated? At the first beginning no doubt there are difficulties in gaining a hearing for all sciences, but English Political Economy has long passed out of its first beginning? Surely, if there were not some intrinsic defect, it would have been firmly and coherently established, just as others are?

In this reasoning there is evident plausibility, and I answer that, in my judgment, there are three defects in the mode in which Political Economy has been treated in England, which have prevented people from seeing what it really is, and from prizing it at its proper value.

First,—It has often been put forward, not as a theory of the principal causes affecting wealth in *certain* societies, but as a theory of the principal, sometimes even of all, the causes affecting wealth in *every* society. And this has occasioned many and strong doubts about it. Travellers fresh from the sight, and historians fresh from the study, of peculiar and various states of society, look with dislike and disbelief on a single set of abstract propositions which claim, as they think, to be applicable to all such societies, and to explain a most important part of most of them. I cannot here pause to say how far particular English Economists have justified this accusation; I only say that, taking the whole body of them, there is much ground for it, and that in almost every one of them there is some ground. No doubt almost every one—every one of importance—has admitted that there is a "friction" in society which counteracts the effect of the causes treated of. But in general they leave their readers with the idea that, after all, this friction is but subordinate; that probably in the course of years it may be neglected; and, at any rate, that the causes assigned in the science of Political Economy, as they treat it, are the main and principal ones. Now I hold that these causes are only the main ones in a single kind of society—a society of grown-up competitive commerce, such as we have in England; that it is only in such societies that the other and counteractng forces can be set together under the minor head of "friction"; but that in other societies these other causes—in some cases one, and in some another—are the most effective ones, and that the greatest confusion arises if you try to fit on *un*-economic societies the theories only true of, and only proved as to, economic ones. In my judgment, we need—not that the authority of our Political Economy should be impugned, but that it should be *minimised;* that we should realise distinctly where it is established, and where not; that its sovereignty should be upheld, but its frontiers marked. And until this is done, I am sure that there will remain the same doubt and hesitation in many minds about the science that there is now.

Secondly,—I think in consequence of this defect of conception Economists have been far more abstract, and in consequence much more dry, than they need have been. If they had distinctly set before themselves that they were dealing only with the causes of wealth in a single set of societies, they might have effectively pointed their doctrines with facts from those societies. But, so long as the vision of universal theory vaguely floated before them they shrank from particular illustrations. Real societies are plainly so many and so unlike, that an instance from one kind does not show that the same thing exists in other societies; it rather raises in the mind a presumption that it does not exist there; and therefore speculators aiming at an all-embracing doctrine refrain from telling cases, because those cases are apt to work in unexpected ways, and to raise up the image not only of the societies in which the tenet illustrated is true, but also of the opposite group in which it is false.

Thirdly,—It is also in consequence, as I imagine, of this defective conception of their science, that English Economists have not been as fertile as they should have been in verifying it. They have been too content to remain in the "abstract," and to shrink from concrete notions, because they could not but feel that many of the most obvious phenomena of many nations did not look much like their abstractions. Whereas in the societies with which the science is really concerned, an almost infinite harvest of verification was close at hand, ready to be gathered in; and because it has not been used, much confidence in the science has been lost, and it is thought "to be like the stars which give no good light because they are so high."

Of course this reasoning implies that the boundaries of this sort of Political Economy are arbitrary, and might be fixed here or there. But this is already implied when it is said that Political Economy is an abstract science. All abstractions are arbitrary; they are more or less convenient fictions made by the mind for its own purposes. An abstract idea means a concrete fact or set of facts *minus* something thrown away. The fact or set of facts were made by nature; but how much you will throw aside of them and how much you will keep for consideration you settle for yourself. There may be any number of political economies according as the subject is divided off in one way or in another, and in this way all may be useful if they do not interfere with one another, or attempt to rule further than they are proved.

The particular Political Economy which I have been calling the English Political Economy, is that of which the first beginning was made by Adam Smith. But what he did was much like the rough view of the first traveller who discovers a country; he saw some great outlines well, but he mistook others and left out much. It was Ricardo who made the first map; who reduced the subjects into consecutive shape, and constructed what you can call a science. Few greater efforts of mind have been made, and not many have had greater fruits. From Ricardo the science passed to a whole set of minds—James Mill, Senior, Torrens, MacCulloch, and others, who busied themselves with working out his ideas, with elaborating and with completing them. For five and twenty years the English world was full of such discussions. Then Mr. J. S. Mill—the Mr. Mill whom the present generation know so well, and who has had so much influence—shaped with masterly literary skill the confused substance of those discussions into a compact whole. He did not add a great deal which was his own, and some of what is due to him does not seem to me of great value. But he pieced the subjects together, showed where what one of his predecessors had done had fitted on to that of another, and adjusted this science to other sciences according to the notions of that time. To many students his book is the Alpha and Omega of Political Economy; they know little of what was before, and imagine little which can come after in the way of improvement. But it is not given to any writer to occupy such a place. Mr. Mill would have been the last to claim it for himself. He well knew, that, taking his own treatise as the standard, what he added to Political Economy was not a ninth of what was due to Ricardo, and that for much of what is new in his book he was rather the *Secrétaire de la Rédaction*, expressing and formulating the current views of a certain world, than producing by original thought from his own brain. And his remoteness from mercantile life, and I should say his enthusiastic character, eager after things far less sublunary than money, made him little likely to give finishing touches to a theory of "the great commerce." In fact he has not done so; much yet remains to be done in it as in all sciences. Mr. Mill, too, seems to me open to the charge of having widened the old Political Economy either too much or not enough. If it be as I hold, a theory proved of, and applicable to, particular societies only, much of what is contained in Mr. Mill's book should not be there; if it is, on the contrary, a theory holding good for all societies, as far as they are concerned with wealth, much more ought to be there, and much which is there should be guarded and limited. English Political Economy is not a finished and completed theory, but the first lines of a great analysis which has worked out much, but which still leaves much unsettled and unexplained.

There is nothing capricious, we should observe, in this conception of Political Economy, nor, though it originated in England, is there anything specially English in it. It is the theory of commerce, as commerce tends more and more to be when capital increases and competition grows. England was the first—or one of the first—countries to display these characteristics in such vigour and so isolated as to suggest a separate analysis of them, but as the world goes on, similar characteristics are being evolved in one society after another. A similar money market, a similar competing trade based on large capital, gradually tends to arise in all countries. As "men of the world" are the same everywhere, so the great commerce is the same everywhere. Local peculiarities and ancient modi-

fying circumstances fall away in both cases; and it is of this one and uniform commerce which grows daily, and which will grow, according to
every probability, more and more, that English Political Economy aspires
to be the explanation.

And our Political Economy does not profess to prove this growing
world to be a good world—far less to be the best. Abroad the necessity of
contesting socialism has made some writers use the conclusions brought
out by our English science for that object. But the aim of that science is
far more humble; it says these and these forces produce these and these
effects, and there it stops. It does not profess to give a moral judgment on
either; it leaves it for a higher science, and one yet more difficult, to
pronounce what ought and what ought not to be.

The first thing to be done for English Political Economy, as I hold, is
to put its aim right. So long as writers on it do not clearly see, and as
readers do not at all see, the limits of what they are analysing, the result
will not satisfy either. The science will continue to seem what to many
minds it seems now, proved perhaps but proved *in nubibus;* true, no doubt,
somehow and somewhere, but that somewhere a *terra incognita,* and that
somehow an unknown quantity. As a help in this matter I propose to
take the principal assumptions of Political Economy one by one, and to
show, not exhaustively, for that would require a long work, but roughly,
where each is true and where it is not. We shall then find that our Political
Economy is not a questionable thing of unlimited extent, but a most
certain and useful thing of limited extent. By marking the frontier of our
property we shall learn its use, and we shall have a positive and reliable
basis for estimating its value.

The Preliminaries of Political Economy

It is on account of its abstract character that Political Economy
is often, and justly described, as a science of "tendencies" only; that is,
the object of it is to work out and ascertain the result of certain great
forces, as if these alone operated, and as if nothing else had any effect
in the matter. But as in matter of fact many other forces have an effect,
the computed results of the larger isolated forces will never exactly happen; they will only, as it is said, tend more or less to happen; that is, they
happen more and more nearly in proportion as the resisting and perturb-
ing causes in each case happen to be less and less.

The very refined nature of the modern science of Political Economy
has naturally led to many mistakes about it. The mere idea of such a
science has evidently never crossed the minds of many able writers, and
persons who have given but slight consideration to the matter are much
puzzled. Analogous sciences of physical subjects are, as has been said, easy
to find, but illustrations from them do not tell much where effectual
description of Political Economy is most wanted. A science occupied with

human things, and professedly with a part of human things profoundly interesting, awakens a great curiosity among multitudes of little cultivation. They begin to think about it, and to read about it, and the better the books they read, the more likely are they to be puzzled by what they find. They know that they are reading words which are constantly used in common life, and about things resembling, at least, those of that life, but nevertheless the reasonings and the conclusions do not seem to belong to real life at all. Such persons know nothing about statics or dynamics; and any attempt to explain the nature of statics or dynamics, is only explaining *obscurum per obscurius*. As might be expected, the worst offenders are the uncultured moralists. They see all manner of reasonings framed, and of conclusions drawn, apparently about subjects with which morality itself is concerned deeply—about (say) industry and wealth, population and poverty, and they never dream that there is anything peculiar about these conclusions. They apply the "rules of morality" to them at once; they ask: "Is argument B true of good persons? Would not conclusion C augment wickedness?" whereas, in fact, the economic writers under consideration did not mean (and rightly did not mean) to deal with ethics at all. They only evolved a hypothesis; they did not intend that their arguments should be thought to be taken from real life, or that their conclusions should be roughly, and as they stood, applied to real life. They considered not the whole of actual human nature, but only a part of it. They dealt not with man, the moral being, but with man, the money-making animal.

Naturally, too, the cultivators of the abstract science itself (even those who fully understood its peculiar nature), did not always in practice remember the remoteness to practice of that nature. On the contrary, they rushed forth into the world with hasty recommendations to instant action; whereas the very justification of their reasonings, and the very ground of their axioms, was the necessity of beginning the investigation of the subject in a simple theory, and far away from the complexities of practice and action. But so much are the practical impulses of man stronger than his theoretical tastes, that the cultivators of an abstract science are always in great danger of forgetting its abstract nature; they rush and act on it at once. In the abstract physical sciences there is an effectual penalty. A person who acted on abstract dynamics would soon break his head, but in mental and physical sciences unhappily there are no instant tests of failure. Whatever happens, a man can always argue that he was right; and thus an abstract science of human things is more delicate to handle, and more likely to be misused, than a similar science of external nature.

A sort of uncertainty likewise seems, even in the better-informed minds, to creep over the subject. If it is so remote from practice, they say, how can you test it, and how can you tell that it is true? But this is exactly so also in the corresponding physical sciences. One of the shrewd-est observers of intellectual matters of the generation, the late Sir G. C. Lewis, used to say: "My experience in this office" (he was then Secretary of State for War) "has convinced me that when you come to practice, physics are just as uncertain as metaphysics. The abstract theory of physics is unquestionably much more complete, but if you want to deal with an instance in life, you will always find that there is a 'tension,' or a 'friction,' or some other cause, which is not accurately measured and does not figure in the abstract theory. And this is the reason why, on all such questions, scientific evidence is so conflicting. You can always obtain an eminent engineer on any side to set against an eminent engineer on the other side, because the scientific and certain part of the subject is not the whole, and there still remains an imperfectly explored *residuum* on which there may be different opinions." All this is as true of Political Economy as of any physical science; its deductions may be incontro-vertible, and its results precisely true, whenever its assumptions are true, but these results will be very imperfect guides, wherever those assumptions are impaired by contradictory matter.

On the other side, however, it should also be said that "abstract" Political Economy is not by any means the unnatural thing which, from the account of it on paper, and the description of its difficulties, it would seem to be. Many people on the matter have "talked prose all their lives without knowing it"; many people have given admirable arguments on Political Economy, and have been more or less precisely aware of the difference of their assumptions from those of the real world, though they have never studied the specially abstract science, and could have given no sufficient delineation of it. The notion of investigating how much money persons would make, who simply wished to make it, and how they would best do so, is a very simple idea. The desire for wealth—using wealth in the largest sense, so as to include not only the means of luxury, but the means of subsistence—is so preponderant in very many minds, that it is very easy, if necessary, to regard it as the sole object. As far as people are what we now always call men of business, money, the thing they look for and the thing they want, is their sole object, and in that sense of the phrase, Political Economy may be fairly called the science of "business."

On that account, in some very large scenes of our present English life, Political Economy is exactly true. The primary assumption on which it rests is precisely realised. On the Stock Exchange everybody does act from a love of money; men come there to make it, and they try to make as much of it as they can. Of Lombard Street the same may be said; the pecuniary phenomena of Lombard Street may be investigated with quite sufficient accuracy, on the assumption that bankers come there only to make money, and when there, make as much of it as they can.

All markets are scenes nearly similar; so long as they are at the market all dealers try to make the best bargain they can. As the principal nations of the world at present are nations of business—commercial nations— and as the mass of men in such nations are mainly occupied in business, it follows that with respect to those nations a simple analysis of the unchecked consequences of the "business motive" will be a near approximation to a large part of their life, though it will not be a perfect account of their complete career, for there is very much also in every nation besides business and besides money—but it will be a useful hint to a predominant characteristic of that career. Having investigated the effects of this principal motive, we may when we please, and as far as it is necessary, investigate the effects of the almost infinite number of the secondary and interfering motives.

As, too, it is at present necessary for all nations to be rich in order to be influential in the world, it follows further, that an account of the commercial motive of action, taken by itself, is, as the world now stands, an analysis of the results of a principal ingredient in the days that are gone by, when poor barbarians, if warlike, were more powerful than rich civilised people. The times are gone by when civilisation enervated energy, or when wealth impeded valour. At present, courage without money is courage without guns; and courage without guns is useless. Political Economy traces, in an abstract way, the effects of the desire to be rich, and nations must now-a-days abound in that passion if they are to have much power or much respect in the world.

On the other hand, no intellectual attempt can be more absurd than the attempt to apply the conclusions of our Political Economy to the lives of nations at an non-commercial stage of their existence. A great military nation, based on slavery, like the Romans; a nation bound by fixed customs like so many Oriental nations; tribes in a state of barbarism —are not guided principally by the commercial spirit. The money-getting element is a most subordinate one in their minds; its effects are very subordinate ones in their lives. As the commercial element is all but necessary to considerable combinations of men, that element will amost always have effects, and usually important effects, in the destiny of these combinations. But only in communities where the commercial element is the greatest element, will these effects be the greatest. In so far as nations are occupied in "buying and selling," in so far will Political Economy, the exclusive theory of men buying and selling, come out right, and be true of them.

But it will be good as far as it goes, and, though it is not my business to say it, I think it will be the fault of the writer if the curious interest of the facts does not lead many readers to a further study of the subject.

And, though what has been explained is the principal difference between the hypothetical science of Political Economy and the **real**

world, it is by no means the only difference. Just as this science takes
an abstract and one-sided view of man, who is one of its subjects, so it
also takes an abstract and one-sided view of wealth, which is its other
subject. Wealth is infinitely various; as the wants of human nature are
almost innumerable, so the kinds of wealth are various. Why men want
so many things is a great subject fit for inquiry. Which of them it would
be wise for men to want more of, and which of them it would be wise to
want less of—are also great subjects equally fit. But with these subjects
Political Economy does not deal at all; it leaves the first to the meta-
physician, who has to explain, if he can, the origin and the order of human
wants; and the second to the moralist, who is to decide, to the best of
his ability, which of these tastes are to be encouraged, and when—which
is to be discouraged, and when. The only peculiarity of wealth with
which the economist is concerned is its *differentia specifica*—that which
makes it wealth. To do so it must gratify some want of man, or it would
not be desirable, or it would not be wealth. But whence that want comes,
whether from a low part of man, or from a high, is to the economist
immaterial; whether it is a desirable want for man to gratify he cares as
little, so long as that gratification does not hurt man as a wealth-producing machine. He regards a pot of beer and a picture, a book of religion
and a pack of cards, as all equally "wealth," and therefore, for his
purpose, equally worthy of regard. The only division of wealth in his
mind is, if I may use the words, the division between sterile and not
sterile. Some things will help men to make new things; some things will
induce men to work and make new things; both these classes of things
are in the eyes of the economist capital or reproductive. On the other
hand, other things have no similar reproductive power; if they were taken
out of the world all work would go on with equal efficiency, and as many
things would be produced. And these last are, in the eyes of the economist,
unproductive opulence, just as the first were productive capital.

*   *   *   *   *

And, lastly, Political Economy declines to investigate all the causes
which determine the rate of increase of man, and assumes an avowedly
incomplete and approximate formula as to it. From the very nature of
the case, Political Economy must do this. The causes which regulate the
increase of mankind are little less than all the causes outward and inward
which determine human action. Climate, social customs, political government, inherited race-nature, and other things beside, affect, as we all
know, the rate at which population grows. Political Economy would have
to discuss half physiology, half the science of government, and half
several other sciences too, if it attempted to investigate the real laws
which regulate the multiplication of mankind; it has necessarily to make
an assumption, to assume as a dictum some approximation to the complex

truth, which is at once simple enough to be manageable, and true enough to be useful. Political Economy, therefore, assumes that in any particular society the power of parents to produce children exceeds the power to provide for them in what those parents think sufficient comfort; whence it comes that either parents must not produce all the children that they can, or that, if they do, the standard of comfort in the population must deteriorate, and if the multiplication continue, and the deterioration augment, that the population must die off. There is no difficulty in showing that this assumption embodies accurately enough the ordinary experience of mankind as history records it, and as present facts evince it. An immense "reserve power" of multiplication is certainly to be found in most countries, which is kept down by one obstacle or other, but which is ready to start forward when that obstacle is removed. No two countries can differ more in every respect important for this purpose than Great Britain and British India. Yet both of them seem to prove the same result. At home, the people of Great Britain increase only at the rate of 1.01 per cent. per annum, and double in fifty-eight years; but if you take the very same population to the Colonies or the United States, it is believed to increase at a much more rapid rate, and to double itself more rapidly, though the relative increase is not nearly so great as is sometimes assumed when no sufficient account is taken of the continual immigration into those countries. The lesson of Hindostan is still more remarkable. The population of the Peninsula is ordinarily supposed not to have augmented since the time of Alexander; there is conclusive evidence that for centuries preceding the English conquest it augmented very slowly, if at all. But now, under the influence of long peace, and long good government, the population is beginning to augment rapidly. In the North-West Provinces, where the *data* are the best, it is said to be augmenting almost as rapidly as the population of Great Britain. Here, as before, there is an immense acceleration of the rate of multiplication, because a repressive force has, as before, been withdrawn. No one can doubt that the same experiment would have a like result in other cases.

It may be said that out of Europe there is very much unoccupied land, and that even if Europe produced all the people it could, those people might be sent thither. But emigration on such a scale, though imaginable in speculation, is not possible in practice. To create very rapidly new colonies, or to extend very rapidly old ones, requires the migration not only of persons but of capital. You must send thither the means of subsistence if the emigrants are to be subsisted, and the means of employment if they are to be employed, and capital will not go unless you pay it. It must have its regular percentage; and as yet no capital employed in founding colonies—no capital, that is, of a founding company, or of founders as such—has ever paid a farthing. The capital so expended has been a great benefit to the emigrants and to the colony, but it has never paid a dividend; on the contrary, the whole capital has commonly been lost. There are no means by which owners at home can be sure of their interest, nor will very many owners of capital go themselves to the colonies, only because it would much help the poor there if they did so. Capital must be propelled by self-interest; it cannot be enticed by benevolence. The sudden foundation of a colony so huge as to contain all the *possible* children—all those that might be in excess of those which are—is impossible; the bare idea of it is ridiculous.

ARNOLD TOYNBEE

(1852–1883)

Toynbee's work was twofold: first that of a writer on economics, and second that of a social reformer. His early death, at the age of thirty-one, cut short a useful life in service to his fellow men and destroyed the intellectual promise of a brilliant career.

As an economist, Toynbee was an important figure in the British Historical School. His only existing work is a volume of lectures on "The Industrial Revolution." In it are included also lectures on "Ricardo and the Old Political Economy," as well as some popular addresses on "Wages and Natural Law," "Industry and Democracy," and "Are Radicals Socialists?"

Toynbee's chief aim was to show how each writer was influenced by his own environment, and how each school of thought grew out of its particular historical setting. This viewpoint is old today, but it was novel then.

In the second place, Toynbee sought to bring economics from the clouds down to the earth. In short, he sought to supplement theory with fact, and to test statistically the truth of some deductive principles. Indeed, he even dared to do battle with the great Ricardian law of wages. He succeeded in demonstrating that the "iron law of wages" could not stand historical criticism. His method of attack was not that of deductive logic, but rather the accumulation of numerous, reliable statistics as to the course of wages of the English workingman during the past generation or more. The plain facts of the case were that real wages had risen. They had not remained constant at either a bare subsistence or a minimum standard level.

The following selections are taken from "The Industrial Revolution" (1884). The student is asked to note Toynbee's point of view, his method of approach, his references to other writers, and, finally, his specific arguments.

Toynbee was important also as a social worker. Indeed, he was a pioneer in what was later called settlement work. Toynbee had a sincere love for the workingman, and a burning passion for social reform. He was particularly interested in labor problems, and frequently addressed meetings of the workers. To him the war against poverty was a sacred crusade. He believed that economic inequality should be reduced and that the social effects of poverty could be mitigated.

ARNOLD TOYNBEE

SELECTIONS FROM "THE INDUSTRIAL REVOLUTION OF THE EIGHTEENTH CENTURY IN ENGLAND"

CHAPTER I. INTRODUCTORY

Division of the subject.—Advantages of combining the study of History and Political Economy.—The deductive method.—The historical method.— Importance of a discussion of method.—Laws and precepts relative.—The social problems of the present to be borne in mind in studying the history of the past.

The subject of these lectures is the Industrial and Agrarian Revolution at the end of the eighteenth and beginning of the nineteenth centuries. The course is divided into three parts. The first deals with Adam Smith and the England of his time. It will describe England on the eve of the industrial revolution, and the system of regulation and protection of industry as it existed in 1760. It will give also an outline of Smith's book, its aims and character, and especially his theory of trade. The second part will group itself round the work of Malthus, who dealt not so much with the causes of wealth as with the causes of poverty, with the distribution of wealth rather than with its production. It will describe England in the midst of the Industrial Revolution, and will inquire into the problem of pauperism and the subjects connected with it. The third part will be associated with the name of Ricardo, and will deal with England at the time of peace. It will discuss the doctrine of rent and wages together with certain theories of economic progress, *and will cover the questions of currency, so much agitated at that period, and the history of the commercial and financial changes which followed the Peace.*

I have chosen the subject because it was in this period that modern Political Economy took its rise. It has been a weakness of the science, as pursued in England, that it has been too much dissociated from history. Adam Smith and Malthus, indeed, had historical minds; but the form of modern text books is due to Ricardo, whose mind was entirely unhistorical. Yet there is a double advantage in combining the two studies. In the first place Political Economy is better understood by this means. Abstract propositions are seen in a new light when studied in relation to the facts which were before the writer at the time when he formulated them. So regarded they are at once more vivid and less likely to mislead. Ricardo becomes painfully interesting when we read the history of his time. And, in the second place, History also is better understood when studied in connection with Political Economy; for the latter not only teaches us in reading History to look out for the right kind of facts, but enables us to explain many phenomena like those attending the introduction of enclosures and machinery, or the effects of different systems of currency, which without its assistance would remain unintelligible. The careful deductive reasoning, too, which Political Economy teaches is of great importance to the historian, and the habits of mind acquired from it are even more valuable than the knowledge of principles which it gives, especially to students of facts, who might otherwise be overwhelmed by the mass of their materials.

Of late years, however, there has been a steady sustained attack upon the abstract Deductive Method of Political Economy pursued by Ricardo and Mill, and an attempt to set up historical investigation in its place as the only true method of economic inquiry. This attack rests on a misconception of the function of the Deductive Method. The best exposition of the place of Abstract Political Economy is to be found in Bagehot's *Economic Studies*. Bagehot points out that this abstract science holds good only upon certain assumptions, but though the assumptions are often not entirely correct, the results may yet be approximately true. Thus the economists, firstly, regard only one part of man's nature, and treat him simply as a money-making animal; secondly, they disregard the influence of custom, and only take account of competition. Certain laws are laid down under these assumptions; as, for instance, that the rate of wages always tends to an equality, the permanent difference obtaining in various employments being only sufficient to balance the favourable or unfavourable circumstances attending each of them—a law which is only true after a certain stage of civilisation and in so far as the acquisition of wealth is the sole object of men. Such hypothetical laws, though leading only to rough conclusions, are yet useful in giving us a point of view from which to observe and indicate the existence of strong overmastering tendencies. Advocates of the Historical Method, like Mr. Cliffe Leslie, therefore, go too far when they condemn the Deductive Method as radically false. There is no real opposition between the two. The apparent opposition is due to a wrong use of deduction; to a neglect on the part of those employing it to examine closely their assumptions and to bring their conclusions to the test of fact; to arguments based on premises which are not only not verified but absolutely untrue (as in the wage-fund theory); and generally to the failure to combine induction with deduction. But this misuse of the method does not imply any radical faultiness in it. The right method in any particular case must be largely determined by the nature of the problem. Neither is it fair to make abstract Political Economy responsible for the confusion in many minds between its laws and the precepts which are based on them. It is a pure science, and its end is knowledge. But the Political Economy of the press and the platform is a practical science, that is, a body of rules and maxims to guide conduct. Journalists and members of Parliament confound the laws of the pure science with the maxims of the practical science. It was thus that Mr. Gladstone in the Land Act controversy of 1881 was constantly accused of violating the laws of Political Economy. It was impossible for Mr. Gladstone to do any such thing. The laws of Political Economy can no more be violated than those of physical science. What the journalists meant was that he had departed from a great economic precept—that which recommends freedom of contract.

The Historical Method pursues a different line of investigation. It examines the actual causes of economic development and considers the influence of institutions, such as the mediaeval guilds, our present landlaws, or the political constitution of any given country, in determining the distribution of wealth. Without the aid of the Historical Method it would be impossible, for instance, to understand why one-half of the land in the United Kingdom is owned by 2512 persons.

And not only does it investigate the stages of economic development in a given country, but it compares them with those which have obtained in other countries and times, and seeks by such comparison to discover laws of universal application. Take, as an instance of the discoveries of this Comparative Political Economy, the tendency which Sir H. Maine and M. de Laveleye have pointed out to pass from collective to individual ownership of land. This is a law which is true of nearly all civilised countries. We must be careful, however, not to generalise too hastily in these matters. A clever pamphlet lately published in Dublin appeals to another generalisation of Sir H. Maine—"Maine's Law," as it is denominated—in condemnation of recent legislation. "Sir H. Maine," says the writer, "in his *Ancient Law* has remarked that the movement of all progressive societies has hitherto been a movement from status to contract. The demand of this agitation is that Ireland should be legislatively declared a retrograde society, and that the social movement should be from contract back again to status." "Is it expedient," asks another, "to reform our laws so as to assimilate them to those in use among nations of an inferior social development?" A deeper study of existing civilisation in England, and of other civilisations, past and present, would have shown that the step was not a retrograde one—that whilst the sphere of contract has been widening, it has been also narrowing, and that such a condition of things as we see in Ireland has never existed anywhere else without deep social misery, outrage, and disturbance. Custom or law or public opinion, or all three, have intervened in the past, and will intervene in the future. It is true that there is a movement from status to contract; yet if we look closely, we find that the State has over and over again had to interfere to restrict the power of individuals in which this movement results. The real course of movement has been first from status to contract, then from contract to a new kind of status determined by the law—or, in other words, from unregulated to regulated contract.

The Historical Method is also of value because it makes us see where economic laws and precepts are relative. The old economists were wont to speak as if these laws and precepts were universal. Free trade, for instance, is a sound policy, no doubt, for England, and for all nations at a certain stage of development; but it is open to any one to say that free trade is only good under certain conditions.

No English economist, it is true, has dared to say this. Mr. Jevons, to take an example, would admit restrictions only for considerations of the most paramount importance. But it is an unjustifiable prejudgment of the question to lay down that this policy must be wise at all times and places. I do not mean to assert, however, that there are not some laws which are universally true, such as the law of diminishing returns.

This discussion about method may seem barren, but it is not really so. Take such a question as the functions of the State. Mr. Senior spent much time in attempting to discover an universal formula which should define their proper limit all the world over. Such an attempt must be abandoned. The proper limits of Government interference are relative to the nature of each particular state and the stage of its civilisation. It is a matter of great importance at the present day for us to discover what these limits are in our own case, for administration bids fair to claim a large share of our attention in the future. It would be well if, in studying the past, we could always bear in mind the problems of the present, and go to that past to seek large views of what is of lasting importance to the human race. It is an old complaint that histories leave out of sight those vital questions which are connected with the condition of the people. The French Revolution has indeed profoundly modified our views of history, but much still remains to be done in that direction. If I could persuade some of those present to study Economic History, to follow out the impulse originally given by Malthus to the study of the history of the mass of the people, I should be indeed glad. Party historians go to the past for party purposes; they seek to read into the past the controversies of the present. You must pursue facts for their own sake, but penetrated with a vivid sense of the problems of your own time. This is not a principle of perversion, but a principle of selection. You must have some principle of selection, and you could not have a better one than to pay special attention to the history of the social problems which are agitating the world now, for you may be sure that they are problems not of temporary but of lasting importance.

Chapter VIII. The Chief Features of the Revolution

Growth of economic science.—Competition.—Its uses and abuses.—The symptoms of the Industrial Revolution.—Rapid growth of population.—Its relative density in North and South.—The agrarian revolution.—Enclosures.—Consolidation of farms and agricultural improvements.—The revolution in manufacturers.—The factory system.—Expansion of trade.—Rise in rents.—Change in the relative position of classes.

The essence of the Industrial Revolution is the substitution of competition for the mediaeval regulations which had previously controlled the production and distribution of wealth. On this account it is not only one of the most important facts of English history, but Europe owes to it the growth of two great systems of thought—Economic Science, and its antithesis, Socialism. The development of Economic Science in England has four chief landmarks, each connected with the name of one of the four great English economists. The first is the publication of Adam Smith's *Wealth of Nations* in 1776, in which he investigated the causes of wealth and aimed at the substitution of industrial freedom for a system of restriction. The production of wealth, not the welfare of man, was what Adam Smith had primarily before his mind's eye; in his own words, "the great object of the Political Economy of every country is to increase the riches and power of that country." His great book appeared on the eve of the Industrial Revolution. A second stage in the growth of the science is marked by Malthus's *Essay on Population*, published in 1798, which may be considered the product of that revolution, then already in full swing. Adam Smith had concentrated all his attention on a large production; Malthus directed his inquires, not to the causes of wealth but to the causes of poverty, and found them in his theory of population. A third stage is marked by Ricardo's *Principles of Political Economy and Taxation*, which appeared in 1817, and in which Ricardo sought to ascertain the laws of the distribution of wealth. Adam Smith had shown how wealth could be produced under a system of industrial freedom, Ricardo showed how wealth is distributed under such a system, a problem which could not have occurred to any one before his time. The fourth stage is marked by John Stuart Mill's *Principles of Political Economy*, published in 1848, Mill himself asserted that "the chief merit of his treatise" was the distinction drawn between the laws of production and those of distribution, and the problem he tried to solve was, how wealth *ought to be* distributed. A great advance was made by Mill's attempt to show what was and what was not inevitable under a system of free competition. In it we see the influence which the rival system of Socialism was already beginning to exercise upon the economists. The whole spirit of Mill's book is quite different from that of any economic works which had up to his time been written in England. Though a re-statement of Ricardo's system, it contained the admission that the distribution of wealth is the result of "particular social arrangements," and it recognised that competition alone is not a satisfactory basis of society.

Competition, heralded by Adam Smith, and taken for granted by Ricardo and Mill, is still the dominant idea of our time; though since the publication of the *Origin of Species*, we hear more of it under the name of the "struggle for existence." I wish here to notice the fallacies involved in the current arguments on this subject. In the first place it is assumed that all competition is a competition for existence. This is not true. There is a great difference between a struggle for mere existence and a struggle for a particular kind of existence. For instance, twelve men are struggling for employment in a trade where there is only room for eight; four are driven out of that trade, but they are not trampled out of existence. A good deal of competition merely decides what kind of work a man is to do; though of course when a man can only do one kind of work, it may easily become a struggle for bare life. It is next assumed that this struggle for existence is a law of nature, and that therefore all human interference with it is wrong. To that I answer that the whole meaning of civilisation is interference with this brute struggle. We intend to modify the violence of the fight, and to prevent the weak being trampled under foot.

Competition, no doubt, has its uses. Without competition no progress would be possible, for progress comes chiefly from without; it is external pressure which forces men to exert themselves. Socialists, however, maintain that this advantage is gained at the expense of an enormous waste of human life and labour, which might be avoided by regulation. But here we must distinguish between competition in production and competition in distribution, a difference recognised in modern legislation, which has widened the sphere of contract in the one direction, while it has narrowed it in the other. For the struggle of men to outvie one another in production is beneficial to the community; their struggle over the division of the joint produce is not. The stronger side will dictate its own terms; and as a matter of fact, in the early days of competition the capitalists used all their power to oppress the labourers, and drove down wages to starvation point. This kind of competition has to be checked; there is no historical instance of its having lasted long without being modified either by combination or legislation, or both. In England both remedies are in operation, the former through Trades-Unions, the latter through factory legislation. In the past other remedies were applied. It is this desire to prevent the evils of competition that affords the true explanation of the fixing of wages by Justices of the Peace, which seemed to Ricardo a remnant of the old system of tyranny in the interests of the strong. Competition, we have now learnt, is neither good nor evil in itself; it is a force which has to be studied and controlled; it may be compared to a stream whose strength and direction have to be observed, that embankments may be thrown up within which it may do its work harmlessly and beneficially.

But at the period we are considering it came to be believed in as a gospel, and, the idea of necessity being superadded, economic laws deduced from the assumption of universal unrestricted competition were converted into practical precepts, from which it was regarded as little short of immoral to depart.

Coming to the facts of the Industrial Revolution, the first thing that strikes us is the far greater rapidity which marks the growth of population. Before 1751 the largest decennial increase, so far as we can calculate from our imperfect materials, was 3 per cent. For each of the next three decennial periods the increase was 6 per cent.; then between 1781 and 1791 it was 9 per cent.; between 1791 and 1801, 11 per cent.; between 1801 and 1811, 14 per cent.; between 1811 and 1821, 18 per cent. This is the highest figure ever reached in England, for since 1815 a vast emigration has been always tending to moderate it; between 1815 and 1880 over eight millions (including Irish) have left our shores. But for this our normal rate of increase would be 16 or 18 instead of 12 per cent. in every decade.

Next we notice the relative and positive decline in the agricultural population. In 1811 it constituted 35 per cent. of the whole population of Great Britain; in 1821, 33 per cent.; in 1831, 28 per cent. And at the same time its actual numbers have decreased. In 1831 there were 1,243,057 adult males employed in agriculture in Great Britain; in 1841 there were 1,207,989. In 1851 the whole number of persons engaged in agriculture in England was 2,084,153; in 1861 it was 2,010,454, and in 1871 it was 1,657,138. Contemporaneously with this change, the centre of density of population has shifted from the Midlands to the North; there are at the present day 458 persons to the square mile in the countries north of the Trent, as against 312 south of the Trent. And we have lastly to remark the change in the relative population of England and Ireland. Of the total population of the three kingdoms, Ireland had in 1821 32 per cent., in 1881 only 14.6 per cent.

An agrarian revolution plays as large part in the great industrial change of the end of the eighteenth century as does the revolution in manufacturing industries, to which attention is more usually directed. Our next inquiry must therefore be: What were the agricultural changes which led to this noticeable decrease in the rural population? The three most effective causes were: the destruction of the common-field system of cultivation; the enclosure, on a large scale, of common and waste lands; and the consolidation of small farms into large. We have already seen that while between 1710 and 1760 some 300,000 acres were enclosed, between 1760 and 1843 nearly 7,000,000 underwent the same process. Closely connected with the enclosure system was the substitution of large for small farms. In the first half of the century Laurence, though approving of consolidation from an economic point of view, had thought that the odium attaching to an evicting landlord would operate as a strong check upon it. But these scruples had now disappeared. Eden in 1795 notices how constantly the change was effected, often accompanied by the conversion of arable to pasture; and relates how in a certain Doretshire village he found two farms where twenty years ago there had been thirty. The process went on uninterruptedly into the present century. Cobbett, writing in 1826, says: "In the parish of Burghclere one single farmer holds, under Lord Carnarvon, as one farm, the lands that those now living remember to have formed fourteen farms, bringing up in a respectable way fourteen families." The consolidation of farms reduced the number of farmers, while the enclosures drove the labourers off the land, as it became impossible for them to exist without their rights of pasturage for sheep and geese on common lands.

Severely, however, as these changes bore upon the rural population, they wrought, without doubt, distinct improvement from an agricultural point of view. They meant the substitution of scientific for unscientific culture. "It has been found," says Laurence, "by long experience, that common or open fields are great hindrances to the public good, and to the honest improvement which every one might make of his own." Enclosures brought an extension of arable cultivation and the tillage of inferior soils; and in small farms of 40 to 100 acres, where the land was exhausted by repeated corn crops, the farm buildings of clay and mud walls and three-fourths of the estate often saturated with water, consolidation into farms of 100 to 500 acres meant rotation of crops, leases of nineteen years, and good farm buildings. The period was one of the great agricultural advance; the breed of cattle was improved, rotation of crops was generally introduced, the steam-plough was invented, agricultural societies were instituted. In one respect alone the change was injurious. In consequence of the high prices of corn which prevailed during the French war, some of the finest permanent pastures were broken up. Still, in spite of this, it was said in 1813 that during the previous ten years agricultural produce had increased by one-fourth, and this was an increase upon a great increase in the preceding generation.

Passing to manufactures, we find here the all-prominent fact to be the substitution of the factory for the domestic system, the consequence of the mechanical discoveries of the time. Four great inventions altered the character of the cotton manufacture; the spinning-jenny, patented by Hargreaves in 1770; the water-frame, invented by Arkwright the year before; Crompton's mule introduced in 1779, and the self-acting mule, first invented by Kelly in 1792, but not brought into use till Roberts improved it in 1825. None of these by themselves would have revolutionised the industry. But in 1769—the year in which Napoleon and Wellington were born—James Watt took out his patent for the steam-engine. Sixteen years later it was applied to the cotton manufacture.

In 1785 Boulton and Watt made an engine for a cotton-mill at Papple-wick in Notts, and in the same year Arkwright's patent expired. These two facts taken together mark the introduction of the factory system. But the most famous invention of all, and the most fatal to domestic industry, the power-loom, though also patented by Cartwright in 1785, did not come into use for several years, and till the power-loom was introduced the workman was hardly injured. At first, in fact, machinery raised the wages of spinners and weavers owing to the great prosperity it brought to the trade. In fifteen years the cotton trade trebled itself; from 1788 to 1803 has been called its "golden age"; for, before the power-loom but after the introduction of the mule and other mechanical improvements by which for the first time yarn sufficiently fine for muslin and a variety of other fabrics was spun, the demand became such that "old barns, carthouses, out-buildings of all descriptions were repaired, windows broke through the old blank walls, and all fitted up for loom-shops; new weavers' cottages with loom-shops arose in every direction, every family bringing home weekly from 40 to 120 shillings per week." At a later date, the condition of the workman was very different. Meanwhile, the iron industry had been equally revolutionised by the invention of smelting by pit-coal brought into use between 1740 and 1750, and by the application in 1788 of the steam-engine to blast furnaces. In the eight years which followed this later date, the amount of iron manufactured nearly doubled itself.

A further growth of the factory system took place independent of machinery, and owed its origin to the expansion of trade, an expansion which was itself due to the great advance made at this time in the means of communication. The canal system was being rapidly developed through-out the country. In 1777 the Grand Trunk canal, 96 miles in length, con-necting the Trent and Mersey, was finished; Hull and Liverpool were connected by one canal while another connected them both with Bristol; and in 1792, the Grand Junction canal, 90 miles in length, made a water-way from London through Oxford to the chief midland towns. Some years afterwards, the roads were greatly improved under Telford and Macadam; between 1818 and 1829 more than a thousand additional miles of turnpike road were constructed; and the next year, 1830, saw the opening of the first railroad. These improved means of communication caused an extra-ordinary increase in commerce, and to secure a sufficient supply of goods it became the interest of the merchants to collect weavers around them in great numbers, to get looms together in a workshop, and to give out the warp themselves to the work-people. To these latter this system meant a change from independence to dependence; at the beginning of the century the report of a committee asserts that the essential difference between the domestic and the factory system is, that in the latter the work is done "by persons who have no property in the goods they manufacture." Another direct consequence of this expansion of trade was the regular recurrence of

periods of over-production and of depression, a phenomenon quite unknown under the old system, and due to this new form of production on a
large scale for a distant market.

These altered conditions in the production of wealth necessarily
involved an equal revolution in its distribution. In agriculture the prominent fact is an enormous rise in rents. Up to 1795, though they had risen
in some places, in others they had been stationary since the Revolution.
But between 1790 and 1833, according to Porter, they at least doubled.
In Scotland, the rental of land, which in 1795 had amounted to £2,000,000,
had risen in 1815 to £5,278,685. A farm in Essex, which before 1793 had
been rented at 10s. an acre, was let in 1812 at 50s., though six years after,
this had fallen again to 35s. In Berks and Wilts, farms which in 1790
were let at 14s., were let in 1810 at 70s., and in 1820 at 50s. Much of this
rise, doubtless, was due to money invested in improvements—the first
Lord Leicester is said to have expended £400,000 on his property—but it
was far more largely the effect of the enclosure system, of the consolidation of farms, and of the high price of corn during the French war. Whatever may have been its causes, however, it represented a great social
revolution, a change in the balance of political power and in the relative
position of classes. The farmers shared in the prosperity of the landlords;
for many of them held their farms under beneficial leases, and made large
profits by them. In consequence, their character completely changed;
they ceased to work and live with their labourers, and became a distinct
class. The high prices of the war time thoroughly demoralised them, for
their wealth then increased so fast, that they were at a loss what to do with
it. Cobbett has described the change in their habits, the new food and
furniture, the luxury and drinking, which were the consequences of more
money coming into their hands than they knew how to spend. Meanwhile,
the effect of all these agrarian changes upon the condition of the labourer
was an exactly opposite and most disastrous one. He felt all the burden
of high prices, while his wages were steadily falling, and he had lost his
common-rights. It is from this period, viz., the beginning of the present
century, that the alienation between farmer and labourer may be dated.

Exactly analogous phenomena appeared in the manufacturing world.
The new class of great capitalist employers made enormous fortunes, they
took little or no part personally in the work of their factories, their
hundreds of workmen were individually unknown to them; and as a
consequence, the old relations between masters and men disappeared, and
a "cash nexus" was substituted for the human tie. The workmen on their
side resorted to combination, and Trade-Unions began a fight which
looked as if it were between mortal enemies rather than joint producers.
The misery which came upon large sections of the working people at this
epoch was often, though not always, due to a fall in wages, for as I said
above, in some industries they rose. But they suffered likewise from the

conditions of labour under the factory system, from the rise of prices, especially from the high price of bread before the repeal of the corn-laws, and from those sudden fluctuations of trade, which, ever since production has been on a large scale, have exposed them to recurrent periods of bitter distress. The effects of the Industrial Revolution prove that free competition may produce wealth without producing well-being. We all know the horrors that ensued in England before it was restrained by legislation and combination.

CHAPTER XIII. TWO THEORIES OF ECONOMIC PROGRESS

Distribution of wealth the problem of the present time.—Ricardo's theory that wages will remain stationary and interest fall.—Facts disprove both propositions.—Henry George's theory of economic progress likewise contradicted by facts.

Since Mill, in 1848, wrote his chapter on the future of the working classes, the question of the distribution of wealth has become of still greater importance. We cannot look around on the political phenomena of to-day without seeing that this question is at the root of them. We see the perplexity in which men stand, and the divisions springing up in our great political parties, because of the uncertainty of politicians how to grapple with it. Political power is now widely diffused; and whatever may be the evils of democracy, this good has come of it, that it has forced men to open their eyes to the misery of the masses, and to inquire more zealously as to the possibility of a better distribution of wealth. Economists have to answer the question whether it is possible for the mass of the working classes to raise themselves under the present conditions of competition and private property. Ricardo and Henry George have both answered, No; and the former has formulated a law of economic development, according to which, as we have seen, rent must rise, profits and interest fall, and wages remain stationary, or perhaps fall. Now is there any relation of cause and effect between this rise in rent and fall in wages? Ricardo thought not. Acording to his theory, profits and wages are fixed independently of rent; a rise in rent and a fall in wages might be due to the same cause, but the one was not the result of the other, and the rise in rent would not be at the expense of the labourers. Yet practical opinion goes in the opposite direction. From the evidence of farmers and land-agents we see that it is widely believed that the high rents exacted from farmers have been partly taken out of the pockets of the labourers. "If there is a fall in the price of corn, agricultural wages will fall, unless there is a corresponding fall in rent," was said before a Parliamentary Commission in 1834. Ten years ago the connection was admitted in Ireland; and the Land Act of 1870 was founded on the belief that rack-rents were not really the surplus left when capital and labour had received their fair returns, and that the only limit to the rise of rents was the bare necessities of the peasantry. In England it has been assumed that wages and profits have fixed lines of their own independent of rent, but this is not universally true; where the farmers have suffered from high rents, they in their turn have ground down the labourers. Thus even in England rent has been exacted from the labourer; and this is not an opinion but a fact, testified by the evidence of agents, clergy, and farmers themselves. What appears accurate to say about the matter is, that high rents have in some cases been one cause of low wages.

This direct effect of rent on wages under certain conditions is quite distinct from the "brazen law of wages" which Lassalle took from Ricardo. It is impossible, according to Ricardo, for labourers to improve their position under existing industrial conditions, for if wages rise, population will advance also, and wages return to their own level; there cannot therefore be any permanent rise in them. Ricardo, indeed, did not deny that the standard of comfort varied in different countries, and in the same country at different times; but these admissions he only made parenthetically, he did not seem to think they seriously touched the question of population, and they did not affect his main conclusions. For instance, he argues that a tax on corn will fall entirely on profits, since the labourer is already receiving the lowest possible wages. This statement may be true with regard to the very lowest class of labourers, but it certainly does not apply to artisans, nor to a large proportion of English working men at the present time. With them, at any rate, it is not true that they are already receiving the lowest possible wage, nor that there is an invincible bar to their progress. Let us turn to the test of facts and see if wages have risen since 1846. Henry George says that free trade has done nothing for the labourer; Mill, in 1848, predicted the same. Professor Cairnes came to a very similar conclusion; writing in 1874 he said, that "the large addition to the wealth of the country has gone neither to profit nor to wages, nor yet to the public at large, but to swell . . . the rent-roll of the owner of the soil." Yet it is a fact that though the cost of living has undoubtedly increased, wages have risen in a higher ratio. Take the instance of a carpenter as a fair average specimen of the artisan class. The necessaries of a carpenter's family in 1839 cost 24s. 10d. per week; in 1875 they cost 29s. But meanwhile the money wages of a carpenter had risen from 24s. to 35s. Thus there had been not only a nominal but a real rise in his wages. Turning to the labourer, his cost of living was about 15s. in 1839, it was a little under 15s. in 1875. The articles he consumes have decreased in cost, while in the case of the artisan they have increased, because the labourer spends a much larger proportion of his wages on bread. The labourer's wages meanwhile have risen from 8s. to 12s. or 14s.; in 1839 he could not properly support himself on his wages alone. These facts seem conclusive, but certainty is difficult from the very varying estimates of consumption and money wages. For strong proof of a rise in agricultural wages we may

take a particular instance. On an estate of Forfar the yearly wages of a
first ploughman were by the wages-book, in

1840	£28	2	0	1870	£42	5	0
1850	28	15	0	1880	48	9	0
1860	39	7	0				

According to his own admission the standard of comfort of the first
ploughman employed on this estate in 1810 had risen, for he complained,
in a letter describing his position, of his increased expenditure, increased
not because things were dearer, but because he now needed more of them.

We may take as further evidence the statistics of the savings of the
working classes; it is impossible to get more than an approximate estimate
of them, but they probably amount to about £130,000,000. To these we
may add the savings actually invested in houses. In Birmingham there are
13,000 houses owned by artisans. All this is small compared with the
whole capital of the country, which, in 1875, was estimated at £8,500,000,-
000 at least, with an annual increase of £235,000,000—this latter sum far
exceeding the total savings of the working classes. The comparison will
make us take a sober view of their improvement; yet the facts make it
clear that the working classes can raise their position, though not in the
same ratio as the middle classes. Mr. Mulhall also estimates that there is
less inequality between the two classes now than forty years ago. He calculates that the average wealth of a rich family has decreased from £28,-
820 to £25,803, or 11 per cent.; that of a middle-class family has decreased
from £1439 to £1005, or 30 per cent.; while that of a working-class family
has *increased* from £44 to £86, or nearly 100 per cent. But without
pinning our faith to any particular estimate, we can see clearly enough
that the facts disprove Ricardo's proposition that no improvement is
possible; and there are not wanting some who think that the whole tendency of modern society is towards an increasing equality of condition.

Was Ricardo any more correct in saying that interest and profits
(between which he never clearly distinguished) must fall? As a matter of
fact, for the last century and a half interest in England has been almost
stationary, except during the great war. In Walpole's time it was three
per cent.; during the war it doubled, but after the peace it dropped to
four per cent., and has remained pretty steady at that rate ever since.
Ricardo thought that the cost of the labourer's subsistence would necessarily increase, owing to the necessity of cultivating more land, and as
he would thus require a greater share of the gross produce, less wealth
would be left for the capitalist. He overlooked the fact that the rate of
interest depends not merely on the cost of labour, but on the field of
employment as well. As civilization advances, new inventions and new
enterprises create a fresh demand for capital: some £700,000,000 have
been invested in English railways alone. No doubt, if the field for English

capital were confined to England, the rate of interest might fall; but Ricardo forgot the possibility of capital emigrating on a large scale. Thus Ricardo's teaching on this point is deficient both in abstract theory and as tested by facts. What we really find to have taken place is, that though rent has risen, there is good reason to suppose that in the future it may fall; that interest has not fallen much; and that the standard of comfort and the rate of wages, both of artisans and labourers—of the former most decidedly, and to a certain extent also of the latter, has risen.

I wish next to examine Mr. George's theory of economic progress. Mr. George is a disciple of Ricardo, both in his method and his conclusions; he has as great a contempt for facts and verification as Ricardo himself. By this method he succeeds in formulating a law, according to which, in the progress of civilisation, interest and wages will fall together, and rents will rise. Not only is the labourer in a hopeless condition, but the capitalist is equally doomed to a stationary or declining fortune. "Rent," he says, "depends upon the margin of cultivation, rising as it falls, and falling as it rises. Interest and wages depend on the margin of cultivation, falling as it falls, and rising as it rises." The returns which the capitalist obtains for his capital and the labourer for his work, depend on the returns from the worst land cultivated; that is, on the quality of land accessible to capital and labour without payment of rent.

Now Mr. George's observations are derived from America, and what he has done is to generalise a theory, which is true of some parts of America, but not of old countries. His book seems conclusive enough at first sight. There is little flaw in the reasoning, if we grant the premises; but there are great flaws in the results when tested by facts. Do interest and wages always rise and fall together? As an historical fact they do not. Between 1715 and 1760, while rents (according to Professor Rogers) rose but slowly (Arthur Young denies that they rose at all), interest fell, and wages rose. Between 1790 and 1815 rent doubled, interest doubled, wages fell. Between 1846 and 1882 rents have risen, interest has been stationary, wages have risen. Thus in all these three periods the facts contradict Mr. George's theory. Rent indeed has generally risen, but neither profits nor wages have steadily fallen, nor have their variations borne any constant relation to one another. Coming to Mr. George's main position, that rent constantly tends to absorb the whole increase of national wealth, how does this look in the light of fact? Does all the increase of wealth, for instance in the Lancashire cotton manufactures, go simply to raise rents? Evidently not. Wages have risen owing to improvements in machinery; and in most cases profits have also risen. We can prove by statistics that in England the capitalists' wealth has increased faster than that of the landowners'; for in the assessments to the income-tax there has been a greater increase under Schedule D, which comprises the profits of capitalists and the earnings of professional men, than under Schedule A, which comprises revenues from land. At the same time, Mr. George has made out a strong case against private property in land in great towns; but here he has only restated more forcibly what Adam Smith and Mill advocated, when they recommended taxes on ground rents as the least objectionable of all taxes. Under the existing conditions the working people in great towns may be said to be taxed in the worst of ways by the bad condition of their houses. An individual or a corporation lets a block of buildings for a term of years; the lessee sublets it, and the sub-lessee again for the third time. Each class is here oppressing the one beneath it, and the lowest unit suffers most. This is why the problem of the distribution of wealth is sure, in the near future, to take the form of the question, how to house the labourers of our towns.

PART VII

SOCIAL REFORMERS AND IDEALISTS

1. Jean Charles L. Simonde de Sismondi: "Political Economy and Philosophy of Government."

2. John Ruskin: (*a*) "Essays on Political Economy."
   (*b*) Letters from "Fors Clavigera."

JEAN CHARLES L. SIMONDE DE SISMONDI

(1773–1842)

Sismondi was born in Geneva, Switzerland, of French and Italian ancestry. His father was a Protestant clergyman, and young Sismondi grew up in the city of John Calvin. Most of his life was spent in literary activities and in minor governmental positions. He wrote in both Italian and French.

The literary career of Sismondi may be divided into three parts: first, his early economic writings, second, his work as a historian, and third, his later economic writings. It is hard to reconcile the young economist with the older; his early work was neither important nor original. Like his contemporary, Say, he might have been classified as a French follower of Adam Smith. On the other hand, the later writings of Sismondi were those of a strongly dissenting nonconformist. Perhaps this was due to his intermediate study of history and to his travels, especially in England, where he was much impressed by the effects of the Industrial Revolution on the workers and by several economic crises.

Sismondi's two important historical works were "The History of France" and "The History of the Italian Republics." His first economic writing was "Table of Tuscan Agriculture" (1801), which was followed by the more important "Principles of Political Economy Applied to the Regulation of Commerce," commonly known as "Commercial Wealth" (1803). The later works of Sismondi included "New Principles of Political Economy," or Wealth in Its Relation to Population," which appeared first in 1819, but which was followed by important revisions in 1827 and 1836. It is ordinarily considered his greatest work. The last important work of Sismondi was "Studies in Political Economy" (1837 to 1838).

The following selections are taken from "Introduction to Inquiries into Political Economy," which was one of a number of Sismondi's essays which were collected, translated and published in 1847 under the title, "Political Economy and the Philosophy of Government."

Although Sismondi considered himself a follower of Adam Smith, his later writings bitterly attacked the classical school, as represented by Malthus, Ricardo, and Say. To him economics was a moral science, and its subject was not wealth but man. By method Sismondi was a historian, but by inclination he was a social reformer. Because of these fundamental differences in concepts and methods of approach, there was rarely a meeting of minds on specific points between Sismondi on the one hand and the classicists on the other. The one exception is the famous argument in which Sismondi affirmed the existence of over-production, which Say and his English allies, Malthus and Ricardo, vigorously denied.

To the student of the history of economic though, Sismondi is important because he stands at the parting of the ways. Classical economy was proceeding along its deductive, abstract, and "unmoral" lines. Sismondi insisted that economics was social in character, ethical in its objectives, and historical in its methods. Sismondi's work may be regarded as an intermediate step between the great schisms yet to come. In his work the student can easily trace the beginning of the historical school, and can glimpse some foreshadowing of the socialistic groups of thinkers.

JEAN CHARLES L. SIMONDE DE SISMONDI

SELECTIONS FROM "POLITICAL ECONOMY AND THE PHILOSOPHY OF GOVERNMENT"

INTRODUCTION TO INQUIRIES INTO POLITICAL ECONOMY

The first attention of society must be given to the securing of its material interests, of its subsistence; and we wish to endeavour to discover what path must be followed in order that the material wealth which labour creates may procure and maintain the greatest well-being for all: it is this, which, according to the etymology of the word, we call political economy, for it is the law or the rule of the house or of the city.

Let us not be reproached with lowering man to the level of the brutes by proposing, as the first object of his efforts, the direction of that labour which secures his subsistence, in calling the attention of society, before everything else, to advantages simply material: it will soon be seen that, more than any of our forerunners, we consider political economy in its relation with the soul, and with the intellect. But subsistence is necessary to life, and with life, to all the moral developments, all the intellectual developments, of which the human race is susceptible. Society, as well as individuals, must consider bodily health before any thing else, must provide in the first place for its wants and its development; for without the vigour which this health supplies, without the leisure, which only begins when these wants are satisfied, the health of the mind is impossible. Facts present themselves on every side to convince us that the manner in which society provides for its subsistence, decides at the same time on the wretchedness or comfort of the greatest number; on the health, the beauty, the vigour of the race, or its degeneracy; on the feelings of sympathy or jealously with which fellow men look upon one another as brothers eager to assist one another, or as rivals furious to destroy one another; on that activity of mind, lastly, which is developed by a happy mixture of leisure, and which puts all on the way of progress in intelligence, imagination, and taste; or that enervating languor which luxury produces in some, and the brutishness which results to others from the abuse of physical strength and from fatigue.

That product of human labour, which, with subsistence, represents all the material good which man can enjoy, and almost all the intellectual good to which he can only attain by the help of the first, has been called wealth. Wealth, or the theory of the increase of wealth, has been regarded as the special object of political economy, an object better designated, since the time of Aristotle, by the name of *chresmatistique* (chresmatistic). Ideas are not made clearer by disputes upon words, and we should not bring this forward, if it did not serve to define precisely the course of the false direction which has been followed, in our time, in one branch of social science. This science has always had, and must always have for its object, men gathered together in society; economy, according to the proper sense of the word, is the regulation of the house; political economy is the regulation of the house applied to the city: these are the two great human associations, the primitive associations which are the object of the science; all proceeds from man, all must relate to man, and to man united by a common tie. But wealth is an attribute, shall we say, of man, or of things? Wealth is a term of comparison which has no sense, if it is not distinctly expressed at the same time to what it relates. Wealth, which is an appreciation of material things, is at the same time an abstraction, and chresmatistics, or the science of the increase of wealth, having considered it abstractly and not with relation to man and to society, has raised its edifice on a basis which is dissipated into air.

Wealth, we have said, is the product of human labour, which procures for man all the material good which he wishes to enjoy; it is the representation of all physical enjoyments, and also of all the moral enjoyments which proceed from them. Very well; but for whom? This question should never be lost sight of, whilst, on the contrary, it never presents itself to theorists. For whom? According to the answer which is given to this question, man himself belongs to wealth, or wealth belongs to man.

The Shah of Persia esteems himself rich, because he reckons as his wealth all the inhabitants of his vast empire, who are his slaves, and all their goods, which he can take from them whenever he chooses. St. Domingo was formerly called a rich colony, because only the forty thousand whites who inhabited it were considered, and the four hundred thousand slaves who laboured for them were reckoned as their property. The cotton trade in England is called a rich business, for it brings colossal fortunes to the merchant who imports it, to the manufacturer who fabricates it in immense factories, to the seller who sends it all over the world; but no account is taken of the cultivator, who, whilst producing cotton, remains in slavery or indigence; of the weaver, who scarcely satisfies his hunger whilst he works, or dies of hunger when work is interrupted. In our eyes, we do not hesitate to say so, national wealth is the participation of ALL in the advantages of life. It is in various proportions, without doubt, that the members of the community are called upon to divide the product of social labour, but we shall never call wealth the share which one member takes from another.

At the first view of the question, every one thinks he comprehends clearly what wealth is, and the effects of wealth on society; every one thinks he comprehends how it modifies the condition of the poorest and of the richest; but the more closely it is looked at, the more do contradictory phenomena, which to a certain point balance one another, embarrass the judgment. It is because wealth is not an essence, but an attribute, and its nature changes with the persons and the things to which it is attributed. As satisfying our wants, as the source of our physical enjoyments, the idea which we form of it is sufficiently precise, but then it admits of very few degrees. To form a conception of the increase of wealth when our wants are satisfied, we must go out of ourselves and consider the value of things, either by the distinction they confer by marking rank in society, or by the labour which has been devoted to obtaining them; and as these two appreciations are not even commensurable, as our minds continually vibrate from one to the other, we often end by asking ourselves what there is in wealth which is real, and whether, after having enriched ourselves, we do not remain poorer than we were before.

In fact, all artificial productions are valued more cheaply in a rich nation than in a poor nation: thus, whilst we call ourselves richer than our forefathers, all our manufactured commodities cost us much less. Is it true, then, that we have become richer by accumulating more? How shall we compare, for example, the different kinds of stuffs which have succeeded one another in our dress? How shall we decide, by what we spend on them, whether we are richer or poorer? So far as they satisfy real wants, their utility is nearly the same, but since they have been obtained with less labour, they are of less value; since they can be exchanged for less of the means of subsistence, they are also of less value; and under that point of view in which they principally flatter the passions of the rich as a distinction of rank, they are still less value, for the price of the most magnificent dress is more within reach of the inferior conditions of society than it was at any preceding period. It is asserted, however, that the introduction of a new manufacture enriches the country; that when, with the same labour, ten times, a hundred times more yards of stuff have been produced, ten times, a hundred times more wealth has been created; but what becomes of this wealth in its application to the wants of society? what becomes of it if we endeavour to draw up a balance sheet of the affairs of the nation? Does it really diminish in proportion as its exchangeable value diminishes? and then what is the real utility of all those modern inventions of art, of which we are so proud?

In fact, we lose ourselves whenever we attempt to consider wealth abstractedly. Wealth is a modification of the state of man: it is only by referring to man that we can form a clear idea of it. Wealth is the abundance of things which the labour of man produces, and which the wants of man consume. A truly rich nation would be one in which this abundance would produce the most material enjoyment, to the poor on one side, to the rich on the other.

Let us endeavour to form a rather more precise idea of these wants, of these desires, of these enjoyments of the human race. to which is attached the happiness of communities. The enjoyments of the poor are composed of the abundance, of the variety, and of the wholesomeness of their nourishment, of the sufficiency of clothes relative to the climate, and of their cleanliness; of the convenience and of the salubrity of their lodging, also as regards the climate and the quantity of fuel which it requires; lastly, of the certainty that the future will not be inferior to the present, and that a poor man can by the same labour obtain at least the same enjoyment. No nation can be considered as prosperous, if the condition of the poor, who form a part of it, is not secure under the four relations which we have just enumerated. Subsistence in this degree is the common right of man, and should be secured to all those who do what they can to forward common labour; and the nation is so much the more prosperous, the more every individual is assured of having a share in these comforts of the poor.

The enjoyments of the rich are composed, in the first place, of these same three wants being satisfied in regard to food, clothing, and lodging, and by the same security for the future continuance of this well-being; but they comprehend a new element, leisure: the subsistence of the rich must be independent of their labour. In satisfying wants, there is no doubt a sufficiently large latitude. Food, clothing, and lodging may be infinitely better for some than for others. We must not, however, be under an illusion with regard to the enjoyment which is attached to the satisfying of the wants even of the richest. Some are purely sensual, and the philosopher who wishes to appreciate the advantages of wealth to a nation, will not attach too much importance to these, without, however, denying their existence. Others exist only as distinctions, as giving to him who is in possession of them a feeling of superiority over his fellow-creatures. We do not deny this distinction, nor that the respect with which opulence inspires the vulgar, when it is seen displayed on a sumptuous table, in magnificent dresses and equipages, in vast and solid buildings, may not have some political utility; but in appreciating the happiness of a nation, the happiness which wealth gives to the rich, the philosopher will not make more account of the enjoyments of vanity than of those of the senses. He will perhaps make still less account of the third prerogative of wealth in regard to the wants of the human race, that of satisfying its love of change.

But wealth secures to the rich two prerogatives, the advantages of which are reflected throughout the whole of society; one is the employment of their leisure in the development of their intellectual faculties; the other, the employment of their superfluity in the relief of all kinds of wretchedness. It is from these two prerogatives that rich men are necessary to the progress of every nation; whilst a nation which had no rich men, that is to say, no men who can dispose of their leisure and of their superfluity, would rapidly fall into ignorance, barbarism, and selfishness. Let us not be deluded as to the necessarily stupifying consequences of bodily labour and fatigue. Were all the individuals of the nation called upon to exert their muscular force, it would soon be deprived not only of all progress in science and in the fine arts, but in intelligence, taste, mind, and grace. The human cattle might without doubt continually get fatter in their stables, but they would always approach nearer the brutes, they would continually get farther from celestial intelligences. Intellectual progress, however, gives rise to new wants among the rich, and opens a new employment for wealth. Intelligence, imagination, sensibility, require to be satisfied as well as the body, and the search of aesthetic beauty, or moral beauty, or intellectual beauty, attracts toward them a superfluity of human activity, as well as of the wealth which man has produced, and which would otherwise have been unemployed. Charity is another prerogative of wealth, still more important to society than to the poor themselves. It is charity which must repair the accidental disorders which disturb the regular distribution of wealth; but it is charity which, much more, must connect different ranks, substitute affection and gratitude for the contention of interests, spread knowledge with benefits, render all individuals equally participators in the moral superiority acquired by some; lastly, give to the nation that stability which she can only preserve by love among fellow citizens.

To appreciate the influence of the enjoyments of the rich on national happiness, we must take an account not only of their intensity, but of the number of those who participate in them. If we suppose that, after having provided for the necessities of all, the superfluity of the nation is reserved to endow the rich, and if it be then asked in what proportion it is desirable to see them rise above the rest, it is easy to answer, in the first place, that it is better to make many happy than only one; that he who united ten shares sufficient to secure ease and leisure to ten families, will not himself be as happy as these ten families would have been; but it will soon be acknowledged also, that for the nation, for the social object of their pre-eminence, many moderately rich are worth more than one rich man in opulence. If the vocation of the rich man is especially to develop his intelligence for the good of all, it must not be forgotten that though labour brutifies, it is true, yet that luxury enervates, so that the beneficial influence of the rich on society diminishes not only with the diminution of their number, but with the increase of their wealth, when it goes beyond a certain point. If the second prerogative of wealth is to bind society together by charity, it will be equally felt that the more the number of rich men scattered over the country is diminished, the more distant their residences are by their patrimonies being increased, the more also will they be strangers to the poor whom they ought to assist; the more will the bonds of sympathy be broken by distance of place or of rank; so that even should we suppose that the charities of a *millionaire* would equal those of the ten or the hundred rich men whose patrimonies were united in one, still their moral effect, their social effect, would not be the same.

After having thus endeavoured to appreciate at their just value the advantages of wealth, both as regards the poor and the rich, we shall a little better understand, perhaps, what is the distribution of wealth most desirable for happiness and for moral progress, but we shall scarcely have advanced so far as to be able to form a judgment on what enriches or impoverishes a nation, or to discover what effect that which at first appears a progress in wealth must have on general prosperity.

The phenomena which we see before our eyes, far from enlightening our doubts, seem as if they must increase them. In our times, man has made a gigantic progress in industry. With the assistance of the sciences which he cultivates, he has learned to employ as a master the powers of nature; and seconded by the wealth which he has previously accumulated, or by his capital, he produces every year a great mass of things destined for the enjoyment of the human race. The works of man multiply, and change the face of the earth; warehouses are filled; in workshops we admire the power which man has borrowed from the wind, from water, from fire, from steam, to accomplish his own work; the genius with which he has subdued nature, and the rapidity with which he executes industrial labours which formerly would have required ages. Each city, each nation, overflows with wealth, each one wishes to send to its neighbours those commodities which are superabundant, and new discoveries in science allow of their being transported, in spite of the immensity of their weight and of their bulk, with a rapidity truly confounding. It is the triumph of chresmatistics; never has the art of producing and accumulating wealth been pushed so far.

But is it equally the triumph of political economy? Has this rule of the house and of the city provided for the happiness of both one and the other? Man, for whom this wealth is destined, human society, whose material enjoyments it ought to increase, have these gained in ease, have they gained in security, in proportion to this immense development? At the first aspect of this question, it seems so certain that the more things there are destined for the enjoyments of man, the greater share will each one be able to obtain, that we do not give ourselves the trouble to weigh our answer. Nevertheless, if we look at men, and not at things, if we detail human conditions and the advantages which each one of them can reap from wealth, doubt may perhaps enter our minds. Is each man, in his own sphere, we shall ask, more secure of his subsistence, than he was before this great development of industry? Has he more repose at present, more security for the future? Does he enjoy more independence? Is he not only better lodged, better clothed, better fed, but has he gained by the development of the irrational powers more leisure and more apti-

tude for intellectual developments? Has the proportion between different
conditions changed to the advantage or disadvantage of the greater
number? Are those who occupy the lowest steps of the scale more or less
numerous than formerly? Are there more steps than formerly between the
rich and the poor, or are there fewer; and is it more or less easy for
the first successively to pass over them? For example, in the country, is it
the number of day-labourers, or of that of *métayers*, of small farmers, of
small proprietors, which has proportionably increased? In towns, is it the
number of those who work by the day, or of masters and journeymen, of
small heads of workshops, of retail and wholesale dealers, of intermedi-
ates between the producer and the consumer, which has in the same way
increased? Let us feel well the importance of all these questions, when
it is the sum of social happiness at two different periods that we wish to
compare. Wealth is realized in enjoyment; but to estimate the mass of
national enjoyment, it is almost always at the number of those who
participate in it that we must stop, for the enjoyment of the rich man
does not increase with his wealth.

We have infinite difficulty in conceiving a social organisation different from our own, and in seeing a past in which we did not live. However,
the monuments alone of a country sometimes speak a language to which
we cannot refuse to listen. Those which surround us in the place where we
are writing this, revivfy the past with a power which presents it entire to
the imagination. In Italy, from the most opulent city to the lowest village,
there is scarcely a house which does not appear superior to the condition
of those who inhabit it at this day; not a house which is not superior to
what would be required now, even in the most prosperous countries, for
men in the condition of those who have built it. Superb Genoa, the city
of palaces, was raised by commerce, but let the palaces of Paris and
London, which have been raised by modern commerce, be counted, let
those in all the provinces of England and France be added to them, there
will not be found so large a number as decorate this one city; there will not
be found one that has the same imposing character of grandeur and magnificence. The opulence of the commercial men of our days has neither
past nor future; thus it does not raise monuments. A single state amongst
the republics of Italy seems to have reckoned more rich merchants than
the two empires which, at this day, hold the sceptre of commerce. But the
palaces of the merchants of Venice, of Florence, of Bologna, of Sienna,
rivalled in magnificence those of Genoa; whilst the palaces of the military
nobility ornamented Milan, Turin, Naples, Placentia, Modena, and
Ferrara, more than Paris or London are now ornamented.

* * * * *

What then is the end of human society? Is it to dazzle the eyes by the
immense production of useful and elegant things; to astonish the under-

standing by the empire which man exercises over nature, and by the precision and rapidity with which inanimate machines execute human work? Is it to cover the sea with vessels, and the land with railways, distributing in every way the productions of an ever-increasing industrial activity? Is it to give to two or three individuals in a hundred thousand the power of disposing of an opulence which would give comfort to all these hundred thousand? In this case we have, without doubt, made immense progress, in comparison with our ancestors; we are rich in invention, rich in activity, rich in scientific power, rich especially in merchandize; for every nation has not only enough for itself, but for all its neighbours. But if the end which society ought to propose to itself, in favouring labour, and securing its fruits, should rather be to secure the development of man, and of all men; to spread with a beneficent hand through the whole community, though in different proportions, the fruits of the labour of man, those fruits which we call wealth; if these fruits, which comprise moral and intellectual as well as material benefits, ought to be a means of improvement as well as of enjoyment, is it sure that we have approached nearer the object? Is it sure that in searching after wealth we have not forgotten the order and regulation of the house, and of the city, Political Economy?

In all the military monarchies of Europe, property, as well as all the other rights of citizens, was ill protected, those of the weak not at all. The possessions of poor peasants, of poor artisans, were subjected to vexations and exactions, now only known in the despotic monarchies of the East; it is not by this state of violence, the fruit of a detestable political organization, that we must judge of the reward formerly secured to labour. We have seen that the lowest rank among the inhabitants of the country, the cultivators, were in general proprietors loaded with dues, it is true, but with dues which would have left them a superfluity, if the rapaciousness of the powerful had not often snatched it from them: the lowest rank among the inhabitants of towns, the apprentices and journeymen, were in general well clothed, well fed, well lodged in the house of the master with whom they worked; and they were sure, by assiduity, of becoming masters in their turn, and being then for the rest of their lives sheltered from want.

The order which we have substituted for this, and which the chresmatistic school considers as its triumph, is founded on quite other principles. This school, pursuing as it were abstractedly the increase of wealth, without asking in whose favour this wealth ought to be accumulated, has proposed as the object of nations the production of the greatest possible quantity of work at the cheapest rate. Wealth, it says, is so much of the useful product of labour as is not consumed, which accumulates on the earth: this wealth accumulates in two ways, by more being produced, and less spent. Each member of the community wishes to enrich himself, each one therefore endeavours to increase what he produces, or to diminish the expense of it; each one, individually, thus tends to the common object of human society. Give to all these individual actions their free spring. Far from restraining men either in what they produce or in what they save, let them on the contrary be excited by universal rivalry and competition; let these reign equally amongst all conditions, and all men of every condition: wealth will then be seen to increase, either by the augmentation of production, or the diminution of expense, with an activity which former ages have never known. From hence, in fact, the chresmatistics, or all those who in our time have become celebrated as political economists, have held out to the industrials, to all the undertakers of work of every kind, discourses in favour of the indefinite liberty of industry and trade, in favour of the most animated competition, which may be thus translated: "Seek your own interest before every things else; you will find it in being preferred to your rivals, whether as relates to selling or to working; you will find it in making the most lucrative conditions you can with those who wish to serve you; whether they relate to purchasing from them, or to making them work for you. Perhaps you will thus reduce them to indigence, perhaps you will ruin them, perhaps you will destroy their health or their lives. That is not your business: you represent the interest of the consumers; now each one is a consumer in his turn; therefore you represent the interest of all, the national interest. Thus listen to no consideration, let no pity stop you, for perhaps you will be called on to say to your rivals, your death is our life."

This language will appear harsh, no doubt, but it is not more so than the conduct of those rivals who throughout the whole of Europe have been called on by this new doctrine to supplant one another, to destroy one another. Two modes of acting, equally encouraged by chresmatistism, have begun, wherever free scope has been granted to individual interests. On one hand the object was to create more wealth, more of those things which labour makes, and which man desires to consume. Now, as things only become wealth when they find the consumer who is willing to purchase them in order to use them, and as wants do not increase with production, each industrial wished to occupy the place of his rival, and to take away his customers. Nations rival one another in production, and glory in it. If a Frenchman can dispose of his merchandize in a foreign market, till then reserved to the English, or if the Englishman can exclude the Frenchman, each praises himself, and demands the applause of his countrymen, not merely as having made a good speculation, but as having performed a patriotic action. The same rivalship exists between towns of the same empire, between workshop and workshop of the same town. Everywhere it is equally war to the death: its consequences are the ruin of the heads, the mortality of the subalterns; it overthrows as many fortunes as it raises, and the branch of commerce which flourishes the most, is probably that in which, taken altogether, there have been the most failures, for new fortunes have only risen from the overthrow of older ones. In fact, before the introduction of universal competition, the celebrity of manufactures belonged to their age; the name of the great fabricators was like a title of nobility which they transmitted with pride to their descendants; now antiquity is a title to distrust, and a prognostic of ruin; it is only beginners who are enterprizing, industrious, and who know how to undersell their rivals.

But if each one labours to increase production, each one labours also to produce cheaper, and one of these is the necessary consequence, the completion of the other. Now wealth, we have said, is the fruit of labour: economy in the expense of production can be nothing but economy in the quantity of labour employed to produce, or economy in the payment of this labour, In fact, from one extremity to the other of the countries in which free competition is admitted, the governing idea which is excited, in whoever undertakes productive labour, or whoever pays for it, is to make more things with the same quantity of human labour, or to obtain human labour at a lower price. Now whenever these two first conditions are obtained, the third necessarily follows, for all superabundant hands are thrown on the market, and are obliged to offer themselves at a cheaper rate. Let whatever is called progress in the arts, in manufactures, in agriculture, be examined, and it will be found that every discovery, every improvement, may be reduced to doing as much with less labour, or more with the same labour; all progress tends also to reduce the value and reward of labour, or the ease of those who live only to labour.

The fundamental change which has taken place in society, amidst the universal struggle created by competition, is the introduction of the *proletary* among human conditions, the name of whom, borrowed from the Romans, is ancient, but whose existence is quite new. The proletaries were in the Roman republic men who had nothing, who paid no taxes, and who belonged to the country only by the *proles*, by the offspring which they produced for it; for the Romans, as well as ourselves, had observed that they have the most numerous families, who having nothing, take no care to rear them. For the rest, the Roman proletary did not labour, for in a community which admits slavery, labour is dishonourable to free men; he lived almost entirely at the expense of the community, on the distribution of provisions made by the republic. It may almost be said, that in modern times the community lives at the expense of the proletary, on that share of the remuneration of his labour which it deducts from him. The proletary, in fact, according to the order which chresmatistism tends to establish, ought alone to be loaded with all the labour of the community, and ought to be a stranger to all property, and live only on wages. The community, according to the chresmatistic school, is divided, as regards that labour which produces wealth, into three classes of persons: landed proprietors, capitalists, and day-labourers or proletaries. The first give land, the second employment, and the third hand-labour; in return, the first receive rent, the second profit, and the third wages; each endeavours to retain as much as he can of the total product, and their reciprocal struggle fixes the proportion between rent, profit, and wages.

* * * * *

As by the power of great capital all independent trades have been attacked, and the man who was formerly a master in a trade has been forced to descend to the rank of a man who works by the day, of a proletary, so also have been attacked the domestic labours of the inferior members of the family; and the chresmatistic school has, by its arguments, seconded the power of money, and the seduction of cheapness. Why, it says, should the housewife spin, weave, and prepare all the linen of the family? All this work would be done infinitely cheaper at the manufactory; with much less money the housewife would have more stuffs, and of a finer quality. Why should she knead the bread? she cannot make it so light, she cannot bake it to such an exact point, she cannot make it so cheaply as the baker. Why should she make the pot boil? An establishment on a great scale, with supplies made beforehand, a considerable capital and a common inspection, would procure her better food with great saving of time and fuel. Omnibus kitchens might even every day bring her soup to her door. Why? Why, because reciprocal cares and duties form and strengthen domestic ties; because the wife endears herself to the family of the poor man by the solicitude with which she provides for its first necessities; because love is often in a labouring man only a brutal and transient passion; but his affection for her who every day prepares for him the only enjoyment which he can obtain in the day, thus increases also every day. It is the wife who foresees, and who remembers, in the midst of that life passed so rapidly in labour, and physical wants; it is she who knows how to combine economy, neatness, and order, with abundance. It is in the happiness she gives that she finds strength to resist, if it is necessary, the imperious demand of drunkenness and gluttony. When the wife has nothing to do in the house but to produce children, can it be supposed that the sacred bond of marriage is not more broken, than by the lessons and the example of the most reprehensible immorality?

Manufactures have, however, in those nations which are called the most prosperous, gained the advantage over domestic labours, as well as over independent trades. Their success has been announced as a prodigious conquest of industry, and publicists as well as the heads of the chresmatistic school, rivalled one another in felicitations on the rapid increase of public wealth. But a frightful reality suddenly appeared, disturbing all minds, and shaking all the principles which had been announced in so dogmatic a tone: it was the appearance of *pauperism*, its rapid and threatening increase, and the confession of the oracles of the science that they felt themselves powerless to remedy it. *Pauperism* is a calamity which began by making itself felt in England, and which has at present no other name but what the English have given it, though it begins to visit also other industrial countries. Pauperism is the state to which proletaries are necessarily reduced when work fails. It is the condition of men who must live by their labour, who can only work when capitalists employ them, and who, when they are idle, must become a burden on the community. This community, which gives all its support to the rich, does not allow the proletary to labour on the land, unless the proprietor of his tenant wants him for this purpose. It does not allow him to work at trades, if the manufacturer or his foreman does not want him. Justice and humanity equally proclaim the necessity of legal charity, or of a provision made by social authority in favour of the poor, whose distress would be no less alarming than grievous. No community has believed that it could refuse this legal charity, but it is only very recently that experience and calculation have equally demonstrated that the community has not the power to support such a burden. The Poor Law increases the wretchedness of the poor, their dependence, and their vices, at the same time that it is capable of raising them from indigence only in proportion as it absorbs the clear net income of the richest nation.

What then is become of this opulence so long cried up? Where is this progress towards prosperity which we are called on to admire? Since nations became richer, are they more in a state to feed themselves? By forgetting man for things, by unceasingly multiplying material wealth, has only poverty then been created? By exciting each one to seek only his own advantage at the expense of all those with whom he has any transactions, have we gained, instead of the equilibrium of all individual powers, only the combined action of each one, for his own advantage no doubt, but to the disadvantage of all. We have long said so, it is true, but writing makes little impression when it attacks a dominant system. Facts are more obstinate and more rebellious. They do not manifest themselves less from its being supposed that they can be refuted without being heard, as if they were only writings; they often increase from having been neglected, and then they fall with their whole weight on the most skilfully constructed theory, crushing and overthrowing it at the very moment when its author was congratulating himself on having victoriously refuted all his adversaries.

JOHN RUSKIN

(1819–1900)

The career of John Ruskin is too familiar to warrant an outline here of his life and work. It is sufficient merely to note that he was not only a man of letters and a student of art, but also a social reformer and a lecturer on economic topics.

Ruskin's works of interest to students of economics included: "Unto This Last" (1862); "Munera Pulveris" (1872); and "Fors Clavigera, Letters to the Workmen and Labourers of Great Britain" (1871–1884). Many of these lectures and essays, some of which had first appeared as magazine articles, were subsequently brought together under the title "Essays in Political Economy."

In 1871, Ruskin founded the Guild of St. George, an experiment with the English workers. He remained all his life the friend of those who toiled with their hands. An uncompromising foe of the Industrial Revolution and the Machine age, he constantly sought to revive and to stimulate craftsmanship.

Ruskin was not an economist in the strict sense of the term, but rather an essayist, a lecturer, and a social reformer. He was an artist rather than a scientist. He loved to play with words and even to coin them, as, for illustration, his term "illth." He delighted not in the logician's precision, but, instead, he sought to warm the souls of his readers about the ideals of the good and the beautiful. As with the ancient Greeks, these ideals of goodness and beauty were fused into one noble concept.

The student will be somewhat confused by Ruskin's radically different use of terms, some of which he did attempt to define. Again, he will find his writings full of beautiful platitudes which are difficult to translate with specific meaning. Because of this ambiguity, as well as because of his insistence on the ethical and spiritual character of economics, Ruskin, like Tolstoy and Gandhi, may be termed a mystic.

The chief economic influences of Ruskin have been indirect in the form of workers' education and perhaps in raising the social morality of business. One of his disciples is the great English economist, John A. Hobson, whose book entitled "Work and Wealth" attempts to develop the ideals of Ruskin into an economic system of human valuation. Again, Clay's familiar text entitled "Economics for the General Reader" shows some influence of Ruskin.

JOHN RUSKIN

ESSAYS ON POLITICAL ECONOMY

MUNERA PULVERIS

I. Maintenance of Life: Wealth, Money and Riches

As domestic economy regulates the acts and habits of a household, political economy regulates those of a society or state, with reference to the means of its maintenance.

Political economy is neither an art nor a science,[1] but a system of conduct and legislature, founded on the sciences, directing the arts, and impossible, except under certain conditions of moral culture.

By the "maintenance" of a state is to be understood the support of its population in healthy and happy life; and the increase of their numbers, so far as that increase is consistent with their happiness. It is not the object of political economy to increase the numbers of a nation at the cost of common health or comfort; nor to increase indefinitely the comfort of individuals, by sacrifice of surrounding lives, or possibilities of life.

The assumption which lies at the root of nearly all erroneous reasoning on political economy,—namely, that its object is to accumulate money or exchangeable property,—may be shown in few words to be without foundation. For no economist would admit national economy to be legitimate which proposed to itself only the building of a pyramid of gold. He would declare the gold to be wasted, were it to remain in the monumental form, and would say it ought to be employed. But to what end? Either it must be used only to gain more gold, and build a larger pyramid, or to some purpose other than the gaining of gold. And this other purpose, however at first apprehended, will be found to resolve itself finally into the service of

[1] The science which in modern days has been called Political Economy is in reality nothing more than the investigation of the phenomena of commercial operations. It has no connexion with political economy, as understood and treated of by the great thinkers of past ages; and as long as it is allowed to pass under the same name every word written by those thinkers—and chiefly the words of Plato, Xenophon, Cicero, and Bacon—must be either misunderstood or misapplied. The reader must not, therefore, be surprised at the care and insistence with which I have retained the literal and earliest sense of all important terms used in these papers; for a word is usually well made at the time it is first wanted; its youngest meaning has in it the full strength of its youth; subsequent senses are commonly warped or weakened; and as a misused word always is liable to involve an obscured thought, and all careful thinkers, either on this or any other subject, are sure to have used their words accurately, the first condition, in order to be able to avail ourselves of their sayings at all, is a firm definition of terms.

man—that is to say, the extension, defence, or comfort of his life. The golden pyramid may perhaps be providently built, perhaps improvidently; but, at all events, the wisdom or folly of the accumulation can only be determined by our having first clearly stated the aim of all economy, namely, the extension of life.

If the accumulation of money, or of exchangeable property, were a certain means of extending existence, it would be useless, in discussing economical questions, to fix our attention upon the more distant object— life—instead of the immediate one—money. But it is not so. Money may sometimes be accumulated at the cost of life, or by limitations of it; that is to say, either by hastening the deaths of men, or preventing their births. It is therefore necessary to keep clearly in view the ultimate object of economy; and to determine the expediency of minor operations with reference to that ulterior end.

It has been just stated that the object of political economy is the continuance not only of life, but of healthy and happy life. But all true happiness is both a consequence and cause of life: it is a sign of its vigour, and means of its continuance. All true suffering is in like manner a consequence and cause of death. I shall therefore in future, use the word "Life" singly: but let it be understood to include in its signification the happiness and power of the entire human nature, body and soul.

That human nature, as its Creator made it, and maintains it wherever His laws are observed, is entirely harmonious. No physical error can be more profound, no moral error more dangerous, than that involved in the monkish doctrine of the opposition of body to soul. No soul can be perfect in an imperfect body; no body perfect without perfect soul. Every right action and true thought sets the seal of its beauty on person and face; every wrong action and foul thought its seal of distortion; and the various aspects of humanity might be read as plainly as a printed history, were it not that the impressions are so complex that it must always in some cases—and, in the present state of our knowledge, in all cases—be impossible to decipher them completely. Nevertheless, the face of a consistently just, and of a consistently unjust person, may always be rightly discerned at a glance; and if the qualities are continued by descent through a generation or two, there arises a complete distinction of race. Both moral and physical qualities are communicated by descent, far more than they can be developed by education (though both may be destroyed for want of education), and there is as yet no ascertained limit to the nobleness of person and mind which the human creature may attain, by persevering observance of the laws of God respecting its birth and training.

We must therefore yet farther define the aim of political economy to be "The multiplication of human life at the highest standard." It might at first seem questionable whether we should endeavour to maintain a small number of persons of the highest type of beauty and intelligence, or a larger number of an inferior class. But I shall be able to show in the sequel, that the way to maintain the largest number is first to aim at the highest standard. Determine the noblest type of man, and aim simply at maintaining the largest possible number of persons of that class, and it will be found that the largest possible number of every healthy subordinate class must necessarily be produced also.

The perfect type of manhood, as just stated, involves the perfections (whatever we may hereafter determine these to be) of his body, affections, and intelligence. The material things, therefore, which it is the object of political economy to produce, and use (or accumulate for use), are things which serve either to sustain and comfort the body, or exercise rightly the affections and form the intelligence. Whatever truly serves either of these purposes is "useful" to man, wholesome, healthful, helpful, or holy. By seeking such things, man prolongs and increases his life upon the earth.

On the other hand, whatever does not serve either of these purposes,— much more whatever counteracts them,—is in like manner useless to man, unwholesome, unhelpful, or unholy; and by seeking such things man shortens and diminishes his life upon the earth. And neither with respect to things useful or useless can man's estimate of them alter their nature. Certain substances being good for his food, and others noxious to him, what he thinks or wishes respecting them can neither change their nature, nor prevent their power. If he eats corn, he will live; if nightshade, he will die. If he produce or make good and beautiful things, they will "re-create" him; (note the solemnity and weight of the word); if bad and ugly things, they will "corrupt" or break in pieces—that is, in the exact degree of their power, kill him. For every hour of labour, however enthusiastic or well intended, which he spends for that which is not bread, so much possibility of life is lost to him. His fancies, likings, beliefs, however brilliant, eager, or obstinate, are of no avail if they are set on a false object. Of all that he has laboured for, the eternal law of heaven and earth measures out to him for reward, to the utmost atom, that part which he ought to have laboured for, and withdraws from him (or enforces on him, it may be) inexorably that part which he ought not to have laboured for. The dust and chaff are all, to the last speck, winnowed away, and on his summer threshing-floor stands his heap of corn; little or much, not according to his labour, but to his discretion. No "commercial arrangements," no painting of surfaces nor alloying of substances, will avail him a pennyweight. Nature asks of him calmly and inevitably, What have you found, or formed—the right thing or the wrong? By the right thing you shall live; by the wrong you shall die.

To thoughtless persons it seems otherwise. The world looks to them as if they could cozen it out of some ways and means of life. But they cannot cozen IT: they can only cozen their neighbours. The world is not to be cheated of a grain; not so much as a breath of its air can be drawn surreptitiously. For every piece of wise work done, so much life is granted; for every piece of foolish work, nothing; for every piece of wicked work, so much death. This is as sure as the courses of day and night. But when the means of life are once produced, men, by their various struggles and industries of accumulation or exchange, may variously gather, waste, restrain, or distribute them; necessitating, in proportion to the waste or restraint, accurately so much more death. The rate and range of additional death is measured by the rate and range of waste, and is inevitable;—the only question (determined mostly by fraud in peace, and force in war) is, Who is to die, and how?

Such being the everlasting law of human existence, the essential work of the political economist is to determine what are in reality useful or life-giving things, and by what degrees and kinds of labour they are attainable and distributable. This investigation divides itself under three great heads;—the studies, namely, of the phenomena, first, of WEALTH; secondly, of MONEY; and thirdly, of RICHES.

These terms are often used as synonymous, but they signify entirely different things. "WEALTH" consists of things in themselves valuable; "MONEY," of documentary claims to the possession of such things; and "RICHES" is a relative term, expressing the magnitude of the possessions of one person or society as compared with those of other persons or societies.

The study of Wealth is a province of natural science:—it deals with the essential properties of things.

The study of Money is a province of commercial science:—it deals with conditions of engagement and exchange.

The study of Riches is a province of moral science:—it deals with the due relations of men to each other in regard of material possessions; and with the just laws of their association for purposes of labour.

I shall in this paper shortly sketch out the range of subjects which will come before us as we follow these three branches of inquiry.

Section 1. *Wealth*

Wealth, it has been said, consists of things essentially valuable. We now, therefore, need a definition of "value."

Value signifies the strength or "availing" of anything towards the sustaining of life, and is always two-fold; that is to say, primarily, INTRINSIC, and secondarily, EFFECTUAL.

The reader must, by anticipation, be warned against confusing value with cost, or with price. Value is the life-giving power of anything; cost, the quantity of labour required to produce it; price, the quantity of labour which its possessor will take in exchange for it. Cost and price are commercial conditions, to be studied under the head of money.

Intrinsic value is the absolute power of anything to support life. A sheaf of wheat of given quality and weight has in it a measurable power of sustaining the substance of the body; a cubic foot of pure air, a fixed power of sustaining its warmth; and a cluster of flowers of given beauty a fixed power of enlivening or animating the senses and heart.

It does not in the least affect the intrinsic value of the wheat, the air, or the flowers, that men refuse or despise them. Used or not, their own power is in them, and that particular power is in nothing else.

But, in order that this value of theirs may become effectual, a certain state is necessary in the recipient of it. The digesting, breathing, and perceiving functions must be perfect in the human creature before the food, air, or flowers can become of their full value to it. The production of effectual value, therefore, always involves two needs: first, the production of a thing essentially useful; then the production of the capacity to use it. Where the intrinsic value and acceptant capacity come together there is Effectual value, or wealth; where there is either no intrinsic value, or no acceptant capacity, there is no effectual value; that is to say, no wealth. A horse is no wealth to us if we cannot ride, nor a picture if we cannot see, nor can any noble thing be wealth, except to a noble person. As the aptness of the user increases, the effectual value of the thing used increases; and in its entirety can co-exist only with perfect skill of use, or harmony of nature. The effectual value of a given quantity of any commodity existing in the world at any moment is therefore a mathematical function of the capacity existing in the human race to enjoy it. Let its intrinsic value be represented by x, and the recipient faculty by y; its effectual value is $x\,y$, in which the sum varies as either coefficient varies, is increased by either's increase, and cancelled by either's absence.

Valuable material things may be conveniently referred to five heads:

1. Land, with its associated air, water, and organisms.

2. Houses, furniture, and instruments.

3. Stored or prepared food and medicine, and articles of bodily luxury, including clothing.

4. Books.

5. Works of art.

* * * * *

Section 2. Money

Under this head, we shall have to examine the laws of currency and exchange; of which I will note here the first principles.

Money has been inaccurately spoken of as merely a means of circulation. It is, on the contrary, an expression of right. It is not wealth, but a documentary claim to wealth, being the sign of the relative quantities of it, or of the labour producing it, to which, at a given time, persons or societies are entitled.

If all the money in the world, notes and gold, were destroyed in an instant, it would leave the world neither richer nor poorer than it was. But it would leave the individual inhabitants of it in different relations.

Money is, therefore, correspondent in its nature to the title-deed of an estate. Though the deed be burned, the estate still exists, but the right to it has become disputable.

The worth of money remains unchanged, as long as the proportion of the quantity of existing money to the quantity of existing wealth or available labour which it professes to represent, remains unchanged.

If the wealth increases, but not the money, the worth of the money increases; if the money increases, but not the wealth, the worth of the money diminishes.

Money, therefore, cannot be arbitrarily multiplied, any more than title-deeds can. So long as the existing wealth or available labour is not fully represented by the currency, the currency may be increased without diminution of the assigned worth of its pieces. But when the existing wealth, or available labour is once fully represented, every piece of money thrown into circulation diminishes the worth of every other existing piece, in the proportion it bears to the number of them, provided the new piece be received with equal credit; if not, the depreciation of worth takes place exclusively in the new piece, according to the inferiority of its credit.

When, however, new money, composed of some substance of supposed intrinsic value (as of gold), is brought into the market, or when new notes are issued which are supposed to be deserving of credit, the desire to obtain the money will, under certain circumstances, stimulate industry: an additional quantity of wealth is immediately produced, and if this be in proportion to the new claims advanced, the value of the existing currency is undepreciated. If the stimulus given be so great as to produce more goods than are proportioned to the additional coinage, the worth of the existing currency will be raised.

Arbitrary control and issues of currency affect the production of wealth, by acting on the hopes and fears of men, and are, under certain circumstances, wise. But the issue of additional currency to meet the exigencies of immediate expense, is merely one of the disguised forms of borrowing or taxing. It is, however, in the present low state of economical knowledge, often possible for Governments to venture on an issue of currency, when they could not venture on an additional loan or tax, because the real operation of such issue is not understood by the people, and the pressure of it is irregularly distributed, and with an unperceived gradation.

Finally. The use of substances of intrinsic value as the materials of a currency, is a barbarism;—a remnant of the conditions of barter, which alone can render commerce possible among savage nations. It is, however, still necessary, partly as a mechanical check on arbitrary issues; partly as a means of exchanges with foreign nations. In proportion to the extension of civilization, and increase of trustworthiness in Governments, it will cease. So long as it exists, the phenomena of the cost and price of the articles used for currency, are mingled with those of currency itself, in an almost inextricable manner; and the worth of money in the market is affected by multitudinous accidental circumstances, which have been traced, with more or less success by writers on commercial operations: but with these variations the true political economist has no more to do than an engineer fortifying a harbour of refuge against Atlantic tide, has to concern himself with the cries or quarrels of children who dig pools with their fingers for its ebbing currents among the sand.

Section 3. Riches

According to the various industry, capacity, good fortune, and desires of men, they obtain greater or smaller share of, and claim upon, the wealth of the world.

The inequalities between these shares, always in some degree just and necessary, may be either restrained by law (or circumstance) within certain limits; or may increase indefinitely.

Where no moral or legal restraint is put upon the exercise of the will and intellect of the stronger, shrewder, or more covetous men, these differences become ultimately enormous. But as soon as they become so distinct in their extremes as that, on one side, there shall be manifest redundance of possession, and on the other manifest pressure of need,—the terms "riches" and "poverty" are used to express the opposite states; being contrary only in the manner of the terms "warmth" and "cold"; which neither of them imply an actual degree, but only a relation to other degrees, of temperature.

Respecting riches, the economist has to inquire, first, into the advisable modes of their collection; secondly, into the advisable modes of their administration.

Respecting the collection of national riches, he has to inquire, first, whether he is justified in calling the nation rich, if the quantity of money it possesses relatively to that possessed by other nations be large, irrespectively of the manner of its distribution. Or does the mode of distribution in any wise affect the nature of the riches? Thus, if the king alone be rich—suppose Croesus or Mausolus—are the Lydians and Carians therefore a rich nation? Or if one or two slavemasters be rich, and the nation be otherwise composed of slaves, is it to be called a rich nation? For if not, and the ideas of a certain mode of distribution or operation in the riches, and of a certain degree of freedom in the people, enter into our idea of riches as attributed to a people, we shall have to define the degree of fluency or circulative character which is essential to their vitality; and the degree of independence of action required in their possessors. Questions which look as if they would take time in answering. And farther. Since there are two modes in which the inequality, which is indeed the condition and constituent of riches, may be established—namely, by increase of possession on the one side, and by decrease of it on the other— we have to inquire, with respect to any given state of riches, precisely in what manner the correlative poverty was produced: that is to say, whether by being surpassed only, or being depressed also; and if by being depressed, what are the advantages, or the contrary, conceivable in the depression. For instance, it being one of the commonest advantages of being rich to entertain a number of servants, we have to inquire, on the one side, what economical process produced the riches of the master; and on the other, what economical process produced the poverty of the persons who serve him; and what advantages each (on his own side) derives from the result.

These being the main questions touching the collection of riches, the next, or last, part of the inquiry is into their administration.

They have in the main three great economical powers which require separate examination: namely, the powers of selection, direction, and provision.

A. Their power of SELECTION relates to things of which the supply is limited (as the supply of best things is always). When it becomes matter of question to whom such things are to belong, the richest person has necessarily the first choice, unless some arbitrary mode of distribution be otherwise determined upon. The business of the economist is to show how this choice may be a wise one.

B. Their power of DIRECTION arises out of the necessary relation of rich men to poor, which ultimately, in one way or another, involves the direction of, or authority over, the labour of the poor; and this nearly as much over their mental as their bodily labour. The business of the economist is to show how this direction may be a Just one.

C. Their power of PROVISION or "preparatory sight" (for pro-accumulation is by no means necessarily provision), is dependent upon their redundance, which may of course by active persons be made available in preparation for future work or future profit; in which function riches have generally received the name of capital; that is to say, of head-, or source-material. The business of the economist is to show how this provision may be a Distant one.

The examination of these three functions of riches will embrace every final problem of political economy;—and, above, or before all, this curious and vital problem,—whether, since the wholesome action of riches in these three functions will depend (it appears), on the Wisdom, Justice, and Farsightedness of the holders; and it is by no means to be assumed that persons primarily rich, must therefore be just and wise,— it may not be ultimately possible so, or somewhat so, to arrange matters, as that persons primarily just and wise, should therefore be rich?

Such being the general plan of the inquiry before us, I shall not limit myself to any consecutive following of it, having hardly any good hope of being able to complete so laborious a work as it must prove to me; but from time to time, as I have leisure, shall endeavour to carry forward this part or that, as may be immediately possible; indicating always with accuracy the place which the particular essay will or should take in the completed system.

IV. Laws and Governments: Labour and Riches

* * * * *

There are, therefore, let me finally enforce, and leave with the reader this broad conclusion,—three things to be considered in employing any poor person. It is not enough to give him employment. You must employ him first to produce useful things; secondly, of the several (suppose equally useful) things he can equally well produce, you must set him to make that which will cause him to lead the healthiest life; lastly, of the things produced, it remains a question of wisdom and conscience how much you are to take yourself, and how much to leave to others. A large quantity, remember, unless you destroy it, *must* always be so left at one time or another; the only questions you have to decide are, not what you will give, and what you will keep, but when, and how, and to whom, you will give. The natural law of human life is, of course, that in youth a man shall labour and lay by store for his old age, and when age comes, should use what he has laid by, gradually slackening his toil, and allowing himself more frank use of his store, taking care always to leave himself as much as will surely suffice for him beyond any possible length of life. What he has gained, or by tranquil and unanxious toil continues to gain, more than is enough for his own need, he ought so to administer, while he yet lives, as to see the good of it again beginning, in other hands; for thus he has himself the greatest sum of pleasure from it, and faithfully uses his sagacity in its control. Whereas most men, it appears, dislike the sight of their fortunes going out into service again, and say to themselves,— "I can indeed nowise prevent this money from falling at last into the hands of others, nor hinder the good of it, such as it is, from becoming theirs, not mine; but at least let a merciful death save me from being a witness of their satisfaction; and may God so far be gracious to me as to let no good come of any of this money of mine before my eyes." Supposing this feeling unconquerable, the safest way of rationally indulging it would be for the capitalist at once to spend all his fortune on himself, which might actually, in many cases, be quite the rightest as well as the pleasantest thing to do, if he had just tastes and worthy passions. But, whether for himself only, or through the hands and for the sake of others also, the law of wise life is, that the maker of the money should also be the spender of it, and spend it, approximately, all, before he dies; so that his true ambition as an economist should be, to die, not as rich, but as poor, as possible, calculating the ebb tide of possession in true and calm proportion to the ebb tide of life. Which law, checking the wing of accumulative desire in the mid volley, and leading to peace of possession and fulness of fruition in old age, is also wholesome, in that by the freedom of gift, together with present help and counsel, it at once endears and dignifies age in the sight of youth, which then no longer strips the bodies of the dead, but receives the grace of the living. Its chief use would (or will be, for men are indeed capable of attaining to this much use of their reason), that some temperance and measure will be put to the acquisitiveness of commerce. For as things stand, a man holds it his duty to be temperate in his food, and of his body, but for no duty to be temperate in his riches, and of his mind. He sees that he ought not to waste his youth and his flesh for luxury; but he will waste his age, and his soul, for money, and think it no wrong, nor the *delirium tremens* of the intellect any evil. But the law of life is, that a man should fix the sum he desires to make annually, as the food he desires to eat daily; and stay when he has reached the limit, refusing increase of business, and leaving it to others, so obtaining due freedom of time for better thoughts. How the gluttony of business is punished, a bill of health for the principals of the richest city houses, issued annually, would show in a sufficiently impressive manner.

I know, of course, that these statements will be received by the modern merchant as an active border rider of the sixteenth century would have heard of its being proper for men of the Marches to get their living by the spade instead of the spur. But my business is only to state veracities and necessities; I neither look for the acceptance of the one, nor promise anything for the nearness of the other. Near or distant, the day will assuredly come when the merchants of a state shall be its true "ministers of exchange," its porters, in the double sense of carriers and gate-keepers, bringing all lands into frank and faithful communication, and knowing for their master of guild, Hermes the herald, instead of Mercury the gain-guarder.

And now, finally, for immediate rule to all whom it concerns.

The distress of any population means that they need food, house-room, clothes, and fuel. You can never, therefore, be wrong in employing any labourer to produce food, house-room, clothes, or fuel: but you are *always* wrong if you employ him to produce nothing, (for then some other labourer must be worked double time to feed him); and you are generally wrong, at present, if you employ him (unless he can do nothing else) to produce works of art, or luxuries; because modern art is mostly on a false basis, and modern luxury is criminally great.

The way to produce more food is mainly to bring in fresh ground, and increase facilities of carriage;—to break rock, exchange earth, drain the moist, and water the dry, to mend roads, and build harbours of refuge. Taxation thus spent will annihilate taxation, but spent in war, it annihilates revenue.

The way to produce house-room is to apply your force first to the humblest dwellings. When your bricklayers are out of employ, do not build splendid new streets, but better the old ones; send your paviours and slaters to the poorest villages, and see that your poor are healthily lodged before you try your hand on stately architecture. You will find its stateliness rise better under the trowel afterwards; and we do not yet build so well as that we need hasten to display our skill to future ages. Had the labour which has decorated the Houses of Parliament filled, instead, rents in walls and roofs throughout the county of Middlesex; and our deputies met to talk within massive walls that would have needed no stucco for five hundred years,—the decoration might have been better afterwards, and the talk now. And touching even our highly conscientious church building, it may be well to remember that in the best days of church plans, their masons called themselves "logeurs du bon Dieu"; and that since, according to the most trusted reports, God spends a good deal of His time in cottages as well as in churches, He might perhaps like to be a little better lodged there also.

The way to get more clothes is—not, necessarily, to get more cotton. There were words written twenty years ago which would have saved many of us some shivering had they been minded in time. Shall we read them?

"The Continental people, it would seem, are importing our machinery, beginning to spin cotton and manufacture for themselves, to cut us out of this market and then out of that! Sad news indeed; but irremediable. By no means the saddest news—the saddest news is, that we should find our national existence, as I sometimes hear it said, depend on selling manufactured cotton at a farthing an ell cheaper than any other people. A most narrow stand for a great nation to base itself on! A stand which, with all the Corn-Law abrogations conceivable, I do not think will be capable of enduring.

"My friends, suppose we quitted that stand; suppose we came honestly down from it and said—'This is our minimum of cotton prices; we care not, for the present, to make cotton any cheaper. Do you, if it seem so blessed to you, make cotton cheaper. Fill your lungs with cotton fur, your heart with copperas fumes, with rage and mutiny; become ye the general gnomes of Europe, slaves of the lamp!' I admire a nation which fancies it will die if it do not undersell all others to the end of the world. Brothers, we will cease to undersell them; we will be content to equal-sell them; to be happy selling equally with them! I do not see the use of underselling them: cotton-cloth is already two-pence a yard, or lower; and yet bare backs were never more numerous among us. Let inventive men cease to spend their existence incessantly contriving how cotton can be made cheaper; and try to invent a little how cotton at its present cheapness could be somewhat justlier divided among us.

"Let inventive men consider—whether the secret of this universe does after all consist in making money. With a hell which means—'failing to make money, I do not think there is any heaven possible that would suit one well. In brief, all this Mammon gospel of supply-and-demand, competition, *laissez faire*, and devil take the hindmost' (foremost, is it not, rather, Mr. Carlyle?), 'begins to be one of the shabbiest gospels ever preached.'" (In the matter of clothes, decidedly.)

The way to produce more fuel is first to make your coal mines safer, by sinking more shafts; then set all your convicts to work in them, and if, as is to be hoped, you succeed in diminishing the supply of that sort of labourer, consider what means there may be, first of growing forest where its growth will improve climate; then of splintering the forests which now make continents of fruitful land pathless and poisonous, into faggots for fire;—so gaining at once dominion sunwards and icewards. Your steam power has been given you (you will find eventually) for work such as that; and not for excursion trains, to give the labourer a moment's breath, at the peril of his breath for ever, from amidst the cities which you have crushed into masses of corruption. When you know how to build cities, and how to rule them, you will be able to breathe in their streets, and the "excursion" will be the afternoon's walk or game in the fields round them. Long ago, Claudian's peasant of Verona knew, and we must yet learn, in his fashion, the difference between *via* and *vita*.

"But nothing of this work will pay?"

No; no more than it pays to dust your rooms, or wash your doorsteps. It will pay; not at first in currency, but in that which is the end and the source of currency,—in life; (and in currency richly afterwards). It will pay in that which is more than life,—in "God's first creature, which was light," whose true price has not yet been reckoned in any currency, and yet into the image of which all wealth, one way or other, must be cast. For your riches must either be as the lightning, which,

> begot but in a cloud,
> Though shining bright, and speaking loud,
> Whilst it begins, concludes its violent race;
> And, where it gilds, it wounds the place;

or else as the lightning of the sacred sign, which shines from one part of the heaven to the other. There is no other choice; you must either take dust for deity, spectre for possession, fettered dream for life, and for epitaph, this reversed verse of the great Hebrew hymn of economy (Psalm cxii.):—"He hath gathered together, he hath stripped the poor, his iniquity remaineth for ever." Or else, having the sun of justice to shine on you, and the sincere substance of good in your possession, and the pure law and liberty of life within you, leave men to write this better legend over your grave:—

"He hath dispersed abroad. He hath given to the poor. His righteousness remaineth for ever."

JOHN RUSKIN

SELECTION FROM LETTERS FROM "FORS CLAVIGERA," II, LETTER XXXVII

THE ST. GEORGE EXPERIMENT

* * * * *

I have not hitherto stated, except in general terms, the design to which these letters point, though it has been again and again defined, and it seems to me explicit enough—the highest possible education, namely, of English men and women living by agriculture in their native land. . . . It is time now to say more clearly what I want them to do.

The substantial wealth of man consists in the earth he cultivates, with its pleasant or serviceable animals and plants, and in the rightly produced work of his own hands. I mean to buy, for the St. George's Company, the first pieces of ground offered to me at fair price (when the subscriptions enable me to give *any* price),—to put them as rapidly as possible into order, and to settle upon them as many families as they can support, of young and healthy persons, on the condition that they do the best they can for their livelihood with their own hands, and submit themselves and their children to the rules written for them.

I do not care where the land is, nor of what quality. I would rather it should be poor, for I want space more than food. I will make the best of it I can, at once, by wage-labour, under the best agricultural advice. It is easy now to obtain good counsel, and many of our landlords would willingly undertake such operations occasionally, but for the fixed notion that every improvement of land should at once pay, whereas the St. George's Company is to be consistently monastic in its principles of labour, and to work for the redemption of any desert land, without other idea of gain than the certainty of future good to others. I should best like a bit of marsh land of small value, which I would trench into alternate ridge and canal, changing it all into solid land, and deep water, to be farmed in fish. If, instead, I get a rocky piece, I should first arrange reservoirs for rain, then put what earth is sprinkled on it into workable masses; and ascertaining, in either case, how many mouths the gained spaces of ground will easily feed, put upon them families chosen for me by old landlords, who know their people, and can send me cheerful and honest ones, accustomed to obey orders, and live in the fear of God. Whether the fear be Catholic, or Church-of-England, or Presbyterian, I do not in the least care, so that the family be capable of any kind of sincere devotion; and conscious of the sacredness of order. If any young couples of the higher classes choose to accept such rough life, I would rather have them for tenants than any others.

Tenants, I say, and at long lease, if they behave well: with power eventually to purchase the piece of land they live on for themselves, if they can save the price of it; the rent they pay, meanwhile, being the tithe of the annual produce, to St. George's fund. The modes of the cultivation of the land are to be under the control of the overseer of the whole estate, appointed by the Trustees of the fund; but the tenants shall build their own houses to their own minds, under certain conditions as to material and strength; and have for themselves the entire produce of the land, except the tithe aforesaid.

The children will be required to attend training schools for bodily exercise, and music, with such other education as I have already described. Every household will have its library, given it from the fund, and consisting of a fixed number of volumes,—some constant, the others chosen by each family out of a list of permitted books, from which they afterwards may increase their library if they choose. The formation of this library for choice, by a republication of classical authors in standard forms, has long been a main object with me. No newspapers, nor any books but those named in the annually renewed lists, are to be allowed in any household. In time I hope to get a journal published, containing notice of any really important matters taking place in this or other countries, in the closely sifted truth of them.

The first essential point in the education given to the children will be the habit of instant, finely accurate, and totally unreasoning, obedience to their fathers, mothers, and tutors; the same precise and unquestioning submission being required from heads of families to the officers set over them. The second essential will be the understanding of the nature of honour, making the obedience solemn and constant; so that the slightest wilful violation of the laws of the society may be regarded as a grave breach of trust, and no less disgraceful than a soldier's recoiling from his place in a battle.

In our present state of utter moral disorganization, it might indeed seem as if it would be impossible either to secure obedience, or explain the sensation of honour; but the instincts of both are native in man, and the roots of them cannot wither, even under the dust-heap of modern liberal opinions. My settlers, you observe, are to be young people, bred on old estates; my commandants will be veteran soldiers; and it will be soon perceived that pride based on servitude to the will of another is far loftier and happier than pride based on servitude to humour of one's own.

Each family will at first be put on its trial for a year, without any lease of the land: if they behave well, they shall have a lease for three years; if through that time they satisfy their officers, a life-long lease, with power to purchase.

I have already stated that no machines moved by artificial power are to be used on the estates of the society; wind, water, and animal force are to be the only motive powers employed, and there is to be as little trade or importation as possible; the utmost simplicity of life, and restriction of possession, being combined with the highest attainable refinement of temper and thought. Everything that the members of any household can sufficiently make for themselves, they are so to make, however clumsily; but the carpenter and smith, trained to perfectest work in wood and iron, are to be employed on the parts of houses and implements in which finish is essential to strength. The ploughshare and spade must be made by the smith, and the roof and floors by a carpenter; but the boys of the house must be able to make either a horseshoe, or a table.

Simplicity of life without coarseness, and delight in life without lasciviousness, are, under such conditions, not only possible to human creatures, but natural to them. I do not pretend to tell you straight-forwardly all laws of nature respecting the conduct of men; but some of those laws I know, and will endeavour to get obeyed; others, as they are needful, will be in the sequel of such obedience ascertained. What final relations may take place between masters and servants, labourers and employers, old people and young, useful people and useless, in such a society, only experience can conclude; nor is there any reason to anticipate the conclusion. Some few things the most obstinate will admit, and the least credulous believe: that washed faces are healthier than dirty ones, whole clothes decenter than ragged ones, kind behaviour more serviceable than malicious, and pure air pleasanter than foul. Upon that much of "philosophic positive" I mean to act; and, little by little, to define in these letters the processes of action. That it should be left to me to begin such a work, with only one man in England—Thomas Carlyle—to whom I can look for steady guidance, is alike wonderful and sorrowful to me; but as the thing is so, I can only do what seems to me necessary, none else coming forward to do it. For my own part, I entirely hate the whole business: I dislike having either power or responsibility; am ashamed to ask for money, and plagued in spending it. I don't want to talk, nor to write, nor to advise or direct anybody. I am far more provoked at being thought foolish by foolish people, than pleased at being thought sensible by sensible people; and the average proportion of the numbers of each is not to my advantage. If I could find any one able to carry on the plan instead of me, I never should trouble myself about it more; and even now, it is only with extreme effort and chastisement of my indolence that I go on: but, unless I am struck with palsy, I do not seriously doubt my perseverance, until I find somebody able to take up the matter in the same mind, and with a better heart.

The laws required to be obeyed by the families living on the land will be,—with some relaxation and modification, so as to fit them for English people,—those of Florence in the fourteenth century. In what additional rules may be adopted, I shall follow, for the most part, Bacon, or Sir Thomas More, under sanction always of the higher authority which of late the English nation has wholly set its strength to defy—that of the Founder of its Religion;

*   *   *   *   *

PART VIII

RISE OF SOCIALISM AND ECONOMIC RADICALISM

1. Charles Fourier: "The Social Destiny of Man."

2. Pierre Joseph Proudhon: "What Is Property."

3. Marx and Engels: "Manifesto of the Communist Party."

4. Karl Marx: (*a*) "Critique of Political Economy."
   (*b*) "Eighteenth *Brumaire* of Louis Bonaparte."
   (*c*) "*Das Kapital.*"

CHARLES FOURIER

(1772–1837)

Fourier was a Frenchman, whose life covered the interesting periods of the French Revolution, the Napoleonic Era, the Restoration of the Bourbons, and the Revolution of 1830. He was, in turn, a soldier, a business man, and a writer. He was somewhat pedantic in mind and dissolute in character, but withal he possessed a mild disposition and a vivid imagination.

Fourier is to be classified with the Englishman, Robert Owen, as one of the associationists, who formed a school among the early Utopian or bourgeois socialists. To this group, association was a social principle analogous to the law of gravitation in the physical world. Harmony was to be achieved by the formation of a colony, or some isolated social group, which would practice division of labor within itself.

This revolutionary period produced numerous fantastic or Utopian schemes similar to those of Owen and Fourier. The whole social structure seemed to be in need of making over, and the formation of little colonies provided an excellent method of trying out new schemes of social organization. Even staid New England felt the influence of Fourier, as reflected in the Brook Farm experiment in which several literary figures participated.

The chief works of Fourier were "The Theory of the Four Movements and of General Destinies" (1808); "Treatise on Domestic Agricultural Association, or Industrial Attraction" (1822); and "New Industrial and Social World" (1829).

The following selection has been taken from the first of these works, which is ordinarily referred to as "The Social Destiny of Man." The English translation by Clapp, published in 1857, has been followed. It will be noted that not only are political and economic institutions to be revamped, but also the present form of family life is to be altered. Indeed, the institution of permanent monogamy was Fourier's chief target.

CHARLES FOURIER

SELECTIONS FROM "THE SOCIAL DESTINY OF MAN" OR "THE THEORY OF THE FOUR MOVEMENTS"

PART II

DESCRIPTION OF VARIOUS BRANCHES OF PRIVATE AND DOMESTIC DESTINIES

SECTION I. ON THE COMBINED HOUSEHOLD OF THE SEVENTH AND TWENTY-SIXTH PERIODS, AND THE ENNUIS EXPERIENCED BY BOTH SEXES IN THE ISOLATED HOUSEHOLD

II. *The Combined Household.*

I shall now speak of the method which may be substituted for our present Domestic Order. It is a measure borrowed from the seventh Social Period. I shall call it the *Combined Household, or Series of Nine Groups.* It may be organized in eight or ten groups, but the number nine is better adapted for a regular balance in the play of the passions.

To organize this Household, an edifice should be constructed suitable for the accommodation of a hundred persons of different degrees of wealth; eighty persons of one sex, and twenty domestics of the two sexes. There should be suites of apartments of different prices, so that every person can choose according to his means; there should also be halls and saloons for various public purposes.

The Series in its internal relations should be formed, so far as is possible, of nine Groups, each containing nine persons. (It should be borne in mind that these numbers are not imperative, and that I indicate everything approximatively.) For example, for the repasts, there should be nine tables distributed three and three in the respective halls of the first, second and third class of prices; and in each hall the three tables should be served at consecutive hours—say at one, two, and three o'clock in order in every respect to avoid uniformity; for uniformity, tameness, and mediocrity are the three natural enemies of the passions of Harmony, since the equilibrium of the passions can not be established except by a regular contrast of opposites.

The Series should have three compatible occupations. For instance, one Series of artisans could carry on the three trades of carpentry, joinery, and cabinet-making. This Society should have a name and an escutcheon —say the Oak. Further on should be the Series of the Lilac, composed of women, carrying on the business of mantua-making, millinery, and shirt-making.

Each associate should furnish an amount of capital regulated by a progressive scale, for instance, 4,000, 8,000, 12,000 francs; or 0, 1,000, 2,000; or if the founders are rich and wish to establish a magnificent Series, their subscriptions might extend to 100,000, 200,000, 300,000 francs, taking care always that the first class furnish triple that furnished by the third. This capital will serve as a guarantee for all the advances made by the Series in the way of rent, provisions, etc., to each member.

These Societies admit no coercive statutes, no monastic constraints. For example, the groups of individuals of the third class may sometimes order the fare of the second or of the first class, the directors giving credit to all who do not abuse it. The palaces or mansions of neighboring Series should intercommunicate by means of covered galleries protected from the air, so that in the relations of pleasure and business there may be a guarantee against the inclemency of the weather, from which so much inconvenience is experienced in Civilization. The members should be able to go day and night from one palace to the other by means of passages well heated or ventilated according to the season and without any risk, as in the present Order, of being constantly wet, bespattered, and exposed to colds and inflammations by passing suddenly from hot rooms to the open streets. On leaving a ball or banquet, persons wishing to sleep away from their apartments should be able to pass from one edifice to another under cover, and without overshoes or furs, or even the bother of taking a carriage. Instead of having to traverse three or four streets, as in Civilization, they would merely have to go through the public galleries of three or four contiguous edifices, without being exposed to either the cold or the heat, the wind or the rain. This system of sheltered communications is one of the thousand conveniences reserved for the Combined Order, of which the Unitary Palace of the Series gives a partial idea.

To organize the Series in balanced rivalry with each other, there should be formed eighteen in regular gradation; namely nine masculine and nine feminine; but this organization would be more costly than a Phalanx of the Combined Order. The trial might be made with six Series, three of men, and three of women. By means of this rivalry, though it would be on a small scale, the Series would put an end to the three philosophic virtues—uniformity, tameness, and mediocrity—at once. For example, the Series of the Willow, being the poorest of the six, would pique itself on carrying neatness, dexterity, politeness and the other qualities compatible with its small fortune, to the highest degree, while in matters in which it could attain only to mediocrity, it would make no pretension.

Societies of this kind will not, like the Combined Order, admit of extreme contrasts, such as that which exists between the poor man and the millionaire; these disparities which will be harmonized in the eighth Period, are not adapted to the seventh which is here in question.

In the eighth Period, Association is *contrasted*, and in the seventh *shaded;* thus the Combined Household, or Series of nine Groups, though composed of members unequal in fortune and in other respects, should not have too great a dissimilarity between them, whereas a Phalanx of the eighth Period would bring together the most extreme contrasts.

We see in our large cities a germ of the Combined Household, as in the case of the Clubs and Casinos, which already cause the insipid family group to be deserted. They afford relaxations and amusements of various kinds at less than a tenth of what they would cost in the private household. Every kind of pleasure becomes economical both in respect to money and trouble, all the preparations being carefully made by persons specially appointed for the purpose, as will be the case in the Combined Household. But Clubs and Casinos are based on a principle of equality which interferes with the development of ambition, whereas the Combined Household, being subdivided into nine rivalized and unequal groups, will open a vast field to it in the three characters of patron, patronized, and independent. I do not speak of the arrangements relative to children, nor of their education in such a household, because to explain such details, it would be necessary to give a synopsis of the whole Period. Let us confine ourselves to reasoning on the hypothesis that six Combined households are established; two composed of the opulent class, two of the middle class, and two of the poorer class. And let us suppose these six Series placed at once in the midst of Civilization—in a city like Paris or London. What would be the result of a domestic innovation so foreign to our old customs of social incoherence and isolation?

Observe, first, that in order to found these Series, it will not be necessary to overthrow and devastate empires as happens whenever an attempt is made to carry out the visionary schemes of the philosophers. On the contrary, the work will be entirely a pacific one; and instead of ravaging the earth to establish the rights of man, we shall peaceably establish the rights of woman by allotting to her three of the proposed Associations which will admit of nine classes of fortunes for each sex.

As for the results which this social inoculation would produce, these are enigmas which I leave to the inquisitive, but I will endeavor to furnish the key to them.

In administrative economy, what advantage would not a government find in dealing with a Series which paid its taxes on a fixed day and on simple notice, instead of treating with twenty isolated families, half of whom would defraud the government, and the other half refuse to pay till forced to by law. In case of contravention of the laws, no penalties would be inflicted except those which are simply humiliating.

such as removing the escutcheon from over the entrance of the edifice. What increase of revenue and what facility of administration would be secured in case a whole nation should be organized in Associations or Series of this kind! Might not governments, while diminishing the taxes by a third, find themselves one half richer owing to the economy in collecting, and in the increase of taxable products which would result from combined Industry?

In domestic economy, how great would be the diminution of individual expenses! Might not a person in the Combined Household live on a thousand francs income much better than on three thousand in the Isolated Household, and avoid, in addition, the trouble of marketing, supervision, and other details which would be attended to by the group of major-domos of each tribe?

Persons who have no inclination for the functions of major-domo or other domestic employments, would not be in any way occupied with the details of the household, and on quitting work would think of nothing but enjoying themselves at the various tables and parties of the Series, and of the neighboring Series of both sexes which would reciprocate invitations and visits. In this way, parties so expensive among us would in the end cost but little or nothing to the respective hosts. In fact an Association would not levy a profit either upon its members, whom it would indemnify every time they were absent from a meal, nor on its guests whom it would treat on the same terms as its own members, so that, balancing the account, every one could pass his time at social parties without expending a stiver more than if he had remained alone in his own room. As for the fare, I have stated that by means of combined labor, it would cost only a third of the trouble and expense which it costs in our isolated household.

To judge of the variety and charms afforded by the meetings of guests from various Series, it is necessary to understand the relations of Industry and of Love in the Seventh Period, to explain which here would require too much space.

In respect to manners and customs, it will be seen that in each Series, however poor, there will reign an *esprit de corps*—a jealousy of the honor of the Series; and that the first of the three classes will become the standard for the two others who will aim to imitate it. This *esprit de corps* will suffice to do away with the most offensive habits of the civilized populace, such as rudeness, vulgarity, untidiness, meanness, etc., by which a Series would consider itself disgraced. It would instantly dismiss any member who should be guilty of them.

These results would be due to the rivalry between the two sexes. The feminine Series would always be eager to distinguish themselves by courtesy, and to make up for deficiency of fortune, by excess of urbanity. Such a spirit would be incompatible with the popular institutions of the Civilizees, who do not possess either of the three following means for polishing the manners of men.

1. Competition between feminine and masculine corporations.

2. Emulation between the three classes of the same Series and the groups of each class.

3. The pecuniary independence which will be enjoyed in the seventh Period, in which the subordinate functions will be three times as lucrative as they are in the incoherent Order.

Our present Societies being destitute of these three means of social refinement and elevation, we should not be astonished that they tend to rudeness and vulgarity in all the trades and professions of the middle and lower classes. Nevertheless we find some among them, the soldiers for instance, who already have very noble tendencies, and are ready to sacrifice their lives for the honor of the corps in which they have little or no enjoyment. This enthusiasm common among soldiers, shows what advantage might be derived from *esprit de corps*, if it existed between the two sexes, as will be the case in the seventh Period, when all the domestic and social evils of Civilization will disappear. Among those evils must be mentioned domestic servitude, or *personal service*, which will not be admitted in the seventh Period. In this Order, as a rule, domestics will not be in the service of individuals but of the Institution; each of them will devote himself to the associates whose characters are most in sympathy with his own; this privilege of choice will render domestic service agreeable to inferiors as well as superiors. It is friendship rather than interest which will bring the parties together, and this is another charm unknown in Societies organized in families, in which domestics are generally the secret enemies of their employers. The three principal causes of this are:—

1. *The low rate of wages*, which are so reduced in the incoherent Order. Domestic service in this Order being very complicated, requires three times as many agents as in the Combined Household, and their pay must in consequence be reduced to a third what it would be in the latter.

2. *Incompatibility of character between the employer and the employed*, which renders the former tyrannical and establishes in domestic relations an extreme coldness which is augmented by fear of theft and other frauds, which can not occur in the Series.

3. *Multiplicity and Complication of Domestic Functions.* This will cease to exist in the Combined Household, in which every domestic will choose a function suited to his taste, and will devote only a portion of his time to domestic service. In the present Order, servants being compelled to perform twenty different functions, half of which are disagreeable to them, conceive a disgust for their calling and often hate their employers, even before knowing them. On the other hand, domestic service in the Series will offer numerous advantages to both servant and

master; so that in all respects this Order will have the faculty of converting occupations which are a constant source of vexation in the Civilized Order, into positive pleasures.

The old especially will be delighted with this new Order. There is nothing more sad than the condition of the old and of children in Civilization; this Society does not admit of functions adapted to either of the two extremes of life, so that infancy and old age become a burden to the community. Children, however, receive a certain degree of attention in anticipation of their future services; but the old, from whom nothing is expected but their property, are neglected, importuned, secretly railed at, and often hurried to the grave. Some respect is paid to them among the rich, but among the peasantry, nothing is more afflicting than the treatment they receive. They are slighted, thrust aside without ceremony, and reproached every hour with their useless existence.

These scandalous abuses will cease in the Combined Household in which the old will have functions not less useful than those of men in the prime of life; and, when in good health, they will enjoy an existence as delightful as during the best periods of their lives. To judge how marvellously the Combined Order will be found suited to the human passions, it should be observed that Nature has distributed to us our various tastes in a proportion and variety adapted to this new Order and in constant disproportion to the requirements of the Civilized Order.

I will give a proof of this which has already been presented, but which it is well to repeat. I have said that the majority of women have no taste nor aptitude for the cares of the household. Most of them are annoyed and harassed even by the cares of a small family. Others of them, on the contrary, make mere sport of domestic labors, and excel in them to such a degree that we should judge them competent to conduct a household of a hundred persons. Nevertheless Civilization requires of all women that they have a uniform taste for domestic labors which they all may be called on to perform. How happens it, then, that Nature refuses this taste and aptitude to three fourths of them? It is to preserve the proportion suitable for the Combined Order which will employ but one fourth of them in such functions.

If we continue our analysis of the inconveniences connected with our present domestic life, with the isolated household, it will be seen that all its vexations spring from one cause, namely, from *social incoherence*, which requires of every man and woman capacities and tastes which Nature has given to but a very small number, in order not to exceed the wants of the Combined Order which is our Destiny, and which ordinarily will employ but ten persons where we employ a hundred. It would have been useless, therefore, for Nature to have distributed in profusion such and such tastes which we consider so praiseworthy, such as that for housekeeping, which tastes, if they were as common as is required by Civilization, would become superfluous and inconvenient in the Combined Order.

I dwell on these facts in order to reproduce and enforce a conclusion which I have several times announced, namely, that there is nothing vicious or defective in our natural tastes and characters; that they are distributed in a variety and proportion adapted to our future Destiny; and that there is nothing vicious or defective on the earth but our incoherent Order that can not in any way accommodate itself to the nature of the passions, all of which are adapted to the wants of the Combined Order, the germs of which will be found in the Combined Household.

III. *Debasement of Woman in Civilization.*

Is there a shadow of justice to be found in the position forced upon woman in Civilization? Is not the young girl an article of merchandise offered for sale to any one who wishes to negotiate for her possession and exclusive ownership? Is not the consent she gives to the conjugal tie a mere mockery? Is it not forced upon her by the prejudices which beset her from infancy? Society would persuade her that the chain she is about to wear is woven of flowers. In respect to the rights of woman, is public opinion any more advanced at the present day than in that rude age when a certain Council of Macon discussed the question whether women have souls?—a question which was decided in the affirmative by a majority of only three votes!

The laws of England, so much vaunted by the moralists, accord to men various rights equally dishonoring to the female sex; such is the right of pecuniary indemnity given to the husband as a compensation for the infidelity of the wife. The forms are less gross in France, but the system is essentially the same. Here, as everywhere, young women languish, fall sick, and die for want of a union imperatively commanded by Nature, but which prejudice forbids them under penalty of ignominy and ruin, until they have been legally sold. Such events, though rare, are still sufficiently frequent to attest the slavery of the weaker sex, a contempt for the demands of Nature, and the absence of all justice in respect to woman.

The happy results which would have followed the extension of the rights of woman may be judged of by the experience of all countries. We find that the noblest nations have always been those which have accorded to woman the most liberty. We see this among the Barbarians and Savages as well as among the Civilizees. The Japanese, who are the most industrious, the most brave, and the most honorable among Barbaric nations, are also the least jealous of and the most indulgent toward woman. So true is this, that the wealthy Chinese make the voyage to Japan to indulge in amatory pleasures forbidden them by the hypocritical customs of their own nation.

The Otaheitans, for the same reason, were the best of all Savage tribes. Considering their limited resources, no tribe ever carried industry to such an extent. The French, who are the most liberal in many respects toward woman, are also among the best of the Civilizees, from the fact that they are the nation the most flexible—the one which can be the most easily excited by enthusiasm to do great things. And despite certain faults, such as frivolity, individual vanity, and uncleanliness, they are nevertheless the first Civilized nation, from this simple fact of their flexibility of character, which is the quality most opposed to the character of Barbarians.

We may observe, in the same sense, that the most vicious nations have always been those which have reduced woman to the greatest subjection. Witness the Chinese, who are the refuse of the globe—the most knavish, the most cowardly, the most wretched of all industrial nations; accordingly they are the most jealous and the most intolerant in respect to woman.

Among modern Civilizees, the least indulgent to the female sex are the Spaniards; hence they have remained behind all the other European nations, and have acquired no lustre in the arts or sciences.

As for Savage tribes, examination will prove that the most vicious are those which have the least respect for woman, and among whom her condition is the most miserable.

We may lay it down as a general rule, then, that *social progress and changes of Period are accomplished in proportion to the progress of Woman toward Liberty, and that the decline of society takes place in proportion to the diminution of her liberty.*

Other events influence these political vicissitudes and changes, but there is nothing which leads so rapidly to social progress or decline as modifications in the condition of woman. I have already said that the simple adoption of the harem or the seclusion of women, would change the Civilizees in a short time into Barbarians, while the simple abolition of the harem would cause the Barbarians to become Civilizees. In a word, *the extension of the rights of Woman is the fundamental principle of all social progress.*

Section II. On the Splendors of the Combined Order

VII. *Lustre of the Arts and Sciences.*

To judge to what degree of splendor the arts and sciences will be carried in the Combined Order, we must first understand what honors and rewards it will bestow upon the scientific men and artists.

Every Association will prepare, annually, according to the decision of the majority, a table of the inventions and compositions which have appeared and been accepted during the year. Each of these productions will be judged by the competent Series; as, for instance, a tragedy by the Series of Literature and Poetry.

If a work is esteemed worthy of recompense, a sum will be fixed upon to be adjudged to the author; for example twenty cents to Racine for his tragedy of *Phèdre*.

Each Phalanx having made up the list of prizes or recompenses to be adjudged, will forward it to the Central Administration, which counts the votes of the different Associations and makes up the list for the whole Province. This is sent to a higher administration by which the provincial returns arrive by degrees to the Supreme Administration at Constantinople —the future capital of the Globe—where the final verification takes place, and where are proclaimed the names of the authors crowned by the suffrages of the majority of the Associations of the globe. The author or inventor has adjudged to him the average of the sums voted by this majority. If a million Phalanxes vote ten cents, a million twenty cents, and a million thirty cents, the recompense will be fixed at twenty cents. Suppose twenty cents are awarded to Racine for his tragedy of Phèdre, and sixty cents to Franklin for the invention of the lightning-rod, the Administration would send Racine drafts for the sum of $600,000, and to Franklin the sum of $1,800,000 drawn on the Congress of their respective nations. This sum would be paid by the three million Phalanxes of the globe.

In addition, Franklin and Racine would receive the triumphal decoration and be declared Citizens of the Globe, and wherever they travelled they would enjoy in every Phalanx the same privileges and prerogatives which are accorded to its highest authorities.

These awards, the payments of which would be trifling for each Association, would be immense for the authors and inventors, especially as they may be frequently repeated. It might happen that Racine and Franklin would earn a similar sum the following year for having distinguished themselves by some other production obtaining the suffrages of the Globe.

The smallest works, provided they were received with general favor, would bring immense sums to their authors; for if the globe should adjudge to Haydn one cent for a given symphony, to Lebrun two cents for a given ode, Haydn would receive $30,000 and Lebrun $60,000 for a work which might not have cost them a month's labor. They might earn this sum several times in a single year.

For works like those of the sculptor, which can not be exhibited to the whole globe, other means of recompense will be devised.

It follows from what has been said, that in the Combined Order superior talent, of whatever kind, will assure to its possessor an immense fortune, and artists and men of science will have no occasion for soliciting protection or patronage; far from this, anything of the kind would serve only to humiliate both the patron and the patronized.

Suppose that Pradon, after much solicitation, succeeds in interesting in his tragedy of *Phèdre* twenty neighboring Associations in which he has friends, and where he has secured the performance of his piece; suppose even that these Associations have had the weakness to award a recompense to Pradon, of what account would be the vote of twenty Phalanxes out of three millions? And what mortification would be experienced by these twenty Phalanxes when the returns should come to be published at the capital of the globe! It would be seen, from the whole number of votes, that an unknown play called *Phèdre*, and composed by one Pradon, had found acceptance in twenty Associations, all compeers and neighbors of the said Pradon. It will easily be conceived that such an announcement would cause alike the author and the twenty Associations which had patronized him to be covered with disgrace all over the globe. But what would happen despite all the intrigues of Pradon? Simply that the twenty Associations whose support he had solicited would not care to expose themselves to mortification and disgrace, by giving their suffrage to a play of such little merit; that far from being able to count on half the suffrages of the globe, such a play would not be accepted at twenty leagues distance in any Association where Pradon had no particular friends.

It is thus that in the Combined Order all patronage and favoritism will serve only to mortify an author, without being of any advantage to him, while the man of real talent will rise at once, without the aid of either intrigue or solicitation, to immense reputation and fortune. There will be but one means of success, namely that of delighting a majority of the Phalanxes of the globe.

After this digression on the unitary recompenses which will be awarded to men of science and art in the Combined Order, let us examine what will be the effect of such a system on some particular branch of art—say the *Opera*.

PIERRE JOSEPH PROUDHON

(1809–1865)

Proudhon was a literary radical who belonged to the generation after Fourier. He may be classified as a realistic or proletarian socialist in contrast to the earlier Utopian and bourgeois socialists. Perhaps it is more correct to regard him as one of the earliest anarchists; at least that is how he classified himself.

Proudhon's chief work of interest to students of the history of economic thought is "What is Property?" (1840). His answer is that property, as distinguished from possession, is robbery. Moreover, according to him, property owners are thieves. Truly the thunder before the storm of 1848 was even deeper than that before the revolution of 1789.

Proudhon's writing showed the change in the character of socialism from a bourgeois to a proletarian type. The way was paved for Marxism. Again, Proudhon foreshadowed the development of anarchism and the split between socialism and anarchistic communism.

The following selections are taken from "What is Property," translated from the French by Tucker. The student will be interested to note Proudhon's egotism and bombastic style.

PIERRE JOSEPH PROUDHON

SELECTIONS FROM "WHAT IS PROPERTY?" OR "AN INQUIRY INTO THE PRINCIPLE OF RIGHT AND OF GOVERNMENT"

FIRST MEMOIR

Chapter I. Method Pursued in This Work. The Idea of a Revolution.

If I were asked to answer the following question: *What is slavery?* and I should answer in one word, *It is murder,* my meaning would be understood at once. No extended argument would be required to show that the power to take from a man his thought, his will, his personality, is a power of life and death; and that to enslave a man is to kill him. Why, then, to this other question: *What is property?* may I not likewise answer, *It is robbery,* without the certainty of being misunderstood; the second proposition being no other than a transformation of the first?

I undertake to discuss the vital principle of our government and our institutions, property: I am in my right. I may be mistaken in the conclusion which shall result from my investigations: I am in my right. I think best to place the last thought of my book first: still am I in my right.

Such an author teaches that property is a civil right, born of occupation and sanctioned by law; another maintains that it is a natural right, originating in labor,—and both of these doctrines, totally opposed as they may seem, are encouraged and applauded. I contend that neither labor, nor occupation, nor law, can create property; that it is an effect without a cause: am I censurable?

But murmurs arise!

Property is robbery? That is the war-cry of '93! That is the signal of revolutions!

Reader, calm yourself: I am no agent of discord, no firebrand of sedition. I anticipate history by a few days; I disclose a truth whose development we may try in vain to arrest; I write the preamble of our future constitution. This proposition which seems to you blasphemous— *property is robbery*—would, if our prejudices allowed us to consider it, be recognized as the lightning-rod to shield us from the coming thunderbolt; but too many interests stand in the way! . . . Alas! philosophy will not change the course of events: destiny will fulfill itself regardless of prophecy. Besides, must not justice be done and our education be finished?

Property is robbery! . . . What a revolution in human ideas! *Proprietor* and *robber* have been at all times expressions as contradictory as the beings whom they designate are hostile; all languages have perpetuated this opposition. On what authority, then, do you venture to attack universal consent, and give the lie to the human race? Who are you, that you should question the judgment of the nations and the ages?

Of what consequence to you, reader, is my obscure individuality? I live, like you, in a century in which reason submits only to fact and to evidence. My name, like yours, is TRUTH-SEEKER. My mission is written in these words of the law: *Speak without hatred and without fear; tell that which thou knowest!* The work of our race is to build the temple of science, and this science includes man and Nature. Now, truth reveals itself to all; to-day to Newton and Pascal, to-morrow to the herdsman in the valley and the journeyman in the shop. Each one contributes his stone to the edifice; and, his task accomplished, disappears. Eternity precedes us, eternity follows us: between two infinites, of what account is one poor mortal that the century should inquire about him?

Disregard then, reader, my title and my character, and attend only to my arguments. It is in accordance with universal consent that I undertake to correct universal error; from the *opinion* of the human race I appeal to its *faith*. Have the courage to follow me; and, if your will is untrammelled, if your conscience is free, if your mind can unite two propositions and deduce a third therefrom, my ideas will inevitably become yours. In beginning by giving you my last work, it was my purpose to warn you, not to defy you; for I am certain that, if you read me, you will be compelled to assent. The things of which I am to speak are so simple and clear that you will be astonished at not having perceived them before, and you will say: "I have neglected to think." Others offer you the spectacle of genius wresting Nature's secrets from her, and unfolding before you her sublime messages: you will find here only a series of experiments upon *justice* and *right*, a sort of verification of the weights and measures of your conscience. The operations shall be conducted under your very eyes; and you shall weigh the result.

Nevertheless, I build no system. I ask an end to privilege, the abolition of slavery, equality of rights, and the reign of law. Justice, nothing else; that is the alpha and omega of my arguments: to others I leave the business of governing the world.

One day I asked myself: Why is there so much sorrow and misery in society? Must man always be wretched? And not satisfied with the explanations given by the reformers,—these attributing the general distress to governmental cowardice and incapacity, those to conspirators and *émeutes*, still others to ignorance and general corruption,—and weary of the interminable quarrels of the tribune and the press, I sought to fathom the matter myself. I have consulted the masters of science; I have read a hundred volumes of philosophy, law, political economy, and history: would to God that I had lived in a century in which so much reading had been useless! I have made every effort to obtain exact information, comparing doctrines, replying to objections, continually constructing equations and reductions from arguments, and weighing thousands of syllogisms in the scales of the most rigorous logic. In this laborious work, I have collected many interesting facts which I shall share with my friends and the public as soon as I have leisure. But I must say that I recognized at once that we had never understood the meaning of these words, so common and yet so sacred: *Justice, equity, liberty;* that concerning each of these principles our ideas have been utterly obscure, and, in fact, that this ignorance was the sole cause, both of the poverty that devours us, and of all the calamities that have ever afflicted the human race.

My mind was frightened by this strange result: I doubted my reason. What! said I, that which eye has not seen, nor ear heard, nor insight penetrated, you have discovered! Wretch, mistake not the visions of your diseased brain for the truths of science! Do you not know (great philosophers have said so) that in points of practical morality universal error is a contradiction?

I resolved then to test my arguments; and in entering upon this new labor I sought an answer to the following questions: Is it possible that humanity can have been so long and so universally mistaken in the application of moral principles? How and why could it be mistaken? How can its error, being universal, be capable of correction?

These questions, on the solution of which depended the certainty of my conclusions, offered no lengthy resistance to analysis. It will be seen, in chapter V. of this work, that in morals, as in all other branches of knowledge, the gravest errors are the dogmas of science; that, even in the works of justice, to be mistaken is a privilege which ennobles man; and that whatever philosophical merit may attach to me is infinitely small. To name a thing is easy: the difficulty is to discern it before its appearance. In giving expression to the last stage of an idea,—an idea which permeates all minds, which to-morrow will be proclaimed by another if I fail to announce it to-day,—I can claim no merit save that of priority of utterance. Do we eulogize the man who first perceives the dawn?

Yes: all men believe and repeat that equality of conditions is identical with equality of rights; that *property* and *robbery* are synonymous terms; that every social advantage accorded, or rather usurped, in the name of superior talent or service, is iniquity and extortion. All men in their hearts, I say, bear witness to these truths; they need only to be made to understand it.

* * * * *

Is property just?

Everybody answers without hesitation, "Yes, property is just." I say everybody, for up to the present time no one who thoroughly understood the meaning of his words has answered no. For it is no easy thing to reply understandingly to such a question; only time and experience can furnish an answer. Now, this answer is given; it is for us to understand it. I undertake to prove it.

We are to proceed with the demonstration in the following order:—

I. We dispute not at all, we refute nobody, we deny nothing; we accept as sound all the arguments alleged in favor of property, and confine ourselves to a search for its principle, in order that we may then ascertain whether this principle is faithfully expressed by property. In fact, property being defensible on no ground save that of justice, the idea, or at least the intention, of justice must of necessity underlie all the arguments that have been made in defence of property; and, as on the other hand the right of property is only exercised over those things which can be appreciated by the senses, justice, secretly objectifying itself, so to speak, must take the shape of an algebraic formula. By this method of investigation, we soon see that every argument which has been invented in behalf of property, *whatever it may be*, always and of necessity leads to equality; that is, to the negation of property.

The first part covers two chapters: one treating of occupation, the foundation of our right; the other, of labor and talent, considered as causes of property and social inequality.

The first of these chapters will prove that the right of occupation *obstructs* property; the second that the right of labor *destroys* it.

II. Property, then, being of necessity conceived as existing only in connection with equality, it remains to find out why, in spite of this necessity of logic, equality does not exist. This new investigation also covers two chapters: in the first, considering the fact of property in itself, we inquire whether this fact is real, whether it exists, whether it is possible; for it would imply a contradiction, were these two opposite forms of society, equality and inequality, both possible. Then we discover, singularly enough, that property may indeed manifest itself accidentally; but that, as an institution and principle, it is mathematically impossible. So that the axiom of the school—*ab actu ad posses valet consecutio:* from the actual to the possible the inference is good—is given the lie as far as property is concerned.

Finally, in the last chapter, calling psychology to our aid, and probing man's nature to the bottom, we shall disclose the principle of *justice*— its formula and character; we shall state with precision the organic law of society; we shall explain the origin of property, the causes of its establishment, its long life, and its approaching death; we shall definitively establish its identity with robbery. And, after having **shown** that these three prejudices—*the sovereignty of man, the inequality of conditions, and property*—are one and the same; that they may be taken for each other, and are reciprocally convertible,—we shall have no trouble in inferring therefrom, by the principle of contradiction, the basis of government and right. There our investigations will end, reserving the right to continue them in future works.

* * * * *

Chapter V. Psychological Exposition of the Idea of Justice and Injustice, and a Determination of the Principle of Government and of Right

Part II. Section 1. Of the Causes of Our Mistakes. The Origin of Property.

* * * * *

Thus, moral evil, or in this case, disorder in society, is naturally explained by our power of reflection. The mother of poverty, crime, insurrection, and war was inequality of conditions, which was the daughter of property, which was born of selfishness, which was engendered by private opinion, which descended in a direct line from the autocracy of reason. Man, in his infancy, is neither criminal nor barbarous, but ignorant and inexperienced. Endowed with imperious instincts which are under the control of his reasoning faculty, at first he reflects but little, and reasons inaccurately; then, benefiting by his mistakes, he rectifies his ideas, and perfects his reason. In the first place, it is the savage sacrificing all his possessions for a trinket, and then repenting and weeping; it is Esau selling his birthright for a mess of pottage, and afterwards wishing to cancel the bargain; it is the civilized workman laboring in insecurity, and continually demanding that his wages be increased, neither he nor his employer understanding that, in the absence of equality, any salary, however large, is always insufficient. Then it is Naboth dying to defend his inheritance; Cato tearing out his entrails that he might not be enslaved; Socrates drinking the fatal cup in defence of liberty of thought; it is the third estate of '89 reclaiming its liberty; soon it will be the people demanding equality of wages and an equal division of the means of production.

Man is born a social being,—that is, he seeks equality and justice in all his relations, but he loves independence and praise. The difficulty of satisfying these various desires at the same time is the primary cause of the despotism of the will, and the appropriation which results from it. On the other hand, man always needs a market for his products; unable to compare values of different kinds, he is satisfied to judge approximately, according to his passion and caprice; and he engages in dishonest commerce, which always results in wealth and poverty. Thus, the greatest evils which man suffers arise from the misuse of his social nature, of this same justice of which he is so proud, and which he applies with such deplorable ignorance. The practice of justice is a science which, when once discovered and diffused, will sooner or later put an end to social disorder, by teaching us our rights and duties.

* * * * *

Property, born of the reasoning faculty, intrenches itself behind comparisons. But, just as reflection and reason are subsequent to spontaneity, observation to sensation, and experience to instinct, so property is subsequent to communism. Communism—or association in a simple form—is the necessary object and original aspiration of the social nature, the spontaneous movement by which it manifests and establishes itself. It is the first phase of human civilization. In this state of society,—which the jurists have called *negative communism,*—man draws near to man, and shares with him the fruits of the field and the milk and flesh of animals. Little by little this communism—negative as long as man does not produce—tends to become positive and organic through the development of labor and industry. But it is then that the sovereignty of thought, and the terrible faculty of reasoning logically or illogically, teach man that, if equality is the *sine qua non* of society, communism is the first species of slavery.

To express this idea by an Hegelian formula, I will say:

Communism—the first expression of the social nature—is the first term of social development,—the *thesis;* property, the reverse of communism, is the second term,—the *antithesis.* When we have discovered the third term, the *synthesis,* we shall have the required solution. Now this synthesis necessarily results from the correction of the thesis by the antithesis. Therefore it is necessary, by a final examination of their characteristics, to eliminate those features which are hostile to sociability. The union of the two remainders will give us the true form of human association.

Section 2. *Characteristics of Communism and of Property.*

I. I ought not to conceal the fact that property and communism have been considered always the only possible forms of society. This deplorable error has been the life of property. The disadvantages of communism are so obvious that its critics never have needed to employ much eloquence to thoroughly disgust men with it. The irreparability of the injustice which it causes, the violence which it does to attractions and repulsions, the yoke of iron which it fastens upon the will, the moral torture to which it subjects the conscience, the debilitating effect which it has upon society; and, to sum it all up, the pious and stupid uniformity which it enforces upon the free, active, reasoning, unsubmissive personality of man, have shocked common sense, and condemned communism by an irrevocable decree.

The authorities and examples cited in its favor disprove it. The communistic republic of Plato involved slavery; that of Lycurgus employed Helots, whose duty it was to produce for their masters, thus enabling the latter to devote themselves exclusively to athletic sports and to war. Even J. J. Rousseau—confounding communism and equality —has said somewhere that, without slavery, he did not think equality of conditions possible. The communities of the early Church did not last the first century out, and soon degenerated into monasteries. In those of the Jesuits of Paraguay, the condition of the blacks is said by all travellers to be as miserable as that of slaves; and it is a fact that the good Fathers were obliged to surround themselves with ditches and walls to prevent their new converts from escaping. The followers of Baboeuf— guided by a lofty horror of property rather than by any definite belief— were ruined by exaggeration of their principles; the St. Simonians, lumping communism and inequality, passed away like a masquerade. The greatest danger to which society is exposed to-day is that of another shipwreck on this rock.

Singularly enough, systematic communism—the deliberate negation of property,—is conceived under the direct influence of the proprietary prejudice; and property is the basis of all communistic theories.

The members of a community, it is true, have no private property; but the community is proprietor, and proprietor not only of the goods, but of the persons and wills. In consequence of this principle of absolute property, labor, which should be only a condition imposed upon man by Nature, becomes in all communities a human commandment, and therefore odious. Passive obedience, irreconcilable with a reflecting will, is strictly enforced. Fidelity to regulations, which are always defective, however wise they may be thought, allows of no complaint. Life, talent, and all the human faculties are the property of the State, which has the right to use them as it pleases for the common good. Private associations are sternly prohibited, in spite of the likes and dislikes of different natures, because to tolerate them would be to introduce small communities within the large one, and consequently private property; the strong work for the weak, although this ought to be left to benevolence, and not enforced, advised, or enjoined; the industrious work for the lazy, although this is unjust; the clever work for the foolish, although this is absurd; and, finally, man—casting aside his personality, his spontaneity, his genius, and his affections—humbly annihilates himself at the feet of the majestic and inflexible Commune.

Communism is inequality, but not as property is. Property is the exploitation of the weak by the strong. Communism is the exploitation of the strong by the weak. In property, inequality of conditions is the result of force; under whatever name it be disguised: physical and mental force; force of events, chance, *fortune;* force of accumulated property, &c.

In communism, inequality springs from placing mediocrity on a level with excellence. This damaging equation is repellent to the conscience, and causes merit to complain; for, although it may be the duty of the strong to aid the weak, they prefer to do it out of generosity,—they will never endure a comparison. Give them equal opportunities of labor, and equal wages, but never allow their jealousy to be awakened by mutual suspicion of unfaithfulness in the performance of the common task.

Communism is oppression and slavery. Man is very willing to obey the law of duty, serve his country, and oblige his friends; but he wishes to labor when he pleases, where he pleases, and as much as he pleases. He wishes to dispose of his own time, to be governed only by necessity, to choose his friendships, his recreation, and his discipline; to act from judgment, not by command; to sacrifice himself through selfishness, not through servile obligation. Communism is essentially opposed to the free exercise of our faculties, to our noblest desires, to our deepest feelings. Any plan which could be devised for reconciling it with the demands of the individual reason and will would end only in changing the thing while preserving the name. Now, if we are honest truth-seekers, we shall avoid disputes about words.

Thus, communism violates the sovereignty of the conscience, and equality: the first, by restricting spontaneity of mind and heart, and freedom of thought and action; the second, by placing labor and laziness, skill and stupidity, and even vice and virtue on an equality in point of comfort. For the rest, if property is impossible on account of the desire to accumulate, communism would soon become so through the desire to shirk.

* * * * *

In recapitulation:

Justice, after passing through the state of negative communism, called by the ancient poets the *age of gold*, commences as the right of the strongest. In a society which is trying to organize itself, inequality of faculties calls up the idea of merit; *équité* suggests the plan of proportioning not only esteem, but also material comforts, to personal merit; and since the highest and almost the only merit then recognized is physical strength, the strongest, αριστος, and consequently the best, αριστος, is entitled to the largest share; and if it is refused him, he very naturally takes it by force. From this to the assumption of the right of property in all things, it is but one step.

Such was justice in the heroic age, preserved, at least by tradition, among the Greeks and Romans down to the last days of their republics. Plato, in the "Gorgias," introduces a character named Callicles, who spiritedly defends the right of the strongest, which Socrates, the advocate of equality, τον ισον, seriously refutes. It is related of the great Pompey that he blushed easily, and, nevertheless, these words once escaped his lips: "Why should I respect the laws, when I have arms in my hand?" This shows him to have been a man in whom moral sense and ambition were struggling for the mastery, and who sought to justify his violence by the motto of the hero and the brigand.

From the right of the strongest springs the exploitation of man by man, or bondage; usury, or the tribute levied upon the conquered by the conqueror; and the whole numerous family of taxes, duties, monarchical prerogatives, house-rents, farm rents, &c.; in one word,—property.

Force was followed by artifice, the second manifestation of justice, which was detested by the ancient heroes, who, not excelling in that direction, were heavy losers by it. Force was still employed, but mental force instead of physical. Skill in deceiving an enemy by treacherous propositions seemed deserving of reward; nevertheless, the strong always prided themselves upon their honesty. In those days, oaths were observed and promises kept according to the letter rather than the spirit: *Uti lingua nuncupassit, ita jus esto,*—"As the tongue has spoken, so must the right be," says the law of the Twelve Tables. Artifice, or rather perfidy, was the main element in the politics of ancient Rome. Among other examples, Vico cites the following, also quoted by Montesquieu: The Romans had guaranteed to the Carthaginians the preservation of their goods and their *city,*—intentionally using the word *civitas,* that is, the society, the State; the Carthaginians, on the contrary, understood them to mean the material city, *urbs,* and accordingly began to rebuild their walls. They were immediately attacked on account of their violation of the treaty, by the Romans, who, acting upon the old heroic idea of right, did not imagine that, in taking advantage of an equivocation to surprise their enemies, they were waging unjust war.

From artifice sprang the profits of manufactures, commerce, and banking, mercantile frauds, and pretensions which are honored with the beautiful names of *talent* and *genius,* but which ought to be regarded as the last degree of knavery and deception; and, finally, all sorts of social inequalities.

In those forms of robbery which are prohibited by law, force and artifice are employed alone and undisguised; in the authorized forms, they conceal themselves within a useful product, which they use as a tool to plunder their victim.

The direct use of violence and stratagem was early and universally condemned; but no nation has yet got rid of that kind of robbery which acts through talent, labor, and possession, and which is the source of all the dilemmas of casuistry and the innumerable contradictions of jurisprudence.

The right of force and the right of artifice—glorified by the rhapsodists in the poems of the "Iliad" and the "Odyssey"—inspired the legislation of the Greeks and Romans, from which they passed into our morals and codes. Christianity has not changed at all. The Gospel should not be blamed, because the priests, as stupid as the legists, have been unable either to expound or to understand it. The ignorance of councils and popes upon all questions of morality is equal to that of the market-place and the money-changers; and it is this utter ignorance of right, justice, and society, which is killing the Church, and discrediting its teachings for ever. The infidelity of the Roman church and other Christian churches is flagrant; all have disregarded the precept of Jesus; all have erred in moral and doctrinal points; all are guilty of teaching false and absurd dogmas, which lead straight to wickedness and murder. Let it ask pardon of God and men,—this church which called itself infallible, and which has grown so corrupt in morals; let its reformed sisters humble themselves, . . . and the people, undeceived, but still religious and merciful, will begin to think.

The development of right has followed the same order, in its various expressions, that property has in its forms. Every where we see justice driving robbery before it and confining it within narrower and narrower limits. Hitherto the victories of justice over injustice, and of equality over inequality, have been won by instinct and the simple force of things; but the final triumph of our social nature will be due to our reason, or else we shall fall back into feudal chaos. Either this glorious height is reserved for our intelligence, or this miserable depth for our baseness.

The second effect of property is despotism. Now, since despotism is inseparably connected with the idea of legitimate authority, in explaining the natural causes of the first, the principle of the second will appear.

What is to be the form of government in the future? I hear some of my younger readers reply: "Why how can you ask such a question? You are a republican." "A republican! Yes; but that word specifies nothing. *Res publica;* that is, the public thing. Now, whoever is interested in public affairs—no matter under what form of government—may call himself a republican. Even kings are republicans."—"Well! you are a democrat?"—"No."—"What! you would have a monarchy."—"No." —"A constitutionalist?"—"God forbid!"—"You are then an aristocrat?"—"Not at all."—"You want a mixed government?"—"Still less."—"What are you, then?"—"I am an anarchist."

* * * * *

In proportion as society becomes enlightened, royal authority diminishes. That is a fact to which all history bears witness. At the birth of nations, men reflect and reason in vain. Without methods, without principles, not knowing how to use their reason, they cannot judge of the justice of their conclusions. Then the authority of kings is immense, no knowledge having been acquired with which to contradict it. But.

little by little, experience produces habits, which develop into customs; then the customs are formulated in maxims, laid down as principles,—in short, transformed into laws, to which the king, the living law, has to bow. There comes a time when customs and laws are so numerous that the will of the prince is, so to speak, entwined by the public will; and that, on taking the crown, he is obliged to swear that he will govern in conformity with established customs and usages; and that he is but the executive power of a society whose laws are made independently of him.

Up to this point, all is done instinctively, and, as it were, unconsciously; but see where this movement must end.

By means of self-instruction and the acquisition of ideas, man finally acquires the idea of *science*, that is, of a system of knowledge in harmony with the reality of things, and inferred from observation. He searches for the science, or the system, of inanimate bodies,—the system of organic bodies, the system of the human mind, and the system of the universe: why should he not also search for the system of society? But, having reached his height, he comprehends that political truth, or the science of politics, exists quite independently of the will of sovereigns, the opinion of majorities, and popular beliefs,—that kings, ministers, magistrates, and nations, as wills, have no connection with the science, and are worthy of no consideration. He comprehends, at the same time, that, if man is born a sociable being, the authority of his father over him ceases on the day when, his mind being formed and his education finished, he becomes the associate of his father; that his true chief and his king is the demonstrated truth; that politics is a science, not a stratagem; and that the function of the legislator is reduced, in the last analysis, to the methodical search for truth.

Thus, in a given society, the authority of man over man is inversely proportional to the stage of intellectual development which that society has reached; and the probable duration of that authority can be calculated from the more or less general desire for a true government,—that is, for a scientific government. And just as the right of force and the right of artifice retreat before the steady advance of justice, and must finally be extinguished in equality, so the sovereignty of the will yields to the sovereignty of the reason, and must at last be lost in scientific socialism. Property and royalty have been crumbling to pieces ever since the world began. As man seeks justice in equality, so society seeks order in anarchy.

Anarchy,—the absence of a master, of a sovereign,—such is the form of government to which we are every day approximating, and which our accustomed habit of taking man for our rule, and his will for law, leads us to regard as the height of disorder and the expression chaos. The story is told, that a citizen of Paris in the seventeenth century having heard it said that in Venice there was no king, the good man could not recover from his astonishment, and nearly died from laughter at the mere mention of so ridiculous a thing. So strong is our prejudice. As long as we live, we want a chief or chiefs; and at this very moment I hold in my hand a *brochure*, whose author—a zealous communist— dreams, like a second Marat, of the dictatorship. The most advanced among us are those who wish the greatest possible number of sovereigns,— their most ardent wish is for the royalty of the National Guard. Soon, undoubtedly, some one, jealous of the citizen militia, will say, "Everybody is king." But, when he has spoken, I will say, in my turn, "Nobody is king; we are, whether we will or no, associated." Every question of domestic politics must be decided by departmental statistics; every question of foreign politics is an affair of international statistics. The science of government rightly belongs to one of the sections of the Academy of Sciences, whose permanent secretary is necessarily prime minister; and, since every citizen may address a memoir to the Academy, every citizen is a legislator. But, as the opinion of no one is of any value until its truth has been proven, no one can substitute his will for reason,— nobody is king.

All questions of legislation and politics are matters of science, not of opinion. The legislative power belongs only to the reason, methodically recognized and demonstrated. To attribute to any power whatever the right of veto or of sanction, is the last degree of tyranny. Justice and legality are two things as independent of our approval as is mathematical truth. To compel, they need only to be known; to be known, they need only to be considered and studied. What, then, is the nation, if it is not the sovereign,—if it is not the source of the legislative power? The nation is the guardian of the law—the nation is the *executive power*. Every citizen may assert: "This is true; that is just"; but this opinion controls no one but himself. That the truth which he proclaims may become a law, it must be recognized. Now, what is it to recognize a law? It is to verify a mathematical or a metaphysical calculation; it is to repeat an experiment, to observe a phenomenon, to establish a fact. Only the nation has the right to say, "Be it known and decreed."

I confess that this is an overturning of received ideas, and that I seem to be attempting to revolutionize our political system; but I beg the reader to consider that, having begun with a paradox, I must, if I reason correctly, meet with paradoxes at every step, and must end with paradoxes. For the rest, I do not see how the liberty of citizens would be endangered by entrusting to their hands, instead of the pen of the legislator, the sword of the law. The executive power, belonging properly to the will, cannot be confided to too many proxies. That is the true sovereignty of the nation.

The proprietor, the robber, the hero, the sovereign—for all these titles are synonymous—imposes his will as law, and suffers neither contradiction nor control; that is, he pretends to be the legislative and executive power at once. Accordingly, the substitution of the scientific and true law for the royal will is accomplished only by a terrible struggle; and this constant substitution is, after property, the most potent element in history, the most prolific source of political disturbances. Examples are too numerous and too striking to require enumeration.

Now, property necessarily engenders despotism,—the government of caprice, the reign of libidinous pleasure. That is so clearly the essence of property that, to be convinced of it, one need but remember what it is, and observe what happens around him. Property is the right to *use* and *abuse*. If, then, government is economy,—if its object is production and consumption, and the distribution of labor and products,—how is government possible while property exists? And if goods are property, why not the proprietors be kings, and despotic kings—kings in proportion to their *facultes bonitaires?* And if each proprietor is sovereign lord within the sphere of his property, absolute king throughout his own domain, how could a government of proprietors be any thing but chaos and confusion?

Section 3. Determination of the third form of Society. Conclusion.

Then, no government, no public economy, no administration, is possible, which is based upon property.

Communism seeks *equality* and *law*. Property, born of the sovereignty of the reason, and the sense of personal merit, wishes above all things *independence* and *proportionality*.

But communism, mistaking uniformity for law, and levelism for equality, becomes tyrannical and unjust. Property, by its despotism and encroachments, soon proves itself oppressive and anti-social.

The objects of communism and property are good—their results are bad. And why? Because both are exclusive, and each disregards two elements of society. Communism rejects independence and proportionality; property does not satisfy equality and law.

Now, if we imagine a society based upon these four principles,— equality, law, independence, and proportionality,—we find:

1. That *equality*, consisting only in *equality of conditions*, that is, of *means*, and not in *equality of comfort*,—which it is the business of the laborers to achieve for themselves, when provided with equal means, —in no way violates justice and *équité*.

2. That *law*, resulting from the knowledge of facts, and consequently based upon necessity itself, never clashes with independence.

3. That individual *independence*, or the autonomy of the private reason, originating in the difference in talents and capacities, can exist without danger within the limits of the law.

4. That *proportionality*, being admitted only in the sphere of intelligence and sentiment, and not as regards material objects, may be observed without violating justice or social equality.

This third form of society, the synthesis of communism and property, we call *liberty*.

In determining the nature of liberty, we do not unite communism and property indiscriminately; such a process would be absurd eclecticism. We search by analysis for those elements in each which are true, and in harmony with the laws of Nature and society, disregarding the rest altogether; and the result gives us an adequate expression of the natural form of human society,—in one word, liberty.

Liberty is equality, because liberty exists only in society; and in the absence of equality there is no society.

Liberty is anarchy, because it does not admit the government of the will, but only the authority of the law; that is, of necessity.

Liberty is infinite variety, because it respects all wills within the limits of the law.

Liberty is proportionality, because it allows the utmost latitude to the ambition for merit, and the emulation of glory.

We can now say, in the words of M. Cousin: "Our principle is true; it is good, it is social; let us not fear to push it to its ultimate."

Man's social nature becoming *justice* through reflection, *équité* through the classification of capacities, and having *liberty* for its formula, is the true basis of morality,—the principle and regulator of all our actions. This is the universal motor, which philosophy is searching for, which religion strengthens, which egotism supplants, and whose place pure reason never can fill. *Duty* and *right* are born of need, which, when considered in connection with others, is a *right*, and when considered in connection with ourselves, a *duty*.

We need to eat and sleep. It is our right to procure those things which are necessary to rest and nourishment. It is our duty to use them when Nature requires it.

We need to labor in order to live. To do so is both our right and our duty.

We need to love our wives and children. It is our duty to protect and support them. It is our right to be loved in preference to all others. Conjugal fidelity is justice. Adultery is high treason against society.

We need to exchange our products for other products. It is our right that this exchange should be one of equivalents; and since we consume before we produce, it would be our duty, if we could control the matter, to see to it that our last product shall follow our last consumption. Suicide is fraudulent bankruptcy.

We need to live our lives according to the dictates of our reason. It is our right to maintain our freedom. It is our duty to respect that of others.

We need to be appreciated by our fellows. It is our duty to deserve their praise. It is our right to be judged by our works.

Liberty is not opposed to the rights of succession and bequest. It contents itself with preventing violations of equality. "Choose," it tells us, "between two legacies, but do not take them both." All our legislation concerning transmissions, entailments, adoptions, and, if I may venture to use such a word, *coadjutoreries*, requires remodelling.

Liberty favors emulation, instead of destroying it. In social equality, emulation consists in accomplishing under like conditions; it is its own reward. No one suffers by the victory.

Liberty applauds self-sacrifice, and honors it with its votes, but it can dispense with it. Justice alone suffices to maintain the social equilibrium. Self-sacrifice is an act of supererogation. Happy, however, the man who can say, "I sacrifice myself."

Liberty is essentially an organizing force. To insure equality between men and peace among nations, agriculture and industry, and the centres of education, business, and storage, must be distributed according to the climate and the geographical position of the country, the nature of the products, the character and natural talents of the inhabitants, &c., in proportions so just, so wise, so harmonious, that in no place shall there ever be either an excess or a lack of population, consumption, and products. There commences the science of public and private right, the true political economy. It is for the writers on jurisprudence, henceforth unembarrassed by the false principle of property, to describe the new laws, and bring peace upon earth. Knowledge and genius they do not lack; the foundation is now laid for them.

I have accomplished my task; property is conquered, never again to arise. Wherever this work is read and discussed, there will be deposited the germ of death to property; there, sooner or later, privilege and servitude will disappear, and the despotism of will will give place to the reign of reason. What sophisms, indeed, what prejudices (however obstinate) can stand before the simplicity of the following propositions:

I. Individual *possession* is the condition of social life; five thousand years of property demonstrate it. *Property* is the suicide of society. Possession is a right; property is against right. Suppress property while maintaining possession, and, by this simple modification of the principle, you will revolutionize law, government, economy, and institutions; you will drive evil from the face of the earth.

II. All having an equal right of occupancy, possession varies with the number of possessors; property cannot establish itself.

III. The effect of labor being the same for all, property is lost in the common prosperity.

IV. All human labor being the result of collective force, all property becomes, in consequence, collective and unitary. To speak more exactly, labor destroys property.

V. Every capacity for labor being, like every instrument of labor, an accumulated capital, and a collective property, inequality of wages and fortunes (on the ground of inequality of capacities) is, therefore, injustice and robbery.

VI. The necessary conditions of commerce are the liberty of the contracting parties and the equivalence of the products exchanged. Now, value being expressed by the amount of time and outlay which each product costs, and liberty being inviolable, the wages of laborers (like their rights and duties) should be equal.

VII. Products are bought only by products. Now, the condition of all exchange being equivalence of products, profit is impossible and unjust. Observe this elementary principle of economy, and pauperism, luxury, oppression, vice, crime, and hunger will disappear from our midst.

VIII. Men are associated by the physical and mathematical law of production, before they are voluntarily associated by choice. Therefore, equality of conditions is demanded by justice; that is, by strict social law; esteem, friendship, gratitude, admiration, all fall within the domain of *equitable* or *proportional* law only.

IX. Free association, liberty—whose sole function is to maintain equality in the means of production and equivalence in exchanges—is the only possible, the only just, the only true form of society.

X. Politics is the science of liberty. The government of man by man (under whatever name it be disguised) is oppression. Society finds its highest perfection in the union of order with anarchy.

KARL MARX (1818–1883) AND FRIEDRICH ENGELS (1820–1895)

It is almost impossible to separate the careers and the contributions of Karl Marx and Friedrich Engels. The two men were inseparable friends and coworkers in the formation of the Socialist Party and in the presentation of their views in written form. It was the modesty of Engels which kept him in the background, and which led him constantly to give full credit to Marx.

Karl Marx was born in the German city of Treves of Jewish parents, who later passed from Judaism to Protestantism, in order that the father might secure a governmental position. Young Marx studied philosophy at the University of Bonn, where he came under the dominating influence of Hegelian thought.

Marx showed an early interest in the social, political, and intellectual movements of his day, carefully observing the influences of the tremendous economic changes which had been taking place. He became the editor of various radical journals, and was driven successively from Germany, France, and Belgium. Marx finally became a political exile in England, where he spent his life in study, in writing, and in organizing the Social Democratic Party.

Important works of Marx were: "Introduction to a Critique of Hegel's Philosophy of Rights" (1843), which contained a statement of the materialistic interpretation of history; "The Poverty of Philosophy" (1847), which was largely a criticism of Proudhon; "Discourse on the Question of Free Exchange" (1848); and "Toward a Critique of Political Economy" (1859). His great masterpiece, of course, was "Capital." The first volume appeared in 1867, and the two remaining volumes were brought out in 1885 and 1894 (after the death of Marx in 1885) by his friend and collaborator, Friedrich Engels.

Karl Marx was the founder of Marxism, or scientific and proletarian socialism, as opposed to the earlier Utopian and bourgeois socialism. Moreover, he represented revolutionary socialism, as compared with the later evolutionary socialism of Bernstein and the English Fabians.

"Das Kapital," known as the Bible of socialism, gives the theoretical basis of the elaborate economic system of Marx. It contains his labor theory of value, derived, mind you, from classical, Ricardian sources, but developed by Marx into a theory of surplus value and a philosophy of exploitation. "Das Kapital" also contains Marx's materialistic interpretation of history, his Hegelian dialectics of thesis, antithesis, and synthesis, and the famous "vampire" cycle from money to capital and from capital back to money. The following selections from Marx touch these points. In general, the translation by More and Aveling of the third German edition of *"Das Kapital"* has been followed.

"Manifesto of the Communist Party" was the party platform of the socialists at the time of the revolution of 1848. The student is asked to note how many of these proposals have subsequently come into effect, and which of them would be considered radical today.

KARL MARX AND FRIEDRICH ENGELS

SELECTIONS FROM "MANIFESTO OF THE COMMUNIST PARTY"

A spectre is haunting Europe—the spectre of Communism. All the Powers of old Europe have centered into a Holy Alliance to exercise this spectre; Pope and Czar, Metternich and Guizot, French Radicals and German police-spies.

Where is the party in opposition that has not been decried as communistic by its opponents in power? Where the opposition that has not hurled back the branding reproach of Communism against the more advanced opposition parties, as well as against its reactionary adversaries?

Two things result from this fact.

I. Communism is already acknowledged by all European Powers to be itself a Power.

II. It is high time that Communists should openly, in the face of the whole world, publish their views, their aims, their tendencies, and meet this nursery tale of the Spectre of Communism with a Manifesto of the party itself.

To this end, Communists of various nationalities have assembled in London and sketched the following Manifesto, to be published in the English, French, German, Italian, Flemish, and Danish languages.

I. Bourgeois and Proletarians

The history of all hitherto existing society is the history of class struggles.

Freeman and slave, patrician and plebeian, lord and serf, guild-master and journeyman, in a word, oppressor and oppressed, stood in constant opposition to one another, carried on uninterrupted, now hidden, now open fight, a fight that each time ended, either in a revolutionary reconstitution of society at large, or in the common ruin of the contending classes.

In the earlier epochs of history we find almost everywhere a complicated arrangement of society into various orders, a manifold gradation of social rank. In ancient Rome we have patricians, knights, plebeians, slaves; in the middle ages, feudal lords, vassals, guild-masters, journeymen, apprentices, serfs; in almost all of these classes, again, subordinate gradations.

The modern bourgeois society that has sprouted from the ruins of feudal society has not done away with class antagonisms. It has but established new classes, new conditions of oppression, new forms of struggle in place of the old ones.

Our epoch, the epoch of the bourgeoisie, possesses, however, this distinctive feature; it has simplified the class antagonisms. Society as a whole is more and more splitting up into two great hostile camps, into two great classes directly facing each other: Bourgeoisie and Proletariat.

From the serfs of the Middle Ages sprang the chartered burghers of the earliest towns. From these burgesses the first elements of the bourgeoisie were developed.

The discovery of America, the rounding of the Cape, opened up fresh ground for the rising bourgeoisie. The East Indian and Chinese markets, the colonization of America, trade with the colonies, the increase in the means of exchange and in commodities generally, gave to commerce, to navigation, to industry, an impulse never before known, and thereby, to the revolutionary element in the tottering feudal society, a rapid development.

The feudal system of industry, under which industrial production was monopolized by close guilds, now no longer sufficed for the growing wants of the new market. The manufacturing system took its place. The guild-masters were pushed on one side by the manufacturing middle class; division of labor between the different corporate guilds vanished in the face of division of labor in each single workshop.

Meantime the markets kept ever growing, the demand ever rising. Even manufacture no longer sufficed. Thereupon, steam and machinery revolutionized industrial production. The place of manufacture was taken by the giant Modern Industry, the place of the industrial middle-class, by industrial millionaires, the leaders of whole industrial armies, the modern bourgeois.

Modern industry has established the world-market, for which the discovery of America paved the way. This market has given an immense development to commerce, to nagivation, to communication by land. This development has, in its turn, reacted on the extension of industry; and in proportion as industry, commerce, navigation, railways extended, in the same proportion the bourgeoisie developed, increased its capital, and pushed into the background every class handed down from the Middle Ages.

We see, therefore, how the modern bourgeoisie is itself the product of a long course of development, of a series of revolutions in the modes of production and of exchange.

Each step in the development of the bourgeoisie was accompanied by a corresponding political advance of that class. An oppressed class under the sway of the feudal nobility; an armed and self-governing association in the medieval commune, (here independent urban republic, as in Italy and Germany, there taxable "third estate" of the monarchy, as in France); afterwards, in the period of manufacture proper, serving either the semi-feudal or the absolute monarchy as a counterpoise against the nobility, and in fact corner stone of the great monarchies in general— the bourgeoisie has at last, since the establishment of modern industry and of the world-market, conquered for itself, in the modern representative state, exclusive political sway. The executive of the modern state is but a committee for managing the common affairs of the whole bourgeoisie.

The bourgeoisie, historically, has played a most revolutionary part.

The bourgeoisie, wherever it has got the upper hand, has put an end to all feudal, patriarchal, idylic relations. It has pitilessly torn asunder the motley feudal ties that bound man to his "natural superiors," and has left no other nexus between man and man than naked self-interest, than callous "cash payment." It has drowned the most heavenly ecstasies of religious fervor, of chivalrous enthusiasm, of philistine sentimentalism, in the icy water of egotistical calculation. It has resolved personal worth into exchange value, and in place of the numberless indefeasible chartered freedoms, has set up that single, unconscionable freedom—Free Trade. In one word, for exploitation, veiled by religious and political illusions, it has substituted naked, shameless, direct, brutal exploitation.

The bourgeoisie has stripped of its halo every occupation hitherto honored and looked up to with reverent awe. It has converted the physician, the lawyer, the priest, the poet, the man of science, into its paid wage laborers.

The bourgeoisie has torn away from the family its sentimental veil, and has reduced the family relation to a mere money relation.

The bourgeoisie has disclosed how it came to pass that the brutal display of vigor in the Middle Ages, which reactionists so much admire, found its fitting complement in the most slothful indolence. It has been the first to show what man's activity can bring about. It has accomplished wonders far surpassing Egyptian pyramids, Roman aqueducts, and Gothic cathedrals; it has conducted expeditions that put in the shade all former exoduses of nations and crusades.

The bourgeoisie cannot exist without constantly revolutionizing the instruments of production, and thereby the relations of production, and with them the whole relations of society. Conservation of the old modes of production in unaltered form was, on the contrary, the first condition of existence for all earlier industrial classes. Constant revolutionizing of production, uninterrupted disturbance of all social conditions, everlasting uncertainty and agitation distinguish the bourgeois epoch from all earlier ones. All fixed, fast-frozen relations, with their train of ancient and venerable prejudices and opinions, are swept away, all new-formed ones become antiquated before they can ossify. All that is solid melts into the air, all that is holy is profaned, and man is at last compelled to face with sober senses, his real conditions of life, and his relations with his kind.

The need of a constantly expanding market for its products drives the bourgeoisie over the whole surface of the globe. It must elbow-in everywhere, settle everywhere, establish connections everywhere.

The bourgeoisie has through its exploitation of the world-market given a cosmopolitan character to production and consumption in every country. To the great chagrin of reactionists, it has drawn from under the feet of industry the national ground on which it stood. All old-established national industries have been destroyed or are daily being destroyed. They are dislodged by new industries, whose introduction becomes a life and death question for all civilized nations, by industries that no longer work up indigenous raw material, but raw material drawn from the remotest zones; industries whose products are consumed, not only at home, but in every quarter of the globe. In place of the old wants, satisfied by the productions of the country, we find new wants, requiring for their satisfaction the products of distant lands and climes. In place of the old local and national seclusion and self sufficiency, we have inter-course in every direction, universal interdependence of nations. And as in material, so also in intellectual production. The intellectual creations of individual nations become common property. National one-sidedness and narrowmindedness become more and more impossible, and from the numerous national and local literatures there arises a world-literature.

The bourgeoisie, by the rapid improvement of all instruments of production, by the immensely facilitated means of communication, draws all, even the most barbarian nations, into civilization. The cheap prices of its commodities are the heavy artillery with which it batters down all Chinese walls, with which it forces the barbarians' intensely obstinate hatred of foreigners to capitulate. It compels all nations, on pain of extinction, to adopt the bourgeois mode of production; it compels them to introduce what it calls civilization into their midst, *i.e.*, to become bourgeois themselves. In a word, it creates a world after its own image.

The bourgeoisie has subjected the country to the rule of the towns. It has created enormous cities, has greatly increased the urban population as compared with the rural, and has thus rescued a considerable part of the population from the idiocy of rural life. Just as it has made the country dependent on the towns, so it has made barbarian and semi-barbarian countries dependent on civilized ones, nations of peasants on nations of bourgeois, the East on the West.

The bourgeoisie keeps more and more doing away with the scattered state of the population, of the means of production, and of property. It has agglomerated population, centralized means of production, and has concentrated property in a few hands. The necessary consequence of this was political centralization. Independent, or but loosely connected provinces, with separate interests, laws, governments, and systems of taxation, became lumped together in one nation, with one government, one code of laws, one national class-interest, one frontier and one customs' tariff.

The bourgeoisie, during its rule of scarce one hundred years, has created more massive and more colossal productive forces than have all preceding generations together. Subjection of nature's forces to man, machinery, application of chemistry to industry and agriculture, steam-navigation, railways, electric telegraphs, clearing of whole continents for cultivation, canalization of rivers, whole populations conjured out of the ground—what earlier century had even a presentiment that such productive forces slumbered in the lap of social labor?

We see then, the means of production and of exchange on whose foundation the bourgeoisie built itself up, were generated in feudal society. At a certain stage in the development of these means of production and of exchange, the conditions under which feudal society produced and exchanged, the feudal organization of agriculture and manufacturing industry—in one word, the feudal relations of property—became no longer compatible with the already developed productive forces; they became so many fetters. They had to burst asunder; they were burst asunder.

Into their places stepped free competition, accompanied by a social and political constitution adapted to it, and by the economical and political sway of the bourgeois class.

A similar movement is going on before our own eyes. Modern bourgeois society with its relations of production, of exchange, and of property, a society that has conjured up such gigantic means of production and of exchange, is like the sorcerer, who is no longer able to control the powers of the nether world whom he has called up by his spells. For many a decade past, the history of industry and commerce is but the history of the revolt of modern productive forces against modern conditions of production, against the property relations that are the conditions for the existence of the bourgeoisie and of its rule. It is enough to mention the commercial crises that by their periodical return put on its trial, each time more threateningly, the existence of the entire bourgeois society. In these crises a great part not only of the existing products, but also of the previously created productive forces, are periodically destroyed. In these crises there breaks out an epidemic that, in all earlier epochs would have seemed an absurdity—the epidemic of over-production. Society suddenly finds itself put back into a state of momentary barbarism; it appears as if a famine, a universal war of devastation, had cut off the supply of every means of subsistence; industry and commerce seem to be destroyed; and why? Because there is too much civilization, too much means of subsistence, too much industry, too much commerce. The productive forces at the disposal of society no longer tend to further the development of the conditions of bourgeois property; on the contrary, they have become too powerful for these conditions by which they are confined, and as soon as they overcome these limitations they bring disorder into the whole of bourgeois society, endanger the existence of bourgeois property. The conditions of bourgeois society are too narrow to comprise the wealth created by them. And how does the bourgeoisie get over these crises? On the one hand by enforced destruction of a mass of productive forces; on the other, by the conquest of new markets, and by the more thorough exploitation of the old ones. That is to say, by paving the way for more extensive and more destructive crises, and by diminishing the means whereby crises are prevented.

The weapons with which the bourgeoisie felled feudalism to the ground are now turned against the bourgeoisie itself.

But not only has the bourgeoisie forged the weapons that bring death to itself; it has also called into existence the men who are to wield those weapons—the modern working class—the proletarians.

In proportion as the bourgeoisie,—that is, as capital, is developed, in the same proportion is the proletariat, the modern working class, developed, a class of laborers who live only so long as they find work, and who find work only so long as their labor increases capital. These laborers, who must sell themselves piecemeal, are a commodity, like every other article of commerce, and are consequently exposed to all the vicissitudes of competition, to all the fluctuations of the market.

Owing to the extensive use of machinery and to division of labor, the work of the proletarians has lost all individual character, and, consequently, all charm for the workman. He becomes an appendage of the machine, and it is only the most simple, most monotonous, and most easily acquired knack that is required of him. Hence, the cost of production of a workman is restricted almost entirely to the means of subsistence that he requires for his maintenance, and for the propagation of his race. But the price of a commodity, and also of labor, is equal to its cost of production. In proportion, therefore, as the repulsiveness of the work increases the wage decreases. Nay more, in proportion as the use of machinery and division of labor increase, in the same proportion the burden of toil increases, whether by prolongation of the working hours, by increase of the work enacted in a given time, or by increased speed of the machinery, and so forth.

Modern industry has converted the little workshop of the patriarchal master into the great factory of the industrial capitalist. Masses of laborers, crowded into factories, are organized like soldiers. As privates of the industrial army they are placed under the command of a perfect hierarchy of officers and sergeants. Not only are they the slaves of the bourgeois class and of the bourgeois state, they are daily and hourly enslaved by the machine, by the foreman, and, above all, by the individual bourgeois manufacturer himself. The more openly this despotism proclaims gain to be its end and aim, the more petty, the more hateful and the more embittering it is.

The less the skill and exertion or strength implied in manual labor, in other words, the more modern industry becomes developed, the more is the labor of men superseded by that of women. Differences of age and sex have no longer any distinctive social validity for the working class. All are instruments of labor, more or less expensive to use, according to their age and sex.

No sooner is the exploitation of the laborer by the manufacturer so far at an end that he receives his wages in cash, than he is set upon by the other portions of the bourgeoisie, the landlord, the shopkeeper, the pawnbroker, and so forth.

The lower strata of the middle class—the small tradespeople, shopkeepers and retired tradesmen generally, the handicraftsmen and peasants—all these sink gradually into the proletariat, partly because their diminutive capital does not suffice for the scale on which modern industry is carried on, and is swamped in the competition with the large capitalists, partly because their specialized skill is rendered worthless by new methods of production. Thus the proletariat is recruited from all classes of the population.

The proletariat goes through various stages of development. With its birth begins its struggle with the bourgeoisie. At first the contest is carried on by individual laborers, then by the workpeople of a factory, then by the operatives of one trade, in one locality, against the individual bourgeois who directly exploits them. They direct their attacks not against the bourgeois conditions of production, but against the instruments of production themselves; they destroy imported wares that compete with their labor, they smash machinery, they set factories ablaze, they seek to restore by force the vanished status of the workman of the Middle Ages.

At this stage the laborers still form an incoherent mass scattered over the whole country, and broken up by their mutual competition. If anywhere they unite to form more compact bodies, this is not yet the consequence of their own active union, but of the union of the bourgeoisie, which class, in order to attain its own political ends, is compelled to set the whole proletariat in motion, and is moreover, for a time, still able to do so. At this stage, therefore, the proletarians do not fight their enemies, but the enemies of their enemies, the remnants of absolute monarchy, the landowners, the non-industrial bourgeois, the petty bourgeoisie. Thus the whole historical movement is concentrated in the hands of the bourgeoisie, every victory so obtained is a victory for the bourgeoisie.

But with the development of industry the proletariat not only increases in number; it becomes concentrated in greater masses, its strength grows and it feels that strength more. The various interests and conditions of life within the ranks of the proletariat are more and more equalized, in proportion as machinery obliterates all distinctions of labor, and nearly everywhere reduces wages to the same low level. The growing competition among the bourgeois, and the resulting commercial crises, make the wages of the workers ever more fluctuating; the unceasing improvement of machinery, ever more rapidly developing, makes their livelihood more and more precarious; the collisions between individual workmen and individual bourgeois take more and more the character of collisions between two classes. Thereupon the workers begin to form combinations (trade unions) against the bourgeois; they club together in order to keep up the rate of wages; they found permanent associations in order to make provision beforehand for these occasional revolts. Here and there the contest breaks out into riots.

Now and then the workers are victorious, but only for a time. The real fruit of their battle lies not in the immediate result, but in the ever expanding union of workers. This union is helped on by the improved means of communication that are created by modern industry, and that places the workers of different localities in contact with one another. It was just this contact that was needed to centralize the numerous local struggles, all of the same character, into one national struggle between classes. But every class struggle is a political struggle. And that union, to attain which the burghers of the Middle Ages with their miserable highways, required centuries, the modern proletarians, thanks to railways, achieve in a few years.

This organization of the proletarians into a class, and consequently into a political party, is continually being upset again by the competition between the workers themselves. But it ever rises up again, stronger, firmer, mightier. It compels legislative recognition of particular interests of the workers by taking advantage of the divisions among the bourgeoisie itself. Thus the Ten-Hours-Bill in England was carried.

Altogether collisions between the classes of the old society further, in many ways, the development of the proletariat. The bourgeoisie finds itself involved in a constant battle—at first with the aristocracy; later on, with those portions of the bourgeoisie itself whose interests have become antagonistic to the progress of industry; at all times, with the bourgeoisie of foreign countries. In all these battles it sees itself compelled to appeal to the proletariat, to ask for its help, and thus to drag it into the political arena. The bourgeoisie itself, therefore, supplies the proletariat with its own elements of political and general education; in other words, it furnishes the proletariat with weapons for fighting the bourgeoisie.

Further, as we have already seen, entire sections of the ruling classes are, by the advance of industry, precipitated into the proletariat, or are at least threatened in their conditions of existence. These also supply the proletariat with fresh elements of enlightenment and progress.

Finally, in times when the class-struggle nears the decisive hour, the process of dissolution going on within the ruling class, in fact within the whole range of an old society, assumes such a violent, glaring character that a small section of the ruling class cuts itself adrift and joins the revolutionary class, the class that holds the future in its hands. Just as, therefore, at an earlier period, a section of the nobility went over to the bourgeoisie, so now a portion of the bourgeoisie goes over to the proletariat, and in particular, a portion of the bourgeois ideologists, who have raised themselves to the level of comprehending theoretically the historical movements as a whole.

Of all the classes that stand face to face with the bourgeoisie today the proletariat alone is a really revolutionary class. The other classes decay and finally disappear in the face of modern industry; the proletariat is its special and essential product.

The lower middle-class, the small manufacturer, the shopkeeper, the artisan, the peasant, all these fight against the bourgeoisie, to save fron extinction their existence as fractions of the middle class. They are therefore not revolutionary, but conservative. Nay, more; they are reactionary, for they try to roll back the wheel of history. If by chance they are revolutionary, they are so only in view of their impending transfer into the proletariat; they thus defend not their present, but their future interests; they desert their own standpoint to place themselves at that of the proletariat.

The "dangerous class," the social scum, that passively rotting mass thrown off by the lowest layers of the old society, may here and there be swept into the movement by a proletarian revolution; its conditions of life, however, prepare it far more for the part of a bribed tool of reactionary intrigue.

In the conditions of the proletariat, those of old society at large are already virtually swamped. The proletarian is without property; his relation to his wife and children has no longer anything in common with the bourgeois family relations; modern industrial labor, modern subjection to capital, the same in England as in France, in America as in Germany, has stripped him of every trace of national character. Law, morality, religion, are to him so many bourgeois prejudices, behind which lurk in ambush just as many bourgeois interests.

All the preceding classes that got the upper hand sought to fortify their already acquired status by subjecting society at large to their conditions of appropriation. The proletarians cannot become masters of the productive forces of society, except by abolishing their own previous mode of appropriation, and thereby also every other previous mode of appropriation. They have nothing of their own to secure and to fortify; their mission is to destroy all previous securities for and insurances of individual property.

All previous historical movements were movements of minorities, or in the interest of minorities. The proletarian movement is the self-conscious, independent movement of the immense majority. The proletariat, the lowest stratum of our present society, cannot stir, cannot raise itself up without the whole superincumbent strata of official society being sprung into the air.

Though not in substance, yet in form, the struggle of the proletariat with the bourgeoisie is at first a national struggle. The proletariat of each country must, of course, first of all settle matters with its own bourgeoisie.

In depicting the most general phases of the development of the proletariat, we have traced the more or less veiled civil war, raging within existing society, up to the point where that war breaks out into open revolution, and where the violent overthrow of the bourgeoisie, lays the foundation for the sway of the proletariat.

Hitherto every form of society has been based, as we have already seen, on the antagonism of oppressing and oppressed classes. But in order to oppress a class, certain conditions must be assured to it under which it can at least continue its slavish existence. The serf, in the period of serfdom, raised himself to membership in the commune, just as the petty bourgeois, under the yoke of feudal absolutism, managed to develop into a bourgeois. The modern laborer, on the contrary, instead of rising with the progress of industry, sinks deeper and deeper below the conditions of existence of his own class. He becomes a pauper, and pauperism develops more rapidly than population and wealth. And here it becomes evident that the bourgeoisie is unfit any longer to be the ruling class in society, and to impose its conditions of existence upon society as an over-riding law. It is unfit to rule, because it is incompetent to assure an existence to its slave within his slavery, because it cannot help letting him sink into such a state that it has to feed him, instead of being fed by him. Society can no longer live under this bourgeoisie; in other words, its existence is no longer compatible with society.

The essential condition for the existence, and for the sway of the bourgeois class, is the formation and augmentation of capital; the condition for capital is wage-labor. Wage-labor rests exclusively on competition between the laborers. The advance of industry, whose involuntary promoter is the bourgeoisie, replaces the isolation of the laborers, due to competition, by their revolutionary combination, due to association. The development of modern industry, therefore, cuts from under its feet the very foundation on which the bourgeoisie produces and appropriates products. What the bourgeoisie therefore produces, above all, are its own grave-diggers. Its fall and the victory of the proletariat are equally inevitable.

II. PROLETARIANS AND COMMUNISTS

In what relation do the Communists stand to the proletarians as a whole?

The Communists do not form a separate party opposed to other working-class parties.

They have no interests separate and apart from those of the proletariat as a whole.

They do not set up any sectarian principles of their own, by which to shape and mould the proletarian movement.

The Communists are distinguished from the other working class parties by this only: 1. In the national struggles of the proletarians of the different countries, they point out and bring to the front the common interests of the entire proletariat, independently of all nationality. 2. In the various stages of development which the struggle of the working class against the bourgeoisie has to pass through, they always and everywhere represent the interests of the movement as a whole.

The Communists, therefore, are on the one hand practically the most advanced and resolute section of the working class parties of every country, that section which pushes forward all others; on the other hand, theoretically, they have over the great mass of the proletariat the advantage of clearly understanding the line of march, the conditions, and the ultimate general results of the proletarian movement.

The immediate aim of the Communists is the same as that of all the other proletarian parties—formation of the proletariat into a class, overthrow of the bourgeois supremacy, conquest of political power by the proletariat.

The theoretical conclusions of the Communists are in no way based on ideas or principles that have been invented or discovered by this or that would-be universal reformer.

They merely express, in general terms, actual relations springing from an existing class struggle, from a historical movement going on under our very eyes. The abolition of existing property-relations is not at all a distinctive feature of Communism.

All property relations in the past have continually been subject to historical change consequent upon the change in historical conditions.

The French Revolution, for example, abolished feudal property in favor of bourgeois property.

The distinguishing feature of Communism is not the abolition of property generally, but the abolition of bourgeois property. But modern bourgeois private property is the final and most complete expression of the system of producing and appropriating products, based on class antagonism, on the exploitation of the many by the few.

In this sense, the theory of the Communists may be summed up in the single sentence: Abolition of private property.

We Communists have been reproached with the desire to abolish the right of personally acquiring property as the fruit of a man's own labor, which property is alleged to be the groundwork of all personal freedom, activity, and independence.

Hard-won, self-acquired, self-earned property! Do you mean the property of the petty artisan and of the small peasant, a form of property that preceded the bourgeois form? There is no need for us to abolish that; the development of industry has to a great extent already destroyed it, and is still destroying it daily.

Or do you mean modern bourgeois private property?

But does wage-labor create any property for the laborer? Not a bit. It creates capital,—that is, the kind of property which exploits wage-labor, and which cannot increase except upon condition of getting a new supply of wage-labor for fresh exploitation. Property, in its present form, is based on the antagonism of capital and wage-labor. Let us examine both sides of this antagonism.

To be a capitalist is to have not only a purely personal, but a social status in production. Capital is a collective product, and only by the united action of many members, nay, in the last resort, only by the united action of all members of society, can it be set in motion.

Capital is therefore not a personal, it is a social power.

When, therefore, capital is converted into common property, into the property of all members of society, personal property is not thereby transformed into social property. It is only the social character of the property that is changed. It loses its class-character.

Let us now take wage-labor.

The average price of wage-labor is the minimum wage, that quantum of the means of subsistence which is absolutely requisite to keep the laborer in bare existence as a laborer. What, therefore, the wage-laborer appropriates by means of his labor, merely suffices to prolong and reproduce a bare existence. We by no means intend to abolish this personal appropriation of the products of labor, an appropriation that is made for the maintenance and reproduction of human life, and that leaves no surplus wherewith to command the labor of others. All that we want to do away with is the miserable character of this appropriation, under which the laborer lives merely to increase capital and is allowed to live only in so far as the interest of the ruling class requires it.

In bourgeois society, living labor is but a means to increase accumulated labor. In communist society accumulated labor is but a means to widen, to enrich, to promote the existence of the laborer.

In bourgeois society, therefore, the past dominates the present; in communist society the present dominates the past. In bourgeois society capital is independent and has individuality, while the living person is dependent and has no individuality.

And the abolition of this state of things is called by the bourgeois abolition of individuality and freedom! And rightly so. The abolition of bourgeois individuality, bourgeois independence, and bourgeois freedom is undoubtedly aimed at.

By freedom is meant, under the present bourgeois conditions of production, free trade, free selling and buying.

But if selling and buying disappears, free selling and buying disappears also. This talk about free selling and buying, and all the other "brave words" of our bourgeoisie about freedom in general, have a meaning, if any, only in contrast with restricted selling and buying, with the fettered traders of the Middle Ages, but have no meaning when opposed to the communistic abolition of buying and selling, of the bourgeois conditions of production, and of the bourgeoisie itself.

You are horrified at our intending to do away with private property. But in your existing society private property is already done away with for nine-tenths of the population; its existence for the few is solely due to its non-existence in the hands of those nine-tenths. You reproach us, therefore, with intending to do away with a form of property, the necessary conditions for whose existence is the non-existence of any property for the immense majority of society.

In one word, you reproach us with intending to do away with your property. Precisely so; that is just what we intend.

From the moment when labor can no longer be converted into capital, money, or rent, into a social power capable of being monopolized, —that is, from the moment when individual property can no longer be transformed into bourgeois property, into capital—from that moment, you say, individuality vanishes.

You must, therefore, confess that by "individual" you mean no other person than the bourgeois, than the middle-class owner of property. This person must, indeed, be swept out of the way and made impossible.

Communism deprives no man of the power to appropriate social products; all that it does is to deprive him of the power to subjugate the labor of others by means of such appropriation.

It has been objected that upon the abolition of private property all work will cease and universal laziness will overtake us.

According to this, bourgeois society ought long ago to have gone to the dogs through sheer idleness; for those of its members who work acquire nothing, and those who acquire anything do not work. The whole of this objection is but another expression of the tautology, that there can no longer be any wage-labor when there is no longer any capital.

All objections urged against the communistic mode of producing and appropriating material products have, in the same way, been urged against the communistic modes of producing and appropriating intellectual products. Just as, to the bourgeois, the disappearance of class property is the disappearance of production itself, so the disappearance of class culture is to him identical with the disappearance of all culture.

That culture, the loss of which he laments, is, for the enormous majority, a mere training to act as a machine.

But do not argue with us by applying to our intended abolition of bourgeois property, the standard of your bourgeois notions of freedom, culture, law, etc. Your very ideas are but the outgrowth of the conditions of your bourgeois production and bourgeois property, just as your jurisprudence is but the will of your class made into a law for all, a will whose essential character and direction are determined by the economic conditions of existence of your class.

The selfish misconception that induces you to transform into eternal laws of nature and of reason the social forms springing from your present mode of production and form of property—historical relations that rise and disappear in the progress of production—this misconception you share with every ruling class that has preceded you. What you see clearly in the case of ancient property, what you admit in the case of feudal property, you are of course forbidden to admit in the case of your own bourgeois form of property.

Abolition of the family? Even the most radical flare up at this infamous proposal of the Communists.

On what foundation is the present family, the bourgeois family, based? On capital, on private gain. In its completely developed form this family exists only among the bourgeoisie. But this state of things finds its complement in the practical absence of the family among the proletarians, and in public prostitution.

The bourgeois family will vanish as a matter of course when its complement vanishes, and both will vanish with the vanishing of capital.

Do you charge us with wanting to stop the exploitation of children by their parents? To this crime we plead guilty.

But, you will say, we destroy the most hallowed of relations when we replace home education by social.

And your education! Is not that also social, and determined by the social conditions under which you educate, by the intervention, direct or indirect, of society by means of schools, and the like? The Communists have not invented the intervention of society in education; they do but seek to alter the character of that intervention, and to rescue education from the influence of the ruling class.

The bourgeois clap-trap about the family and education, about the hallowed co-relation of parent and child, becomes all the more disgusting.

the more, by the action of modern industry, all family ties among the proletarians are torn asunder and their children transformed into simple articles of commerce and instruments of labor.

But you Communists would introduce community of women, screams the whole bourgeois chorus.

The bourgeois sees in his wife a mere instrument of production. He hears that the instruments of production are to be exploited in common, and, naturally, can come to no other conclusion than that the lot of being common to all will likewise fall to the women.

He has not even a suspicion that the real point aimed at is to do away with the status of women as mere instruments of production.

For the rest, nothing is more ridiculous than the virtuous indignation of our bourgeois at the community of women which, they pretend, is to be openly and officially established by the Communists. The Communists have no need to introduce community of women; it has existed almost from time immemorial.

Our bourgeois, not content with having the wives and daughters of their proletarians at their disposal, not to speak of common prostitutes, take the greatest pleasure in seducing each others' wives.

Bourgeois marriage is in reality a system of wives in common, and thus, at the most, what the Communists might possibly be reproached with, is that they desire to introduce, in substitution for a hypocritically concealed, an openly legalized community of women. For the rest, it is self-evident that the abolition of the present system of production must bring with it the abolition of the community of women springing from that system,—that is, of prostitution both public and private.

The Communists are further reproached with desiring to abolish countries and nationalities.

The working men have no country. We cannot take from them what they have not got. Since the proletariat must first of all acquire political supremacy, must rise to be the leading class of the nation, must constitute itself the nation, it is, so far, itself national, though not in the bourgeois sense of the word.

National differences and antagonisms between peoples are daily more and more vanishing, owing to the development of the bourgeoisie, to freedom of commerce, to the world-market, to uniformity in the mode of production and in the conditions of life corresponding thereto.

The supremacy of the proletariat will cause them to vanish still faster. United action, of the leading civilized countries at least, is one of the first conditions for the emancipation of the proletariat.

In proportion as the exploitation of one individual by another is put an end to, the exploitation of one nation by another will also be put an end to. In proportion as the antagonism between classes within the nation vanishes, the hostility of one nation to another will come to an end

The charges against Communism made from a religious, a philosophical, and generally, from an ideological standpoint, are not deserving of serious examination.

Does it require deep intuition to comprehend that man's ideas, views, and conceptions, in one word, man's consciousness, changes with every change in the conditions of his material existence, in his social relations, and in his social life?

What else does the history of ideas prove than that intellectual production changes in character in proportion as material production is changed? The ruling ideas of each age have ever been the ideas of its ruling class.

When people speak of ideas that revolutionize society they do but express the fact that within the old society the elements of a new one have been created, and that the dissolution of the old ideas keeps even pace with the dissolution of the old conditions of existence.

When the ancient world was in its last throes the ancient religions were overcome by Christianity. When Christian ideas succumbed in the eighteenth century to rationalist ideas, feudal society fought its death-battle with the then revolutionary bourgeoisie. The ideas of religious liberty and freedom of conscience merely gave expression to the sway of free competition within the domain of knowledge.

"Undoubtedly," it will be said, "religious, moral, philosophical, and judicial ideas have been modified in the course of historical development. But religion, morality, philosophy, political science, and law, constantly survived this change."

"There are, besides, eternal truths, such as Freedom, Justice, and so forth, that are common to all states of society. But Communism abolishes eternal truth, it abolishes all religion and all morality, instead of constituting them on a new basis; it therefore acts in contradiction to all past historical experience."

What does this accusation reduce itself to? The history of all past society has consisted in the development of class antagonisms, antagonisms that assumed different forms at different epochs.

But whatever form they may have taken, one fact is common to all past ages—namely, the exploitation of one part of society by the other. No wonder, then, that the social consciousness of past ages, despite all the multiplicity and variety it displays, moves within certain common forms, or general ideas, which cannot completely vanish except with the total disappearance of class antagonisms.

The Communist revolution is the most radical rupture with traditional property-relations; no wonder that its development involves the most radical rupture with traditional ideas.

But let us have done with the bourgeois objections to Communism.

We have seen above that the first step in the revolution by the working class is to raise the proletariat to the position of ruling class, to win the battle of democracy.

The proletariat will use its political supremacy to wrest, by degrees, all capital from the bourgeoisie, to centralize all instruments of production in the hands of the state,—that is, of the proletariat organized as a ruling class; and to increase the total productive forces as rapidly as possible.

Of course, in the beginning, this cannot be effected except by means of despotic inroads on the rights of property, and on the conditions of bourgeois production; by means of measures, therefore, which appear economically insufficient and untenable, but which in the course of move-ment outstrip themselves, necessitate further inroads upon the old social order, and are unavoidable as a means of entirely revolutionizing the mode of production.

These measures will of course be different in different countries.

Nevertheless in the most advanced countries the following will be pretty generally applicable:

1. Abolition of property in land and application of all rents of land to public purposes.

2. A heavy progressive or graduated income tax.

3. Abolition of all right of inheritance.

4. Confiscation of the property of all emigrants and rebels.

5. Centralization of credit in the hands of the state, by means of a national bank with state capital and an exclusive monopoly.

6. Centralization of the means of communication and transport in the hands of the state.

7. Extension of factories and instruments of production owned by the state; the bringing into cultivation of waste lands, and the improve-ment of the soil generally in accordance with a common plan.

8. Equal liability of all to labor. Establishment of industrial armies, especially for agriculture.

9. Combination of agriculture with manufacturing industries; gradual abolition of the distinction between town and country by a more equable distribution of the population over the country.

10. Free education for all children in public schools. Abolition of children's factory labor in its present form. Combination of education with industrial production, and so forth.

When, in the course of development, class distinctions have disap-peared, and all production has been concentrated in the hands of a vast association of the whole nation, the public power will lose its political character. Political power, properly so called, is merely the organization power of one class for oppressing another. If the proletariat during its contest with the bourgeoisie is compelled, by the force of circumstances, to organize itself as a class, if, by means of a revolution, it makes itself the ruling class, and, as such, sweeps away by force the old conditions of production, then it will, along with these conditions, have swept away the conditions for the existence of class antagonisms, and of classes generally, and will thereby have abolished its own supremacy as a class.

In place of the old bourgeois society, with its classes and class antagonisms, we shall have an association in which the free development of each is the condition for the free development of all.

III. Socialist and Communist Literature

1. *Reactionary Socialism*

A. Feudal Socialism.—Owing to their historical position, it became the vocation of the aristocracies of France and England to write pamphlets against modern bourgeois society. In the French revolution of July, 1830, and in the English reform agitation, these aristocracies again succumbed to the hateful upstart. Thenceforth, a serious political contest was altogether out of the question. A literary battle alone remained possible. But even in the domain of literature the old cries of the Restoration period had become impossible.

In order to arouse sympathy the aristocracy were obliged to lose sight, apparently, of their own interests and to formulate their indictment against the bourgeoisie in the interest of the exploited working class alone. Thus the aristocrats took their revenge by singing lampoons on their new master, and whispering in his ears sinister prophecies of coming catastrophe.

In this way arose feudal socialism: half lamentation, half lampoon; half echo of the past, half menace of the future; at times, by its bitter, witty, and incisive criticism, striking the bourgeoisie to the very hearts' core, but always ludicrous in its effect, through total incapacity to comprehend the march of modern history.

The aristocracy, in order to rally the people to them, waved the proletarian alms-bag in front as a banner. But the people, so often as it joined them, saw on their hindquarters the old feudal coat of arms, and deserted with loud and irreverent laughter.

One section of the French Legitimists, and "Young England," excelled in this spectacle.

In pointing out that their mode of exploitation was different to that of the bourgeoisie, the feudalists forget that they exploited under circumstances and conditions that were quite different, and that are now antiquated. In showing that, under their rule, the modern proletariat never existed, they forget that the modern bourgeoisie is the necessary offspring of their own form of society.

For the rest, so little do they conceal the reactionary character of their criticism that their chief accusation against the bourgeoisie amounts to this, that under the bourgeois regime a class is being developed which is destined to cut up root and branch the old order of society.

What they upbraid the bourgeoisie with is not so much that it creates a proletariat, as that it creates a revolutionary proletariat.

In political practice, therefore, they join in all coercive measures against the working-class; and in ordinary life, despite their high-falutin phrases, they stoop to pick up the golden apples dropped from the tree of industry, and to barter truth, love, and honor for traffic in wool, sugar beets, and potato alcohol.

As the parson has ever gone hand in hand with the landlord, so has clerical socialism with feudal socialism.

Nothing is easier than to give Christian asceticism a socialistic tinge. Has not Christianity declaimed against private property, against marriage, against the state? Has it not preached, in the place of these, charity and poverty, celibacy and mortification of the flesh, monastic life and Mother Church? Christian socialism is but the holy water with which the priest consecrates the heartburnings of the aristocrat.

B. Petty Bourgeois Socialism.—The feudal aristocracy was not the only class that was ruined by the bourgeoisie, not the only class whose conditions of existence pined and perished in the atmosphere of modern bourgeois society. The medieval burgesses and the small peasant bourgeoisie were the precursors of the modern bourgeoisie. In those countries which are but little developed, industrially and commercially, these two classes still vegetate side by side with the rising bourgeoisie.

In countries where modern civilization has become fully developed, a new class of petty bourgeois has been formed, fluctuating between proletariat and bourgeoisie, and ever renewing itself as a supplementary part of bourgeois society. The individual members of this class, however, are being constantly hurled down into the proletariat by the action of competition, and, as modern industry develops, they even see the moment approaching when they will completely disappear as an independent section of modern society, to be replaced, in manufactures, agriculture, and commerce, by managers, superintendents, and foremen.

In countries like France, where the peasants constitute far more than half of the population, it was natural that writers who sided with the proletariat against the bourgeoisie should use, in their criticism of the bourgeois regime, the standard of the peasant and petty bourgeois, and from the standpoint of these intermediate classes should take up the cudgels for the working class. Thus arose petty bourgeois socialism. Sismondi was the head of this school, not only in France, but also in England.

This school of socialism dissected with great acuteness the contradictions in the conditions of modern production. It laid bare the hypocritical apologies of economists. It proved incontrovertibly the disastrous effects of machinery and division of labor; the concentration of capital and land in a few hands; overproduction and crises; it pointed out the inevitable ruin of the petty bourgeois, and peasant, the misery of the proletariat, the anarchy in production, the crying inequalities in the distribution of wealth, the industrial war of extermination between nations, the dissolution of old moral bonds, of the old family relations, of the old nationalities.

In its positive aims, however, this form of Socialism aspires either to restoring the old means of production and of exchange, and with them the old property relations and the old society, or to cramping the modern means of production and of exchange within the framework of the old property relations that have been, and were bound to be, exploded by those means. In either case it is both reactionary and utopian.

Its last words are—corporate guilds for manufacture, patriarchal relations in agriculture.

Ultimately, when stubborn historical facts had dispersed all intoxicating effects of self-deception, this form of socialism ended in a miserable fit of the blues.

C. German or "True" Socialism.—The Socialist and Communist literature of France, a literature that originated under the pressure of a bourgeoisie in power, and that was the expression of the struggle against this power, was introduced into Germany at a time when the bourgeoisie in that country had just begun its contest with feudal absolutism.

German philosophers, would-be philosophers, and *beaux esprits* eagerly seized on this literature, only forgetting that, when these writings immigrated from France into Germany, French social conditions had not immigrated along with them. In contact with German social conditions this French literature lost its immediate practical significance and assumed a purely literary aspect. Thus, to the German philosophers of the eighteenth century, the demands of the first French Revolution were nothing more than the demands of "Practical Reason" in general, and the utterance of the will of the revolutionary French bourgeoisie signified in their eyes the laws of pure Will, of Will as it was bound to be, of true human Will generally.

The work of the German literati consisted solely in bringing the new French ideas into harmony with their ancient philosophical conscience, or rather, in annexing the French ideas without deserting their own philosophical point of view.

This annexation took place in the same way in which a foreign language is appropriated, namely by translation.

It is well known how the monks wrote silly lives of Catholic saints over the manuscripts on which the classical works of ancient heathendom had been written. The German literati reversed this process with the profane French literature. They wrote their philosophical nonsense beneath the French original. For instance, beneath the French criticism of the economic functions of money they wrote "Alienation of Humanity," and beneath the French criticism of the bourgeois state they wrote "Dethronement of the Category of the General," and so forth.

The introduction of these philosophical phrases at the back of the French historical criticisms they dubbed "Philosophy of Action," "True Socialism," "German Science of Socialism," "Philosophical Foundation of Socialism," and so on.

The French Socialist and Communist literature was thus completely emasculated. And, since it ceased in the hands of the German to express the struggle of one class with the other, he felt conscious of having overcome "French one-sidedness" and of representing, not true requirements, but the requirements of Truth, not the interests of the proletariat, but the interests of Human Nature, of Man in general, who belongs to no class, has no reality, who exists only in the misty realm of philosophical phantasy.

This German socialism, which took its school-boy task so seriously and solemnly, and extolled its poor stock-in-trade in such mountebank fashion, meanwhile gradually lost its pedantic innocence.

The fight of the German, and especially of the Prussian, bourgeoisie against feudal aristocracy and absolute monarchy, in other words the liberal movement, became more earnest.

By this, the long-wished-for opportunity was offered to "True Socialism" of confronting the political movement with the socialist demands, of hurling the traditional anathemas against liberalism, against representative government, against bourgeois competition, bourgeois freedom of the press, bourgeois legislation, bourgeois liberty and equality, and of preaching to the masses that they had nothing to gain and everything to lose by this bourgeois movement. German socialism forgot in the nick of time that the French criticism, whose silly echo it was, presupposed the existence of modern bourgeois society, with its corresponding economic conditions of existence, and the political constitution adapted thereto, the very things whose attainment was the object of the pending struggle in Germany.

To the absolute governments, with their following of parsons, professors, country squires, and officials, it served as a welcome scarecrow against the threatening bourgeoisie.

It was a sweet finish after the bitter pills of floggings and bullets with which these same governments, just at that time, dosed the German working class risings.

While this "True Socialism" thus served the governments as a weapon for fighting the German bourgeoisie, it at the same time directly represented a reactionary interest, the interest of the German philistines. In Germany the petty bourgeois class, a relic of the sixteenth century, and since then constantly cropping up again under various forms, is the real social basis of the existing state of things.

To preserve this class is to preserve the existing state of things in Germany. The industrial and political supremacy of the bourgeoisie threatens it with certain destruction; on the one hand, from the concentration of capital; on the other, from the rise of a revolutionary proletariat. "True Socialism" appeared to kill these two birds with one stone. It spread like an epidemic.

The robe of speculative cobwebs, embroidered with flowers of rhetoric, steeped in the dew of sickly sentiment, this transcendental robe in which the German socialists wrapped their sorry "eternal truths," all skin and bone, served wonderfully to increase the sale of their goods amongst such a public.

And on its part, German socialism recognized more and more its own calling as the bombastic representative of the petty bourgeois philistine.

It proclaimed the German nation to be the model nation, and the German petty philistine to be the typical man. To every villainous meanness of this model man it gave a hidden, higher, socialistic interpretation, the exact contrary of its true character. It went to the extreme length of directly opposing the "brutally destructive" tendency of Communism, and of proclaiming its supreme and impartial contempt of all class struggles. With very few exceptions, all the so-called Socialist and Communist publications that now (1847) circulate in Germany belong to the domain of this foul and enervating literature.

2. *Conservative or Bourgeois Socialism*

A part of the bourgeoisie is desirous of redressing social grievances, in order to secure the continued existence of bourgeois society.

To this section belong economists, philanthropists, humanitarians, improvers of the condition of the working class, organizers of charity, members of societies for the prevention of cruelty to animals, temperance fanatics, hole-and-corner reformers of every imaginable kind. This form of socialism has, moreover, been worked out into complete systems.

We may cite Proudhon's *Philosophy of Poverty* as an example of this form.

The socialistic bourgeois want all the advantages of modern social conditions without the struggles and dangers necessarily resulting therefrom. They desire the existing state of society minus its revolutionary and disintegrating elements. They wish for a bourgeoisie without a proletariat. The bourgeoisie naturally conceives the world in which it is supreme to be the best; and bourgeois socialism develops this comfortable conception into various more or less complete systems. In requiring the proletariat to carry out such a system, and thereby to march straightway into the social New Jerusalem, it but requires in reality that the proletariat should remain within the bounds of existing society, but should cast away all its hateful ideas concerning the bourgeoisie.

A second and more practical, but less systematic, form of this socialism ought to depreciate every revolutionary movement in the eyes of the working class by showing that no mere political reform, but only a change in the material conditions of existence, in economical relations, could be of any advantage to them. By changes in the material conditions of existence this form of Socialism, however, by no means understands abolition of the bourgeois relations of production, an abolition that can be effected only by a revolution, but administrative reforms, based on the continued existence of these relations; reforms, therefore, that in no respect affect the relations between capital and labour, but, at the best, lessen the cost, and simplify the administrative work, of bourgeois government.

Bourgeois socialism attains adequate expression when, and only when, it becomes a mere figure of speech.

Free trade—for the benefit of the working class. Protective duties— for the benefit of the working class. Prison reform—for the benefit of the working class. This is the last word and the only seriously meant word of bourgeois socialism.

It is summed up in the phrase: The bourgeois is a bourgeois—for the benefit of the working class.

3. *Critical-Utopian Socialism and Communism*

We do not here refer to that literature which, in every great modern revolution, has always given voice to the demands of the proletariat, such as the writings of Babeuf and others.

The first direct attempts of the proletariat to attain its own ends, made in times of universal excitement, when feudal society was being overthrown, these attempts necessarily failed, owing to the then undeveloped state of the proletariat, as well as to the absence of the economic conditions for its emancipation, conditions that had yet to be produced, and could be produced by the impending bourgeois epoch alone. The revolutionary literature that accompanied these first movements of the proletariat had necessarily a reactionary character. It inculcated universal asceticism and social leveling in its crudest form.

The Socialist and Communist systems properly so called, those of St. Simon, Fourier, Owen, and others, spring into existence in the early undeveloped period, described above, of the struggle between proletariat and bourgeoisie.

The founders of these systems see, indeed, the class antagonisms, as well as the action of the decomposing elements in the prevailing form of society. But the proletariat, as yet in its infancy, offers to them the spectacle of a class without any historical initiative or any independent political movement.

Since the development of class antagonism keeps even pace with the development of industry, the economic situation, as they find it, does not as yet offer to them the material conditions for the emancipation of the proletariat. They therefore search after a new social science, after new social laws, that are to create these conditions.

Historical action is to yield to their personal inventive action, historically created conditions of emancipation to fantastic ones, and the gradual, spontaneous class-organization of the proletariat to an organization of society specially contrived by these inventors. Future history resolves itself, in their eyes, into the propaganda and the practical carrying out of their social plans.

In the formation of their plans they are conscious of caring chiefly for the interests of the working class, as being the most suffering class. Only from the point of view of being the most suffering class does the proletariat exist for them.

The undeveloped state of the class struggle, as well as their own surroundings, cause socialists of this kind to consider themselves far superior to all class antagonisms. They want to improve the condition of every member of society, even that of the most favored. Hence, they habitually appeal to society at large, without distinction of class; nay, by preference, to the ruling class. For how can people, when once they understand their system, fail to see in it the best possible plan of the best possible state of society?

Hence, they reject all political, and especially all revolutionary action; they wish to attain their ends by peaceful means, and endeavor, by small experiments, necessarily doomed to failure, and by the force of example, to pave the way for the new social gospel.

Such fantastic pictures of future society, painted at a time when the proletariat is still in a very undeveloped state and has but a fantastic conception of its own position, correspond with the first instinctive yearnings of that class for a general reconstruction of society.

But these Socialist and Communist publications contain also a critical element. They attack every principle of existing society. Hence they are full of the most valuable materials for the enlightenment of the working class. The practical measures proposed in them, such as the abolition of the distinction between town and country, of the family, of the carrying on of industries for the account of private individuals, and of the wage system, the proclamation of social harmony, the conversion of the functions of the state into a mere superintendence of production, all these proposals point solely to the disappearance of class antagonisms which were at that time only just cropping up, and which, in these publications, are recognized under the earliest, indistinct, and undefined forms only. These proposals, therefore, are of a purely utopian character.

The significance of Critical-Utopian Socialism and Communism bears an inverse relation to historical development. In proportion as the modern class struggle develops and takes definite shape, this fantastic standing apart from the contest, these fantastic attacks on it, lose all practical value and all theoretical justification. Therefore, although the originators of these systems were in many respects revolutionary, their disciples have in every case formed mere reactionary sects. They hold fast by the original views of their masters, in opposition to the progressive historical development of the proletariat. They therefore endeavor, and that consistently, to dull the edge of the class struggle and to reconcile the class antagonisms. They still dream of experimental realization of their social Utopias, of founding isolated "phalansteries," of establishing "Home Colonies," of setting up a "Little Icaria"—duodecimo editions of the New Jerusalem—and to realize all these castles in the air they are compelled to appeal to the feelings and purses of the bourgeois. By degrees they sink into the category of the reactionary or conservative socialists depicted above, differing from these only by more systematic pedantry, and by their fanatical and superstitious belief in the miraculous effects of their social science.

They therefore violently oppose all political action on the part of the working class; such action, according to them, can only result from blind unbelief in the New Gospel.

The Owenites in England, and the Fourierists in France, respectively oppose the Chartists and the Reformists.

IV. POSITION OF THE COMMUNISTS IN RELATION TO THE VARIOUS EXISTING OPPOSITION PARTIES

Section II has made clear the relations of the Communists to the existing working class parties, such as the Chartists in England and the Agrarian Reformers in America.

The Communists fight for the attainment of the immediate aims, for the enforcement of the momentary interests of the working class; but in the movement of the present they also represent and take care of the future of that movement.

In France the Communists ally themselves with the Social-Democrats against the conservative and radical bourgeoisie, reserving, however, the right to take up a critical position in regard to phrases and illusions traditionally handed down from the Great Revolution.

In Switzerland they support the Radicals, without losing sight of the fact that this party consists of antagonistic elements, partly of Democratic Socialists, in the French sense, partly of radical bourgeois.

In Poland they support the party that insists on an agrarian revolution, as the prime condition for national emancipation, that party which fomented the insurrection of Cracow in 1846.

In Germany they fight side by side with the bourgeoisie whenever it acts in a revolutionary way, against the absolute monarchy, the feudal squirearchy, and the petty bourgeoisie.

But they never cease for a single instant to instill into the working class the clearest possible recognition of the hostile antagonism between bourgeoisie and proletariat, in order that the German workers may straightway use, as so many weapons against the bourgeoisie, the social and political conditions that the bourgeoisie must necessarily introduce along with its supremacy, and in order that, after the fall of the reactionary classes in Germany, the fight against the bourgeoisie itself may immediately begin.

The Communists turn their attention chiefly to Germany, because that country is on the eve of a bourgeois revolution, that is bound to be carried out under more advanced conditions of European civilization, and with a more developed proletariat, than that of England was in the seventeenth and of France in the eighteenth century, and because the bourgeois revolution in Germany will be but the prelude to an immediately following proletarian revolution.

In short, the Communists everywhere support every revolutionary movement against the existing social and political order of things.

In all these movements they bring to the front, as the leading question in each, the property question, no matter what its degree of development at the time.

Finally, they labor everywhere for the union and agreement of the democratic parties of all countries.

The Communists disdain to conceal their views and aims. They openly declare that their ends can be attained only by the forcible overthrow of all existing social conditions. Let the ruling classes tremble at a Communistic revolution. The proletarians have nothing to lose but their chains. They have a world to win.

Working men of all countries, unite!

KARL MARX

SELECTION FROM "CRITIQUE OF POLITICAL ECONOMY"

I. The Materialistic Conception of History

I was led by my studies to the conclusion that legal relations as well as forms of the state could neither be understood by themselves nor explained by the so-called general progress of the human mind, but that they are rooted in the material conditions of life. . . . The general conclusion at which I arrived and which, once reached, continued to serve as the leading thread in my studies, may be briefly summed up as follows:

In the social production which men carry on they enter into definite relations which are indispensable and independent of their will; these relations of production correspond to a definite stage of development of their material powers of production. The sum total of these relations of production constitutes the economic structure of society—the real foundation, on which rise legal and political forms of social consciousness.

The mode of production in material life determines the general character of the social, political, and spiritual processes of life. It is not the consciousness of men that determines their existence, but on the contrary their social existence determines their consciousness.

At a certain stage in their development, the material forces of production in society come into conflict with the existing relations of production, or—what is but a legal expression for the same thing—with the property relations within which they had been at work before. From forms of development of the forces of production, these turn into their fetters. Then comes the period of social revolution. With the change of the economic foundation, the entire immense superstructure is more or less rapidly transformed.

In considering such transformations the distinction should always be made between the material transformation of the economic conditions of production, which can be determined with the precision of natural science, and the legal, political, religious, aesthetic, or philosophical—in short, the ideological forms in which men become conscious of this conflict and fight it out. Just as our opinion of an individual is not based on what he thinks of himself, so can we not judge of such a period of transformation by its own consciousness; on the contrary, this consciousness must rather be explained from the contradictions of material life, from the existing conflict between the social forces of production and the relations of production.

No social order ever disappears before all the productive forces for which there is room within it have been developed; and new higher relations of production never appear before the material conditions of their existence have matured in the womb of the old society. Therefore, mankind always takes up only such problems as it can solve; since, looking at the matter more closely, we will always find that the problem itself arises only when the material conditions necessary for its solution already exist or are at least in process of formation.

KARL MARX

SELECTION FROM "EIGHTEENTH BRUMAIRE OF LOUIS BONAPARTE"

II. The Proletarian Revolution

Man makes his own history, but he does not make it out of the whole cloth; he does not make it out of conditions chosen by himself, but out of such as he finds close at hand. The tradition of all past generations weighs like an alp upon the brain of the living. At the very time when men appear engaged in revolutionizing things and themselves, in bringing about what never was before, at such very epochs of revolutionary crisis do they anxiously conjure up into their service the spirits of the past, assume their names, their battle cries, their costumes, to enact a new historic scene in such time-honored disguise and with such borrowed language. . . . Thus does the beginner, who has acquired a new language, keep on translating it back into his own mother tongue; only then has he grasped the spirit of the new language and is able freely to express himself therewith, when he moves in it without recollections of the old one and has forgotten in its use his own hereditary tongue. . . .

The social revolution of the nineteenth century cannot draw its poetry from the past, it can draw that only from the future. It cannot start upon its work before it has stricken off all superstition concerning the past. Former revolutions required historic reminiscences in order to intoxicate themselves with their own issues. The revolution of the nineteenth century must let the dead bury their own dead in order to reach its issue. With the former, the phrase surpassed the substance; with this one, the substance surpasses the phrase. . . .

Bourgeois revolutions, like those of the eighteenth century, rush onward rapidly from success to success, their stage effects outbid one another, men and things seem to be set in flaming brilliants, ecstasy is the prevailing spirit; but they are short-lived, they reach their climax speedily, and then society relapses into a long fit of nervous reaction before it learns how to appropriate the fruits of its period of feverish excitement. Proletarian revolutions, on the contrary, such as those of the nineteenth century, criticize themselves constantly; constantly interrupt themselves in their own course; come back to what seems to have been accomplished, in order to start anew; scorn with cruel thoroughness the half-measures, weaknesses, and meannesses of their first attempts; seem to throw down their adversary only to enable him to draw fresh strength from the earth and again to rise up against them in more gigantic stature; constantly recoil in fear before the undefined monster magnitude of their own objects—until finally that situation is created which renders all retreat impossible, and conditions themselves cry out: "Hic Rhodus, hic salta!"

KARL MARX

SELECTIONS FROM "DAS KAPITAL"

Book I. Capitalist Production

Part I. Commodities and Money

Chapter I. Commodities

Section 1.—The Two Factors of a Commodity; Use-value and Value (The Substance of Value and the Magnitude of Value).

The wealth of those societies in which the capitalist mode of production prevails, presents itself as "an immense accumulation of commodities," its unit being a single commodity. Our investigation must therefore begin with the analysis of a commodity.

A commodity is, in the first place, an object outside us, a thing that by its properties satisfies human wants of some sort or another. The nature of such wants, whether, for instance, they spring from the stomach or from fancy, makes no difference. Neither are we here concerned to know how the object satisfies these wants, whether directly as means of subsistence, or indirectly as means of production.

Every useful thing, as iron, paper, &c., may be looked at from the two points of view of quality and quantity. It is an assemblage of many properties, and may therefore be of use in various ways. To discover the various use of things is the work of history. So also is the establishment of socially-recognized standards of measure for the quantities of these useful objects. The diversity of these measures has its origin partly in the diverse nature of the objects to be measured, partly in convention.

The utility of a thing makes it a use-value. But this utility is not a thing of air. Being limited by the physical properties of the commodity, it has no existence apart from that commodity. A commodity, such as iron, corn, or a diamond, is therefore, so far as it is a material thing, a use-value, something useful. This property of a commodity is independent of the amount of labor required to appropriate its useful qualities. When treating of use-value, we always assume to be dealing with definite quantities, such as dozens of watches, yards of linen, or tons of iron. The use-values of commodities furnish the material for a special study, that of the commercial knowledge of commodities. Use-values become a reality only by use or consumption: they also constitute the substance of all wealth, whatever may be the social form of that wealth. In the form of society we are about to consider, they are, in addition, the material depositories of exchange value.

Exchange value, at first sight, presents itself as a quantitative relation as the proportion in which values in use of one sort are exchanged for those of another sort, a relation constantly changing with time and place. Hence exchange value appears to be something accidental and purely relative, and consequently an intrinsic value, *i. e.*, an exchange value that is inseparably connected with, inherent in commodities, seems a contradiction in terms. Let us consider the matter a little more closely.

A given commodity, *e. g.*, a quarter of wheat is exchanged for x blacking, y silk, or z gold, &c.—in short, for other commodities in the most different proportions. Instead of one exchange value, the wheat has, therefore, a great many. But since x blacking, y silk, or z gold, &c., each represent the exchange value of one quarter of wheat, x blacking, y silk, z gold, &c., must as exchange values be replaceable by each other, or equal to each other. Therefore, first: the valid exchange values of a given commodity express something equal; secondly, exchange value, generally, is only the mode of expression, the phenomenal form, of something contained in it, yet distinguishable from it.

Let us take two commodities, *e. g.*, corn and iron. The proportions in which they are exchangeable, whatever those proportions may be, can always be represented by an equation in which a given quantity of corn is equated to some quantity of iron: *e. g.*, 1 quarter corn = x cwt. iron. What does this equation tell us? It tells us that in two different things—in 1 quarter of corn and x cwt. of iron, there exists in equal quantities something common to both. The two things must therefore be equal to a third, which in itself is neither the one nor the other. Each of them, so far as it is exchange value, must therefore be reducible to this third.

A simple geometrical illustration will make this clear. In order to calculate and compare the areas of rectilinear figures, we decompose them into triangles. But the area of the triangle itself is expressed by something totally different from its visible figure, namely, by half the product of the base into the altitude. In the same way the exchange values of commodities must be capable of being expressed in terms of something common to them all, of which thing they represent a greater or less quantity.

This common "something" cannot be either a geometrical, a chemical, or any other natural property of commodities. Such properties claim our attention only in so far as they affect the utility of those commodities, make them use-values. But the exchange of commodities is evidently an act characterised by a total abstraction from use-value. Then one use-value is just as good as another, provided only it be present in sufficient quantity. Or, as old Barbon says, "one sort of wares are as good as another, if the values be equal. There is no difference or distinction in things of equal value .... An hundred pounds' worth of lead or iron, is of as great value as one hundred pounds' worth of silver or gold." As use-values, commodities are, above all, of different qualities, but as exchange values they are merely different quantities, and consequently do not contain an atom of use-value.

If then we leave out of consideration the use-value of commodities, they have only one common property left, that of being products of labor. But even the product of labor itself has undergone a change in our hands. If we make abstraction from its use-value, we make abstraction at the same time from the material elements and shapes that make the product a use-value; we see in it no longer a table, a house, yarn, or any other useful thing. Its existence as a material thing is put out of sight. Neither can it any longer be regarded as the product of the labor of the joiner, the mason, the spinner, or of any other definite kind of productive labor. Along with the useful qualities of the products themselves, we put out of sight both the useful character of the various kinds of labor embodied in them, and the concrete forms of that labor; there is nothing left but what is common to them all; all are reduced to one and the same sort of labor, human labor in the abstract.

Let us now consider the residue of each of these products; it consists of the same unsubstantial reality in each, a mere congelation of homogeneous human labor, of labor-power expended without regard to the mode of its expenditure. All that these things now tell us is, that human labor-power has been expended in their production, that human labor is embodied in them. When looked at as crystals of this social substance, common to them all, they are— Values.

We have seen that when commodities are exchanged, their exchange value manifests itself as something totally independent of their use-value. But if we abstract from their use-value, there remains their Value as defined above. Therefore, the common substance that manifests itself in the exchange value of commodities, whenever they are exchanged, is their value. The progress of our investigation will show that exchange value is the only form in which the value of commodities can manifest itself or be expressed. For the present, however, we have to consider the nature of value independently of this, its form.

A use-value, or useful article, therefore, has value only because human labor in the abstract has been embodied or materialised in it. How, then, is the magnitude of this value to be measured? Plainly, by the quantity of the value-creating substance, the labor, contained in the article. The quantity of labor, however, is measured by its duration, and labor-time in its turn finds its standard in weeks, days, and hours.

Some people might think that if the value of a commodity is determined by the quantity of labor spent on it, the more idle and unskilful the laborer, the more valuable would his commodity be, because more time would be required in its production. The labor, however, that forms the substance of value, is homogeneous human labor, expenditure of one uniform labor-power. The total labor-power of society, which is embodied in the sum total of the values of all commodities produced by that society, counts here as one homogeneous mass of human labor-power, composed though it be of innumerable individual units. Each of these units is the same as any other, so far as it has the character of the average labor-power of society, and takes effect as such; that is, so far as it requires for producing a commodity, no more time than is needed on an average, no more than is socially necessary. The labor-time socially necessary is that required to produce an article under the normal conditions of production, and with the average degree of skill and intensity prevalent at the time. The introduction of power looms into England probably reduced by one half the labor required to weave a given quantity of yarn into cloth. The hand-loom weavers, as a matter of fact, continued to require the same time as before; but for all that, the product of one hour of this labor represented after the change only half an hour's social labor, and consequently fell to one-half its former value.

We see then that that which determines the magnitude of the value of any article is the amount of labor socially necessary, or the labor-time socially necessary for its production. Each individual commodity, in this connection, is to be considered as an average sample of its class. Commodities, therefore, in which equal quantities of labor are embodied, or which can be produced in the same time, have the same value. The value of one commodity is to the value of any other, as the labor-time necessary for the production of the one is to that necessary for the production of the other. "As values, all commodities are only definite masses of congealed labor-time."

The value of a commodity would therefore remain constant, if the labor-time required for its production also remained constant. But the latter changes with every variation in the productiveness of labor. This productiveness is determined by various circumstances, amongst others, by the average amount of skill of the workmen, the state of science, and the degree of its practical application, the social organisation of production, the extent and capabilities of the means of production, and by physical conditions. For example, the same amount of labor in favourable seasons is embodied in eight bushels of corn, and in unfavourable, only in four. The same labor extracts from rich mines more metal than from poor mines. Diamonds are of very rare occurrence on the earth's surface, and hence their discovery costs, on an average, a great deal of labor-time. Consequently much labor is represented in a small compass. Jacob doubts whether gold has ever been paid for at its full value. This applies still more to diamonds. According to Eschwege, the total produce of the Brazilian diamond mines for the eighty years, ending in 1823, had not realised the price of one-and-a-half years' average produce of the sugar and coffee plantations of the same country, although the diamonds cost much more labor, and therefore represented more value. With richer mines, the same quantity of labor would embody itself in more diamonds and their value would fall. If we could succeed at a small expenditure of labor, in converting carbon into diamonds, their value might fall below that of bricks. In general, the greater the productiveness of labor, the less is the labor-time required for the production of an article, the less is the amount of labor crystallised in that article, and the less is its value; and *vice versâ*, the less the productiveness of labor, the greater is the labor-time required for the production of an article, and the greater is its value. The value of a commodity, therefore, varies directly as the quantity, and inversely as the productiveness, of the labor incorporated in it.

A thing can be a use-value, without having value. This is the case whenever its utility to man is not due to labor. Such are air, virgin soil, natural meadows, &c. A thing can be useful, and the product of human labor, without being a commodity. Whoever directly satisfies his wants with the produce of his own labor, creates, indeed, use-values, but not commodities. In order to produce the latter, he must not only produce use-values, but use-values for others, social use-values. Lastly, nothing can have value, without being an object of utility. If the thing is useless, so is the labor contained in it; the labor does not count as labor, and therefore creates no value.

Part II. The Transformation of Money into Capital

Chapter IV. The General Formula for Capital

The circulation of commodities is the starting point of capital. The production of commodities, their circulation, and that more developed form of their circulation called commerce, these form the historical groundwork from which it rises. The modern history of capital dates from the creation in the 16th century of a world-embracing commerce and a world-embracing market.

If we abstract from the material substance of the circulation of commodities, that is, from the exchange of the various use-values, and consider only the economic forms produced by this process of circulation, we find its final result to be money: this final product of the circulation of commodities is the first form in which capital appears.

As a matter of history, capital, as opposed to landed property, invariably takes the form at first of money; it appears as moneyed wealth, as the capital of the merchant and of the usurer. But we have no need to refer to the origin of capital in order to discover that the first form of appearance of capital is money. We can see it daily under our very eyes. All new capital, to commence with, comes on the stage, that is, on the market, whether of commodities, labor, or money, even in our days in the shape of money that by a definite process has to be transformed into capital.

The first distinction we notice between money that is money only, and money that is capital, is nothing more than a difference in their form of circulation.

The simplest form of the circulation of commodities is C—M—C, the transformation of commodities into money, and the change of the money back again into commodities; or selling in order to buy. But alongside of this form we find another specifically different form: M—C—M, the transformation of money into commodities, and the change of commodities back again into money; or buying in order to sell. Money that circulates in the latter manner is thereby transformed into, becomes capital, and is already potentially capital.

Now let us examine the circuit M—C—M a little closer. It consists, like the other, of two antithetical phases. In the first phase, M—C, or the purchase, the money is changed into a commodity. In the second phase, C—M, or the sale, the commodity is changed back again into money. The combination of these two phases constitutes the single movement whereby money is exchanged for a commodity and the same commodity is again exchanged for money; whereby a commodity is bought in order to be sold, or, neglecting the distinction in form between buying and selling, whereby a commodity is bought with money, and then money is bought with a commodity. The result, in which the phases of the process vanish, is the exchange of money for money, M—M. If I purchase 2,000 lbs. of cotton for £100, and resell the 2,000 lbs. of cotton for £110, I have, in fact, exchanged £100 for £110, money for money.

Now it is evident that the circuit M—C—M would be absurd and without meaning if the intention were to exchange by this means two equal sums of money, £100 for £100. The miser's plan would be far simpler and surer; he sticks to his £100 instead of exposing it to the dangers of circulation. And yet, whether the merchant who has paid £100 for his cotton sells it for £110, or lets it go for £100, or even £50, his money has, at all events, gone through a characteristic and original movement, quite different in kind from that which it goes through in the hands of the peasant who sells corn, and with the money thus set free buys clothes. We have therefore to examine first the distinguishing characteristics of the forms of the circuits M—C—M and C—M—C, and in doing this the real difference that underlies the mere difference of form will reveal itself.

Let us see, in the first place, what the two forms have in common.

Both circuits are resolvable into the same two antithetical phases, C—M, a sale, and M—C, a purchase. In each of these phases the same material elements—a commodity, and money, and the same economical *dramatis personae*, a buyer and a seller—confront one another. Each circuit is the unity of the same two antithetical phases, and in each case this unity is brought about by the intervention of three contracting parties, of whom one only sells, another only buys, while the third both buys and sells.

What, however, first and foremost distinguishes the circuit C—M—C from the circuit M—C—M, is the inverted order of succession of the two phases. The simple circulation of commodities begins with a sale and ends with a purchase, while the circulation of money as capital begins with a purchase and ends with a sale. In the one case both the starting-point and the goal are commodities, in the other they are money. In the first form the movement is brought about by the intervention of money, in the second by that of a commodity.

In the circulation C—M—C, the money is in the end converted into a commodity, that serves as a use-value; it is spent once for all. In the inverted form, M—C—M, on the contrary, the buyer lays out money in order that, as a seller, he may recover money. By the purchase of his commodity he throws money into circulation, in order to withdraw it again by the sale of the same commodity. He lets the money go, but only with the sly intention of getting it back again. The money, therefore, is not spent, it is merely advanced.

In the circuit C—M—C, the same piece of money changes its place twice. The seller gets it from the buyer and pays it away to another seller. The complete circulation, which begins with the receipt, concludes with the payment, of money for commodities. It is the very contrary in the circuit M—C—M. Here it is not the price of money that changes its place twice, but the commodity. The buyer takes it from the hands of the seller and passes it into the hands of another buyer. Just as in the simple circulation of commodities the double change of place of the same piece of money effects its passage from one hand into another, so here the double change of place of the same commodity brings about the reflux of the money to its point of departure.

Such reflux is not dependent on the commodity being sold for more than was paid for it. This circumstance influences only the amount of the money that comes back. The reflux itself takes place, so soon as the purchased commodity is resold, in other words, so soon as the circuit M—C—M is completed. We have here, therefore, a palpable difference between the circulation of money as capital, and its circulation as mere money.

The circuit C—M—C comes completely to an end, so soon as the money brought in by the sale of one commodity is abstracted again by the purchase of another.

If, nevertheless, there follows a reflux of money to its starting point, this can only happen through a renewal or repetition of the operation. If I sell a quarter of corn for £3, and with this £3 buy clothes, the money, so far as I am concerned, is spent and done with. It belongs to the clothes merchant. If I now sell a second quarter of corn, money indeed flows back to me, not however as a sequel to the first transaction, but in consequence of its repetition. The money again leaves me, so soon as I complete this second transaction by a fresh purchase. Therefore, in the circuit C—M—C, the expenditure of money has nothing to do with its reflux. On the other hand, in M—C—M, the reflux of the money is conditioned by the very mode of its expenditure. Without this reflux, the operation fails, or the process is interrupted and incomplete, owing to the absence of its complementary and final phase, the sale.

The circuit C—M—C starts with one commodity, and finishes with another, which falls out of circulation and into consumption. Consumption, the satisfaction of wants, in one word, use-value, is its end and aim. The circuit M—C—M, on the contrary, commences with money and ends with money. Its leading motive, and the goal that attracts it, is therefore mere exchange value.

In the simple circulation of commodities, the two extremes of the circuit have the same economic form. They are both commodities, and commodities of equal value. But they are also use-values differing in their qualities, as, for example, corn and clothes. The exchange of products, of the different materials in which the labor of society is embodied, forms here the basis of the movement. It is otherwise in the circulation M—C—M, which at first sight appears purposeless, because tautological. Both extremes have the same economic form. They are both money, and therefore are not qualitatively different use-values; for money is but the converted form of commodities, in which their particular use-values vanish. To exchange £100 for cotton, and then this same cotton again for £100, is merely a roundabout way of exchanging money for money, the same for the same, and appears to be an operation just as purposeless as it is absurd. One sum of money is distinguishable from another only by its amount. The character and tendency of the process M—C—M, is therefore not due to any qualitative difference between its extremes, both being money, but solely to their quantitative difference. More money is withdrawn from circulation at the finish than was thrown into it at the start. The cotton that was bought for £100 is perhaps resold for £100+ £10 or £110. The exact form of this process is therefore M—C—M′, where $M' = M + \Delta M =$ the original sum advanced, plus an increment. This increment or excess over the original value I call "surplus-value." The value originally advanced, therefore, not only remains intact while in circulation, but adds to itself a surplus-value or expands itself. It is this movement that converts it into capital.

Of course it is also possible, that in C—M—C, the two extremes C—C, say corn and clothes, may represent different quantities of value. The farmer may sell his corn above its value, or may buy the clothes at less than their value. He may, on the other hand, "be done" by the clothes merchant. Yet, in the form of circulation now under consideration, such differences in value are purely accidental. The fact that the corn and the clothes are equivalents, does not deprive the process of all meaning, as it does in M—C—M. The equivalence of their values is rather a necessary condition to its normal course.

The repetition or renewal of the act of selling in order to buy, is kept within bounds by the very object it aims at, namely, consumption or the satisfaction of definite wants, an aim that lies altogether outside the sphere of circulation. But when we buy in order to sell, we, on the contrary, begin and end with the same thing, money, exchange-value; and thereby the movement becomes interminable. No doubt, M. becomes M+Δ M, £100 become £110. But when viewed in their qualitative aspect alone, £110 are the same as £100, namely money; and considered quantitatively, £110 is, like £100, a sum of definite and limited value. If now, the £110 be spent as money, they cease to play their part. They are no longer capital. Withdrawn from circulation, they become petrified into a hoard, and though they remained in that state till doomsday, not a single farthing would accrue to them. If, then, the expansion of value is once aimed at, there is just the same inducement to augment the value of the £110 as that of the £100; for both are but limited expressions for ex-change-value, and therefore both have the same vocation to approach, by quantitative increase, as near as possible to absolute wealth. Momentarily, indeed, the value originally advanced, the £100 is distinguishable from the surplus value of £10 that is annexed to it during circulation; but the distinction vanishes immediately. At the end of the process we do not receive with one hand the original £100, and with the other, the surplus-value of £10. We simply get a value of £110, which is in exactly the same condition and fitness for commencing the expanding process, as the original £100 was. Money ends the movement only to begin it again. Therefore, the final result of every separate circuit, in which a purchase and consequent sale are completed, forms of itself the starting point of a new circuit. The simple circulation of commodities—selling in order to buy—is a means of carrying out a purpose unconnected with circulation, namely, the appropriation of use-values, the satisfaction of wants. The circulation of money as capital is, on the contrary, an end in itself, for the expansion of value takes place only within this constantly renewed movement. The circulation of capital has therefore no limits. Thus the conscious representative of this movement, the possessor of money becomes a capitalist. His person, or rather his pocket, is the point from which the money starts and to which it returns. The expansion of value, which is the objective basis or main-spring of the circulation M—C—M, becomes his subjective aim, and it is only in so far as the appropriation of ever more and more wealth in the abstract becomes the sole motive of his operations, that he functions as a capitalist, that is, as capital personified and endowed with consciousness and a will. Use-values must therefore never be looked upon as the real aim of the capitalist; neither must the profit on any single transaction. The restless never-ending process of profit-making alone is what he aims at. This boundless greed after riches, this passionate chase after exchange-value, is common to the capitalist and the miser; but while the miser is merely a capitalist gone mad, the capitalist is a rational miser. The never-ending augmentation of exchange-value, which the miser strives after, by seeking to save his money from circulation, is attained by the more acute capitalist, by constantly throwing it afresh into circulation.

The independent form, *i.e.*, the money-form, which the value of commodities assumes in the case of simple circulation, serves only one purpose, namely, their exchange, and vanishes in the final result of the movement. On the other hand, in the circulation M—C—M, both the money and the commodity represent only different modes of existence of value itself, the money its general mode, and the commodity its particular, or, so to say, disguised mode. It is constantly changing from one form to the other without thereby becoming lost, and thus assumes an automatically active character. If now we take in turn each of the two different forms which self-expanding value successively assumes in the course of its life, we then arrive at these two propositions: Capital is money: Capital is commodities. In truth, however, value is here the active factor in a process, in which, while constantly assuming the form in turn of money and commodities, it at the same time changes in magnitude, differentiates itself by throwing off surplus-value from itself; the original value, in other words, expands spontaneously. For the movement, in the course of which it adds surplus value, is its own movement, its expansion, therefore, is automatic expansion. Because it is value, it has acquired the occult quality of being able to add value to itself. It brings forth living offspring, or, at the least, lays golden eggs.

Value, therefore, being the active factor in such a process, and assuming at one time the form of money, at another that of commodities, but through all these changes preserving itself and expanding, it requires some independent form, by means of which its identity may at any time be established. And this form it possesses only in the shape of money. It is under the form of money that value begins and ends, and begins again, every act of its own spontaneous generation. It began by being £100, it is now £110, and so on. But the money itself is only one of the two forms of value. Unless it takes the form of some commodity, it does not become capital. There is here no antagonism, as in the case of hoarding, between the money and commodities. The capitalist knows that all commodities, however scurvy they may look, or however badly they may smell, are in faith and in truth money, inwardly circumcised Jews, and what is more, a wonderful means whereby out of money to make more money.

In simple circulation, C—M—C, the value of commodities attained at the most a form independent of their use-values, *i. e.*, the form of money; but that same value now in the circulation M—C—M, or the circulation of capital, suddenly presents itself as an independent substance, endowed with a motion of its own, passing through a life-process of its own, in which money and commodities are mere forms which it assumes and casts off in turn. Nay, more: instead of simply representing the relations of commodities, it enters now, so to say, into private relations with itself. It differentiates itself as original value from itself as surplus-value; as the father differentiates himself from himself quâ the son, yet both are one and of one age: for only by the surplus value of £10 does the £100 originally advanced become capital, and so soon as this takes place, so soon, as the son, and by the son, the father, is begotten, so soon does their difference vanish, and they again become one, £110.

Value therefore now becomes value in process, money in process, and, as such, capital. It comes out of circulation, enters into it again, preserves and multiplies itself within its circuit, comes back out of it with expanded bulk, and begins the same round ever afresh. M—M′, money which begets money, such is the description of Capital from the mouths of its first interpreters, the Mercantilists.

Buying in order to sell, or, more accurately, buying in order to sell dearer, M—C—M′, appears certainly to be a form peculiar to one kind of capital alone, namely, merchants' capital. But industrial capital too is money, that is changed into commodities, and by the sale of these commodities, is reconverted into more money. The events that take place outside the sphere of circulation, in the interval between the buying and selling, do not affect the form of this movement. Lastly, in the case of interest-bearing capital, the circulation M—C—M′ appears abridged. We have its result without the intermediate stage, in the form M—M′, "en style lapidaire" so to say, money that is worth more money, value that is greater than itself.

M—C—M′ is therefore in reality the general formula of capital as it appears prima facie within the sphere of circulation.

Part III. The Production of Absolute Surplus-value

Chapter VII. The Labor-process and the Process of Producing Surplus-value

Section 1.—*The Labor-process or the Production of Use-values.*

The capitalist buys labor-power in order to use it; and labor-power in use is labor itself. The purchaser of labor-power consumes it by setting the seller of it to work. By working, the latter becomes actually, what before he only was potentially, labor-power in action, a laborer. In order that his labor may reappear in a commodity, he must, before all things, expend it on something useful, on something capable of satisfying a want of some sort. Hence, what the capitalist sets the laborer to produce, is a particular, use-value, a specified article. The fact that the production of use-values, or goods, is carried on under the control of a capitalist and on his behalf, does not alter the general character of that production. We shall, there-fore, in the first place, have to consider the labor-process independently of the particular form it assumes under given social conditions.

Labor is, in the first place, a process in which both man and Nature participate, and in which man of his own accord starts, regulates, and controls the material re-actions between himself and Nature. He opposes himself to Nature as one of her own forces, setting in motion arms and legs, head and hands, the natural forces of his body, in order to appro-priate Nature's productions in a form adapted to his own wants. By thus acting on the external world and changing it, he at the same time changes his own nature. He develops his slumbering powers and compels them to act in obedience to his sway. We are not now dealing with those primitive instinctive forms of labor that remind us of the mere animal. An immeasurable interval of time separates the state of things in which a man brings his labor-power to market for sale as a commodity, from that state in which human labor was still in its first instinctive stage. We presuppose labor in a form that stamps it as exclusively human. A spider conducts operations that resemble those of a weaver, and a bee puts to shame many an architect in the construction of her cells. But what dis-tinguishes the worst architect from the best of bees is this, that the archi-tect raises his structure in imagination before he erects it in reality. At the end of every labor-process, we get a result that already existed in the imagination of the laborer at its commencement. He not only effects a change of form in the material on which he works, but he also realises a purpose of his own that gives the law to his *modus operandi*, and to which he must subordinate his will. And this subordination is no mere momentary act. Besides the exertion of the bodily organs, the process demands that, during the whole operation, the workman's will be steadily in consonance with his purpose. This means close attention. The less he is attracted by the nature of the work, and the mode in which it is carried on, and the less, therefore, he enjoys it as something which gives play to his bodily and mental powers, the more close his attention is forced to be.

The elementary factors of the labor-process are 1, the personal activity of man, *i.e.*, work itself, 2, the subject of that work, and 3, its instruments.

The soil (and this, economically speaking, includes water) in the virgin state in which it supplies man with necessaries or the means of subsistence ready to hand, exists independently of him, and is the uni-versal subject of human labor. All those things which labor merely sepa-rates from immediate connection with their environment, are subjects of labor spontaneously provided by Nature. Such are fish which we catch and take from their element, water, timber which we fell in the virgin forest, and ores which we extract from their veins. If, on the other hand, the subject of labor has, so to say, been filtered through previous labor, we call it raw material; such is ore already extracted and ready for washing. All raw material is the subject of labor, but not every subject of labor is raw material; it can only become so, after it has undergone some alteration by means of labor.

An instrument of labor is a thing, or a complex of things, which the laborer interposes between himself and the subject of his labor, and which serves as the conductor of his activity. He makes use of the mechanical, physical, and chemical properties of some substances in order to make other substances subservient to his aims. Leaving out of consideration such ready-made means of subsistence as fruits, in gathering which a man's own limbs serve as the instruments of his labor, the first thing of which the laborer possesses himself is not the subject of labor but its instrument. Thus Nature becomes one of the organs of his activity, one that he annexes to his own bodily organs, adding stature to himself in spite of the Bible. As the earth is his original larder, so too it is his original tool house. It supplies him, for instance, with stones for throwing, grinding, pressing, cutting, &c. The earth itself is an instrument of labor, but when used as such in agriculture implies a whole series of other instruments and a comparatively high development of labor. No sooner does labor undergo the least development, than it requires specially prepared instruments. Thus in the oldest caves we find stone implements and weapons. In the earliest period of human history domesticated animals, *i.e.*, animals which have been bred for the purpose, and have undergone modifications by means of labor, play the chief part as instruments of labor along with specially prepared stones, wood, bones, and shells. The use and fabrication of instruments of labor, although existing in the germ among certain species of animals, is specifically characteristic of the human labor-process, and Franklin therefore defines man as a tool-making animal. Relics of by-gone instruments of labor possess the same importance for the investigation of extinct economical forms of society, as do fossil bones for the determination of extinct species of animals. It is not the articles made, but how they are made, and by what instruments, that enables us to distinguish different economical epochs. Instruments of labor not only supply a standard of the degree of development to which human labor has attained, but they are also indicators of the social conditions under which that labor is carried on. Among the instruments of labor, those of a mechanical nature, which, taken as a whole, we may call the bone and muscles of production, offer much more decided characteristics of a given epoch of production, than those which, like pipes, tubs, baskets, jars, &c., serve only to hold the materials for labor, which latter class, we may in a general way, call the vascular system of production. The latter first begins to play an important part in the chemical industries.

In a wider sense we may include among the instruments of labor, in addition to those things that are used for directly transferring labor to its subject, and which therefore, in one way or another, serve as conductors of activity, all such objects as are necessary for carrying on the labor-process. These do not enter directly into the process, but without them it is either impossible for it to take place at all, or possible only to a partial extent. Once more we find the earth to be a universal instrument of this sort, for it furnishes a *locus standi* to the laborer and a field of employment for its activity. Among instruments that are the result of previous labor and also belong to this class, we find workshops, canals, roads, and so forth.

In the labor-process, therefore, man's activity, with the help of the instruments of labor, effects an alteration, designed from the commencement, in the material worked upon. The process disappears in the product; the latter is a use-value, Nature's material adapted by a change of form to the wants of man. Labor has incorporated itself with its subject: the former is materialised, the latter transformed. That which in the laborer appeared as movement, now appears in the product as a fixed quality without motion. The blacksmith forges and the product is a forging.

If we examine the whole process from the point of view of its result, the product, it is plain that both the instruments and the subject of labor, are means of production, and that the labor itself is productive labor.

Though a use-value, in the form of a product, issues from the labor-process, yet other use-values, products of previous labor, enter into it as means of production. The same use-value is both the product of a previous process, and a means of production in a later process. Products are therefore not only results, but also essential conditions of labor.

With the exception of the extractive industries, in which the material for labor is provided immediately by nature, such as mining, hunting, fishing, and agriculture (so far as the latter is confined to breaking up virgin soil), all branches of industry manipulate raw material, objects already filtered through labor, already products of labor. Such is seed in agriculture. Animals and plants, which we are accustomed to consider as products of nature, are in their present form, not only products of, say last year's labor, but the result of a gradual transformation, continued through many generations, under man's superintendence, and by means of his labor. But in the great majority of cases, instruments of labor show even to the most superficial observer, traces of the labor of past ages.

Raw material may either form the principal substance of a product, or it may enter into its formation only as an accessory. An accessory may be consumed by the instruments of labor, as coal under a boiler, oil by a wheel, hay by draft-horses, or it may be mixed with the raw material in order to produce some modification thereof, as chlorine into unbleached linen, coal with iron, dye-stuff with wool, or again, it may help to carry on the work itself, as in the case of the materials used for heating and lighting workshops. The distinction between principal substance and accessory vanishes in the true chemical industries, because there none of the raw material reappears, in its original composition, in the substance of the product.

Every object possesses various properties, and is thus capable of being applied to different uses. One and the same product may therefore serve as raw material in very different processes. Corn, for example, is a raw material for millers, starch-manufacturers, distillers, and cattle-breeders. It also enters as raw material into its own production in the shape of seed: coal, too, is at the same time the product of, and a means of production in, coal-mining.

Again, a particular product may be used in one and the same process, both as an instrument of labor and as raw material. Take, for instance, the fattening of cattle, where the animal is the raw material, and at the same time an instrument for the production of manure.

A product, though ready for immediate consumption, may yet serve as raw material for a further product, as grapes when they become the raw material for wine. On the other hand, labor may give us its product in such a form, that we can use it only as raw material, as is the case with cotton, thread, and yarn. Such a raw material, though itself a product, may have to go through a whole series of different processes: in each of these in turn, it serves, with constantly varying form, as raw material, until the last process of the series leaves it a perfect product, ready for individual consumption, or for use as an instrument of labor.

Hence we see, that whether a use-value is to be regarded as raw material, as instrument of labor, or as product, this is determined entirely by its function in the labor process, by the position it there occupies: as this varies, so does its character.

Whenever therefore a product enters as a means of production into a new labor-process, it thereby loses its character of product, and becomes a mere factor in the process. A spinner treats spindles only as implements for spinning, and flax only as the material that he spins. Of course it is impossible to spin without material and spindles; and therefore the existence of these things as products, at the commencement of the spinning operation, must be presumed: but in the process itself, the fact that they are products of previous labor, is a matter of utter indifference; just as in the digestive process, it is of no importance whatever, that bread is the produce of the previous labor of the farmer, the miller, and the baker. On the contrary, it is generally by their imperfections as products, that the means of production in any process assert themselves in their character as products. A blunt knife or weak thread forcibly remind us of Mr. A., the cutler, or Mr. B., the spinner. In the finished product the labor by means of which it has acquired its useful qualities is not palpable, has apparently vanished.

A machine which does not serve the purposes of labor is useless. In addition, it falls a prey to the destructive influence of natural forces. Iron rusts and wood rots. Yarn with which we neither weave nor knit, is cotton wasted. Living labor must seize upon these things and rouse them from their death-sleep, change them from mere possible use-values into real and effective ones. Bathed in the fire of labor, appropriated as part and parcel of labor's organism, and, as it were, made alive for the performance of their functions in the process, they are in truth consumed, but consumed with a purpose, as elementary constituents of new use-values, of new products, ever ready as means of subsistence for individual consumption, or as means of production for some new labor-process.

If then, on the one hand, finished products are not only results, but also necessary conditions, of the labor-process, on the other hand, their assumption into that process, their contact with living labor, is the sole means by which they can be made to retain their character of use-values, and be utilised.

Labor uses up its material factors, its subject and its instruments, consumes them, and is therefore a process of consumption. Such productive consumption is distinguished from individual consumption by this, that the latter uses up products, as means of subsistence for the living individual; the farmer, as means whereby alone, labor, the labor-power of the living individual, is enabled to act. The product, therefore, of individual consumption, is the consumer himself; the result of productive consumption, is a product distinct from the consumer.

In so far then, as its instruments and subjects are themselves products, labor consumes products in order to create products, or in other words, consumes one set of products by turning them into means of production for another set. But, just as in the beginning, the only participators in the labor-process were man and the earth, which latter exists independently of man, so even now we still employ in the process many means of production, provided directly by nature, that do not represent any combination of natural substances with human labor.

The labor process, resolved as above into its simple elementary factors, is human action with a view to the production of use-values, appropriation of natural substances to human requirements; it is the necessary condition for effecting exchange of matter between man and Nature; it is the everlasting nature-imposed condition of human existence, and therefore is independent of every social phase of that existence, or rather, is common to every such phase. It was, therefore, not necessary to represent our laborer in connexion with other laborers; man and his labor on one side, Nature and its materials on the other, sufficed. As the taste of the porridge does not tell you who grew the oats, no more does this simple process tell you of itself what are the social conditions under which it is taking place, whether under the slave-owner's brutal lash, or the anxious eye of the capitalist, whether Cincinnatus carries it on in tilling his modest farm or a savage in killing wild animals with stones.

Let us now return to our would-be capitalist. We left him just after he had purchased, in the open market, all the necessary factors of the labor-process; its objective factors, the means of production, as well as its subjective factor, labor-power. With the keen eye of an expert, he had selected the means of production and the kind of labor-power best adapted to his particular trade, be it spinning, bootmaking, or any other kind. He then proceeds to consume the commodity, the labor-power that he has just bought, by causing the laborer, the impersonation of that labor-power, to consume the means of production by his labor. The general character of the labor-process is evidently not changed by the fact, that the laborer works for the capitalist instead of for himself; moreover, the particular methods and operations employed in boot-making or spinning are not immediately changed by the intervention of the capitalist. He must begin by taking the labor-power as he finds it in the market, and consequently be satisfied with labor of such a kind as would be found in the period immediately preceding the rise of the capitalists. Changes in the methods of production by the subordination of labor to capital, can take place only at a later period, and therefore will have to be treated of in a later chapter.

The labor-process, turned into the process by which the capitalist consumes labor-power, exhibits two characteristic phenomena. First, the laborer works under the control of the capitalist to whom his labor belongs; the capitalist taking good care that the work is done in a proper manner, and that the means of production are used with intelligence, so that there is no unnecessary waste of raw material, and no wear and tear of the implements beyond what is necessarily caused by the work.

Secondly, the product is the property of the capitalist and not that of the laborer, its immediate producer. Suppose that a capitalist pays for a day's labor-power at its value; then the right to use that power for a day belongs to him, just as much as the right to use any other commodity, such as a horse that he has hired for the day. To the purchaser of a commodity belongs its use, and the seller of labor-power, by giving his labor, does no more, in reality, than part with the use-value that he has sold. From the instant he steps into the workshop, the use-value of his labor-power, and therefore also its use, which is labor, belongs to the capitalist. By the purchase of labor-power, the capitalist incorporates labor, as a living ferment, with the lifeless constituents of the product. From his point of view, the labor-process is nothing more than the consumption of the commodity purchased, *i.e.*, of labor-power; but this consumption cannot be effected except by supplying the labor-power with the means of production. The labor-process is a process between things that the capitalist has purchased, things that have become his property. The product of this process also belongs, therefore, to him, just as much as does the wine which is the product of a process of fermentation completed in his cellar.

Section 2.—The Production of Surplus-value.

The product appropriated by the capitalist is a use-value, as yarn, for example, or boots. But, although boots are, in one sense, the basis of all social progress, and our capitalist is a decided "progressive," yet he does not manufacture boots for their own sake. Use-value is, by no means, the thing *"qu'on aime pour lui-même"* in the production of commodities. Use-values are only produced by capitalists, because, and in so far as, they are the material substratum, the depositaries of exchange-value. Our capitalist has two objects in view: in the first place, he wants to produce a use-value that has a value in exchange, that is to say, an article destined to be sold, a commodity; and secondly, he desires to produce a commodity whose value shall be greater than the sum of the values of the commodities used in its production, that is, of the means of production and the labor-power, that he purchased with his good money in the open market. His aim is to produce not only a use-value, but a commodity also; not only use-value, but value; not only value, but at the same time surplus-value.

It must be borne in mind, that we are now dealing with the production of commodities, and that, up to this point, we have only considered one aspect of the process. Just as commodities are, at the same time, use-values and values, so the process of producing them must be a labor-process, and at the same time, a process of creating value.

Let us now examine production as a creation of value.

We know that the value of each commodity is determined by the quantity of labor expended on and materialised in it, by the working-time necessary, under given social conditions, for its production. This rule also holds good in the case of the product that accrued to our capitalist, as the result of the labor-process carried on for him. Assuming this product to be 10 lbs. of yarn, our first step is to calculate the quantity of labor realised in it.

For spinning the yarn, raw material is required; suppose in this case 10 lbs. of cotton. We have no need at present to investigate the value of this cotton, for our capitalist has, we will assume, bought it at its full value, say of ten shillings. In this price the labor required for the production of the cotton is already expressed in terms of the average labor of society. We will further assume that the wear and tear of the spindle, which, for our present purpose, may represent all other instruments of labor employed, amounts to the value of 2s. If, then, twenty-four hours' labor, or two working days, are required to produce the quantity of gold represented by twelve shillings, we have here, to begin with, two days' labor already incorporated in the yarn.

We must not let ourselves be misled by the circumstance that the cotton has taken a new shape while the substance of the spindle has to a certain extent been used up. By the general law of value, if the value of 40 lbs. of yarn = the value of 40 lbs. of cotton + the value of a whole spindle, *i.e.*, if the same working time is required to produce the commodities on either side of this equation, then 10 lbs. of yarn are an equivalent for 10 lbs. of cotton, together with one-fourth of a spindle. In the case we are considering the same working time is materialised in the 10 lbs. of yarn on the one hand, and in the 10 lbs. of cotton and the fraction of a spindle on the other. Therefore, whether value appears in cotton, in a spindle, or in yarn, makes no difference in the amount of that value. The spindle and cotton, instead of resting quietly side by side, join together in the process, their forms are altered, and they are turned into yarn; but their value is no more affected by this fact than it would be if they had been simply exchanged for their equivalent in yarn.

The labor required for the production of the cotton, the raw material of the yarn, is part of the labor necessary to produce the yarn, and is therefore contained in the yarn. The same applies to the labor embodied in the spindle, without whose wear and tear the cotton could not be spun.

Hence, in determining the value of the yarn, or the labor-time required for its production, all the special processes carried on at various times and in different places, which were necessary, first to produce the cotton and the wasted portion of the spindle, and then with the cotton and spindle to spin the yarn, may together be looked on as different and successive phases of one and the same process. The whole of the labor in the yarn is past labor; and it is a matter of no importance that the operations necessary for the production of its constituent elements were carried on at times which, referred to the present, are more remote than the final operation of spinning. If a definite quantity of labor, say thirty days, is requisite to build a house, the total amount of labor incorporated in it is not altered by the fact that the work of the last day is done twenty-nine days later than that of the first. Therefore the labor contained in the raw material and the instruments of labor can be treated just as if it were labor expended in an earlier stage of the spinning process, before the labor of actual spinning commenced.

The values of the means of production, *i.e.*, the cotton and the spindle, which values are expressed in the price of twelve shillings, are therefore constituent parts of the value of the yarn, or, in other words, of the value of the product.

Two conditions must nevertheless be fulfilled. First, the cotton and spindle must concur in the production of a use-value; they must in the present case become yarn. Value is independent of the particular use-value by which it is borne, but it must be embodied in a use-value of some kind. Secondly, the time occupied in the labor of production must not exceed the time really necessary under the given social conditions of the case. Therefore, if no more than 1 lb. of cotton be requisite to spin 1 lb. of yarn, care must be taken that no more than this weight of cotton is consumed in the production of 1 lb. of yarn; and similarly with regard to the spindle. Though the capitalist have a hobby, and use a gold instead of a steel spindle, yet the only labor that counts for anything in the value of the yarn is that which would be required to produce a steel spindle, because no more is necessary under the given social conditions.

We now know what portion of the value of the yarn is owing to the cotton and the spindle. It amounts to twelve shillings or the value of two days' work. The next point for our consideration is, what portion of the value of the yarn is added to the cotton by the labor of the spinner.

We have now to consider this labor under a very different aspect from that which it had during the labor-process; there, we viewed it solely as that particular kind of human activity which changes cotton into yarn; there, the more the labor was suited to the work, the better the yarn, other circumstances remaining the same. The labor of the spinner was then viewed as specifically different from other kinds of productive labor, different on the one hand in its special aim, viz., spinning, different, on the other hand, in the special character of its operations, in the special nature of its means of production and in the special use-value of its product. For the operation of spinning, cotton and spindles are a necessity, but for making rifled cannon they would be of no use whatever. Here, on the contrary, where we consider the labor of the spinner only so far as it is value-creating, *i.e.*, a source of value, his labor differs in no respect from the labor of the man who bores cannon, or (what here more nearly concerns us), from the labor of the cotton-planter and spindle-maker incorporated in the means of production. It is solely by reason of this identity, that cotton planting, spindle making and spinning, are capable of forming the component parts, differing only quantitatively from each other, of one whole, namely, the value of the yarn. Here, we have nothing more to do with the quality, the nature and the specific character of the labor, but merely with its quantity. And this simply requires to be calculated. We proceed upon the assumption that spinning is simple, unskilled labor, the average labor of a given state of society. Hereafter we shall see that the contrary assumption would make no difference.

While the laborer is at work, his labor constantly undergoes a transformation: from being motion, it becomes an object without motion;

from being the laborer working, it becomes the thing produced. At the end of one hour's spinning, that act is represented by a definite quantity of yarn; in other words, a definite quantity of labor, namely that of one hour, has become embodied in the cotton. We say labor, *i.e.*, the expenditure of his vital force by the spinner, and not spinning labor, because the special work of spinning counts here, only so far as it is the expenditure of labor-power in general, and not in so far as it is the specific work of the spinner.

In the process we are now considering it is of extreme importance, that no more time be consumed in the work of transforming the cotton into yarn than is necessary under the given social conditions. If under normal, *i.e.*, average social conditions of production, *a* pounds of cotton ought to be made into *b* pounds of yarn by one hour's labor, then a day's labor does not count as 12 hours' labor unless 12 *a* pounds of cotton have been made into 12 *b* pounds of yarn; for in the creation of value, the time that is socially necessary alone counts.

Not only the labor, but also the raw material and the product now appear in quite a new light, very different from that in which we viewed them in the labor-process pure and simple. The raw material serves now merely as an absorbent of a definite quantity of labor. By this absorption it is in fact changed into yarn, because it is spun, because labor-power in the form of spinning is added to it; but the product, the yarn, is now nothing more than a measure of the labor absorbed by the cotton. If in one hour $1\frac{2}{3}$ lbs. of cotton can be spun into $1\frac{2}{3}$ lbs. of yarn, then 10 lbs. of yarn indicate the absorption of 6 hours' labor. Definite quantities of product, these quantities being determined by experience, now represent nothing but definite quantities of labor, definite masses of crystallized labor-time. They are nothing more than the materialisation of so many hours or so many days of social labor.

We are here no more concerned about the facts, that the labor is the specific work of spinning, that its subject is cotton and its product yarn, than we are about the fact that the subject itself is already a product and therefore raw material. If the spinner, instead of spinning, were working in a coal mine, the subject of his labor, the coal, would be supplied by Nature; nevertheless, a definite quantity of extracted coal, a hundred weight, for example, would represent a definite quantity of absorbed labor.

We assumed, on the occasion of its sale, that the value of a day's labor-power is three shillings, and that six hour's labor are incorporated in that sum; and consequently that this amount of labor is requisite to produce the necessaries of life daily required on an average by the laborer. If now our spinner by working for one hour, can convert $1\frac{2}{3}$ lbs. of cotton into $1\frac{2}{3}$ lbs. of yarn, it follows that in six hours he will convert 10 lbs. of cotton into 10 lbs. of yarn. Hence, during the spinning process, the cotton absorbs six hours' labor. The same quantity of labor is also embodied in a piece of gold of the value of three shillings. Consequently by the mere labor of spinning, a value of three shillings is added to the cotton.

Let us now consider the total value of the product, the 10 lbs. of yarn. Two and a half days' labor have been embodied in it, of which two days were contained in the cotton and in the substance of the spindle worn away, and half a day was absorbed during the process of spinning. This two and a half days' labor is also represented by a piece of gold of the value of fifteen shillings. Hence, fifteen shillings is an adequate price for the 10 lbs. of yarn, or the price of one pound is eighteen-pence.

Our capitalist stares in astonishment. The value of the product is exactly equal to the value of the capital advanced. The value so advanced has not expanded, no surplus-value has been created, and consequently money has not been converted into capital. The price of the yarn is fifteen shillings, and fifteen shillings were spent in the open market upon the constituent elements of the product, or, what amounts to the same thing, upon the factors of the labor-process; ten shillings were paid for the cotton, two shillings for the substance of the spindle worn away, and three shillings for the labor-power. The swollen value of the yarn is of no avail, for it is merely the sum of the values formerly existing in the cotton, the spindle, and the labor-power; out of such a simple addition of existing values, no surplus-value can possibly arise. These separate values are now all concentrated in one thing; but so they were also in the sum of fifteen shillings, before it was split up into three parts, by the purchase of the commodities.

There is in reality nothing very strange in this result. The value of one pound of yarn being eighteenpence, if our capitalist buys 10 lbs. of yarn in the market, he must pay fifteen shillings for them. It is clear that, whether a man buys his house ready built, or gets it built for him, in neither case will the mode of acquisition increase the amount of money laid out on the house.

Our capitalist, who is at home in his vulgar economy, exclaims: "Oh! but I advanced my money for the express purpose of making more money." The way to Hell is paved with good intentions, and he might just as easily have intended to make money, without producing at all. He threatens all sorts of things. He won't be caught napping again. In future he will buy the commodities in the market, instead of manufacturing them himself. But if all his brother capitalists were to do the same, where would he find his commodities in the market? And his money he cannot cat. He tries persuasion. "Consider my abstinence; I might have played ducks and drakes with the 15 shillings; but instead of that I consumed it productively, and made yarn with it." Very well, and by way of reward he is now in possession of good yarn instead of a bad conscience; and as for playing the part of a miser, it would never do for him to relapse into such bad ways as that; we have seen before to what results such asceticism leads. Besides, where nothing is, the king has lost his rights: whatever may be the merit of his abstinence, there is nothing wherewith specially to remunerate it, because the value of the product is merely the sum of the values of the commodities that were thrown into the process of production. Let him therefore console himself with the reflection that virtue is its own reward. But no, he becomes importunate. He says: "The yarn is of no use to me: I produced it for sale." In that case let him sell it, or, still better, let him for the future produce only things for satisfying his personal wants, a remedy that his physician M'Culloch has already prescribed as infallible against an epidemic of over-production. He now gets obstinate. "Can the laborer," he asks, "merely with his arms and legs, produce commodities out of nothing? Did I not supply him with the materials, by means of which, and in which alone, his labor could be embodied? And as the greater part of society consists of such ne'er-do-wells, have I not rendered society incalculable service by my instruments of production, my cotton and my spindle, and not only society, but the laborer also, whom in addition I have provided with the necessaries of life? And am I to be allowed nothing in return for all this service?" Well, but has not the laborer rendered him the equivalent service of changing his cotton and spindle into yarn? Moreover, there is here no question of service. A service is nothing more than the useful effect of a use-value, be it of a commodity, or be it of labor. But here we are dealing with exchange-value. The capitalist paid to the laborer a value of 3 shillings, and the laborer gave him back an exact equivalent in the value of 3 shillings, added by him to the cotton: he gave him value for value. Our friend, up to this time so purse-proud, suddenly assumes the modest demeanour of his own workman, and exclaims: "Have I myself not worked? Have I not performed the labor of superintendence and of overlooking the spinner? And does not this labor, too, create value?" His overlooker and his manager try to hide their smiles. Meanwhile, after a hearty laugh, he re-assumes his usual mien. Though he chanted to us the whole creed of the economists, in reality, he says, he would not give a brass farthing for it. He leaves this and all such like subterfuges and juggling tricks to the professors of political economy, who are paid for it. He himself is a practical man; and though he does not always consider what he says outside his business, yet in his business he knows what he is about.

Let us examine the matter more closely. The value of a day's labor-power amounts to 3 shillings, because on our assumption half a day's labor is embodied in that quantity of labor-power, *i.e.*, because the means of subsistence that are daily required for the production of labor-power, cost half a day's labor. But the past labor that is embodied in the labor-power, and the living labor that it can call into action; the daily cost of maintaining it, and its daily expenditure in work, are two totally different things. The former determines the exchange-value of the labor-power, the latter is its use-value. The fact that half a day's labor is necessary to keep the laborer alive during 24 hours, does not in any way prevent him from working a whole day. Therefore, the value of labor-power, and the value which that labor-power creates in the labor process, are two entirely different magnitudes; and this difference of the two values was what the capitalist had in view, when he was purchasing the labor-power. The useful qualities that labor-power possesses, and by virtue of which it makes yarn or boots, were to him nothing more than a condition *sine qua non;* for in order to create value, labor must be expended in a useful manner. What really influenced him was the specific use-value which this commodity possesses of being *a source not only of value, but of more value than it has itself*. This is the special service that the capitalist expects from labor-power, and in this transaction he acts in accordance with the "eternal laws" of the exchange of commodities. The seller of labor-power, like the seller of any other commodity, realizes its exchange-value, and parts with its use-value. He cannot take the one without giving the other. The use-value of labor-power, or in other words, labor, belongs just as little to its seller, as the use-value of oil after it has been sold belongs to the dealer who has sold it. The owner of the money has paid the value of a day's labor-power; his, therefore, is the use of it for a day; a day's labor belongs to him. The circumstance, that on the one hand the daily sustenance of labor-power costs only half a day's labor, while on the other hand the very same labor-power can work during a whole day, that consequently the value which its use during one day creates, is double what he pays for that use, this circumstance is, without doubt, a piece of good luck for the buyer, but by no means an injury to the seller.

Our capitalist foresaw this state of things, and that was the cause of his laughter. The laborer therefore finds, in the workshop, the means of production necessary for working, not only during six, but during twelve hours. Just as during the six hours' process our 10 lbs. of cotton absorbed six hours' labor, and became 10 lbs. of yarn, so now, 20 lbs. of cotton will absorb 12 hours' labor and be changed into 20 lbs. of yarn. Let us now examine the product of this prolonged process. There is now materialised in this 20 lbs. of yarn the labor of five days, of which four days are due to the cotton and the lost steel of the spindle, the remaining day having been absorbed by the cotton during the spinning process. Expressed in gold, the labor of five days is thirty shillings. This is therefore the price of the 20 lbs. of yarn, giving, as before, eighteenpence as the price of a pound. But the sum of the values of the commodities that entered into the process amounts to 27 shillings. The value of the yarn is 30 shillings. Therefore the value of the product is ⅒ greater than the value advanced for its production; 27 shillings have been transformed into 30 shillings; a surplus-value of 3 shillings has been created. The trick has at last succeeded; money has been converted into capital.

Every condition of the problem is satisfied, while the laws that regulate the exchange of commodities, have been in no way violated. Equivalent has been exchanged for equivalent. For the capitalist as buyer paid for each commodity, for the cotton, the spindle and the labor-power, its full value. He then did what is done by every purchaser of commodities; he consumed their use-value. The consumption of the labor-power, which was also the process of producing commodities, resulted in 20 lbs. of yarn, having a value of 30 shillings. The capitalist, formerly a buyer, now returns to market as a seller, of commodities. He sells his yarn at eighteenpence a pound, which is its exact value. Yet for all that he withdraws 3 shillings more from circulation than he originally threw into it. This metamorphosis, this conversion of money into capital, takes place both within the sphere of circulation and also outside it; within the circulation, because conditioned by the purchase of the labor-power in the market; outside the circulation, because what is done within it is only a stepping-stone to the production of surplus-value, a process which is entirely confined to the sphere of production. Thus *"tout est pour le mieux dans le meilleur des mondes possibles."*

By turning his money into commodities that serve as the material elements of a new product, and as factors in the labor-process, by incorporating living labor with their dead substance, the capitalist at the same time converts value, *i.e.*, past, materialised, and dead labor into capital, into value big with value, a live monster that is fruitful and multiplies.

If we now compare the two processes of producing value and of creating surplus-value, we see that the latter is nothing but the continuation of the former beyond a definite point. If on the one hand the process be not carried beyond the point, where the value paid by the capitalist for the labor-power is replaced by an exact equivalent, it is simply a process of producing value; if, on the other hand, it be continued beyond that point, it becomes a process of creating surplus-value.

If we proceed further, and compare the process of producing value with the labor-process, pure and simple, we find that the latter consists of the useful labor, the work, that produces use-values. Here we contemplate the labor as producing a particular article; we view it under its qualitative aspect alone, with regard to its end and aim. But viewed as a value-creating process, the same labor-process presents itself under its quantitative aspect alone. Here it is a question merely of the time occupied by the laborer in doing the work; of the period during which the labor-power is usefully expended. Here, the commodities that take part in the process do not count any longer as necessary adjuncts of labor-power in the production of a definite, useful object. They count merely as depositaries of so much absorbed or materialised labor; that labor, whether previously embodied in the means of production, or incorporated in them for the first time during the process by the action of labor-power, counts in either case only according to its duration; it amounts to so many hours or days as the case may be.

Moreover, only so much of the time spent in the production of any article is counted, as, under the given social conditions, is necessary. The consequences of this are various. In the first place, it becomes necessary that the labor should be carried on under normal conditions. If a self-acting mule is the implement in general use for spinning, it would be absurd to supply the spinner with a distaff and spinning wheel. The cotton too must not be such rubbish as to cause extra waste in being worked, but must be of suitable quality. Otherwise the spinner would be found to spend more time in producing a pound of yarn than is socially necessary, in which case the excess of time would create neither value nor money. But whether the material factors of the process are of normal quality or not, depends not upon the laborer, but entirely upon the capitalist. Then again, the labor-power itself must be of average efficacy. In the trade in which it is being employed, it must possess the average skill, handiness and quickness prevalent in that trade, and our capitalist took good care to buy labor-power of such normal goodness. This power must be applied with the average amount of exertion and with the usual degree of intensity; and the capitalist is as careful to see that this is done, as that his workmen are not idle for a single moment. He has bought the use of the labor-power for a definite period, and he insists upon his rights. He has no intention of being robbed. Lastly, and for this purpose our friend has a penal code of his own, all wasteful consumption of raw material or instruments of labor is strictly forbidden, because what is so wasted, represents labor superfluously expended, labor that does not count in the product or enter into its value.

We now see, that the difference between labor, considered on the one hand as producing utilities, and on the other hand, as creating value, a difference which we discovered by our analysis of a commodity, resolves itself into a distinction between two aspects of the process of production.

The process of production, considered on the one hand as the unity of the labor-process and the process of creating value, is production of commodities; considered on the other hand as the unity of the labor-process and the process of producing surplus-value, it is the capitalist process of production, or capitalist production of commodities.

We stated, on a previous page, that in the creation of surplus-value it does not in the least matter, whether the labor appropriated by the capitalist be simple unskilled labor of average quality or more complicated skilled labor. All labor of a higher or more complicated character than average labor is expenditure of labor-power of a more costly kind, labor-power whose production has cost more time and labor, and which therefore has a higher value, than unskilled or simple labor-power. This power being of higher value, its consumption is labor of a higher class, labor that creates in equal times proportionally higher values than unskilled labor does. Whatever difference in skill there may be between the labor of a spinner and that of a jeweller, the portion of his labor by which the jeweller merely replaces the value of his own labor-power, does not in any way differ in quality from the additional portion by which he creates surplus-value. In the making of jewellery, just as in spinning, the surplus-value results only from a quantitative excess of labor, from a lengthening-out of one and the same labor-process, in the one case, of the process of making jewels, in the other of the process of making yarn.

But on the other hand, in every process of creating value, the reduction of skilled labor to average social labor, *e.g.*, one day of skilled to six days of unskilled labor, is unavoidable. We therefore save ourselves a superfluous operation, and simplify our analysis, by the assumption, that the labor of the workman employed by the capitalist is unskilled average labor.

PART IX

MISCELLANEOUS AMERICAN WRITERS

1. Henry George: "Progress and Poverty."
2. Francis A. Walker: "Political Economy."
3. Simon Nelson Patten: "Premises of Political Economy."

HENRY GEORGE

(1839–1897)

Although Henry George has been referred to as the "Prophet of San Francisco," he was born in Philadelphia, a short distance from Independence Hall. His life was as vigorous and as interesting as his writings. At the age of sixteen, he went to sea and served two years before the mast. On his return to Philadelphia, like Franklin and Carey, he learned the printer's trade. But the lure of the sea again enticed him. He became a rover, but a most observant one. His travels led him to Australia and to British Columbia in search of gold. Finally, he returned to San Francisco where he settled for a number of years. He married and had several children.

A life of adventure was followed by a period of dire poverty, for San Francisco suffered severely in the period of reaction which followed the gold boom of 1849. Henry George learned from actual experience the terrible character of poverty. Finally, he secured a position as a printer, and rapidly advanced to the positions of reporter, editor, contributor, and, finally, managing editor. He had a facile pen, a fund of first hand information, and a "nose for news."

In 1867 George was one of the founders of the *San Francisco Post*, the first penny newspaper west of the Rocky Mountains. The business was at first successful and the plant expanded, but disaster came in the panic of 1873. So severe was it that gold ingots were said to have been refused as collateral. In any event, even the Bank of California was forced to suspend payment. A Governor of California, whom George's pen had helped to elect, finally gave him a political appointment. It is also interesting to note in passing that not only had Henry George experienced poverty, but also he had a rare opportunity to witness the rapid increase in land values which accompanied the development of the West after the completion of the first transcontinental railroad.

Meanwhile, George had been working on his famous manuscript "Progress and Poverty," which finally appeared in 1879. This thesis, however, had been developed by him even earlier in a pamphlet entitled "Our Land and Land Policy," which had appeared in 1871. Of course, the suggestion of a tax on land values was not new. In "Progress and Poverty," Henry George himself made acknowledgment to the physiocrats, as the kindlers of the feeble light, which he sought to fan into a great burning flame.

In the latter part of his career, Henry George entered politics. It is only fair to say, however, that he was primarily a social reformer and not a party man. In the famous election of 1886, he was the labor party candidate for mayor of New York City against the Tammany Hall candidate. It is interesting to observe that in this three-cornered fight Theodore Roosevelt was the Republican nominee.

In addition to his famous "Progress and Poverty," other works of George were: "The Irish Question," afterward called "The Irish Land Question" (1881); "Social Problems" (1883); "Protection or Free Trade" (1886); "A Perplexed Philosopher," a criticism of Herbert Spencer (1892); and "The Condition of Labor, an Open Letter to Pope Leo the XIII in Answer to His Encyclical on Labor" (1898). There is also "A Science of Political Economy," finished after his death by his son, and published in 1898.

Henry George was not only a great social reformer, but also a keen thinker on many economic questions. He was a student not merely of practical problems, but also of economic theory. For illustration, he produced a brilliant criticism of the wage fund theory, as well as an ingenious but fanciful theory of distribution. It is strange that an individual whose influence stimulated thousands should be so singularly neglected by students of the history of economic thought. Because of this fact, the following selection has been taken, not from the minor works of Henry George, but from his great masterpiece, "Progress and Poverty." It is of interest as a piece of English composition, if for no other reason. It is hoped that the student will secure a copy of "Progress and Poverty," which is easily accessible in cheap editions, and read the entire work.

One of the most interesting and sympathetic appraisals of the life and work of Henry George is that by Louis F. Post under the title "The Prophet of San Francisco," published in 1930 by the Vanguard Press.

HENRY GEORGE

SELECTIONS FROM "PROGRESS AND POVERTY"

INTRODUCTORY: THE PROBLEM

The present century has been marked by a prodigious increase in wealth-producing power. The utilization of steam and electricity, the introduction of improved processes and labor-saving machinery, the greater subdivision and grander scale of production, the wonderful facilitation of exchanges, have multiplied enormously the effectiveness of labor.

At the beginning of this marvelous era it was natural to expect, and it was expected, that labor-saving inventions would lighten the toil and improve the condition of the laborer; that the enormous increase in the power of producing wealth would make real poverty a thing of the past. Could a man of the last century—a Franklin or a Priestley—have seen, in a vision of the future, the steamship taking the place of the sailing vessel, the railroad train of the wagon, the reaping machine of the scythe, the threshing machine of the flail; could he have heard the throb of the engines that in obedience to human will, and for the satisfaction of human desire, exert a power greater than that of all the men and all the beasts of burden of the earth combined; could he have seen the forest tree transformed into finished lumber—into doors, sashes, blinds, boxes or barrels, with hardly the touch of a human hand; the great workshops where boots and shoes are turned out by the case with less labor than the old-fashioned cobbler could have put on a sole; the factories where, under the eye of a girl, cotton becomes cloth faster than hundreds of stalwart weavers could have turned it out with their hand-looms; could he have seen steam hammers shaping mammoth shafts and mighty anchors, and delicate machinery making tiny watches; the diamond drill cutting through the heart of the rocks, and coal oil sparing the whale; could he have realized the enormous saving of labor resulting from improved facilities of exchange and communication—sheep killed in Australia eaten fresh in England, and the order given by the London banker in the afternoon executed in San Franisco in the morning of the same day; could he have conceived of the hundred thousand improvements which these only suggest, what would he have inferred as to the social condition of mankind?

It would not have seemed like an inference; further than the vision went, it would have seemed as though he saw; and his heart would have leaped and his nerves would have thrilled, as one who from a hight beholds just ahead of the thirst-stricken caravan the living gleam of rustling woods and the glint of laughing waters. Plainly, in the sight of the imagination, he would have beheld these new forces elevating society from its very foundations, lifting the very poorest above the possibilty of want, exempting the very lowest from anxiety for the material needs of life; he would have seen these slaves of the lamp of knowledge taking on themselves the traditional curse, these muscles of iron and sinews of steel making the poorest laborer's life a holiday, in which every high quality and noble impulse could have scope to grow.

And out of these bounteous material conditions he would have seen arising, as necessary sequences, moral conditions realizing the golden age of which mankind have always dreamed. Youth no longer stunted and starved; age no longer harried by avarice; the child at play with the tiger; the man with the muck-rake drinking in the glory of the stars! Foul things fled, fierce things tame; discord turned to harmony! For how could there be greed where all had enough? How could the vice, the crime, the ignorance, the brutality, that spring from poverty and the fear of poverty, exist where poverty had vanished? Who should crouch where all were freemen; who oppress where all were peers?

More or less vague or clear, these have been the hopes, these the dreams born of the improvements which give this wonderful century its preëminence. They have sunk so deeply into the popular mind as to radically change the currents of thought, to recast creeds and displace the most fundamental conceptions. The haunting visions of higher possibilities have not merely gathered splendor and vividness, but their direction has changed—instead of seeing behind the faint tinges of an expiring sunset, all the glory of the daybreak has decked the skies before.

It is true that disappointment has followed disappointment, and that discovery upon discovery, and invention after invention, have neither lessened the toil of those who most need respite, nor brought plenty to the poor. But there have been so many things to which it seemed this failure could be laid, that up to our time the new faith has hardly weakened. We have better appreciated the difficulties to be overcome; but not the less trusted that the tendency of the times was to overcome them.

Now, however, we are coming into collision with facts which there can be no mistaking. From all parts of the civilized world come complaints of industrial depression; of labor condemned to involuntary idleness; of capital massed and wasting; of pecuniary distress among business men; of want and suffering and anxiety among the working classes. All the dull, deadening pain, all the keen, maddening anguish, that to great masses of men are involved in the words "hard times," afflict the word today. This state of things, common to communities differing so widely in situation, in political institutions, in fiscal and financial systems, in density of population and in social organization, can hardly be accounted for by local causes. There is distress where large standing armies are maintained, but there is also distress where the standing armies are nominal; there is distress where protective tariffs stupidly and wastefully hamper trade, but there is also distress where trade is nearly free; there is distress where autocratic government yet prevails, but there is also distress where political power is wholly in the hands of the people; in countries where paper is money, and in countries where gold and silver are the only currency. Evidently, beneath all such things as these, we must infer a common cause.

That there is a common cause, and that it is either what we call material progress or something closely connected with material progress, becomes more than an inference when it is noted that the phenomena we class together and speak of as industrial depression, are but intensifications of phenomena which always accompany material progress, and which show themselves more clearly and strongly as material progress goes on. Where the conditions to which material progress everywhere tends are most fully realized—that is to say, where population is densest, wealth greatest, and the machinery of production and exchange most highly developed—we find the deepest poverty, the sharpest struggle for existence, and the most enforced idleness.

It is to the newer countries—that is, to the countries where material progress is yet in its earlier stages—that laborers emigrate in search of higher wages, and capital flows in search of higher interest. It is in the older countries—that is to say, the countries where material progress has reached later stages—that widespread destitution is found in the midst of the greatest abundance. Go into one of the new communities where Anglo-Saxon vigor is just beginning the race of progress; where the machinery of production and exchange is yet rude and inefficient; where the increment of wealth is not yet great enough to enable any class to live in ease and luxury; where the best house is but a cabin of logs or a cloth and paper shanty, and the richest man is forced to daily work—and though you will find an absence of wealth and all its concomitants, you will find no beggars. There is no luxury, but there is no destitution. No one makes an easy living, nor a very good living; but every one *can* make a living, and no one able and willing to work is oppressed by the fear of want.

But just as such a community realizes the conditions which all civilized communities are striving for, and advances in the scale of material progress—just as closer settlement and a more intimate connection with the rest of the world, and greater utilization of labor-saving machinery, make possible greater economies in production and exchange, and wealth in consequence increases, not merely in the aggregate, but in proportion to population—so does poverty take a darker aspect. Some get an infinitely better and easier living, but others find it hard to get a living at all. The "tramp" comes with the locomotive, and almshouses and prisons are as surely the marks of "material progress" as are costly dwellings, rich warehouses, and magnificent churches. Upon streets lighted with gas and patrolled by uniformed policemen, beggars wait for the passer-by, and in the shadow of college, and library, and museum, are gathering the more hideous Huns and fiercer Vandals of whom Macaulay prophesied.

This fact—the great fact that poverty and all its concomitants show themselves in communities just as they develop into the conditions towards which material progress tends—proves that the social difficulties existing wherever a certain stage of progress has been reached, do not arise from local circumstances, but are, in some way or another, engendered by progress itself.

And, unpleasant as it may be to admit it, it is at last becoming evident that the enormous increase in productive power which has marked the present century and is still going on with accelerating ratio, has no tendency to extirpate poverty or to lighten the burdens of those compelled to toil. It simply widens the gulf between Dives and Lazarus, and makes the struggle for existence more intense. The march of invention has clothed mankind with powers of which a century ago the boldest imagination could not have dreamed. But in factories where labor-saving machinery has reached its most wonderful development, little children are at work; wherever the new forces are anything like fully utilized, large classes are maintained by charity or live on the verge of recourse to it; amid the greatest acumulations of wealth, men die of starvation, and puny infants suckle dry breasts; while everywhere the greed of gain, the worship of wealth, shows the force of the fear of want. The promised land flies before us like the mirage. The fruits of the tree of knowledge turn as we grasp them to apples of Sodom that crumble at the touch.

It is true that wealth has been greatly increased, and that the average of comfort, leisure, and refinement has been raised; but these gains are not general. In them the lowest class do not share.* I do not mean that the condition of the lowest class has nowhere nor in anything been improved; but that there is nowhere any improvement which can be credited to increased productive power. I mean that the tendency of what we call material progress is in nowise to improve the condition of the lowest class in the essentials of healthy, happy human life. Nay, more, that it is to still further depress the condition of the lowest class. The new forces, elevating in their nature though they be, do not act upon the social fabric from underneath, as was for a long time hoped and believed, but

---

* It is true that the poorest may now in certain ways enjoy what the richest a century ago could not have commanded, but this does not show improvement of condition so long as the ability to obtain the necessaries of life is not increased. The beggar in a great city may enjoy many things from which the backwoods farmer is debarred, but that does not prove the condition of the city beggar better than that of the independent farmer.

strike it at a point intermediate between top and bottom. It is as though an immense wedge were being forced, not underneath society, but through society. Those who are above the point of separation are elevated, but those who are below are crushed down.

This depressing effect is not generally realized, for it is not apparent where there has long existed a class just able to live. Where the lowest class barely lives, as has been the case for a long time in many parts of Europe, it is impossible for it to get any lower, for the next lowest step is out of existence, and no tendency to further depression can readily show itself. But in the progress of new settlements to the conditions of older communities it may clearly be seen that material progress does not merely fail to relieve poverty—it actually produces it. In the United States it is clear that squalor and misery, and the vices and crimes that spring from them, everywhere increase as the village grows to the city, and the march of development brings the advantages of the improved methods of production and exchange. It is in the older and richer sections of the Union that pauperism and distress among the working classes are becoming most painfully apparent. If there is less deep poverty in San Francisco than in New York, is it not because San Francisco is yet behind New York in all that both cities are striving for? When San Francisco reaches the point where New York now is, who can doubt that there will also be ragged and barefooted children on her streets?

This association of poverty with progress is the great enigma of our times. It is the central fact from which spring industrial, social, and political difficulties that perplex the world, and with which statesmanship and philanthropy and education grapple in vain. From it come the clouds that overhang the future of the most progressive and self-reliant nations. It is the riddle which the Sphinx of Fate puts to our civilization, and which not to answer is to be destroyed. So long as all the increased wealth which modern progress brings goes but to build up great fortunes, to increase luxury and make sharper the contrast between the House of Have and the House of Want, progress is not real and cannot be permanent. The reaction must come. The tower leans from its foundations, and every new story but hastens the final catastrophe. To educate men who must be condemned to poverty, is but to make them restive; to base on a state of most glaring social inequality political institutions under which men are theoretically equal, is to stand a pyramid on its apex.

All-important as this question is, pressing itself from every quarter painfully upon attention, it has not yet received a solution which accounts for all the facts and points to any clear and simple remedy. This is shown by the widely varying attempts to account for the prevailing depression. They exhibit not merely a divergence between vulgar notions and scientific theories, but also show that the concurrence which should exist between those who avow the same general theories breaks up upon practical questions into an anarchy of opinion. Upon high economic authority we have been told that the prevailing depression is due to over-consumption; upon equally high authority, that it is due to over-production; while the wastes of war, the extension of railroads, the attempts of workmen to keep up wages, the demonetization of silver, the issues of paper money, the increase of labor-saving machinery, the opening of shorter avenues to trade, etc., etc., are separately pointed out as the cause, by writers of reputation.

And while professors thus disagree, the ideas that there is a necessary conflict between capital and labor, that machinery is an evil, that competition must be restrained and interest abolished, that wealth may be created by the issue of money, that it is the duty of government to furnish capital or to furnish work, are rapidly making way among the great body of the people, who keenly feel a hurt and are sharply conscious of a wrong. Such ideas, which bring great masses of men, the repositories of ultimate political power, under the leadership of charlatans and demagogues, are fraught with danger; but they cannot be successfully combated until political economy shall give some answer to the great question which shall be consistent with all her teachings, and which shall commend itself to the perceptions of the great masses of men.

It must be within the province of political economy to give such an answer. For political economy is not a set of dogmas. It is the explanation of a certain set of facts. It is the science which, in the sequence of certain phenomena, seeks to trace mutual relations and to identify cause and effect, just as the physical sciences seek to do in other sets of phenomena. It lays its foundations upon firm ground. The premises from which it makes its deductions are truths which have the highest sanction; axioms which we all recognize; upon which we safely base the reasoning and actions of every-day life, and which may be reduced to the metaphysical expression of the physical law that motion seeks the line of least resistance —viz., that men seek to gratify their desires with the least exertion. Proceeding from a basis thus assured, its processes, which consist simply in identification and separation, have the same certainty. In this sense it is as exact a science as geometry, which, from similar truths relative to space, obtains its conclusions by similar means, and its conclusions when valid should be as self-apparent. And although in the domain of political economy we cannot test our theories by artificially produced combinations or conditions, as may be done in some of the other sciences, yet we can apply tests no less conclusive, by comparing societies in which different conditions exist, or by, in imagination, separating, combining, adding or eliminating forces or factors of known direction.

I propose in the following pages to attempt to solve by the methods of political economy the great problem I have outlined. I propose to seek the law which associates poverty with progress, and increases want with advancing wealth; and I believe that in the explanation of this paradox we shall find the explanation of those recurring seasons of industrial and commercial paralysis which, viewed independent of their relations to more general phenomena, seem so inexplicable. Properly commenced and carefully pursued, such an investigation must yield a conclusion that will stand every test, and as truth will correlate with all other truth. For in the sequence of phenomena there is no accident. Every effect has a cause, and every fact implies a preceding fact.

That political economy, as at present taught, does not explain the persistence of poverty amid advancing wealth in a manner which accords with the deep-seated perceptions of men; that the unquestionable truths which it does teach are unrelated and disjointed; that it has failed to make the progress in popular thought that truth, even when unpleasant, must make; that, on the contrary, after a century of cultivation, during which it has engrossed the attention of some of the most subtle and powerful intellects, it should be spurned by the statesman, scouted by the masses, and relegated in the opinion of many educated and thinking men to the rank of a pseudo-science in which nothing is fixed or can be fixed—must, it seems to me, be due not to any inability of the science when properly pursued, but to some false step in its premises, or overlooked factor in its estimates. And as such mistakes are generally concealed by the respect paid to authority, I propose in this inquiry to take nothing for granted, but to bring even accepted theories to the test of first principles, and should they not stand the test, to freshly interrogate facts in the endeavor to discover their law.

I propose to beg no question, to shrink from no conclusion, but to follow truth wherever it may lead. Upon us is the responsibility of seeking the law, for in the very heart of our civilization to-day women faint and little children moan. But what that law may prove to be is not our affair. If the conclusions that we reach run counter to our prejudices, let us not flinch; if they challenge institutions that have long been deemed wise and natural, let us not turn back.

Chapter I. The Current Doctrine of Wages—Its Insufficiency

Reducing to its most compact form the problem we have set out to investigate, let us examine, step by step, the explanation which political economy, as now accepted by the best authority, gives of it.

The cause which produces poverty in the midst of advancing wealth is evidently the cause which exhibits itself in the tendency, everywhere recognized, of wages to a minimum. Let us, therefore, put our inquiry into this compact form:

Why, in spite of increase in productive power, do wages tend to a minimum which will give but a bare living?

The answer of the current political economy is, that wages are fixed by the ratio between the number of laborers and the amount of capital devoted to the employment of labor, and constantly tend to the lowest amount on which laborers will consent to live and reproduce, because the increase in the number of laborers tends naturally to follow and overtake any increase in capital. The increase of the divisor being thus held in check only by the possibilities of the quotient, the dividend may be increased to infinity without greater result.

In current thought this doctrine holds all but undisputed sway. It bears the indorsement of the very highest names among the cultivators of political economy, and though there have been attacks upon it, they are generally more formal than real.* It is assumed by Buckle as the basis of his generalizations of universal history. It is taught in all, or nearly all, the great English and American universities, and is laid down in text-books which aim at leading the masses to reason correctly upon practical affairs, while it seems to harmonize with the new philosophy, which, having in a few years all but conquered the scientific world, is now rapidly permeating the general mind.

Thus entrenched in the upper regions of thought, it is in cruder form even more firmly rooted in what may be styled the lower. What gives to the fallacies of protection such a tenacious hold, in spite of their evident inconsistencies and absurdities, is the idea that the sum to be distributed in wages is in each community a fixed one, which the competition of "foreign labor" must still further subdivide. The same idea underlies most of the theories which aim at the abolition of interest and the restriction of competition, as the means whereby the share of the laborer in the general wealth can be increased; and it crops out in every direction among those who are not thoughtful enough to have any theories, as may be seen in the columns of newspapers and the debates of legislative bodies.

And yet, widely accepted and deeply rooted as it is, it seems to me that this theory does not tally with obvious facts. For, if wages depend upon the ratio between the amount of labor seeking employment and the amount of capital devoted to its employment, the relative scarcity or abundance of one factor must mean the relative abundance or scarcity of the other. Thus, capital must be relatively abundant where wages are

---

* This seems to me true of Mr. Thornton's objections, for while he denies the existence of a predetermined wage fund, consisting of a portion of capital set apart for the purchase of labor, he yet holds (which is the essential thing) that wages are drawn from capital, and that increase or decrease of capital is increase or decrease of the fund available for the payment of wages. The most vital attack upon the wage fund doctrine, of which I know, is that of Professor Francis A. Walker (The Wages Question: New York, 1876), yet he admits that wages are in large part advanced from capital—which, so far as it goes, is all that the staunchest supporter of the wage fund theory could claim—while he fully accepts the Malthusian theory. Thus his practical conclusions in nowise differ from those reached by expounders of the current theory.

high, and relatively scarce where wages are low. Now, as the capital used in paying wages must largely consist of the capital constantly seeking investment, the current rate of interest must be the measure of its relative abundance or scarcity. So, if it be true that wages depend upon the ratio between the amount of labor seeking employment and the capital devoted to its employment, then high wages (the mark of the relative scarcity of labor) must be accompanied by low interest (the mark of the relative abundance of capital), and reversely, low wages must be accompanied by high interest.

This is not the fact, but the contrary. Eliminating from interest the element of insurance, and regarding only interest proper, or the return for the use of capital, is it not a general truth that interest is high where and when wages are high, and low where and when wages are low? Both wages and interest have been higher in the United States than in England, in the Pacific than in the Atlantic States. Is it not a notorious fact that where labor flows for higher wages, capital also flows for higher interest? Is it not true that wherever there has been a general rise or fall in wages there has been at the same time a similar rise or fall in interest? In California, for instance, when wages were higher than anywhere else in the world, so also was interest higher. Wages and interest have in California gone down together. When common wages were $5 a day, the ordinary bank rate of interest was twenty-four per cent. per annum. Now that common wages are $2 or $2.50 a day, the ordinary bank rate is from ten to twelve per cent.

Now, this broad, general fact, that wages are higher in new countries, where capital is relatively scarce, than in old countries, where capital is relatively abundant, is too glaring to be ignored. And although very lightly touched upon, it is noticed by the expounders of the current political economy. The manner in which it is noticed proves what I say, that it is utterly inconsistent with the accepted theory of wages. For in explaining it such writers as Mill, Fawcett, and Price virtually give up the theory of wages upon which, in the same treatises, they formally insist. Though they declare that wages are fixed by the ratio between capital and laborers, they explain the higher wages and interest of new countries by the greater relative production of wealth. I shall hereafter show that this is not the fact, but that, on the contrary, the production of wealth is relatively larger in old and densely populated countries than in new and sparsely populated countries. But at present I merely wish to point out the inconsistency. For to say that the higher wages of new countries are due to greater proportionate production, is clearly to make the ratio with production, and not the ratio with capital, the determinator of wages.

Though this inconsistency does not seem to have been perceived by the class of writers to whom I allude, it has been noticed by one of the most logical of the expounders of the current political economy. Professor

Cairnes* endeavors in a very ingenious way to reconcile the fact with the theory, by assuming that in new countries, where industry is generally directed to the production of food and what in manufactures is called raw material, a much larger proportion of the capital used in production is devoted to the payment of wages than in older countries where a greater part must be expended in machinery and material, and thus, in the new country, though capital is scarcer (and interest is higher), the amount determined to the payment of wages is really larger, and wages are also higher. For instance, of $100,000 devoted in an old country to manufactures, $80,000 would probably be expended for buildings, machinery and the purchase of materials, leaving but $20,000 to be paid out in wages, whereas in a new country, of $30,000 devoted to agriculture, etc., not more than $5,000 would be required for tools, etc., leaving $25,000 to be distributed in wages. In this way it is explained that the wage fund may be comparatively large where capital is comparatively scarce, and high wages and high interest accompany each other.

In what follows I think I shall be able to show that this explanation is based upon a total misapprehension of the relations of labor to capital—a fundamental error as to the fund from which wages are drawn; but at present it is only necessary to point out that the connection in the fluctuation of wages and interest in the same countries and in the same branches of industry cannot thus be explained. In those alternations known as "good times" and "hard times" a brisk demand for labor and good wages is always accompanied by a brisk demand for capital and stiff rates of interest. While, when laborers cannot find employment and wages droop, there is always an accumulation of capital seeking investment at low rates.† The present depression has been no less marked by want of employment and distress among the working classes than by the accumulation of unemployed capital in all the great centers, and by nominal rates of interest on undoubted security. Thus, under conditions which admit of no explanation consistent with the current theory, do we find high interest coinciding with high wages and low interest with low wages—capital seemingly scarce when labor is scarce, and abundant when labor is abundant.

All these well known facts, which coincide with each other, point to a relation between wages and interest, but it is to a relation of conjunction not of opposition. Evidently they are utterly inconsistent with the theory that wages are determined by the ratio between labor and capital, or any part of capital.

How, then, it will be asked, could such a theory arise? How is it that it has been accepted by a succession of economists, from the time of Adam Smith to the present day?

* Some Leading Principles of Political Economy Newly Expounded, Chapter 1, Part 2.
† Times of commercial panic are marked by high rates of discount, but this is evidently **not a high rate** of interest, properly so-called, but a high rate of insurance against risk.

If we examine the reasoning by which in current treatises this theory of wages is supported, we see at once that it is not an induction from observed facts, but a deduction from a previously assumed theory—viz., that wages are drawn from capital. It being assumed that capital is the source of wages, it necessarily follows that the gross amount of wages must be limited by the amount of capital devoted to the employment of labor, and hence that the amount individual laborers can receive, must be determined by the ratio between their number and the amount of capital existing for their recompense.* This reasoning is valid, but the conclusion, as we have seen, does not correspond with the facts. The fault, therefore, must be in the premises. Let us see.

I am aware that the theorem that wages are drawn from capital is one of the most fundamental and apparently best settled of current political economy, and that it has been accepted as axiomatic by all the great thinkers who have devoted their powers to the elucidation of the science. Nevertheless, I think it can be demonstrated to be a fundamental error— the fruitful parent of a long series of errors, which vitiate most important practical conclusions. This demonstration I am about to attempt. It is necessary that it should be clear and conclusive, for a doctrine upon which so much important reasoning is based, which is supported by such a weight of authority, which is so plausible in itself, and is so liable to recur in different forms, cannot be safely brushed aside in a paragraph.

The proposition I shall endeavor to prove, is:

That wages, instead of being drawn from capital, are in reality drawn from the product of the labor for which they are paid.†

Now, inasmuch as the current theory that wages are drawn from capital also holds that capital is reimbursed from production, this at first glance may seem a distinction without a difference—a mere change in terminology, to discuss which would be but to add to those unprofitable disputes that render so much that has been written upon politico-economic subjects as barren and worthless as the controversies of the various learned societies about the true reading of the inscription on the stone that

---

* For instance McCulloch (Note VI to Wealth of Nations) says: "That portion of the capital or wealth of a country which the employers of labor intend to or are willing to pay out in the purchase of labor, may be much larger at one time than another. But whatever may be its absolute magnitude, it obviously forms the only source from which any portion of the wages of labor can be derived. No other fund is in existence from which the laborer, as such, can draw a single shilling. And hence *it follows* that the average rate of wages, or the share of the national capital appropriated to the employment of labor falling, at an average, to each laborer, must entirely depend on its amount as compared with the number of those amongst whom it has to be divided." Similar citations might be made from all the standard economists.

† We are speaking of labor expended in production, to which it is best for the sake of simplicity to confine the inquiry. Any question which may arise in the reader's mind as to wages for unproductive services had best therefore be deferred.

Mr. Pickwick found. But that it is much more than a formal distinction will be apparent when it is considered that upon the difference between the two propositions are built up all the current theories as to the relations of capital and labor; that from it are deduced doctrines that, themselves regarded as axiomatic, bound, direct, and govern the ablest minds in the discussion of the most momentous questions. For, upon the assumption that wages are drawn directly from capital, and not from the product of the labor, is based, not only the doctrine that wages depend upon the ratio between capital and labor, but the doctrine that industry is limited by capital—that capital must be accumulated before labor is employed, and labor cannot be employed except as capital is accumulated; the doctrine that every increase of capital gives or is capable of giving additional employment to industry; the doctrine that the conversion of circulating capital into fixed capital lessens the fund applicable to the maintenance of labor; the doctrine that more laborers can be employed at low than at high wages; the doctrine that capital applied to agriculture will maintain more laborers than if applied to manufactures; the doctrine that profits are high or low as wages are low or high, or that they depend upon the cost of the subsistence of laborers; together with such paradoxes as that a demand for commodities is not a demand for labor, or that certain commodities may be increased in cost by a reduction in wages or diminished in cost by an increase in wages.

In short, all the teachings of the current political economy, in the widest and most important part of its domain, are based more or less directly upon the assumption that labor is maintained and paid out of existing capital before the product which constitutes the ultimate object is secured. If it be shown that this is an error, and that on the contrary the maintenance and payment of labor do not even temporarily trench on capital, but are directly drawn from the product of the labor, then all this vast superstructure is left without support and must fall. And so likewise must fall the vulgar theories which also have their base in the belief that the sum to be distributed in wages is a fixed one, the individual shares in which must be necessarily decreased by an increase in the number of laborers.

The difference between the current theory and the one I advance is, in fact, similar to that between the mercantile theory of international exchanges and that with which Adam Smith supplanted it. Between the theory that commerce is the exchange of commodities for money, and the theory that it is the exchange of commodities for commodities, there may seem no real difference when it is remembered that the adherents of the mercantile theory did not assume that money had any other use than as it could be exchanged for commodities. Yet, in the practical application of these two theories, there arises all the difference between rigid governmental protection and free trade.

If I have said enough to show the reader the ultimate importance of the reasoning through which I am about to ask him to follow me, it will not be necessary to apologize in advance either for simplicity or prolixity. In arraigning a doctrine of such importance—a doctrine supported by such a weight of authority, it is necessary to be both clear and thorough.

Were it not for this I should be tempted to dismiss with a sentence the assumption that wages are drawn from capital. For all the vast super-structure which the current political economy builds upon this doctrine, is in truth based upon a foundation which has been merely taken for granted, without the slightest attempt to distinguish the apparent from the real. Because wages are generally paid in money, and in many of the operations of production are paid before the product is fully completed, or can be utilized, it is inferred that wages are drawn from pre-existing capital, and, therefore, that industry is limited by capital—that is to say that labor cannot be employed until capital has been accumulated, and can only be employed to the extent capital has been accumulated.

Yet in the very treatises in which the limitation of industry by capital is laid down without reservation and made the basis for the most impor-tant reasonings and elaborate theories, we are told that capital is stored up or accumulated labor—"that part of wealth which is saved to assist future production." If we substitute for the word "capital" this definition of the word, the proposition carries its own refutation, for that labor can-not be employed until the results of labor are saved becomes too absurd for discussion.

Should we, however, with this *reductio ad absurdum*, attempt to close the argument, we should probably be met with the explanation, not that the first laborers were supplied by Providence with the capital necessary to set them to work, but that the proposition merely refers to a state of society in which production has become a complex operation.

But the fundamental truth, that in all economic reasoning must be firmly grasped and never let go, is that society in its most highly devel-oped form is but an elaboration of society in its rudest beginnings, and that principles obvious in the simpler relations of men are merely dis-guised and not abrogated or reversed by the more intricate relations that result from the division of labor and the use of complex tools and methods. The steam grist mill, with its complicated machinery exhibiting every diversity of motion, is simply what the rude stone mortar dug up from an ancient river bed was in its day—an instrument for grinding corn. And every man engaged in it, whether tossing wood into the furnace, running the engine, dressing stones, printing sacks or keeping books, is really devoting his labor to the same purpose that the pre-historic savage did when he used his mortar—the preparation of grain for human food.

And so, if we reduce to their lowest terms all the complex operations of modern production, we see that each individual who takes part in this infinitely subdivided and intricate network of production and exchange is really doing what the primeval man did when he climbed the trees for fruit or followed the receding tide for shellfish—endeavoring to obtain from nature by the exertion of his powers the satisfaction of his desires. If we keep this firmly in mind, if we look upon production as a whole—as the co-operation of all embraced in any of its great groups to satisfy the various desires of each, we plainly see that the reward each obtains for his exertions comes as truly and as directly from nature as the result of that exertion, as did that of the first man.

To illustrate: In the simplest state of which we can conceive, each man digs his own bait and catches his own fish. The advantages of the division of labor soon become apparent, and one digs bait while the others fish. Yet evidently the one who digs bait is in reality doing as much to-wards the catching of fish as any of those who actually take the fish. So when the advantages of canoes are discovered, and instead of all going a-fishing, one stays behind and makes and repairs canoes, the canoe-maker is in reality devoting his labor to the taking of fish as much as the actual fishermen, and the fish which he eats at night when the fishermen come home, are as truly the product of his labor as of theirs. And thus when the division of labor is fairly inaugurated, and instead of each attempting to satisfy all of his wants by direct resort to nature, one fishes, another hunts, a third picks berries, a fourth gathers fruit, a fifth makes tools, a sixth builds huts, and a seventh prepares clothing—each one is, to the extent he exchanges the direct product of his own labor for the direct product of the labor of others, really applying his own labor to the production of the things he uses—is in effect satisfying his particular desires by the exertion of his particular powers; that is to say, what he receives he in reality produces. If he digs roots and exchanges them for venison, he is in effect as truly the procurer of the venison as though he had gone in chase of the deer and left the huntsman to dig his own roots. The common expression, "I made so and so," signifying "I earned so and so," or "I earned money with which I purchased so and so," is, economically speaking, not metaphorically but literally true. Earning is making.

Now, if we follow these principles, obvious enough in a simpler state of society, through the complexities of the state we call civilized, we shall see clearly that in every case in which labor is exchanged for commodities, production really precedes enjoyment; that wages are the earnings—that is to say, the makings of labor—not the advances of capital, and that the laborer who receives his wages in money (coined or printed, it may be, before his labor commenced) really receives in return for the addition his labor has made to the general stock of wealth, a draft upon that general stock, which he may utilize in any particular form of wealth that will best satisfy his desires; and that neither the money, which is but the draft, nor the particular form of wealth which he uses it to call for, represents advances of capital for his maintenance, but on the contrary represents the wealth, or a portion of the wealth, his labor has already added to the general stock.

Keeping these principles in view we see that the draughtsman, who, shut up in some dingy office on the banks of the Thames, is drawing the plans for a great marine engine, is in reality devoting his labor to the production of bread and meat as truly as though he were garnering the grain in California or swinging a lariat on a La Plata pampa; that he is as truly making his own clothing as though he were shearing sheep in Australia or weaving cloth in Paisley, and just as effectually producing the claret he drinks at dinner as though he gathered the grapes on the banks of the Garonne. The miner who, two thousand feet under ground in the heart of the Comstock, is digging out silver ore, is, in effect, by virtue of a thousand exchanges, harvesting crops in valleys five thousand feet nearer the earth's center; chasing the whale through Arctic icefields; plucking tobacco leaves in Virginia; picking coffee berries in Honduras; cutting sugar cane on the Hawaiian Islands; gathering cotton in Georgia or weaving it in Manchester or Lowell; making quaint wooden toys for his children in the Hartz Mountains; or plucking amid the green and gold of Los Angeles orchards the oranges which, when his shift is relieved, he will take home to his sick wife. The wages which he receives on Saturday night at the mouth of the shaft, what are they but the certificate to all the world that he has done these things—the primary exchange in the long series which transmutes his labor into the things he has really been laboring for?

All this is clear when looked at in this way; but to meet this fallacy in all its strongholds and lurking places we must change our investigation from the deductive to the inductive form. Let us now see, if, beginning with facts and tracing their relations, we arrive at the same conclusions as are thus obvious when, beginning with first principles, we trace their exemplification in complex facts.

FRANCIS A. WALKER

(1840–1897)

Amasa Walker (1799–1875) was one of America's pioneer economists. In 1866 appeared his "Science of Wealth," which was a standard, orthodox text for American students, along with Carey's voluminous, unorthodox treatise on social science.

General Francis A. Walker, the equally distinguished son of Amasa Walker, followed in the footsteps of his father. He was the first president of the American Economic Association, which was founded at Saratoga in September, 1885. He also became head of the famous Massachusetts Institute of Technology.

The chief works in economics of General Francis A. Walker were "The Wages Question" (1876); "Money" (1878); and "A General Treatise, Political Economy" (1883). Walker's "Political Economy" immediately won well deserved praise and general acceptance. A second edition appeared in 1887 and a third edition in 1888. Our selections have been taken from the third edition of Walker's "Political Economy."

General Francis Walker is important because of his influence in securing for economics a respected position in institutions of higher learning, and for his clear and systematic treatment of that subject. He also made very definite contributions of both a critical and a constructive character.

Like Henry George, Francis Walker attacked the classical wage fund theory. He also made a rather penetrating analysis of profits. Although Walker made the enterpriser, rather than the landlord, the center of his system, he applied the Ricardian principle to his analysis of profits as a measure of the human differential.

Perhaps Walker's discussion of profits and his stress on the *entrepreneur* are of most interest to the American student. Consequently, our selections from Walker's "Political Economy" center about these topics.

It will be noted that American writers, unlike the British, treat interest as a separate share in distribution, distinct from profits. General Francis Walker was among the first to break up profits into its component parts. He spoke of the four distribution shares, namely, rent, wages, interest, and profits, rather than merely of three shares, rent, wages, and profits.

FRANCIS A. WALKER

SELECTIONS FROM "POLITICAL ECONOMY"

CHAPTER III. INTEREST

285. *Definition of Interest.*—We have seen one share cut off from the product of industry—rent; one claimant satisfied—the landlord. The reader now sees why this topic was first treated. In economic theory, this is ever the first claim to be adjusted and paid. We can make no progress—not so much as by a single step—toward discovering the principles which govern the division of the product of industry among capitalists, employers, and laborers, until rent is taken out, until the claim of the landlord is satisfied. Hence the topic, Rent, comes first, in a treatise on the distribution of wealth.

We are now to speak of Interest: the share of the Capitalist in the product of industry.

In Part II we inquired into the origin and office of capital. We saw that capital consists of savings out of earnings, the native powers of the earth, air and water not being regarded as capital. Wealth having been produced, some of it, much of it, must soon be consumed, in order to sustain the producing classes, and to repair the waste inevitably attendant upon production, and even upon the mere lapse of time. All of it may be so consumed, and will be, under the urgent and constantly recurring desires which wealth alone can satisfy, unless some motive for saving can be found which shall prove strong enough to withstand the impulses to immediate gratification, and to wrest a portion of wealth from the jaws of appetite. We have shown what that motive is, and how it manifests itself in a barbarous condition.

In an advanced state of society, the motive to saving is not so much found in the desire of the individual to accumulate tools and materials for his own handling, as in the desire to obtain interest from some one else, for the use of that portion of wealth whose consumption is thus postponed. To the varying strength of this motive with different men, and different races, we shall have occasion to refer further on.

286. *Interest Not Paid for the Use of Money.*—It has been said that interest is the compensation paid for the use of capital. The usual form of statement is that interest is paid for the use of money. Broadly speaking, this is not true. Money, which is one of the many forms of capital, is, indeed, often the agent in effecting the loan of other species of capital. But in these cases, it is not the money, philosophically considered, that is

borrowed: The interest paid is for the use of the capital obtained through that agency. One borrows $5,000, and gives a note for that sum, with interest. With this money he purchases live stock, machinery for his factory, or goods for his trade: these were what he wanted; these were what he really borrowed; these are what he pays interest upon. The money was solely a means to that end.

But money is not always, it is not in a majority of cases, in a highly advanced state of industrial society it is, indeed, rarely, the agent in effecting the loan of capital. The country merchant buys goods and gives his notes for two, four, and six months, promising to pay the price with interest. Interest on what? On money? No money passed in the transaction. What was borrowed was hardware and crockery, dry goods, and groceries. The young farmer buys cattle to stock his farm, and gives his note, promising to pay, with interest: not interest on money, for he has had none, but interest on the value of cows and working oxen.

287. *The Rate of Interest.*—Let us now inquire how the rate of interest is determined.

Since the use of capital is a matter of bargain and sale, or of exchange, what should determine the rate of interest but the demand for, and the supply of, loanable capital?

Here we see the futility of the notion, which, from time to time, obtains a strong hold on the public mind of America, and, indeed, of all new countries, that the rate of interest is to be lowered by increasing the supply of money through the issue of paper notes. Men wish to borrow that they may get control of the agencies of production: capital in its various forms. The amount to be paid for the use of capital will depend on its abundance compared with the occasions for its productive use. The issue of money will not increase the number of horses and cattle and plows, nor will it build shops and warehouses or construct machinery for manufacture or for transport.

If the people of a community be thriving and progressive, the demand for capital, to start new enterprises, or to enlarge those already established, will be very great. If the community be, also, young, having brought to new fields the social and industrial ideas, tastes and ambitions of an old society, the supply of capital will be scanty, and the rate of interest will rule high.

288. Is this high rate of interest a hardship? No, the hardship lies in the scarcity of capital. The high rate of interest becomes the active means of removing that hardship, through increasing the supply of capital available to meet the demand. A high rate of interest is not an evil, but the cure of an evil. How is this?

Capital is, as we have seen, the result of saving. Interest, then, is the reward of abstinence. A part, a large part, of all produced wealth must be at once consumed to meet the conditions of human existence; but the remaining portion may be consumed or may be accumulated, according to the will of the owner. The strength of the motive to accumulation will vary with the reward of abstinence. If that be high, the disposition to save will be strengthened, and capital will be rapidly accumulated; if that be low, that disposition will be relatively weak, and capital will increase slowly, if, indeed, the body of existing capital be not dissipated at the demands of appetite.

We do not say that the strength of the disposition will increase proportionally to the increase of remuneration; that it will, for instance, be one-fifth greater at six per cent. interest than at five per cent. Moral philosophy has reached no such precision in gauging motives. But it is certain that, among the same people, and at the same time, the higher the rate of interest the stronger will be the motives which lead to saving: the more rapid the accumulation of capital.

So we see that a high rate of interest, instead of being the cause of an evil, is really its cure; and that to depress the rate of interest, as, for example, by force of law, would be to retard the processes by which capital is supplied.

As a high rate of interest is not in itself an evil, so a low rate of interest does not necessarily imply a condition which is a subject of congratulation. A low rate of interest may mean that, in a thriving, progressive community, the accumulation of capital has gone on so rapidly as to outrun the occasions for its productive use. It may mean that the people are so dull, indolent and unambitious, or the state of society so disordered, that commercial and manufacturing enterprises are not undertaken, and no enlargement of traditional industries is looked for. A small amount of capital more than suffices for such scanty needs.

289. *The Rate of Interest Tends to a Decline.*—Despite the urgent and ever-recurring demands for the consumption of wealth in various forms of self-indulgence; despite the occasional reversal of the course of accumulation, in the occurrence of war; despite all the effects of misgovernment and social disorder, wealth tends strongly to increase. Since the application of steam-power to manufactures and transportation, this rate of increase has been so great as even to transcend the demand for the uses of wealth in undertaking new industrial and commercial enterprises, and thus, with some temporary exceptions, interest has tended to decline.

In this respect interest differs markedly, we may say, essentially, from rent. The latter tends to rise, with the lapse of time, the increase of population, the growth of wealth. The former tends to decline under the same conditions. This constitutes one of the two reasons why the economist insists upon treating interest and rent separately in his discussion of the distribution of the product of industry. The second of these reasons will now be stated.

290. *There Is Not Any No-interest Capital.*—We have seen (par. 255) that the whole theory of rent rests on the assumption that there is a body of no-rent lands. These serve as the base from which to measure upwards the successive degrees of productiveness of the lands bearing rent.

In the theory of capital there is nothing to correspond to this. The economist does not find any no-interest capital. In theory, all capital bears an interest, and all portions of capital bear equal interest. If one portion, in fact, brings no interest to its owner, or brings an interest below that obtained by the owners of other portions, this is because of misadventure, due to accident or erroneous calculation, not to the nature of the capital itself.

Of course, it is anticipated by the political economist that the interest realized by portions of capital actually loaned will vary not a little, even within the same market, inasmuch as competition is never perfect in any sphere; but what has been stated shows how fundamentally the theory of interest differs from that of rent.

291. *Is There a Minimum Rate of Interest?*—We have said that the inducement to save diminishes, other things equal, as the rate of interest falls. Is there a point at which the disposition to consume wealth for purposes of comfort or luxury will equal in strength the disposition to acquire an annual income by saving wealth for productive uses, so that no further accumulation will take place, the savings out of earnings thereafter being only sufficient to make good the waste of production and keep up the stock of capital?

If there is a minimum rate of interest, it is very low. Fifteen or twenty years ago, six per cent. was the traditional rate of interest in New England, and probably few of us then thought that, if the rate were to go lower, it really would be worth while to "save." We had become so accustomed to six per cent. that it had come to seem as if there were some law of nature that fixed that rate. Six per cent.? Why of course a man would get six per cent.? Yet since that time we have seen the rate of interest steadily fall, in consequence of the vast accumulation of capital, till now loans of capital are to be had on good security at four and one-half or even four per cent., while the government borrows all it wants at three and one-half or even three. The English government has long borrowed at three per cent. The government of Holland during the most flourishing period of the republic, was even able to borrow at two per cent.

292. *Income from Investments, How Computed.*—Misapprehensions regarding the actual rate of interest are not infrequently occasioned by the failure to note, what would appear very plain, that the amount of interest paid upon bonds or notes, and the amount of dividends declared upon shares of corporate stock, should be compared, not with a nominal par value, but with the sum actually invested in the purchase of such bonds, stocks, notes or shares, or else with the sum for which these would at the time bring, if sold.

Thus, we read in the newspapers, that the Boston and Maine railroad, in May, 1887, declared a semi-annual dividend of five per cent., being at the rate of ten per cent., a year.

This statement, by itself, might create the impression that invest- ment in the stock of this road would be a peculiarly profitable one. A reference, however, to the stock quotations, in another column of the same newspaper, would have shown that the shares of this railroad were then selling at about $230, on the par of $100. A person, therefore, buying a share of this stock, in April, 1887, would have received but a trifle over four per cent., per annum, which was about the rate of interest then prevailing upon "bottom mortgages."

On the other hand, a number of railroad companies, during the great speculative extension, 1868–1873, advertised to sell at seventy dollars, bonds for one hundred dollars, bearing seven per cent. interest. What, then, was the rate of interest promised on this investment? Seven per cent.? No: the rate of interest promised to be paid was ten per cent., and, even, as we shall see, more than that. The investor paid seventy dollars for a bond, to receive upon it annually seven dollars of interest, per year, until the bond should mature, and then to receive $100 in money, whereas he only paid down $70. In other words, he was, on the expiry of the bond, to receive a premium of $30, over and above an annual interest of ten per cent. The "present value" of this premium would depend on the length of time the bond had "to run."

293. *False Interest: Insurance of the Principal.*—A great deal that is paid under the name of interest is not interest in the true sense, but is merely a premium for the insurance of the principal sum lent. Real interest only comprises that part of the payment made which would be paid, were the return of the principal, at the date of the maturity of the obligation, a matter of reasonable certainty. Absolute assurance can be reached in no human transaction; but where the risk is so small that it amounts to nothing in the mind of the lender, as in the case of British consols, or of a "bottom mortgage," where the sum lent is only a half or a third of the value of improved real estate, we have an instance of real interest, pure and simple.

Whatever, in the same market, at the same time, is paid above this, for the use of capital, is of the nature of insurance against the risk of losing the amount lent. If the rate of real interest in London is 3 per cent., as determined by the price of consols, loans on various kinds of fair security may range from that rate up to 5 or 6 per cent.; while all the time note- brokers are "shaving" the "paper" of second and third rate dealers at from 10 to 20 per cent. discount.

294. *Extra-hazardous Risks.*—The operation of the mind of the person who lends capital, at a high interest, upon poor security, is a familiar one. He sees the opportunity to obtain interest proper—the normal remuneration for forbearing to consume in immediate self-indulgence the wealth he has created, or come into possession of—without encountering any appreciable risk of losing the principal sum. But there is offered him a higher, perhaps a much higher, rate of interest, for a loan into which a chance of total loss enters. His mind balances the risk against the prize. The yearly value of the latter is definite. It is three, five or ten per cent. on the sum asked to be lent. Were he to receive this added interest for a sufficient number of years, he could even afford to lose the principal. He may receive the interest during the full term of the obligation, and then have his principal back again. He knows also that he may receive but one or two annual payments of interest, and then be compelled to recognize his investment as a total loss.

Of the degree of risk there is no measure. The ablest statistician, the first financier of the world, could give no mathematical statement of the chances for or against the ultimate repayment of the loan. The matter lies very vaguely even in the mind of the shrewdest banker or broker. He sees that there is great risk or little risk, very great risk or very little risk, or that the elements on which the ability of the borrower is to depend are altogether shrouded in uncertainty; but as to giving a mathematical expression to the value of the loan, based on the chances of loss, the man who does this is deceiving either himself or some one else.

295. With the great majority of lenders no calculation whatever, deserving of the name, enters into the negotiation of loans where more than double interest is paid. The capitalist is simply tempted beyond what he is able to bear, or else, if a man of another temper, the enhanced inducement becomes of itself a reason for refusing to lend his money, and he shuts the door upon negotiation. Look at the hundreds of millions, the thousands of millions, that have been sunk in railway shares and mining stocks by persons who had not the smallest qualifications for estimating the value of the risk, but whose prudence gave way under an offer of ten, or twelve, or twenty per cent. Writers on Interest are too much given to assuming that the losses sustained in extra-hazardous investments are balanced by the gains, and that the "average rate" is somehow maintained. The fact is, few lenders are capable of making any computation of the value of the risks they take; few even go through the form of doing so.

The only thing that can be said with assurance is that the vast majority of lenders on extra-hazardous risks are losers. The high rate of interest proves a snare. Tempted by the offer of 12 or 20 per cent., they take risks for which 40 or 50 would be inadequate. Interest is paid, dividends are declared, just long enough to complete the subscription, just long enough to secure the last gudgeon in the pool. And it is often astonishing to note the class of men who contribute to a scheme which is in its very terms an insult to common-sense. Bought wit is the best wit; but in this matter, experience seldom suffices for wisdom. The susceptibility to humbug is perennial in the human breast. After a dance of folly, in which figure "The Periwig Company, and the Spanish-Jackass Company, and the Quicksilver-fixation Company"; in which prospectus vies with prospectus to see which shall be the more preposterous; and in which investor vies with investor in recklessness, there comes, indeed, a resting spell, more through exhaustion of means than through acquired prudence; but the first tingle of reviving activity in trade starts the fever of speculation anew, and the knaves find the dupes as numerous and as credulous as ever.

296. *The Wreckers of Trade.*—The foregoing remarks apply to the great majority of investors who take extra-hazardous risks. Yet there are in every large commercial community those who reap enormous rates of interest with only rare losses to offset their gains. These are men with preternatural sagacity to know when it is safe to trust a rogue, how far to ride with a spendthrift towards his ruin, just the point at which to leave a tottering house whose foundations they have undermined by drains of exorbitant interest, just the moment at which to "unload" a stock; men with the cunning to secure themselves against loss, whoever may suffer; men who have the hardness to exact the last penny of their dues, at whatever distress to the debtor. Such men are the wreckers of trade. Their gains are great, for they reap the enormous profits of extra-hazardous risks, yet seldom lose in the principal sum lent. Rarely, indeed, is an embarrassed firm saved by their aid. Resort to them is the almost certain precursor of ruin. It serves to delay the catastrophe a little, only to make it utter and remediless at the last.

297. *Double Interest.*—The foregoing remarks apply only to extra-hazardous risks, where, to put it roundly, more than double interest is paid. With investments or temporary loans inside this limit, a different rule obtains. The rates of interest paid are still graded with little real appreciation of the degrees of risk taken; the sums obtained as insurance can not be assumed to be proportioned to the hazard; yet it is generally possible for an investor or lender to say, this is more safe than that: the adverse chances here are few and small; are many and great there.

But there is a more marked difference between extra-hazardous and ordinary risks in the loan of capital. With the former, the rates obtained are, as a whole, taking all classes of investors or lenders together, below the actuarial value of the risks taken, and such loans and investments, in spite of the acuteness of the professional money-lending class, result, as a body, in loss. With ordinary risks, the rates of interest are, on an average, above their true value, as estimated from the basis of bottom mortgages and government loans.

For example, in England, a few years ago, the return from capital invested in government bonds was about 3.3 per cent.; while the savings banks realized on their investments, which may be assumed to have been made in a conservative spirit, $4\frac{1}{2}$ per cent., and the average return to investors in railway stocks was 5 per cent. Now, here is an undeniable case of disproportion. Any shrewd and sensible man, selling £100,000 of consols, investing the proceeds in the shares of ten reputable railways, and compounding through a term of years the extra $1\frac{7}{10}$ per cent., per annum, would create a fund far more than sufficient to offset any losses he might sustain in an individual case. This disproportion is due first, to the estimation, higher than an actuarial value, placed by large classes of investors upon the feeling of security, the absence of all apprehensions and occasional alarms, and, secondly, to the favor extended by the courts to the investment of trust funds in government bonds.

298. *Differing Rates of Interest in the Same Market.*—We have laid down the proposition (par. 132) that in one market, at one time, there can be but one price for equal portions of the same commodity. The plain facts of interest seem to controvert this position. In the same market, at the same moment, the price paid for the use of capital may range from three per cent. upwards, to five, to ten, to twenty. Is this because between the portions of capital so loaned an economic difference exists, which creates a preference for one over the other, as when several different grades of flour are sold at several distinct prices? No, the capital loaned may be, in all economic respects, uniform. A man having $30,000 on deposit in a bank, may, on the same day, buy $10,000 worth of "governments" which pay four per cent., invest in "railways" paying six per cent. dividends, to the same amount; and loan the remainder at ten per cent. on personal security. Manifestly, between the three portions of capital loaned or invested, no economic differences existed.

To what, then, is the phenomenon noted due? In part to the cause discussed under the last head—the insurance of the principal sum lent. Twenty years ago there were on the stock market, in Lombard Street, three kinds of government securities: English consols, bringing, then, three and a quarter per cent. interest on the investment; Russian bonds bringing five and a quarter per cent., and Turkish bonds bringing ten and a half per cent. Every day large amounts of these bonds were bought by Englishmen. Doubtless, some purchasers bought portions of each kind of securities.

Inasmuch as the possibility of the English government becoming bankrupt, or tending to repudiation, is never admitted by an Englishman, the dividends received by holders of the "consols" constituted pure interest, the reward the abstinence. The added two per cent. obtained from the Russian bonds represented the value, as viewed by the purchaser, of the insurance of his capital against the risk of loss attendant

on loaning it to the government of a people, possessing great natural
resources, indeed, and bound together by a strong national feeling, but
rude in manner, primitive in industry, with their political questions largely
unsolved, and having points of possible collision with England. But while
the Englishman demanded five and a quarter per cent. per annum from
the Russian government, as the consideration for his loan, he exacted
just twice that consideration from the Turkish government, though a
government bound to Great Britain by the strongest ties of self-interest,
because both the resources and the good faith of the Turkish government
were reasonably suspected, and its existence was dependent on support
from foreign powers.

299. *Imperfect Competition in the Money Market.*—We have in the
foregoing paragraph used the expression, "as viewed by the purchaser."
Hereby is indicated a consideration, which, while it is of importance in
any market, is of especial importance in the market where capital is
loaned, the so-called money-market. In quoting Prof. Jevons' statement
of the reason, why, in the same market, at the same moment, all equal
portions of a perfectly homogeneous commodity must bring the same
price, we added that this proposition assumed perfect competition, all
the conditions of a good market being fully realized. Now, perfect competition only exists where there is ample and accurate information. In
bargains relating to the use of capital, so little is known by the parties
respecting the supply of and the demand for capital, especially where
usury laws drive borrowers and lenders to shifts and evasions; so much
more are men disposed to conceal the fact and the extent of their borrowing than of their buying; so much does the repayment of the principal
depend, in spite of law, upon the good faith of the borrower, that the
market for the loan of capital can rarely be called a good market.

All bargains in the "money market," as the market for the loan of
capital is popularly called, take place necessarily upon information imperfect at the best, often of a private and confidential nature: hence it frequently happens that, in the same market, at the same moment, loans,
upon equally good security, are made at different rates; while it is not at
all unlikely to occur, that, of two loans of unequal value, as to security,
the more hazardous may be made at the lower rate of interest.

300. *Differing Rates of Interest in Different Markets.*—Of course, all
that has been said of differing rates of interest in the same market holds
good of different markets; but, wholly in addition of the causes which
produce those differences, is reason found for different rates in distinct markets. Thus it is notorious that, for long terms of years, the
loan of capital could be obtained, upon what was locally regarded
as approved security, for 4 per cent. in London as freely as for 6 per
cent. in New York, or 8 per cent. in Chicago, or 12 per cent. in Iowa,
or Kansas.

Whence these differences? In some degree, doubtless, these successive additions of interest, as capital passed westward, were of the nature of insurance on the principal sum lent. In each case, the security might be as good as could ordinarily be obtained in that community. Security, however, is a relative term; what would be deemed ample security in one place would not pass the scrutiny of lenders in another. The older the country the greater, other things equal, the permanence of economic relations; the more does industry settle down within traditional limits, and acquire a definite and calculable rate of increase; the higher the value assigned to commercial reputation, the more carefully are the men selected who are to control the agencies of production and trade, the fewer the chances of revolutionary changes in business.

301. *Disinclination of Capital to Emigrate.*—But not all, or even the greater part of the differences which have been noted, are due to this cause. It is the disinclination of capital to emigrate, which allows such wide differences in the local rates of interest. This disinclination is due to various causes. In part, it is the continuing effect of old laws, now generally abrogated, discriminating against aliens. In part, it is due to the suspicion that strangers may not be fairly dealt with by courts and by officers of the law, in case of seizures or foreclosures. In part, it is due to the apprehension of the effect of international hostilities, which cause a suspension of interest-payments, if not forfeiture of the principal. In part, it is due to the fact that investments made at a distance must generally be made through an agent, upon whose good faith or sound judgment may depend the fate of the principal invested.

While these and other causes may operate, singly or in conjunction, to create local differences of interest, the main cause of such differences is found in the inertia of the owners of capital, making them ready to accept lower rates upon the spot than could perhaps be obtained with no less safety, through inquiry and effort at a distance, and, secondly, in the necessary lack of information as to prevailing rates of interest and existing degrees of security for the principal.

I remember to have read somewhere an estimate by an economist of reputation, fixing this "disinclination of capital to emigrate" at two per cent. It is doubtful, however, whether the matter is subject to any such form of statement. The disinclination to invest capital abroad must differ among men of different races; it must differ with differing conditions respecting the communication of news, and respecting international relations. Indeed, it must differ widely with differing moods of the public mind. At times, it may disappear altogether with the excitement of speculative mania, as in the days of the South Sea Bubble, and in the year preceding the English crisis of 1825. It sometimes seems to be the case that loans and investments are made abroad more freely than at home, probably because it is less easy to detect the fallacy of schemes bearing foreign names, and relating to distant lands.

CHAPTER IV. PROFITS

302. *Definition of Profits.*—We have now seen two shares cut off the product of industry—rent and interest; two claimants satisfied—the landlord and the capitalist.

We now come to inquire respecting the share of the Employer, who organizes and conducts production, deciding what shall be produced; in what amounts, of what varieties, materials and patterns; and to what persons, at what prices, and on what terms of payment, the products shall be sold.

303. *The Entrepreneur or Employing Class.*—We have seen that in a primitive state of industrial society the employer does not appear. When, however, the forms of production become many and complex; when the hand-tool is replaced by the machine; when many persons, of various degrees of skill, strength and intelligence, are united in the same industrial operation; when the materials consumed are gathered from distant lands, and the products, in turn, are distributed widely to consumers not known to the producer, and are sold largely upon credit; when, moreover, a few simple, standard styles give way to ever-varying fashions, in material, in form, in color: in such a state, the employer, the master, the entrepreneur, becomes a necessity of the situation. He performs a function which is indispensable to a large and varied production, and for so doing receives a remuneration which we call profits.

304. Unfortunately, as it seems to me, the entrepreneur or employing function has not been adequately treated, if, indeed, it has been in the smallest degree recognized. English and American economists, in general, have chosen to regard the capitalist as the employer of labor, that is, as employing labor merely because of the possession of capital, and to the extent only to which he possesses capital. We have just now said that, in an early stage of industrial society, the employer does not appear in distinct shape. The possession of capital there constitutes a sufficient qualification for the employment of labor.

In the later stages of industrial development, the mere possession of capital no longer constitutes the sole, or even the main qualification for employing labor. The laborer no longer looks to the employer to furnish merely food and tools and materials, but to furnish, also, technical skill, commercial knowledge and powers of administration; to assume responsibilities and provide against contingencies; to shape and direct production and to organize and control the industrial machinery. So important and difficult are these duties, so rare are the abilities they demand, that he who can discharge these will generally find the capital required. If he be the man to conduct business,* food, tools, and materials will not, under our modern system of credit, long be wanting to him. On the other hand, without these higher qualifications the mere possessor of capital will employ labor at the risk, almost the certainty, of total or partial loss.

The employer, the entrepreneur, thus rises to be the master of the situation. It is no longer true that a man becomes the employer of labor because he is a capitalist. Men command capital because they have the qualifications to employ labor. To men so endowed, capital and labor alike resort, for the opportunity to perform their several functions and to entitle themselves to share in the product of industry. By this is not meant that the employer is not, in any case, or to any extent, a capitalist, but that he is not an employer to the extent only to which he is a capitalist, nor is he an employer at all because he is a capitalist.

305. *Use of the Word Profits by English and American Economists.*—As the English and American economists generally leave the entrepreneur out of their discussion of production, so they leave out of view the share of the entrepreneur in treating of the distribution of wealth. "Profits" come to mean only the remuneration for the use of capital, what we call distinctively interest; or, if it be recognized that the man who organizes and conducts industrial operations receives something over and above the mere return upon that portion of the capital employed by him which he owns in his own right, that something is disparaged by being termed "the wages of supervision and management."

Now it is fundamental in my theory of distribution that the entrepreneur class, the employers of labor, receive a share of the product of industry which is so important, through its amount, that it can not possibly be omitted from consideration, and so widely different in the principles by which it is governed, that the term wages can not be applied thereto without inducing a wholly unnecessary and mischievous confusion of ideas, leading directly to false results.

To the entrepreneur's share of the product of industry I shall strictly apply the term profits. This use of the term, in my judgment, tends to promote clearer conceptions regarding the distribution of wealth in the modern industrial state.

306. *Profits a Species of the Same Genus as Rent.*—In my opinion, profits thus defined bear a strong resemblance to rent. In this view I follow Archbishop Whately, who, in the appendix to his treatise on Logic, declares that the rent of land is only a species of an extensive genus, although, as he complains, the English economists have treated it as constituting a genus by itself, and have either omitted its cognate species, or have included them under genera to which they do not properly belong.

* "Many employers of labor, *in some parts of England more than half,* have risen from the ranks of labor. Every artisan who has exceptional natural abilities has a chance of raising himself to a post of command."—Marshall's "Economics of Industry."

If this view is correct, the principles deduced therefrom will be of very great consequence, not only to political economy, but to social philosophy. Let us, therefore, state again the essential differences between Rent and Interest.

1st. A portion of the land cultivated for the supply of any given market, bears no rent; this we call the no-rent land. The rent paid for any piece of land is exactly measured, in theory, by its excess of advantages in production, over the advantages in production pertaining to the no-rent land. On the other hand, there is not any no-interest capital. It is true that a person lending capital may not only not obtain, in the result, any interest for its use, but may even lose the principal; but this will be due to violence or fraud, to flood or fire or stress of weather, or, else, to the unsuspected incompetency of the borrower to conduct business, all of which we may sum up in the word accident. There is no reason why such accidents should befall one portion of capital and not another, whereas there is a reason, in the nature of the case, why one piece of land should bear a rent and another not; why one piece should bear a high and another a low rent. Theoretically all capital bears interest; and, theoretically also, all capital bears the same rate of interest, exceptions being either, first, apparent only, as when an additional per cent. is charged, not as interest proper, but for the insurance of the principal, or secondly, those arising from the disinclination of capital to emigrate, from the ignorance or inertia of lenders and borrowers, or from the force of laws interfering with contracts of loan.

2nd. It follows that interest forms a part of the price of all products, but that rent forms no part of the price of agricultural produce (for the demonstration of this theorem, see par. 262), and that the amount received by the landlord, as rent, is not paid either by the agricultural laborer, or by the consumer of the produce.

307. *Profits Governed by the Same Law as Rent.*—Having restated the essential distinction between interest and rent, I shall now undertake to show that profits, the remuneration of the entrepreneur or employer, partake largely of the nature of rent, being a species of the same genus. So far as this is the case, profits do not form a part of the price of the products of industry, and do not cause any diminution of the wages of labor.

The successful conduct of business, under free and active competition, is due to exceptional abilities or to exceptional opportunities. Whether due to exceptional abilities or to exceptional opportunities, my proposition could be equally well established, just as it makes no difference in the theory of rent whether a piece of land owes its superior advantages for the purposes of cultivation to higher natural fertility, or to closer proximity to the market to be supplied. Yet it can not be a matter of indifference to social philosophy, whether the power to command profits be due to exceptional abilities or to exceptional opportunities; and I may, therefore, be pardoned for pausing to point out that the former are far more efficient than the latter, in securing profits.

To justify this assertion it will be enough to refer to the well-known fact that a great majority of all business houses which have achieved notable success have been founded by men who owed almost nothing to opportunity. On the other hand, nothing is more familiar than the spectacle of great houses, deeply founded, which have enjoyed high prestige, wide connections and large accumulated capital, dwindling away little by little, if not brought abruptly to their downfall, under the successors of the original founder, simply because the management which had been strong and brave and wise, became commonplace, purposeless, timid and weak. All this is so familiar that I do not fear that any American, at least, will question the assertion that exceptional abilities have far more to do with the successful conduct of business, than exceptional opportunities.

Inasmuch as it would make no difference whether profits were due to exceptional abilities or to exceptional opportunities, while the former are, in fact, much the more important factor in the successful conduct of business, I shall, hereafter, for convenience and simplicity, speak of profits as due to exceptional abilities, just as in discussing the question of the use of the land, we speak of rent as due to differences in fertility, assuming, for convenience of illustration, all the fields under view to be in equal proximity to the market.

308. *A Theoretical No-profits Stage of Production.*—If the number of men of exceptional abilities were sufficient or more than sufficient to do all the business that required to be done, of all sorts and in all places; if (2) these men, however much surpassing all other members of the industrial society, were among themselves equal in all respects which concern the conduct of business; and if (3) this class, so constituted and so endowed, were distinguished from all not of their class so clearly and conspicuously that no one having these exceptional abilities should fail to be recognized, and no one lacking such abilities in the full measure should esteem himself capable of conducting business, or be so esteemed, for the purpose of obtaining credit, we should have a situation closely analogous to that which we described (par. 255) in the case of a community near which was found an amount of good land, of uniform quality, adequate, or more than adequate, to raise all produce required for the support of the community.

The result would be, either that this class would, by forming a combination and scrupulously adhering to its terms and its spirit, create and maintain a monopoly price for their services in conducting the business requiring to be done, which is so improbable as to be altogether out of our contemplation, or they would, by competing among themselves for the amount of business, bring down its rate to so low a point that the remuneration of each and every one of this class would be practically equal to what he would receive if employed by another. This, which we might call the "no-profits" stage of industrial society, corresponds closely to the "no-rent" stage in the cultivation of the soil. The persons remaining in the conduct of business would earn their necessary subsistence, but no more. Economically it would make no difference to them whether they did this, as employers or employed.

309. In fact, however, the qualifications for the conduct of business are not equal throughout all of a sufficiently numerous class. On the contrary, the range of ability is almost world-wide. First, we have those rarely-gifted persons who, in common phrase, seem to turn every thing they touch into gold; whose commercial dealings have the air of magic; who have such insight as almost to seem to have foresight; who are so resolute and firm in temper that apprehension and alarms and repeated shocks of disaster never cause them to relax their hold or change their course; who have such command over men that all with whom they have to do acquire vigor from the contact and work for them as they would not, perhaps could not, work for others.

Next below, though far below, we have that much larger class of men of business, of a high order of talent, though without genius or any thing savoring of magic, whose unqualified success is easily comprehended, even if it can not be imitated: men of natural mastery, sagacious, prompt and resolute.

Then we have the men who, on the whole, do well, or pretty well, in business: men who enjoy a harmonious union of all the qualities of the entrepreneur, though only in moderate degree, or in whom some defect, mental or moral, impairs a higher order of abilities; men who are never masters of their fortunes, are never beyond the imminence of disaster, and yet, by care and pains and diligence, win no small profits from their business, and, if frugality be added to their other virtues, accumulate in time large estates.

Lower down in the industrial order are a multitude of men who are found in the control of business enterprises for no good reason: men of checkered fortunes, sometimes doing well, but more often ill; some of them, perhaps, filling a place that would not otherwise be filled, but, more commonly in business because they have forced themselves into it under a mistaken idea of their own abilities, perhaps encouraged by the partiality of friends who have been willing to place in their hands the agencies of production, or intrust them with commercial or banking capital. The industrial careers of these men are not peculiarly happy, though the degree in which they suffer from the constant imminence of loss, perhaps of bankruptcy, is very much a matter of temperament. Some take it extremely hard, and when they fall make no effort to rise again; others are irrepressible as Harlequin, jumping up, alert as ever, after being apparently hanged, drawn and quartered by the common executioner.

310. *The No-profits Class of Employers.*—Now, in my view of the question of profits, we find, in the lower stratum of the industrial order thus rudely and hastily sketched, a "no-profits" class of employers. Notwithstanding all the magnificent premiums of business success, the men of real business power are not so many but that no small part of the posts of industry and trade are filled by men inadequately qualified, and who, consequently, have a very checkered career and realize for themselves, taking their whole lives together, a meager compensation, so meager that, for purposes of scientific reasoning, we may treat it as constituting no profits at all. Live they do, partly by legitimate toll upon the business that passes through their hands, partly at the cost of their creditors, with whom they make frequent compositions, partly at the expense of friends, or by the sacrifice of inherited means. This bare subsistence, obtained through so much of hard work, of anxiety, and often of humiliation, we regard as that minimum which, in economics, we can treat as *nil*. From this low point upwards, we measure profits.

311. *Profits Do Not Form a Part of the Price of Manufactured Products.* If this view of the employing class be correctly taken, it appears that, under perfect competition, that is, where the conditions of a good market are supplied, manufacturing profits, for instance, are not obtained through any deduction from the wages of mechanical labor; and, secondly, manufacturing profits do not constitute a part of the price of manufactured goods. All profits are drawn from a body of wealth which is created by the exceptional abilities (or opportunities) of those employers who receive profits, measured from the level of those employers who receive no profits, just as all rents are drawn from a body of wealth, which is created by the exceptional fertility (or facilities for transportation of produce) of the rent-lands, measured from the level of the no-rent lands.

The price of manufactured goods of any particular description is determined by the cost of production of that portion of the supply which is produced at the greatest disadvantage (par. 137). If the demand for such goods is so great as to require a certain amount to be produced under the management and control of persons whose efficiency in organizing and supervising the forces of labor and capital is small, the cost of production of that portion of the stock will be large, and the price will be correspondingly high, yet, high as it is, it will not be high enough to yield to the employers of this grade any more than that scant and difficult subsistence which we have taken as the no-profits line.

The price at which these goods are to be sold, however, will determine the price of the whole supply, since, in any one market, at any one time, there is but one price for different portions of the same commodity.

Hence, whatever the cost of production of those portions of the supply which are produced by employers of a higher industrial grade, they will command the same price as those portions which are produced at the greatest disadvantage. The difference, so measured, will go as profits to each individual employer, according to his own success in production.

312. *Profits Are Not Subtracted from Wages.*—Do profits, then, come out of wages? Not at all. The employers of the lowest industrial grade— the no-profits employers, as we have called them—must pay wages sufficient to hire laborers to work under their direction. These wages constitute an essential part of the cost, to the employer, of the production of the goods. The fact that these wages are so high is the reason why these employers are unable (their skill and power in organizing and energizing labor and capital being no greater than they are), to realize any profits for themselves.

The employers of the higher industrial grades will pay the same wages to their laborers. Why, in equity or in economics, should a laborer who works for a strong, prudent and skillful master, receive higher wages than one whose fortune it is to work for a vacillating, weak or reckless employer. The one laborer is as efficient as the other, and works as hard. The difference in production, which, in the one case allows rent to be paid, and in the other enables the employers to secure a profit, is due to no superiority in the quality of the labor or the capital employed, over that of the labor and the capital employed where no rents or no profits are realized. In the one case it is due to the superior fertility of the land, or its greater facilities for the transportation of produce; in the other, to the superior abilities or opportunities of him who conducts industry.

In the latter case, the employer, paying wages at the same rate to his laborers, and interest, at the same rate, to the capitalist, for so much as he has to borrow, and selling his goods, so far as they are of equal quality, at the same price as the employer who makes no profits, is yet able to accumulate a clear surplus after all obligations are discharged, which surplus is called profits. This is effected by his carefully study of the sources of his materials; by his comprehension of the demands of the market; by his steadiness and self-control in the presence of temptations to extravagance or wild ventures; by his organizing force and administrative ability; by his energy, economy and prudence.

313. *The No-profits Employer.*—A failure to discern the true relations of profits to wages has led to a mistaken appreciation of the interests of the community, and especially of the laboring classes, regarding the employers of labor. While the large profits of the successful employer have been the subject of much jealousy, and almost uniformly excite in the minds of the unthinking the sense of personal wrong, there is an entire lack of jealousy exhibited towards the unsuccessful man of business, who often receives a great deal of sympathy from the laboring class.

So far as the sympathy extended towards the unsuccessful man of business is of a personal nature, flowing from a kindly disposition towards the unfortunate, it is, of course, very amiable. But there is reason to believe that this sentiment is not wholly of a good origin, but is quite as largely produced by a misapprehension of economic relations. The laborers appreciate, in some degree, the cares under which the unsuccessful employer labors, the anxieties from which he suffers, the humiliation into which he is occasionally plunged. They know he has a pretty poor time of it on the whole, and they are not envious of him. On the contrary, they use his hard lot to sharpen their envy of the man who reaps large profits from the conduct of business and the employment of labor. They compare the rich rewards of the one, who, perhaps in time, becomes worth his millions, with the meager recompense of the other, who, at the end of a long life of labor, has little to show for it all; and the comparison tends to heighten the feeling of loss and of wrong with which the gains of the former are contemplated.

If, however, we have rightly indicated the source of profits, not only is the unsuccessful employer deserving of no special economic sympathy, but his conduct of business, his control of labor-force and capital-force is at a great cost to the laboring class, as forming a part of the general community.

We saw that rents were measured upward from the productive level of no-rent land. If, therefore, that level is lowered, rents are, (par. 257) by that fact raised. Similarly, profits are measured upwards from the level of the no-profit class of employers; and any cause which brings incompetent persons into the conduct of business, or keeps them there against the natural tendency of trade to throw them out, increases the profits of the successful employers, as a class, by enhancing the cost of production and, consequently, the price of that portion of the supply which is produced at the greatest disadvantage. This enhancement of price is at the expense of all who consume the goods so produced; the laboring class equally with others, in theory; probably in fact more than any other, on account of their limited ability to look out for their own interests in retail trade.

314. *What Causes Help to Swell the Proportion of Incompetent Employers of Labor?*—Shilly-shally laws relating to insolvency do this; bad money does this; truck does this; protection, in my judgment, does this. Each of these causes enables men to escape the consequences of incompetency, and to hang miserably on to business, where they are an obstruction and a nuisance. Slavery, in like manner, enables men to control labor and direct production, who never would become, on an equal scale, the employers of free labor; and it is not more to the inefficiency of the slave than to the incompetency of the master, that the unproductiveness of chattel labor is due.

The lower the industrial quality of free labor, the more ignorant and inert the individual laborer, the lower may be the quality of the men who can just sustain themselves in the position of employers. Men become the employers of cheap labor who would never become the employers of dear labor, and who ought not to be the employers of any sort of labor. The more active becomes the competition among the wages class, the more prompt their resort to market, the more persistent their demand for every possible increase of remuneration, the greater will be the pressure brought to bear upon such employers to drop out of the place into which they have crowded themselves at the cost of the general community, and where they have been able to maintain themselves only because the working classes have failed, through ignorance or inertia, to exact their full terms.

315. *Importance of This View of Profits.*—It is competent to any person to dissent from the view of the origin and measure of business profits I have presented; but it can not be gainsaid that, if that view be accepted as correct, we have here the keystone of the arch, which completes the structure and binds together the other members into a symmetrical whole spanning the entire field of distribution. We shall not, however, be able to appreciate all the consequences of this theory, until we have carried our studies through the subject of wages, the remuneration of labor.

316. *Getting Rid of the Employer.*—In the department of Production we described the function of the entrepreneur, or employer, the person who, hiring labor on the one hand, and borrowing capital on the other, initiates industrial operations according to his own plans, and with a view to his own economic benefit. Coming down to the department of Distribution, we have, but just now, inquired how the contemplated benefit is secured by the employer, and what are the limits of that benefit, which we term profits.

It has been said, in the course of this discussion, that this benefit obtained by the employer, his profits, has been the object of not a little jealousy and envy on the part of the laborers and capitalists to whom he has paid wages or interest. Those wages and that interest the recipients would be glad to see increased by some addition derived from the source from which the employer obtains his profits. This could only be done by the laborers and the capitalists combining to perform the employer's work in production, and thereby becoming entitled, or perhaps we had better say enabled, to claim his share of the product in distribution.

317. *Co-operation.*—Organized and systematic efforts to get rid of the entrepreneur or employer have not been unknown. Among the many schemes for largely and rapidly improving the condition of the masses of the people, which had their birth in the period of social and political fermentation which we call the Revolution of 1848, none had

fairer promise of substantial results than that known by the name of Co-operation.

Generically, co-operation is a term of wide application, and, in its use in political economy, may express the union of industrial agents in production upon any terms and under any system of organization. Since the period referred to, however, the term has come to have a limited signification, confined to an industrial organization from which the entrepreneur is excluded, and under which the product of industry is again to be divided into three principal shares, instead of four as under the entrepreneur system. I here only indicate the place which co-operation occupies in the scheme of Distribution, postponing the discussion of the scheme to Part VI.

SIMON NELSON PATTEN

(1852-1922)

Simon N. Patten was born of pioneer stock in New York State, but his boyhood days were spent on the farm lands of Illinois. Although destined for the law, his inquiring but impractical mind turned toward the study of philosophy and the liberal arts. After preliminary work in school and academy he spent a brief period at Northwestern University. But in those days young students of this country were inclined to seek instruction at the older seats of knowledge in Europe. Consequently, Patten was one of the group of young Americans who sought the ripe scholarship of German universities.

Following the advice of several of his friends, Patten went to the University of Halle in search of higher learning leading toward the degree of doctor of philosophy. These three years from 1875 to 1878 were profitably spent under the instruction of Professor Konrad and under the influence of the German historical school. Again, Patten was particularly impressed by the contrast between the natural and social environments of the older civilizations of Europe and those of America, particularly our own West. The Ricardian concept of the niggardliness of nature was understandable in Europe, but it was not applicable to American conditions.

After his return to the United States in 1878, Patten attempted teaching in the lower schools, but he soon abandoned it for the study of law. Unfortunately, his eyes failed, and for the next three years he was forced to endure inactivity and to live in partial darkness and intermittent pain. In 1882, Patten visited Philadelphia, where his vision was restored by a competent occulist who was able to fit him successfully with glasses.

After another short and varied experience in the schools of the middle West and after the publication of "Premises of Political Economy," Patten was appointed to a professorship of political economy at the University of Pennsylvania in 1888. Here he played an important part in the early history of the Wharton School, the first collegiate school of business in the United States. Dr. Patten remained on the faculty of the University of Pennsylvania until his retirement in 1917. He died five years later in the summer of 1922.

Although writing was a very difficult task for him, Patten was most prolific. He was the author of numerous special articles, most of which appeared in various periodicals, chiefly those of the American Economic

Association and the American Academy of Political and Social Science, in both of which organizations he played an important pioneering role. The chief books of Patten were: "Premises of Political Economy" (1885); "Consumption of Wealth" (1889); "Economic Basis of Protection" (1890); "Theory of Dynamic Economics" (1892); "Theory of Social Forces" (1896); "Development of English Thought" (1899); "Theory of Prosperity" (1902); "Heredity and Social Progress" (1903); "New Basis of Civilization" (1907); "Social Basis of Religion" (1911); "Reconstruction of Economic Theory" (1912); and "Mud Hollow" (1922). After Patten's death some of his papers were published by Tugwell, with an introduction by H. R. Seager, under the title "Essays in Economic Theory" (1924).

Patten has been termed by the late Professor Seager as "the most original and suggestive economist that America has yet produced." Indeed, intellectual originality and economic dissent were among his leading characteristics. His students were numerous and devoted, but he founded no school of thought except in the hearts of his associates.

Patten recognized no barriers among any of the social sciences, nor did he observe any formalities in the organization of his work. Although he knew classical economy, rereading each year his John Stuart Mill, he accepted little of it as applicable to the new dispensation in the New World of America, especially after the Industrial Revolution. Although unorthodox in both content and method, Patten's classroom discussions were a constant source of inspiration to both teacher and student. He was interested not in what a student thought, but how; not in facts, but in ideas; not in the memorization of laws and formulae, but in creation, criticism and evaluation.

Although it is difficult to classify an iconoclast, Patten had most in common with the historical school. If he believed any one economic law, it was that of social change. Different economic environments produced different social conditions, requiring a readjustment to new factors, a restatement of old principles and a redefinition of objectives. This point of view is suggested by such a title as "The New Basis of Civilization." This book radiates optimism, for it is built about his famous concept of the transition from a deficit economy of pain to a surplus economy of pleasure. Again, Patten's stress on consumption was as new as it was important. The old hedonistic concept of the maximum of utility with the minimum of effort was to be secured by social changes in habits of consumption, bringing them into conformity with the new products and greater potentialities of the physical environment of America.

The following selections are taken from one of Patten's earliest works, "Premises of Political Economy." They illustrate the characteristics and concepts just mentioned. Again, the later writings of Patten broadened into sociology, and even strayed into the fields of fiction and versification.

The best account of Patten's life and work is to be found in "Memorial Addresses on the Life and Services of Simon N. Patten," Supplement to the *Annals* of the American Academy of Political and Social Science for May, 1923. Attention should be called also to the Special Supplement of the *American Economic Review* for 1923 and to the article by Rexford G. Tugwell in the *Journal of Political Economy* for April, 1923.

SIMON NELSON PATTEN

SELECTIONS FROM "THE PREMISES OF POLITICAL ECONOMY"

INTRODUCTION

The Science of Economics has had a historical development. At first some of its important truths were dimly perceived, then a theory was formulated, new doctrines from time to time were added, the old doctrines gradually became better known and understood, and errors have been gradually detected and discarded. As a result of this development the doctrines of the science have been formulated in a very objectionable manner, and economic truths have lacked symmetry, the newer doctrines not having been applied to all parts of the science, while old errors, though driven from their strongholds, still lurk in many unsuspected corners. These considerations make a return to the discussion of first principles necessary, and this I take up the more readily because of a conviction that they are not correctly apprehended in the current economic literature.

Since the time of Ricardo the discussion of first principles has been very one-sided, the ultimate premises used by him having been accepted by most subsequent writers. It is true that many economists have rejected the premises of Ricardo, but having done this on other than purely economic grounds, they have had little or no effect on the development of the science. It is my purpose in the following discussion to contest from strictly economic grounds the validity of several fundamental propositions laid down by Ricardo and other writers of the same school.

* * * * *

The present Science of Economics is as imperfect as Astronomy would be if one of the laws of motion were unknown. In each department of Economics all the deductions are based on some one ultimate fact, and the conclusions arrived at are true only on condition that no other ultimate facts exist which influence the phenomena under investigation. The law of rent is usually discussed as though differences of soil were the sole cause of rent, and the law of population only considers the difference between the possible rates of increase of population and food, while free trade and the effects of free competition are discussed from an equally narrow stand-point. It is plain that such discussions are of a very limited value, if many ultimate facts, or even any, are overlooked, and it is my purpose to point out these neglected facts, and to place them in proper relation to those facts at present so much used in deductive Economics.

709

The increase in the price of food accompanying the advance of civilization, is the main point which economic theories have to explain. Is the increased price the result of a single cause, or does it arise from a combination of various causes, and are these causes of a physical or of a social nature? The well-known answer of Ricardo is that there is a single physical cause,—the various degrees of fertility which different lands possess. The best lands are limited in quantity, and as the demand for food increases less fertile lands, having a higher cost of cultivation, must be brought into use, and hence the price of food must rise when more food is required for an increasing population. Ricardo gives this answer in his explanation of rent, and Malthus adopts the same view in discussing the law of population, by assuming that the means of subsistence are exhausted, or nearly so, because the price of food is high. It is no wonder that so simple and apparently self-evident an explanation has found ready acceptance, and one theory of rent having been presented, no one took the trouble to investigate whether some other theory could account for all the facts needing explanation.

In the following chapters I shall endeavor to present a consistent theory, showing that the main causes of rent, and of the increased price of agricultural produce, are not of a physical, but of a social nature. The prevalence of ignorance, and a lack of appreciation of inexclusive pleasures, cause a demand for commodities of which nature can supply but small quantities, waste a large part of what is produced, and at the same time prevent the distribution of population and the increase of capital. The ignorant and inefficient classes displace the skilled and intelligent, because their wants are so limited that they are able to give a greater surplus as rent than the higher classes can do, and whatever class can give the greater surplus gets possession of the field of employment, and thus the survival of other classes is prevented. By these social causes a high price of food can be brought about, but this high price affords no indication of the exhaustion of the food-supply, unless the field of employment is much larger to the ignorant than to the intelligent classes. From the nature of the field of employment, then, must it be determined whether rent has physical or social causes. If the field of employment enlarges as the people become skilled and accumulate wealth, then what may be called the social theory of rent is correct; on the other hand, if the ignorant possess much the larger field of employment, then the physical theory of rent based on the natural obstacles to the increase of food must be accepted. The only condition on which it could be true that the field of employment would be larger to the ignorant than to the intelligent classes, is that the greater portion of the land of the earth has so low a degree of fertility that the higher classes cannot be employed on it. If the greater part of the land has, or can be made to have, a high degree of fertility, there can be no doubt that the intelligent classes, when not prevented by social causes, can obtain a much larger gross produce from the more fertile land, and, while supporting a much larger population, can also increase the average return for labor above what the inefficient classes could get from all the land. Whether the physical or social theory of rent is correct must be determined by the ratio of the superior to the inferior lands, and if I show that most of the land either has, or is capable of having a high degree of fertility, I shall disprove the physical theory of rent, which explains the increased price of agricultural produce from physical causes.

* * * * *

The real cause of the present social distress is to be found in the prevailing sentiment regarding the consumption of wealth, and especially of food. Nature is not equally productive of all kinds of wealth, and men cannot expect to choose those forms of wealth of which nature is least productive and receive the same reward as if they chose for consumption those articles supplied most abundantly by nature. Men complain of the niggardliness of nature, when really the only thing wrong is the universal disposition on the part of men to prefer those forms of wealth of which nature is least productive, instead of other commodities of which nature offers a generous supply. As soon as the productive power of men is increased, it is not used to augment their supply of commodities, but to enable them to obtain articles produced by nature less abundantly than those formerly consumed. Meat is demanded instead of vegetable food, wheat-bread instead of rye-bread, while corn is mainly used as animal food or for making whiskey, and tobacco displaces other crops of which the earth is more productive. The same change in the demand for commodities causes silk to be preferred to the more abundant cotton, seal-skin cloaks to be chosen instead of the equally useful ones made from wool; and on all sides could other examples of a like nature be pointed out.

I am well aware that these changes are often looked upon as the best evidence of an advancing civilization, and that this is especially true in England and in America. The Anglo-Saxon race pride themselves on the fact that they reject the greater part of those articles of food which the land cultivated by them can produce. They love a diet composed almost wholly of beef and white bread, and look down with contempt upon the German with his sausage and black bread, the Frenchman with soup and frogs, and all other nations that have a diet more in harmony with the natural conditions by which they are surrounded.

It is not my purpose to endeavor to determine which of these races has the most resources for happiness. However instructive such a study may be, as an economist I am more interested in studying what are the effects of these different modes of the consumption of wealth on its production and distribution. We can choose any form of consumption, but we cannot avoid the necessary effects which accompany our choice. Every soil is more productive of some one crop than of another, and the same soil will produce more when used for a variety of crops than when one only is raised. The land of any country can produce a certain quantity of each kind of food more advantageously than if a greater or less quantity were demanded for consumption. When all the land is put to its most productive use, there is a fixed relation between the quantities of the various articles produced, and if more or less of any article is produced than its proportional share, the gross produce of the whole country will be diminished.

We have, then, two distinct types of civilizations,—the one in which those things are desired of which nature is least productive, the other in which each individual conforms to those external conditions necessary for the greatest possible production. I desire to point out that the economic laws of these two different civilizations are not the same, and that the doctrines whose universality is asserted by the English school of economists are only true of a civilization where the mass of the people prefer those commodities which can be produced by nature only in relatively small quantities. It is only when the land is used to produce a very few articles of food that the Ricardian theory of rent is true, and it is only in those nations desiring but a small variety of food and having but few sources of pleasure where the tendency to increase of population is so great as to be injurious. Under these conditions the gross and average return for labor is so small that a low class of laborers become a necessity, and they can be utilized only by a large scale of production making the laborers dependent upon their employers and preventing free competition through the combination of the few capitalists who control each industry. As soon as a nation decides the use for which its land shall be employed, it determines for the most part the character of its inhabitants, the scale of its industries, the manner in which its wealth shall be distributed, and the degree in which competition shall be really free.

Just laws for the distribution of wealth cannot compensate for the reduction in the average return for labor necessitated by a choice of those articles of food supplied by nature in but very limited quantities. So long as the present mode of consumption continues, neither the nationalization of land nor even the appropriation of all the means of production can increase the average income to such a degree as to make its possessor comfortable and happy. The losses to the laboring classes occasioned by an unequal distribution of wealth are very small when compared with what is lost through a disregard, on their part, of the conditions by which the food-supply is increased. When they comply with these conditions not only will they obtain all the increase of produce, but they will also set in motion causes which will bring to them the greater part of what is now enjoyed by the other classes. The economic conditions making desirable the nationalization of land and other more socialistic measures are those which also raise rent and bring out such a struggle for food as to reduce wages to a minimum. Nowhere can stronger adherents of the Ricardian doctrines be found than among the socialists, and this is because their conception of natural laws accords with the views of Ricardo. If the doctrines of Ricardo are not universally true, a civilization is possible in which each individual, by complying with the surrounding external conditions, can obtain all that reward which nature offers for labor and abstinence, and when men comply with these conditions they will no longer need the above-mentioned measures to insure a just distribution of wealth.

If the social theory of rent is correct, it is necessary to explain why there is at the present time such an unequal distribution of wealth, and why wages are low when they might be high. I shall show that when two different civilizations contest in the same society for the occupation of the field of employment, the power to survive depends, not on a higher average return for labor, but on the surplus which can be given as rent, the class commanding the larger surplus getting possession of the field of employment. That class of laborers which can pay the highest price for food can deprive others of the necessary means of support, and hence obtain the victory in the contest. For a higher class of laborers to displace a lower, they must, in a state of free competition, be able to pay more for food and still have sufficient incomes remaining to maintain that standard of life to which they are accustomed. When this cannot be done, the intelligence and skill of the laborers are reduced, progress and the increase of population are checked, and society becomes stationary.

The ultimate cause of the present low return for labor is not to be found in the niggardliness of nature, but rather in the combination of cheap labor and low interest, by which the price of food is forced so high, and the value of other commodities so low, that the more intelligent classes are driven from the field of employment, or their numbers so reduced that they only do work with which cheap labor cannot compete. So long as nine-tenths of the labor of any society can be performed by a very low class of laborers, as is the case in our present industrial state, the mass of the people will remain ignorant and degraded, unless society by its laws and customs prevents the success of that combination which is the chief cause of our present evils. A higher social state cannot be attained while free competition results merely in a displacement of the higher classes by their inferiors, who, having no desire for, or appreciation of, better things, can force the price of food so high that no one else can compete with them.

In the first chapters of this work the problems relating to land, population, and the effect of increased production on the average return for labor are discussed; and then free competition, the causes of an unequal distribution of wealth, and the hindrances to social progress are considered, and some of the means of bettering our present social state are pointed out.

Chapter II. The Social Causes Producing a High Price of Food

Thus far only the physical capacities of the earth to produce food, and the conditions on which increased quantites of food can be obtained, have been examined. Now I wish to call attention to the importance of the reaction of the consumption on the production of wealth, and to the influence which the economy of the food-supply exerts on production. The current theory is that consumption has no influence on production, and that a demand for commodities is not a demand for labor. It determines merely the direction of labor, but not the quantity or efficiency of the labor, or the total aggregate of wealth produced. This proposition is set down by most economists as one of the most fundamental and best established doctrines of Political Economy. This subject, like many others in Political Economy, is much obscured by the nature of the attack to which the current doctrine has been subjected, by which the attention of economists has been diverted from the real issue involved to questions almost frivolous. It is against the popular notion that the extravagance of the rich is a blessing to the poor, by giving them employment, that the arguments of economists have been directed, and so doing they have laid down propositions which, while strong enough to withstand the opposition met with on popular grounds, are very weak when examined from another and more reasonable point of view.

I shall first show the influence which changes in the demand for commodities have on the aggregate production whenever the change is from a commodity which nature can produce less abundantly to one capable of being produced more abundantly. Of some commodities nature can produce more than of others, and if the more abundant are demanded a greater population can be supported, and for their labor a greater proportional return can be had, than if something yielded by nature less abundantly was demanded. On a given area more rye can be obtained for the same labor than wheat, and more corn and potatoes than rye, and in many climates more rice than corn or potatoes. Hence if corn or potatoes are demanded for food instead of rice, a much smaller population can be supported, and a still smaller if rye is wanted, while wheat will support the smallest population of all. But this is not all, for by examining the laws of nature more closely we shall find that the abundance in which nature can produce given articles varies with the changes of climate and soil. Some climates and soils are naturally adapted to wheat, some to oats, others to rye, barley, or potatoes, and still others to rice, sugar, and other tropical products, while other parts are best fitted for the pasture of cattle. If this is true, a change in the demand for food, from commodities of which under the circumstances nature can produce but small quantities to those which can be produced in greater abundance, will increase both the gross and average return for labor, and at the same time bring about a more equal distribution of wealth. Let us suppose the demand for wheat has been so great as to cause not only all natural wheat lands to be sown to wheat, but also some of the potato lands. This would not only cause a much greater proportional expenditure of labor than if a less quantity of wheat was demanded, but also a great increase of rent on the good wheat lands, all of which would come out of the consumers' revenue. If the demand for food would change so that less wheat and more potatoes were wanted, the price of wheat would fall, the demand being supplied from a better class of wheat land than before, while the price of potatoes would not rise, or at least not rise as much as the price of wheat fell. The community then would have a double gain, less labor would be required to supply its demand for food, and rent would fall; lands poor in their capacity to produce wheat being no longer cultivated for wheat but for potatoes, for which they are especially adapted.

Ricardo, in discussing the causes of rent, views the whole world as used for the production of a single article, and because any one article cannot be raised on all soils and in every climate at an equal cost of labor, he grades all land according to its power of producing some one article, and then shows that rent will rise as lands less fitted for the production of this article are used for its production. Certainly if the people demand only wheat, for instance, as food, they must pay a high rent; but this does not prove that an increase of population necessitates a rise of rent. Suppose there are four classes of land, of which the first is best adapted for wheat, the second for rye, the third for corn, and the fourth for potatoes. If only one article were in demand, so that all the four classes of land must be used for its production, every extension of cultivation would be accompanied by a rise in the price of food. On the other hand, if all of these articles were desired, and the demand for each article was in proportion to the land best fitted for its production, there would be no rent from differences in fertility, or at least much less rent than if only one article were produced. The rise of rent merely shows that there is too much of some one kind of food demanded, and does not prove that more food cannot be obtained without increasing the cost of production.

Besides the difference of climate and soil, the rotation of crops has a great effect on the quantity produced, and to have a proper rotation there must be a demand for all the products required for the rotation; and a change in the demand for commodities which allows a better rotation of crops causes a much greater quantity of food to be obtained with no greater expenditure of labor.

If nature produces some articles of food more abundantly than others, and some articles grow more advantageously in one climate or soil than in others, and if any soil will produce a variety of articles by a rotation of crops in greater abundance than one article, the population which a country can support cannot be determined without a knowledge of what the inhabitants will demand for food. A much greater population can be provided with subsistence if they demand for food what nature can produce most abundantly than if they demand something of which nature can supply but a very limited quantity. So much has this fact been misunderstood that many economists have maintained that those nations prospered best who used the most expensive food. The use of wheat and beef is regarded as indications of a high standard of life, while the use of potatoes and rice is looked upon as the cause of misery and degradation of the countries which use them as the chief articles of diet. There is a seeming justification of this view in the conditions of those countries which use a cheap and abundant kind of food. India, Egypt, and Ireland, where potatoes, rice and other like articles of food are used, have a much lower standard of life than England, where wheat, beef, and other foodstuffs, which cannot be supplied by nature except in mose limited quantities, are demanded. Wherever the tendencies producing an unequal distribution of wealth are strong there can be no doubt that a nation runs a great danger in the introduction of a cheap article of food, since by the use of such a food the probabilities of increasing the effects of the unequal distribution are much augmented. So long as a dear kind of food is used, those of the laborers who wish to better their condition can, by using a cheaper food themselves, obtain a great advantage, which will aid them much towards their improvement; if, however, all the laborers use the cheaper food, those desiring to save have no advantage, and are thus practically without hope of improvement, and all remain in a low and degraded state, while the few to whom the benefit of an unequal distribution comes enjoy all the produce of the industry of the people. On the other hand, if there is no danger of an unequal distribution, or if a nation adopt proper means to overcome the tendencies in this direction, the advantages of cheap food are very apparent, as a much greater population can be supported with a much less expenditure of labor than when only dear food is used.

The use of cheap food must not be confounded with the use of a single article, such as potatoes or rice, for a diet; for the laws of nature are so arranged that a mixed diet is always the cheapest. For a time land will produce one article, such as potatoes or wheat, very abundantly, but the fertility will soon decrease unless the crop is changed and some other article is raised, since only by a proper rotation of crops can the fertility of the soil be maintained or increased. So, too, as climates and soils are different, nations can supply their wants by exchange, and get many articles of food with less labor than if they attempted to raise them at home. The cheapest food then will contain all the variety necessary to support life, and will be in harmony with the tastes and inclinations of all who are willing to adjust themselves to the natural conditions by which the gross and average return for labor is increased.

Even when the amount of the food-supply is known the number of the population which it supports cannot be determined, unless it is also known what commodities this population will demand. Some commodities are richer in food-material than others, and the consumption of these will create a larger demand for land than the consumption of the others, and if such articles be used, only a much smaller population can be supported. It is usually regarded as axiomatic by economists that each person requires a fixed quantity of food, and when the food-supply is known the amount of the population can be inferred; but this is not true. Food is not only used to support life, but is also largely consumed for the mere pleasure which the consumption gives, so that almost every one, if he has the means, consumes two or three times as much as is needed for the preservation of life and health. Wherever this is done not only is the population much reduced, but also the sum of the pleasures to be obtained by each one is greatly diminished, since other pleasures of a different kind are lost when the food is consumed instead of being converted, as it may be, into other kinds of enjoyment. The pleasure derived from food is exclusive, and is only enjoyed by the person who consumes the food, while many other pleasures can be enjoyed by a great number without any more expenditure of labor than if they were produced for the pleasure of one person. The different sources of enjoyment presented by a pleasant dinner illustrate clearly the various degrees of exclusiveness which different pleasures possess. The floral decorations, the table furniture, and the tasteful preparation of the food can be enjoyed by all alike. These pleasures do not depend on the amount of food as do the pleasures procured by consuming the edible dishes. The latter pleasures are exclusive and demand an increase of food for each additional person enjoying it.

Compare, again, the pleasure derived from beer and music. For each additional glass of beer additional labor is required, and if a double quantity is demanded, twice the amount of labor is needed in general to produce it. This increase of expense is not true of music, since a large number of persons can be entertained with music by an orchestra with no more labor than if the number was small. That one enjoys the music does not debar another from a like enjoyment, but the enjoyment of both is rather increased by the fact that they have a common pleasure. The same lack of exclusiveness in consumption is true of books—a book that would exchange for twenty glasses of beer can be enjoyed in turn by a thousand people, while, if the beer had been purchased instead of the book, but twenty of the thousand would have had any enjoyment, and the rest would have been excluded. Art is also similar to music and books in the amount of pleasure that can be derived from a small expenditure of labor and of the food-supply. So many persons cannot enjoy a painting simultaneously as can enjoy a piece of music, but as the painting lasts for a long time while the music does not, the painting is in time capable of giving as much pleasure at as little cost as can be obtained by any other means.

The examples which have been given lie at the extremes in regard to labor and the consumption of food necessary to produce a given amount of pleasure. Beer and other articles of like character require the greatest amount of labor and consumption of food, while music, books, and art require the least, in proportion to the amount of pleasure obtained. Between these extremes are innumerable other commodities, some requiring more and others less labor and consumption of food in their production, and thus they approximate one or the other of the class of commodities above mentioned.

The number of acres required to produce the food and liquor of each person determines the population of any section and the demand for labor. If the average person requires twenty acres to produce what he eats and drinks, there is but one-half the demand for labor that there would be if he consumed only the produce of ten acres and exchanged the produce of the other ten acres with artisans for other commodities. This fact can be well illustrated by taking many parts of the South, where every farmer has still to make his own liquor, and raises his own tobacco and corn, but has little or no exchange with the outside world. Suppose in such a society there should be a change of demand from liquor and tobacco to clothes. This demand for cloth would cause an increased demand for labor. All the labor formerly employed to produce the tobacco, and grain for liquor, would now be employed in raising food for the cloth-makers, while more cloth must be made to supply the increased demand. If now the people desired good houses, and reduced their consumption of food in the form of liquor and tobacco still more, they would permit the population to increase, and the additional laborers could find employment in building houses.

There is another important circumstance affecting the consumption of food in the degree of exclusiveness of family life. Where each family lives in seclusion, having a private house, preparing its own food, and doing all other work without any co-operation, the consumption of the food-supply is many times greater than it would be if the same families should so live as to allow the proper degree of division of labor. Certainly in the cooking and serving of food alone at least half of it is wasted or rendered worthless by the inefficiency of the labor employed in private life. It is a necessary disadvantage of private life that the labor be unskilled, as no person can wash, cook, and perform all the other work of a family with as little waste and as efficiently as the labor could be performed under conditions where each person is engaged in one occupation only. Where bread is made in a bakery, the same material will make much more bread and of a better quality than where each family bakes for itself. For example, take the difference in this respect between America and Germany. In Germany all bread is made in a bakery, while in America most of it is baked at home. It is no exaggeration to say that German rye-bread is more palatable than the wheat-bread served up on the ordinary American table. It is only when furnished with the finest qualities of wheat-flour that the ordinary cook can produce edible bread, while a baker can produce a better article with the poorest of wheat. The same waste is true of every department of private life, and when the present mode of living becomes modified so as to allow a greater division of labor, there will be an important economy of the food-supply, and a much larger population will be provided with subsistence without an increase of cost.

The amount of labor that can be employed in a country depends on the economy of the food-supply, and any change in consumption from commodities which draw largely on the food-supply to those requiring less land for their production, creates a demand for additional labor, and allows for an increase of population. So also a change in the demand from commodities which give only brief pleasure to those giving pleasure for a longer time, or to more persons at one time, will increase the demand for labor and the gross amount of pleasures to be enjoyed by the people. Clothes last for enjoyment a longer time than tobacco. A change of demand from tobacco to clothes will not only increase the demand for labor, but also the amount of pleasure to be enjoyed, since by the additional labor more is produced, and what is produced gives pleasure for a longer time than the former product. In the same way a demand for beautiful houses instead of fine clothes adds to the amount of the pleasures which any community has to enjoy, since houses last longer than clothes, can be enjoyed by many at the same time, and do not draw so largely on the food-supply, while public parks, museums, libraries, and musical concerts encroach still less on the food-supply, as they are most permanent in their effects, and the enjoyment of them by one person does not exclude the enjoyment of them by others.

As each individual demands commodities that will require the use of additional land for their production, or as he consumes his wealth in a manner which excludes others from enjoying his wealth with him, the demand for land increases and rent and the price of food rise. An unequal distribution of wealth is the result, and this cause brings about other changes, which increase still further the demand for land and raise the price of food. Rich persons, as a class, do not desire commodities so much for the pleasure which can be derived from them as for the display of their wealth. It is the rareness of an article which makes it desirable to them. Cheap things which all may have are passed by, and commodities are sought after of which there are not enough to supply the wants of every person. This spirit soon pervades all classes, each person desiring articles rarer and more costly than those lower in life can afford to purchase. Fashionable articles are desired and new clothes are purchased before utility demands a change, thus causing a great waste of labor and material. The desire to excel others is also visible in the desire of the rich to have all their amusement in private, although a multitude might have the pleasure without increase of cost. Their libraries, their art collections, their parks, must be their exclusive property, not because their pleasure is thereby increased, but because the possession of such treasures is beyond the means of ordinary people. This desire for rare and costly articles, especially when accompanied by the desire of individuals to have them for their exclusive use, creates a demand for land raises the price of food. So long as this spirit prevails to as great a degree as at present, the present high price of food will continue; and this spirit must cease before cheap food and an equal distribution of wealth are possible.

The effect of a change of demand from commodities requiring a large consumption of the food-supply to those better economizing it is as marked on the distribution of wealth as on the production. Let us suppose ten men working together, four of whom produce the food-supply, while six are engaged in making other articles desired for consumption. Each man would have a right to one-tenth of what is produced, and as the amount of food produced is but four-tenths of the gross production, any four of the men could, by taking all their share in food, exhaust the whole supply and leave the other six without food. The knowledge or fear that they would do this would break up the whole social arrangement and cause each one to work by himself, or the price of food would rise and that of other commodities fall until there was no danger that any one would demand more than his share of food. No one could live without food, and every one would give the whole produce of his labor rather than perish; hence if the six engaged in other than agricultural pursuits were determined to exchange what they produced for food alone, they would reduce the value of their produce until the whole produce of each would procure but one-tenth of the food-supply, which is the same amount that they would have received had they in the first place consented to an equitable exchange and not endeavored to obtain only food for their productions, while they have lost the share of one another's production which they would have obtained by a just division.

If each person increases his demand for food, either the number of the people in a country must be reduced, or a greater part of the labor must be devoted to the production of food. In either case there is a decline of civilization, as where nothing but food is produced, however abundant it may be, there is no civilization, and such a society will be low and ignorant. This shows that there is a condition to a high civilization which is nearly always overlooked. A high civilization requires that the labor of each should be exchanged for much more than enough to support the laborer but he must not endeavor to obtain food in exchange for all his labor. The amount of food for which the labor of each will exchange is the measure of his wages. It shows how many of the laborers can be spared from the production of food to produce other articles. For each laborer, however, to endeavor to obtain food for all his wages would destroy the civilization, or cause such an unequal distribution of wealth that the wages of each would only suffice to purchase the amount of food necessary for existence. If the people in any society do not choose to scatter, and each one raise food for himself, they must content themselves with the food necessary for their support, and each take his share of the other commodities produced, or they will force upon themselves such an unequal distribution of wealth that their wages will furnish them but a bare living. The latter alternative is what most societies take, and as a result wages are at a minimum and the price of food high. Every one endeavors to get more than his share of food, and as there is no way in which the part can be made equal to the whole, they obtain no more than if they had consented to take an equitable share, and at the same time they lose all their share of the other products of labor.

The demand for commodities of which nature can produce but very limited quantities, and the desire for food to be consumed for mere pleasure over and above what is sufficient to maintain health, are the important causes of the high price of food. Many times the present amount of food might be obtained, with no increase of the proportional cost, if the people would be content with a diet containing the different articles of food in that proportion which will allow the land to be employed in the production of those commodities for which it is best fitted; and the same food would supply many times the present population if it were only used to preserve health, and not consumed in administering to an appetite for intoxicating drinks or otherwise wasted through ignorance and a lack of appreciation of what inexclusive pleasures are.

In addition to these limitations of the food-supply caused by ignorance and prejudice, there are still greater contractions of the field of employment produced by the lack of appreciation of future as contrasted with present rewards, and hence capital is not accumulated to the proper amount, and the resources of all countries are but partially developed. To emigrate to new countries also requires capital, and where wages are low and the people ignorant, they have not the means, and often not even the desire, to go where wages are high and food is cheap. Thus the very fact that the price of food is high prevents the increase of food, as it causes an unfavorable distribution of wealth and an increase of ignorance, and prevents such a distribution of population as would increase the supply of food and remedy the unequal distribution of wealth.

In this connection only a reference can be made to another important cause of the high price of food, as a subsequent chapter will be devoted to its discussion. When there is free competition, the power of producers to survive does not depend on the gross produce of industry, nor on the efficiency of their labor, but on the surplus which can be given as rent. If the produce of one class of laborers is but one-half that of another class, the first class will displace the second if they demand less than one-half the wages. As the wants of cheap and inefficient laborers are small, and their rate of increase is rapid, they have the power of underselling when furnished with capital at a low rate of interest. Paying a higher price for food, and more as rent, they drive the more efficient classes out of the field of employment, and at the same time they so reduce both the gross return for industry and the field of employment itself that a much smaller population can be supplied with food then would be supported by the more efficient laborers whom they have displaced.

For these reasons it is evident that food is high in price not because any limit to the food-supply has been reached, but because the field of employment is so small to the ignorant and inefficient classes demanding the wrong commodities, and not willing to save for themselves. The obstacles to the increase of food and population are not physical in their nature. They are the result of ignorance and prejudice, and so long as they continue to flourish in their present force there cannot but be a high price for food and an unequal distribution of wealth.

From the foregoing discussion it will be seen a high price of food is not the result of a pressure of population against the means of subsistence that could be utilized if men were willing to conform to the conditions imposed by nature for the increase of the food-supply. Men impose unnatural limitations on themselves, and thus limit their field of employment, and as a result they must pay a high price for food. Men have a tendency to reduce their food-supply below their actual wants, and thus cause an artificial pressure of population upon the means of subsistence which they are willing to utilize.

This tendency to limit the food-supply is true not only of man, but of all animal life. The pressure of the increase of animal life is not on all the means of subsistence, but only on those kinds of food which can be obtained under simple conditions. To use two or more sources of food requires more intelligence and a higher organism than does the use of but one kind of food. An abundance of food induces animals to use only those kinds of food which can be obtained with the least effort, and these are the varieties of food which can be obtained under the simplest conditions. For food obtained under simple conditions a simple organism is the fittest organism, and the instincts which accompany a low form of organic life lead the animal to reject all sources of nourishment except those whose conditions are so simple that only a small effort will supply its wants. Animals, as well as man, have a tendency to economize labor, and an economy of effort causes a decline of intelligence where the wants of an animal can be supplied under simple conditions. The simpler the organism the higher is its rate of increase, and the increase in numbers soon causes a pressure upon the means of subsistence which are utilized. The tendency to increase and the tendency to limit the food-supply are thus brought into conflict, and as a result in those animals in which these tendencies are weakest, some of the instincts and habits which limit the food-supply are broken down and a new species is formed, with a more complex organism, capable of acquiring more kinds of food, or the same food under more varied conditions. The simplest organisms, not the fittest organisms, tend to survive. Only when the increase of simple organisms have exhausted the food-supply that can be obtained under simple conditions will animal life develop and maintain the more complex organisms and that intelligence necessary for their existence where food can be obtained only under complex conditions.

Evolution does not arise from a primary tendency in animal life for the fittest to survive. It is the result of two apparently injurious tendencies—the tendency to increase and the tendency to limit the food-supply. These two tendencies, always operating together, cause the simpler organisms in whom these tendencies are strongest to monopolize the means of subsistence obtainable under simple conditions, thus forcing those animals in whom these tendencies are weaker into more complex environments, where higher organisms and more intelligence are needed.

In the original man the tendency to limit the food-supply can be clearly seen, and in all the various social states through which he has developed up to the present time he has never failed so to limit the supply of food as to check the natural growth of population, and thus bring about an unequal distribution of wealth. The uncivilized races have numberless superstitions about food by which a large part of it must be rejected, and thus the supply is reduced. Each tribe will not eat cattle of a certain color. Here striped cattle are prohibited by one superstition; there the spotted animals are for a similar reason rejected, and travellers among such tribes often have great difficulty in feeding their followers, as no kind of food can be procured which all will eat. Large quatities of food are given by these tribes to their idols or gods: and often their departed ancestors, being supposed still to relish food, must be conciliated by having a portion of what there is to eat set aside for them. At the same time the production of food is greatly limited by other usages and customs, which prevent the use of many tracts of land which otherwise would probably be cultivated.

When these tribes develop into nations having a higher civilization they lose many of these superstitions and customs limiting the food-supply, but others are retained, or adopted, which prevent the use of the greater part of the resources offered by the land of the country for the production of food. There is a strong tendency merely to utilize some one, or at least but very few, of the resources which might be developed. Some nations subsist only on the cattle which they herd, others cultivate some one plant, like rice or potatoes, which grow almost spontaneously in some regions, and still others live almost entirely on bread and meat, neglecting, and often despising, the many other means of subsistence which nature has placed at their disposal.

The original man was a slave to his appetites and passions, and enjoyed only those pleasures which are of a physical nature. As he did not conform in the least to the demands of nature, he had only those means of subsistence, such as berries, fish, and game, which nature furnishes without labor. A partial conformity to nature has caused the cultivation of naturally fertile land where the obstacles to cultivation are few. Here, however, the progress of civilization has been stopped, because no race has yet been willing to subordinate the physical and exclusive pleasures of life to those obtained from the consumption of other kinds of wealth which would so harmonize with all the demands of nature as to allow the use of all land in the most productive manner, and thus cause the removal of the more formidable obstacles to the extension of cultivation.

There is an obvious connection between the field of employment open to any people and the number of qualities in them which are sufficiently developed to influence their consumption. To those who desire but few things which thrive without labor the land of any country can furnish only a small supply of food, and to get this food they must live in small tribes separated so widely from one another that little commerce or division of labor is possible. As the development of the qualities inherent in men cause an appreciation of new modes of consumption, the land is gradually put to more productive uses. Additional men can be employed in agriculture, and the better cultivation of the land will allow a greater proportion of the whole population to be engaged in other work than the production of food. The development of each additional quality in men causes them to value new qualities in land capable of increasing their sources of enjoyment, induces them to economize food so as to be better able to satisfy their new desires, and leads them to a better appreciation of the future, which makes them willing to accumulate more capital and acquire additional skill. It may be truly said that the development of each additional quality puts mankind in a new world. With its aid not only is a new field of employment discovered, but the old one has a different aspect, since all its qualities are valued from an altered and more rational stand-point. Just as the use of larger and more powerful telescopes continually brings into view many-fold more stars than were before visible, and at the same time gives a new and more perfect view of those formerly observed, so also the gradual bringing into activity of new qualities in men causes a great increase of the opportunities to labor, and an enlarged return for labor in the field of employment before in use.

The greater the conformity to nature the more will all the qualities in land be brought into use, and the larger will be the ratio of the good land to the poor. On the other hand, when any nation endeavors to increase production without a greater conformity to natural conditions on the part of the people, there will be an increasing proportion of poor land as compared with the good. A nation first cultivates those soils which are considered by the people to be the best, and these are always those where food can be obtained under the most simple conditions. If their estimate of the land does not change on account of a better adjustment of themselves to nature, they can supply the wants of an increasing population only from soils less fitted than those before in use for the production of the commodities desired by those not conforming to nature. Only the development of those qualities in man which change his estimate of land will cause an increase both of the quantity of land cultivated and of the ratio of the good land to the poor, allowing all land to be used for what it is best fitted.

From the qualities of the soil alone cannot be determined whether or not a given tract of land is good land. The demand for food and the use which is made of capital and skill are likewise important factors in determining our estimate of land. For this reason rent, when accompanied by a high price of food, is not the result of natural monopoly. It is caused by the survival of classes or races who, contrary to nature, endeavor to use the whole world for the production of a few articles of food of which but small quantities can be grown, and who adhere to methods of production which economize to the greatest extent possible the use of capital and skill. When such men survive, a greater conformity to natural conditions being thus prevented, land less productive of the desired articles of food must be cultivated as the demand for food increases. The present high price of food and the artificial pressure of population on the means of subsistence are due to this lack of conformity to nature, and only by a better adjustment to natural conditions can we hope to preserve a low price of food and increase the average return for labor.

APPENDIX

POPULARIZATIONS OF ENGLISH CLASSICAL ECONOMY

Jane Haldimand Marcet: "Conversations on Political Economy"

Harriet Martineau: "Illustrations of Political Economy"

At the present time popularizations of science and philosophy continue to pour from the presses in the form of stories of philosophy, outlines of history, and readable accounts of the nature of the physical universe. Again, much is now being said about the socialization of the curriculum, and economics is finding its way down into the secondary schools. Finally, various attempts are being made to "motivate" our teaching and to substitute play for formal discipline. These tendencies may be good or bad, but they are not new. The student of the history of economic thought is inclined to observe with Solomon that there is nothing—or at least very little—that is new under the sun.

A century ago, MacWickar, writing his "First Lessons in Political Economy," stated: "The principles of political economy are mere truisms which children might well understand and which they ought to be taught. A hundred years ago only savants could fathom them. To-day they are the common places of the nursery and the only real difficulty is their too great simplicity."

This statement of an almost forgotten schoolman is comparable to the still more famous dictum of John Stuart Mill on value, namely, "Happily, there is nothing in the laws of value which remains (1848) for the present or any future writer to clear up; the theory of that subject is complete . . . . "

The classical economists and their followers were inclined to regard the economic truths of their day as rather simple, and to view the science of economics as complete and finished. Such a conception was popularized and crystallized by the work of two English women who sought to render "the dismal science" less dismal in its treatment, if not in its contents. Accordingly, they sought to reduce to story form, for the education of young ladies, the teachings of Smith and Mathus, and even the abstractions of Ricardo.

Literary curiosity impels us to present to the student of the history of economic thought brief selections from "Conversations on Political Economy" (1816) by Mrs. Marcet and "Illustrations of Political Economy" (1832–1834) by Miss Martineau. Their relegation to an appendix was regarded as preferable to an interruption of the serious train of thought carried by the volume itself.

727

(MRS.) JANE HALDIMAND MARCET

(1769–1858)

Jane Haldimand was the daughter of a rich Swiss merchant established in London. In 1799 she married Dr. Alexander Marcet, a prominent London physician of Swiss birth.

The chief claim of Mrs. Marcet to fame is her attempt to popularize science, philosophy, and economics in the form of a series of conversations between an omnivorous child and an omniscient adult. Her first work was "Conversations in Chemistry," which appeared in 1806. Revised editions of this work continued until the sixteenth edition was reached in 1853. It has been said that by this time 160,000 copies of this popular primer of chemistry had been sold in the United States alone.

Even more successful was Mrs. Marcet's attempt to do the same thing for economics. "Conversations in Political Economy" first appeared in 1816 and continued to be reprinted in numerous later editions. Even Lord Macaulay himself wrote, "Every girl who has read Mrs. Marcet's little dialogues on political economy could teach Montagu or Walpole many lessons on finance."

Miss Harriet Martineau's "Illustrations of Political Economy," the first volume of which appeared in 1832, owed its origin to Mrs. Marcet's "Conversations in Political Economy," although the author herself makes no such acknowledgment. Indeed, Mrs. Marcet was so successful in popularizing her chemistry and economics that she had numerous followers. Even today, the century plant has blossomed again, although it prefers to regard itself as a new species.

Mrs. Marcet's conversations continued on uninterrupted in many fields for a generation or more. In addition to those on chemistry and economics, the following of her numerous writings were very popular: "Conversations on Natural Philosophy" (1819), "Conversations on Vegetable Physiology" (1829), "John Hopkin's Notions on Political Economy" (1833), and "Conversations on Land and Water" (1838).

JANE HALDIMAND MARCET

SELECTIONS FROM "CONVERSATIONS ON POLITICAL ECONOMY IN WHICH THE ELEMENTS OF THAT SCIENCE ARE FAMILIARLY EXPLAINED"

CONVERSATION IX

On Wages and Population

High wages not invariably accompanying great capital.—Great capital and low wages in China.—Small capital and high wages in America.—Advantages of new settled countries.—Poverty the natural check to population.—Great population advantageous only when resulting from plenty.—Increasing wealth preferable to any stationary capital.—Mistake in encouraging population.—Population of manufacturing towns.—Industry piece work.

CAROLINE

I have been reflecting a great deal on our last conversation, Mrs. B., and the conclusions I have drawn from it are, that the greater the capital a country possesses, the greater number of people it can maintain, and the higher the wages of labour will be.

MRS. B

The greater the stock of subsistence, the more people may be maintained by it, no doubt; but your second inference is not at all a necessary conclusion. China is a very rich country, and yet wages are I believe, no where so low. The accounts which travellers give of the miserable state of the inferior classes, are painful to hear; and their poverty is not the result of idleness, for they run about the streets with tools in their hands, begging for work.

CAROLINE

This is owing to the immense population of China; so that, though the capital of the country may be very considerable, still it is insufficient for the maintenance of all its inhabitants.

MRS. B

You should therefore always remember that the rate of wages does not depend upon the absolute quantity of capital, but upon its quantity relative to the number of people to be maintained by it. This is a truth which, however simple, is continually lost sight of, and hence arise errors without number in political economy. If China had ten times the wealth it actually possesses, and its population were at the same time tenfold as numerous, the people would not be better fed.

America, on the other hand, is a country of very small capital, and yet wages are remarkably high there.

CAROLINE

How do you account for that? for the demand for labour, you know, can only be in proportion to the extent of capital.

MRS. B

The capital of America, though small when compared with those of the countries of Europe, is very considerable in proportion to the number of people to be maintained by it. In America, and in all newly settled countries as yet thinly inhabited, the wages of labour are high, because capital increases with prodigious rapidity. Where land is plentiful and productive, and the labourers to cultivate it scarce, the competition amongst the landholders to obtain labourers is so great as to enable this class to raise their demands, and the higher the wages the labourer receives, the sooner he has it in his power to purchase a piece of land and become landholder himself. Thus the class of labourers is continually passing into the class of proprietors, and making room for a fresh influx of labourers, both from the rising generation and from emigrations from foreign countries.

CAROLINE

America has then the double advantage, of high wages and low price of land; no wonder that it is so thriving a country.

CONVERSATION X

On the Condition of the Poor

Of the cultivation of commons and waste lands.—Of emigration.—Education of the lower classes.—Benefit clubs.—Saving banks.—Parochial relief.—Alms and private charities.—Rewards.

CAROLINE

In our last conversation, Mrs. B., you pointed out the evils arising from an excess of population; they have left a very melancholy impression on my mind. I have been reflecting ever since whether there might be any means of averting them, and of raising subsistence to the level of population, rather than suffering population to sink to the level of subsistence. Though we have not the same resource in land as America; yet we have large tracts of waste land, which by being brought into cultivation would produce an additional stock of subsistence.

MRS. B

You forget that industry is limited by the extent of capital, and that no more labourers can be employed than we have the means of maintaining; they work for their daily bread, and without obtaining it, they neither could nor would work. All the labourers which the capital of the country can maintain being disposed of, the only question is, whether it be better to employ them on land already in a state of cultivation, or in breaking up and bringing into culture new lands; and this point may safely be trusted to the decision of the landed proprietors, as it is no less their interest than that of the labouring classes that the greatest possible quantity of produce should be raised. To a certain extent it has been found more advantageous to lay out capital in improving the culture of old land, rather than to employ it in bringing new land into tillage; because the soil of the waste land is extremely poor and ungrateful, and requires a great deal to be laid out on it before it brings in a return. But there is often capital sufficient for both these purposes, and of late years we have seen not only prodigious improvements in the processes of agriculture throughout the country, but a great number of commons inclosed and cultivated.

CAROLINE

I fear you will think me inconsistent, but I cannot help regretting the inclosure of commons; they are the only resource of the cottagers for the maintenance of a few lean cattle. Let me once more quote my favorite Goldsmith:

> "Where then, ah where shall poverty reside,
> "To 'scape the pressure of contiguous pride?
> "If to some common's fenceless limits stray'd,
> "He drives his flock to pick the scanty blade,
> "Those fenceless fields the sons of wealth deride,
> "And e'en the bare worn common is deny'd."

MRS. B

You should recollect that we do not admit poets to be very good authority in political economy. If, instead of feeding a few lean cattle, a common can, by being inclosed, fatten a much greater number of fine cattle, you must allow that the quantity of subsistence will be increased, and the poor, though in a less direct manner, will fare the better for it. Labourers are required to inclose and cultivate those commons, the neighbouring cottagers are employed for that purpose, and this additional demand for labour turns to their immediate advantage. They not only receive an indemnity for their loss of right of common, but they find purchasers for the cattle they can no longer maintain, in the proprietors of the new inclosures.

When Finchley Common was inclosed, it was divided amongst the inhabitants of that parish; and the cottagers and little shopkeepers sold the small slips of land which fell to their share to men of greater property, who thus became possessed of a sufficient quantity to make it answer to them to inclose and cultivate it; and the poorer classes were amply remunerated for their loss of commonage by the sale of their respective lots.

CAROLINE

But if we have it not in our power to provide for a redundant population by the cultivation of our waste lands, what objection is there to sending those who cannot find employment at home, to seek a maintenance in countries where it is more easily obtained, where there is a greater demand for labour? Or why should they not found new colonies in the yet unsettled parts of America?

MRS. B

Emigration is undoubtedly a resource for an overstocked population; but one that is adopted in general with greater reluctance by individuals; and is commonly discouraged by governments, from an apprehension of its diminishing the strength of the country.

* * * * *

But to return to the population of England; the more we find ourselves unable to provide for an overgrown population, the more desirous we should be to avail ourselves of those means which tend to prevent the evil—such, for instance, as a generald iffusion of knowledge, which would excite greater attention in the lower classes to their future interests.

CAROLINE

Surely you would not teach political economy to the labouring classes, Mrs. B.?

MRS. B

No; but I would endeavour to give the rising generation such an education as would render them not only moral and religious, but industrious, frugal, and provident. In proportion as the mind is informed, we are able to calculate the consequences of our actions: it is the infant and the savage who live only for the present moment; those whom instruction has taught to think reflect upon the past and look forward to the future. Education gives rise to prudence, not only by enlarging our understandings, but by softening our feelings, by humanizing the heart, and promoting amiable affections. The rude and inconsiderate peasant marries without either foreseeing or caring for the miseries he may entail on his wife and children; but he who has been taught to value the comforts and decencies of life, will not heedlessly involve himself and all that is dear to him in poverty, and its long train of miseries.

CAROLINE

I am very happy to hear that you think instruction may produce this desirable end, since the zeal for the education of the poor that has been displayed of late years gives every prospect of success; and in a few years more, it may perhaps be impossible to meet with a child who cannot read and write.

MRS. B

The highest advantages, both religious, moral, and political, may be expected to result from this general ardour for the instruction of the poor. No great or decided improvement can be effected in the manners of the people but by the education of the rising generation. It is difficult, if not impossible, to change the habits of men whose characters are formed, and settled; the prejudices of ignorance that have grown up with us will not yield to new impressions; whilst youth and innocence may be moulded into any form you chose to give them. But independently of schools and the various institutions for the education of youth, there is an establishment among the lower classes which is peculiarly calculated to inculcate lessons of prudence and economy. I mean the Benefit Clubs, or Friendly Societies; the members of which, by contributing a small stipend monthly, accumulate a fund which furnishes them relief and aid in times of sickness or distress. These associations have spread throughout the country, and their good effects are rendered evident by comparing the condition of such of the labouring classes as belong to them with those of the same district who have no resource in times of distress, but parochial relief or private charity. The former are comparatively cleanly, industrious, sober, frugal, respecting themselves, and respected by others; depending in times of casual sickness or accident on funds created by their own industry, they maintain an honourable pride and independence of character: whilst the latter, in a season of distress, become a prey to dirt and wretchedness; and being dissatisfied with the scantiness of parish reliefs, they are often driven to the commission of crimes. It is above a century since these clubs were first instituted; they have received encouragement both from government and individuals, and have spread throughout the country. I dare say that your prudent gardener Thomas is a member of one of them.

CAROLINE

Yes; and he belongs to one which can boast of peculiar advantages, as most of the gentlemen in the neighbourhood subscribe to it; in order by increasing the fund, and consequently the amount of the relief which the distressed members can receive, to encourage the poor to belong to it.

MRS. B

That is an excellent mode of bestowing charity, for you are not only sure that you relieve the necessitous, but also the industrious poor. A similar plan has been adopted, within these few years, in a village in the neighbourhood of London, and has been attended with the greatest success. Various schemes had been devised by the charitable inhabitants of this village to relieve the necessities of their poor, and so much was done for them by the opulent, that they found little need to exert their own industry; whilst the poor in the neighbouring parishes, attracted by the munificence of the charitable donations, flocked to the place; so that notwithstanding all their bounty, the rich still found themselves surrounded by objects of penury and distress. Convinced at length that they created as much poverty as they relieved, they came to a resolution of completely changing their system. They established benefit clubs, and the sums which they before gave away in alms, were now subscribed to these societies, so as to afford very ample relief to its members in cases of distress. The consequence was, that the idle poor abandoned the place, and the industrious poor were so well provided for that the village has assumed quite a new aspect, and penury and want are scarcely any more to be seen.

Conversation XV

On Value and Price

Of the value of commodities.—Of the distinction between exchangeable value and price.—Of utility considered as essential to value.—Of the cost of production, or natural value of commodities.—Of the component parts of the cost of production, rent, profit, and wages.—Of their imperfection as a measure of value.—Of supply and demand.—Of the component parts of the exchangeable value of commodities.—High price of commodities arising from scarcity.—Low price arising from excessive supply.—Low price arising from diminution of cost of production.

MRS. B

Before we proceed to the subject of trade, it is necessary that you should understand what is meant by the value of commodities.

CAROLINE

That cannot be very difficult; it is one of the first things we learn.

MRS. B

What is learnt at an age when the understanding is not yet well developed, is not always well learnt. What do you understand by the value of commodities?

CAROLINE

We call things valuable which cost a great deal of money; a diamond necklace, for instance, is very valuable.

MRS. B

But if, instead of money, you gave in exchange for the necklace silk or cotton goods, tea, sugar, or any other commodity, would you not still call the necklace valuable?

CAROLINE

Certainly I should; for, supposing the necklace to be worth 1000 l., it is immaterial whether I give 1000 l. in money, or 1000 l. worth of any thing else in exchange for it.

MRS. B

The value of a commodity is therefore estimated by the quantity of other things *generally* for which it will exchange, and hence it is frequently called exchangeable value.

CAROLINE

Or, in other words, the *price* of a commodity.

MRS. B

No, *price* does not admit of so extensive a signification. The price of a commodity is its exchangeable value, estimated in *money only*. It is necessary that you should remember this distinction.

CAROLINE

But what is it that renders a commodity valuable? I always thought that its price was the cause of its value; but I begin to perceive that I was mistaken: for things are valuable independently of money; it is their real intrinsic value which induces people to give money for them.

MRS. B

Certainly; money cannot impart value to commodities; it is merely the scale by which their value is measured; as a yard measures a piece of cloth.

CAROLINE

I think the value of things must consist in their utility, for we commonly value a commodity according to the use we can make of it. Food, clothing, houses, carriages, furniture, have all their several uses.

MRS. B

That is very true; yet there are some things of the most general and important utility, such, for instance, as light, air, and water, which, however indispensable to our welfare, have no exchangeable value; nothing is given for them, nor can any thing be obtained in exchange for them.

No one will give anything for what is so plentiful, and so readily obtained that every one may have as much as he requires, without making any sacrifice; but as light, air, and water, are essential even to our existence, surely they should be esteemed valuable.

In political economy we can consider valuable such commodities only as are susceptible of receiving a value in exchange; for this purpose the commodity must neither be produced in so unlimited a manner, nor so easily obtained that it may be had for nothing. It must, on the contrary, be in such request that men are willing to give something for it. Thus clothes, houses, furniture, though certainly less useful than light, air, and water, have exchangeable value.

Nature works for us gratuitously; and when she supplies us with articles in such abundance that no labour is required to procure them; those articles have no exchangeable value: but no sooner does the labour of man become necessary to procure us the use and enjoyment of any commodity, than that commodity acquires a value; either a price is paid for it in money, or other things are given in exchange for it. Light, air, and water are the free and bountiful gifts of nature, but if man constructs a lamp, we must pay for the light it diffuses: if we are indebted to his labours for a ventilator, or even a fan, we pay for the air they procure us; and when water is conveyed through pipes to our houses, raised by pumps, or brought to us in any manner by the art of man, a price is paid for it.

Workmen must of course be paid for the labour they bestow, whether it be in the production of a commodity, or merely in its conveyance. But it appears to me, Mrs. B., that it is *labour* rather than *utility* that constitutes value, for however we may enjoy the utility, it is the labour we pay for.

That labour, you will observe, is valuable only if it gives utility to an object. Were a man to construct or fabricate commodities which had neither utility, curiosity, or beauty, the labour he bestowed upon them would give them no value, and if he exposed them for sale, he would find no purchasers.

That is true; but the words beauty and curiosity, which you have just used, have raised another objection in my mind, to utility being essential to value. I recollect your defining wealth to be every article of utility, convenience, or luxury; wealth, no doubt, always implies value, but there are many articles of luxury that are perfectly devoid of utility, and which are valued either for their beauty, their curiosity or their rarity. What, for instance, is more valuable than diamonds? and yet they are of no use.

MRS. B

When we say that utility is essential to value, the expression is used in its most enlarged sense. Those who wear diamonds find them useful to gratify their vanity or pride, or to support their rank in life. The utility of luxuries must generally be considered in this point of view. I should, however, tell you, that Adam Smith distinguished two kinds of value; the one arising from utility, the other from what can be obtained in exchange.

* * * * *

HARRIET MARTINEAU

(1802–1876)

Harriet Martineau was an English writer of Huguenot ancestry. She was the older sister of Dr. James Martineau, an eminent clergyman.

In spite of poor health, a neurotic outlook, and a shattered romance in early life, Miss Martineau continued to write special articles for periodicals until success finally crowned her efforts. Poetry and short stories followed, until interrupted by a protracted illness.

After various other vicissitudes of fortune, Miss Martineau turned to the writing of stories illustrating accepted economic doctrines, inspired by the success of Jane Marcet's "Conversations in Political Economy." This series of "Illustrations of Political Economy" began in 1832 and continued until 1834. It comprised nine volumes and contained thirty stories. It was followed by several "Poor Law Tales" and "Illustrations of Taxation."

Miss Martineau soon became one of the literary lights of the day. Statesmen implored her opinion on economic questions. Robert Owen, for illustration, sought unsuccessfully to have her compose a story in defense socialism. On her visit to America she openly took sides with the abolitionists in their struggle against slavery.

Miss Martineau's tales strike us as unreadable fiction, crowded with a mass of erudition, and dedicated to the perpetuation of half truths and unwarranted generalizations. Nevertheless, they struck fire in the early Victorian period as effective popularizations, of the generally accepted economic doctrines of the dominant classical school. Even "the stern Benthamites," to use her own language, thanked her as a faithful expositor of their doctrines.

Miss Martineau's interests extended from the scientific to the occult, and her writings from poetry to prose. She composed numerous special articles on a wide range of subjects from unitarianism to mesmerism. Her longer works go all the way from political economy to fiction. Indeed, she even succeeded in blending the last two to her own satisfaction, as well as that of economists and gentle readers by the thousands. Finally, her devotional experiences passed from one of almost religious fanaticism to agnosticism and even atheism.

HARRIET MARTINEAU

SELECTIONS FROM "ILLUSTRATIONS OF POLITICAL ECONOMY"

TALE No. 1. LIFE IN THE WILDS

Summary of Principles Illustrated in the First Volume

Wealth consists of such commodities as are useful,—that is, necessary or agreeable to mankind.

Wealth is to be obtained by the employment of labour on materials furnished by nature.

As the materials of nature appear to be inexhaustible, and as the supply of labour is continually progressive, no other limits can be assigned to the operations of labour than those of human intelligence. And where are the limits of human intelligence?

Productive labour being a beneficial power, whatever stimulates and directs this power is beneficial also.

Many kinds of unproductive labour do this. Many kinds of unproductive labour are therefore beneficial.

All labour for which there is a fair demand is equally respectable.

Labour being a beneficial power, all economy of that labour must be beneficial

Labour is economized,

I. By division of Labour;—in three ways.
1. Men do best what they are accustomed to do.
2. Men do the most quickly work which they stick to.
3. It is a saving of time to have several parts of a work going on at once.

Labour is economized,

II. By the use of machinery, which
1. Eases man's labour.
2. Shortens man's labour; and thus, by doing his work, sets him at liberty for other work.

Labour should be protected by securing its natural liberty: that is—
1. By showing no partiality.
2. By removing the effects of former partiality.

Chapter II. What Is Wealth?

"Well, my friend," said the captain to Mr. Stone, as they sat watching their fire, "how do you feel at the close of this strange day?"

"Very much as if I were in a dream. When I look round this place and think of all that I have seen and done since morning, I can scarcely believe that we are the same people, living in the same age of the world, as yesterday. We seem to have gone back in the course of a night from a state of advanced civilization to a primitive condition of society."

"Except," interrupted his friend, "that the intelligence belonging to a state of advancement remains."

"True," replied Mr. Stone; "and it is this which makes the present too good an opportunity to be lost of observing what the real wealth of society consists of, and what the unassisted labour of man can do towards producing that wealth."

"I wish," said the captain, "that the people in England, who think that wealth consists in gold, and silver, and bank notes, would come here, and see how much their money is worth in our settlement. A thousand sovereigns would not here buy a hat, nor a roll of bank notes a loaf of bread. Here, at least, money is not wealth."

"Nor any where else," said Mr. Stone, "as we may see by putting a very simple case. Put a man with a bag of gold into an empty house, in England, or any where else, and he will starve in a week, unless he is allowed to give his gold in exchange for what will supply his wants. But give a man, who has not a shilling, a room well stocked with meat, and bread, and beer, and he has wealth enough to maintain him for a week or a fortnight, or as long as his provision lasts. And this is a test which holds good all the world over."

"And yet gold and silver may be called riches," said the captain, "while they procure us things of greater value than themselves."

"Certainly: they are, as long as they can be made use of, a part of wealth, though only one, and that not the greatest part. Wealth is made up of many things—of land, of houses, of clothes, furniture, food, and of the means (whether gold and silver, or any thing else) by which these things may be obtained. Whatever lives, or grows, or can be produced, that is necessary, or useful, or agreeable to mankind, is wealth."

"Then our settlement," said the captain, "is not stripped of all its property. We have some wealth left."

"Poor as we are," said his friend, "we are richer than if we were in the midst of the sandy desert to the north of us, with a wagon full of gold in our possession. We have here what gold could not buy in such a place, food and shelter."

"And other things too," said the captain. "We have clothing, for flax grows in the woods; and there are plenty of animals within reach, whose skins can be dried and cleaned to make us cloaks or beds, or tanned for shoes and caps and aprons for our workmen. We have furniture, for there is plenty of timber in the woods to make tables and chairs. We have . . . "

"Stay," interrupted his friend, "you are getting on too fast. All these things are likely to become ours, I grant you; but before we can call them our own,—before they become wealth to us, something must be added which we have not yet taken into consideration. You forget that there is no wealth without labour, and labour must be applied before the commonest productions can become wealth."

"True," replied the captain. "The flax must be gathered, and dried, and hackled, and woven, before it will make a shirt; and the animals must be caught, and a great deal of labour be spent upon their skins before they become fit for clothing or bedding; and the timber must be felled and sawn, and the pieces put skilfully together, before we possess it in the form of tables and chairs. But surely the case is different with food, of some kinds at least. There is fish in the pond, and fruit on the tree, ready made for man's use. Man spends no labour on the fruit that grows wild in such a climate as this; and yet we daily find that it is wealth to us."

"I beg your pardon," said Mr. Stone. "There is the labour of gathering it. An orange is of no use to any man living unless he puts out his hand to pluck it. And as for the fish in the pond,—think of the carp that Hill told us of this morning. They are no wealth to us till we can catch them, though the pool is within reach, and they belong to nobody else."

"We should have had them by this time if we had but got a net," said the captain.

"The net is one thing wanting, certainly," said his friend, "but labour is another. If the net were now lying ready on the bank, we should be no better for the fish, unless some one took the trouble of drawing them out of the water. I do not say that unassisted labour will furnish us with all that we want; but I do say that nothing can be had without the exertion of getting it; that is, that there is no wealth without labour."

"True," said the captain. "Even the manna in the wilderness would have been of no more use to the Hebrews than the carp in the pool to us, if they had not exerted themselves to gather it up. Food was never yet rained into the mouth of any man."

"And if it had been," said Mr. Stone, "he must have troubled himself to hold back his head and open his mouth. So you see what conclusion we come to, even in an extreme case."

"But with all our labour," said the captain, "how little we can do in comparison with what is done for us! Labour may be necessary to make the productions of Nature useful to us; but how much greater are the powers of Nature in preparing them for us! To look back no farther than to-day,—the antelope could not have been food for us unless human hands had prepared it; but how much was done beforehand! It was nourished, we know not how, by the grass it fed upon; it was made, we know not how, fit food for our bodies; and our bodies were so formed as to be strengthened by this food. Neither do we understand how fire acts upon the flesh so as to make it tender; or even how wood in its turn nourishes the fire. All that human labour has done was to bring together the wood, and the fire, and the animal, and then to eat the food prepared. Nature did the rest."

* * * * *

INDEX

B

C

E

F

G